Lecture Notes in Information Systems and Organisation

Volume 74

Lecture Notes in Information Systems and Organization—LNISO—is a series of scientific books that explore the current scenario of information systems, in particular IS and organization. The focus on the relationship between IT, IS and organization is the common thread of this collection, which aspires to provide scholars across the world with a point of reference and comparison in the study and research of information systems and organization. LNISO is the publication forum for the community of scholars investigating behavioral and design aspects of IS and organization. The series offers an integrated publication platform for high-quality conferences, symposia and workshops in this field. Materials are published upon a strictly controlled double blind peer review evaluation made by selected reviewers.

LNISO is abstracted/indexed in Scopus

Daniel Beverungen · Christiane Lehrer ·
Matthias Trier
Editors

Conceptualizing Digital Responsibility for the Information Age

Proceedings of the 18th International Conference on Wirtschaftsinformatik, Paderborn, Germany, 2023, Vol. 1

Springer

Editors
Daniel Beverungen
Department of Information Systems
Paderborn University
Paderborn, Nordrhein-Westfalen, Germany

Christiane Lehrer
Department of Digitalization
Copenhagen Business School
Frederiksberg, Denmark

Matthias Trier
Department of Information Systems
Paderborn University
Paderborn, Nordrhein-Westfalen, Germany

ISSN 2195-4968 ISSN 2195-4976 (electronic)
Lecture Notes in Information Systems and Organisation
ISBN 978-3-031-80118-1 ISBN 978-3-031-80119-8 (eBook)
https://doi.org/10.1007/978-3-031-80119-8

This Springer imprint is published by the registered company Springer Nature Switzerland AG
The registered company address is: Gewerbestrasse 11, 6330 Cham, Switzerland

Organization

Conference Chairs

Prof. Dr. Daniel Beverungen, Paderborn University, Germany
Prof. Dr. Dennis Kundisch, Paderborn University, Germany
Prof. Dr. Milad Mirbabaie, Paderborn University, Germany
Prof. Dr. Oliver Müller, Paderborn University, Germany
Prof. Dr. Guido Schryen, Paderborn University, Germany
Prof. Dr. Simon Thanh-Nam Trang, Paderborn University, Germany
Prof. Dr. Matthias Trier, Paderborn University, Germany

Program Committee Chairs

Prof. Dr. Daniel Beverungen, Paderborn University, Germany
Prof. Dr. Christiane Lehrer, Copenhagen Business School, Denmark
Prof. Dr. Matthias Trier, Paderborn University, Germany

Doctoral Consortium Chairs

Prof. Dr. Martin Matzner, Friedrich-Alexander-Universität Erlangen-Nuremberg, Germany
Prof. Dr. Guido Schryen, Paderborn University, Germany
Dr. Miriam Stumpe, Paderborn University, Germany
Dr. Sandra Zilker, Friedrich-Alexander-Universität Erlangen-Nuremberg, Germany

Local Arrangement Chair

Prof. Dr. Dennis Kundisch, Paderborn University, Germany

Sustainability Chair

Prof. Dr. Simon Thanh-Nam Trang, Paderborn University, Germany

Website and Social Media Chair

Prof. Dr. Milad Mirbabaie, Paderborn University, Germany

Preface

This volume comprises papers accepted for publication and presented at the 18. Internationale Tagung Wirtschaftsinformatik (Wi23)—the International Conference of the German-speaking Information Systems Community—held from 18 to 21 September 2023 in Paderborn, Germany. Leaving behind 2 years of virtual conferences due to the COVID-19 pandemic, the Wi23 took an important role in re-uniting our community, enabling the attendees to meet "old" colleagues—many of them friends—and new people in an on-premise conference setting. In this sense, the Heinz-Nixdorf MuseumsForum, home to the world's largest computer museum, provided an ideal setting for this conference, in which the history and future of the digital society converged.

The conference theme—Digital Responsibility: Social, Ethical, Ecological Implications of Information Systems—acknowledged the crucial role of normative principles in navigating the rapidly accelerating pace of technological change. While digital technologies offer immense opportunities, they also pose significant risks. As markets and innovations outpace regulations, concerns about privacy, fairness, and societal impact continue to grow. Digital Responsibility addresses how individuals, organizations, and governments can ensure ethical, inclusive, and sustainable digital development. In Information Systems, Digital Responsibility emphasizes moving beyond mere legal compliance, urging stakeholders to consider the broader social, environmental, and ethical consequences of digital transformation. Issues such as avoiding algorithmic bias, assuring data privacy, and providing equitable access to digital services are central to this approach.

The Wi23 program featured 20 scientific tracks. Apart from a track dedicated to the conceptualization and implications of Digital Responsibility itself, many tracks explored the opportunities and challenges digital transformation presents while many also highlighted the importance of responsible practices. The breadth of topics covered research areas such as business models, digital markets, human–computer interaction, service science, enterprise modeling, and business process management. Specific tracks also examined digitalization prospects in industry, retail, smart cities, education, health, and logistics, alongside focused discussions on the philosophy of science, innovative prototypes, and student contributions.

Focusing on these tracks, we received a reassuring number of 214 full paper submissions and 65 research-in-progress papers. Reflecting the WI conference's role as the premier academic conference of the German-speaking Information Systems/ Wirtschaftsinformatik community, all manuscripts were subjected to an in-depth peer-review process. Each manuscript was assigned to at least two reviewers and one associate editor, assessing the manuscript's scientific rigor and relevance in 953 reviews. The review process resulted in acceptance decisions on 86 full papers and 16 research-in-progress papers, reflecting an overall acceptance rate of 33% across all papers submitted.

This selection of high-quality papers is more than can be included in a single volume. Therefore, we decided to split the conference proceedings into three volumes:

1. The first volume, "Conceptualizing Digital Responsibility for the Information Age," comprises papers that focus on establishing and clarifying the conceptual ramifications of digital responsibility and its principles in connecting with information systems. A particular focus is also the role of humans and organizations in a digital transformation that is responsible.
2. The second volume, "Solutions and Technologies for Responsible Digitalization," comprises papers focusing on digital technologies' actual design. It includes not only foundational topics of our discipline, like information modeling, business process management, and digital infrastructures, but also topics that have emerged more recently, such as data science, prescriptive analytics, and distributed trust. This volume also comprises papers from the conference's industry track, presenting innovative prototypes that can provide immediate business value.
3. The third volume, "Transforming the Digitally Sustainable Enterprise," comprises papers that focus on the domain tracks of the conference, bringing concrete perspectives and transformation journeys in different industries to the foreground. This volume includes papers on IT strategy, service innovation, and new business models. A particular focus is set on current opportunities and challenges related to digital technologies in health, education, industry and retail, smart cities, and mobility.

Besides the conference tracks, the scientific program of Wi23 included many other formats for presentation and discussion. These included a keynote presentation, a panel discussion, a Chief Information Officers' (CIO) panel, a doctoral consortium, and various ancillary workshops and community meetings. A particular focus of these events was, once again, establishing Digital Responsibility as a normative guideline for the further digital transformation of society. To initiate and focus discussions, we performed a Delphi study with most of the track chairs before the conference to pinpoint how Digital Responsibility can be positioned in the broader Information Systems community. We posit that these results left a strong mark on the community by introducing the concept of digital responsibility and discussing its ramifications.

Organizing the first post-pandemic conference of our community, we also took the liberty to introduce and prototype some administrative innovations that we envisioned would make the conference more interactive, inspiring, and fun. First, regarding paper presentations, we invited the authors to present their research in three different presentation formats, comprising thought-provoking paper sessions, pitch paper sessions, and classic paper sessions. We take the positive feedback as evidence that the new formats spiced up the presentations while attracting a greater audience and promoting more inspiring discussions. Second, regarding diversity, the Wi23 was the first WI conference to establish diversity in all track chair teams in terms of gender and age. As a program committee, we approached 11 women and 9 men to serve as heads for our 20 tracks and asked them to assemble their track chair teams in line with two guidelines: Each track should include men and women, as well as involve at least one young scientist as track chairs. Third, perhaps most notably, we moved the conference from winter to September to avoid the pandemic's repercussions to interfere with the conference once again.

We want to thank all authors, track chairs, associate editors, reviewers, and committee members for devoting their valuable time to organizing and hosting the Wi23. Particular thanks are also due to the entire organizing team from Paderborn University, who worked with all their hearts and souls to welcome our community to Paderborn for a conference that is inspiring, fun, and an asset for developing strong professional and personal relationships.

Finally, we sincerely thank the sponsors who generously supported our conference. Their commitment made it possible to provide a conference experience that we found unique. Special thanks apply to our gold sponsors DATEV eG and the Software Innovation Campus Paderborn (SICP), our silver sponsors 29FORWARD, Arvato, Finanz Informatik, Heinz Nixdorf Stiftung Westfalen, UNITY, Weidmüller, and our bronze sponsors myConsult, Springer, and SpringerGabler. KONTOR N and Störtebecker Braumanufaktur helped us to make the conference reception a truly memorable event.

As the program committee of the Wi23 conference, we wish you an insightful read of the proceedings. May the research published at this conference stimulate fresh thinking, inspire you to develop new ideas, and build an appreciation for the normative principles that Digital Transformation can offer as guidance for the further progress of digital transformation. We are convinced that in a world that is transforming at incredible speed, it is on us to envision and build the type of society we desire.

Paderborn, Copenhagen
September 2024

Daniel Beverungen
Christiane Lehrer
Matthias Trier

Contents

Digital Innovation, Adoption and Use

Human–Computer Interaction and Social Online Behavior

About the Editors

Daniel Beverungen is a Professor of Information Systems and Enterprise Systems at Paderborn University, Germany. His research interests include service research, business process management, and the design of innovative information systems.

Christiane Lehrer is an Associate Professor at the Department of Digitalization at Copenhagen Business School, Denmark. Her research interests include data-driven innovation, user behavior, and sustainable information systems.

Matthias Trier is a Professor of Information Systems and Social Computing at Paderborn University, Germany, and a Visiting Professor at Copenhagen Business School, Denmark. His research interests include digital social user behavior such as the appropriation of social media and collaboration platforms in companies' digital participation, the influence of electronic discourse, cooperation in virtual reality, and event-driven dynamic network analysis.

Digital Responsibility: Social, Ethical and Ecological Implication of IS

A Picture is Worth a Thousand Words—Exploring Bias in Inclusive Chatbots

Ricarda Schlimbach, Anika Stoppel, Lucas Lampka, and Susanne Robra-Bissantz

Abstract This study examines the impact of different avatar pictures (gender & disability representation) and gendering on students' perceptions of chatbots in an interaction on learning strategies with 180 students from a German university. In the first experiment, we manipulated the chatbot's humanoid profile picture based on gender and the representation of a visible handicap (wheelchair). In the second experiment, we varied its language style. Statistical analysis revealed that displaying a physical disability significantly enhanced trust, credibility, and empathy but reduced perceived competence and dominance. Gender-sensitive language improved perceptions of competence, trust, credibility, and empathy, whereas we did not find significant interaction effects between both factors. Our results imply the necessity of a more inclusive design of information systems and highlight designers' responsibility in raising awareness and mitigating unconscious bias, as digital learning (technologies) continue to advance.

Keywords Inclusiveness · PCA · Bias · Chatbot · Diversity · Social cues

R. Schlimbach (✉) · A. Stoppel · L. Lampka · S. Robra-Bissantz
TU Braunschweig, Chair of Service Information Systems, Braunschweig, Germany
e-mail: r.schlimbach@tu-bs.de

A. Stoppel
e-mail: a.stoppel@tu-bs.de

L. Lampka
e-mail: l.lampka@tu-bs.de

S. Robra-Bissantz
e-mail: s.robra-bissantz@tu-bs.de

R. Schlimbach
Hochschule Heilbronn, Wirtschaftsinformatik, Schwäbisch Hall, Germany

D. Beverungen et al. (eds.), *Conceptualizing Digital Responsibility for the Information Age*, Lecture Notes in Information Systems and Organisation 74,
https://doi.org/10.1007/978-3-031-80119-8_1

1 Introduction

The inclusion of individuals with physical or mental disabilities in learning environments at schools and universities should be viewed as a given, not a privilege (Miyauchi 2020). Inclusion in the context of learning means that all learners, including those with physical or mental disabilities, have the same opportunities to participate in the learning experience (Francisco et al. 2020). However, individuals with physical or mental disabilities are often attributed with less competence; for instance in job application processes, resulting in being less frequently considered for job postings (Bonaccio et al. 2020). Similarly, even young students tend to believe the statements of physically healthy, non-disabled individuals were more credible than those of someone with a physical disability, although they cannot always explain this biased perception that reflects the deeply ingrained prejudices against minorities (Jaffer and Ma 2015; Manzanero et al. 2015). In addition to the inclusion of people with physical or mental disabilities, mitigating gender bias is also an important issue (Bernagozzi et al. 2021; Fossa and Sucameli 2022). Moreover, gender-sensitive language might reduce prejudice and discrimination by integrating everyone equally into language use, especially in learning environments (Formanowicz et al. 2015; Sczesny et al. 2016).

As teaching and learning are increasingly shifting into the digital space and being technologically supported, socially inclusive design of information systems for educational purposes must be taken into greater consideration (Schlimbach and Robra-Bissantz 2022), especially because humans tend to apply social rules, norms, expectations, and attitudes from reality to situations in which they communicate with machines (Lee and Nass, 2010). In this context, the inclusive design of Pedagogical Conversational Agents (PCAs) appears to be particularly relevant, as they embody social cues such as a human identity (e.g., avatar, gender) and verbal cues (Feine et al. 2019; Seeger et al. 2018) like natural and potentially gender-sensitive language, while also gaining attention in research and practice (Khosrawi-Rad et al. 2022). Despite several studies that target minorities as the key user group for interacting with PCAs such as disadvantaged learners (Gupta and Chen 2022) or internationals with language barriers (Schlimbach, Khosrawi-Rad et al. 2022), research that explores the impact of their inclusive design is scarce to find. PCAs neither represent visually disabled people nor do they use gender-sensitive language to foster diversity in education (Schlimbach and Robra-Bissantz 2022). This seems surprising, in that diversity representation has been found to positively influence students' respect towards minorities and results essential for inclusiveness in education (Al-Obaydi 2019; Holoien 2013; Lie et al. 2021). Understanding inclusive PCA design and how it leads to (potentially biased) responses of the PCA's characteristics is thus of high practical relevance. We, therefore, intend to contribute to the following research questions (RQ):

*To what extent does the visual portrayal of a physical disability of a PCA (avatar portrayed with a visible physical disability) influence students' perception of (a) its competence, (b) trust, (c) credibility, (d) dominance, and (e) empathy **(RQ1)**? To* *what extent do the results found in (a) to (e) differ between a female and a male PCA's representation* ***(RQ2)****? How does the use of gender-sensitive language by a PCA influence users' perception of the variables (a) to (e) mentioned before* ***(RQ3)****?*

Findings on how the portrayal of physical disability and the use of gender-sensitive language in PCAs affect students' perception might build upon recent findings (Fossa and Sucameli 2022; Schlimbach and Robra-Bissantz 2022) and create further awareness for the mindful and socially inclusive design of supportive tools (in education).

2 Research Background

2.1 Designing Inclusive PCAs

PCAs facilitate learning by offering interactive support to students in their role of a tutor, peer student, or coach (Hobert and Meyer von Wolff 2019) and mitigate learning content (Weber et al. 2021). In interacting, human users attribute social qualities to their artificial conversation partners according to the computers-are-social-actors theory (CASA), even when they know that they are interacting with a computer (Lee and Nass, 2010). Adapted social cues (Seeger et al. 2018) can intentionally design PCAs to promote inclusiveness in educational technology (Lembcke et al. 2020), and thus, influence human perception in real life (Feine et al. 2020). For instance, a PCA's human identity can be embodied by its name (Cowell and Stanney 2005), gender (Schuetzler et al. 2018), and avatar representation (Gong 2008), while emojis transmit nonverbal cues (Hu et al. 2018) and visual design (Gupta and Chen 2022). Verbal cues, such as language style (Gnewuch et al. 2018), self-references (Schuetzler et al. 2018), and personal introduction (Cafaro et al. 2016), help circumscribe the category of cues. Each of these elements may potentially promote inclusiveness by capturing underrepresented characteristics (Holoien 2013; Ydo 2020). Inclusion begins with the individual perception of differences between people (Boban and Hinz 2009). Therefore, it is of enormous importance to sensitize understanding and to establish inclusive structures both in social life and information systems.

2.2 Gender-Neutral Language

The discussion about the introduction of gender-neutral language has been ongoing in Germany since the 1970s. It deals with the fact that in German grammar, the generic masculine is used when describing a group of both female and male individuals. This means that a group of female and male students is referred to as "Studenten," which implies that both female and male individuals are meant equally. However, this becomes problematic when using the generic masculine causes cognitive exclusion of female individuals ("Studentinnen") and results in their being given less attention in various contexts (Braun et al. 2007). This phenomenon has been confirmed in prior studies (e.g., Heise 2000) and resulted in alternatives to have all genders represented in language use, including neutralization, using both gender forms, or adding symbols like an asterix (*) to represent inclusiveness (Braun et al. 2007).

With the introduction of § 1 Abs. 2 of the Federal Equality Act, which obliges the use of gender-equitable language, the discussion about the necessity of moving away from the generic masculine has shifted to how and in what form the implementation should take place. However, there is also a controversial debate on the use of gender-sensitive language, as it decreases comprehensibility, harms grammatical correctness and thus might set further language barriers (Braun et al. 2007; Chubb and Derrick 2020).

2.3 *Theoretical Foundations that Lead to Bias*

Social identity theory (Tajfel and Turner 1979), focuses on how individuals derive their sense of self and social identity from group membership. It suggests that people tend to categorize themselves and others into social groups and develop a sense of belonging and self-esteem based on their group membership. The theory also addresses the concepts of in-group favoritism, where individuals show a preference for their own group, and out-group aversion, where individuals may exhibit negative attitudes or behaviors towards members of other groups. In addition, the Stigma theory, developed by Erving Goffman in 1963, examines the social process of labeling and devaluing individuals or groups based on perceived differences or deviations from societal norms. It explores how stigmatized individuals may experience social exclusion, discrimination, and the negative effects of stereotypes. A stigma is a usually visible attribute that sets individuals apart from others. For example, this could be skin color or a physical disability. The result of a stigma could be that the affected individual is not being fully accepted within social situations (Goffman 1986).

When people first meet, they tend to perceive each other based on their most prominent characteristics. This phenomenon is known as the *Halo Effect*, when positive characteristics or features lead to a positive assessment of attributes (Landy and Sigall 1974), or as the *Horn Effect*, when negative characteristics or features lead to a negative assessment of attributes (Pohl 2016; Shifrer 2013). Often, other attributes are being overlooked (Domsch et al. 2019). For instance, in the context of this research project, people with physical or mental disabilities are often judged primarily based on this characteristic and are then perceived as less competent in general, even in situations where the handicap is irrelevant (Fiske et al. 2007; Rohmer and Louvet, 2018). People have preconceived notions of social groups and their behaviors and abilities, which are unreflectively applied to every member of that group. Stereotypes, unlike prejudices, are not emotional but rather neutral. Prejudices are internalized and individually confirmed stereotypes that people believe to be true. Bias like gender bias

(Oh et al. 2019) or affinity bias (Trainer et al. 2020) in this context refers to perception distortions that arise, among others, from prejudices, sometimes even arising unconsciously. These biases are evolutionarily determined to quickly process information to survive. For instance, affinity bias makes people prefer others who are similar to themselves or to close associates, while beauty bias associates a person's appearance with certain qualities (Domsch et al. 2019). Gender bias provokes distortions due to the perceived gender of a person (Striebing 2021), whereas confirmation bias describes people searching for confirming information that supports their thought patterns (Domsch et al. 2019). Due to the CASA theory (Nass and Moon 2000), these biases might translate to the perception of PCAs and initial findings prove that gender bias, affinity bias, and unconscious bias towards disabilities are shown towards chatbots as well (Feine et al. 2020; Schlimbach and Robra-Bissantz 2022; Zabel and Otto 2021).

3 Research Design

To understand the relationship between the representation of physical disability and the use of gender-neutral language and the target variables of competence, trust, credibility, dominance, and empathy as variables relevant to learning success (cf. following sections), we designed six PCAs and derived 15 hypotheses to be tested in experiments.

3.1 Deriving Hypotheses

Perceived Competence. The perception of a person's competence in a given activity is determined by the successful integration of their accumulated knowledge, skills, and experience relevant to the situation (Fiske et al. 2007; Schmid et al. 2022). In our experiment, we evaluate the perceived domain expertise of the PCAs in teaching learning strategies. As all PCAs possess the same subject matter knowledge and response repertoire, their expertise is identical. According to studies, 77% of chatbot users expect the technical competence to be at least equivalent to, or even more advanced than that of a human (Furchheim et al. 2021). Individuals with physical or mental disabilities are perceived as less competent in real life (Fiske et al. 2007). Women also appear less competent than men (Oh et al. 2019), whereas users of gender-sensitive language appear more competent in a study than those who do not use it (Hannover and Wolter, 2019; Vervecken and Hannover, 2012). We anticipate that these findings transfer to PCAs. **H1**: The portrayal of a physical handicap has a negative impact on perceived competence. **H2**: Using a female profile picture has a negative impact on the PCA's perceived competence. **H3**: The use of gender-sensitive language has a positive impact on perceived competence.

Trust. Schweer (1996) and Luhmann (1989) describe trust as a fundamental attitude that a person holds towards others. The success of an educational intervention is positively correlated with the level of trust established between the tutor and student, and consequently between the PCA and its user (Schweer 2000). Women are perceived as more trustworthy than men in general (Buchan et al. 2008). Regarding trust in people with physical or mental disabilities, no evidence was found in the literature so we assume this trait has no impact on trust. People also tend to trust initiatives that use gender-sensitive language more, while those that do not are viewed as less competent and less credible (Formanowicz et al. 2015). The same applies to the use of gender-sensitive language. We thus hypothesize **H4**: Depicting physical disability has a positive impact on perceived trust. **H5**: Using a female profile picture has a positive impact on perceived trust. **H6**: Using gender-sensitive language has neither a positive nor negative impact on perceived trust.

Credibility. The variable credibility can be related both to the persons themselves and to the statements made by a person. A person is considered credible when they convey information to another person and believe it to be true, with no intention to deceive the other person. The actual truthfulness of a statement is not a necessary condition for its credibility (Köhnken 1999). There were no indications found that gender or a physical limitation have an impact on perceived credibility, but Formanowicz et al. (2015) found people not using gender-sensitive language are seen as less credible, which is why we assume the following hypotheses: **H7**: Depicting a physical limitation has no positive or negative influence on perceived credibility. **H8**: The gender displayed in the PCA's profile picture has no positive or negative influence on its perceived credibility. **H9**: The use of gender-sensitive language has a positive influence on perceived credibility.

Dominance. Dominant individuals are described as those who take responsibility, influence and control others, enjoy being in the spotlight, and are willing to assert their goals with aggression if necessary (Cheng et al. 2013). A teacher's dominant behavior has a negative impact on learners' motivation to learn (Jiang and Zhang 2021). Typically, the trait of dominance is associated more with male individuals (Wirtz 2021), which is why they are more likely to be perceived as dominant. As described above, inclusion means that society and structures must adapt so that people with and without physical or mental disabilities can operate equally. However, since inclusion has not yet penetrated all areas, people with disabilities still have to adapt to their environment and show consideration (Felder 2017). Concerning the perceived dominance in the use of gender-sensitive language, we hypothesize that the gendering chatbot will be perceived as less dominant because it integrates and includes all users and appears more at eye level. We thus hypothesize **H10**: The representation of a physical limitation has a negative impact on perceived dominance. **H11**: The use of a female profile picture for the PCA has a negative impact on perceived dominance. **H12**: The use of gender-sensitive language in a PCA has a negative impact on perceived dominance.

Empathy. Empathy is ascribed to individuals who can empathize with the feelings of others (Light 2019). In the learning environment, empathy has a positive impact on the learning success of the students as an empathetic teacher motivates them stronger (Tausch 2008). Women are attributed with a more pronounced ability to empathize than men (Greenberg et al. 2018). As described above, people with physical or mental limitations often have to adapt more frequently in their everyday lives, so it is assumed that they deal with their fellow human beings more empathetically due to their own experiences. The argumentation with regard to gender-inclusive language and its influence on the perception of empathy follows that of the dominance variable. The resulting hypotheses are **H13**: The portrayal of a physical limitation has a positive influence on perceived empathy. **H14**: The use of a female profile picture for the PCA has a positive influence on perceived empathy. **H15**: The use of gender-inclusive language in a PCA has a positive influence on empathy ascribed to the PCA.

3.2 *Conducting the Experiment*

Within the framework of this research project, the RQs were investigated in two experiments designed between subjects with a total of 180 participating students. We anticipated a medium effect size (Cohen's d = 0.6), a desired statistical power level of 0.8 and a probability level of $p < 0.05$. The a priori power analysis (Soper 2023) thus resulted in a minimum total sample size (two-tailed hypothesis) of 90 per experiment. This approach is complemented by a quantitative survey with qualitative open questions to leverage the strengths of each method and achieve informative results (Halcomb and Hickman 2015).

First, we created the PCAs 1–4 with *Google Dialogflow* with a consistent communication style but manipulated their profile pictures as shown in Fig. 1. PCA 1 is represented by Ben, a male person without an apparent disability. PCA2 embodies again Ben but displays his physical limitation (a wheelchair). PCA3 shows Lena, a female without apparent disability, while PCA4 represents her with physical limitations (visible wheelchair). Second, we manipulated the gender-sensitive language style. Max uses gender-sensitive language embedded into PCA5, while PCA6 interacts using the generic masculine. The conversation content is identical for all six PCAs, as we provided pre-defined response buttons for users to select from, making them less error-prone and ensuring comparability of all conversations. The topic taught by all chatbots is learning strategies, as it is relevant in the learning context cross-disciplinary. Following a between-subject design, we instructed participants to test only one of the six PCAs by randomly assigning them to one PCA depending on their birth month.

Thirty participants were recruited per PCA, resulting in a total of 180 participants for the study. The probands were students, as the overall goal was to use a PCA as a learning tutor at university. We initially instructed students on how to interact with the PCA. We monitored that they tested the PCA sufficiently before having them answer a follow-up survey. It mainly queries items on a Likert scale from 1 to 7

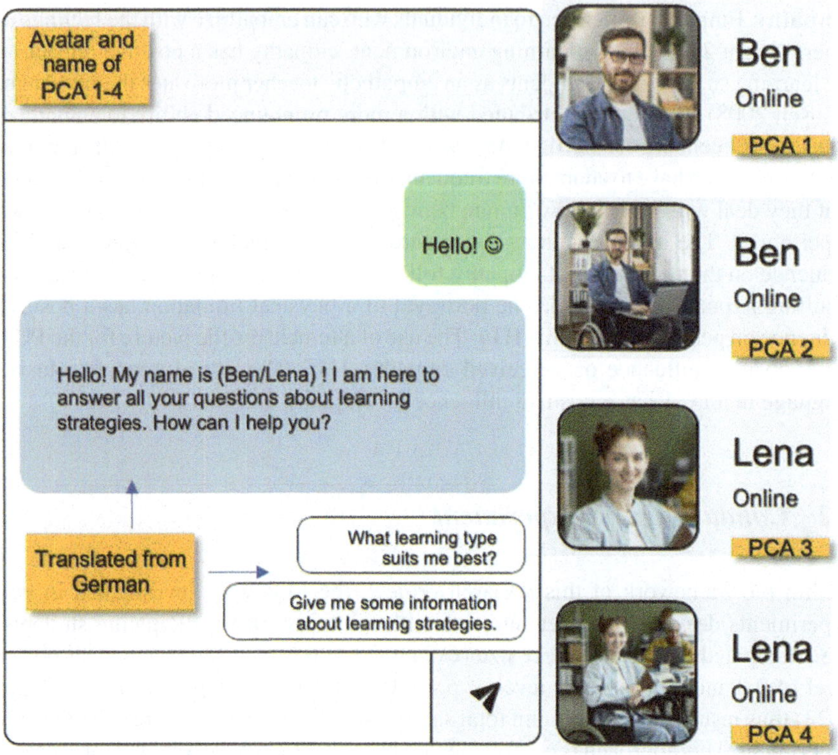

Fig. 1 Visualized PCA manipulations

("strongly agree" to "strongly disagree") to assess their perceptions towards the five target constructs to be then statistically analyzed in Jamovi 2.3.21. More precisely, we measured competence (Toader et al. 2020), trust (Simmel et al. 1992; Toader et al. 2020), credibility (Wirth 1999), empathy (Bodrunova et al. 2019; Früh and Wünsch 2009), and dominance (Gay 2000) with scientifically validated items adapted to the use cases of a PCA that teaches learning strategies. Additionally, the survey queried students about attitudes toward gender-sensitive language in chatbots. Finally, we collected sociodemographic data (age, gender, study level).

4 Results

Among the 180 students, 31% are female and 69% male. 47.8% of all participants had already tried a chatbot in a learning context, while 52.2% of the participants did not. The majority of the participants was pursuing a bachelor's degree, 35% were studying towards a master's degree, and 22 had completed their master's degree,

Table 1 Demographic data

	Gender		Age group				Study level		
	Male	Female	< 20	20–24	25–29	> 29	BSc	MSc	Ph.D.
Group 1	17	13	5	12	8	5	11	13	6
Group 2	21	9	9	11	8	2	12	12	6
Group 3	18	12	5	17	5	3	15	12	3
Group 4	17	13	6	12	9	3	18	8	4
Group 5	25	5	10	14	3	3	23	6	1
Group 6	26	4	10	13	6	1	16	12	2
	124	56	45	79	39	17	95	63	22

among these 1,1% completed a PhD, or graduated from vocational training (1,1%) before. There was a great diversity of majors covered in this study such as Information Systems, Technology Management, Psychology or Engineering.

Demographic data per PCA group (e.g., group 1 tested PCA1) concerning gender, age and study level (Bachelor's (BSc); Master's (MSc) or Ph.D. Students (Ph.D.)) are summarized in Table 1.

4.1 Quantitative Results

First, we performed a reliability analysis in Jamovi to check for internal construct validity. Then, we conducted an exploratory factor analysis to verify that the items correspond to their respective constructs. For each of the five constructs (competence, trust, credibility, empathy, and dominance), a Cronbach's alpha was calculated to assess its reliability. These alpha values were found to be good or even excellent ranging from 0.842 (credibility) to 0.955 (competence). The exploratory factor analysis confirmed that the items were correctly assigned to their respective constructs. Since the Shapiro–Wilk normality test (p (competence, trust, empathy, dominance) < 0.001; p (credibility) $= 0.009$) and Levene's test of homogeneity ($p = 0.157$)) were violated, the use of Student's t-test rendered inappropriate. Therefore, we picked the Welch's t-test for independent samples fur further analysis.

Impact on visible physical disability and gender. The comparison between the portrayal of physical disability (PCA 2&4) and no visible disability (PCA 1&3) is summarized in Table 2 and depicts the results of the Welch's t-test (non-disabled vs. disabled) with 120 participants that judged on the chatbots (between subject design).

In summary, the results show that **not**[1] depicting Ben's and Lena's physical disability had a small positive effect on the competence variable (Cohen's D (CD) = 0.388), a small negative effect on trust (CD = – 0.325), a medium negative effect

[1] The initial publication of this paper in the AIS eLibrary failed to include the negation in this sentence and thus inverted the statement.

Table 2 Welch's t-test comparing disabled versus. non-disabled avatar pictures

Non-disabled versus. disabled		t	df	P	Effect size	
Competence	Welch's t	2.13	103	0.036	Cohens d	0.388
Trust	Welch's t	− 1.78	114	0.078	Cohens d	− 0.325
Credibility	Welch's t	− 3.34	110	0.001	Cohens d	− 0.609
Empathy	Welch's t	− 15.72	118	< 0.001	Cohens d	− 2.870
Dominance	Welch's t	5.13	112	< 0.001	Cohens d	0.937

(CD = − 0.609) on credibility, and a large negative effect on empathy (CD = − 2.87). On the other hand, the perception of dominance was affected largely positively (CD = 0.937). Table 3 additionally presents the descriptive statistics of the variables under investigation.

For the analysis and answering of research questions, it is also of interest whether the gender of the avatar has an influence on the dependent variables. We thus conducted another Welch's t-Test comparing both PCAs' representing Ben with the other two showing Lena. The comparison shows again significant differences (Table 4).

As depicted, the female represSSentation has a small negative effect (CD = − 0.402) on perceived competence. So, Lena is perceived significantly less competent than Ben, although both PCAs mediate the same factual knowledge and differ exclusively regarding their profile picture. Besides, the female representation has a large negative effect on trust (CD = − 1.099), a medium negative effect on credibility (CD = − 0.556), and a small negative effect on empathy (CD = − 0.11). Moreover, the

Table 3 Descriptive statistics on disabled versus non-disabled pcas in comparison

	PCA	Comp	Trust	Cred	Empa	Domi
Mean	1&3	5.91	5.43	5.27	3.47	4.36
	2&4	5.50	5.66	5.68	5.91	3.49
Standard deviation	1&3	1.22	0.65	0.58	0.85	0.81
	2&4	0.82	0.78	0.77	0.85	1.03

Table 4 Welch's t-test comparing avatar pictures of ben versus lena

Ben 1+2 versus Lena 3+4		t	df	P	Effect size	
Competence	Welch's t	−2.200	0.117	0.030	Cohens d	−0.402
Trust	Welch's t	−6.019	0.117	< 0.001	Cohens d	−1.099
Credibility	Welch's t	−3.048	0.115	0.003	Cohens d	−0.556
Empathy	Welch's t	−0.600	0.116	0.550	Cohens d	−0.110
Dominance	Welch's t	−2.384	0.118	0.019	Cohens d	−0.435

Table 5 Welch's t-test comparing gender-sensitive with generic language

PCA 5 versus PCA 6		t	df	P	Effect size	
Competence	Welch's t	1.34	47	0.019	Cohens d	0.346
Trust	Welch's t	2.33	50	0.024	Cohens d	0.601
Credibility	Welch's t	2.61	49	0.012	Cohens d	0.673
Empathy	Welch's t	3.97	39	< 0 .001	Cohens d	1.024
Dominance	Welch's t	−4.52	58	< 0 .001	Cohens d	−1.166

female representation reveals a medium negative effect on the dominance variable (CD = – 0.435).

By conducting a factorial ANOVA analysis, we found no significant interaction effects for either of the five measured constructs between the two factors of gender and (dis)ability.

Impact on gendering. Next, we compare the results between PCA5 and PCA6, which represent the use of gender-inclusive language and the usage of the generic masculinum for PCA Max, respectively. As Table 5 shows, using gender-inclusive language has a moderate positive effect (CD = 0.601) on the variable of competence. Similarly, the effect is also moderate (CD = 0.673) on the variable of credibility. The use of gender-inclusive language has a large positive effect on the variable of empathy (CD = 1.024). Also, the use of gender-inclusive language indicates a large negative effect (CD = – 1.166) on perceived dominance in our experiment.

We could not control for gender, as PCA5 and PCA6 showed both the same male person (Max) in the portrayal of the chat interface.

4.2 *Qualitative Results*

Both PCAs with and without displaying physical limitations appear competent to users because they provide supportive information on learning methods and offer video material beyond the textual conversation, guide the conversation, give detailed answers, and speak error-free. Regarding the comparison of Ben with/without the use of gender-inclusive language, fewer responses were given, but it can be seen that the PCA using gender-inclusive language appears competent because it *"visually exudes confidence"* and provides correct and detailed information. All chatbots were noted as not credible as human tutors, but the credibility of the information provided was confirmed. Students claim that PCAs displaying physical limitations appear empathetic since they embody inclusiveness and *"want others not to feel sorry about their disability"*. In contrast, the PCAs without physical limitations and those without using gender-inclusive language do appear less empathetic as they are perceived more egocentric and the conversation feels *"more mechanic"*. PCAs without displaying physical limitations appear dominant since they control the tone and *"do not allow users to steer the conversation"*.

5 Discussion

In this study, we investigated the effect of different avatar characteristics (gender, physical disability) and the usage of a gender-inclusive language style on six DVs.

Below, in Table 6, we summarize the confirmation (Bold) or rejection (Italics) of our hypotheses and document the eventually measured relations in our experiment.

Table 6 Table on experimental results

H1	The presentation of a physical limitation has a small effect size (Cohen's d = 0.388) and a significant negative impact ($p = 0.036$) on perceived competence
H2	The use of a female gender avatar also has a small effect size (Cohen's d = 0.402) and a significant negative impact ($p = 0.03$) on perceived competence
H3	The use of gender-inclusive language has a small effect size (Cohen's d = 0.346) and a positive but non-significant ($p = 0.186$) impact on perceived competence
H4	The embodiment of a physical limitation has a small effect size (Cohen's d = 0.325) and a significant positive impact ($p = 0.078$) on perceived trust
H5	The use of a female avatar image has a large effect size (Cohen's d = 1.099) and a highly significant ($p < 0.001$) negative impact on perceived trust
H6	The use of gender-inclusive language has a medium effect size (Cohen's d = 0.601) and a significant ($p = 0.024$) positive impact on perceived trust
H7	The embodiment of a physical limitation has a medium effect size (Cohen's d = 0.609) and a highly significant ($p = 0.001$) positive impact on perceived credibility
H8	The use of a female avatar also has a medium effect size (Cohen's d = 0.556) and a highly significant ($p = 0.003$) negative impact on perceived credibility
H9	The use of gender-inclusive language has a medium effect size (Cohen's d = 0.673) and a significant ($p = 0.012$) positive impact on perceived credibility
H10	The presentation of a physical limitation has a large effect size (Cohen's d = 0.939) and a highly significant ($p < 0.001$) negative impact on perceived dominance
H11	The use of a female avatar image has a small effect size (Cohen's d = 0.435) and a significant ($p = 0.019$) negative impact on perceived dominance
H12	Gender-inclusive language has a large effect size (Cohen's d = 1.166) and a highly significant ($p < 0.001$) negative impact on perceived dominance
H13	The portrayal of a physical limitation has a very large effect size (Cohen's d = 2.870) and a highly significant ($p < 0.001$) positive impact on perceived empathy
H14	The influence of a female avatar image has no statistically significant effect on perceived empathy ($p = 0.550$)
H15	The use of gender-inclusive language has a large effect size (Cohen's d = 1.024) and a highly significant ($p < 0.001$) positive impact on perceived empathy

The physical world abounds with biases towards people with disabilities, gender, and affinity (Fiske et al. 2007; Oh et al. 2019; Rohmer and Louvet, 2018; Trainer et al., 2020). Our study builds on initial evidence from Schlimbach and Robra-Bissantz (2022) that these biases also apply to virtual information systems like PCAs, consistent with CASA and social response theory (Nass and Moon 2000). The implications of these findings are relevant for the design of PCAs, chatbots, and other information systems, as inclusive design and its implications need to be considered from the outset.

Although positive discrimination in the virtual world offers the potential to represent diversity characteristics in avatar design, practical implementation is still limited (Schlimbach, Rinn, et al. 2022). However, PCAs can facilitate dialogic encounters between minorities, address discrimination, and contribute to the reflection on diversity (Gupta and Chen 2022; Lie et al. 2021). Our findings suggest that avatars should be designed carefully to enhance the perceived effectiveness of the PCA. For example, empathy has a positive effect on learners' success, but dominant behavior by a teacher has a negative impact on learners' motivation (Jiang and Zhang 2021; Tausch 2008). However, designing only toward desirable learning outcomes risks excluding diversity and perpetuating unconscious bias. We suggest increasing the visibility of different genders and avatars with physical disabilities in the PCA landscape to enhance diversity awareness and mitigate bias.

Our research implications are significant for designing and developing PCAs and other virtual information systems. By highlighting the impact of avatar design on users' perceptions, our findings underscore the importance of inclusive design practices from the outset. Designers and developers should consider the representation of diverse genders and visible physical disabilities in the PCA landscape to foster diversity awareness and mitigate bias. Furthermore, our study highlights the potential of PCAs to facilitate dialogic encounters, address discrimination, and promote reflection on diversity. Educators and policymakers can leverage this potential to create inclusive learning environments that promote empathy, trust, and credibility. By integrating inclusive design principles and fostering diversity awareness, PCAs and other information systems can play a crucial role in promoting equity and inclusivity in various contexts.

It is important to acknowledge some limitations of our study. First, our research focused on the visual portrayal of a physical disability and gender-sensitive language in PCAs within an educational context. However, avatars can possess various other characteristics, such as age, race, or clothing, which could also influence users' perceptions. Future research should explore the effects of these additional factors and their interactions to provide a more comprehensive understanding of avatar design and its impact on user perception. Second, our study was conducted with German university students, and the results may not generalize to other populations or cultural contexts. Replicating the experiments with diverse participant groups and in different cultural settings would enhance the external validity of the findings. Moreover, while our research focused on PCAs in educational settings, the implications of avatar design and inclusive language extend beyond education. Further investigations in different domains and target groups will contribute to a more comprehensive understanding of the potential limitations and benefits of diverse avatar representation. In addition, gender-inclusive language showed positive effects on the perceived trust and credibility of our PCAs, but the sample size for that specific t-test was below the calculated 90 probands in the a priori power analysis and should thus be repeated with a larger sample.

In summary, future studies could investigate how different avatar characteristics (e.g., age, race, clothing) impact the perceived effectiveness of a PCA and whether certain groups respond differently to manipulated factors. Mitigating social and algorithmic bias is particularly challenging since underrepresented characteristics and perceptions of diversity are context-specific and diverge widely between cultures, application fields, and target groups (Koopmans and Schaeffer 2017). Further studies are needed to address this challenge and promote inclusion and diversity in PCAs and other information systems. Designers and developers should mindfully consider social cues (Feine et al. 2019), i.e. gendering and inclusiveness to mitigate bias without harming variables relevant to learning with PCAs.

References

Al-Obaydi, L. (2019). Cultural Diversity, Awareness and Teaching: A Study in an EFL Context. Journal of Asia TEFL, 16, 987–995. https://doi.org/10.18823/asiatefl.2019.16.3.15.987

Bernagozzi, M., Srivastava, B., Rossi, F., & Usmani, S. (2021). Gender Bias in Online Language Translators: Visualization, Human Perception, and Bias/Accuracy Tradeoffs. IEEE Internet Computing, 25(5), 53–63. https://doi.org/10.1109/MIC.2021.3097604

Boban, I., & Hinz, A. (2009). Der Index für Inklusion: Lernen und Teilhabe in der Schule der Vielfalt entwickeln. Sozial Extra, 33(9–10), 12–16. https://doi.org/10.1007/s12054-009-0078-4

Bodrunova, S. S., Koltsova, O., Følstad, A., Halpin, H., Kolozaridi, P., Yuldashev, L., Smoliarova, A., & Niedermayer, H. (Eds.). (2019). Internet Science: INSCI 2018 International Workshops, St. Petersburg, Russia, October 24–26, 2018, Revised Selected Papers (Vol. 11551). Springer International Publishing. https://doi.org/10.1007/978-3-030-17705-8

Bonaccio, S., Connelly, C. E., Gellatly, I. R., Jetha, A., & Martin Ginis, K. A. (2020). The Participation of People with Disabilities in the Workplace Across the Employment Cycle: Employer Concerns and Research Evidence. Journal of Business and Psychology, 35(2), 135–158. https://doi.org/10.1007/s10869-018-9602-5

Braun, F., Oelkers, S., Rogalski, K., Bosak, J., & Sczesny, S. (2007). "Aus Gründen der Verständlichkeit ...": Der Einfluss generisch maskuliner und alternativer Personenbezeichnungen auf die kognitive Verarbeitung von Texten. Psychologische Rundschau, 58(3), 183–189. https://doi.org/10.1026/0033-3042.58.3.183

Buchan, N. R., Croson, R. T. A., & Solnick, S. (2008). Trust and gender: An examination of behavior and beliefs in the Investment Game. Journal of Economic Behavior & Organization, 68(3–4), 466–476. https://doi.org/10.1016/j.jebo.2007.10.006

Cafaro, A., Vilhjálmsson, H. H., & Bickmore, T. (2016). First impressions in human-agent virtual encounters. ACM Transactions on Computer-Human Interaction, 23(4), 1–40. https://doi.org/10.1145/2940325

Cheng, J. T., Tracy, J. L., Foulsham, T., Kingstone, A., & Henrich, J. (2013). Two ways to the top: Evidence that dominance and prestige are distinct yet viable avenues to social rank and influence. Journal of Personality and Social Psychology, 104(1), 103–125. https://doi.org/10.1037/a0030398

Chubb, J., & Derrick, G. E. (2020). The impact a-gender: Gendered orientations towards research Impact and its evaluation. Palgrave Communications, 6(1), Article 1. https://doi.org/10.1057/s41599-020-0438-z

Cowell, A. J., & Stanney, K. M. (2005). Manipulation of non-verbal interaction style and demographic embodiment to increase anthropomorphic computer character credibility. International Journal of Human-Computer Studies, 62(2), 281–306. https://doi.org/10.1016/j.ijhcs.2004.11.008

Domsch, M. E., Ladwig, D. H., & Weber, F. C. (2019). UNCONSCIOUS BIAS – Eine Einführung zu Vorurteilen im Arbeitsleben. In M. E. Domsch, D. H. Ladwig, & F. C. Weber (Eds.), Vorurteile im Arbeitsleben (pp. 3–20). Springer Berlin Heidelberg. https://doi.org/10.1007/978-3-662-59232-8_1

Feine, J., Gnewuch, U., Morana, S., & Maedche, A. (2019). A Taxonomy of Social Cues for Conversational Agents. International Journal of Human-Computer Studies, 132, 138–161. https://doi.org/10.1016/j.ijhcs.2019.07.009

Feine, J., Gnewuch, U., Morana, S., & Maedche, A. (2020). Gender Bias in Chatbot Design: Vol. 11970 LNCS (p. 93). Scopus. https://doi.org/10.1007/978-3-030-39540-7_6

Felder, F. (2017). Inklusion und Arbeit: Was steht auf dem Spiel? In C. Misselhorn & H. Behrendt (Eds.), Arbeit, Gerechtigkeit und Inklusion (pp. 99–119). J.B. Metzler. https://doi.org/10.1007/978-3-476-04374-0_7

Fiske, S. T., Cuddy, A. J. C., & Glick, P. (2007). Universal dimensions of social cognition: Warmth and competence. Trends in Cognitive Sciences, 11(2), 77–83. https://doi.org/10.1016/j.tics.2006.11.005

Formanowicz, M. M., Cisłak, A., Horvath, L. K., & Sczesny, S. (2015). Capturing socially motivated linguistic change: How the use of gender-fair language affects support for social initiatives in Austria and Poland. Frontiers in Psychology, 6. https://doi.org/10.3389/fpsyg.2015.01617

Fossa, F., & Sucameli, I. (2022). Gender Bias and Conversational Agents: An ethical perspective on Social Robotics. Science and Engineering Ethics, 28(3). Scopus. https://doi.org/10.1007/s11948-022-00376-3

Francisco, M. P. B., Hartman, M., & Wang, Y. (2020). Inclusion and Special Education. Education Sciences, 10(9), 238. https://doi.org/10.3390/educsci10090238

Früh, W., & Wünsch, C. (2009). Empathie und Medienempathie. Publizistik, 54(2), 191–215. https://doi.org/10.1007/s11616-009-0038-9

Furchheim, P., Monard, F., Uebersax, H.-P., Müller, M., Hannich, F., & Kaya, T. (2021). Chatbot Studie '21. Institut für Marketing Management. https://www.intre.cc/wp-content/uploads/2021/09/Chatbot-Studie-2021_aiaibot_ZHAW.pdf

Gay, F. (Ed.). (2000). DISG-Persönlichkeitsprofil: Verstehen Sie sich selbst besser , schöpfen Sie Ihre Möglichkeiten aus, entdecken Sie Ihre Stärken und Schwächen; [mit dem Original DISG-Testmaterial zur Selbstauswertung] (16. Aufl., 106.-110 Tsd). DISG-Training.

Gnewuch, U., Morana, S., Adam, M., & Maedche, A. (2018). "The Chatbot is typing …" – The Role of Typing Indicators in Human-Chatbot Interaction.

Goffman, E. (1986). Stigma: Notes on the management of spoiled identity (1. Touchstone ed). Simon & Schuster.

Gong, L. (2008). How social is social responses to computers? The function of the degree of anthropomorphism in computer representations. Computers in Human Behavior, 24(4), 1494–1509. https://doi.org/10.1016/j.chb.2007.05.007

Greenberg, D., Warrier, V., Allison, C., & Baron-Cohen, S. (2018). Testing the Empathizing-Systemizing theory of sex differences and the Extreme Male Brain theory of autism in half a million people. Proceedings of the National Academy of Sciences, 115, 1811032115. https://doi.org/10.1073/pnas.1811032115

Gupta, S., & Chen, Y. (2022). Supporting Inclusive Learning Using Chatbots? A Chatbot-Led Interview Study. Journal of Information Systems Education, 33(1), 98–108.

Halcomb, E., & Hickman, L. (2015). Mixed methods research. Nursing Standard, 29(32), 41–47. https://doi.org/10.7748/ns.29.32.41.e8858
Hannover, B., & Wolter, I. (2019). Geschlechtsstereotype: Wie sie entstehen und sich auswirken. In B. Kortendiek, B. Riegraf, & K. Sabisch (Eds.), Handbuch Interdisziplinäre Geschlechterforschung (pp. 201–210). Springer Fachmedien. https://doi.org/10.1007/978-3-658-12496-0_16
Heise, E. (2000). Sind Frauen mitgemeint? Eine empirische Untersuchung zum Verständnis des generischen Maskulinums und seiner Alternativen. Sprache & Kognition, 19(1/2), 3–13. https://doi.org/10.1024//0253-4533.19.12.3
Hobert, S., & Meyer von Wolff, R. (2019, February 24). Say Hello to Your New Automated Tutor – A Structured Literature Review on Pedagogical Conversational Agents. 14th International Conference on Wirtschaftsinformatik, Siegen, Germany.
Holoien, D. S. (2013). Do Differences Make A Difference? The Effects of Diversity on Learning, Intergroup Outcomes, and Civic Engagement. Princetion University Reports, 18.
Hu, T., Xu, A., Liu, Z., You, Q., Guo, Y., Sinha, V., Luo, J., & Akkiraju, R. (2018). Touch Your Heart: A Tone-aware Chatbot for Customer Care on Social Media. 1–12. https://doi.org/10.1145/3173574.3173989
Jaffer, S., & Ma, L. (2015). Preschoolers show less trust in physically disabled or obese informants. Frontiers in Psychology, 5. https://doi.org/10.3389/fpsyg.2014.01524
Jiang, A. L., & Zhang, L. J. (2021). University Teachers' Teaching Style and Their Students' Agentic Engagement in EFL Learning in China: A Self-Determination Theory and Achievement Goal Theory Integrated Perspective. Frontiers in Psychology, 12, 704269. https://doi.org/10.3389/fpsyg.2021.704269
Khosrawi-Rad, B., Rinn, H., Schlimbach, R., Gebbing, P., Yang, X., Lattemann, C., Markgraf, D., & Robra-Bissantz, S. (2022). Conversational Agents in Education – A Systematic Literature Review. ECIS 2022 Research Papers. https://aisel.aisnet.org/ecis2022_rp/18
Köhnken, G. (1999). Glaubwürdigkeit. In R. Lempp, G. Schütze, & G. Köhnken (Eds.), Forensische Psychiatrie und Psychologie des Kindes- und Jugendalters (pp. 318–341). Steinkopff. https://doi.org/10.1007/978-3-662-21913-3_29
Koopmans, R., & Schaeffer, M. (2017). Statistical and Perceived Diversity and Their Impacts on Neighborhood Social Cohesion in Germany, France and the Netherlands. https://doi.org/10.31235/osf.io/64p3z
Landy, D., & Sigall, H. (1974). Beauty is talent: Task evaluation as a function of the performer's physical attractiveness. Journal of Personality and Social Psychology, 29(3), 299–304. https://doi.org/10.1037/h0036018
Lee, J.-E. R., & Nass, C. I. (Eds.). (2010). Trust in Computers: The Computers-Are-Social-Actors (CASA) Paradigm and Trustworthiness Perception in Human-Computer Communication. IGI Global. https://doi.org/10.4018/978-1-61520-901-9.ch001
Lembcke, T.-B., Diederich, S., & Brendel, A. B. (2020). Supporting Design Thinking Through Creative and Inclusive Education Facilitation: The Case of Anthropomorphic Conversational Agents for Persona Building. ECIS 2020 Research Papers. https://aisel.aisnet.org/ecis2020_rp/27
Lie, R., Boogaard, B., & Witteveen, L. (2021). Towards design principles for diversity sensitive learning (pp. 134–146). https://doi.org/10.4324/9781003112525-12
Light, S. N. (2019). The Heterogeneity of Empathy: Possible Treatment for Anhedonia? Frontiers in Psychiatry, 10, 185. https://doi.org/10.3389/fpsyt.2019.00185
Luhmann, N. (1989). Vertrauen: Ein Mechanismus der Reduktion sozialer Komplexität (3., durchgesehene Aufl). F. Enke.
Manzanero, A. L., Alemany, A., Recio, M., Vallet, R., & Aróztegui, J. (2015). Evaluating the Credibility of Statements Given by Persons With Intellectual Disability. [Evaluación de la credibilidad de relatos de personas con discapacidad intelectual]. Anales de Psicología, 31(1), 338–344. https://doi.org/10.6018/analesps.31.1.166571

Miyauchi, H. (2020). A Systematic Review on Inclusive Education of Students with Visual Impairment. Education Sciences, 10(11), 346. https://doi.org/10.3390/educsci10110346

Nass, C., & Moon, Y. (2000). Machines and Mindlessness: Social Responses to Computers. Journal of Social Issues, 56(1), 81–103. https://doi.org/10.1111/0022-4537.00153

Oh, D., Buck, E. A., & Todorov, A. (2019). Revealing Hidden Gender Biases in Competence Impressions of Faces. Psychological Science, 30(1), 65–79. https://doi.org/10.1177/095679761 8813092

Pohl, R. F. (Ed.). (2016). Cognitive Illusions (0 ed.). Psychology Press. https://doi.org/10.4324/978 1315696935

Rohmer, O., & Louvet, E. (2018). Implicit stereotyping against people with disability. Group Processes & Intergroup Relations, 21(1), 127–140. https://doi.org/10.1177/1368430216638536

Schlimbach, R., & Robra-Bissantz, S. (2022). Exploring the Impact of Inclusive PCA Design on Perceived Competence, Trust and Diversity. SIGHCI 2022 Proceedings. https://aisel.aisnet.org/sighci2022/9

Schlimbach, R., Khosrawi-Rad, B., & Robra-Bissantz, S. (2022, June 26). Deriving Design Knowledge for eLearning Companions to Support International Students. 35th Bled eConference - Digital Restructuring and Human (Re)Action, Bled, Slovenia. https://doi.org/10.18690/um.fov.4.2022.2

Schlimbach, R., Rinn, H., Markgraf, D., & Robra-Bissantz, S. (2022). A Literature Review on Pedagogical Conversational Agent Adaptation. PACIS 2022 Proceedings. https://aisel.aisnet.org/pacis2022/20

Schmid, D., Staehelin, D., Bucher, A., Dolata, M., & Schwabe, G. (2022). Does Social Presence Increase Perceived Competence? Evaluating Conversational Agents in Advice Giving through a Vido-Based Survey. 26, ACM Human Computer Interaction(6). https://doi.org/10.1145/349 2845

Schuetzler, R. M., Giboney, J. S., Grimes, G. M., & Nunamaker, J. F. (2018). The Influence of Conversational Agents on Socially Desirable Responding. In Hawaii International Conference on System Sciences 2018 (HICSS-51). https://aisel.aisnet.org/hicss-51/cl/hci/8

Schweer, M. K. W. (1996). Vertrauen in der pädagogischen Beziehung (1. Aufl). Huber.

Schweer, M. K. W. (2000). Vertrauen als basale Komponente der Lehrer-Schüler-Interaktion. In M. K. W. Schweer (Ed.), Lehrer-Schüler-Interaktion (pp. 129–138). VS Verlag für Sozialwissenschaften. https://doi.org/10.1007/978-3-322-97477-8_6

Sczesny, S., Formanowicz, M., & Moser, F. (2016). Can Gender-Fair Language Reduce Gender Stereotyping and Discrimination? Frontiers in Psychology, 7. https://doi.org/10.3389/fpsyg.2016.00025

Seeger, A.-M., Pfeiffer, J., & Hinzl, A. (2018). Deigning Anthropromorphic Conversational Agents: Development and Empirical Evaluation of a Design Framework.

Shifrer, D. (2013). Stigma of a Label: Educational Expectations for High School Students Labeled with Learning Disabilities. Journal of Health and Social Behavior, 54(4), 462–480. https://doi.org/10.1177/0022146513503346

Simmel, G., Rammstedt, O., & Simmel, G. (1992). Soziologie: Untersuchungen über die Formen der Vergesellschaftung (1. Aufl). Suhrkamp.

Soper, D. (2023). Free A-priori Sample Size Calculator for Student t-Tests—Free Statistics Calculators. https://www.danielsoper.com/statcalc/calculator.aspx?id=47

Striebing, C. (2021, May 18). Karriere-Killer Gender Bias. https://blog.iao.fraunhofer.de/karriere-killer-gender-bias/

Tajfel, H., & Turner, J. C. (1979). An Integrative Theory of Intergroup Conflict. In W. G. Austin & S. Worchel (Eds.), The Social Identity Theory of Intergroup Behavior (pp. 33–47). Brooks/Cole Pub. Co.

Tausch, R. (2008). Personzentriertes Verhalten von Lehrern in Unterricht und Erziehung. In M. K. W. Schweer (Ed.), Lehrer-Schüler-Interaktion (pp. 155–176). VS Verlag für Sozialwissenschaften. https://doi.org/10.1007/978-3-531-91104-5_6

Toader, D.-C., Boca, G., Toader, R., Măcelaru, M., Toader, C., Ighian, D., & Rădulescu, A. T. (2020). The Effect of Social Presence and Chatbot Errors on Trust. Sustainability, 12(1), Article 1. https://doi.org/10.3390/su12010256

Trainer, T., Taylor, J., & Stanton, C. (2020, November 18). Choosing the Best Robot for the Job: Affinity Bias in Human-Robot Interaction. https://doi.org/10.1007/978-3-030-62056-1_41

Vervecken, D., & Hannover, B. (2012). Ambassadors of gender equality? How use of pair forms versus masculines as generics impacts perception of the speaker: Perception of speakers of gender fair language. European Journal of Social Psychology, 42(6), 754–762. https://doi.org/10.1002/ejsp.1893

Weber, F., Rüttimann, D., Wambsganss, T., & Söllner, M. (2021, December). Pedagogical Agents for Interactive Learning: A Taxonomy of Conversational Agents in Education.

Wirth, W. (1999). Methodologische und konzeptionelle Aspekte der Glaubwürdigkeitsforschung. In Glaubwürdigkeit in der Marketingkommunikation: Konzeption, Einflussfaktoren und Wirkungspotenzial. (pp. 47–66). Deutscher Universitätsverlag.

Wirtz, M. A. (2021). Maskulinität. In Dorsch Lexikon der Psychologie. https://dorsch.hogrefe.com/stichwort/maskulinitaet

Ydo, Y. (2020). Inclusive education: Global priority, collective responsibility. PROSPECTS, 49(3), 97–101. https://doi.org/10.1007/s11125-020-09520-y

Zabel, S., & Otto, S. (2021). Bias in, Bias Out – the Similarity-Attraction Effect Between Chatbot Designers and Users: Vol. 12764 LNCS (p. 197). Scopus. https://doi.org/10.1007/978-3-030-78468-3_13

Ensuring Energy Affordability Through Digital Technology: A Research Model and Intervention Design

Saskia Bluhm, Philipp Staudt, Christina Speck, and Christof Weinhardt

Abstract In order to ensure energy affordability, we propose a design-oriented behavioral research study with the aim of helping low-income tenants to develop an efficient energy behavior by increasing their energy self-efficacy. We propose to compare different digital interventions in field tests to understand, in an un filtered way, what helps low-income tenants to be able to reduce their energy costs. We thereby contribute towards understanding how the vulnerable group of low-income tenants with their limitations and needs regarding their energy consumption behavior can be effectively supported digitally. In addition, we con tribute initial measurement instruments for energy worries, energy literacy and energy self-efficacy to evaluate the effects of digital interventions.

Keywords Self-efficacy · Energy justice · Digital intervention · Green IS

1 Motivation

While increasing energy access has arguably led to higher living standards for billions of people (Energy Access Targets Working Group (2016)), the rising energy costs have also widened the gap between poor and rich (Wewerinke-Singh (2022)). Several influencing factors lead to a higher risk of energy poverty for low-income households, such as higher incidence of energy cutoffs due to the inability to pay their bill: *First*, while economies are expanding their renewable energy generation as part of a

S. Bluhm (✉) · C. Speck · C. Weinhardt
Institute of Information Systems and Marketing, Karlsruhe Institute of Technology, Karlsruhe, Germany
e-mail: christina.speck@kit.edu

C. Weinhardt
e-mail: weinhardt@kit.edu

P. Staudt
University of Oldenburg, Oldenburg, Germany
e-mail: philipp.staudt@uol.de

D. Beverungen et al. (eds.), *Conceptualizing Digital Responsibility for the Information Age*, Lecture Notes in Information Systems and Organisation 74,
https://doi.org/10.1007/978-3-031-80119-8_2

sustainable energy transition to combat climate change, opportunities are unevenly distributed in a world of an increasingly cheap, renewable energy supply (Levy and Patz (2015)). On the one hand, wealthy homeowners can become self-sufficient by using, for example, photovoltaic (PV) panels, smart home technology (including smart meters) and battery systems. On the other hand, under-resourced tenants remain dependent on the electric grid, which exposes them to further rising wholesale prices caused, for instance, by the necessarily rising prices of fossil fuels due to carbon pricing. *Second*, the currently rising energy prices have a stronger effect on poorer households, which is shown by various studies proving that the relative cost-of-living increase for the poorest households has been larger than for the richest households in different countries (Zhao et al. (2022)). *Third*, low-income households might not be able to get favorable retail contracts based on their poor credit rating. *And fourth*, previous studies show that low-income residents often obtain lower levels of energy literacy (EL), meaning that they might not be aware of their options to reduce their energy costs (van den Broek (2019), Richards et al. (2018)). This may also prevent them from understanding government programs designed to help them (Adams et al. (2022)). These inequities across socioeconomic groups underscore the need for new approaches for advancing energy transitions that address distributive justice (costs and benefits) and recognition justice (vulnerable groups) (Sovacool et al. (2019)) in order to reduce energy poverty and mitigate climate change at the same time. It has been shown that if adequately designed, Information Systems (IS) have the power to induce sustainable (economical and environmental) behavioral changes (Elliot (2011), Melville (2010)). Given its disciplinary purview, it is therefore important and timely for us to confront our responsibility as Green IS scholars to find ways to mitigate the negative consequences of the energy transition for poorer households, i.e. helping to ensure energy affordability for all while at the same time reducing carbon emissions (Mihale-Wilson et al. (2022)). The current study is part of a bigger research project, in which we aim to support low-income tenants—as opposed to homeowners, who have more options when it comes to becoming more energy efficient—to develop an efficient energy behavior by using low-threshold smart meters and an accompanying web-based app. Within the current study, we present the first steps of this full study. Specifically, here we (1) present the theoretical foundations and the targeted research gap of our research study, (2) derive hypotheses and the describe the resulting research model, (3) report on the empirical results towards measurement instruments for energy worries (EW), energy self-efficacy (ESE) and EL.

2 Prior Research and Theoretical Background

In recent years, there has been an increased awareness of ensuring energy affordability within society and politics. Due to the increases in energy costs in 2022, the proportion of households at risk of energy poverty increased even in wealthier countries like Germany (Henger and Stockhausen (2022)). There is a variety of definitions for the term *energy poverty*. For our purposes, it is useful to understand energy poverty as a situation in which households are not able to adequately access required energy services in their homes such as heating, cooking and lightning at affordable costs (Pye et al. (2017), Turai et al. (2021)). We thus understand energy affordability as the counterpart of energy poverty. Following previous work describing the drivers of energy poverty (e.g., Pye et al. (2017)), we present a non-exhaustive overview of influencing factors that lead to energy poverty in Fig. 1 and show where we add value with our study. On the left side of Fig. 1, the three main drivers identified (low income, poor energy efficiency and high energy bills) are shown as a circle, as they individually lead to energy poverty, but also influence each other. Furthermore, they are influenced by additional factors, which are shown by the blue boxes connected to the respective main factors. Since low income is fixed for the purpose of this study, further factors influencing low income are omitted. To the right of the factors, red-bordered gray boxes list exemplary studies that relate to the respective factor and either focus on low-income households or use (non-)digital interventions. In the following, we describe those factors and related studies in more detail to finally address the resulting research gap.

High energy bills are caused by the level of energy consumption and energy prices and can be influenced by energy policies like financial incentive programs. High energy bills are especially damning for low-income tenants as affording for energy makes up a larger share of their budget and as they have no option of supplying themselves with low-cost renewable generation or of changing the apartment structure, which potentially causes high baseline energy consumption (Gawel et al. (2015), Kröger et al. (2022)). Various studies elaborate on this by concentrating on different influencing factors of energy costs for low-income households, e.g., Murray & Mills

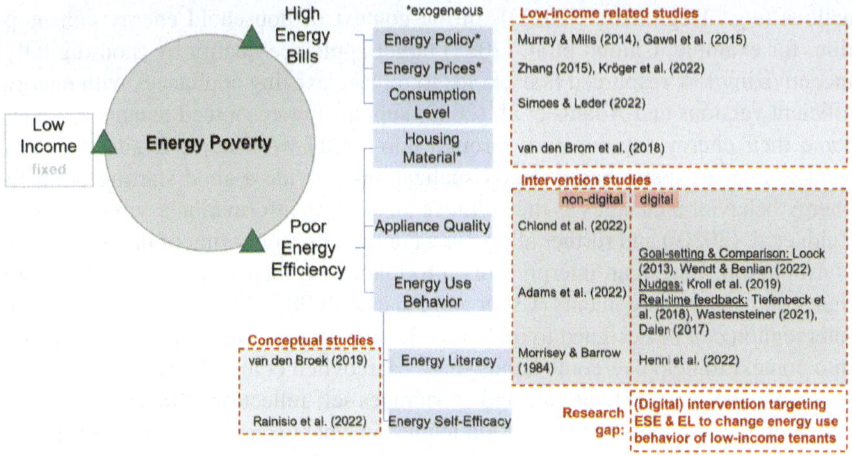

Fig. 1 Relevant selected drivers influencing energy poverty

(2014) on energy policy, Zhang (2015) on energy prices, Simões & Leder (2022) on energy consumption levels at home, van den Brom et al. (2018)) on housing material (red-bordered gray box in the upper right of Fig. 1). While housing material, energy policies and energy prices are exogenous and cannot be influenced by tenants, they can influence their consumption level, which has links to energy efficiency that can be influenced as a driver of the energy bill. If real-time pricing and time-of-use tariffs become widespread in the future, the energy price to be paid will also be directly influenceable by tenants by shifting their energy consumption to times when energy is cheaper. In the long term, it is therefore necessary to equip them with the relevant knowledge about their energy consumption to enable them to react to these price signals.

Energy efficiency itself is driven by energy use behavior, the quality of the used appliances and the housing material (e.g., insulation). As people with low income have limited options regarding their housing choices, are not able to improve insulation or install PV panels and heat pumps, their energy efficiency suffers due to material factors (e.g., Sovacool et al. (2019)). In addition to such material factors, people's energy use behavior might lead to an unnecessary high consumption level and therefore poor energy efficiency. It has been shown that households have limited knowledge about their energy consumption at home and therefore do not know how to be more energy efficient (e.g., Boateng et al. (2020), Hernández (2016), van den Broek (2019)). As depicted in the lower red-bordered gray box on the right in Fig. 1, there are previous studies, which target an improvement of energy efficiency through interventions (e.g., Morrisey and Barrow (1984)).

Intervention can be defined as "purposeful action by an agent to create change" (Midgley (2000), p.156). There are digital and non-digital interventions, which are often designed for changing certain behavioral patterns (e.g., Michie et al. (2015)). This is done by including behavior-based incentives to motivate users to take certain actions (e.g., Degirmenci (2021)). In the context of household energy consumption, for example, Chlond et al. (2022) target appliance quality by (non-digitally) incentivizing low-resourced households to replace existing appliances with energy-efficient versions and Adams et al. (2022) support low-resourced tenants to understand their energy use behavior through non-digital workshops. Digital interventions like smart meter based data visualizations provide a good starting point for energy behavioral changes as they remove an existing information asymmetry (e.g., Zeidi et al. (2020)) and further allow for a continuous monitoring of the own energy consumption. Users can interpret this information on their own to create or revise their competence judgements (Usher and Pajares (2008)). To go one step further, an intervention can be designed to include reflection aspects. Reflection puts an action into context to help overcome habits (e.g., Marcovitch et al. (2008)). This supports users to make sense of their data and encourages self-reflection of their (energy use) behavior to equip them with better guidelines on what to change. To go even further, a third stage of intervention can be designed by including active support elements. Thereby, users are not on their own in the evaluation of their behavior, but receive external support, like supervision or concrete recommendations. Previous studies show that this helps to reinforce the effect towards goal achievement (e.g., Knebel et al. (2009)). Recent smart meter studies have been using a Design Science Research approach to develop user-centric digital interventions with the aim of changing the users' energy behavior, e.g., through goal-setting and comparison functionalities (Loock et al. (2013), Wendt and Benlian (2022)), digital nudges (Kroll et al. (2019)) or real-time feedback (Tiefenbeck et al. (2018), Wastensteiner et al. (2021), Dalén and Krämer (2017)).

Energy literacy has previously been studied as an antecedent of energy behavior at home, but existing studies struggle to generate energy behavior change by solely focusing on increasing EL (van den Broek (2019)). A reason for this could be the lack of a specific and concrete definition of EL related to the household consumption context. EL is often defined broadly and includes, for example, knowledge about energy sources (DeWaters and Powers (2013)), which is not relevant when analysing household energy consumption. Therefore, we define EL based on previous definitions (e.g., van den Broek (2019), Martins et al. (2020)), but specific to household energy consumption as *the knowledge and expertise regarding personal household energy consumption.*

Self-efficacy has been introduced by Bandura (1977) as an antecedent of behavior and can be adapted to different contexts. Self-efficacy describes the confidence in personal capabilities and is related to the perceived individual skills and the ability to handle new emerging situations, i.e., the ease of performing a certain behavior, which is influenced by factors like prior experiences. According to Bandura (1986), there are four different sources of self-efficacy, which are (1) mastery experiences (own previous performance in a certain context), (2) vicarious experiences of observing others or putting one's performance into relation, (3) verbal persuasions received from others and (4) emotional and physiological states such as stress or mood. Therefore, self-efficacy can be explicitly strengthened by addressing these antecedents, which makes it powerful when behavioral changes, like in our case, are targeted (Bandura (1977), Pakarinen et al. (2017)). Self efficacy has been conceptualized in various contexts within the IS literature. Early on, it was used to describe the behavioral intention to use a system, similar to the technology acceptance model. The first conceptualization to the IS domain was framed as computer self-efficacy and a related construct is introduced in Compeau and Higgins (1995). While their construct is aimed at a particular domain of self-efficacy, the authors develop their scale closely to its original conceptualization by Bandura (1986). Agarwal et al. (2000) provide an overview of a broad range of studies employing the construct of computer self-efficacy and Thatcher and Perrewe (2002) study antecedents of computer self-efficacy empirically. Since then, IS scholars have used self-efficacy conceptualizations in other contexts. For instance, Kankanhalli et al. (2005) introduce knowledge self-efficacy as an antecedent to the likelihood of contributing to knowledge repositories, Keith et al. (2015) introduce mobile-computing self-efficacy to explain trust in location-based mobile apps and Spruill et al. (2021) conceptualize creative self-efficacy as an antecedent to problem solving skills. In the energy domain, Lee and Tanusia

(2016) show that energy education and ESE lead to more sustainable energy behavioral intentions. Rainisio et al. (2022) even show that the domain-specific ESE leads to actual energy saving behavior, but do not provide an intervention to target ESE (conceptual studies on the left of Fig. 1). Just as for EL, there is no uniform definition for ESE. Previous studies define the concept either more broadly (e.g., Lee and Tanusia (2016)) or within another (e.g., work) context (Zierler et al. (2017)), which makes a specific definition of the concept necessary. Based on these previous definitions of ESE (e.g., Lee and Tanusia (2016), Zierler et al. (2017)) and the guidelines of Bandura (2006), we therefore define ESE within our concrete context as *the confidence in one's own ability to be energy efficient at home.*

Research gap While we have identified a variety of studies either highlighting disadvantages for low-income households or using (digital) interventions to help people in general with regard to their energy consumption, none of them makes the link. Particularly, no study specifically designs and evaluates digital interventions considering the circumstances of low-income tenants or seeking to strengthen their EL and ESE in order to bring about behavior change with respect to their energy use. In contrast to richer households, these households face special challenges and greater limitations in their efforts to reduce (the risk of) energy poverty. Mani et al. (2013), for example, state that low-income households have less cognitive bandwidth available that can be used to focus on improving their (energy) literacy. While the material factors and energy prices are kept as fixed external constraints, which cannot be changed by an intervention study, our study targets ESE (and EL) of low-income tenants as antecedents of their energy behavior. Our aim is to improve low-income tenants' individual ESE and EL level with the consequence of an increased energy efficiency through customized digital interventions. For providing a helpful solution, which is being used, we aim to understand what is necessary to enable our specific target group of low-income tenants to develop an efficient energy behavior. As an addition to existing studies, we therefore derive and compare three digital interventions with an increasing size of intervention based on theory. In the current paper, we describe the theoretical basis, the research model and the results of necessary measurement scale developments.

3 Research Model and Hypotheses Development

We presume that digital interventions can be designed to achieve an efficient energy behavior for low-income tenants and the effect increases with the size of intervention.

In the following, we describe our research model in Fig. 2 and all underlying hypotheses. Previous studies have shown that IS activity intensity differs depending on the amount of provided helpful features. For example, Ableitner et al. (2020) have shown within energy communities that IS usage decreases when user functionalities within the IS were limited (in their case due to an increased price-setting automation). Another study found slightly higher IS activity intensity for prosumers (who could

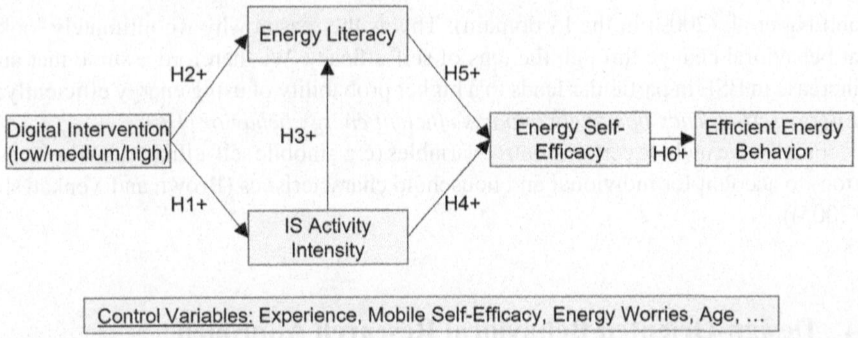

Fig. 2 Proposed research model

use more functionalities within the provided IS) compared to consumers (Richter et al. (2022)). We therefore hypothesize that a higher amount of helpful features within a user-centric developed IS, i.e., targeting low-income tenants, will increase IS activity intensity: *A higher size of the digital intervention will positively influence the IS activity intensity (H1).*

If the level of information depth within an IS increases, and thus more information asymmetry is removed, more cognitive processes can be triggered and the learning experience can be enhanced (e.g., Herrmann et al. (2021), Zeidi et al. (2020)). The information depth can be increased by increasing the amount of relevant functionalities included in the artifact. We thereby deduce that the inclusion of a higher amount of goal-oriented features can lead to greater EL increases: *A higher size of the digital intervention will positively influence energy literacy (H2).*

In order for any effects to be triggered, the IS must of course be used in the first place. It has been shown that using an IS can lead to higher EL (e.g., Henni et al. (2022)) and (educational) interventions in general have been shown to have positive effects on EL (Morrisey & Barrow (1984)). Therefore, we can assume that the effect on energy awareness and knowledge is higher if the IS activity intensity, i.e., the amount of using the IS, is higher: *IS activity intensity will positively influence energy literacy (H3).*

We further assume that IS activity intensity also boosts the users' confidence in the presented context. This is supported, for example, by Dillon et al. (2003) showing that.

the amount of using a computer leads to higher levels of computer self-efficacy: *IS activity intensity will positively influence energy self-efficacy (H4).* Studies in other domains have looked at antecedents to self-efficacy finding that an increase in literacy leads to an increase in self-efficacy (e.g., for financial literacy and financial self-efficacy Danes and Haberman (2007)), which is why we hypothesize: *Energy literacy will positively influence energy self-efficacy (H5).*

Self-efficacy is a frequently used construct in behavioral research and has been proven to be a precursor of behavioral change in different areas (e.g., Rainisio et al. (2022), Zierler et al. (2017), Białynicki-Birula et al. (2022) in the energy domain and Ng et al. (2009) in the IS domain). This is the reason why we ultimately look at behavioral change through the lens of self-efficacy. We therefore assume that an increase in ESE in particular leads to a higher probability of using energy efficiently: *Energy self-efficacy positively impacts efficient energy behavior (H6).*

Finally, we include certain control variables (e.g., mobile self-efficacy, EW, education) to account for individual and household characteristics (Brown and Venkatesh (2005)).

4 Design-Oriented Behavioral Research Approach

To test these hypotheses, we will conduct field tests, in which each participant is equipped with one of the three digital interventions. In addition, we will track the personal devel opments (e.g., regarding energy knowledge, confidence and behavior) of the participants during the intervention period. To be certain that the provided digital intervention in cludes features that help the target users (low-resourced tenants of apartment buildings) in achieving the goal (reaching an efficient energy behavior), we design the IS in a user-centric way. To accomplish the goal of providing user-centric IS, we make use of the methodologies of the "design-oriented behavioral research approach" (Maedche et al. (2021)). This approach offers the possibility of building on knowledge from behavioral sciences and design-oriented IS research. Hence, it can expand the knowledge base for understanding both the user behavior within the IS context and the broader user decisions within the domain under study, in our case energy decisions made offline in real-life. IS granting direct access to fine-grained behavioral data, as smart meter IS do for electricity consumption, offer the possibility of measuring the effects of behavioral interventions over time for a large number of users in the real-world with little interference between measurement activity and the object being measured (Loock et al. (2013)). For such IS, design-oriented behavioral research can therefore serve as important source of fun damental knowledge (Niiniluoto (1993)). We position our study as a "manipulation" study following the design research activity framework of Maedche et al. (2021), where creativity and ingenuity are needed for the treatment design. In a manipulation study, different manipulable causes of behavioral change are included through the designed artifact. This distinguishes this approach from traditional behavioral research, where the explanatory factors cannot be manipulated. While the design of a manipulation study comes with a high degree of freedom as the treatments are "creatively designed" (Maed che et al. (2021)), we aim to propose treatments that contribute to the overarching goal. Therefore, we propose to build on existing knowledge to design three treatments, which increase in their size of intervention (low, medium, high). This increase in intervention size can be achieved through the integration of an increasing number of features, which are target-oriented and tailored to the target group. The increasing size of intervention is not intended to be a measurable variable, but rather represents that the treatments are ranked by building on each other, meaning that the second (third) treatment includes all features of the first (second) treatment plus additional helpful features. In our case, these features should therefore be selected based on existing design knowledge regarding smart home energy apps (e.g., Bluhm et al. (2022), Ableitner et al. (2020), Herrmann et al. (2018)), include the limitations and requirements of low-income tenants, and target the previously mentioned four antecedents of self-efficacy (Bandura (1986)) to achieve the goal of efficient energy behavior. The first treatment shall represent the lowest size of digital intervention. In our context of energy use behavior, we propose a pure provision of information to provide transparency, i.e., to only include the high-resolution visualiza tions of individual energy consumption behavior. The second treatment of the artifact shall represent a medium sized digital intervention. In our context, it shall encourage the users' self-reflection of their energy use behavior (e.g., through goal settings and regular queries) to help them evaluate their behavior in context. The third treatment of the artifact shall finally represent the highest size of digital intervention. We propose to the provide supportive features like individual energy saving recommendations based on the current behavior.

5 Measurement Instruments

To ensure that we can actually measure the intervention effects, valid measurement scales are necessary for all variables under investigation. Based on screening the literature, we either use existing scales or develop appropriate scales by following the approach of MacKenzie and Podsakoff (2011). To check for the manipulation of the treatments, we include three items (Hauser et al. (2018)): "To what extent has the app given you transparency about your electricity consumption?" (to check for the lowest intervention dimension of providing information), "To what extent has the app encouraged you to self reflect on your electricity consumption behavior?" (to check for the medium intervention dimension of encouraging reflection) and "To what extent has the app supported you in improving your electricity consumption behavior?" (to check for the highest intervention dimension of providing active support). *IS activity intensity* is measured with objective measures, i.e., click behavior and time spent in the app. As the users' level of concern and characteristics like confidence for using the provided app will probably influence how they are able to interact with the IS (Keith et al. (2015)), measures for mobile computing self-efficacy, energy worries and previous experience with energy apps are included as control variables. For measuring *Mobile-computing self-efficacy*, the 4-item scale from Keith et al. (2015) is used and *prior energy app experience* is queried with a single-item. Energy worries have previously not been conceptualized, which is why we define EW as *the extent to which the expected cost of energy to be paid causes concern and affects personal well-being*. The *energy behavior* can be analyzed objectively by using the smart meter time series or subjectively through a survey-based approach. We have carefully diverged between the two approaches and finally decided to take the survey-based approach due to three main reasons. Firstly, it has the advantage of providing comparability regardless of how much energy can actually be saved in a household during the two week testing time period. Secondly, the conduction of the study during different environmental seasons does not influence the results for the same reason, which makes it possible to reach a larger sample size. Thirdly, we expect users to change their energy behavior for the sake of testing the app (e.g., using different appliances during the first few days just to know how much energy they consume). That would distort the benefit of the app when comparing the artificially increased power consumption at the beginning with the power consumption at the end of the test period. The energy behavior will therefore be queried by behavioral items (e.g., "Since using the app, I've been more efficient with electricity at home."), which still gives us the option to validate these statements with the real data. As mentioned in Chapter 2, EL and ESE are only broadly defined in literature and we did not find any adequate, validated scales of EL and ESE for the household energy use case. As self-efficacy as well as literacy measures can generally be adapted to different contexts (Bandura (2006)), we develop adequate measurement scales for the home energy consumption context. Another aim is to ensure that we use measurement instruments that distinct the constructs from each other, so that the instruments measure different things (i.e., for energy literacy and energy self-efficacy). This comparison is also a novelty in literature. First, we develop initial item sets meeting the construct definitions, which are then rated and improved by experts. Second, those item sets are pre-tested within an online survey. Third, the items for the final scales are selected and their validity is evaluated.

Initial item set development Based on the recommendations of DeVellis (2017), we develop initial item sets for the three constructs energy self-efficacy, energy literacy and energy worries according to the construct definitions, i.e., ESE: "the confidence in one's own ability to be energy efficient at home", EL: "the knowledge and expertise regarding personal household energy consumption", EW: "the extent to which the expected cost of energy to be paid causes concern and affects personal well-being". For developing the initial ESE item set, the guidelines from Bandura (2006) are further taken into account. Self-efficacy scales should also reflect the level of confidence to overcome certain obstacles, which make it more difficult to perform the required activity (Bandura (2006)). The items need to reflect the current state of confidence, should be phrased in terms of "can do" rather than "will do" and should ensure concordance to the outcome measure, in our case efficient energy behavior. Our initial item sets are then extended, specified and adjusted within a discussion of five researchers from an energy IS research group.

After the discussion, the full list of items is sent to the expert discussants to receive their individual scores on a 5-point Likert scale from 0 (not at all) to 4 (extremely good) for each of the items regarding their ability to measure the corresponding construct. The items which have scored an average of at least 3/4 in the expert rating are then selected for a pre-testing survey (Table 1). Six items for EW, nine items for EL, and seven items for ESE are selected.

The **online survey for item pretesting** consists of a short introduction, followed by six socio-demographic questions and the 22 selected items to be tested (Table 1) in random order. The pretest survey was not incentivized and distributed via various

Table 1 Remaining item list for the three tested constructs

Item	ESE	EL	EW
EW1 The current costs of electricity are having a negative impact on my			0.838
personal well-being			
EW2 Current electricity prices are forcing me to make severe comfort cuts			0.821
EW6 I am afraid of rising electricity costs			0.798
EW4 I currently have to reduce my electricity consumption so much that it			
is having a negative impact on my well-being			
EW3* I am afraid of not being able to pay my electricity bill soon	−0.103		0.730
EW5 I am concerned about the rising electricity prices	−0.129	0.693	
EL2 I know how much electricity my refrigerator consumes	0.882		
EL8 I know roughly what percentage of my electricity consumption is lighting	0.859		
EL3 I know my current average electricity price per kilowatt hour	0.718		
EL7* I know approximately how much [energy] electricity my household			
uses per year	0.141	0.663	
EL10 I know roughly what percentage of my electricity consumption is			
accounted for by entertainment devices		0.898	
EL9 I know approximately what percentage of my electricity consumption			
is heat supply	0.140	0.568	
EL1 Currently, I know very well about my personal electricity consumption			
behavior	0.399	0.472	
EL4 I know what I can do to reduce my electricity consumption	0.522	0.205	
EL11 I know what is used for heating in my household	0.299	0.113	
ESE1 I am confident that I am currently able to be electricity efficient at home	0.851		
ESE5 I have confidence in my ability to use electricity efficiently at home			
right now	0.844		
ESE8* I feel I am currently able to use electricity efficiently at home	0.863	−0.144	
ESE10* I am confident that I can currently use electricity efficiently			
at home even when I have other things to worry about	0.794		−0.150
ESE3 I think I have the knowledge I need to be electricity efficient at home			
right now	0.809		

(continued)

Table 1 (continued)

Item	ESE	EL	EW
ESE14 I am confident that I can currently be electricity efficient at home even			
if my electricity costs are calculated on a fixed basis	0.784		0.146
ESE12 I am confident that I can currently be electricity efficient at home even			
if I have to justify my electricity efficient behavior to others	0.629		−0.133
dropped, **included, *conditionally included**			

social media platforms. 159 persons started taking the survey, of which 128 fully completed it. Eight participants were dropped because they completed the survey in less than 120.

seconds, so it is assumed that they did not answer the survey carefully. Therefore, the an alyzed sample consists of 120 participants, which is above the commonly used threshold of 100 and within the range of three to ten participants per tested item (MacKenzie and Podsakoff (2011)). 53% of participants are male, the average age is 31.5 years (between 17 and 89 years). The majority of the sample lives in an apartment (87.5%), which is the category of people we aim to target for the full study. 46% of participants are in school or university, 49% are (self-)employed. While 51% of respondents take care of their electricity contract themselves, someone else is responsible for the rest.

Factor analysis To check whether the tested items form the three constructs we want to measure, a factor analysis is used, which has the goal to model the relationships between items with fewer factors (i.e., extract latent variables) and provides outcomes like inter-item-correlations between all individual items and factor loadings. For each construct, we would like to find a similarity between the items corresponding to this construct and a difference to items supposedly belonging to another construct. The Bartlett test shows a significant effect meaning that correlations are large enough to continue the analysis ($\chi\hat{}2 = 1508.883$, p-value $= 0.000$, df $= 190$) and the KMO factor adequacy test reveals a good mean sampling adequacy of 0.84 (Kaiser (1974)), which is large enough to run an exploratory factor analysis (EFA) (Tucker & MacCallum (1997)). To interpret the results of the factor analysis, we use a factor extraction where the number of factors to be extracted is given as input, followed by a factor rotation to obtain a simple structure and improve interpretability. Principal Component Analysis (PCA) or Principal Factor Analysis (PFA) can be chosen for factor extraction. PCA assumes that the common variance of the items makes up all of the total variance, while PFA distinguishes between common and unique variance. We choose PFA as it does not only explain why there are correlations among the individual items, but by including unique variance additionally acknowledges that the latent variables do not explain all the shared variance among items. To check whether the theoretical 3-factor structure (EW, EL, ESE) of our items can be confirmed non-theoretically and data-wise, we run a parallel factor analysis using a maximum likelihood procedure. The 3-factor structure can be proven by all tests, i.e., the parallel analysis suggests three factors, the scree plot in Fig. 3 shows three factors left of the elbow (Cattell (1966)) and the new KMO rule is fulfilled (three eigenvalues above 0.7). Next, we run the PFA with three factors to be extracted followed by a promax rotation, which does an orthogonal (uncorrelated) rotation and then translates the results into a simple oblique (correlated) factor solution (Hendrickson & White (1964)). The resulting pattern matrix (right side in Table 1) reveals which items to drop as they load higher on another construct (e.g., EL4, EL11), or load on two constructs and comparatively low on the targeted construct (e.g., EL1, EL9, ESE12, ESE14, EW5). The items EW3, EL7, ESE8 and ESE10 have small loadings to one of the other constructs, but still load high on the target construct, which is why they are not dropped. As we intend to keep the scales short, i.e., for not disturbing participants unnecessarily long and do not want to include redundant items, we analyze inter-item correlations to eliminate highly correlated items as they express the same thing. We find very high correlations between EL8 and EL10 (0.75) and between ESE1 and ESE3 (0.708). As EL10 loads negatively on ESE and ESE3 loads less on ESE than ESE1, we eliminate EL10 and ESE3 (which mentions knowledge and could therefore be confused with energy literacy).

Resulting scales Finally, the scales to be used within the field study consist of the items EL2, EL3, EL7, EL8 for EL with a high Cronbach's alpha of 0.84, the items ESE1, ESE5, ESE8, ESE10 for ESE with a high Cronbach's alpha of 0.88 and EW1, EW2, EW3, EW4, EW6 for EW with a high Cronbach's alpha of 0.89 (Table 1). EW3, EL7, ESE8 and ESE10 are conditionally included in the final measurement scales. The scales are generally to be validated within the field tests, with more attention to these items.

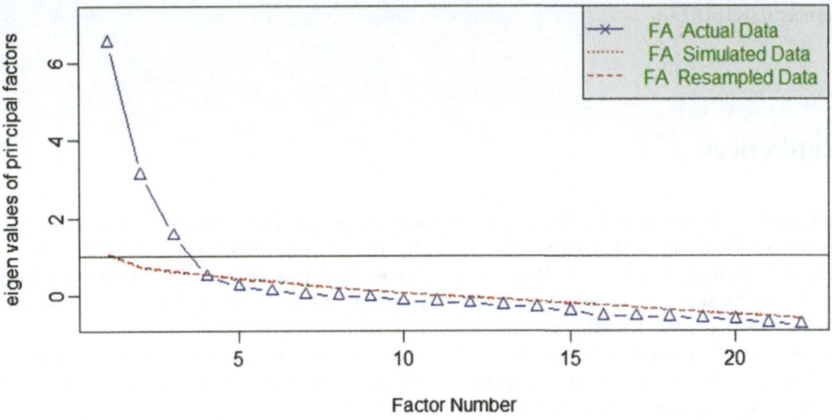

Fig. 3 Parallel analysis scree plot

6 Conclusion and Outlook

Within the current study we describe the first steps within a bigger research project with the aim of developing a design theory for digital self-efficacy intervention that specifically addresses the circumstances of the low-income tenant population. Involv ing the target audience in the design process puts the research directly into practice, assesses the practical feasibility of the proposed solution and ensures that it contributes to an improvement of their energy consumption behavior. We propose an approach for understanding this vulnerable population with their special limitations and needs with regards to their energy consumption behavior. Within the current paper, we contribute by presenting a theory-deducted research model whose hypotheses will be tested in a field study. We further contribute by using this understanding to provide the foundations of designing digital interventions customized to the low-income target group in order to bring them along in the energy transition. Since the evaluation of a solution depends not least on the accuracy of the measurement instruments, we place special emphasis in an early stage of the study on the measurement of all constructs included in the research model. As the constructs energy worries, energy literacy and energy self-efficacy are too imprecisely defined in literature, no or hardly any validated measurement instruments are available. Therefore, we report on the results of a development and evaluation study of such measurement instruments providing scales that distinct the constructs from each other, so that the instruments measure different things. On the one hand, we will now use and validate these measurement instruments within the field study. On the other hand, they can also be taken up by other scientists.

Acknowledgements This research is funded by the German Federal Ministry of Education and Research (BMBF) within the Innovations for Tomorrow's Production, Services and Work (funding number 02K18D000).

References

Ableitner, L., Tiefenbeck, V., Meeuw, A., Wörner, A., Fleisch, E. & Wortmann, F. (2020), 'User behavior in a real-world peer-to-peer electricity market', Applied Energy 270, 115061.

Adams, J., Kenner, A., Leone, B., Rosenthal, A., Sarao, M. & Boi-Doku, T. (2022), 'What is energy literacy? responding to vulnerability in philadelphia's energy ecologies', En-ergy Research & Social Science 91, 102718.

Agarwal, R., Sambamurthy, V. & Stair, R. M. (2000), 'Research report: The evolv ing re-lationship between general and specific computer self-efficacy—an empirical assess-ment', Information Systems Research 11(4), 418–430.

Bandura, A. (1977), 'Self-efficacy: Toward a unifying theory of behavioral change', Psychological Review 84(2), 191–215.

Bandura, A. (1986), 'Social foundations of thought and action', *Englewood Cliffs, NJ* 1986(23–28).

Bandura, A. (2006), 'Guide for constructing self-efficacy scales', *Self-efficacy beliefs of adolescents* 5(1), 307–337.

Białynicki-Birula, P., Makieła, K. & Mamica, Ł. (2022), 'Energy literacy and its deter minants among students within the context of public intervention in poland', *Energies* 15(15), 5368.

Bluhm, S., Staudt, P. & Weinhardt, C. (2022), 'Towards designing smart home energy ap plications for effective use', *The Transdisciplinary Reach of Design Science Research. DESRIST 2022.* pp. 303–314.

Boateng, G. O., Balogun, M. R., Dada, F. O. & Armah, F. A. (2020), 'Household energy insecurity: dimensions and consequences for women, infants and children in low- and middle-income countries', *Social science & medicine (1982)* 258, 113068.

van den Brom, P., Meijer, A. & Visscher, H. (2018), 'Performance gaps in energy consumption: household groups and building characteristics', *Building Research & Information* 46(1), 54–70.

Brown & Venkatesh (2005), 'Model of adoption of technology in households: A base line model test and extension incorporating household life cycle', *MIS Quarterly* 29(3), 399.

Cattell, R. B. (1966), 'The scree test for the number of factors', *Multivariate Behavioral Research* 1(2), 245–276.

Chlond, B., Goeschl, T. & Kesternich, M. (2022), 'Energy efficiency for the poor: Vary ing subsidies and procedures in a refrigerator replacement program', *13th Toulouse Conference on The Economics of Energy and Climate.*

Compeau, D. R. & Higgins, C. A. (1995), 'Computer self-efficacy: Development of a measure and initial test', *MIS Quarterly* 19(2), 189.

Czajkowski, K., Fitzgerald, S., Foster, I. & Kesselman, C. (2001), Grid Information Services for Distributed Resource Sharing, *in* 'Proceedings 10th IEEE International Symposium on High Performance Distributed Computing', IEEE, pp. 181–194.

Dalén, A. & Krämer, J. (2017), 'Towards a user-centered feedback design for smart meter interfaces to support efficient energy-use choices - a design science approach', *Business & Information Systems Engineering* 59(5), 361–373.

Danes, S. M. & Haberman, H. (2007), 'Teen financial knowledge, self-efficacy, and behavior: A gendered view', *Journal of Financial Counseling and Planning* 18(2).

Degirmenci, K. (2021), 'Toward digital interventions to overcome intergenerational discounting: A design science approach', *AMCIS 2021 Proceedings.*

DeVellis, R. F. (2017), *Scale development: Theory and applications*, fourth edition edn, SAGE, Los Angeles.

DeWaters, J. & Powers, S. (2013), 'Establishing measurement criteria for an energy literacy questionnaire', *The Journal of Environmental Education* 44(1), 38–55.

Dillon, T. W., Lending, D., Crews, II, T. R. & Blankenship, R. A. (2003), 'Nursing self-efficacy of an integrated clinical and administrative information system', *CIN: Computers, Informatics, Nursing* 21(4), 198.

Elliot (2011), 'Transdisciplinary perspectives on environmental sustainability: A resource base and framework for it-enabled business transformation', *MIS Quarterly* 35(1), 197.

Energy Access Targets Working Group (2016), 'More than a lightbulb: Five recommendations to make modern energy access meaningful for people and prosperity'.

Gawel, E., Korte, K. & Tews, K. (2015), 'Distributional challenges of sustainability policies—the case of the german energy transition', *Sustainability* 7(12), 16599– 16615.

Hauser, D. J., Ellsworth, P. C. & Gonzalez, R. (2018), 'Are manipulation checks neces sary?', *Frontiers in Psychology* 9, 998.

Hendrickson, A. E. & White, P. O. (1964), 'Promax: A quick method for rotation to oblique simple structure.', *British journal of statistical psychology* 17(1), 65–70.

Henger, R. & Stockhausen, M. (2022), 'Gefahr der energiearmut wächst', *Henger IW Kurzbericht* (55).

Henni, S., Franz, P., Staudt, P., Peukert, C. & Weinhardt, C. (2022), 'Evaluation of an interactive visualization tool to increase energy literacy in the building sector', *Energy and Buildings* 266, 112116.

Hernández, D. (2016), 'Understanding 'energy insecurity' and why it matters to health', *Social science & medicine (1982)* 167, 1–10.

Herrmann, M. R., Brumby, D. P. & Oreszczyn, T. (2018), 'Watts your usage? a field study of householders' literacy for residential electricity data', *Energy Efficiency* 11(7), 1703–1719.
Herrmann, M. R., Brumby, D. P., Cheng, L., Gilbert, X. M. & Oreszczyn, T. (2021), 'An empirical investigation of domestic energy data visualizations', *International Journal of Human-Computer Studies* 152, 102660.
Kaiser, H. F. (1974), 'An index of factorial simplicity', *Psychometrika* 39(1), 31–36.
Kankanhalli, Tan & Wei (2005), 'Contributing knowledge to electronic knowledge repositories: An empirical investigation', *MIS Quarterly* 29(1), 113.
Keith, M. J., Babb, J. S., Lowry, P. B., Furner, C. P. & Abdullat, A. (2015), 'The role of mobile-computing self-efficacy in consumer information disclosure', *Information Systems Journal* 25(6), 637–667.
Knebel, U., Leimeister, J., Esch, S., Pressler, A. & Krcmar, H. (2009), 'Problem solv ing patterns in design science research - learning from engineering', *ECIS 2009 Proceedings*.
Kröger, M., Longmuir, M., Neuhoff, K. & Schuetze, F. (2022), 'The costs of natural gas dependency: Price shocks, inequality, and public policy', *DIW Berlin Discussion Paper No. 2010*.
Kroll, T., Paukstadt, U., Kreidermann, K. & Mirbabaie, M. (2019), 'Nudging people to save energy in smart homes with social norms and self-commitment', *Research-in Progress Papers*.
Lee, J. W. C. & Tanusia, A. (2016), 'Energy conservation behavioural intention: attitudes, subjective norm and self-efficacy', *IOP Conference Series: Earth and Environmental Science* 40(1), 012087.
Levy, B. S. & Patz, J. A. (2015), 'Climate change, human rights, and social justice', *Annals of Global Health* 81(3), 310–322.
Loock, C.-M., Staake, T. & Thiesse, F. (2013), 'Motivating energy-efficient behavior with green is: An investigation of goal setting and the role of defaults', *MIS Quarterly* 37(4), 1313–1332.
MacKenzie & Podsakoff (2011), 'Construct measurement and validation procedures in mis and behavioral research: Integrating new and existing techniques', *MIS Quarterly* 35(2), 293.
Maedche, A., Gregor, S. & Parsons, J. (2021), 'Mapping design contributions in infor mation systems research: The design research activity framework', *Communications of the Association for Information Systems* 49(1), 355–378.
Mani, A., Mullainathan, S., Shafir, E. & Zhao, J. (2013), 'Poverty impedes cognitive function', *Science* 341(6149), 976–980.
Marcovitch, S., Jacques, S., Boseovski, J. J. & Zelazo, P. D. (2008), 'Self-reflection and the cognitive control of behavior: Implications for learning', *Mind, Brain, and Education* 2(3), 136–141.
Martins, A., Madaleno, M. & Dias, M. F. (2020), 'Energy literacy: What is out there to know?', *Energy Reports* 6, 454–459.
Melville (2010), 'Information systems innovation for environmental sustainability', *MIS Quarterly* 34(1), 1.
Michie, S., Wood, C., Johnston, M., Abraham, C., Francis, J. J. & Hardeman, W. (2015), 'Behaviour change techniques: the development and evaluation of a taxonomic method for reporting and describing behaviour change interventions (a suite of five studies involving consensus methods, randomised controlled trials and analysis of qualitative data)', *Health technology assessment (Winchester, England)* 19(99), 1–188.
Midgley, G. (2000), Systemic intervention, *in* 'Systemic Intervention', Springer, Boston, MA, pp. 113–133.
Mihale-Wilson, C., Hinz, O., van der Aalst, W. & Weinhardt, C. (2022), 'Corporate digital responsibility', *Business & Information Systems Engineering* 64(2), 127–132.
Morrisey, J. T. & Barrow, L. (1984), 'A review of energy education: 1975 to need 1981', *Science Education* 68(4), 365–379.
Murray, A. G. & Mills, B. F. (2014), 'The impact of low-income home energy assistance program participation on household energy insecurity', *Contemporary Economic Policy* 32(4), 811–825.
Ng, B.-Y., Kankanhalli, A. & Xu, Y. (2009), 'Studying users' computer security behavior: A health belief perspective', *Decision Support Systems* 46(4), 815–825.
Niiniluoto, I. (1993), 'The aim and structure of applied research', *Erkenntnis* 38(1), 1–21.

Pakarinen, A., Parisod, H., Smed, J. & Salanterä, S. (2017), 'Health game interventions to enhance physical activity self-efficacy of children: a quantitative systematic review', *Journal of Advanced Nursing* 73(4), 794–811.

Pye, S., Dobbins, A., Baffert, C., Brajkovic, J., Deane, P. & de Miglio, R. (2017), Chapter ´ 30 - energy poverty across the eu: Analysis of policies and measures, *in* M. Welsch, ed., 'Europe's energy transition', Academic Press, London, pp. 261–280.

Rainisio, N., Boffi, M., Pola, L., Inghilleri, P., Sergi, I. & Liberatori, M. (2022), 'The role of gender and self-efficacy in domestic energy saving behaviors: A case study in lombardy, italy', *Energy Policy* 160, 112696.

Richards, E., Swan, G. & Case, D. (2018), 'National energy literacy among high school seniors and recent graduates'.

Richter, B., Staudt, P. & Weinhardt, C. (2022), 'Citizen energy communities - insights into long-term participant behavior from a field study'.

Simões, G. M. F. & Leder, S. M. (2022), 'Energy poverty: The paradox between low income and increasing household energy consumption in brazil', *Energy and Buildings* 268, 112234.

Sovacool, B. K., Martiskainen, M., Hook, A. & Baker, L. (2019), 'Decarbonization and its discontents: a critical energy justice perspective on four low-carbon transitions', *Climatic Change* 155(4), 581–619.

Spruill, A., Keith, M. & Babb, J. (2021), 'Augmenting information systems creative self-efficacy through video gaming', *ICIS 2021 Proceedings* .

Thatcher, J. B. & Perrewe, P. L. (2002), 'An empirical examination of individual traits as antecedents to computer anxiety and computer self-efficacy', *MIS Quar terly* 26(4), 381.

Tiefenbeck, V., Goette, L., Degen, K., Tasic, V., Fleisch, E., Lalive, R. & Staake, T. (2018), 'Overcoming salience bias: How real-time feedback fosters resource conserva tion', *Management Science* 64(3), 1458–1476.

Tucker, L. R. & MacCallum, R. C. (1997), *Exploratory factor analysis*, Unpublished manuscript.

Turai, E., Schmatzberger, S. & Broer, R. (2021), 'Overview report on the energy poverty concept: Energy poverty in the privately-owned, multi-family environment'.

Usher, E. L. & Pajares, F. (2008), 'Sources of self-efficacy in school: Critical review of the literature and future directions', *Review of Educational Research* 78(4), 751–796.

van den Broek, K. L. (2019), 'Household energy literacy: A critical review and a conceptual typology', *Energy Research & Social Science* 57, 101256.

Wastensteiner, J., Weiss, T. M., Haag, F. & Hopf, K. (2021), 'Explainable ai for tailored electricity consumption feedback–an experimental evaluation of visualizations', *ECIS 2021 Research Papers* .

Wendt, C. & Benlian, A. (2022), 'Motivating sustainable resource consumption through the design of goal setting in smart meter user interfaces', *ECIS 2022 Research Papers* .

Wewerinke-Singh, M. (2022), 'A human rights approach to energy: Realizing the rights of billions within ecological limits', *Review of European, Comparative & International Environmental Law* 31(1), 16–26.

Zeidi, I. M., Morshedi, H. & Otaghvar, H. (2020), 'A theory of planned behavior enhanced intervention to promote health literacy and self-care behaviors of type 2 diabetic patients', *Journal of Preventive Medicine and Hygiene* 61(4), E601–E613.

Zhang, F. (2015), 'Energy price reform and household welfare: The case of turkey', *The Energy Journal* 36(2).

Zhao, X., Ramzan, M., Sengupta, T., Deep Sharma, G., Shahzad, U. & Cui, L. (2022), 'Impacts of bilateral trade on energy affordability and accessibility across europe: Does economic globalization reduce energy poverty?', *Energy and Buildings* 262, 112023.

Zierler, R., Wehrmeyer, W. & Murphy, R. (2017), 'The energy efficiency behaviour of individuals in large organisations: A case study of a major uk infrastructure operator', *Energy Policy* 104, 38–49.

The Motivation of Companies to Implement Corporate Digital Responsibility Activities Voluntarily: An Empirical Assessment

K. Valerie Carl, Michael Kubach, and Cristina Mihale-Wilson

Abstract Technological advancements such as Artificial Intelligence afford new opportunities and pose new challenges. In this context, Corporate Digital Responsibility (CDR) has gained increasing attention. CDR presents a comprehensive and well-structured approach to companies' responsibilities in the digital setting. While the threats of digitalization start to materialize, research on CDR is still in its infancy, with little empirical understanding of whether and why companies engage in CDR practices. This qualitative study addresses the motivation of companies to pursue CDR by conducting 29 expert interviews. In practice, firms implement CDR activities to follow their inner motivation or to satisfy external expectations. Our results indicate that motivation differs primarily according to the company size and the addressees of efforts. Motivational sources for conducting CDR activities are rather company-specific while allowing for some generalization based on company types. In this way, this study enables several future research avenues worth pursuing.

Keywords Corporate digital responsibility · Company activities · Qualitative research · Expert interviews · Future research avenues

K. V. Carl (✉) · C. Mihale-Wilson
Chair of Information Systems and Information Management, Goethe University, Frankfurt/Main, Germany
e-mail: kcarl@wiwi.uni-frankfurt.de

C. Mihale-Wilson
e-mail: mihale-wilson@wiwi.uni-frankfurt.de

M. Kubach
Fraunhofer IAO, Stuttgart, Germany
e-mail: michael.kubach@iao.fraunhofer.de

D. Beverungen et al. (eds.), *Conceptualizing Digital Responsibility for the Information Age*, Lecture Notes in Information Systems and Organisation 74,
https://doi.org/10.1007/978-3-031-80119-8_3

1 Introduction

The impact of digitalization is widespread and affects organizations of all sizes and industries (Tarafdar et al., 2015). In many areas, adopting digital technologies creates new business opportunities and lays the foundation for long-term success (Bharadwaj, 2000). With progress in digitally advanced technologies, digital goods and services' productivity and complexity increase. While these advances are beneficial for many reasons, they also present various challenges and dangers for businesses and consumers. However, this work focuses on businesses as our main subject of interest.

The continuous digital evolution alters the requirements for a company's management, agility, and organizational culture (Sambamurthy et al., 2003; Grover, Tseng and Pu, 2022). Companies must implement effective management strategies to navigate the digital landscape, address the risks and challenges it presents, and take opportunities. The concept of Corporate Digital Responsibility (CDR) has arisen in response to this need. Despite sharing similar objectives with Corporate Social Responsibility (CSR), CDR and CSR differ in their focus areas. While CSR emphasizes environmental and social concerns, CDR specifically addresses the impacts of a company's digital activities. Especially "exponential growth in technological development, malleability of technologies and data in use, and pervasiveness of technology and data" (Lobschat et al., 2021, p. 876) manifest particularities of digital technologies. Therefore, CDR aims to promote ethical and accountable digitalization by offering guiding principles for corporations.

Currently, research on digitalization is expanding, but only a limited number of scholars have explored ethical considerations in this field (Grover, Carter and Jiang, 2019). In this context, the discussion surrounding CDR is attracting growing interest in academia and practical applications as it builds on ethical norms for corporate behavior and translates them into business practice. Previous research attempted to clarify the definition and responsibilities of CDR (e.g., Herden et al., 2021; Lobschat et al., 2021), explored its applications in managing Artificial Intelligence (AI) (e.g., Elliott et al., 2021), and assessed its implementation across different industries (e.g., Etter et al., 2019; Jones and Comfort, 2021). However, most of the research on the concept of CDR is rather conceptual (Mueller, 2022). The concept's definition continues to become more refined, underscoring the need for a more empirical understanding (Mihale-Wilson et al., 2022; Mueller, 2022).

First empirical research efforts concerning CDR are dedicated to the assessment of the consumers' point of view towards the topic (e.g., Mihale-Wilson et al., 2021; Carl et al., 2024), whereas the company's perspective on CDR is relatively scarce in research. To advance the empirical investigation of the CDR concept sustainably, this study focuses on the company's view on CDR. We aim to explore companies' initiatives regarding ethical and responsible digital business practices, thereby paving the way for future research on the corporate perspective. In this context, we are particularly interested in strategic drivers motivating companies to adopt and establish a CDR culture in their organization voluntarily. For companies, it is vital that their strategic initiatives also yield a corresponding return. The strategic goals pursued with such engagement must first be evaluated empirically to assess whether CDR engagement is worthwhile from a research perspective compared to a company's expectations, supporting the operationalization of the concept in practice.

Varying motivations influence the implementation of CDR in practice following differing strategic goals. These motivations can be intrinsic (i.e., internally driven) or extrinsic (i.e., stakeholder-oriented) (Schaltegger and Burritt, 2018). Employees and managers drive intrinsic motivation according to their moral and ethical beliefs, whereas extrinsic motivation is directed at or induced by relevant stakeholder groups (Schaltegger and Burritt, 2018).

To the best of our knowledge, this is one of the first studies to assess companies' strategic considerations that motivate CDR implementation in practice empirically. In this way, we can inform and empower future research to empirically evaluate the corporate perspective on CDR. We conducted an extensive qualitative study with companies of different sizes and industries. We assessed whether the engagement is internally or externally driven and the specific motivation behind the voluntary CDR commitment. To gain an in-depth understanding of the various motivating factors for implementing CDR, the next chapter first introduces CSR and CDR in detail and thereby differentiates them from one another for a better understanding of the topic. Section 3 illustrates the employed methodology and provides details on the study sample. In Sect. 4, we present quantitative and qualitative analyses of the data obtained. We conclude with a discussion of the results, the theoretical and managerial implications, limitations, as well as future research avenues.

2 Corporate Social and Digital Responsibility

As already noted, the concepts of CDR and CSR are intertwined and belong to the broader concept of Corporate Responsibility. One commonly accepted definition (Pirsch et al., 2007) describes CSR as encompassing society's expectations of firms regarding: (i) economic (e.g., achieving profits and creating sustainability), (ii) legal (e.g., adhering to laws and regulations), (iii) ethical (e.g., proper and fair behavior), and (iv) philanthropic (e.g., wellbeing of associated communities) matters (Carroll, 1979; Matten and Moon, 2007). Therefore, CSR initiatives fulfill these expectations and responsibilities towards society voluntarily. Nevertheless, various organizations and individuals have differing interpretations of the concept leading to a wide range of CSR activities getting executed depending on the individual perception and the organization's priorities (van Marrewijk, 2003). For instance, these activities can encompass the environment, human rights and dignity, sustainability, community development, or economic development (Kesavan et al., 2013).

Advancements in technology have made corporate responsibility more complex and require managing both the risks and opportunities that come with these developments (Lobschat et al., 2021). Dealing with these advancements requires a solid technological focus. To account for the ubiquity of digital products, services, and technologies, CDR is centered around technology and its impact on society and companies. In contrast, CSR follows a broader goal towards society and covers some technological developments but does not make technology its main focus (Mihale-Wilson et al., 2022). Still, the interrelation of both concepts is under discussion (e.g., Mueller, 2022; Trittin-Ulbrich and Böckel, 2022). One stream of research argues that CDR is a subsequent concept belonging to CSR (e.g., Herden et al., 2021; Pelters, 2021). In contrast, a second parallel stream considers CDR as an (independent) addition to CSR with some overlaps (e.g., Elliott et al., 2021; Lobschat et al., 2021; Trittin-Ulbrich and Böckel, 2022), at least in such an early stage of research (Mueller, 2022). We follow the second stream of research in this study, considering CDR and CSR separately due to the emphasis on technology that distinguishes CDR as well as the inherent opportunity to establish cross-functional cooperation in companies that CDR requires for a successful operationalization in practice (Mihale-Wilson et al., 2022; Trittin-Ulbrich and Böckel, 2022). We follow the view that these concepts are interrelated with some overlaps and separating them is unfeasible (Lobschat et al., 2021), such as in the areas of eco-efficiency, human rights, social equity, inclusion, and working conditions. Still, the two concepts approach these issues differently, conditioning CDR as an independent concept.

CDR is attracting increasing attention both in research and in practice. The scholarly discussion shares a mutual comprehension of different CDR activities aimed at consumers despite different nomenclature developing in parallel (Mihale-Wilson et al., 2022). Among experts, a general understanding prevails about the importance of everyone having access to essential digital products, being informed on their correct usage, and being cognizant of the consequences of their consumption decisions. Furthermore, experts emphasize the requirement for greater transparency concerning algorithmic decisions, data privacy and security incidents, or data flows (Nofer et al., 2014). The expert discourse also concentrates on the issue of product safety and accountability in the digital age, as well as the need for adapted governance and participation mechanisms (Mihale-Wilson et al., 2022).

In conclusion, these perspectives share CDR's underlying understanding and scope and vary primarily in terms of specific emphasis. As a result of the converging definition of CDR, research calls for an enhanced empirical understanding of the subject (Mihale-Wilson et al., 2022; Mueller, 2022). While some research developed a better empirical understanding of CDR from the consumers' perspective (e.g., Mihale-Wilson et al., 2021; Carl et al., 2024), there is a lack of knowledge concerning the companies' viewpoint. This publication aims to empirically assess the motivational drivers of companies pursuing CDR following the call for a better empirical understanding of the concept and its drivers in practice (Mihale-Wilson et al., 2022; Mueller, 2022). In this way, this study enables future research to investigate the degree of fulfillment of the found motivators empirically, thus supporting companies in the profitability consideration of such CDR activities. Drawing on prior insights from CSR and sustainability research, the motivation behind responsibility commitment has adverse effects on success, e.g., in terms of financial performance (e.g., Tang et al., 2012).

3 Methodology and Sample

To study companies' motivation to conduct CDR activities, we used a qualitative research approach employing the works and following the principles articulated by Myers and Newman (2007) and Myers (2009).

The data was collected through semi-structured interviews using a guideline with a set of questions to gain insight into the participants' general knowledge and understanding of CDR, as well as the CDR practices implemented in the companies included in the sample and their specific motivational drivers. The guideline included a definition of CDR and sample activities. We tested the guidelines in a pretest and adjusted them based on the results.

The data collection for this study involved 29 individuals who were interviewed for 30 to 60 min each. These interviews took place in 2020 and the early months of 2021 and were performed remotely due to the COVID-19 pandemic. We conducted the interviews via telephone, Zoom, or MS Teams and recorded them with the interviewees' consent. Afterward, we transcribed the recordings for analysis.

We utilized the software MAXQDA to support two experts from our project team who carried out the coding process for qualitative content analysis (Krippendorff, 2004). The first expert initiated the process by establishing a two-layer coding system (i.e., aggregate dimensions) based on the motivational drivers (intrinsic vs. extrinsic) for CDR commitment and corresponding, inductively developed specific motivators. Subsequently, we conducted our coding in three rounds, beginning with the first expert extending the code system, when necessary, in the first round. Next, the experts held a joint discussion to ensure a shared and consistent understanding of the interpretation of the codes. To ensure impartiality, the second expert independently conducted the coding process (coding round 2), extending the coding system when needed. The output from both rounds of coding was then combined to evaluate the intercoder reliability between the experts. After the results of both coding sessions were reviewed and discussed by both experts, the first expert carried out the coding process again, considering the updates made to the coding system by expert two and the insights gathered from the discussion (coding round 3).

The coding process led to a refinement of the initial two-layer coding process. Thus, we inductively developed the coding scheme: The analyzed data led to splitting up extrinsic motivation (i.e., second-order concepts) into active measures (e.g., fostering active firm positioning and increase in sales by considering stakeholder preferences and demands) and reactive measures (e.g., acting due to external pressure, e.g., regulations or public pressure, and risk avoidance). In this way, the coders developed the following coding scheme. Thereby, corresponding (inductively developed) motivators (i.e., first-order concepts) supplement the motivational sources (see Fig. 1).

The information on the sample companies, including the position of the interviewees, industry, customer segment, and size, is listed in Table 2 in the Appendix. The interviewees represent a range of companies from small and medium enterprises (SMEs) to large corporations located in Germany that offer products and/or services

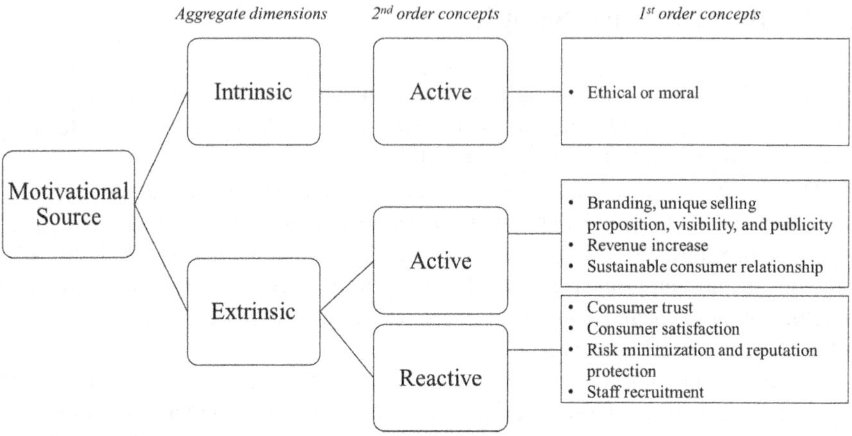

Fig. 1 Motivational sources

that apply digital technologies and for whom CDR is, therefore, a relevant concept. To attract a heterogeneous sample of SMEs and large enterprises active in business-to-business (B2B) and business-to-consumer (B2C) contexts, we performed our recruitment through web research, personal contacts, and snowball sampling through interviewees. To this end, this study strived to evaluate a heterogeneous sample in terms of size and customer types to provide a more comprehensive understanding of motivational drivers for conducting CDR-related activities. Especially in terms of SMEs, conducted CDR activities as well as motivational drivers behind such engagement are less visible since corporate communication is often less pronounced than in large companies. Still, motivations can differ vastly between different company types. To this end, we did not focus on one particular company type for initial empirical insights into motivational drivers for conducting CDR commitment. Instead, we aimed to provide a mixed sample of different company types and shapes.

The interview participants held various roles in their respective companies, ranging from founders to department heads. The key criterion was not the specific job title but rather the individuals' knowledge and expertise about the company and motivation for CDR activities, which made them knowledgeable experts on the subject within their company (Homburg et al., 2012). The sample in our study includes 5 large corporations, 23 SMEs, and 1 company coordinating a network of smaller manufacturers. Of these, 18 are primarily focused on B2B operations, 8 on B2C operations, and 3 consider themselves to have a dual focus on both B2B and B2C.

4 Firms' Motivational Drivers for the Implementation of Corporate Digital Responsibility Activities

When first assessing the derived motivational sources quantitatively, we developed a ranking of motivators by importance across the sample (see Table 1). Over the entire sample, branding (41%) and consumer trust (41%) are crucial motivations for establishing CDR in the company. Regarding branding, an active and extrinsic motivational driver for CDR activities, representant #5 of a car manufacturer puts it that way: "Data protection [as a dimension of CDR] is not only a legal question but also a strategic one […]. Customer data security is clearly one of the company's core brand values […]. Our vehicles should offer our customers the highest level of safety and comfort […] and we want to transfer the brand essence from the analog world to the digital one." Consumer trust, in contrast, can be classified as a reactive extrinsic motivational source of CDR activities. The answer of respondent #3 from an ERP software company combines the branding and the trust aspect and illustrates that CDR activities can also be motivated by customer's concerns and to counter a potential loss of trust: "As we are now slowly making the transformation to the cloud business, there are many questions. It is important for us not only to meet the legal standards, but also to be very transparent, for example, regarding the location of our servers. With this we aim to regain trust in our brand and our products." The transfer from the analogue to the digital world, as already mentioned by interviewee #5 for branding, is relevant for the trust aspect as well. An example gives interviewee #1 from an IT service provider: "In terms of the motivation for the CDR project, data protection [as compliance with legal requirements] is only a small matter. In concrete terms, it is about bringing customer trust and a comprehensible value system over into the digital world."

Besides, the data illustrate the heterogeneity in motivational sources according to the company size (see Table 1). The motivations vary greatly between large companies and SMEs in our sample, showing some heterogeneity between the two groups. Particularly remarkable are the different foci between large companies and SMEs in this study. Interviewed SMEs implement CDR activities primarily due to intrinsic motivation (39%), or as interviewee #13 from a business e-learning SMEs puts it "My motivation is the or my vision of a good company.", and risk minimization (i.e., extrinsic and reactive, 39%). Interviewee #23 explains the reasoning that their smart home startup decided they had to be particularly cautious when it comes to security and privacy due to their limited resources as a small firm: "We just thought, we're just too small to secure a cloud as we envision it […]. Otherwise, we would have had a lot more options in the early stages of these [products] than with [this privacy-friendly solution]. […] a lot of things, especially with automation, didn't work […]. But we said we'd never get it right anyway, to secure something like that with 35 people. Then we said that this solution would give us the privacy we wanted." Large firms on the other hand have differing motivational sources. Companies in this group implement CDR activities primarily due to extrinsic motivational sources, employing active and reactive approaches to the subject (i.e., branding (active, 80%), consumer

Table 1 Ranking of the motivational sources across the sample

Rank	Motivators	Firm size		Customer segment		Total
		SMEs (%)	**Large firms** (%)	**B2C** (%)	**B2B** (%)	
1	Branding, unique selling proposition, visibility, and publicity**	35	**80**	27	**43**	41
2	Consumer trust***	30	**80**	**55**	**43**	41
3	Risk minimization and reputation protection***	**39**	40	**36**	33	38
4	Consumer satisfaction***	30	**80**	27	**38**	38
5	Ethical or moral*	**39**	20	27	33	35
6	Sustainable consumer relationship**	26	20	18	24	24
7	Revenue increase**	21	20	27	19	21
8	Staff recruitment***	4	**60**	0	**19**	14

Note * Intrinsic motivational source, active; ** Extrinsic motivational source, active; *** Extrinsic motivational source, reactive

trust (reactive, 80%), and consumer satisfaction (reactive, 80%)). The difference in the motivator of employee recruitment is particularly noteworthy: While only 4% of SMEs in the sample implement CDR due to this motivation, the share of large companies is 60%. In addition, the results indicate some heterogeneity within the group of SMEs. While the interviewed large firms mainly concentrate on a few motivational sources they share across the sample, SMEs' motivational sources are rather individual in this study, indicating that there might not be such coinciding motivators.

In addition, motivation sources differ between the addressees of the CDR commitment (B2C vs. B2B) (see Table 1) in our sample. While B2C companies apply CDR to increase consumer trust (55%) and to minimize risks (36%), B2B companies implement CDR-related activities for branding (43%), consumer trust (43%), and consumer satisfaction (38%) purposes in this study. Surprisingly, none of the B2C companies in the sample reported staff recruitment as a motivator for performing CDR activities compared to 19% of the B2B companies. A reason might be that it is more challenging for B2B companies to gain public visibility and present themselves and their jobs as attractive to potential new employees. This is reflected in the comment by respondent #1 from a B2B company: "We've had an incredible demand for staff for the last 5 years [...]. The baby boomers are slowly leaving now [...]. [And it works,] we see young colleagues who enjoy working for us, although [our topics] don't necessarily look sexy to young people." The difference in the importance of staff recruitment and the deviating top-ranked motivators indicate a high degree of heterogeneity between the interviewed B2C and B2B companies.

To sum up, the empirical results illustrate the diverging motivational sources for companies to pursue CDR activities voluntarily. Results differ between company size, customer segment (B2C vs. B2B), and within some company types in our sample. Hence, the motivational sources underpinning the integration of CDR efforts in companies seem to be company dependent. One size does not seem to fit all companies equally. However, the results allow for some generalization due to the observed homogeneity of motivational sources within some company-type groups. Finally, what sticks out over all subgroups is that the importance of revenue increase as a motivational source is generally low in this sample. A reason might be that the relationship between CDR activities and a revenue increase is indirect or as participant #11 from an e-commerce software company—one of the few making the connection at all—states: "If e-commerce is trusted in Germany, we can sell our software. Hence, we don't only follow ethical motives, [these activities] fulfil our business policy."

5 Discussion, Future Research Avenues, and Conclusion

Research on CDR is currently rather conceptual, moving towards a joint agreement on the definition and understanding of the concept (Mihale-Wilson et al., 2022; Mueller, 2022). Hence, an empirical understanding of CDR and related stakeholder behavior is crucial for research and practice alike. So far, there is only little empirical knowledge concerning the company's perspective on CDR—a gap this study aims to close—to develop future research paths worthwhile pursuing. Evaluating the motivation for pursuing CDR commitment allows for future research on the company-internal perspective on the concept (e.g., operationalization in practice, alignment of company motives and consumer perception, degree of fulfillment of the found motivators). The results illustrate that companies act both intrinsically and extrinsically (active and reactive) motivated. When driven by extrinsic motivations, the extent to which CDR activities can enhance a company's image is dependent on how consumers perceive them. Therefore, companies following extrinsic motivational drivers should strive to design CDR initiatives that fit consumers' needs and preferences, aligning the internal perspective on the issue with external perceptions. However, external perception (usually by consumers) can also be important in shaping the engagement for intrinsically motivated CDR implementation. Accordingly, it is interesting for future research how consumers perceive and value these different motivational drivers. Drawing on renowned knowledge of CSR, such activities can indeed influence firm outcomes, e.g., in terms of increased brand sales and enhanced financial performance (e.g., Wickert, 2021; Nickerson et al., 2022). However, no empirical research is dedicated to CDR that evaluates whether the motivation to pursue CDR engagement materializes. Consequently, this study's inductively derived motivational factors should motivate future research to assess whether CDR engagement can improve, e.g., financial performance. In this way, IS research can investigate the extent to which findings from CSR research can be transferred to CDR.

Besides, the results suggest that a company's motivation to pursue CDR activities is rather individual but can be approximated by company types. For example, the results suggest a certain homogeneity for large companies in our sample, while SMEs reveal rather individual motivations in this study. Thus, our study provides first empirical insights into the different motivational drivers that condition the implementation of CDR in organizations according to the size of the company or the addressees of the CDR engagement. The results emphasize the diversity of motivational drivers within companies. In our sample, most companies pursue CDR activities based on multiple motivations. Hence, future research should not take an isolated perspective concerning one pursued motivational driver but rather evaluate the interplay of different motivators within a company. In this way, future inquiries can explore the causal relationship of these potentially effective dimensions.

This study makes several theoretical and practical contributions. Firstly, this study illustrates initial empirical insights into motivational drivers for conducting CDR activities. In this way, the results can ignite future research when assessing the benefitting effect of a company's motivational drivers for pursuing CDR activities on consumer perception. Secondly, the results emphasize some heterogeneity between different company types (i.e., size and addressees of engagement) as well as within certain groups of company types (e.g., SMEs). For future research, the study results illustrate the importance of focusing on specific groups of companies in the study since one motivation obviously does not cover all types of companies equally. Thirdly, this study uncovers that companies implement CDR activities usually due to various motivators and goals. This implies the need to consider motivators not in isolation but in interaction, as they may have halo effects (positive and negative) on each other.

For practice, this study can serve as an orientation of potential benefitting effects of pursuing CDR activities. In this way, the results should motivate companies to assess whether these motivations account for an exceeded CDR commitment and implementation in practice. Moreover, this study paves the way to investigate actual effects based on these motivators and thus help companies determine which activities can be profitable and how. As a rule, additional CDR activities are associated with additional costs, whereby consumers' increased willingness to pay often does not cover the costs incurred (e.g., Carl et al., 2024). Accordingly, companies need to know to what extent CDR engagement can still pay off, e.g., through an improved financial performance. Thus, this study paves the way for future research and, building on that, the support of corporate practice in implementing CDR.

Despite our efforts, the study we conducted and the results we derived have some limitations. One limitation concerns the origin of our sample. We conducted our study with a focus on companies in Germany. Therefore, further testing should consider possible regional differences in company motivation. Furthermore, we sought to achieve a balanced mix of different company types in the sample. Future studies can conduct accentuated detailed studies for specific company types based on the derived results to assess the findings in the light of larger samples. In this way, future research can assess whether the insights for specific company types hold for larger samples (e.g., less represented large companies). While the sample size is appropriate for a qualitative interview study, more company-type or industry-specific research in the future can add to the overall understanding of whether the observed results also hold for an overall larger combined sample.

Nevertheless, this research serves as a starting point for future (predominantly empirical) research on CDR, providing essential insights into companies' motivation to implement CDR activities. This way, we add the company's perspective to the CDR discourse by revealing empirical insights into different motivational sources. This paves the way for a detailed empirical investigation and verification of the transferability of findings from CSR research.

Acknowledgements This work was supported by the Federal Ministry for Economic Affairs and Energy [grant numbers 01MD16009F (ENTOURAGE), 01MD16009F (ForeSight)]; and the Hessian State Chancellery—Hessian Minister of Digital Strategy and Development [grant number 6/493/71574093 (CDR-CAT)].

Appendix

See Table 2.

Table 2 Study sample

#	Interviewee position	Industry	Customer segment	Firm size
1	Corporate data protection supervisor	IT service provider	B2B	Large company
2	Department head for support, training, and IT	Project management software	B2B	Large company
3	Global volunteering and impact measurement lead	ERP software	B2B	Large company
4	Team member product management	Comparison shopping portal	B2C	Large company
5	Coordination digital and data governance	Car manufacturing	B2C	Large company
6	Consultant / partner	IT consulting	B2B	SME
7	Product lead	Enterprise software	B2B	SME
8	Public relations manager	Enterprise software	B2B	SME
9	Product portfolio manager	IT service provider	B2B	SME
10	Founder and CEO	Software as a service developer and provider	B2B	SME
11	Founder and CEO	E-commerce software	B2B	SME
12	Chief information officer	IT project management	B2B	SME
13	CEO	Business e-learning software	B2B	SME
14	Head global sales	IT consulting	B2B	SME
15	Co-founder	E-commerce software	B2B	SME
16	Head customer relations	Enterprise software	B2B	SME
17	Chief sales officer	Enterprise software	B2B	SME
18	Manager sales, consulting	Enterprise software	B2B	SME
19	CEO	IT and risk management consulting	B2B	SME
20	CEO	IT service provider	B2B	SME
21	Head PR and marketing	E-commerce platform	B2B, B2C	SME
22	Founder and CEO	Talent management and training software	B2B, B2C	SME
23	Head of service	Smart home devices	B2C	SME

(continued)

Table 2 (continued)

#	Interviewee position	Industry	Customer segment	Firm size
24	Chief marketing officer	Online gaming platform	B2C	SME
25	Co-founder	Smart home devices	B2C	SME
26	CSR manager	E-commerce	B2C	SME
27	Founder	E-learning platform	B2C	SME
28	CEO	Smart home devices	B2C	SME
29	Head of marketing	Smart home devices	B2B, B2C	Company network

N = 29

References

Bharadwaj, A.S. (2000), 'A Resource-Based Perspective on Information Technology Capability and Firm Performance: An Empirical Investigation', *MIS Quarterly*, 24(1), pp. 169–196. https://doi.org/10.2307/3250983.

Carl, K.V. *et al.* (2024), 'A Consumer Perspective on Corporate Digital Responsibility: An Empirical Evaluation of Consumer Preferences', *Journal of Business Economics*, forthcoming. https://doi.org/10.1007/s11573-023-01142-y.

Carroll, A.B. (1979), 'A Three-Dimensional Conceptual Model of Corporate Performance', *Academy of Management Review*, 4(4), pp. 497–505. https://doi.org/10.5465/amr.1979.4498296.

Elliott, K. *et al.* (2021), 'Towards an Equitable Digital Society: Artificial Intelligence (AI) and Corporate Digital Responsibility (CDR)', *Society*, 58(3), pp. 179–188. https://doi.org/10.1007/s12115-021-00594-8.

Etter, M., Fieseler, C. and Whelan, G. (2019), 'Sharing Economy, Sharing Responsibility? Corporate Social Responsibility in the Digital Age', *Journal of Business Ethics*, 159(4), pp. 935–942. https://doi.org/10.1007/s10551-019-04212-w.

Grover, V., Carter, M. and Jiang, D. (2019), 'Trends in the Conduct of Information Systems Research', *Journal of Information Technology*, 34(2), pp. 160–177. https://doi.org/10.1177/0268396219834122.

Grover, V., Tseng, S.-L. and Pu, W. (2022), 'A Theoretical Perspective on Organizational Culture and Digitalization', *Information & Management*, 59(4), p. 103639. https://doi.org/10.1016/j.im.2022.103639.

Herden, C. *et al.* (2021), '"Corporate Digital Responsibility": New Corporate Responsibilities in the Digital Age', *Sustainability Management Forum*, 29, pp. 13–29. https://doi.org/10.1007/s00550-020-00509-x.

Homburg, C. *et al.* (2012), 'What Drives Key Informant Accuracy?', *Journal of Marketing Research*, 49(4), pp. 594–608. https://doi.org/10.1509/jmr.09.0174.

Jones, P. and Comfort, D. (2021), 'Corporate Digital Responsibility in the Hospitality Industry', *Athens Journal of Tourism*, 8(1), pp. 9–18. https://doi.org/10.30958/ajt.8-1-1.

Kesavan, R., Bernacchi, M.D. and Mascarenhas, O.A.J. (2013), 'Word of Mouse: CSR Communication and the Social Media', *International Management Review*, 9(1), pp. 58–66.

Krippendorff, K. (2004), *Content Analysis: An Introduction to Its Methodology*. Thousand Oaks, CA, U.S.: Sage Publications Ltd.

Lobschat, L. *et al.* (2021), 'Corporate Digital Responsibility', *Journal of Business Research*, 122, pp. 875–888. https://doi.org/10.1016/j.jbusres.2019.10.006.

van Marrewijk, M. (2003), 'Concepts and Definitions of CSR and Corporate Sustainability: Between Agency and Communion', *Journal of Business Ethics*, 44(2), pp. 95–105. https://doi.org/10.1007/978-94-007-4126-3_32.

Matten, D. and Moon, J. (2007), 'Pan-European Approach: A Conceptual Framework for Understanding CSR', in W.Ch. Zimmerli, K. Richter, and M. Holzinger (eds) *Corporate Ethics and Corporate Governance*. Berlin, Heidelberg: Springer, pp. 179–199

Mihale-Wilson, C. *et al.* (2021), 'Corporate Digital Responsibility – Extended Conceptualization and a Guide to Implementation', in F. Rowe et al. (eds) *Proceedings of the 29th European Conference on Information Systems (ECIS)*. Marrakech, Morocco.

Mihale-Wilson, C. *et al.* (2022), 'Corporate Digital Responsibility: Relevance and Opportunities for Business and Information Systems Engineering', *Business & Information Systems Engineering*, 64(2), pp. 127–132. https://doi.org/10.1007/s12599-022-00746-y.

Mueller, B. (2022), 'Corporate Digital Responsibility', *Business & Information Systems Engineering*, 64(5), pp. 689–700. https://doi.org/10.1007/s12599-022-00760-0.

Myers, M.D. (2009), *Qualitative Research in Business and Management*. Sage Publications Ltd.

Myers, M.D. and Newman, M. (2007), 'The Qualitative Interview in IS Research: Examining the Craft', *Information and Organization*, 17(1), pp. 2–26. https://doi.org/10.1016/j.infoandorg.2006.11.001.

Nickerson, D. *et al.* (2022), 'The Impact of Corporate Social Responsibility on Brand Sales: An Accountability Perspective', *Journal of Marketing*, 86(2), pp. 5–28. https://doi.org/10.1177/00222429211044155.

Nofer, M. *et al.* (2014), 'The Economic Impact of Privacy Violations and Security Breaches', *Business & Information Systems Engineering*, 6, pp. 339–348. https://doi.org/10.1007/s12599-014-0351-3.

Pelters, E. (2021), 'Corporate Digital Responsibility—Understanding and Applying', in T.A. Herberger and J.J. Dötsch (eds) *Digitalization, Digital Transformation and Sustainability in the Global Economy*. Cham: Springer International Publishing (Springer Proceedings in Business and Economics), pp. 71–84. https://doi.org/10.1007/978-3-030-77340-3_6.

Pirsch, J., Gupta, S. and Grau, S.L. (2007), 'A Framework for Understanding Corporate Social Responsibility Programs as a Continuum: An Exploratory Study', *Journal of Business Ethics*, 70(2), pp. 125–140. https://doi.org/10.1007/s10551-006-9100-y.

Sambamurthy, V., Bharadwaj, A. and Grover, V. (2003), 'Shaping Agility Through Digital Options: Reconceptualizing the Role of Information Technology in Contemporary Firms', *MIS Quarterly*, 27(2), pp. 237–263. https://doi.org/10.2307/30036530.

Schaltegger, S. and Burritt, R. (2018), 'Business Cases and Corporate Engagement with Sustainability: Differentiating Ethical Motivations', *Journal of Business Ethics*, 147(2), pp. 241–259. https://doi.org/10.1007/s10551-015-2938-0.

Tang, Z., Hull, C.E. and Rothenberg, S. (2012), 'How Corporate Social Responsibility Engagement Strategy Moderates the CSR–Financial Performance Relationship', *Journal of Management Studies*, 49(7), pp. 1274–1303. https://doi.org/10.1111/j.1467-6486.2012.01068.x.

Tarafdar, M., Gupta, A. and Turel, O. (2015), 'Special issue on "Dark side of information technology use":an introduction and a framework for research', *Information Systems Journal*, 25(3), pp. 161–170.

Trittin-Ulbrich, H. and Böckel, A. (2022), 'Institutional Entrepreneurship for Responsible Digital Innovation: The Case of Corporate Digital Responsibility', *Creativity and Innovation Management*, 31(3), pp. 447–459. https://doi.org/10.1111/caim.12513.

Wickert, C. (2021), 'Corporate Social Responsibility Research in the Journal of Management Studies: A Shift from a Business-Centric to a Society-Centric Focus', *Journal of Management Studies*, 58(8), pp. E1–E17. https://doi.org/10.1111/joms.12775.

Human Perceptions of Fairness: A Survey Experiment

Julian Sengewald, Anissa Schlichter, Markus Siepermann, and Richard Lackes

Abstract Algorithmic decision-making (ADM) through automation has benefits but must be implemented responsibly. Several mathematical definitions of fair outcomes exist, but it remains unclear how these align with human perceptions of fairness. We conducted a survey experiment (N = 258) examining common machine-learning definitions of fairness (demographic parity, equal opportunity, and equalized odds) in the context of algorithmic job interview invitations. We find that humans perceive the simple fairness definition of demographic parity as less fair than a more complex one that considers whether the invitees were eligible.

Keywords Perceived fairness · Survey experiment · Algorithmic decision-making

1 Introduction

Nowadays, algorithmic decision-making (ADM) is being used prominently in business operations with high visibility and high liability. A prime example is recruitment, where ADM is used for candidate selection and resume screening (Linkedin Talent Solutions 2018, 40–50)—where nondiscriminatory behavior is a concern.

Organizations prefer ADM because they deem it a more objective hiring process (Linkedin Talent Solutions 2018, 40; van den Broek et al. 2019, 3–4). However, ADM

J. Sengewald (✉) · A. Schlichter · R. Lackes
Business Informatics, Technical University Dortmund, Dortmund, Germany
e-mail: julian.sengewald@tu-dortmund.de

A. Schlichter
e-mail: anissa.schlichter@tu-dortmund.de

R. Lackes
e-mail: richard.lackes@tu-dortmund.de

M. Siepermann
Mathematics, Natural Sciences and Computer Science, University of Applied Sciences, Giessen, Germany
e-mail: markus.siepermann@mni.thm.de

D. Beverungen et al. (eds.), *Conceptualizing Digital Responsibility for the Information Age*, Lecture Notes in Information Systems and Organisation 74,
https://doi.org/10.1007/978-3-031-80119-8_4

can perpetuate bias and discrimination in recruitment because it relies on historical data that may not represent a diverse workforce (Dastin 2018; Köchling et al. 2021; Köchling and Wehner 2020; Mehrabi et al. 2021). As a result, ADM performance can be impaired and unfair for different demographic groups. Despite the existence of various computational approaches to address this problem (Friedler et al. 2019), these approaches currently lack a behavioral empirical foundation.

While humans have an innate sense of what constitutes fair treatment from an early age (Sloane et al. 2012), incorporating this sense into an algorithm is challenging. Previous studies (Cheng et al. 2021; Harrison et al. 2020; Srivastava et al. 2019; Wang et al. 2020) have used an empirical approach to identify mathematical definitions of fairness that correlate with *perceived fairness*. By identifying the moral standard that people use to evaluate the distributive outcome of ADM, a machine learning (ML) model can then be "tuned" accordingly, e.g., to choose more equitably to improve its perceived fairness. However, perceptions of fairness are highly context-dependent and subject to varying moral standards. But the existing literature has primarily examined the perceived fairness of ADM in criminal justice and health care while recruitment is a distinct domain. First, a large applicant pool may make it necessary to reject even qualified candidates, a trade-off that organizations must balance. Furthermore, ADM errors in high-stakes domains such as bail, pretrial release, or cancer detection can have irrevocable and serious consequences. In recruitment, errors have less of an impact because candidates who are rejected can re-apply to other companies. Consequently, findings from the areas examined in the prior literature, where decision-making is typically one-off, may not be directly applicable to ADM recruitment. Therefore, we pose the following research question:

RQ: *Which mathematical definition of fairness in ML most closely correlates to people's empirical perception of fairness in ADM-based recruitment?*

By answering this research question, we contribute to the research on how to leverage the potential of ADM in recruitment (Langer et al. 2019; Lee 2018; Suen et al. 2019; van Esch et al. 2019). For this, we explore how mathematical fairness definitions for ML (Harrison et al. 2020; Srivastava et al. 2019; Wang et al. 2020) are perceived in a novel application domain and address to the recent demand for more responsible and ethical ADM (van der Aalst 2017). This paper is organized as follows: In Sect. 2, we describe how ADM can be used in recruitment and provide the technical background for the mathematical definition of fairness. The experimental setup and design are outlined in Sect. 3.1. Section 3.2 describes how perceived fairness was measured, and Sect. 3.3 describes the empirical strategy. The results are presented in Sect. 4 and discussed in Sect. 5.

2 Background

2.1 Fairness in ADM and ML

Advances in ML have enabled widespread ADM adoption. Yet, ML models use probabilistic rules, which can lead to biased-erroneous decisions that treat individuals unfairly (Feuerriegel et al. 2020). Ethical issues arise when these errors disparately affect certain demographic groups. ADM's connection to fairness lies in the benefit allocated by its decision-making, e.g., when making hiring decisions (benefit = job) or deciding about university admissions (benefit = study place); all areas where unfair treatment would be problematic. If an ML classifier assigns a benefit (e.g., a hiring decision), we denote this as $\hat{Y} = 1$ and otherwise as $\hat{Y} = 0$, if no benefit is assigned. The classifier is learned from historical data, where $Y = 1$ indicates that an individual with characteristics X was eligible for the benefit and $Y = 0$ if the individual was ineligible. The decision-making of the ML classifier and eligibility is naturally linked to a confusion matrix; therefore, some authors also use the expression *predictive fairness* when discussing the matter, e.g., (Haas 2019).

There are three ways to ensure that the output of an ML classifier is fair:

- **Pre-processing**: alters data before training, e.g., by reweighting (Kamiran and Calders 2012). This works with any ML classifier.
- **At training time/in-processing**: a method that achieves high utility by simultaneously optimizing the classifier and fairness, e.g., using regularization (Kamishima et al. 2011). The downside is the need for specialized software.
- **Post-processing**: adjusting the predicted label of a classifier after prediction, e.g. using a linear program (Hardt et al. 2016).

For each method, the user must specify a mathematical fairness definition, a *fairness metric*, which can be classified in group- and individual-based metrics (Hutchinson and Mitchell 2019, 52). Group-based metrics are prevalent in software tools (e.g., IBM's AI Fairness 360, Bellamy et al. 2019, Microsoft's Fairlearn, Bird et al. 2020, and Google's What-If tool, Wexler et al. 2020). These metrics calculate the distribution of benefits between groups $g_1, \ldots, g_i, \ldots, g_G$. Gender, age, or ethnicity are examples of attributes used to form groups. If the benefit is allocated equally across the groups, according to a fairness metric, we say that *parity* is achieved for this metric.

Demographic Parity (DP) asserts that an ML classifier is fair if it gives the benefit to all demographic groups at the same rate τ^{DP}:

$$P\big(\hat{Y} = 1 | Group = g_i\big) = \tau^{DP} \forall g_i, i \in 1, \ldots, G$$

A DP classifier does not systematically disadvantage, or advantage individuals based on what group they are in. Unlike a quota system, which is common in the workplace (for example, requiring at least 20% of an executive board to be women), DP requires equal allocation rates for all groups. Although DP ensures the independence of the group and benefit allocation, it does not consider eligibility. The allocation rate among eligible individuals is measured by true-positive-rate ($TPR := P(\hat{Y} = 1|, Y = 1)$), among non-eligible by false-positive-rate, ($FPR := P(\hat{Y} = 1|, Y = 0)$). Allocation rates can be conditioned on eligibility and group to define yet another notion of fairness.

Equal Opportunity/True-Positive Parity (TPP) requires an equal benefit distribution over demographic groups conditioned on eligibility (Hardt et al. 2016). That means that equal opportunity holds if the group-specific TPR has the same value τ^{OP} across groups. True positive parity (TPP) holds when TPR is the same for all groups:

$$P(\hat{Y} = 1|Y = 1, g_i) = \tau^{OP}, \forall g_i \text{with} i \in \{1, \ldots, G\}$$

Equalized Odds (*TPP* + *FPP*) entails, in addition to TPP, also equalized False-Positive Rate (FPR), i.e. False Positive Parity (FPP) holds (Hardt et al. 2016): $P(\hat{Y} = 1|Y = 1, g_i) = \tau_1^{OD}$ and $P(\hat{Y} = 1|Y = 0, g_i) = \tau_2^{OD}, \forall g_i i \in \{1, \ldots, G\}$.

Other parity metrics are Accuracy Parity (ACCP), $P(\hat{Y} = \text{Y}|Group = g_i) = \tau^{acc}$, and False Negative Parity (FNP), $P(\hat{Y} = 0|Y = 1, Group = g_i) = \tau^{\text{FNP}}, \forall g_i i \in \{1, \ldots, G\}$.

2.2 Review of the Literature

The literature has increasingly focused on the issue of the perceived fairness of ADM. While perceived fairness is a broad concept (Dolata et al. 2022), the fourfold model (procedural, interpersonal, informational and distributive) is an empirically supported conceptualization of it (Colquitt and Shaw 2005). Studies have examined procedural features of ADM in terms of perceived fairness, such as how it compares to human decision-making depending on the task being automated (Lee 2018) and the role of data sources (Albach and Wright, James, R. 2021; Grgic-Hlaca et al. 2018). Also, informational aspects such as providing explanations and transparency contribute to perceived fairness (Binns et al. 2018; Dodge et al. 2019; Wang et al. 2020). Providing explanations to improve perceived fairness, while not significant in the case of being self-affected (Wang et al. 2020), can increase the perceived fairness of the overall ADM if designed as global explanations, whereas local explanations tailored to a specific outcome are more appropriate to justify a particular decision (Dodge et al. 2019). Another line of research focuses on distributive fairness, concerning how well ADM is perceived to treat those affected by its decision (Hannan et al. 2021; Harrison et al. 2020; Saxena et al. 2020; Srivastava et al. 2019; Wang et al. 2020). This study contributes to the distributive fairness and group-based metrics literature. Distributive fairness is measured by fairness metrics, which can be categorized into individual-based fairness metrics (Hannan et al. 2021; Saxena et al. 2020), and group-based metrics (Harrison et al. 2020; Srivastava et al. 2019; Wang et al. 2020).

A summary of the research on group-based metrics is shown in Table 1. The first study used two settings and an adaptive design (see Table 1), where the fairness metrics were generated to match the participant's preferred fairness metric. Participants preferred DP in both scenarios (Srivastava et al. 2019). Harrison et al. (2020) investigated how people perceive the fairness of different ways to make an ML model fair, by group metrics (ACCP and FNP[1]) or by the raw model score (i.e., no fairness definition). The study was conducted in the context of deciding whether to grant bail. The experiment was designed as a binary comparison between two models that had one or both properties equalized. Their data indicate a small, but statistically significant, preference for FNP rates between demographic groups (Harrison et al. 2020). Wang et. al. (2020) considered how (un-) equal error rates affect the fairness perception of ML algorithms. As equal error rates imply equal accuracy across groups, we remapped the results of Wang et. al. to ACCP in Table 1. Furthermore, the results showed that the perception of being self-disadvantaged by a biased algorithm was independent of the participant demographics. Also, participants perceived the algorithm as unfair if they received an unfavorable outcome, even though the algorithm was unbiased. Lastly, recent research has chosen a purely qualitative approach (Cheng et al. 2021). When comparing DP and EOP, their finding suggests a preference for EOP (Cheng et al. 2021). Most studies involving perceived fairness of group-based metrics deal with relatively high stake settings (e.g., crime and health) (Cheng et al. 2021; Harrison et al. 2020; Srivastava et al. 2019), and just a few studies deal with low-stakes settings (Wang et al. 2020). Participants are mostly required to select among two ML models satisfying either one/some (conflicting) fairness definitions. Their role was mainly a passive rater not self-affected by the ADM (Harrison et al. 2020; Srivastava et al. 2019). Typically, the fairness definitions were preset (Harrison et al. 2020, 396; Wang et al. 2020, 5), but an adaptive design has also been chosen (Srivastava et al. 2019).

In contrast, we use a new domain in a low stake setting, in which using ADM is well accepted (Langer et al. 2019). Unlike prior studies, we also utilize anonymous groupings to promote neutral responses. In addition, the set of metrics has not be shown to participants in this combination.

[1] In general, in binary ML classification the positive class can be arbitrary assigned to one of the classes. In the study of Harrison et al. (2020) a FP was labelled as "A defendant that is mistakenly denied bail [...]" (p. 4). In this case the decision linked to the positive class is "deny bail" and the beneficial outcome for the defendant would be "grant bail" is the negative class here. Most other studies labelled the beneficial outcome as the positive class (Srivastava et al. 2019). To be consistent across the literature we define in the positive class as the beneficial outcome and decided to remap FP to FN accordingly when necessary.

Table 1 Literature review

Literature	Setting	Approach	Predictive fairness					
			ACCP	FPP	FNP	DP	FPP and TPP	Sample
(Srivastava et al. 2019)	Crime, Health	• Options: Model trade-offs • Measurement: Binary choice • Perspective: Passive rater • Groups: Gender, race • Visualization: Confusion Matrix	○	○	○	●		Online AMT N = 200
(Harrison et al. 2020)	Bail	• Options: Model trade-offs • Measurement: 5-point Likert scale • Perspective: Passive rater • Groups: Race • Visualization: Diagram/ Percentage	○		●			Online AMT N = 502
(Wang et al. 2020)	Training	• Options: Overall rating • Measurement: 7-point Likert scale • Perspective: Personal affected • Groups: Gender, age, race • Visualization: Diagram/ Percentage	●					Online AMT N = 590

(continued)

Table 1 (continued)

Literature	Setting	Approach	Predictive fairness					
			ACCP	FPP	FNP	DP	FPP and TPP	Sample
(Cheng et al. 2021)	Social care	• Qualitative Study • Perspective: Active • Groups: Gender, age, race • Visualization: Multidimensional				○	●	Experts N = 12
This study	Recruitment	• Options: Overall rating • Measurement: 5-point Likert scale • Perspective: Passive rater • Groups: anonymous • Visualization: Confusion matrix		x		x	x	Online volunteers N = 258

○ Not-most-preferred, ● most preferred. Abbreviations:
ACCP Accuracy Parity.
FNP False Negative Parity.
FPP False Positive Parity.
DP Demographic Parity.

3 Methods

3.1 Experiment

Experimental Approach. We use an online survey experiment as our study method which is—according to the literature—the established method (see Fig. 1). We conducted a factorial survey, also known as "vignette experiments" (Atzmüller and Steiner 2010), to determine what the most preferred fairness definition is. In a factorial survey, participants are shown a full description of the scenario and are therefore well suited for studying social norms (Alves and Rossi 1978).

Four vignettes were presented to each participant in a within-subject design (see Fig. 1 panel (a)). Each vignette showed the outcome of an ADM using a confusion matrix. We generated each confusion matrix by a constraint optimization problem, maximizing either the equalized false positive rate, equalized chances, or demographic parity while holding overall accuracy and the number of invitations constant.

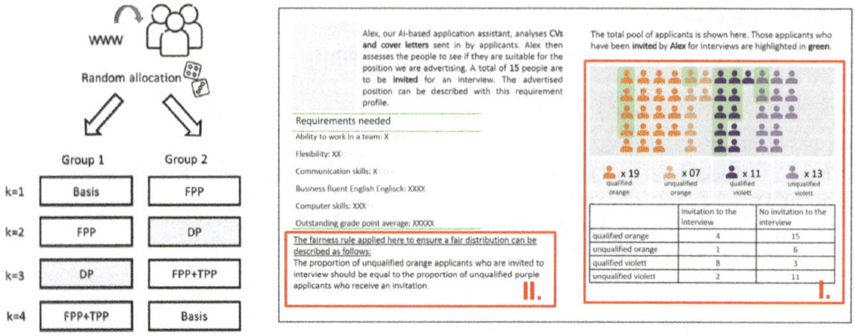

(a) Experimental layout (b) Exemplary vignette[2] maximized for DP

Fig. 1 Experimental structure and vignette design **a** Experimental layout **b** Exemplary vignette[2] maximized for DP

By fixing accuracy, we ensure that participants only evaluate distributive changes not the overall algorithm performance (Srivastava et al. 2019). We also supplied a fairness-unoptimized baseline case. Participants scored three fairness criteria and the baseline scenario. The vignettes were built on each other, so their sequencing was not randomized. FPP was displayed first because it is nested within FPP + TPP. The case DP, unrelated to the nested scenarios, was added between them to hide the nesting. This allowed participants to easily transition between vignettes.

Setting. As the usage domain of ADM, we used candidate prescreening for an advertised job offer. To make the setting realistic, the number of job candidates invited to a personal interview is limited, and therefore only the most qualified candidates should be invited. This use of ADM is one where decision-making is fully automated (Langer et al. 2019). The scenario was chosen for two reasons: first, the experiment's participants would presumably be familiar with the setting of a job interview. This increases the internal validity of the given answers. Furthermore, candidate prescreening for interview invites provides study participants with a realistic and compelling scenario.

Vignette Design. Figure 1 panel (b) shows an exemplary vignette. The vignette begins with a general description: Using ADM for candidate prescreening along with an imaginary job profile. Whether a job candidate is invited to an interview depends on whether the ADM system deems them qualified. The vignette also shows two groups and their corresponding ADM outcomes. Selected job candidates are highlighted in green, while their qualification level is depicted by intense or non-intense shading. Additionally, the algorithmic outcome is also depicted using two group-specific confusion matrices. The confusion matrix was varied as follows (Fig. 1, panel (b), I.) (Table 2):

[2] A grey box represents the graphically visualized AI in the user study; however, the image is not available for online publication due to legal reasons.

Table 2 Variation of invitation (Rows: vignettes. Columns: Confusion matrices)

	TP		TN		FP		FN	
	orange	violet	orange	violet	orange	violet	orange	violet
Basis	9	3	4	13	3	0	10	8
FPP	4	8	6	11	1	2	15	3
DP	5	7	4	13	3	0	14	4
FPP + TPP	8	4	6	11	1	2	11	7

We also give a short explanation of the related fairness definition (Fig. 1, panel (b), II.), to rule out that some definitions are harder for participants to understand (Saha et al. 2020). These descriptions are (translated from German):

- *Basis*. "The ratio of invited qualified applicants to the not-invited qualified applicants should be significantly greater than the ratio of unqualified applicants who receive an invitation to unqualified applicants who are not invited to interview".
- *FFP*. "The proportion of unqualified orange applicants who are invited to interview should be equal to the proportion of invited unqualified purple applicants".
- *FPP + TPP.* FPP and "The proportion of not-invited qualified orange applicants should equal the proportion of not-invited qualified purple applicants".
- *DP*. "The proportion of orange applicants who receive an invitation to interview should be equal to the proportion of purple applicants who receive an invitation".

We depicted both groups solely by color (orange/purple) to maintain anonymity and prevent response biases. In-group favoritism (e.g., male participants give a higher rating to outcomes favoring male depicted candidates) (Harrison et al. 2020, 401) or support for affirmative action (Harrison et al. 2020, 398; Saxena et al. 2020, 5–6), are known predictors of response bias. Blinding the group mitigates the response bias.

3.2 Measurement

We use "overall fairness" to measure the perceived fairness among study participants. Perceived overall fairness can be measured by the individual's experience of fairness and the overall entity perception (Colquitt and Shaw 2005). We use a reduced version of an existing scale that combines both types of fairness ratings (Colquitt and Shaw 2005), with a total of three measurement items. For each item, participants reported on a six-point Likert scale ranging from 1 ('*Completely disagree*') to 6 ('*Completely agree*'). Table 3 shows the items and participants' average ratings for each item.

The overall fairness perception scale is reflective and gives the measurement model: $y_j = \lambda_j \eta + \varepsilon_j$. Each reflective measurement y_j obtained by item j measures with a correlation λ_j the underlying construct η plus an item-specific error term ε_j. To evaluate the reflective model, two factors were examined: 1) the internal consistency

Table 3 Overall fairness, (Colquitt and Shaw 2005), $\alpha = 0.81$, $\rho_c = 0.89$, AVE = 0.72

Item	Text	Mean	Std. dev
1	I feel that the way the decision was made was fair	3.48	1.07
2	Overall, the decision-making process treats every candidate fair	3.46	1.01
3	Most candidates would say that they were treated fair in the decision-making process	3.34	1.06

reliability, and 2) convergent validity (Hair et al. 2021). First, using the criteria of composite reliability ρ_c and Cronbach's α, we assess the internal consistency. The composite reliability ρ_c is reported to be 0.89, indicating that there is a high level of internal consistency (Hair et al. 2021). We also calculated Cronbach's α, the average inter-item correlation, which has a value of 0.81, indicating that there is a high level of consistency between the items (Robinson 2018). Next, we assess the convergent validity. For this validation, we use the average variance extracted (AVE). The AVE is 0.72, which is higher than the required minimum of 0.5 (Hair et al. 2016).

3.3 *Empirical Strategy*

For our analysis, we used an *ordinal mixed-effects* regression model. An ordinal model is a reliable method for estimating the effect of categorical, ordinal, and metric variables on an ordinal outcome (McCullagh 1980). In contrast to a linear model, the ordinal model is more robust against false alarms and false omissions when applied to ordinal data (Liddell and Kruschke 2018). We use a *multinomial logistic* model using a logistic link function, e.g., (Christensen 2018). In our context, the multinomial logistic model assumes a latent fairness perception score y^* for which only categorical realization on the Likert scale is observable. This means participants choose a particular value c on the Likert scale if their latent fairness perception resides in the interval (θ_{c-1}, θ_c). The observed distribution of the fairness ratings, conditioned on the vector of observable characteristics, can therefore be expressed as $P\left(y_{ij,k} = c|x\right) = P\left(\theta_{c-1} < y^*_{ij,k} \leq \theta_c|x\right)$. For answering our research question, we explore how the different trade-offs of optimizing the fairness definitions are perceived.

Owing to the peculiar experimental structure, repeated measurements, we construct an appropriate empirical model. There are repeated measurements for the items and participants. Participants rated a total of four different vignettes. The response pattern of the participant may depend not only on the vignette and observable demographics but also on many unobserved participant characteristics. These unobserved characteristics are modeled by a participant-specific error term $\dot{u}_i$. We also included a random effect for each of the four repeated measures for the item j and those repeated measures share an error term from the reflective measurement model $y_j = \lambda_j \eta + \varepsilon_j$. For repeated measurements, a mixed-effects model is better suited, ensuring more efficient estimates and sound statistical inference (Atzmüller and Steiner 2010). We denote individuals by i, with $i \in 1, \ldots, N$, the item j, with $j \in 1, 2, 3$, and trial k, with $k \in 1, 2, 3, 4$. The full mixed-effects model is given as follows:

$$y_{ij,k} = \beta_o + \beta_1 case + \beta_2 age + \beta_3 sex + \beta_4 education + \dot{u}_i + \varepsilon_j + u_{ij,k}$$

Besides the mixed effects model, we include a linear model in the results, because it is widely used, and to illustrate the robustness of our findings. The linear model is estimated by OLS. Because of repeated measurements, we report clustered standard errors using the sandwich package in R (Zeileis et al. 2020). Standard errors are clustered by the participant, and we use a degree-of-freedom correction of $n/(n-k)$ for the covariance matrix (MacKinnon and White 1985; Zeileis et al. 2020, 7–9). The dependent variable is based on averaging the reflective items $y_{i,k}^{OLS} = \frac{1}{3}\sum_{j=1}^{3} y_{ij,k}$.

4 Results

4.1 Sample

Study participants were voluntarily recruited on social media (Facebook, and WhatsApp) and via e-mail lists. To encourage participation, each participant was offered an incentive in the form of a charitable donation. In total, 523 answered the online questionnaire. 258 participants completed the fairness ratings. The analysis sample was these 258 participants. The sample consists of 58% female, 36% male, and 6% of an undisclosed gender. The age distribution is young, with 64% of the participants being 23–30 years old and 16% being 22 years of age or younger. About 6% did not disclose their gender. The sample is highly educated, with 78% having finished or currently pursuing a university education, which is a higher level of education than the German average (DeStatis 2020). We also asked how frequently study participants had experienced discrimination in work-related decisions such as hiring or job promotion. Female study participants reported being discriminated against in 46% whereas male ones reported 42%. For the entire sample, 42% of the participants had experienced discrimination, and 11% had experienced 'often' discrimination 'often' in the workplace. Therefore, the sample shows awareness of the study topic.

4.2 Fairness Preferences

We now turn to the empirical results. Table 4 reports the results of four regression models. In the first model, we include the main explanatory variable, "optimizing for a mathematical fairness definition", and no further controls. According to the computed coefficients, the TPP fairness criterion stands out as the most well-received option, as it is widely seen as the only agreement that meets the criteria of high perceived fairness. In contrast, other options were found to fall short of these requirements.

Next, we included control variables for demographic characteristics. Overall, the estimated coefficients remain robust in terms of their relative ranking and numerically. The combined effect of the definition of fairness of equalized odds (FPP and TPP) is positive (beta = 0.9, se = 0.133, $p < 0.05$), which we obtained from conducting an ordinal regression containing an appropriately specified dummy coefficient.

In general, all demographic control variables (age, gender, and education) are not statistically significant. Unlike the other models, Model 3 controls for participants' perceived fairness with fixed effects. We found that the previous results hold regardless of whether the reflective measure is included as a fixed or random effect term. The fixed effects for the measurement items are not significantly different from those for the intercept, which includes one of the measurement items. The non-significant result can be interpreted as indicating that the items behave similarly, demonstrating the good properties of our reflective scale for measuring perceived fairness. Finally, we also include a linear model that specifies the Likert scale as the metric variable. The estimated coefficients can now be interpreted directly on a scale from 1 to 7. We again find that the TPP is perceived as more fair than the baseline case. The signs of demographic parity and FPP are negative, indicating that they are perceived as less fair. The effect size is small, and the coefficient is not statistically significant. We also examined possible heterogeneity and tested for interaction effects between demographics and fairness definitions but found no significant effect. In sum, to ensure fairness in simple decisions, TPP criterion is preferable over others.

5 Discussion

The analysis suggests that participants perceive the definitions of equalized odds (FPP and TPP) to be fairer than the remaining definitions. Similar results to ours were obtained in the experiment by Cheng et al. (2021) with qualitative methods. Our approach supports this finding using a quantitative approach and in a recruitment context. Furthermore, we find that DP is the second most preferred fairness metric. These results are not in line with those of Srivastava et al. (2019), who found that DP was considered the fairest. We also find that FPP is the least preferred fairness definition. This finding can be interpreted as follows: participants understood the experiment well because the unqualified would have been invited at the expense of the qualified. It also means that participants considered the business utility of the selection procedure, although we hold accuracy constant. We include FPP in the researched set of fairness metrics because FPP can reduce workplace discrimination by detecting phenomena such as in-group favoritism and nepotism (offering resources preferably to family and friends). We find mixed significance in the results

Table 4 Regression results

	Ordinal (Coefficients are log odds)			OLS
Variables\model	(1)	(2)	(3)	(4)
Fairness definitions (dummy coded)				
True positive parity (TPP)	1.218***	1.218***	1.219***	0.660***
	(0.097)	(0.097)	(0.097)	(0.094)
Demographic parity (DP)	−0.162*	−0.161*	−0.161*	−0.067
	(0.093)	(0.093)	(0.093)	(0.079)
False positive parity (FPP)	−0.301***	−0.301***	−0.302***	−0.140**
	(0.093)	(0.093)	(0.093)	(0.067)
Controls				
Age				
< = 30		−0.343	−0.343	−0.119
		(0.329)	(0.329)	(0.185)
> 30		−0.221	−0.222	−0.119
		(0.386)	(0.386)	(0.185)
Missing		−0.195	−0.195	−0.130
		(0.601)	(0.601)	(0.315)
Gender				
Female		0.390*	0.390*	0.184*
		(0.207)	(0.207)	(0.104)
Missing		1.515**	1.516***	0.747**
		(0.649)	(0.648)	(0.297)
Education				
Bachelor or in-education		0.037	0.037	0.045
		(0.268)	(0.268)	(0.125)
Master and above		0.012	0.012	0.011
		(0.324)	(0.324)	(0.160)
Missing		−1.125	−1.125	−0.557*
		(0.811)	(0.811)	(0.304)
Items	RE	RE	FE	Averaged
Participants	RE	RE	RE	RE
N	3096	3096	3096	1032
Nakagawa's conditional R2	0.465	0. 463	0.463	–
R2	–	–	–	0.06

Significance levels: *** $p \leq 0.01$, **$p \leq 0.05$, *$p \leq 0.1$

for demographics; similar to previous work (Wang et al. 2020). In summary, the results show that perceived fairness can be increased by choosing an appropriate fairness definition to make ML fair; enterprises can increase the perceived fairness of their ADM-based recruitment processes to meet organizational objectives like organizational attractiveness, job satisfaction, commitment, and turnover intentions (Ambrose and Schminke 2009; McCarthy et al. 2017). The fairness definition DP is the second fairest, and therefore may be regarded as a good and easy-to-realize proxy for fairness in the recruitment process. However, the introduction of a quota system into recruitment processes based solely on this definition appears not recommendable. In addition, the DP fairness definition may not accurately capture the fairness perception of participants. It is also possible that participants were predisposed to engage in the DP fairness definition because of their familiarity with government employment advertisements, where the promotion of equality (e.g., between genders) is commonplace. Altogether, what is noticeable is that even for the most regarded fairness definition, equalized odds, the overall fairness perception of the ADM outcome is low. This finding somewhat implies that the set of fairness metrics is not exhaustive and future research is needed. Lastly, we did not find significant age which is line (Wang et al. 2020). The same holds for education which stands in contrast to previous studies (Wang et al. 2020). This could be due to the sample composition.

As with any study, there are limitations. First, the study participants did not rate the actual use of ADM in recruitment. However, due to the realistic scenario, the overall setting is very believable to participants. Furthermore, we used an online volunteer sample, and a different population may provide different ratings. However, students have a higher thematic involvement in the scenario because they will likely encounter ADM-based recruitment. We studied a small set of fairness definitions, and the inclusion of a new fairness metric in the experiment may give another ranking. Overall, the sample is characterized by people of young age and higher education and a large proportion of women. Therefore, the findings would need to be validated with a broader sample. To increase the generalizability of our findings, we propose that future research tests our findings in a different cultural setting because social norms could influence what is perceived as fair (Awad et al. 2018). Also, the organization should consider that solely optimizing for a fairness definition is not enough, because the impacted parties should also be informed about how fairness was ensured, as in our experiment. It would be interesting to study how the design of the information impacts the perception of fairness. Organizations should also consider procedural factors when designing their ADM-based recruitment (Langer et al. 2019; Lee 2018; Ochmann et al. 2020).

6 Conclusion

In particular, ADM has been accepted in less complex decision-making scenarios, such as the prescreening of candidates (Langer et al. 2019). However, while ADM raises ethical concerns, it also allows us to think more deeply about previously implicit processes. Human decisions have more variability and subjectivity than ADM. Algorithmic processes, on the other hand, can be used to make algorithms behave according to societal norms when combined with crowdsourced perceptions of fairness. Therefore, this research can help companies make ADM-based hiring perceived as fair. In line with regulations such as the European Union's proposed AI Act, companies can mitigate the societal impact of AI while increasing efficiency through the use of automation. However, we also believe that excessive crowdsourcing should be scrutinized. Crowdsourcing fairness perceptions are consistent with characterizing existing societal norms (descriptive ethics), but embedding crowdsourced norms into algorithms also has normative implications that require caution.

References

Albach, Michele/Wright, James, R. (2021). The role of accuracy in algorithmic process fairness across multiple domains. Proceedings of the 22nd ACM Conference on Economics and Computation, 29–49. https://doi.org/10.1145/3465456.3467620.

Alves, Wayne M./Rossi, Peter H. (1978). Who Should Get What? Fairness Judgments of the Distribution of Earnings. American Journal of Sociology 84 (3), 541–564. https://doi.org/10.1086/226826.

Ambrose, Maureen L./Schminke, Marshall (2009). The role of overall justice judgments in organizational justice research: a test of mediation. The Journal of applied psychology 94 (2), 491–500. https://doi.org/10.1037/a0013203.

Atzmüller, Christiane/Steiner, Peter M. (2010). Experimental Vignette Studies in Survey Research. Methodology 6 (3), 128–138. https://doi.org/10.1027/1614-2241/a000014.

Awad, Edmond/Dsouza, Sohan/Kim, Richard/Schulz, Jonathan/Henrich, Joseph/Shariff, Azim/Bonnefon, Jean-François/Rahwan, Iyad (2018). The Moral Machine experiment. Nature 563 (7729), 59–64. https://doi.org/10.1038/s41586-018-0637-6.

Bellamy, Rachel K. E./Dey, Kuntal/Hind, Michael/Hoffman, Samuel C./Houde, Stephanie/Kannan, Kalapriya/Lohia, Pranay/Martino, Jacquelyn/Mehta, Sameep/Mojsilović, Aleksandra (2019). AI Fairness 360: An extensible toolkit for detecting and mitigating algorithmic bias. IBM Journal of Research and Development 63 (4/5), 4: 1–4: 15.

Binns, Reuben/van Kleek, Max/Veale, Michael/Lyngs, Ulrik/Zhao, Jun/Shadbolt, Nigel (2018). 'It's Reducing a Human Being to a Percentage'. In: Regan Mandryk/Mark Hancock (Eds.). Engage with CHI. CHI 2018 : proceedings of the 2018 CHI Conference on Human Factors in Computing Systems : April 21 -26, 2018, Montréal, QC, Canada, CHI '18: CHI Conference on Human Factors in Computing Systems, Montreal QC Canada, 21 04 2018 26 04 2018. New York, New York, The Association for Computing Machinery, 1–14.

Bird, Sarah/Dudík, Miro/Edgar, Richard/Horn, Brandon/Lutz, Roman/Milan, Vanessa/Sameki, Mehrnoosh/Wallach, Hanna/Walker, Kathleen (2020). Fairlearn: A toolkit for assessing and improving fairness in AI. Microsoft. MSR-TR-2020–32. Available online at https://www.

microsoft.com/en-us/research/publication/fairlearn-a-toolkit-for-assessing-and-improving-fairness-in-ai/.

Cheng, Hao-Fei/Stapleton, Logan/Wang, Ruiqi/Bullock, Paige/Chouldechova, Alexandra/Wu, Zhiwei Steven Steven/Zhu, Haiyi (2021). Soliciting Stakeholders' Fairness Notions in Child Maltreatment Predictive Systems. In: Yoshifumi Kitamura/Aaron Quigley/Katherine Isbister et al. (Eds.). Proceedings of the 2021 CHI Conference on Human Factors in Computing Systems, CHI '21: CHI Conference on Human Factors in Computing Systems, Yokohama Japan, 08 05 2021 13 05 2021. New York, NY, USA, ACM, 1–17.

Christensen, Rune Haubo B. (2018). Cumulative link models for ordinal regression with the R package ordinal. Submitted in J. Stat. Software 35.

Colquitt, Jason/Shaw, John (2005). How Should Organizational Justice Be Measured? In: Jerald Greenberg/Jason Colquitt (Eds.). Handbook of organizational justice. Mahwah, N.J, Lawrence Erlbaum Associates, 113–152.

Dastin, Jeffrey (2018). Amazon scraps secret AI recruiting tool that showed bias against women. Reuters. Available online at https://www.reuters.com/article/us-amazon-com-jobs-automation-insight-idUSKCN1MK08G (accessed 6/5/2022).

DeStatis (Ed.) (2020). Bildungsstand der Bevölkerung - Ergebnisse des Mikrozensus 2019 - Ausgabe 2020.

Dodge, Jonathan/Liao, Q. Vera/Zhang, Yunfeng/Bellamy, Rachel K. E./Dugan, Casey (2019). Explaining models. In: Wai-Tat Fu/Shimei Pan/Oliver Brdiczka et al. (Eds.). IUI '19, IUI '19: 24th International Conference on Intelligent User Interfaces, Marina del Ray California, 17 03 2019 20 03 2019. New York (NY), ACM, 275–285.

Dolata, Mateusz/Feuerriegel, Stefan/Schwabe, Gerhard (2022). A sociotechnical view of algorithmic fairness. Information Systems Journal 32 (4), 754–818. https://doi.org/10.1111/isj.12370.

Feuerriegel, Stefan/Dolata, Mateusz/Schwabe, Gerhard (2020). Fair AI. Business & Information Systems Engineering 62 (4), 379–384. https://doi.org/10.1007/s12599-020-00650-3.

Friedler, Sorelle A./Scheidegger, Carlos/Venkatasubramanian, Suresh/Choudhary, Sonam/Hamilton, Evan P./Roth, Derek (2019). A comparative study of fairness-enhancing interventions in machine learning. In: Proceedings of the Conference on Fairness, Accountability, and Transparency. Atlanta, GA, USA, Association for Computing Machinery, 329–338.

Grgic-Hlaca, Nina/Redmiles, Elissa M./Gummadi, Krishna P./Weller, Adrian (2018). Human Perceptions of Fairness in Algorithmic Decision Making. In: Pierre-Antoine Champin/Fabien Gandon/Mounia Lalmas et al. (Eds.). Proceedings of the 2018 World Wide Web Conference, the 2018 World Wide Web Conference, Lyon, France, 23.04.2018 - 27.04.2018. Republic and Canton of Geneva, International World Wide Web Conferences Steering Committee, 903–912.

Haas, Christian (2019). The price of fairness. A framework to explore trade-offs in algorithmic fairness. ICIS 2019 Proceedings 19. Available online at https://aisel.aisnet.org/icis2019/data_science/data_science/19/ (accessed 9/21/2020).

Hair, Joseph F./Hult, G. Tomas M./Ringle, Christian M./Sarstedt, Marko (2016). A Primer on Partial Least Squares Structural Equation Modeling (PLS-SEM). 2nd ed. Thousand Oaks, SAGE Publications, Incorporated.

Hair, Joseph F./Hult, G. Tomas M./Ringle, Christian M./Sarstedt, Marko/Danks, Nicholas P./Ray, Soumya (2021). Evaluation of Reflective Measurement Models. In: Joseph F. Hair/Tomas M. Hult/Christian M. Ringle et al. (Eds.). Partial least squares structural equation modeling (PLS-SEM) using R. A workbook. Cham, Springer, 75–90.

Hannan, Jacqueline/Winnie Chen, Huei-Yen/Joseph, Kenneth (2021). Who Gets What, According to Whom? An Analysis of Fairness Perceptions in Service Allocation. In: Proceedings of the 2021 AAAI/ACM Conference on AI, Ethics, and Society. Virtual Event, USA, Association for Computing Machinery, 555–565.

Hardt, Moritz/Price, Eric/Srebro, Nathan (2016). Equality of opportunity in supervised learning. In: Proceedings of the 30th International Conference on Neural Information Processing Systems. Barcelona, Spain, Curran Associates Inc, 3323–3331.

Harrison, Galen/Hanson, Julia/Jacinto, Christine/Ramirez, Julio/Ur, Blase (2020). An empirical study on the perceived fairness of realistic, imperfect machine learning models. In: Proceedings of the 2020 Conference on Fairness, Accountability, and Transparency. New York, NY, USA, Association for Computing Machinery, 392–402.

Hutchinson, Ben/Mitchell, Margaret (2019). 50 Years of Test (Un)fairness: Lessons for Machine Learning. In: Proceedings of the Conference on Fairness, Accountability, and Transparency. Atlanta, GA, USA, Association for Computing Machinery, 49–58.

Kamiran, Faisal/Calders, Toon (2012). Data preprocessing techniques for classification without discrimination. Knowledge and Information Systems 33 (1), 1–33. https://doi.org/10.1007/s10115-011-0463-8.

Kamishima, Toshihiro/Akaho, Shotaro/Sakuma, Jun (2011). Fairness-aware Learning through Regularization Approach. 2011 IEEE 11th International Conference on Data Mining Workshops, 643–650.

Köchling, Alina/Riazy, Shirin/Wehner, Marius Claus/Simbeck, Katharina (2021). Highly accurate, but still discriminatory. Business & Information Systems Engineering 63 (1), 39–54. https://doi.org/10.1007/s12599-020-00673-w.

Köchling, Alina/Wehner, Marius Claus (2020). Discriminated by an algorithm: a systematic review of discrimination and fairness by algorithmic decision-making in the context of HR recruitment and HR development. Business Research 13 (3), 795–848. https://doi.org/10.1007/s40685-020-00134-w.

Langer, Markus/König, Cornelius J./Papathanasiou, Maria (2019). Highly automated job interviews: Acceptance under the influence of stakes. International Journal of Selection and Assessment 27 (3), 217–234. https://doi.org/10.1111/ijsa.12246.

Lee, Min Kyung (2018). Understanding perception of algorithmic decisions: Fairness, trust, and emotion in response to algorithmic management. Big Data & Society 5 (1), 1-16.

Liddell, Torrin M./Kruschke, John K. (2018). Analyzing ordinal data with metric models: What could possibly go wrong? Journal of Experimental Social Psychology 79, 328–348. https://doi.org/10.1016/j.jesp.2018.08.009.

Linkedin Talent Solutions (2018). Global recruiting trends 2018. The 4 ideas changing how you hire. Available online at https://business.linkedin.com/content/dam/me/business/en-us/talent-solutions/resources/pdfs/linkedin-global-recruiting-trends-2018-en-us.pdf (accessed 6/5/2022).

MacKinnon, James G./White, Halbert (1985). Some heteroskedasticity-consistent covariance matrix estimators with improved finite sample properties. Journal of Econometrics 29 (3), 305–325. https://doi.org/10.1016/0304-4076(85)90158-7.

McCarthy, Julie M./Bauer, Talya N./Truxillo, Donald M./Anderson, Neil R./Costa, Ana Cristina/Ahmed, Sara M. (2017). Applicant Perspectives During Selection: A Review Addressing "So What?," "What's New?," and "Where to Next?". Journal of Management 43 (6), 1693–1725. https://doi.org/10.1177/0149206316681846.

McCullagh, Peter (1980). Regression Models for Ordinal Data. Journal of the Royal Statistical Society: Series B (Methodological) 42 (2), 109–127. https://doi.org/10.1111/j.2517-6161.1980.tb01109.x.

Mehrabi, Ninareh/Morstatter, Fred/Saxena, Nripsuta/Lerman, Kristina/Galstyan, Aram (2021). A survey on bias and fairness in machine learning. ACM Computing Surveys 54 (6), Article 115. https://doi.org/10.1145/3457607.

Ochmann, Jessica/Michels, Leonard/Zilker, Sandra/Tiefenbeck, Verena/Laumer, Sven (2020). The influence of algorithm aversion and anthropomorphic agent design on the acceptance of AI-based job recommendations. ICIS 2020 Proceedings. Available online at https://aisel.aisnet.org/icis2020/is_workplace_fow/is_workplace_fow/4.

Robinson, Mark A. (2018). Using multi-item psychometric scales for research and practice in human resource management. Human Resource Management 57 (3), 739–750. https://doi.org/10.1002/hrm.21852.

Saha, Debjani/Schumann, Candice/Mcelfresh, Duncan/Dickerson, John/Mazurek, Michelle/Tschantz, Michael (2020). Measuring non-expert comprehension of machine learning fairness metrics. In: International Conference on Machine Learning. PMLR, 8377–8387.

Saxena, Nripsuta Ani/Huang, Karen/DeFilippis, Evan/Radanovic, Goran/Parkes, David C./Liu, Yang (2020). How do fairness definitions fare? Testing public attitudes towards three algorithmic definitions of fairness in loan allocations. artificial intelligence 283. https://doi.org/10.1016/J.ARTINT.2020.103238.

Sloane, Stephanie/Baillargeon, Renée/Premack, David (2012). Do infants have a sense of fairness? Psychological Science 23 (2), 196–204. https://doi.org/10.1177/0956797611422072.

Srivastava, Megha/Heidari, Hoda/Krause, Andreas (2019). Mathematical Notions vs. Human Perception of Fairness: A Descriptive Approach to Fairness for Machine Learning. In: Proceedings of the 25th ACM SIGKDD International Conference on Knowledge Discovery & Data Mining. Anchorage, AK, USA, Association for Computing Machinery, 2459–2468.

Suen, Hung-Yue/Chen, Mavis Yi-Ching/Lu, Shih-Hao (2019). Does the use of synchrony and artificial intelligence in video interviews affect interview ratings and applicant attitudes? Computers in Human Behavior 98, 93–101

van den Broek, Elmira/Sergeeva, Anastasia/and Huysman, Marleen (2019). Hiring Algorithms: An Ethnography of Fairness in Practice. ICIS 2019 Proceedings. 6.

van der Aalst, Wil M. P. (2017). Responsible data science: Using event data in a "People Friendly" Manner. In: Slimane Hammoudi/Leszek A. Maciaszek/Michele M. Missikoff et al. (Eds.). Enterprise Information Systems, Cham, 2017. Cham, Springer International Publishing, 3–28.

van Esch, Patrick/Black, J. Stewart/Ferolie, Joseph (2019). Marketing AI recruitment: The next phase in job application and selection. Computers in Human Behavior 90, 215–222. https://doi.org/10.1016/j.chb.2018.09.009.

Wang, Ruotong/Harper, F. Maxwell/Zhu, Haiyi (2020). Factors influencing perceived fairness in algorithmic decision-making. In: Regina Bernhaupt (Ed.). Proceedings of the 2020 CHI Conference on Human Factors in Computing Systems, CHI '20: CHI Conference on Human Factors in Computing Systems, Honolulu HI USA. New York, NY, United States, Association for Computing Machinery, 1–14.

Wexler, J./Pushkarna, M./Bolukbasi, T./Wattenberg, M./Viégas, F./Wilson, J. (2020). The What-If Tool: Interactive Probing of Machine Learning Models. IEEE Transactions on Visualization and Computer Graphics 26 (1), 56–65. https://doi.org/10.1109/TVCG.2019.2934619.

Zeileis, Achim/Köll, Susanne/Graham, Nathaniel (2020). Various Versatile Variances: An Object-Oriented Implementation of Clustered Covariances in R. Journal of Statistical Software 95 (1). https://doi.org/10.18637/jss.v095.i01.

Unraveling Information-Limiting Environments: An Empirical Review of Individual, Social, and Technological Filters in Social Media

Kian Schmalenbach, Eva Gengler, Sebastian Schötteler, and Sven Laumer

Abstract Social media platforms offer a convenient way for people to interact and exchange information. However, there are sustained concerns that filter bubbles and echo chambers create information-limiting environments (ILEs) for their users. Despite a well-developed conceptual understanding, the empirical evidence regarding the causes and supporting conditions of these ILEs remains inconclusive. This paper addresses this gap by applying the triple-filter-bubble model developed by (Geschke et al. 2019) to analyze empirical literature on the individual, social, and technological causes of ILEs. While we identify some factors that increase the probability of ILEs under certain conditions, our findings do not suffice to thoroughly validate conceptual models that explain why ILEs emerge. Therefore, we call for future research to investigate the causes of ILEs with higher external validity to develop a more comprehensive understanding of this phenomenon.

Keywords Echo chambers · Filter bubbles · Information-limiting environments · Social media · Triple-filter-bubble model

---

K. Schmalenbach (✉) · E. Gengler · S. Schötteler · S. Laumer
FAU Erlangen-Nürnberg, Institut für Wirtschaftsinformatik, Nuremberg, Germany
e-mail: kian.schmalenbach@fau.de

E. Gengler
e-mail: eva.gengler@fau.de

S. Schötteler
e-mail: sebastian.schoetteler@th-nuernberg.de

S. Laumer
e-mail: sven.laumer@fau.de

S. Schötteler
Technische Hochschule Nürnberg, Nuremberg, Germany

D. Beverungen et al. (eds.), *Conceptualizing Digital Responsibility for the Information Age*, Lecture Notes in Information Systems and Organisation 74,
https://doi.org/10.1007/978-3-031-80119-8_5

1 Introduction

Social media platforms play a crucial role in our society, facilitating global connection, interaction, and information sharing. However, they also pose significant risks, such as misinformation spread, public opinion manipulation, and polarization (Abouzeid et al. 2019; Kitchens et al. 2020; Vicario et al. 2016a, b). The Club of Rome has even identified the propagation of misinformation as the most urgent challenge of our time (Dixson-Decleve et al. 2022). The term "filter bubble," coined by Eli Pariser (2011), highlights the dangers associated with social media. Personalization and filtering algorithms create this phenomenon by presenting users with content that aligns with their past behavior and inferred personality traits. This approach discourages users from encountering information that challenges their beliefs, leading to a limited understanding of available information (Helberger et al. 2018). Consequently, users may be exposed mainly to content that reinforces their existing opinions, resulting in polarization and the formation of "echo chambers" where like-minded individuals continuously reinforce each other's beliefs (Sunstein 2002). These phenomena collectively give rise to an *information-limiting environment (ILE)* that significantly restricts the quantity, diversity, and perspectives of information accessible to social media users (Kitchens et al. 2020).

Understanding the causes of ILEs in social media platforms is complex due to factors such as rapid content growth driven by network effects (Van Alstyne & Brynjolfsson 2005), personalized mechanisms shaping available information (Eg et al. 2023), and social phenomena like homophily and group polarization (Bakshy et al. 2015). The intricate nature of these factors hinders both theoretical and empirical analysis of specific antecedents leading to ILE emergence. To address this challenge, Geschke et al. (2019) propose a framework that categorizes ILE antecedents into three types: individual, social, and technological filters. Individual filters encompass cognitive processes influencing users' information consumption behavior, social filters involve network structure and dynamics contributing to ILEs, and technological filters refer to algorithmic causes of ILEs in social media (Geschke et al. 2019).

While such conceptual frameworks are useful for classifying ILE antecedents, their explanatory power is often limited due to the absence of empirical validation. The complex nature of ILEs, involving sociotechnical interactions and human psychology, necessitates empirical investigation with real individuals instead of relying solely on data obtained from computer simulations (Geschke et al. 2019). In this vein, a recent comprehensive review of empirical research on ILEs by Terren & Borge (2021) highlights the inconclusive nature of empirical findings on antecedents causing ILE emergence, as they appear to depend on context-specific factors such as data collection methods. These observations indicate a lack of a comprehensive overview of empirical evidence on the diverse causes of ILE emergence in the existing literature. To address this gap, we conduct a structured literature review to systematically analyze and synthesize existing empirical findings related to individual users, social contexts, and technological factors associated with ILE emergence. Therefore, we formulate the following research question: *What is the current empirical evidence regarding the role of individual users, social context, and technological factors in the emergence of ILEs in social media?*

In addressing this research question, our objective is to provide a comprehensive and well-structured overview of the existing empirical research on ILE antecedents. Through this analysis, we will assess the adequacy of the aggregated empirical literature for validating conceptual frameworks that explain the emergence of ILEs. If the current empirical evidence is sufficient for validation, our paper will contribute by offering researchers a valuable and comprehensive overview of empirically supported data for explaining ILE emergence. Alternatively, if the literature lacks the necessary empirical support, our study will still make a significant contribution by systematically highlighting this limitation and making the case for future research aimed at empirically deriving and testing the concepts proposed in conceptual papers.

This paper is structured as follows. Section 2 introduces the relationship between ILEs and social media platforms, and the theoretical background of the three ILE antecedents. Section 3 describes the methodology. Section 4 presents the findings, and Sect. 5 concludes the paper by discussing the results.

2 Theoretical Background

2.1 Information-Limiting Environments in Social Media

Social media can be defined as "a group of Internet-based applications that build on the ideological and technological foundations of Web 2.0, and that allow the creation and exchange of user-generated content" (Kaplan & Haenlein 2010). Common social media types are social networking sites (e.g., Facebook), content communities (e.g., YouTube), and (micro)blogs (e.g., Twitter) (Kaplan & Haenlein 2010). Social media enable users to access diverse user-generated information from a large information universe (Boyd & Ellison 2007). However, the emergence of echo chambers and filter bubbles on social media can limit this diversity (Kitchens et al. 2020). Filter bubbles and echo chambers are often used as synonyms. However, they are intertwined yet ultimately distinct concepts. A filter bubble is "the outcome of different processes of information search, perception, selection, and remembering the sum of which causes individual users to receive from the universe of available information only a tailored selection that fits their pre-existing attitudes" (Geschke et al. 2019). An echo chamber is "a social phenomenon where the filter bubbles of interacting individuals strongly overlap" (Geschke et al. 2019).

Put differently, filter bubbles are the individual information spaces social media users maintain, whereas echo chambers refer to the overlap of individual information spaces. For instance, Reddit relies on its users' characteristics, such as locations or interests, to provide them with relevant subreddits (e.g., subreddits about local sports clubs or political orientations). Further, Reddit provides a personalized timeline by which its users are regularly updated with popular posts from their subreddits. Thus, the information users see on Reddit is influenced by their subreddits followed, leading to the emergence of filter bubbles (Linder et al. 2018). Further, Reddit enables its users to discuss in subreddits dedicated to particular topics. Thus, subreddits can be echo chambers in which mainly like-minded individuals with overlapping filter bubbles interact. This phenomenon is further reinforced by the fact that interacting in specific subreddits is sometimes reserved for users following these subreddits. In general, filter bubbles and echo chambers can emerge on various social media platforms next to Reddit, including Facebook (Bechmann & Nielbo 2018) and Twitter (Bozdag et al. 2014).

Despite the conceptual differences between filter bubbles and echo chambers, the commonality between these concepts is that they are ILEs: "We propose the concept of information-limiting environments as encapsulating the primary concerns regarding echo chambers and filter bubbles—namely, that social network homophily and algorithmic filtering constrain the information sources that individuals choose to consume, shielding them from opinion-challenging information and encouraging them to adopt more extreme viewpoints" (Kitchens et al. 2020). We adopt this definition for our paper.

2.2 *Individual, Social, and Technological Filters in Social Media*

Social media platforms provide valuable opportunities for participatory deliberation in democratic societies, enabling users to access, create, and evaluate vast amounts of content (Bernstein et al. 2021). However, due to the overwhelming volume of information available on the internet, the need for information limitation and filtering has arisen (Bruckner et al. 2022). These techniques aim to enhance relevance by curating and prioritizing content based on individual interests and needs (Eg et al. 2023). Nonetheless, the emergence of ILEs poses a significant threat to the democratic process of participation. By constraining the quantity, diversity, and bias of information users encounter, ILEs can undermine fundamental rights such as freedom of speech, expression, and opinion formation (Bernstein et al. 2021; Committee 2011). Moreover, ILEs can introduce biases into users' political and factual perspectives on socially relevant issues, contributing to societal polarization through the reinforcement of echo chambers (Arora et al. 2022). Hence, it is crucial for users, platform operators, and policymakers to comprehend the conditions under which ILEs arise and the reasons behind their emergence.

While the existence of network effects and social homophily in both offline and online networks is well-known (Bakshy et al. 2015), the complexity of the phenomenon is heightened by algorithmic personalized filtering at the individual level and the ease with which users, including bots, can contribute to or influence information flow within a network. In this vein, Geschke et al. (2019) proposed the *triple-filter-bubble model* as a theoretical framework to categorize the filtering processes that give rise to ILEs. This model provides a conceptual understanding of why ILEs, as defined by Kitchens et al. (2020), emerge by identifying three key antecedents. Firstly, *individual filters* encompass cognitive biases at the individual level that influence how users search for, process, and remember information. Secondly, *social filters* pertain to the influence of social connections and interactions in forming close relationships among user subgroups who share similar characteristics or beliefs, which can affect the flow of information through a network. Lastly, *technological filters* are algorithmic in nature and arise from monetary incentives or technological constraints, leading algorithms to filter information based on their perceived relevance in the recommendations provided to users.

Recent reviews have revealed inconclusive empirical findings regarding respective ILE antecedents, emphasizing the need for further investigations into the causes of ILE emergence (Arora et al. 2022; Terren & Borge 2021). Therefore, we conduct a structured literature review of empirical papers addressing ILE antecedents, utilizing the triple-filterbubble model as a theoretical framework. We argue that this model is well-suited for examining the emergence of ILEs from an Information Systems perspective, as it allows for the exploration of socio-technical interaction processes while explicitly differentiating between individual and group-level phenomena. In doing so, our objective is to provide a comprehensive understanding of the factors contributing to ILE development, thereby evaluating the adequacy of the existing empirical literature in validating conceptual frameworks that elucidate the emergence of ILEs.

3 Method

The goal of this paper is twofold. The first goal is to quantitatively and qualitatively review the literature on the antecedents of filter bubbles and echo chambers on social media. The second is to derive future research directions. Both goals comply with literature review research (Webster & Watson 2002). Thus, we adapted the literature review research methodology from vom Brocke et al. (2009). Consequently, our method encompasses four steps. In the first step, we defined this paper's scope and conceptualized our topic within this scope to establish a concept matrix (Webster & Watson 2002). As discussed so far, we set our scope on filter bubble and echo chamber antecedents on social media. Within this scope, we used the framework from Geschke et al. (2019) to conceptualize such antecedents into individual, social, and technological antecedents. We used this conceptualization as it has the potential to provide nuanced insights that exceed single empirical domains and resolve possible conflicting findings. Hence, our resulting matrix enabled categorizing literature findings based on the underlying type of filter bubble or echo chamber antecedent.

In the second step, we populated our concept matrix with relevant literature findings using a systematic literature search approach. Here, we initially defined four inclusion criteria. First, we only included peer-reviewed papers to increase the validity of our findings inferred from the papers. Second, we only included papers published no earlier than 2000 because the first social media papers emerged around this time (Mazlish 2000). Third, in line with our goal to evaluate the adequacy of the existing empirical literature in establishing and validating conceptual frameworks explaining ILE emergence, we specifically focused on empirical papers that examined individual, social, or technological filter bubble or echo chamber antecedents on social media. Fourth, we only included English papers to ensure a sufficient understanding of the papers. As social media is a global and dynamic phenomenon (Kaplan & Haenlein 2010), we included papers irrespective of their underlying publication country or outlet type (i.e., journals or conferences).

After defining the inclusion criteria, we selected three multidisciplinary databases and a list of search terms to derive papers from these databases. We selected Scopus, Web of Science, and EBSCOhost as the databases due to their high level of reproducibility and coverage (Gusenbauer & Haddaway 2019). To query these databases, we selected the central search terms "social media", "echo chamber", and "filter bubble". This list was augmented by synonymous and further relevant terms, namely "social network", "social software", "selective exposure", and "content diversity". For greater coverage, the plural forms of the search terms were also included in the search term list (e.g., "echo chambers"). Our list of search terms is largely congruent with the terms and wordings used in related literature reviews (e.g., Wehner et al. 2017; Terren & Borge 2021) and empirical papers (e.g., Huellmann & Sensmeier 2022). A preliminary study revealed that our scope was highly interdisciplinary. Thus, rather than relying on a predefined set of literature sources—such as the Senior Scholar's List of Premier Journals (AIS 2023)—we applied the list of search terms to query relevant papers from all sources indexed in all three databases. This query revealed 804 papers whose titles, abstracts, or keywords contained both a social media-related and an ILE-related search term.

Next, we scrutinized each paper to infer whether it met the inclusion criteria. Doing so reduced the initial list of 804 to a list of 52 papers. Then, two raters conducted an interrater check to cross-validate whether the papers in this list fulfilled all inclusion criteria. 48 papers received inclusion votes from both raters, while the remaining 4 only received inclusion votes from one of the raters. We used the rater information to calculate Gwet's interrater reliability coefficient (Gwet 2014). Here, we achieved a value of 0.92, indicating substantial validity (Gwet 2014). After internal discussion, we decided to include 1 of the conflicting 4 papers, whereas the residual 3 papers were excluded. Hence, our final list consisted of 49 papers. The most relevant literature sources were the "Social Media and Society" source with 5 papers, followed by the "PLOS ONE" and "ACM Web Conference" sources with 4 papers each, followed by the "Computers in Human Behavior" and "Social Science Computing Review" sources with 3 papers each.

In the last two steps, we established the quantitative and qualitative literature review and inferred directions for future research. For the quantitative literature review, we classified the papers' underlying findings based on publication year, outlet type, antecedent type, addressed social media platform, and social media type (note that a paper can reveal more than one finding). For the qualitative literature review, we used a thematic analysis approach (Braun & Clarke 2006). First, one of the authors categorized each finding into the concept matrix based on its type of addressed filter bubble or echo chamber antecedent (i.e., individual, social, or technological). The author then abstracted conceptually similar findings within each category into higher-level, conceptually distinct antecedents. Overall, this led to 11 higher-level antecedents. To increase methodological rigor, the coding approach was subsequently cross-validated by another author. Lastly, we synthesized the findings belonging to each distinct antecedent as well as how these findings conflict or corroborate with the findings from the other antecedents. To infer directions for future research, we studied the concept matrix as well as the quantitative and qualitative literature reviews.

4 Results

The final set of 49 papers formed the basis for the description of the results in the following sections. Firstly, we present the results of our quantitative analysis. Secondly, we present the results of our qualitative analysis, focusing on the three types of ILE antecedents.

4.1 Quantitative Analysis

Table 1 provides a distribution of the paper findings published per year and overarching antecedent type. Although our sample included papers from various years, all papers were published between 2013 and 2023.

Individual antecedent findings were inferred from 26 papers. Moreover, social antecedent findings were inferred from 25 papers. Lastly, technological antecedent findings were inferred from nine papers. Regarding the empirical methods used in the papers, we observed that data analyses from social media platforms were utilized in 22, surveys in 11, experiments in 11, field studies in five, and focus group research in one of the papers. One paper used a combination of data analysis and

Table 1 Distribution of literature findings from the 41 journal and 8 conference articles reviewed

Year*	2013	2014	2015	2016	2017	2018	2019	2020	2021	2022	2023	Total
Individual	1	2		6		1	4	6	1	4	1	26
Social	1	2	1	6	2	5	3	2	1	1	1	25
Technological		1	1					2	1	3	1	9
Total	2	5	2	12	2	6	7	10	3	8	3	60

* *The annual distribution concerns publication years and does not account for the duration of the research and publication process*

a survey. Notably, less than a quarter of the papers applied experiments despite the method's potential higher suitability in testing assumptions on the impact of specific antecedents on ILEs in comparison with the other methods (Gregor & Hovorka 2011). The platforms examined in the studies included Twitter in 17, Facebook in 14, YouTube in three, Reddit in two, Instagram in one, and TikTok in one case. Five articles relied on other websites (e.g., experimental mockups). Further 12 articles conducted their research independently of any particular platform. Note that some papers addressed more than one social media platform. The unequal representation of platforms may indicate potential gaps in understanding ILEs in social media types beyond text-based ones, such as Instagram and TikTok.

Table 2 presents a concept matrix that summarizes the number of findings per antecedent type and social media platform type. This table provides an overview of the distribution of findings and will be discussed in more detail in subsequent sections. Noticeably, the number of findings in Table 2 may exceed the number of findings in Table 1, as each antecedent type finding can be further operationalized into multiple findings based on the specific antecedents and social media platforms addressed.

4.2 *Individual Antecedents of ILEs*

As defined by Geschke et al. (2019), individual filters are antecedents that pertain to the cognitive or behavioral traits of individual users and contribute to ILEs. Among the papers in our sample, 26 provided evidence regarding the impact of user traits or behaviors on information-filtering processes, which we have further classified as follows.

Demographics. In our sample, six studies examined the relationship between demographic characteristics and the emergence of ILEs. While evidence suggests that certain demographics, such as females, young people, and those with a low education level, may be more likely to encounter ILEs, none of these findings were definitively confirmed. Specifically, three studies (Chan et al. 2022; Parmelee & Roman 2020; Sindermann et al. 2020) found a possible association between female gender and ILEs. One study (An et al. 2013) found a correlation between liberal males and ILE emergence, and another study (Parmelee & Roman 2020) indicated that Caucasian race and young age may be antecedents for ILEs. Two studies (Boulianne & Koc-Michalska 2022; Chan et al. 2022) suggested that a low education level may increase the probability of ILEs.

Personality Traits. Our review examined four studies investigating the association between the "Big Five" personality traits and ILEs. However, conclusive evidence for any specific personality trait was not found. The first study (Bessi 2016) indicated a negative impact of agreeableness, conscientiousness, and extraversion on ILEs, while emotional stability and openness had a positive impact. The second study (Boulianne & Koc-Michalska 2022) reported a positive impact of conscientiousness

Table 2 Concept matrix summarizing the literature findings based on antecedent and platform

Antecedent	Social Networking		Microblogs	Content Communities			General
	Facebook	Instagram	Twitter	Reddit	TikTok	YouTube	
Individual	19	2	9	2	0	1	18
Demographics	2	1	1	0	0	0	3
Personality traits	3	0	1	0	0	0	1
Cognitive factors	4	0	1	0	0	0	4
Political attitude	5	1	3	1	0	0	8
Usage behavior	5	0	3	1	0	1	2
Social	8	0	13	0	0	2	5
Network structure	1	0	4	0	0	0	3
Subgroup formation	1	0	5	0	0	2	0
Interaction patterns	6	0	4	0	0	0	2
Technological	1	0	1	0	2	3	4
algorithmic interaction	0	0	0	0	1	1	1
Network influence	0	0	1	0	1	0	2
Content characteristics	1	0	0	0	0	2	1

and a negative impact of extraversion on ILEs. The third study (Sindermann et al. 2020) found a negative effect of emotional stability and openness on ILEs. Lastly, the fourth study (An et al. 2013) did not observe any effects related to personality traits.

Cognitive Factors. Nine studies in our sample investigated the impact of cognitive processes on ILEs. Consistent evidence emerged for the positive impact of confirmation bias (An et al. 2014; Brugnoli et al. 2019; Sülflow et al. 2019) and negative emotions (Del Vicario et al. 2016; Jeong et al. 2019) on ILE emergence. Gullibility (Mosleh et al. 2021), perceived information overload (Auxier & Vitak 2019), and general trust in media (Chan et al. 2022) increased the likelihood of ILEs, while cognitive reflection (Mosleh et al. 2021) and anxiety (Auxier & Vitak 2019) were associated with a decrease. Additionally, accuracy-based motivation for seeking information did not have an effect, while a defense-oriented motivation had a positive impact (Winter et al. 2016).

Political Attitude. In our sample, 14 studies investigated the relationship between political views and ILEs. Overall, it was found that political knowledge increased the likelihood of encountering an ILE (An et al. 2014), while the impact of political interest varied, with some studies showing a negative effect (Boulianne & Koc-Michalska 2022; Sindermann et al. 2020) and others finding no effect (Ohme & Mothes 2020). Regarding political opinion, conflicting evidence was found for conservatism, with two studies reporting a positive impact (Parmelee & Roman 2020; Sindermann et al. 2020) and two others indicating a negative impact (An et al. 2014; Shin 2020). Moreover, partisanship in general was identified as a significant antecedent of ILEs by three studies (Auxier & Vitak 2019; Chan et al. 2022; Robertson et al. 2023), while one study found no effect (Boulianne & Koc-Michalska 2022), and another study suggested a platform-dependent positive effect (Kitchens et al. 2020). Consistent evidence supported a positive effect of polarization (Beam et al. 2018; Reiter et al. 2022), but only one study found a positive effect of ideological orientation (Shin 2020), while three others did not observe this effect (Cargnino & Neubaum 2022, Chan et al. 2022; Parmelee & Roman 2020). Finally, political congruence was identified as an antecedent of ILEs by one study (Vraga 2016), while another study did not find a respective effect (Cargnino & Neubaum 2022).

Usage Behavior. Eight studies explored the influence of usage behavior on ILEs. Early interaction with new content (Bessi et al. 2016) and active re-sharing behavior (An et al. 2014; Bozdag et al. 2014) were identified as significant predictors of ILEs. However, the number of posts a user generates did not correlate with ILE emergence (An et al. 2013). Moreover, the impact of usage frequency on ILEs varied across platforms, with frequent Twitter use showing a partial association with increased risk, while frequent use of Facebook and Reddit appeared to decrease the risk (Chan et al. 2022; Cinelli et al. 2020; Kitchens et al. 2020; Vaccari et al. 2016). Considering the partially contradictory platform-specific findings, usage frequency may not reliably predict ILEs overall.

4.3 Social Antecedents of ILEs

As per Geschke et al. (2019), ILEs are caused by social filters formed by homogeneous network structures, where individuals connect with others who share similar characteristics or beliefs. In this section, we present our findings on the social factors contributing to ILEs on social media, based on an analysis of the 25 relevant papers from our sample.

Network Structure. Eight studies in our sample explored the characteristics of the network structure and their influence on ILEs. Network diversity (Wohn & Bowe 2016) and network stability (Yang et al. 2021) were found to have a negative effect on ILEs. The presence of gatekeepers, such as popular users or opinionated journalists, was identified as a catalyst for ILEs in three studies focused on the Twitter network

(Garimella et al. 2018; Hong & Kim 2016; Vergeer 2015). Additionally, a platform-independent study revealed the role of strategic content dissemination agents in creating a skewed perception of majority opinion among readers, contributing to ILEs (Kim 2019). The impact of network size on ILE emergence varied, with one study suggesting that large networks may support ILEs (Yang et al. 2021), while two others found no significant effect (An et al. 2013; Reiter et al. 2022).

Subgroup Formation. Eight studies identified the formation of homophilic subgroups as a significant contributor to ILEs at the social level. Proximity in terms of demographics (Monti et al. 2023), geography (Bastos et al. 2018; Kaiser & Rauchfleisch 2020), and ideology (Boutyline & Willer 2017; Bright 2018) demonstrated a positive impact on ILE emergence. Moreover, homophilic offline networks (Vaccari et al. 2016) and right-leaning ideological subgroups (Boutyline & Willer 2017) were particularly associated with ILEs, especially on Twitter. Conflicting narratives also predicted ILEs on Facebook and YouTube (Bessi 2016). Finally, research indicated that multilingual users held central positions in the information network, while monolingual users were more likely to encounter ILEs (Bodrunova et al. 2018; Kaiser & Rauchfleisch 2020).

Interaction Patterns. Twelve studies investigated the impact of social interaction motivation or behavior on ILEs. Regarding motivation, approval seeking correlated with ILE emergence in two studies (Awobamise & Jarrar 2019; Wohn & Bowe 2016). Similarly, the receipt of endorsements or likes was found to foster ILEs in two studies (Anspach 2017; Awobamise & Jarrar 2019), although two other studies did not observe this effect (An et al. 2013; Ohme & Mothes 2020). One study also revealed that an increase in negative comments on posts heightened the risk of ILEs (Del Vicario et al. 2016). In terms of behavior, one study found a positive influence of homophilic peer influence on ILEs (Brugnoli et al. 2019), while another study found no impact of peer-induced mainstreaming or polarization on ILEs (Shore et al. 2018). Additionally, two studies focused on Twitter reported a negative association between cascading information dissemination among non-connected users (Liang 2018) and the frequency of inter-group exchange (Yang et al. 2021), and ILE emergence. However, direct interaction with seed users demonstrated a positive impact on ILEs, both on Facebook and Twitter (Bozdag et al. 2014; Shore et al. 2018). Finally, one study found that users who extensively share posts are more likely to encounter ILEs on both Facebook and Twitter (An et al. 2014).

4.4 Technological Antecedents of ILEs

According to Geschke et al. (2019), technological filters refer to algorithms that yield a selective subset of the information available on a platform. Given our focus on empirical studies utilizing actual social media platforms, we did not expect to discover purely technical explanations or remedies for these phenomena. Instead, our analysis of the nine relevant studies from our sample highlights factors that unintentionally contribute to algorithmic conditions on social media platforms, potentially fostering ILEs.

Algorithmic Interaction. Three studies investigated the unintended influence of users on algorithmically induced ILEs, primarily focusing on video platforms such as YouTube and TikTok. These studies revealed that interaction duration and content liking significantly trigger TikTok's recommender algorithm to promote ILE emergence (Boeker & Urman 2022), while the user's location on YouTube does not contribute to algorithmically induced the emergence of ILEs (Kaiser & Rauchfleisch 2020). Furthermore, one study demonstrated that the user's consumption preferences greatly influence the extent of ILEs caused by content-based recommender algorithms (Han et al. 2022).

Network Influence. Four studies have examined how network characteristics contribute to ILEs. A cross-platform study revealed that social media users are more susceptible to being trapped in ILEs compared to users of other websites (Nikolov et al. 2015). Homophilic network structures were found to influence algorithms in filtering information (Ferrara et al. 2022), and popular content creators on Twitter were identified as contributors to algorithmically induced ILEs (Bozdag et al. 2014). However, one study focused on TikTok found that following a larger number of users increases diversity in recommended videos, thereby mitigating ILEs (Boeker & Urman 2022).

Content Characteristics. Four studies revealed that the content itself can inadvertently contribute to algorithmically induced ILEs. Content with a strong political bias, particularly favoring right-wing ideologies, was found to foster ILEs on Facebook and YouTube (Ali et al. 2021; Kaiser & Rauchfleisch 2020; Röchert et al. 2020). Additionally, content with negative sentiment was observed to increase ILE occurrence, albeit the strength of this effect decreases over time (Ludwig et al. 2023).

4.5 Literature Synthesis

Social media can contribute to ILEs via filter bubbles and echo chambers (Kitchens et al. 2020), although empirical evidence on their causes remains inconclusive. In our literature review utilizing the triple-filter-bubble model (Geschke et al. 2019), we analyzed 49 empirical papers investigating individual, social, and technological factors contributing to the emergence of ILEs. Our findings reveal that specific antecedents of ILEs often yield inconclusive or contradictory results. Concerning individual antecedents of ILEs, the impact of political attitude shows conflicting findings, with political knowledge increasing ILE risk (An et al. 2014) while political interest decreasing it (e.g., Sindermann et al. 2020) and conservative beliefs showing ambiguous effects (e.g., Parmelee & Roman 2020; Shin 2020). Similarly, most demographic factors and none of the big five personality traits show a clear influence (e.g., Bessi 2016). Regarding social antecedents, there is a bias towards Facebook and

Twitter in the literature, and contradictory findings are observed between these platforms. For instance, network size significantly affects ILEs on Twitter (Yang et al. 2021) but not on Facebook (An et al. 2013), and homophilic peer influence creates ILEs on Facebook (Brugnoli et al. 2019) but not on Twitter (Shore et al. 2018). Finally, technological antecedents are overall underrepresented in the literature, with a focus on specific platforms like YouTube (Kaiser & Rauchfleisch 2020; Röchert et al. 2020) and TikTok (Boeker & Urman 2022), limiting generalizability due to different algorithms used by each platform.

Concerning research methodology, the majority of studies (22 out of 49) adopted a data-driven approach using social media datasets. Hence, inconsistent results were observed across platforms and contexts, making it difficult to develop a unified theory of ILE emergence without knowledge of the missing moderating factors. Furthermore, many combinations of antecedents and platforms are still understudied or unexplored, as can be seen in Table 2. Therefore, our findings indicate that, despite evidence regarding some factors that contribute to the emergence of ILEs, the limited and ambiguous nature of the evidence hampers the development of a sound explanatory theory based on cause-effect relationships. As a result, we are unable to provide sufficient empirical validation for findings derived from conceptual models such as the triple-filter-bubble model. Instead, we conclude our study by emphasizing the need for future research to (i) systematically classify potential antecedents of ILEs, (ii) collect context-independent empirical data, and (iii) integrate these findings into a unified causal theory of ILE emergence.

5 Discussion

5.1 Theoretical and Practical Implications

Concerning theory, our interdisciplinary literature review reveals a lack of generalizability of empirical evidence on ILEs in social media, with studies primarily correlational, focusing on individual events (e.g., Bodrunova et al. 2018) or specific social media (e.g., Beam et al. 2018; Röchert et al. 2020). This limited scope hinders reconciling conflicting or inconclusive evidence and identifying explanatory factors. Moreover, heavy reliance on data from social media APIs raises concerns about data representativeness. Hence, future research should include more counterfactual or experimental studies to validate reproducible direct or moderated effects on ILEs. We also encourage IS researchers to intensify efforts in theorizing the causes of ILEs in social media. Our results align with past reviews in displaying that the subject area is highly context-sensitive, promoting conflicting results (e.g., Arora et al. 2022; Terren & Borge 2021). However, in contrast to these reviews, our study is the first to explicitly investigate antecedents of ILEs.

Concerning practice, we emphasize the significance of digital literacy for social media users. Given the lack of conclusive evidence regarding the factors contributing to the occurrence of ILEs in social media, we suggest exploring the potential of social media literacy as a promising avenue (Cho et al. 2022). Secondly, we urge policy-makers to monitor the emergence of ILEs in social media and other platforms. The proliferation of data-driven applications, including advanced AI-based tools like ChatGPT, raises concerns about the dissemination of online misinformation and fake news, which pose threats to democratic societies (Bernstein et al. 2021; Helberger 2019). Hence, it is crucial to have clearer evidence of the conditions that lead to ILEs in online networks, particularly in social media, in order to uphold free and informed online discourse.

5.2 Limitations and Future Research Opportunities

While the triple-filter-bubble model provides valuable insights into ILE antecedents, our review is constrained by the three factors encompassed by this model, potentially excluding other causes of ILEs (Geschke et al. 2019). Future research should expand the theoretical framework to incorporate additional potential factors contributing to ILEs. Additionally, our search procedure, relying on selected multidisciplinary databases and predefined search terms, may have representative rather than exhaustive coverage, possibly overlooking relevant papers. To address this limitation, future studies could employ more comprehensive search methods. Lastly, our review exclusively focused on empirical papers, potentially neglecting evidence from alternative approaches such as agent-based modeling or design-oriented studies. Future research could broaden the selection criteria to include articles utilizing these methodologies.

Acknowledgements This research was funded by the German Federal Ministry of Education and Research (BMBF) through grants 01IS17045 Software Campus 2.0 (FAU Erlangen-Nürnberg).

References

Abouzeid, A., Granmo, O., Webersik, C. & Goodwin, M. (2019), Causality-Based Social Media Analysis for Normal Users Credibility Assessment in a Political Crisis, in Niemi V. & Tyutina T., eds, 'Proceedings of the 24th Conference of Open Innovations Association', IEEE Computer Society, pp. 3–14.

AIS (2023), 'Senior Scholar's List of Premier Journals'. **URL:** https://aisnet.org/page/SeniorScholarListofPremierJournals

Ali, M., Sapiezynski, P., Korolova, A., Mislove, A. & Rieke, A. (2021), Ad Delivery Algorithms: The Hidden Arbiters of Political Messaging, *in* 'Proceedings of the 14th ACM International Conference on Web Search and Data Mining', Association for Computing Machinery, pp. 13–21.

An, J., Quercia, D. & Crowcroft, J. (2013), Fragmented Social Media: A Look into Selective Exposure to Political News, *in* 'Proceedings of the 2013 ACM Web Conference', Association for Computing Machinery, pp. 51–52.

An, J., Quercia, D. & Crowcroft, J. (2014), Partisan Sharing: Facebook Evidence and Societal Consequences, *in* 'Proceedings of the 2014 ACM Conference on Online Social Networks', Association for Computing Machinery, pp. 13–23.

Anspach, N. (2017), 'The New Personal Influence: How Our Facebook Friends Influence the News We Read', *Political Communication* **34**(4), 590–606.

Arora, S., Singh, G., Chakraborty, A. & Maity, M. (2022), 'Polarization and Social Media: A Systematic Review and Research Agenda', *Technological Forecasting and Social Change* **183**(1), 121942.

Auxier, B. & Vitak, J. (2019), 'Factors Motivating Customization and Echo Chamber Creation Within Digital News Environments', *Social Media and Society* **5**(2), 1–13.

Awobamise, A. & Jarrar, Y. (2019), 'Exploring the Impact of Social and Source Cues on News Selection', *Plaridel* **16**(1), 141–160.

Bakshy, E., Messing, S. & Adamic, L. (2015), 'Exposure to Ideologically Diverse News and Opinion on Facebook', *Science* **348**(6239), 1130–1132.

Bastos, M., Mercea, D. & Baronchelli, A. (2018), 'The Geographic Embedding of Online Echo Chambers: Evidence from the Brexit Campaign', *PLOS ONE* **13**(11), 1–16.

Beam, M., Hutchens, M. & Hmielowski, J. (2018), 'Facebook News and (De)polarization: Reinforcing Spirals in the 2016 US Election', *Information Communication and Society* **21**(7), 940–958.

Bechmann, A. & Nielbo, K. (2018), 'Are We Exposed to the Same "News" in the News Feed?', *Digital Journalism* **6**(8), 990–1002.

Bernstein, A., de Vreese, C., Helberger, N., Schulz, W., Zweig, K., Baden, C., Beam, M., Hauer, M., Heitz, L., Jürgens, P., Katzenbach, C., Kille, B., Klimkiewicz, B., Loosen, W., Moeller, J., Radanovic, G., Shani, G., Tintarev, N., Tolmeijer, S., van Atteveldt, W., Vrijenhoek, S. & Zueger, T. (2021), 'Diversity in News Recommendation', *Dagstuhl Manifestos* **9**(1), 43–61.

Bessi, A. (2016), 'Personality Traits and Echo Chambers on Facebook', *Computers in Human Behavior* **65**(1), 319–324.

Bessi, A., Zollo, F., Del Vicario, M., Puliga, M., Scala, A., Caldarelli, G., Uzzi, B. & Quattrociocchi, W. (2016), 'Users Polarization on Facebook and Youtube', *PLOS ONE* **11**(8), 1–24.

Bodrunova, S., Smoliarova, A., Blekanov, I., Zhuravleva, N. & Danilova, Y. (2018), 'A Global Public Sphere of Compassion? #jesuischarlie and #jenesuispascharlie on Twitter and Their Language Boundaries', *The Monitoring of Public Opinion Economic & Social Changes* **1**(143), 267–295.

Boeker, M. & Urman, A. (2022), An Empirical Investigation of Personalization Factors on Tiktok, *in* 'Proceedings of the 2022 ACM Web Conference', Association for Computing Machinery, Inc, pp. 2298–2309.

Boulianne, S. & Koc-Michalska, K. (2022), 'The Role of Personality in Political Talk and Like-Minded Discussion', *International Journal of Press/Politics* **27**(1), 285–310.

Boutyline, A. & Willer, R. (2017), 'The Social Structure of Political Echo Chambers: Variation in Ideological Homophily in Online Networks', *Political Psychology* **38**(3), 551–569.

Boyd, D. & Ellison, N. (2007), 'Social Network Sites: Definition, History, and Scholarship', *Journal of Computer-Mediated Communication* **13**(1), 210–230.

Bozdag, E., Gao, Q., Houben, G.-J. & Warnier, M. (2014), 'Does Offline Political Segregation Affect the Filter Bubble? An Empirical Analysis of Information Diversity for Dutch and Turkish Twitter Users', *Computers in Human Behavior* **41**(1), 405–415.

Braun, V. & Clarke, V. (2006), 'Using Thematic Analysis in Psychology', *Qualitative Research in Psychology* **3**(1), 77–101.

Bright, J. (2018), 'Explaining the Emergence of Political Fragmentation on Social Media: The Role of Ideology and Extremism', *Journal of Computer-Mediated Communication* **23**(1), 17–33.

Bruckner, M., Grüning, M., Lindenmayr, M. & Schmalenbach, K. (2022), 'Mind the Gap: A Theory Development Approach for Explaining the Divergence of Human Information Processing Capacity and Information Amount'.

Brugnoli, E., Cinelli, M., Quattrociocchi, W. & Scala, A. (2019), 'Recursive Patterns in Online Echo Chambers', *Scientific Reports* **9**(1), 1–18.

Cargnino, M. & Neubaum, G. (2022), 'Is It Better to Strike a Balance? How Exposure to Congruent and Incongruent Opinion Climates on Social Networking Sites Impacts Users' Processing and Selection of Information', *New Media and Society* **0**(0), 1–19.

Chan, C., Zhao, M. & Lee, P. (2022), 'Determinants of Escape from Echo Chambers: The Predictive Power of Political Orientation, Social Media Use, and Demographics', *Global Media and China* **0**(0), 1–19.

Cho, H., Cannon, J., Lopez, R. & Li, W. (2022), 'Social Media Literacy: A Conceptual Framework', *New Media and Society* **0**(0), 1–20.

Cinelli, M., Brugnoli, E., Lucia Schmidt, A., Zollo, F., Quattrociocchi, W. & Scala, A. (2020), 'Selective Exposure Shapes the Facebook News Diet', *PLOS ONE* **15**(3), 1–17.

Committee, U. N. H. R. (2011), 'International Covenant on Civil and Political Rights'. **URL:** https://www.refworld.org/docid/4ed34b562.html

Del Vicario, M., Vivaldo, G., Bessi, A., Zollo, F., Scala, A., Caldarelli, G. & Quattrociocchi, W. (2016), 'Echo Chambers: Emotional Contagion and Group Polarization on Facebook', *Scientific Reports* **6**(1), 1–12.

Dixson-Decleve, S., Gaffney, O., Ghosh, J., Randers, J., Rockstrom, J. & Stoknes, P. (2022), Earth for All: A Survival Guide for Humanity, 1 edn, *New Society Publishers.*

Eg, R., Demirkol, O. & Tennfjord, M. (2023), 'A Scoping Review of Personalized User Experiences on Social Media: The Interplay Between Algorithms and Human Factors', *Computers in Human Behavior Reports* **9**(1), 1–17.

Ferrara, A., Espin-Noboa, L., Karimi, F. & Wagner, C. (2022), Link Recommendations: Their Impact on Network Structure and Minorities, *in* 'Proceedings of the 14th ACM Web Science Conference', Association for Computing Machinery, pp. 228–238.

Garimella, K., De Francisci Morales, G., Gionis, A. & Mathioudakis, M. (2018), Political Discourse on Social Media: Echo Chambers, Gatekeepers, and the Price of Bipartisanship, *in* 'Proceedings of the 2018 ACM Web Conference', Association for Computing Machinery, pp. 913–922.

Geschke, D., Lorenz, J. & Holtz, P. (2019), 'The Triple-Filter Bubble: Using Agent-Based Modelling to Test a Meta-Theoretical Framework for the Emergence of Filter Bubbles and Echo Chambers', *British Journal of Social Psychology* **58**(1), 129–149.

Gregor, S. & Hovorka, D. (2011), Causality: The Elephant in the Room in Information Systems Epistemology, *in* 'Proceedings of the 19th European Conference on Information Systems', Association for Information Systems, pp. 1–12.

Gusenbauer, M. & Haddaway, N. (2019), 'Which Academic Search Systems Are Suitable for Systematic Reviews or Meta-Analyses? Evaluating Retrieval Qualities of Google Scholar, Pubmed, and 26 Other Resources', *Research Synthesis Methods* **11**(2), 181– 217.

Gwet, K. (2014), *Handbook of Inter-Rater Reliability: The Definitive Guide to Measuring the Extent of Agreement Among Raters*, 4 edn, Advanced Analytics.

Han, H., Wang, C., Zhao, Y., Shu, M., Wang, W. & Min, Y. (2022), 'SSLE: A Framework for Evaluating the "Filter Bubble" Effect on the News Aggregator and Recommenders', *World Wide Web* **25**(3), 1169–1195.

Helberger, N. (2019), 'On the Democratic Role of News Recommenders', *Digital Journalism* **7**(8), 993–1012.

Helberger, N., Karppinen, K. & D'Acunto, L. (2018), 'Exposure Diversity as a Design Principle for Recommender Systems', *Information, Communication & Society* **21**(2), 191–207.

Hong, S. & Kim, S. (2016), 'Political Polarization on Twitter: Implications for the Use of Social Media in Digital Governments', *Government Information Quarterly* **33**(4), 777–782.

Huellmann, J. & Sensmeier, L. (2022), No Filter Bubbles? Evidence from an Online Experiment on the News Diversity of Personalizing News Aggregators, *in* 'Proceedings of the 2022 Pacific Asia Conference on Information Systems', Association for Information Systems, pp. 1–17.

Jeong, M., Zo, H., Lee, C. & Ceran, Y. (2019), 'Feeling Displeasure from Online Social Media Postings: A Study Using Cognitive Dissonance Theory', *Computers in Human Behavior* **97**(1), 231–240.

Kaiser, J. & Rauchfleisch, A. (2020), 'Birds of a Feather Get Recommended Together: Algorithmic Homophily in Youtube's Channel Recommendations in the United States and Germany', *Social Media and Society* **6**(4), 1–15.

Kaplan, A. & Haenlein, M. (2010), 'Users of the World, Unite! The Challenges and Opportunities of Social Media', *Business Horizons* **53**(1), 59–68.

Kim, S. (2019), 'Directionality of Information Flow and Echoes Without Chambers', *PLOS ONE* **14**(5), 1–22.

Kitchens, B., Johnson, S. & Gray, P. (2020), 'Understanding Echo Chambers and Filter Bubbles: The Impact of Social Media on Diversification and Partisan Shifts in News Consumption', *MIS Quarterly: Management Information Systems* **44**(4), 1619–1650.

Liang, H. (2018), 'Broadcast Versus Viral Spreading: The Structure of Diffusion Cascades and Selective Sharing on Social Media', *Journal of Communication* **68**(3), 525–546.

Linder, R., Stacy, A., Lupfer, N., Kerne, A. & Ragan, E. (2018), Pop the Feed Filter Bubble: Making Reddit Social Media a VR Cityscape, *in* 'Proceedings of the 2018 IEEE Conference on Virtual Reality and 3D User Interfaces', IEEE Computer Society, pp. 619–620.

Ludwig, K., Grote, A., Iana, A., Alam, M., Paulheim, H., Sack, H., Weinhardt, C. & Müller, P. (2023), 'Divided by the Algorithm? The (Limited) Effects of Contentand Sentiment-Based News Recommendation on Affective, Ideological, and Perceived Polarization', *Social Science Computer Review* **0**(0), 1–23.

Mazlish, B. (2000), 'Invisible Ties: From Patronage to Networks', Theory, *Culture and Society* **17**(1), 1–19.

Monti, C., D'Ignazi, J., Starnini, M. & Morales, G. (2023), Evidence of Demographic Rather Than Ideological Segregation in News Discussion on Reddit, in 'Proceedings of the 2023 ACM Web Conference', *Association for Computing Machinery*, pp. 1–10.

Mosleh, M., Pennycook, G., Arechar, A. & Rand, D. (2021), 'Cognitive Reflection Correlates with Behavior on Twitter', *Nature Communications* **12**(1), 1–10.

Nikolov, D., Oliveira, D., Flammini, A. & Menczer, F. (2015), 'Measuring Online Social Bubbles', *PeerJ Computer Science* **2015**(12), 1–14.

Ohme, J. & Mothes, C. (2020), 'What Affects Firstand Second-Level Selective Exposure to Journalistic News? A Social Media Online Experiment', *Journalism Studies* **21**(9), 1220–1242.

Pariser, E. (2011), *The Filter Bubble: How the New Personalized Web Is Changing What We Read and How We Think*, 1 edn, Penguin.

Parmelee, J. & Roman, N. (2020), 'Insta-Echoes: Selective Exposure and Selective Avoidance on Instagram', *Telematics and Informatics* **52**(1), 1–10.

Reiter, F., Heiss, R. & Matthes, J. (2022), 'Explaining Attitude-Consistent Exposure on Social Network Sites: The Role of Ideology, Political Involvement, and Network Characteristics', *Social Science Computer Review* **0**(0), 1–20.

Robertson, R., Green, J., Ruck, D., Ognyanova, K., Wilson, C. & Lazer, D. (2023), 'Users Choose to Engage with More Partisan News Than They Are Exposed to on Google Search', *Nature* **618**(1), 342–348.

Röchert, D., Weitzel, M. & Ross, B. (2020), The Homogeneity of Right-Wing Populist and Radical Content in Youtube Recommendations, *in* 'Proceedings of the 2020 International Conference on Social Media and Society', Association for Computing Machinery, pp. 245–254.

Shin, J. (2020), 'How Do Partisans Consume News on Social Media? A Comparison of Self-Reports with Digital Trace Measures Among Twitter Users', *Social Media and Society* **6**(4), 1–12.

Shore, J., Baek, J. & Dellarocas, C. (2018), 'Network Structure and Patterns of Information Diversity on Twitter', *MIS Quarterly: Management Information Systems* **42**(3), 849–872.

Sindermann, C., Elhai, J., Moshagen, M. & Montag, C. (2020), 'Age, Gender, Personality, Ideological Attitudes and Individual Differences in a Person's News Spectrum: How Many and Who Might Be Prone to "Filter Bubbles" and "Echo Chambers" Online?', *Heliyon* **6**(1), 1–10.

Sunstein, C. (2002), 'The Law of Group Polarization', *Journal of Political Philosophy* **10**(2), 40.

Sülflow, M., Schäfer, S. & Winter, S. (2019), 'Selective Attention in the News Feed: An Eye-Tracking Study on the Perception and Selection of Political News Posts on Facebook', *New Media and Society* **21**(1), 168–190.

Terren, L. & Borge, R. (2021), 'Echo Chambers on Social Media: A Systematic Review of the Literature', *Review of Communication Research* **9**(1), 1–39.

Vaccari, C., Valeriani, A., Barberá, P., Jost, J., Nagler, J. & Tucker, J. (2016), 'Of Echo Chambers and Contrarian Clubs: Exposure to Political Disagreement Among German and Italian Users of Twitter', *Social Media and Society* **2**(3), 1–24.

Van Alstyne, M. & Brynjolfsson, E. (2005), 'Global Village or Cyber-Balkans? Modeling and Measuring the Integration of Electronic Communities', *Management Science* **51**(6), 851–868.

Vergeer, M. (2015), 'Peers and Sources as Social Capital in the Production of News: Online Social Networks as Communities of Journalists', *Social Science Computer Review* **33**(3), 277–297.

Vicario, M., Bessi, A., Zollo, F., Petroni, F., Scala, A., Caldarelli, G., Stanley, H. & Quattrociocchi, W. (2016), 'The Spreading of Misinformation Online', *Proceedings of the National Academy of Sciences of the United States of America* **113**(3), 554–559.

vom Brocke, J., Simons, A., Niehaves, B., Riemer, K., Plattfaut, R. & Cleven, A. (2009), Reconstructing the Giant: On the Importance of Rigour in Documenting the Literature Search Process, *in* 'Proceedings of the 17th European Conference on Information Systems', Association for Information Systems, pp. 1–14.

Vraga, E. (2016), 'Party Differences in Political Content on Social Media', *Online Information Review* **40**(5), 595–609.

Webster, J. & Watson, R. (2002), 'Guest Editorial: Analyzing the Past to Prepare for the Future: Writing a Literature Review', *MIS Quarterly* **26**(2), xiii–xxiii.

Wehner, B., Ritter, C. & Leist, S. (2017), 'Enterprise Social Networks: A Literature Review and Research Agenda', *Computer Networks* **114**(1), 125–142.

Winter, S., Metzger, M. & Flanagin, A. (2016), 'Selective Use of News Cues: A MultipleMotive Perspective on Information Selection in Social Media Environments', *Journal of Communication* **66**(4), 669–693.

Wohn, D. & Bowe, B. (2016), 'Micro Agenda Setters: The Effect of Social Media on Young Adults' Exposure to and Attitude Toward News', *Social Media and Society* **2**(1), 1–12.

Yang, A., Choi, I., Abeliuk, A. & Saffer, A. (2021), 'The Influence of Interdependence in Networked Publics Spheres: How Community-Level Interactions Affect the Evolution of Topics in Online Discourse', *Journal of Computer-Mediated Communication* **26**(3), 148–166.

Power Imbalances in Society and AI: On the Need to Expand the Feminist Approach

Eva Johanna Gengler, Marco Wedel, Alexandra Wudel, and Sven Laumer

Abstract Recent advances in artificial intelligence have brought novel opportunities for businesses, societies, and individuals alike, yet they also raise complex questions on inequitable power distribution. We see contemporary AI systems, that reinforce power imbalances and disadvantage marginalized, underrepresented, and underprivileged people. Current approaches to advancing AI, such as ethical, fair, or trustworthy AI, have not included the effects of power in their considerations. As feminism has a long history of doing so, we introduce an intersectional and inclusive feminist approach to shape AI in a more equitable way. We approach this by building on recent information systems and interdisciplinary research as well as on evidence from expert interviews in focus groups, which we conducted in 2022 and 2023. Our study reveals that utilizing a feminist approach could be effective firstly, to shape AI systems and secondly, to change prevailing power structures in societal systems to become more equitable.

Keywords Artificial intelligence · Power imbalances · Feminist philosophy of technology · Socio-technical-systems · Beyond AI ethics

E. J. Gengler (✉) · S. Laumer
Institute of Information Systems, FAU Erlangen-Nürnberg, Nuremberg, Germany
e-mail: eva.gengler@fau.de; eva.gengler@enableYou.de

S. Laumer
e-mail: sven.laumer@fau.de

E. J. Gengler
enableYou Consulting GmbH, Neunkirchen a.Br., Germany

M. Wedel
TU Berlin, Chair for Work, Technology and Participation, Berlin, Germany
e-mail: marco.wedel@tu-berlin.de

A. Wudel
FemAI—Center for Feminist Artificial Intelligence GmbH, Berlin, Germany
e-mail: alexandra.wudel@fem-ai.com

D. Beverungen et al. (eds.), *Conceptualizing Digital Responsibility for the Information Age*, Lecture Notes in Information Systems and Organisation 74,
https://doi.org/10.1007/978-3-031-80119-8_6

1 Introduction

In our societies we have a long history of an inequitable distribution of power. Recently, artificial intelligence (AI) has become power, too, which reinforces traditional power structures (Kim, 2021; Zajko, 2022). Therefore, marginalized, underrepresented, and underprivileged people (MUUP) frequently do not benefit from AI, but are disadvantaged even further. This needs to be recognized, challenged, and changed. Consequently, complex questions around accountability, discrimination, and bias have been raised (Berente et al., 2021) and it becomes necessary to reflect upon the interdependencies between societal and AI systems.

Our research is motivated by numerous cases of biased and discriminatory AI (Feuerriegel et al., 2020). This includes applications in hiring (Jago & Laurin, 2022), lending (Bertrand & Weill, 2021), and recidivism prediction (Angwin et al., 2016; Chouldechova, 2017; Malek, 2022). Certain groups of people have been structurally disadvantaged including women, People of Color, and gender queer people (Buolamwini & Gebru, 2018; Chouldechova, 2017; Jethwani et al., 2022). These and other groups face numerous disadvantages in our societies, and recently these have been mirrored by AI systems.

Structural power imbalances influence the outcomes of AI, further perpetuating the inequities of the analog world. Shifting existing power relations in favor of creating an inclusive society, which is increasingly influenced by AI, becomes a twofold challenge: One must continuously improve societal systems of the analog world, while simultaneously shaping a nexus of AI systems that does not recreate the deeply rooted structural deficiencies of the modern era of twentieth century societies or counteract the positive achievements reached to this day.

One approach to improve societal systems, by identifying i.e., the patriarchy as a focal point of intervention to overcome power imbalances, oppression, and exploitation in modern societies, is feminism (Allen, 1998; Oksala, 2017). For this paper we define patriarchy as a system of social structures, and practices which oppresses, dominates, and exploits MUUP (Walby, 1989). A society is patriarchal if it promotes male privilege "by being male-dominated, male-identified, male-centered, and control-obsessed" (Johnson, 2007, p. 5). Power (to control others) is at its core. In that, the (mis)use of power, the patriarchy is harmful to women and men alike (Johnson, 2007). It is these structures that are reproduced in today's AI systems (Siapka, 2022; Weinberg, 2020).

Feminism seeks to challenge and change societal systems towards equality, freedom, and justice for all e.g., through intersectionality, interdisciplinarity, and evidence-based activism (Ferguson, 2017). It includes aspects of diversity such as gender, age, religion and belief, disability, sexual identity, ethnicity, and appearance (Ferguson, 2017). While it is beyond the scope of this paper to describe the many faces and various facets of feminism, its overall impact can be regarded as one of the most influential contributions to the creation of more inclusive and equitable societal systems in the post-modern era (Carbado et al., 2013; Crenshaw, 1989, 1991). In this study, we decisively incorporate the intersectional and inclusive feminist approach.

Based on that deduction and considering the twofold challenge described above, a question arises: Can the success of the intersectional feminist approach in shaping societal systems be translated into the world of AI to model a nexus of AI systems that does not recreate the structural deficiencies and power imbalances of the patriarchy still and predominantly enshrined in the analog world? Following this idea, the overall assumption of our research is that by building an effective feminist approach for AI, it can a) diminish the recreation of patriarchal power distribution in AI systems and b) reduce the negative influence of such systems on the analogue world and its societal systems.

This research in progress constitutes first theoretical principles and results, by asking:

***RQ**: Can the feminist approach shaping societal systems in the analog world be utilized to shape AI systems?*

Berente et al. (2021) call for less siloed research on AI and to realize this through the boundary-spanning and interdisciplinary nature of information systems (IS). Consequently, this research in progress builds on existing IS research (Berente et al., 2021; Chouldechova, 2017; Feuerriegel et al., 2020; Mikalef et al., 2022; Mikalef & Gupta, 2021), and on research concerning societal approaches to governing and designing AI in a social way (Riedl, 2019; Shneiderman, 2020), computer science (Floridi, 2019; Hagendorff, 2020; Mittelstadt, 2019) as well as social science research (Arrieta et al., 2020; Carbado et al., 2013; Johnson, 2007; Wellner & Rothman, 2020). It extends the discussion through an empirical study (expert interviews in focus groups) on the benefits of a feminist approach to shaping AI. We will illustrate our preliminary findings of how this can challenge and change prevailing power structures (PPS) and thus, enable true participation of and equity for MUUP.

This paper is structured as follows: We motivate our research question in Sect. 2 by providing an overview of current societal approaches to AI and the intersectional feminist approach. We then illustrate our research method in Sect. 3 and present our preliminary results in Sect. 4. Our paper concludes with the outlook in Sect. 5.

2 Theoretical Background

2.1 Societal Approaches to Shape AI

Due to the numerous fields in which AI is utilized, the importance of an impact assessment of AI systems in research, politics, and business is imperative. When analyzing the current discussions on AI's impact on societies and humanity, a variety of different debates emerge: e.g., ethical AI (Hagendorff, 2020; Mittelstadt, 2019), fair AI (Binns, 2017; Feuerriegel et al., 2020), trustworthy AI (European Commission, 2019; Floridi, 2019), responsible AI (Arrieta et al., 2020; Mikalef et al., 2022; Peters et al., 2020), or human-centered AI (Riedl, 2019; Shneiderman, 2020).

These concepts generally reference a value-based approach, which in itself is subject to controversial debates on how to create universal ethical norms, principles and frameworks alongside local, culturally variable identities and traditions (Ess, 2020). However, they do not take into account the socio-structural practices and social relations of the underlying societies, groups, and individuals that shape, interact or are confronted by AI (Weinberg, 2020). Socio-technical, human-centered AI debates, such as ethical AI, do in their normative nature neither question nor take into account the status quo of underlying societal systems and therefore risk translating undesired aspects of their social constitutionality and habitude into the digital world (Hagendorff, 2020; Mittelstadt, 2019; Siapka, 2022). D'Ignazio and Kein (2020) elaborate: They present the widely used concepts *ethics*, *bias*, *fairness*, *accountability*, *transparency*, and the *understanding of algorithms* as concepts that secure power, "[b]ecause they locate the source of the problem in individual or technical systems" (D'Ignazio & Klein, 2020, p. 60).

2.2 The Intersectional and Inclusive Feminist Approach

Existing societal approaches to AI currently do not address the phenomenon of mirrored patriarchal structures and practices in AI models and systems (Michelfelder et al., 2017; Wellner & Rothman, 2020). Feminism contextualizes prevailing power imbalances that currently tend to foster discrimination from the non-digital into the digital world (Weinberg, 2020). Thus, we introduce a feminist approach.

Feminism has a long history of challenging and changing our societies towards more equity and justice. Over the centuries, feminism has evolved. Today there is not one understanding of feminism, but a plurality of feminisms. Feminism has its origin in fighting for equal rights of women and men, however, one of the dominant contemporary directions of feminism is inclusive and intersectional (Ferguson, 2017). This feminism envisions equity for all people, while focusing on power imbalances and MUUP (Ferguson, 2017). This is the concept we use as *feminism* in this paper.

Intersectionality, as one of feminism's greatest achievements, is an open and relentlessly critical approach to power (Ferguson, 2017). It grasps the complex nature of the patriarchal functioning in our societies that impacts people in diverse ways. Intersectionality incorporates the variety of MUUP: e.g., gender, age, religion and belief, disability, sexual identity, ethnicity, and appearance (Ferguson, 2017). Thus, it demonstrates how individuals and groups can face discrimination through more than one attribute. This overlap of more than one disadvantaged feature, potentially results in extensive discrimination (Crenshaw, 1989). E.g., Black women are misclassified by face recognition systems to a high extent, because they are women and at the same time Black (Buolamwini & Gebru, 2018; Perkowitz, 2021). Thus, they face far stronger disadvantages than both Black men and white women (Buolamwini & Gebru, 2018). As AI reflects traits that are devalued in the patriarchal system, e.g., Women of Color particularly suffer from discrimination of AI systems (Buolamwini & Gebru, 2018; Crenshaw, 1989). Therefore, MUUP must be at the core, when deciding upon and building AI. Intersectional and inclusive feminism can be used to analyze and change AI's functioning on the AI system level, as well as on the societal system level.

3 Research Method

The sketched discourses and considerations mentioned above are the guiding deductions for a working hypothesis that has been the starting point for this research in progress. The initial reflections upon the theme have been derived by way of qualitative deliberations informed by past research projects, literature review (Webster & Watson, 2002), and horizon scanning (Cuhls, 2019). The resulting working hypothesis and the research questions have recently been—throughout 2022 and 2023—being tested empirically by way of monthly online roundtables serving as expert focus groups. This participatory form of data collection, based on semi-structured interviews, stimulates discussions between different groups of people and diverse opinions. It is a moderated discourse procedure in which a small group of individuals is inspired to discuss a specific topic based on an input (Kamberelis & Dimitriadis, 2013; Morgan, 1996; Schulz et al., 2012).

We have deliberately emphasized diversity in the composition of participants in terms of MUUP, multi-dimensionality, trans-disciplinarity, and intersectionality, to bring in and discuss different perspectives (Sundermeier et al., 2020). The experts' lenses have been shaped through professional occupations in numerous domains, e.g.: human rights, IS, political science, and policy. The pool of experts has been established as a research effort over the last three years through professional networks and by way of individual recruitment (e.g., conferences, publications, social media, research projects). It currently consists of about one hundred individuals (and counting).

Eight English speaking focus groups sessions were conducted between July 2022 and March 2023. The group size averaged ten people. The sessions were scheduled for 1–15 min and conducted in an online video call format. Participants joined the sessions from around the globe.

We used an iterative method, creating a working hypothesis or a sketched model based on literature, past research, and existing gaps, challenging it within the focus groups, consolidating the outcomes afterwards, and integrating the intermediate results into the next meeting. In practical terms, this means, that e.g., a definition of feminism has been proposed to the group in order to start a discussion on the existence, benefits, and limits of varying feminist approaches. The process of each session was facilitated by one of the authors of this paper who initiated and moderated each discussion. In line with the focus group method, the moderator did not engage actively in the discussion but merely ensured an inclusive, respectful, and on-topic debate. The sessions were either recorded by video (if all participants agreed) or by minutes. The recordings were transcribed and coded in an iterative and explorative way until concepts emerged (Corbin & Strauss, 2014).

4 Preliminary Results

Based on the research process so far, the answer to RQ is: Yes, it is likely that the feminist approach can be utilized to shape AI systems, e.g.: *"Feminism [...] can help to be a foundation with which to analyze and address the threat and potential of AI."* We identified power as an important concept in shaping AI systems, as participants repeatedly mentioned the perpetuation of current patriarchal power structures, e.g.: *"Again the people on top continue to get power, because they already have the power."* Moreover, rather than focusing only on technical and individual influences on AI as emphasized by e.g., the concept of air AI (Feuerriegel et al., 2020), participants argued for a broader context with regard to the people behind its data, design, and context, e.g.: *"We need to encourage more marginalized people and minorities to access this field."* Thus, the three concepts, *data & design*, *people*, and *context* evolved.

Consequently, we introduce our framework depicted in Fig. 1. It illustrates the interdependence of the societal (S1) and AI system (S2): The PPS of S1 influence S2. The intersection of S1 and S2 is shaped by three conceptual areas where the social and analogue is translated into the artificial and digital. As mentioned above these are currently subsumed under the following designators 1) data and design of AI, e.g., the input data, 2) people, e.g., the diversity of people designing AI, and 3) context, e.g., the environment in which AI is built. These proposed main influences of AI systems reinforce and perpetuate the prevailing distribution of power (currently almost exclusively shaped through the patriarchy) within S2, linking back to S1. Therefore, we hypothesize that a feminist approach could break that circle and lead to a more inclusive distribution of power. Thus, AI could become a driver for equity and justice gradually changing S1 including its PPSs.

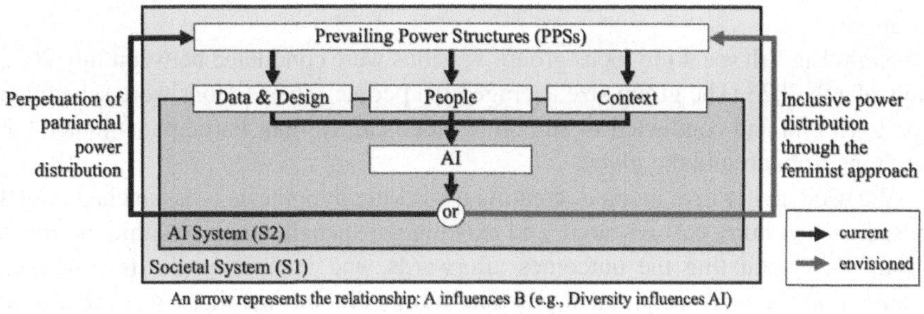

Fig. 1 The interdependence of the societal and AI system

5 Discussion, Limitations, and Outlook

Research displays the exacerbation of existing inequalities by AI (Kim, 2021; Zajko, 2022), however, it remains scarce on how to address this societal challenge. Much research focuses on its normative aspects (e.g., ethical AI). Consequently, the importance of the social practice—being embossed by the patriarchy—is systematically being omitted. Without taking it into account, these efforts will remain normative ideals. To address this gap, we conducted expert focus groups and present intersectional feminism as a means to disrupt this circle. Our framework extends current research through its boundary-spanning and interdisciplinary nature and as such connects previously siloed achievements (Berente et al., 2021). To our knowledge it is the first to integrate and address the root cause of discriminatory AI: the patriarchal society and its PPSs. However, there are limitations to consider: We are limited due to a self-selection bias of focus group participants, with a high percentage of people interested in the topic. Thus, the diversity of answers might have been affected. We aim to create a better balance for future research. Moreover, the methodological approach should be further consolidated. To do so, we envision another seven focus group sessions in 2023. In addition, we will integrate elements of the Delphi method (Niederberger & Renn, 2019) and draw on the existing body of knowledge more comprehensively. The goal is to derive a tested hypothesis leading the way to substantiated theoretical paradigms on how the feminist AI approach can shape both the societal and AI systems as well as their interdependence as a basis for developing applicable practices. Results from the focus groups underline this, e.g.: *"How can we practically address this?"* and *"How can we turn this around so that AI benefits those who are not privileged?"*. Thus, to further expand this body of knowledge, we propose two research questions for this project and future iterations:

RQ 1*: How can the feminist approach to shaping AI systems be conceptualized?*

RQ 2*: How can the feminist approach to shaping AI systems work in practice*?

References

Allen, A. (1998). Rethinking Power. *Hypatia, 13*(1), 21–40. JSTOR. http://www.jstor.org/stable/3810605

Angwin, J., Larson, J., Surya, M., & Lauren, K. (2016). *Machine Bias*. ProPublica. https://www.propublica.org/article/machine-bias-risk-assessments-in-criminal-sentencing

Arrieta, A. B., Díaz-Rodríguez, N., Ser, J. D., Bennetot, A., Tabik, S., Barbado, A., Garcia, S., Gil-Lopez, S., Molina, D., Benjamins, R., Chatila, R., & Herrera, F. (2020). Explainable Artificial Intelligence (XAI): Concepts, taxonomies, opportunities and challenges toward responsible AI. *Information Fusion, 58*, 82–115. https://doi.org/10.1016/j.inffus.2019.12.012

Berente, N., Gu, B., Recker, J., & Santhanam, R. (2021). Managing artificial intelligence. *MIS Quarterly*, 1433–1450. https://doi.org/10.25300/MISQ/2021/16274

Bertrand, J., & Weill, L. (2021). Do algorithms discriminate against African Americans in lending? *Economic Modelling, 104*, 105619. https://doi.org/10.1016/j.econmod.2021.105619

Binns, R. (2017). Fairness in Machine Learning: Lessons from Political Philosophy. *Proceedings of Machine Learning Research 81*, 1–11. http://arxiv.org/abs/1712.03586}

Buolamwini, J., & Gebru, T. (2018). Gender Shades: Intersectional Accuracy Disparities in Commercial Gender Classification. *Proceedings of the 1st Conference on Fairness, Accountability and Transparency*, 77–91. https://proceedings.mlr.press/v81/buolamwini18a.html

Carbado, D., Devon, Crenshaw, K., Mays, V., & Tomlinson, B. (2013). Intersectionality: Mapping the Movements of a Theory. *Du Bois Review: Social Science Research on Race, 10*, 303-312. https://doi.org/10.1017/S1742058X13000349

Chouldechova, A. (2017). Fair Prediction with Disparate Impact: A Study of Bias in Recidivism Prediction Instruments. *Big Data, 5*(2), 153–163. https://doi.org/10.1089/big.2016.0047

Corbin, J. M., & Strauss, A. (2014). *Basics of Qualitative Research: Techniques and Procedures for Developing Grounded Theory* (4th ed.). SAGE Publications, Inc.

Crenshaw, K. (1989). Demarginalizing the Intersection of Race and Sex: A Black Feminist Critique of Antidiscrimination Doctrine, Feminist Theory and Antiracist Politics. *University of Chicago Legal Forum, 1989*(1), 139–167.

Crenshaw, K. (1991). Mapping the Margins: Intersectionality, Identity Politics, and Violence against Women of Color. *Stanford Law Review, 43*(6), 1241–1299. https://www.jstor.org/stable/1229039

Cuhls, K. E. (2019). Horizon Scanning in Foresight – Why Horizon Scanning is only a part of the game. *Futures & Foresight Science, 2*(1), 1–21. https://doi.org/10.1002/ffo2.23

D'Ignazio, C., & Klein, L. F. (2020). *Data Feminism*. MIT Press.

Ess, C. M. (2020). Interpretative Pros Hen Pluralism: From Computer-Mediated Colonization to a Pluralistic Intercultural Digital Ethics. *Philosophy & Technology, 33*(4), 551–569. https://doi.org/10.1007/s13347-020-00412-9

European Commission. (2019). *Ethics Guidelines for Trustworthy AI* (pp. 1–39). https://ec.europa.eu/futurium/en/ai-alliance-consultation.1.html

Ferguson, K. E. (2017). Feminist Theory Today. *Annual Review of Political Science, 20*(1), 269–286. https://doi.org/10.1146/annurev-polisci-052715-111648

Feuerriegel, S., Dolata, M., & Schwabe, G. (2020). Fair AI. *Business & Information Systems Engineering, 62*(4), 379–384. https://doi.org/10.1007/s12599-020-00650-3

Floridi, L. (2019). Establishing the rules for building trustworthy AI. *Nature Machine Intelligence, 1*(6), 261–262. https://doi.org/10.1038/s42256-019-0055-y

Hagendorff, T. (2020). The Ethics of AI Ethics: An Evaluation of Guidelines. *Minds and Machines, 30*, 99–120. https://doi.org/10.1007/s11023-020-09517-8

Jago, A. S., & Laurin, K. (2022). Assumptions About Algorithms' Capacity for Discrimination. *Personality and Social Psychology Bulletin, 48*(4), 582–595. https://doi.org/10.1177/01461672211016187

Jethwani, H., Subramonian, A., Agnew, W., Bleile, M., Arora, S., Ryskina, M., & Xiong, J. (2022). Queer in AI. *XRDS: Crossroads, The ACM Magazine for Students, 28*(4), 18–21. https://doi.org/10.1145/3538543

Johnson, A. G. (2007). *The Gender Knot*. Pearson Education India.

Kamberelis, G., & Dimitriadis, G. (2013). *Focus Groups: From structured interviews to collective conversations*. Routledge. https://doi.org/10.4324/9780203590447

Kim, P. (2021). AI and Inequality. In *Forthcoming in The Cambridge Handbook on Artificial Intelligence & the Law, Kristin Johnson & Carla Reyes, eds. (2022), Washington University in St. Louis Legal Studies Research Paper No. 21–09–03*. Available at SSRN: https://ssrn.com/abstract=3938578

Malek, Md. A. (2022). Criminal courts' artificial intelligence: The way it reinforces bias and discrimination. *AI and Ethics, 2*(1), 233–245. https://doi.org/10.1007/s43681-022-00137-9

Michelfelder, D. P., Wellner, G., & Wiltse, H. (2017). Designing differently: Toward a methodology for an ethics of feminist technology design. In *The Ethics of Technology: Methods and Approaches* (pp. 193–218). Rowman & Littlefield International.

Mikalef, P., Conboy, K., Lundström, J. E., & Popovič, A. (2022). Thinking responsibly about responsible AI and 'the dark side' of AI. *European Journal of Information Systems, 31*(3), 257–268. https://doi.org/10.1080/0960085X.2022.2026621

Mikalef, P., & Gupta, M. (2021). Artificial intelligence capability: Conceptualization, measurement calibration, and empirical study on its impact on organizational creativity and firm performance. *Information & Management, 58*(3). https://doi.org/10.1016/j.im.2021.103434

Mittelstadt, B. (2019). Principles alone cannot guarantee ethical AI. *Nature Machine Intelligence, 1*(11), 501–507. https://doi.org/10.1038/s42256-019-0114-4

Morgan, D. L. (1996). Focus Groups. *Annual Review of Sociology, 22*(1), 129–152. https://doi.org/10.1146/annurev.soc.22.1.129

Niederberger, M., & Renn, O. (Eds.). (2019). *Delphi-Verfahren in den Sozial- und Gesundheitswissenschaften: Konzept, Varianten und Anwendungsbeispiele.* Springer VS.

Oksala, J. (2017). Feminism and Power. In *The Routledge Companion to Feminist Philosophy.* Routledge.

Perkowitz, S. (2021). The Bias in the Machine: Facial Recognition Technology and Racial Disparities. *MIT Case Studies in Social and Ethical Responsibilities of Computing.* https://doi.org/10.21428/2c646de5.62272586

Peters, D., Vold, K., Robinson, D., & Calvo, R. A. (2020). Responsible AI—Two Frameworks for Ethical Design Practice. *IEEE Transactions on Technology and Society, 1*(1), 34–47. https://doi.org/10.1109/TTS.2020.2974991

Riedl, M. O. (2019). Human-centered artificial intelligence and machine learning. *Human Behavior and Emerging Technologies, 1*(1), 33–36. https://doi.org/10.1002/hbe2.117

Schulz, M., Mack, B., & Renn, O. (Eds.). (2012). *Fokusgruppen in der empirischen Sozialwissenschaft.* VS Verlag für Sozialwissenschaften. https://doi.org/10.1007/978-3-531-19397-7

Shneiderman, B. (2020). Human-Centered Artificial Intelligence: Reliable, Safe & Trustworthy. *International Journal of Human–Computer Interaction, 36*(6), 495–504. https://doi.org/10.1080/10447318.2020.1741118

Siapka, A. (2022). Towards a Feminist Metaethics of AI. *Proceedings of the 2022 AAAI/ACM Conference on AI, Ethics, and Society*, 665–674. https://doi.org/10.1145/3514094.3534197

Sundermeier, J., Birkner, S., Ettl, K., Kensbock, J., & Tegtmeier, S. (2020). Hello Diversity! Opportunities and Challenges of Entrepreneurial Diversity in the Digital Age. *Communications of the Association for Information Systems, 47*(1). https://doi.org/10.17705/1CAIS.04732

Walby, S. (1989). Theorising Patriarchy. *Sociology, 23*(2), 213–234. https://doi.org/10.1177/0038038589023002004

Webster, J., & Watson, R. (2002). Analyzing the Past to Prepare for the Future: Writing a Literature Review. *MIS Quarterly, 26.* https://doi.org/10.2307/4132319

Weinberg, L. (2020). Feminist Research Ethics and Student Privacy in the Age of AI. *Catalyst: Feminism, Theory, Technoscience, 6*(2), Article 2. https://doi.org/10.28968/cftt.v6i2.32943

Wellner, G., & Rothman, T. (2020). Feminist AI: Can We Expect Our AI Systems to Become Feminist? *Philosophy & Technology, 33*(2), 191–205. https://doi.org/10.1007/s13347-019-00352-z

Zajko, M. (2022). Artificial intelligence, algorithms, and social inequality: Sociological contributions to contemporary debates. *Sociology Compass, 16*(3). https://doi.org/10.1111/soc4.12962

Digital Innovation, Adoption and Use

Investigating the Use of Augmented Reality and Machine Learning in Electrical Engineering Courses

Miles Al Mehdawi, Tobias Dreesbach, Henning Gösling, and Marcel Brinkmann

Abstract The use of augmented reality (AR) in education and training is growing increasingly. However, applications to integrate augmented reality learning content into training for basic electrical engineering courses are scarce. The individual learning objectives of trainees complicate the digitalization of learning content, particularly for the drawing of circuit diagrams. To increase trainees' learning outcome while simultaneously relieving instructors of classroom supervision, we designed and developed an AR-based prototype, to enhance hand-drawn circuit diagrams in vocational training. The context sensitivity is achieved by combining AR with image recognition. In an experiment with twelve participants, a positive impact of the prototype on trainees' learning outcomes was observed, in comparison to a control group that received instructions without the prototype.

Keywords Augmented reality · Vocational training · Circuit diagrams · Object recognition

---

M. Al Mehdawi (✉) · T. Dreesbach · H. Gösling
German Research Centre for Artificial Intelligence, Smart Enterprise Engineering, Hamburger Straße 24, 49084 Osnabrück, Germany
e-mail: miles97.al@web.de

T. Dreesbach
e-mail: tobias.dreesbach@dfki.de

H. Gösling
e-mail: henning.goesling@dfki.de

M. Brinkmann
KME Germany GmbH, Klosterstraße 29, 49074 Osnabrück, Germany
e-mail: marcel.brinkmann@kme.com

D. Beverungen et al. (eds.), *Conceptualizing Digital Responsibility for the Information Age*, Lecture Notes in Information Systems and Organisation 74,
https://doi.org/10.1007/978-3-031-80119-8_7

1 Introduction

Scientific research in the domain of vocational education and training (VET) shows that the use of augmented reality (AR) can offer learning advantages, compared to books or desktop computer applications (Garzón et al. 2019; Radu, 2014). By using AR in VET, it is possible to enhance the learners' motivation as well as the learners' understanding of the presented learning materials (Li et al. 2011). Especially in practice-oriented training, AR devices can support knowledge transfer and prepare learners for complex tasks (Buehler & Kohne, 2020). Numerous studies on the combination of AR with pedagogical approaches, such as situated or collaborative learning, indicate a positive impact on learning outcome (Garzón et al. 2020). In a three-year consortium research project, we have examined the use of AR in an electrical engineering course. Electrical engineering is a discipline in VET, in which trainees learn the basics of electrical equipment, devices, and systems. Drawing circuit diagrams is also part of the curriculum. The diagrams allow to uniquely determine the dependency relationships between the different symbols of the circuit (Pando Cerra et al. 2014). The training sessions examined in the research project are part of a mandatory three-week course for technical apprenticeships in the company. The trainees independently draw a two-way circuit diagram. As the trainees do not have knowledge about circuit diagrams beforehand, the task can be challenging. Going through the provided workbooks is time-consuming and the abstract concepts in workbooks often lead to a mismatch between theory and practice among students and trainees (Wang, 2016). Consequently, the transfer of specialized knowledge to the real application context in the course requires frequent assistance from the instructor. However, most of the instructor's time is spent correcting drawings rather than assisting individual learners. The instructor has little time to focus on individual trainees. Hence, during a meeting with the instructor, we defined the objective to reduce personal support for checking hand-drawn circuit diagrams and to increase the learning outcomes of trainees by a use of an AR-based application.

The digitization of hand-drawn circuit diagrams proved to be advantageous, enabling virtual interaction with teaching content and dynamic representation (Lakshman Naika et al. 2019; Liu et al. 2020), as well as simplified analysis of relationships (Dey et al. 2021). Existing AR-based solutions for circuit symbol recognition rely predominantly on computers (Abdel-Majeed et al. 2020; Bhattacharya et al. 2020; Dewangan, 2018) or smartphones (Hernández Mesa et al. 2017). However, a significant drawback of these approaches is that the creation of sketches is interrupted by the need to capture images and switch to the respective device, impeding the learners' workflow. The goal of this contribution is to provide trainees with context-sensitive augmentation through AR glasses. The underlying research question is: How augmented reality (AR) can support training sessions in electrical engineering courses within the framework of hand- drawn circuit diagrams? By using an AR based application, we try to achieve a more immersive and independent learning experience for the trainees.

To generalize the results, we discuss the design and evaluation of the prototype to facilitate the transfer of the results to future prototypes that support hand-drawn learning activities. But first, in the following section two, the current state of research regarding AR and artificial intelligence (AI) in electrical engineering education is presented. The third section provides a description of the applied Design Science Research (DSR) method and related research. In the fourth section, the derived requirements for an AR-based application are described, along with the subsequent translation of these requirements into a prototype which uses AI-based object recognition to identify hand-drawn circuit symbols. The application was subsequently evaluated for learning outcomes in a regular training session through a quantitative study. The results of the evaluation are shown in chapter five. The discussion of the findings is presented in section six, followed by the conclusion in section seven.

2 Related Work

VET aims to equip students and trainees with skills and competences but require continuous adaptation towards new technological developments (Kazancoglu and Ozkan-Ozen, 2018). The spatial virtual representations provided by AR devices can be used in VET to convey three-dimensional learning materials (Radu, 2014). The digital extension of the real environment with virtual content in real time is the fundamental characteristic of AR (Vogel et al. 2020). A literature review by Avila-Garzon et al. (2021) identified a total of 3475 studies on educational context related to AR between the years of 1995 and 2020, demonstrating the relevance of AR in VET. Numerous other studies in the educational field concluded that AR learning materials can be effective in increasing the learning outcome for students (Ibáñez and Delgado-Kloos, 2018; Radu, 2014). AR can effectively reduce the occurrence of misconceptions in subjects that involve spatial relationships, which are often difficult to comprehend, by making complex concepts more accessible and understandable. (Ozdemır et al. 2018; Sirakaya and Cakmak, 2018). It is also broadly used in natural sciences, mathematics, and statistics (Garzón et al. 2019; Li et al. 2011). A commonly used pedagogical approach in the field of AR is the theory of situated learning, which refers to AR training materials in authentic environments (Garzón et al. 2020).

In a review by Radu (2014), 26 empirical studies in education were analyzed to compare AR with non-AR applications. Most of the studies of the review indicate that AR applications lead to positive learning outcomes for students in compare to media such as books or desktop computers. It is shown that learning content stays longer in memory and information can be transferred more efficiently to physical tasks (Radu, 2014). However, further evaluations of AR applications in education are still needed (Garzón et al. 2019; Saltan & Arslan, 2016; Wu et al. 2013), e.g., regarding the optimal presentation of information (Phon et al. 2014). When measuring the learning outcome, different parameters are used in the literature: e.g., the completion time for the task, the number of mistakes made, perceived feedback, and a pre-post-test design with questions about the learning content. However, the completion time for the task or the number of mistakes made, are not sufficient measurement criteria for the learning outcome. They do not provide information if learners gained an understanding of the performed task (Wuttke et al. (2022).

Current research emphasizes the need to further explore AR in VET to facilitate a better understanding of learning materials among trainees (Hernández Mesa et al. 2017; Liu et al. 2020). In the VET field of teaching circuit diagrams, instructors bear the responsibility of correcting hand-drawn circuit diagrams made by learners and providing subsequent feedback on the individual drawings. This tedious process can be streamlined by employing automated recognition of diagrams and digital verification of logical correctness (Lakshman Naika et al. 2019).

In addition to AR, AI is already being employed in VET to address domain-specific challenges across a wide range of applications (Chen et al. 2020; Goksel and Bozkurt, 2019; McArthur et al. 2005; Yang and Bai, 2020). The recognition of objects in a camera stream is one of the key topics of AI. In non-VET applications, recognition of circuit diagrams is used for digitizing concept drawings (Liu & Xiao, 2013; Pravalpruk & Dailey, 2016). The topic of object recognition is highly coupled with another key topic of AI: Machine Learning (ML). Through ML, new (artificial) knowledge is derived from empirical data and used for future predictions or decision making (Ongsulee, 2017; Provost & Kohavi, 1998). The methods currently used by AR applications to capture, analyze, and interpret incoming information are still dominated by traditional, non-AI approaches, but can be significantly improved through the use of AI (Sahu et al. 2021).

3 Research Approach

The research in this paper is conducted according to the DSR method of Peffers et al. (2007). With this DSR method, the complete process from the definition of a problem to the evaluation of a corresponding artifact and the discussion of the results can be performed systematically. Hence, it provides a consistent and clearly structured approach to develop IT artifacts. The six phases of the selected DSR method are shown in Fig. 1.

The DSR described in this paper started with the selection of use cases at two companies and two vocational schools that took place in a three-year consortium research project. Within the project, we are aiming to integrate AR into the curricula of vocational schools and companies. The investigation of the use cases have been conducted to support instructors and create innovative educational opportunities (Dreesbach et al. 2021). A focus session with all project partners at the beginning of the research identified four distinct scenarios for the application of AR. The investigated use cases comprise the familiarization with a woodworking center and the configuration of servo motors in the two vocational schools. In the two companies they include the manual assembly of an air conditioning module as well as the design and development of a two-way circuit.

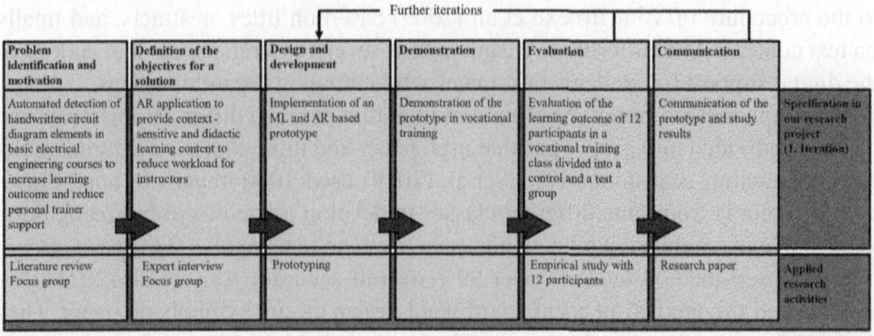

Fig. 1 DSR activities adapted from Peffers et al. (2007)

The design and development of a two-way circuit is part of a basic electrical engineering course and takes place at a market-leading German manufacturer of semi-finished copper products. We identified the need for automated recognition and verification of handwritten circuit drawings (problem identification and motivation). Within the company-specific training, the basic electrical engineering course is mandatory for industrial mechanics, machinists, materials testers, and process engineers. As a part of this basic course, trainees learn how to plan, draw, and assemble an alternating circuit. Firstly, the necessary equipment is explained, and the trainees must answer theoretical questions about it. They have to find the answers to these questions independently, either from books or provided spreadsheets. Then the instructor specifies the necessary equipment for the assembly of an alternating circuit. For each type of equipment, the corresponding circuit symbol is presented and discussed. Then, in the following lesson, the trainees must draw a circuit diagram for the alternating circuit. While drawing, they are supported by the instructor, who answers arising questions and checks the progress of the drawings. More precisely, the instructor checks the selection and correct representation of the circuit symbols as well as the line thickness. So far, the drawings are done with the use of pen and ruler.

Based on the identified need for an automated recognition and verification of handwritten circuit drawings, we conducted a systematic literature review to identify related work. According to Cooper's (1988) definition, a literature review is intended to be a complete and selective coverage of the knowledge base in order to find research results on practical applications. We used the following search term and its German equivalent, too: ((*"Circuit Symbol*" OR "Electr* Symbol*" OR "Circuit Diagram*" OR "Electrical Diagram") AND ("*recogni*" OR "*detect*" OR "identificat*" OR "classificat*") AND ("hand-drawn" OR "handwritten" OR "sketched"*)). We screened the databases Springer Link, IEEE-Xplore, Wiley Online Library, Elsevier Scopus, and Elsevier ScienceDirect. We performed a forward and backward search and removed all duplications (Vom Brocke et al. 2009). The results were checked for (1) implementations, with particular emphasis on (2) prototypes that were implemented and utilized in lessons. Papers were sorted out largely according to the procedure of Vom Brocke et al. (2009) based on titles, abstracts, and finally on text content. After filtering, we came across seven research papers that addressed the digital support for students or trainees while drawing circuit diagrams.

The implemented prototypes found in literature pursued different objectives and can be subdivided into prototypes that used paper and those that used a digital tablet for the drawings. Lakshman Naika et al. (2019) used 1000 images of hand-drawn circuit symbols from nine different classes to develop a circuit symbol recognition algorithm and combined it with a finite state machine to recognize the type of circuit. The proposed method leads to over 99% overall accuracy. Dey et al. (2021) also investigated the prediction accuracy of hand-drawn circuit symbols on paper. They evaluated a two-stage neural network and an extended training dataset for recognizing circuit symbols on paper. The two-stage neuronal network achieved significantly more accurate predictions than a single-stage neural network (Dey et al. 2021).

The tablet-based prototypes developed by Valois et al. (2001) and Ejofodomi et al. (2004) recognized hand-drawn circuits and their symbols on the tablet and presented them in a graphical form afterwards. With the developed prototypes of Liwicki & Knipping (2005) and Liu et al. (2020), learners also draw circuit symbols freely on a digital screen. Furthermore, these applications include a linked virtual simulation of the recorded circuit symbols. Hernández Mesa et al. (2017) developed the prototype "ElectAR" to support basic electrical engineering courses, a smartphone-based application for the recognition and AR-based enrichment of circuit symbols. With ElectAR, students capture circuit symbols on a sheet of paper with the smartphone camera. The application extends the symbols with subject-related learning content (Hernández Mesa et al. 2017). However, the learners do not draw the circuit themselves. Instead, prefabricated drawings are overlaid with learning content in the form of images, videos, and texts. These contents describe how each component of the circuit works in detail (Hernández Mesa et al. 2017). We did not encounter papers that evaluate prototypes designed to support hand-drawn circuit diagrams in VET.

In the second step of the DSR (definition of the objectives for a solution), we established the design and necessary functionalities of the prototype. Therefore, we talked to the instructor of the basic electronics course in a guided interview. The instructor was considered an expert because of his relevant knowledge in theoretical and practical training (Liebold & Trinczek, 2009). He has been teaching the basic electronics course for five years that includes the drawing of electrical circuit diagrams. The interview lasted 30 min and covered the relevance of the problem, the current state of the lesson, potential measures, and environmental factors. In accordance with the qualitative content analysis of Kuckartz (2018), the recorded interview was transcribed, content categories were abstracted, and statement frequencies per content category were documented. The abstracted content categories included the problem relevance, target group, procedure of the training unit, circuit symbol types, teaching content, and the tasks of the instructor. Based on the interview results, the interviewing researcher developed requirements for the AR application. In a following step, he then initiated a focus group to discuss the requirements with two other researchers from the fields of computer science and augmented reality to compare the developed requirements with the results of the literature review. In a moderated discussion he presented each of the requirements to the focus group. Afterwards, the implementation of the prototype started as the third phase of the DSR (Design and Development). Then, the demonstration of the prototype in the basic electrical engineering course was conducted in the fourth phase of the DSR (Demonstration). In the fifth phase of the DSR (Evaluation), we tested the prototype with twelve trainees from the course, in a study with a between-subjects design as described in Sect. 5.

4 Prototype Development

4.1 Consolidation of the Requirements for the Prototype

The focus group in the second step of the DSR consolidated the findings from the expert interview and the literature review, consequently determined the design and functionalities of the AR prototype to support basic electrical engineering courses. In total, three functional requirements (FR) and one non-functional requirement (non-FR) for the development of AR learning elements were collected.

The trainees were already familiar with the circuit symbols required for the drawing, as they had been introduced to them in a previous lesson. The required symbols are as follows: the four symbols luminaire, socket, junction box with fuse, and changeover switch. The first requirement for the prototype is that the AR-based supplements for the symbols shall contain the instructional content from the regular electrical engineering course (**FR 1**). The content includes the details of the functions of the components, examples of specific use-cases, a reference image, and a statement of information about the connection marking of each symbol, completed with a checklist of inspection points used by the instructor. Since the symbols drawn by trainees may contain minor errors in the representation, the second requirement is that the prototype considers correctly drawn circuit symbols as well as those that contain minor errors (**FR 2**). However, it was clear from the interview with the instructor that the prototype should not explicitly illustrate the required circuit diagram drawings. Instead, the trainees should plan the drawing on their own, select necessary circuit symbols, and sketch them on a blank sheet of paper before the AR-based verification and support becomes active. Once they completed the drawing, the prototype should provide context-sensitive supplementation to verify the results (**FR 3**). In addition to the three FRs, the interview also revealed one non-FR. The application should be intuitive for trainees to use (**non-FR 1**).

As part of the electrical engineering course, the instructor asks the trainees to draw the lines between the circuit symbols after they correctly drew the four circuit symbols. To keep the implementation effort low for the first iteration in the DSR, the focus group initially did not consider the evaluation of the lines between the symbols. A computer-based prototype developed by Agarwal et al. (2017) can recognize the lines connecting them in addition to the individual circuit symbols, but in this prototype, too, the circuit symbols are first extracted from the image (Agarwal et al. 2017).

The focus group was followed by the prototype development and a study together with the instructor.

4.2 Model for Object Recognition of Circuit Symbols

We performed an ML-based object recognition during prototype development, so that the AR device recognizes the four symbols required for the circuit diagram to meet FR 1. The trainees themselves created the training dataset by drawing the circuit symbols by hand on a white DIN A4 paper. In total, the trainees and the instructor created fifteen sketches for the dataset. Ten of the sketches contain correct circuit symbols. The other five sketches were intentionally prepared in such a way that they contain common mistakes, such as missing or incorrectly drawn components, to include incorrectly drawn symbols in the training data set (FR 2). We took 317 photos of the sketches with different distances and angles using a 25-megapixel camera. Light sources and backgrounds also varied. Subsequently, we labelled all pictures.

After creating the training dataset, we undertook a one-hour training of the model for object recognition using Microsoft Custom Vision. We exported the model to the Open Neural Network Exchange (ONNX) format. ONNX is an open format for representing ML models. The threshold for the probability of a correct prediction (Probability Threshold) is 50%. The model marks predictions that have probability equal to or greater than 50% as correct forecast. It considers all other predictions incorrect. The overlap threshold, which was 30% in our use case, is the value that indicates that the model considers a prediction correct only when the bounding box of the prediction overlaps at least 30% of the actual bounding box stored in the training dataset. When training the model, we aimed for high ratios of the values because of the potential degradation of these values when running the model on HoloLens 2 due to the restrictive computational resources of the processor and graphics card. The precision of it, which indicates the overall performance of the object recognition for all labels (Henderson & Ferrari, 2017), is 97.1%. The recall, in our use case 97.1%, is the value that indicates that 97,1% of the actual recorded circuit symbols are correctly recognized by the model (Powers, 2011). To conclude, the mean average precision of 99.1% indicates the overall performance of the object recognition for all labels (Henderson & Ferrari, 2017). For the present use case, we judged the evaluated metrics to be sufficient for the recognition of hand-drawn circuit symbols, as all values are in the high upper percentage range.

The two Unity-compatible frameworks Unity Barracuda and Windows Machine Learning (WinML) were available for running the trained model on HoloLens 2. We compared the two frameworks using statistics performed by Lazar (2021). Unity Barracuda computational performance is significantly faster than WinML because it uses the HoloLens 2 graphics card for computation, whereas this is not yet possible with WinML (Lazar, 2021). However, Barracuda requires additional pre-processing steps to the training model. This includes processes such as cropping, scaling, and normalization of the images captured by the HoloLens 2 camera. We used the WinML framework v19041 for the prototype to be able to import the trained model into Unity without further modifications.

4.3 Graphical User Interface

We developed the elements of the graphical user interface (GUI) in the Unity 3D development environment in conjunction with the Microsoft Mixed Reality Toolkit framework. To implement the non-FR of intuitive operation of the application, all menu windows have the same structure and recurring elements appear at the same positions. They also have a header that bears a textual title and describes the contents of the respective window. The title background is additionally colored purple to distinguish it more strongly from the other contents of the environment. A button in the header allows back navigation to the previous window and a menu provides structured navigation. In addition, it is possible to reach into the header of a window to reposition the respective window with a hand movement. The user can adjust the size of the window by grasping a corner and making a diagonal hand movement. Below the header of a window the different contents are displayed. When starting the prototype, a sliding button allows the trainee to take a picture of their circuit diagram. The prototype performs object recognition with the help of the trained model and identifies the four circuit symbols for the electrical engineering course (FR 1). After a symbol was identified, it provides a menu that obtains more information on the recognized symbols. The trainees can select one of the circuit symbols to view the associated information. Figure 2 shows the GUI elements after the AR application recognized the symbol of a socket. The GUI provides a checklist, and a reference image of the socket. The checklist includes the inspection points used by the instructor in the regular training session to support the learner with some hints in a checklist on how to draw the symbol correctly. Therefore, the trainees can themselves perform the verification for each of their hand-drawn circuit symbols (FR 3).

The learners can select a second menu option, where a text box provides examples of specific applications for the circuit symbol. If the trainee checks off all the boxes on the checklist regarding the identified circuit symbols, a success message appears.

5 Prototype Evaluation

To evaluate the prototype, we conducted a study as a pre-post-test design with a total of twelve trainees from different training areas (industrial mechanics, machinists, materials testers, and process engineers). We paid special attention to creating a realistic setting and adopting a structured approach for our evaluation. This allowed us to explore the feasibility of the implemented features in our AR prototype and gain a deeper understanding of the developed design, despite the limitations of our

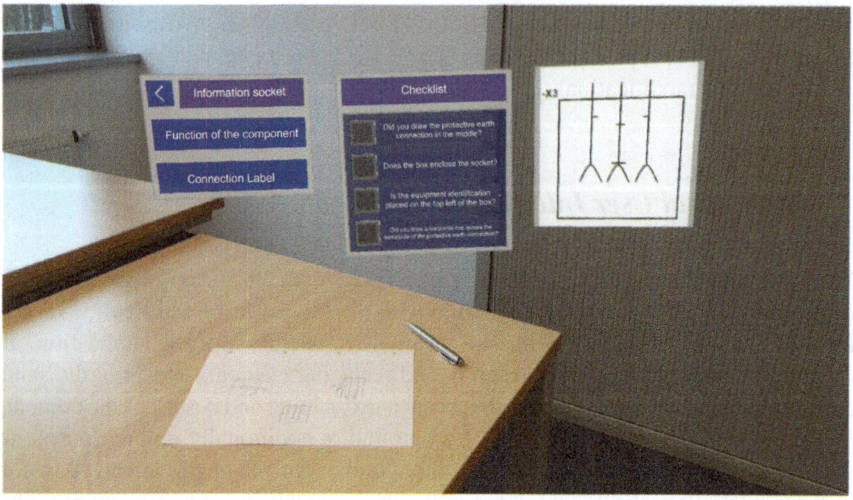

Fig. 2 GUI elements for the checklist and a reference image of the socket (translated)

small sample size. Up to this point, all participants haven't previously taken any other modules in the field of electrical engineering in their respective training programs. All trainees completed a multiple-choice questionnaire (MCQ-1) at the beginning of the study, which included 21 knowledge questions of varying difficulty about the mechanisms and operating equipment of a two-way circuit. The questionnaire was prepared in advance by the instructor according to the learning materials. The treatment afterwards includes the recording of a two-way circuit. For the treatment trainees were randomly separated into two groups with one group using the developed AR prototype and the other group using the conventional workbooks of the training session to acquire the necessary expertise. The group without prototype support was directed by the instructor to draw a two-way circuit while the instructor was available to address any questions arising. This setup remained consistent with the previous course instruction and undergo no further modifications. The other group was individually guided to enter the room. The instructor provided instructions on how to use the AR glasses, allowing for a brief trial period to become familiar with the device. Subsequently, the participants in the group were instructed to draw a two-way circuit. The individual session ended once the two-way circuit was completed, along with a final questionnaire. The entire evaluation process with the prototype took approximately 20 min per participant. Upon completing the task, participants in both groups were instructed to complete a clearly assignable multiple-choice questionnaire (MCQ-2), which asks the same questions as MCQ-1. The results taken from the group-specific MCQ-1 and MCQ-2, in the form of scores, were subsequently evaluated with a mixed ANOVA and used to measure the learning outcome.

As a precondition for the Mixed ANOVA, the Kolmogorov–Smirnov test showed that the data from the survey are normally distributed. Likewise, there are no outliers. The Levene test confirmed the equality of the error variances, and the Box test confirmed the equality of the covariance matrices. The alternative hypothesis H1 states a positive correlation between the use of the developed prototype and the total scores achieved in answering the MCQs by the participants in the study ($p <= 0.05$). To finally answer the research question posed in this paper the H1 is examined using the results of the Mixed ANOVA.

In the following, the measure of a potential interaction effect between time (before and after treatment) and groups (control group versus experimental group) is examined. Since there are no more than two measurement time points for the total scores, sphericity can be assumed. Therefore, the interaction between time and group is significant with a result of 13.412 for the F statistic ($F(1.0; 10.0)$ with $p = 0.004$). Thus, from the within-subjects effects tests for the interaction between time and group on the total score achieved, it appears that there was a statistically significant interaction with an effect size of 0.573 between time (before, $I = 1$; after, $J = 2$) and the two groups. Looking at time separately for both groups, it is noticeable that there was a statistically significant effect ($\eta^2 = 0.914$) of time on the total scores of the experimental group with the AR prototype (at $\alpha = 0.05$). Likewise, the F statistic for the experimental group with AR prototype shows significancy with a result of 52.826 ($F(1.0; 5.0)$ with $p = 0.001$). For the control group without AR prototype, there was no statistically significant effect of time on total score, as seen in the F statistics with a result of 0.741 ($F(1.0; 5.0)$ with $p = 0.741$).

The researchers calculated the pairwise comparison of the estimated marginal means by group and time. Accordingly, the significant effect ($p = 0.001$, at $\alpha = 0.05$) on the total scores of the experimental group arose from task processing (interval between $I = 1$ and $J = 2$) with the AR prototype. As illustrated earlier, there is no significant effect on the total scores of the group without the AR prototype. In the pairwise comparison for the time points before and after task processing, the significance ($p = 0.741$) for the group without AR prototype is above the reference level of $\alpha = 0.05$. Based on the statistical analysis, the alternative hypothesis H1 is accepted because of a positive relationship between the use of the developed prototype and the total scores achieved in answering the MCQs by the participants of the study.

Following the evaluation sessions, the prototype received overwhelmingly positive feedback from participants. The prompt presentation of didactic content coupled with the interaction with virtual elements during circuit symbol recording was deemed exciting. The results indicate that it was beneficial to design the prototype in a way that allows trainees to draw an individual circuit diagram on their own and illustrate the results afterwards using the AR glasses. This approach is consistent with the constructivist perspective that leaves room for learners to actively build their own expertise (Shuell, 1986). Furthermore, the design of the prototype including a checklist and an illustration of the detected circuit symbol to verify the drawing, was adequate for the study and showed promising results.

6 Discussion

A demonstration of AR applications as in our DSR is important to evaluate the use of AR in education and to further discuss the existence of significant benefits (Garzón et al. 2019; Saltan and Arslan, 2016; Wu et al. 2013). The conducted study indicates a positive learning outcome for the AR application. The trainees who used the AR prototype in our study were able to achieve a higher score in answering the questionnaire on the basics of a two-way circuit, than those who used the conventional learning materials. Due to the use of AR glasses, the trainees can easily compare the learning materials displayed with their drawings. By having both hands free, they can also easily make changes to their drawings during the review. Therefore, the results from our conducted study support the findings of Hernández Mesa et al. (2017) that AR applications in circuit diagram drawings have an advantage over previous teaching methods.

Based on the results of our research, the intended reduction of the workload for the instructor was not initially achieved by the prototype. This is due to intensive support provided during the presentation of the AR glasses and familiarization of the trainees. Towards the end of the study, the trainees knew the relevant forms of interaction with the AR glasses. Therefore, their familiarization time for future applications is reduced. However, the company benefits because AR devices are increasingly finding their way into professional practice and trainees are introduced to the technology at an early stage through the prototype. Our impression during the implementation of the study was that both technological knowledge and acceptance towards AR were promoted among the trainees through the application. The positive learning outcome and the successful combination of AR and object recognition indicate a transferability of our results to other use cases, such as assisting with the circuit assembly after the trainees have independently validated their hand-drawn circuit diagrams.

Our study includes three limitations. The first one is the limited scope of the prototype, which is restricted to the two-way circuit. However, through an already implemented interface for the extension of individual information and test points into the prototype, further content can be efficiently integrated in the future. The second limitation is the sample size of twelve trainees in total, which does not ensure general validity of the proven learning outcome. The third limitation is the absence of a supplementary study conducted at a later stage to investigate potential divergences in long-term learning outcomes between the two approaches.

At a technical level, further research can transfer the results to future prototypes that support hand-drawn learning activities. The training dataset created to recognize the drawn circuit symbols was able to achieve a high-performance result for the trained model. The full (offline) execution of the trained model using an ONNX model on HoloLens 2 achieved adequate results during the study. Similar use cases at the technical level could be the drawing of machine elements or physical drawings as well as support in the acquisition of written language for children or persons with low language skills or a writing disability. The results underline the use of an object recognition which considers both correctly drawn circuit symbols and those containing minor errors (FR 2). Nevertheless, one drawback of the prototype was sporadically evident during the study. The application does not provide indications when the trainees cannot replicate the required circuit symbols from the previous lesson or cannot replicate them sufficiently. In that case, the application does not recognize them. Accordingly, a hint function should be integrated into the application to support trainees in the event of start-up difficulties. Further research is needed regarding the dependency relations between the different symbols of the circuit. Due to the high number of possible solutions, a training data set for the dependency relations will be significantly larger.

7 Conclusion

Within the context of this paper, we designed and developed an AR-based prototype to enhance hand-drawn circuit diagrams in vocational training with supportive learning content. Two developers and an instructor, supported by relevant literature, defined the requirements of the prototype for didactic enrichment of circuit diagrams. The implementation of the prototype considered the established requirements pertaining to design and learning content. Following that, the prototype underwent training using AI-based object recognition to accurately identify hand-drawn circuit symbols. In a between-subjects study designed for learning outcome, the experimental group with the prototype was found to have higher learning outcome than the controlled group. The results from the evaluation of the developed prototype demonstrated the potential of AR to improve education and training in the field of electrical engineering. Considering that our research identified further work involving the demand and investigation of systems to recognize and verify hand-drawn circuit diagrams. The scientific relevance of the results are already evident in the first iteration of our DSR. The outcome of our study justifies further investigation to establish a practical use of the prototype in vocational education. In additional iterations of the DSR, the prototype should be more developed, especially with respect to the evaluation of the lines between the circuit symbols.

Acknowledgements This work is part of the research project AdEPT (FKZ: 01PV18008E). The project is funded by the German Federal Ministry of Education and Research (BMBF).

References

Abdel-Majeed, M., Almousa, T., Alsalman, M. & Yosf, A. (2020), "Sketic: a machine learning-based digital circuit recognition platform", *Turkish Journal of Electrical Engineering and Computer Sciences*, Vol. 28 No. 4, pp. 2030–2045.

Agarwal, S., Agrawal, M. & Chaudhury, S. (2017), "Recognizing Electronic Circuits to Enrich Web Documents for Electronic Simulation", in Lamiroy, B. and Dueire Lins, R. (Eds.),

Graphic Recognition. Current Trends and Challenges: 11th International Workshop, Springer International Publishing, Nancy, France, pp. 60–74.

Avila-Garzon, C., Bacca-Acosta, J., Kinshuk, Duarte, J. & Betancourt, J. (2021), "Augmented Reality in Education: An Overview of Twenty-Five Years of Research", *Contemporary Educational Technology*, Vol. 13 No. 3.

Bhattacharya, A., Roy, S., Sarkar, N., Malakar, S. & Sarkar, R. (2020), "Circuit Component Detection in Offline Handdrawn Electrical/Electronic Circuit Diagram", *2020 IEEE Calcutta Conference (CALCON)*, pp. 80–84.

Vom Brocke, J., Simons, A., Niehaves, B., Riemer, K., Plattfaut, R. & Cleven, A. (2009), "Reconstructing the giant: On the importance of rigour in documenting the literature search process", *17th European Conference on Information Systems, ECIS 2009*.

Buehler, K. & Kohne, A. (2020), "Besser Lernen mit VR/AR Anwendungen", in Orsolits, H. and Lackner, M. (Eds.), *Virtual Reality Und Augmented Reality in Der Digitalen Produktion*, Springer Fachmedien, Wiesbaden, pp. 75–97.

Chen, L., Chen, P. & Lin, Z. (2020), "Artificial Intelligence in Education: A Review", *IEEE Access*, Vol. 8, pp. 75264–75278.

Cooper, H.M. (1988), "Organizing knowledge syntheses: A taxonomy of literature reviews", *Knowledge in Society*, Vol. 1 No. 1, p. 104.

Dewangan, A. (2018), "KNN based hand drawn electrical circuit recognition", *International Journal for Research in Applied Science and Engineering Technology*, Vol. 6, pp. 1–6.

Dey, M., Mia, S.M., Sarkar, N., Bhattacharya, A., Roy, S., Malakar, S. & Sarkar, R. (2021), "A two-stage CNN-based hand-drawn electrical and electronic circuit component recognition system", *Neural Computing and Applications*, Vol. 33, pp. 13367–13390.

Dreesbach, T., Berg, M., Gösling, H., Walter, T., Thomas, O. & Knopf, J. (2021), "A Methodology to Enhance Learning Processes with Augmented Reality Glasses", in Ahlemann, F., Schütte, R. and Stieglitz, S. (Eds.), *Innovation Through Information Systems (WI 2021). Lecture Notes in Information Systems and Organisation*, Vol. 48, Springer, Cham.

Ejofodomi, O., Ross, S., Jendoubi, A., Chouikha, M. & Zeng, J. (2004), "Online handwritten circuit recognition on a tablet PC", *33rd Applied Imagery Pattern Recognition Workshop (AIPR'04)*, pp. 241–245.

Garzón, J., Kinshuk, Baldiris, S., Gutiérrez, J. & Pavón, J. (2020), "How do pedagogical approaches affect the impact of augmented reality on education? A meta-analysis and research synthesis", *Educational Research Review*, Elsevier Ltd, Vol. 31, p. 100334.

Garzón, J., Pavón, J. & Baldiris, S. (2019), "Systematic review and meta-analysis of augmented reality in educational settings", *Virtual Reality*, Springer, Vol. 23 No. 4, pp. 447–459.

Goksel, N. & Bozkurt, A. (2019), "Artificial Intelligence in Education: Current Insights and Future Perspectives", in Sisman-Ugur, S. and Kurubacak, G. (Eds.), *Handbook of Research on Learning in the Age of Transhumanism*, IGI Global, pp. 224–236.

Henderson, P. & Ferrari, V. (2017), "End-to-End Training of Object Class Detectors for Mean Average Precision", in Lai, S.-H., Lepetit, V., Nishino, K. and Sato, Y. (Eds.), *Computer Vision – ACCV 2016*, Springer International Publishing, Cham, pp. 198–213.

Hernández Mesa, A., Fabiani Bendicho, M.P. & Martín-Gutiérrez, J. (2017), "ElectAR, an Augmented Reality App for Diagram Recognition", in Stephanidis, C. (Ed.), *HCI International 2017 – Posters' Extended Abstracts*, Springer International Publishing, Vancouver, Canada, pp. 435–440.

Ibáñez, M.-B. & Delgado-Kloos, C. (2018), "Augmented reality for STEM learning: A systematic review", *Computers & Education*, Vol. 123, pp. 109–123.

Kazancoglu, Y. & Ozkan-Ozen, Y.D. (2018), "Analyzing Workforce 4.0 in the Fourth Industrial Revolution and proposing a road map from operations management perspective with fuzzy DEMATEL", *Journal of Enterprise Information Management*, Emerald Publishing Limited, Vol. 31 No. 6, pp. 891–907.

Kuckartz, U. (2018), *Qualitative Inhaltsanalyse: Methoden, Praxis, Computerunterstützung*, 4th ed., Beltz Juventa, Weinheim.

Lakshman Naika, R., Dinesh, R. & Prabhanjan, S. (2019), "Handwritten electric circuit diagram recognition: An approach based on finite state machine", *International Journal of Machine Learning and Computing*, Vol. 9 No. 3, pp. 374–380.

Lazar, L. (2021), *Neural Networks on Microsoft HoloLens 2*, University of Stuttgart.

Li, N., Gu, Y.X., Chang, L. & Duh, H.B.-L. (2011), "Influences of AR-Supported Simulation on Learning Effectiveness in Face-to-face Collaborative Learning for Physics", *2011 IEEE 11th International Conference on Advanced Learning Technologies*, pp. 320–322.

Liebold, R. & Trinczek, R. (2009), "Experteninterview", in Kühl, S., Strodtholz, P. and Taffertshofer, A. (Eds.), *Handbuch Methoden Der Organisationsforschung: Quantitative Und Qualitative Methoden*, VS Verlag für Sozialwissenschaften, Wiesbaden, pp. 32–56.

Liu, S., Lee, L., Jiu, F. & Feng, G. (2020), "Graph-Based Locality-Sensitive Circuit Sketch Recognizer", *IEEE Access*, Vol. 8, pp. 204183–204193.

Liu, Y. & Xiao, Y. (2013), *Circuit Sketch Recognition*, Department of Electrical Engineering Stanford University Stanford, CA, Stanford, CA.

Liwicki, M. & Knipping, L. (2005), "Recognizing and Simulating Sketched Logic Circuits", in Khosla, R., Howlett, R.J. and Jain, L.C. (Eds.), *Knowledge-Based Intelligent Information and Engineering Systems*, Springer, Berlin, Heidelberg, pp. 588–594.

McArthur, D., Lewis, M. & Bishary, M. (2005), "The Roles of Artificial Intelligence in Education: Current Progress and Future Prospects", *Journal of Educational Technology*, Vol. 1 No. 4, pp. 42–80.

Ongsulee, P. (2017), "Artificial intelligence, machine learning and deep learning", *15th International Conference on ICT and Knowledge Engineering (ICT KE)*, pp. 1–6.

Ozdemır, M., Sahın, C., Arcagok, S. & Demır, M.K. (2018), "The Effect of Augmented Reality Applications in the Learning Process: A Meta-Analysis Study", *Eurasian Journal of Educational Research*, Vol. 18 No. 74, pp. 165–186.

Pando Cerra, P., Higuera Garrido, A., Fombona Cadavieco, J. & González Lamar, D. (2014), "Schematics Trainer: An interactive computer tool to study schematic diagrams in engineering education", *Computer Applications in Engineering Education*, Vol. 22 No. 1, pp. 99–109.

Peffers, K., Tuunanen, T., Rothenberger, M.A. & Chatterjee, S. (2007), "A design science research methodology for information systems research", *Journal of Management Information Systems*, Vol. 24 No. 3, pp. 45–77.

Phon, D.N.E., Ali, M.B. & Halim, N.D.A. (2014), "Collaborative Augmented Reality in Education: A Review", *2014 International Conference on Teaching and Learning in Computing and Engineering*, pp. 78–83.

Powers, D.M.W. (2011), "Evaluation: from precision, recall and F-measure to ROC, informedness, markedness and correlation", *International Journal of Machine Learning Technology*, Vol. 2 No. 1, pp. 37–63.

Pravalpruk, B. & Dailey, M.M. (2016), "Offline Text and Non-text Segmentation for Hand-Drawn Diagrams", in Booth, R. and Zhang, M.-L. (Eds.), *PRICAI 2016: Trends in Artificial Intelligence*, Springer International Publishing, Phuket, Thailand, pp. 380–392.

Provost, F. & Kohavi, R. (1998), "Glossary of terms", *Journal of Machine Learning*, Vol. 30 No. 2–3, pp. 271–274.

Radu, I. (2014), "Augmented reality in education: a meta-review and cross-media analysis", *Personal and Ubiquitous Computing*, Vol. 18 No. 6, pp. 1533–1543.

Sahu, C.K., Young, C. & Rai, R. (2021), "Artificial intelligence (AI) in augmented reality (AR)-assisted manufacturing applications: a review", *International Journal of Production Research*, Vol. 59 No. 16, pp. 4903–4959.

Saltan, F. & Arslan, Ö. (2016), "The Use of Augmented Reality in Formal Education: A Scoping Review", *Eurasia Journal of Mathematics, Science and Technology Education*, Vol. 13 No. 2, pp. 503–520.

Shuell, T.J. (1986), "Cognitive Conceptions of Learning", *Review of Educational Research*, Sage Publications, Vol. 56 No. 4, pp. 411–436.

Sirakaya, M. & Cakmak, E.K. (2018), "The effect of augmented reality use on achievement, misconception and course engagement", *Contemporary Educational Technology*, Vol. 9 No. 3, pp. 297–314.

Valois, J.-P., Cote, M. & Cheriet, M. (2001), "Online recognition of sketched electrical diagrams", *Proceedings of Sixth International Conference on Document Analysis and Recognition*, pp. 460–464.

Vogel, J., Koßmann, C., Schuir, J., Kleine, N. & Sievering, J. (2020), "Virtual- und Augmented-Reality-Definitionen im interdisziplinären Vergleich", in Thomas, O. and Ickerott, I. (Eds.), *Smart Glasses: Augmented Reality Zur Unterstützung von Logistikdienstleistungen*, Springer, Berlin, Heidelberg, pp. 19–50.

Wang, J. (2016), "Analysis and Exploration on qDigital Circuitq Course Teaching Reform of the Vocational Colleges", *4th International Conference on Management Science, Education Technology, Arts, Social Science and Economics*, Atlantis Press, pp. 33–36.

Wu, H.K., Lee, S.W.Y., Chang, H.Y. & Liang, J.C. (2013), "Current status, opportunities and challenges of augmented reality in education", *Computers and Education*, Elsevier Ltd, Vol. 62, pp. 41–49.

Wuttke, D., Upadhyay, A., Siemsen, E. & Wuttke-Linnemann, A. (2022), "Seeing the Bigger Picture? Ramping up Production with the Use of Augmented Reality", *Manufacturing & Service Operations Management*, Vol. 24 No. 4, pp. 2349–2366.

Yang, S. & Bai, H. (2020), "The integration design of artificial intelligence and normal students' Education", *Journal of Physics: Conference Series*, Vol. 1453, p. 12090.

Barriers Along the Digital Social Innovation Process: A Structured Literature Review

Christoph Buck, Laura Kempf, Katharina Kneissel, and Anna Krombacher

Abstract Digital social innovation (DSI) is an emerging phenomenon drawing knowledge from digital innovation (DI) and social innovation (SI), offering opportunities to contribute to societal change by leveraging the potential of digital technologies. Although DSI has evoked increasing interest, research and practice are far from realising its full potential as many barriers arise along the DSI process. Thus, holistic insights into DSI process and its barriers are essential. Therefore, we identify barriers along the DSI process through a structured literature review considering DI, SI, and DSI literature. As a result, we identified 28 barriers and classified them into the DSI barrier framework. The DSI barrier framework builds on the DI framework of Kohli and Melville (2019) and extends it by including the societal environment. We thus shed light on the DSI process and provide holistic insights into the barriers along the DSI process.

C. Buck
University of Applied Sciences Augsburg, Augsburg, Germany

Centre for Future Enterprise, Queensland University of Technology, Brisbane, Australia

C. Buck
e-mail: christoph.buck@fim-rc.de; christoph.buck@fit.fraunhofer.de; christoph.buck@qut.edu.au; christoph.buck@tha.de

C. Buck · L. Kempf · K. Kneissel (✉) · A. Krombacher
FIM Research Center for Information Management, University of Bayreuth, Bayreuth, Germany
e-mail: katharina.kneissel@fim-rc.de; katharina.kneissel@tum.de

L. Kempf
e-mail: laura.kempf@fim-rc.de; laura.kempf@fit.fraunhofer.de

A. Krombacher
e-mail: anna.krombacher@fim-rc.de; anna.krombacher@fit.fraunhofer.de

C. Buck · L. Kempf · A. Krombacher
Branch Business & Information Systems Engineering of the Fraunhofer FIT, Bayreuth, Germany

K. Kneissel
Technical University of Munich, Munich, Germany

D. Beverungen et al. (eds.), *Conceptualizing Digital Responsibility for the Information Age*, Lecture Notes in Information Systems and Organisation 74,
https://doi.org/10.1007/978-3-031-80119-8_8

Keywords Digital social innovation · Digital innovation · Social innovation · Barriers

1 Introduction

Societal challenges like climate change, health issues, or racial injustice receive increasing attention and become more pressing each day. As an emerging phenomenon, digital social innovation (DSI), which draws knowledge from digital innovation (DI) and social innovation (SI), appears as a ray of hope in addressing these challenges using digital technologies (Bonina et al. 2021; Yoo et al. 2010). For example, the DSI initiative Child Growth Monitor uses AI to efficiently detect whether a child is malnourished enabling timely help before a child's health is impaired (Welthungerhilfe, 2023) .

While DSI is already highly relevant in practice, research is still in an embryonic stage, and organisations are far from realising its full potential (Bonina et al. 2021; Tim et al. 2021). So far, organisations have failed to successfully develop and implement DSI in the long term, as many barriers arise along the DSI process (Oeij et al. 2019). In the context of this paper, we understand barriers as something that hinders, challenges, or risks the progress of the DSI process, thereby inhibiting DSI's effective implementation (Fuchs and Hess, 2018; Ramilo et al. 2015).

Kohli and Melville (2019) describe a theoretical framework that structures the DI process, encompassing DI actions, environments, and outcomes. While Kohli and Melville (2019) offer a valuable contribution to understanding the DI process, addressing societal challenges has not yet been considered in this context. As we can learn a lot from the barriers that arise in the development of DSI to reach DSI's full potential (Lettice and Parekh, 2010; Neumeier, 2017), we aim to identify these barriers and thus provide insights into the DSI process. Thereby, we focus on barriers that arise along the DSI process from the perspective of the implementing organisation and aim to answer the following research question: *What are the barriers along the DSI process?*

To identify the barriers along the DSI process, we conduct a structured literature review considering DI, SI, and DSI literature (Sharma and Bansal, 2023; Wolfswinkel et al. 2013). A structured literature review is particularly suited to draw a holistic picture of the barriers along the DSI process by integrating fragmented research results across disciplines (Sharma and Bansal, 2023). To profoundly anchor our work in previous research, we use Kohli and Melville's (2019) DI framework as a basis for structuring the identified barriers. We extend this framework in the case of DSI to include the societal environment, which describes the overarching environment, i.e., society, within which DSI takes place. By classifying the 28 identified barriers into this extended framework, we build the DSI barrier framework (DBF). We thus contribute to the emerging phenomenon of DSI by identifying the barriers along the DSI process and laying the foundations for an initial framework of the DSI process. In doing so, the DBF additionally guides practitioners in implementing DSI.

2 Conceptual Framing of Digital Social Innovation

DSI is an emerging phenomenon at the interface between DI and SI (Bonina et al. 2021; Buck et al. 2020). Therefore, to define DSI it is essential to understand both underlying concepts.

DI describes the novel combination of digital and physical components (Yoo et al. 2010) and is conceptualised as consisting of DI actions, DI environments, and DI outcomes. The DI actions consist of four phases (i.e., initiation, development, implementation, exploitation) and are influenced by the internal organisational and external competitive environment (Kohli and Melville, 2019). DI strives to address unfulfilled market and consumer demands and create economic value, by offering solutions that leverage digital technologies (Fichman et al. 2014; Kohli and Melville, 2019; Lettice and Parekh, 2010; Vega and Chiasson, 2019). Digital technologies are a crucial element of DI (Hund et al. 2021). Digital technologies have specific characteristics distinguishing them from conventional technologies, i.e., homogeneity, re-programmability, and self-referential nature (Yoo et al. 2010), as well as embeddedness, connectedness, communicability, editability, identifiability, and associability (Benbya et al. 2020). These unique characteristics of digital technologies are changing the way innovation is conducted, thus opening up new opportunities for value creation, while at the same time creating new barriers, such as the need for novel skills (Hund et al. 2021; Nambisan et al. 2017). Moreover, digital technologies are widely available and affordable, enabling broad scalability and accessibility by large parts of the population (Bonina et al. 2021; Yoo et al. 2010).

SI are innovation activities aiming to drive societal change by introducing novel solutions to societal challenges (Cajaiba-Santana, 2014; Phills et al. 2008). The motivation to improve people's well-being and to create value for society rather than satisfying economic needs drives SI (Phills et al. 2008; Solis-Navarrete et al. 2021). To unfold SI's impact, acceptance and implementation by society are crucial (Eichler and Schwarz, 2019; Purtik and Arenas, 2019). SI addresses "wicked" societal challenges, i.e., deeply rooted problems that have existed for a long time, e.g., poverty, inequality, and climate change (Deserti and Rizzo, 2020; Tracey and Stott, 2017). These challenges are unstructured, complex, and continuous. Thus, they lack a clear problem definition, involve many stakeholders, and have no "once and for all" solution (Tracey and Stott, 2017; Weber and Khademian, 2008).

Especially the wide availability and affordability of digital technologies (Yoo et al. 2010) offer new opportunities to address societal challenges at a previously unimaginable scale and speed (Bonina et al. 2021; Caridà et al. 2022; Qureshi et al. 2021). Thus, using the opportunities of digital technologies as key component of DI, while creating both social and economic value has led to DSI (Bonina et al. 2021; Dong and Götz, 2021). In the context of this paper, we follow Bonina et al. (2021) in defining DSI as using digital technologies to develop new products, services, or processes that meet societal needs or stimulate societal change. Since DSI is an emerging phenomenon, developing a theoretical understanding has only just begun (Qureshi et al. 2021). While Bonina et al. (2021) consider DSI as a whole and explore its dual value orientation (i.e., collectivistic and utilitarian), Buck et al. (2020) conceptualises the characteristics of DSI outcomes in the context of incumbents. Furthermore, Rodrigo and Palacios (2021) illustrate which factors influence employees to commit to DSI in the long-term, and Suseno and Abbott (2021) focus on the perspective of women's entrepreneurship on DSI. Moreover, various contributions explore specific use cases of DSI, e.g., how to design a digital donation system for homeless people (Gebken et al. 2021), or how open-source software can support the economically disadvantaged (Dong and Götz, 2021). While there are already initial approaches to conceptualise the DSI outcomes (e.g. Bonina et al. 2021; Buck et al. 2020), there is a lack of research regarding the DSI process. To gain insights into barriers along the DSI process, we build on the established DI framework by Kohli and Melville (2019) introduced earlier and add the societal environment. The societal environment describes the overarching environment, where DSI occurs and extends beyond the individual organisation and its direct stakeholders. As DSI addresses wicked societal challenges, acceptance and implementation by society are crucial for DSI to unfold its impact (Eichler and Schwarz, 2019; Purtik and Arenas, 2019). During the DSI process, organisations face several barriers, such as failure to achieve societal change or the lack of credibility, hindering the progress of the DSI process (e.g. Roundy and Bonnal, 2017). Thus, holistic insights into the DSI process and the barriers involved are crucial to successfully develop DSI initiatives and unleash their full potential (Bonina et al. 2021; Qureshi et al. 2021).

3 Research Design

We conducted a structured literature review to create a holistic overview of the barriers along the DSI process, building on the approaches of Wolfswinkel et al. (2013) and Sharma and Bansal (2023).

(1) **Define**: We started by defining our search protocol (Sharma and Bansal, 2023; Wolfswinkel et al. 2013). As little DSI research exists so far and DSI draws knowledge from DI and SI (Bonina et al. 2021), we build on the keywords *digital innovation* and *social innovation* for our search string, already including results for *digital social innovation*. Since we want to identify the *barriers* along the DSI process, we include this keyword and its synonyms, *challenge*, and *risk*, in our search string. Consequently, the complete search string is defined as ("digital innovation*" OR "social innovation*") AND (barrier OR challenge OR risk), which we used for title, abstract, and keyword search. We selected the Web of Science Core Collection (WoS) for the literature search to cover the whole picture of DSI as WoS contains high-quality and peer-reviewed articles from a wide range of scientific disciplines such as information systems, business, and social sciences (Clarivate, 2023). Thus, WoS is a widely used database at the intersection of digital and social topics (e.g. Di Vaio et al. 2021; Eichler and Schwarz, 2019; Guandalini, 2022). Furthermore, to identify studies eligible for

our review (Sharma and Bansal, 2023), we defined inclusion criteria: (i) articles taking on a DI, SI, or DSI process perspective, (ii) articles describing at least one barrier, as well as exclusion criteria: (i) articles neither written in German or English, (ii) articles not referring to an organisational context (e.g., referring to forestry).

(2) **Search**: We conducted the literature search across WoS, yielding 1.128 results.

(3) **Select**: We selected the literature, i.e., we gradually excluded irrelevant articles, following the defined search protocol (Sharma and Bansal, 2023; Wolfswinkel et al. 2013). To ensure a representative set of articles, we carried out a three-stage selection process, including title (n = 498), abstract (n = 177), and full-text screening (n = 33). For instance, we excluded the papers Ludvig et al. (2020) and Arts et al. (2020) as they do not refer to an organisational context, but to forestry and aid conservation management, whereas we included the papers Battistella et al. (2021) and Ramilo and Embi (2014) as they cover barriers arising along the DSI process. We concluded the structured literature review with a backward search (Wolfswinkel et al. 2013) including two additional articles, leading to a final set of 35 articles. An overview of the final article set is included in Appendix A.[1]

(4) **Analyse**: We extracted and analysed the data, using open, axial, and selective coding (Sharma and Bansal, 2023; Wolfswinkel et al. 2013). Following Wolfswinkel et al. (2013) one author employed open coding, marking relevant passages referring to barriers along the DSI process, to extract 326 codes. To derive the barriers from the identified codes, we used axial coding and iteratively clustered similar codes into common concepts (Wolfswinkel et al. 2013), leading to 28 barriers. For instance, the barrier *lack of marketing and branding* is a compilation of the codes "*Misbelief of not investing in marketing*", "*Resource scarcity for marketing*" (Roundy, 2017), "*less attention is paid (…) to brand design*" (Komatsu Cipriani, 2017), and "*lack of proper branding strategy*" (Tim et al. 2021). To ensure reliability in deriving the barriers, three authors assigned 80 randomly selected codes out of the 326 codes to the 28 barriers. Inter-coder reliability is satisfactory, with a substantial Cohen's kappa of 0,7875 (Landis and Koch, 1977). We further grouped the 28 barriers into 12 categories, which we derived inductively from the barriers, using selective coding (Wolfswinkel et al. 2013). For instance, the category *resources* is a compilation of the barriers "*lack of financial resources*", "*lack of skilled personnel*", and "*lack of digital infrastructure*". A detailed overview of the identified barriers and corresponding categories can be found in Appendix B1. Finally, we used the DI framework of Kohli and Melville (2019), extended by the societal environment, as a basis to assign these categories to the different elements of the DSI process, leading to the DBF. At all stages, all authors reviewed the barriers and their descriptions to discuss ambiguities and reclassify or rename barriers or categories to ensure the same level of understanding and abstraction.

(5) **Present**: We present and explain the final DBF in the next chapter.

[1] Online-Appendix: https://figshare.com/s/79c7fd2724adeb7aaa00.

4 Digital Social Innovation Barrier Framework

We identified 28 barriers (grouped into 12 categories and five main elements) along the DSI process. Figure 1 depicts our resulting DBF. An overview of the identified barriers with short descriptions and associated references can be found in Appendix B[1].

4.1 Societal Environment

The societal environment describes barriers in the overarching environment, extending beyond individual organisations and their direct stakeholders. The societal environment comprises two barriers: poor digital literacy and triggering societal rethinking.

Poor digital literacy refers to society, i.e., the intended users, not understanding digital technologies and the missing skills to use them, leading to the DSI being rejected and thus failing its purpose (Ramilo and Embi, 2014; Rosa, 2017). Furthermore, *triggering societal rethinking* is challenging for DSI, as it involves questioning deeply rooted informal institutions, i.e., implicit norms, values, and paradigms that emerge and establish unconsciously over time and guide actions (Scott, 2005). Such informal institutions reflect the societal mentality and attitude, for example, conservative thinking, focus on economic profit, or lack of proactive thinking (e.g. Battistella et al. 2021; Oganisjana et al. 2015). Informal institutions are widely accepted and difficult to change (Scott, 2005). However, DSI requires rethinking existing informal institutions to trigger societal change (Purtik and Arenas, 2019), as otherwise it contradicts the objective of societal change and hinders the implementation

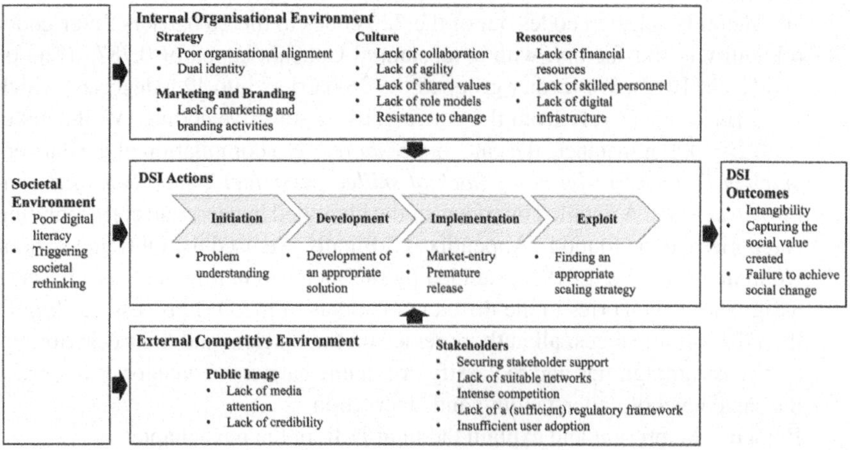

Fig. 1 Digital social innovation barrier framework (based on Kohli and Melville (2019))

and social value creation of DSI (Cajaiba-Santana, 2014; Purtik and Arenas, 2019; Westley et al. 2014).

4.2 Internal Organisational Environment

The internal organisational environment describes organisational barriers (Kohli and Melville, 2019) and comprises eleven barriers in four categories: strategy, culture, resources, and marketing and branding.

Strategy refers to the organisation's strategic focus, determining its use of resources for value creation (Bharadwaj et al. 2013). At the strategic level, organisations must deal with the *dual identity* of DSI, i.e., the simultaneous creation of social impact and economic viability. As both objectives usually strongly interact, the barrier is to deal with the resulting tensions (e.g. Battistella et al. 2021; Deserti and Rizzo, 2020). For example, satisfying the enormous diversity of stakeholders, e.g., financial investors and societal beneficiaries (Deserti and Rizzo, 2020), or dividing scarce resources reasonably between both objectives (Roundy, 2017). Furthermore, the lack of visionary leadership, managerial support, and the resulting lack of strategic focus reflect poor *organisational alignment* for DSI (e.g. Ramilo and Embi, 2014; Vicente et al. 2020). A visionary leader takes responsibility for DSI and drives DSI in the organisation (Westley et al. 2014). In addition, managerial support is critical to create an enabling environment promoting DSI in the organisation, for example, by providing resources or increasing personnel commitment to DSI (Hsu et al. 2019). However, the novelty of integrating social, digital, and economic target dimensions makes developing a strategic focus, and thus organisational alignment, challenging (Ribeiro et al. 2021; Tim et al. 2021; Westley et al. 2014). Additionally, poor organisational alignment leads to poor allocation of scarce resources and a lack of time allocated to DSI alongside day-to-day business (Bharadwaj et al. 2013; Moriggi, 2020; Muhos et al. 2019).

Culture describes the overall working environment and the organisation's attitude towards DSI. The *lack of collaboration* within and between different organisational units and the lack of communication and mutual alignment lead to missing trust and different development schedules (e.g. Brock et al. 2020; Dufour et al. 2014). As DSI development is highly interdisciplinary, the collaboration between different organisational units (e.g., innovation department, legal department, IT) is essential (Charalabidis et al. 2014; Guinan et al. 2019). The lack of collaboration makes it challenging to unify different organisational units working on DSI (Brock et al. 2020; Dufour et al. 2014), which leads, for example, to the technical development not matching the digital literacy of the target group. The *lack of shared values* regarding the attitude toward societal challenges, the use of digital technologies, and innovation in general (Newth and Woods, 2014; Solov'eva et al. 2018; Vicente et al. 2020) is challenging as it reduces the individual's motivation and commitment to DSI (Rodrigo and Palacios, 2021) and weakens trust in collaboration (Arena et al. 2018).

For example, social and economic thinking often represent trade-offs in the DSI process, leading to the potential for conflict. However, creating a shared value base is particularly challenging for DSI, as DSI requires rethinking conventional values and business practices to achieve societal change (e.g. Solov'eva et al. 2018; Vicente et al. 2020). Furthermore, a *lack of agility* due to rigid rules and processes impedes, as requirements and circumstances can change throughout the process (e.g. Brock et al. 2020; Kayser et al. 2018). The increasing speed of digital technologies and rapid changes in societal challenges require organisations to react quickly to external changes (Battistella et al. 2021; Chalmers, 2013; Ramilo and Embi, 2014). Otherwise, DSI might fail to achieve its desired impact, e.g., by not correctly considering changed societal contexts and needs in development (Battistella et al. 2021). Due to a *lack of role models* exemplifying social responsibility and the use of digital technologies, an essential source of inspiration to pursue DSI is missing. As DSI is novel and brings uncertainty, the lack of role models leads to missing encouragement and confidence to take on the responsibility for DSI (e.g. Brock et al. 2020; Suseno and Abbott, 2021). *Resistance to change* is particularly prevalent in DSI through novel digital technologies and the questioning of informal institutions (e.g. Battistella et al. 2021; Newth and Woods, 2014). The novelty of DSI is often associated with fears, uncertainties, and a lack of openness to change (e.g. Ramilo and Embi, 2014; Roundy, 2017). DSI questions deeply rooted economic attitudes within the organisation and thus norms of "proper" business, where economic value creation is central (Battistella et al. 2021; Newth and Woods, 2014). Thus, a DSI idea might be rejected out of the fear of diminishing economic success.

Resources describe the assets and capabilities of an organisation, which are essential in detecting and pursuing DSI ideas (Wade and Hulland, 2004). Missing required resources hinder the DSI process as it leads to the organisation discarding a relevant DSI idea or implementing a DSI idea only in a limited way (e.g. Battistella et al. 2021; Cichosz et al. 2020). The *lack of financial resources* limits necessary investments, e.g., investments in digital infrastructure (e.g. Chalmers, 2013; Grant, 2017). Especially the dual identity of DSI makes acquiring financial resources challenging. Due to its commercial nature, it is difficult to obtain donations. Due to its social nature, it is difficult to attract (private) investors, which are usually mainly interested in financial returns (Newth and Woods, 2014; Popov et al. 2016). In addition, the *lack of skilled personnel* (i.e., managers and employees) (e.g. Arena et al. 2018; Battistella et al. 2021) is caused by the lack of appropriate education and training (e.g. Dufour et al. 2014; Kayser et al. 2018). The lack of digital, social, and managerial expertise hinders identifying new opportunities and implementing DSI (e.g. Muhos et al. 2019; Ramilo and Embi, 2014). This mainly includes understanding and using digital technologies reasonably (e.g. Brock et al. 2020; Kayser et al. 2018) as well as comprehending societal challenges and handling them appropriately (Battistella et al. 2021; Schartinger et al. 2020). Apart from that, as DSI is often mainly driven by a social mission, there is a common lack of knowledge about the commercial side of the business, for instance, funding, networking, and leadership. Without managerial expertise, it is challenging to ensure that DSI stays financially viable (e.g. Deserti and Rizzo,

2020; Živojinović et al. 2019). Finally, the *lack of digital infrastructure* hinders the DSI process. DSI uses digital technologies as a means or purpose in the DSI process and the outcomes (Bonina et al. 2021; Nambisan et al. 2017). Thus, the availability and functionality of digital technologies as a functioning digital infrastructure are fundamental to the DSI process, and their absence inhibits DSI implementation (e.g. Tim et al. 2021; Vicente et al. 2020).

Marketing and branding refer to developing strategies to communicate the value of DSI to the customer (Roundy, 2017). The *lack of marketing and branding* activities arises partly due to a lack of experience (Tim et al. 2021). Their importance is mainly underestimated because of the misconception that it would be contrary to the social mission to invest resources in marketing and branding activities instead of directly devoting them to societal challenges. The lack of investment in marketing activities and the failure to build a brand result in a lack of visibility of DSI in public, i.e., to potential customers and users (Komatsu Cipriani, 2017; Roundy, 2017; Tim et al. 2021).

4.3 *External Competitive Environment*

The external competitive environment describes barriers outside the organisation influencing the DSI process (Kohli and Melville, 2019). The external competitive environment comprises seven barriers in two categories: *stakeholders* and *public image.*

Every organisation interacts with **stakeholders** in its external competitive environment, including regulatory, organisational, and community stakeholders, as well as mass media (Henriques and Sadorsky, 1999). As DSI is highly interdisciplinary and involves different societal groups, organisations must deal with many stakeholders, which must be considered individually (Battistella et al. 2021; Živojinović et al. 2019). Stakeholder support is essential for DSI's existence by providing resources or contributing to its social value through DSI usage (Tanimoto, 2012). However, *securing stakeholder support* is challenging as stakeholders must be convinced of the value created by DSI. Moreover, the stakeholders' economic, social, and technological expectations must be constantly met (e.g. Solov'eva et al. 2018; Wood, 2012). Due to the novelty of DSI, however, it is challenging to properly communicate the mission of DSI and the benefits that each stakeholder will receive (Muhos et al. 2019). Furthermore, in pursuing DSI, organisations often experience a *lack of suitable networks* (Chalmers, 2013; Lettice and Parekh, 2010; Sammut et al. 2020). Networks enable better handling of the complexity of the wicked societal challenges DSI seeks to address by engaging partners for mutual support and exchange (e.g. Qureshi et al. 2021; Sammut et al. 2020). However, due to DSI's dual identity, an organisation neither belongs entirely to the commercial nor the social side. Both networks have reservations about DSI as DSI questions their fundamental principles of either creating social or economic value, but not simultaneously (Battistella et al. 2021). In addition, the *lack of a (sufficient) governmental framework* results in DSI taking place in an institutional void, i.e., there are no or no sufficient rules, regulations, or laws concerning DSI (e.g. Newth and Woods, 2014; Popov et al. 2016). Missing supportive regulations lead, for example, to a lack of public funding (Newth and Woods, 2014; Živojinović et al. 2019) or a deficiency of suitable organisational and legal forms, limiting applicable business and investment models (Newth and Woods, 2014). Furthermore, DSI faces *intense competition* (Tim et al. 2021). Through digital technologies, which enable accelerated dissemination independent of time and place (Nambisan et al. 2017; Yoo et al. 2010), competition occurs locally and globally (Ramilo and Embi, 2014). In addition, DSI competes both in ethical markets, i.e., with social objectives (Nicholls 2007), and traditional markets, i.e., with economic objectives (Komatsu Cipriani, 2017). Moreover, *insufficient user adoption* is a barrier for DSI. Across different user groups, the novelty of DSI causes uncertainty and hesitation (Purtik and Arenas 2019; Roundy 2017). For instance, there are often doubts about technical functionality and usability or the fear of sacrificing privileges (Purtik and Arenas, 2019). In addition, many users presume lower quality and attractiveness for products and services generating social value and view these products and services with great scepticism (Roundy, 2017). If the user does not adopt DSI, it cannot unfold its social value (Eichler and Schwarz, 2019; Purtik and Arenas, 2019).

Public image describes how society perceives DSI. The individual DSI often experiences a *lack of media attention* as it competes with other DSIs for media attention. This leads to the concept and relevance of the individual DSI remaining unknown by the public, thus limiting awareness of the DSI and its social impact. This results in fewer customers, users, or partners becoming aware of DSI, leading to less growth and support (Schartinger et al. 2020; Solov'eva et al. 2018). Furthermore, DSI often *lacks credibility*, which results from the social aspect often being misused as a marketing measure to improve an organisation's image. In doing so, the organisation's communication is misleading as it presents its societal engagement more positively than the truth (Roundy, 2017; Roundy and Bonnal, 2017). As a result, if the customer does not believe in an honest link between DSI and the societal challenge, the customer loses trust and denies DSI's legitimacy (Roundy, 2017).

4.4 DSI Actions

The DSI actions comprise five barriers in four categories: *initiation, development, implementation,* and *exploitation* (Kohli and Melville, 2019).

The **initiation** phase identifies new business opportunities and creates novel ideas for DSI (Kohli and Melville, 2019). The central barrier is *problem understanding*, i.e., understanding the underlying problem and its ecosystem from both a social and an economic perspective and ultimately developing a corresponding DSI idea (Lettice and Parekh, 2010; Roundy and Bonnal, 2017). Understanding the underlying problem in-depth and finding its root cause is difficult due to the multi-layered nature of the wicked societal challenges DSI seeks to address (Chalmers, 2013). However, a thorough understanding of the problem is crucial to not only alleviate symptoms but ultimately drive societal change (Lettice and Parekh, 2010).

The DSI idea is realised in the **development** phase by building a new solution or adapting an existing one (Kohli and Melville, 2019). However, *developing an appropriate solution* is challenging and requires economic and technical feasibility to ensure DSI's long term success (e.g. Kayser et al. 2018; Roundy and Bonnal, 2017). Economic feasibility is questionable if it is not sure that the DSI can build a viable business, for instance, in the case of a niche challenge. DSI cannot survive in the long term, if economic feasibility is not ensured (Roundy and Bonnal, 2017). Technical feasibility is questionable if it is uncertain that the DSI idea can be technically implemented (Kayser et al. 2018). Barriers in technical implementation include, for instance, selecting a suitable digital technology (Cichosz et al. 2020) or considering relevant data processing and data protection regulations (Kayser et al. 2018). If the technical feasibility is not adequately assessed, it leads to subsequent implementation problems and the unnecessary consumption of scarce resources (Dufour et al. 2014; Rosa, 2017).

The **implementation** phase describes the launch of DSI (Kohli and Melville, 2019). As DSI enters conventional market structures and approaches societal challenges in a new way, *market-entry*, i.e., placing a new solution in the market and finding customers, is challenging (Lettice and Parekh 2010). If the customer does not understand the value of using digital technologies to address societal challenges, is unaware of, or does not understand the societal challenge, it becomes difficult to convey DSI's value proposition (Battistella et al. 2021; Purtik and Arenas, 2019; Ramilo and Embi, 2014). The lack of awareness and understanding of the societal challenge leads to questioning DSI's relevance (Schartinger et al. 2020). If DSI is not granted legitimacy, it will not attract customers (Lettice and Parekh, 2010; Ramilo and Embi, 2014; Schartinger et al. 2020), thus, leading to the DSI not surviving financially in the long term (Roundy and Bonnal, 2017). Furthermore, a *premature release* is a barrier to DSI. A hastily introduced solution that does not sufficiently consider interrelationships might have a negative impact by exacerbating the societal challenge or causing adverse side effects (Roundy and Bonnal, 2017). Moreover, DSI should only be introduced to the customer once a certain level of technical maturity has been reached and the business model has been sufficiently elaborated. Otherwise, DSI could fail critical evaluations due to significant technical bugs or contradictions in the business model (Muhos et al. 2019).

Finally, **exploitation** refers to DSI's utilisation (Kohli and Melville, 2019). The barrier with exploitation is *finding an appropriate scaling strategy* that leverages the easy scalability of digital technologies while considering the environmental context, for instance, local regulations (Deserti and Rizzo, 2020), and the organisational context, for instance, access to resources (Deserti and Rizzo, 2020; Tim et al. 2021). In the context of DSI, scaling refers to reaching more and more users and aiming at solving the underlying societal challenge. If an appropriate scaling strategy is not found, societal change may not be achieved, or only to a limited extent (Westley et al. 2014).

4.5 DSI Outcomes

The DSI outcomes are either a product, a service, or a process (Bonina et al. 2021). The DSI outcomes comprise three barriers: *intangibility, capturing social value,* and *failure to achieve societal change.*

Intangibility refers to the digital materiality of DSI, which makes it difficult to perceive the outcome as such. Digital materiality, which enables and requires continuous development even after market entry, leads to difficulty in clearly defining the outcome, which triggers uncertainty (Brock et al. 2020). Furthermore, as social value creation cannot be expressed in economic figures, *capturing social value* is challenging (Battistella et al. 2021; Geobey et al. 2012). While economic value can be measured and uniformly represented by figures, social value is individual, highly subjective, and often deferred and implicit, restricting uniform valuation (Geobey et al. 2012; Popov et al. 2016). This is particularly challenging for funding as most investors are interested in clearly measurable and consistently recorded figures, but these often cannot reflect the impact and value of DSI (Antadze and Westley, 2012; Battistella et al. 2021). Ultimately, the *failure to achieve societal change* contradicts DSI's central objective (Bonina et al. 2021). Societal change is challenging to achieve as often only symptoms are alleviated instead of reaching the societal challenge's core (Lettice and Parekh, 2010; Westley et al. 2014). Furthermore, due to the complexity of societal challenges (Chalmers, 2013), there is a risk of neglecting systemic interrelationships and thus exacerbating the societal challenge to be addressed or triggering adverse side effects, i.e., solving one problem might cause or worsen another one (Roundy and Bonnal, 2017).

5 Contribution and Implication

To unleash the full potential of DSI, capturing the barriers along the DSI process to prevent and counteract them timely is crucial (Bonina et al. 2021; Neumeier, 2017; Qureshi et al. 2021). Addressing this issue and following the call for further DSI research (Qureshi et al. 2021), we contribute the DBF. The DBF includes 28 barriers in 12 categories along the DSI process, structured around five main elements (i.e., societal environment, internal organisational environment, external competitive environment, DSI actions, and DSI outcomes).

Our theoretical implications are twofold. First, we contribute to research on factors influencing the DSI process by identifying 28 barriers along the DSI process. While literature describes capturing and counteracting barriers as crucial for successfully developing DSI, these barriers have not yet been comprehensively identified

(Neumeier, 2017; Ribeiro et al. 2021). With the DBF, we contribute descriptive knowledge, which provides a holistic overview of the barriers along the DSI process and thus lays the foundation for further descriptive, explanatory, and prescriptive knowledge (Gregor, 2006). Second, we extend existing DSI research by laying the foundations for theorising the DSI process. So far, the focus has been on the DSI outcome (Bonina et al. 2021; Buck et al. 2020), whereas the DSI process has been insufficiently explored. To profoundly anchor our work in previous research, we build on the DI framework of Kohli and Melville (2019) and extend it to a DSI framework. To this end, we introduce the societal environment as an additional element in the DSI process, as acceptance and implementation by society are crucial for DSI to unfold its impact (Eichler and Schwarz, 2019; Purtik and Arenas, 2019). In this way, we propose an initial framework of the DSI process.

Additionally, our research offers two valuable recommendations for practitioners. First, our DBF provides an overview of and thus raises awareness for, the various barriers organisations face in the DSI process. For example, organisations can use the DBF to analyse their organisation-specific barriers and thus identify and understand their weaknesses and threats in developing DSI. Such an assessment, in turn, allows considering possible barriers in advance and taking countermeasures at an early stage, enabling organisations to allocate their scarce resources wisely. Second, our DBF offers organisations insights into the DSI process. The five elements of the DSI process serve as a guide to delineate the individual process steps and reflect on possible influences. Guiding organisations in the DSI process, our framework supports practitioners in developing strategies to implement DSI and thus realise the full potential of DSI.

6 Conclusion

DSI is an emerging phenomenon that enables organisations to address societal challenges by leveraging the opportunities of digital technologies (Bonina et al. 2021). To realise the full potential of DSI, it is essential to gain insights into the DSI process and its barriers to address them timely and adequately (Neumeier 2017). Therefore, we derived the DBF, including 28 barriers in 12 categories assigned to the five elements of the DSI process, i.e., societal environment, internal organisational environment, external competitive environment, DSI actions, and DSI outcomes.

Further research can broaden the scope of the literature search and include additional articles to get a more comprehensive picture. Furthermore, due to our research's qualitative nature, all barriers must be treated as hypotheses and propositions. Thus, although each barrier is based on a theoretical foundation, we do not provide validation. Therefore, the explanatory power of the DBF has yet to be investigated through confirmatory research. Further research should employ quantitative approaches as an opportunity to generalise and validate our findings. Moreover, we have treated all barriers equally important, as we cannot deduce from the literature that some barriers are generally more critical than others. Additionally, we did not investigate interactions between different barriers. Therefore, further research should determine the barriers' relevance and interactions across different industries and organisational contexts. Finally, we noted a lack of knowledge regarding systematic recommendations for organisations to manage DSI. Accordingly, we call for future research on DSI in general.

References

Antadze, N. and Westley, F. R. (2012) 'Impact Metrics for Social Innovation: Barriers or Bridges to Radical Change?', Journal of Social Entrepreneurship, vol. 3, no. 2, pp. 133–150.

Arena, M., Bengo, I., Calderini, M. and Chiodo, V. (2018) 'Unlocking finance for social tech start-ups: Is there a new opportunity space?', Technological Forecasting and Social Change, vol. 127, pp. 154–165.

Arts, K., Melero, Y., Webster, G., Sharma, N., Tintarev, N., Tait, E., Mellish, C., Sripada, S., MacMaster, A.-M., Sutherland, H., Horrill, C., Lambin, X. and van der Wal, R. (2020) 'On the merits and pitfalls of introducing a digital platform to aid conservation management: Volunteer data submission and the mediating role of volunteer coordinators', Journal of environmental management, vol. 265, p. 110497.

Battistella, C., Dangelico, R. M., Nonino, F. and Pessot, E. (2021) 'How social start-ups avoid being falling stars when developing social innovation', Creativity and Innovation Management, vol. 30, no. 2, pp. 320–335.

Benbya, H., Nan, N., Tanriverdi, H. and Yoo, Y. (2020) 'Complexity and Information Systems Research in the Emerging Digital World', MIS Quarterly, vol. 44, no. 1, pp. 1–17.

Bharadwaj, A., El Sawy, O. A., Pavlou, P. A. and Venkatraman, N. (2013) 'Digital Business Strategy: Toward a Next Generation of Insights', MIS Quarterly, vol. 37, no. 2, pp. 471–482.

Bonina, C., López-Berzosa, D. and Scarlata, M. (2021) 'Social, commercial, or both? An exploratory study of the identity orientation of digital social innovations', Information Systems Journal, vol. 31, no. 5, pp. 695–716.

Brock, K., Ouden, E. den, Langerak, F. and Podoynitsyna, K. (2020) 'Front End Transfers of Digital Innovations in a Hybrid Agile-Stage-Gate Setting', Journal of Product Innovation Management, vol. 37, no. 6, pp. 506–527.

Buck, C., Krombacher, A. and Wyrtki, K. (2020) 'How Digital is Social? Taking Advantage of Digital for Social Purposes', Proceedings of the 28th European Conference on Information Systems (ECIS).

Cajaiba-Santana, G. (2014) 'Social innovation: Moving the field forward. A conceptual framework', Technological Forecasting and Social Change, vol. 82, pp. 42–51.

Caridà, A., Colurcio, M. and Melia, M. (2022) 'Digital platform for social innovation: Insights from volunteering', Creativity and Innovation Management, vol. 31, no. 4, pp. 755–771.

Chalmers, D. (2013) 'Social innovation: An exploration of the barriers faced by innovating organizations in the social economy', Local Economy: The Journal of the Local Economy Policy Unit, vol. 28, no. 1, pp. 17–34.

Charalabidis, Y., Loukis, E. and Androutsopoulou, A. (2014) 'Fostering Social Innovation through Multiple Social Media Combinations', Information Systems Management, vol. 31, no. 3, pp. 225–239.

Cichosz, M., Wallenburg, C. M. and Knemeyer, A. M. (2020) 'Digital transformation at logistics service providers: barriers, success factors and leading practices', The International Journal of Logistics Management, vol. 31, no. 2, pp. 209–238.

Clarivate (2023) Web of Science Core Collection [Online]. Available at https://clarivate.com/products/scientific-and-academic-research/research-discovery-and-workflow-solutions/web-of-science/web-of-science-core-collection/#benefits (Accessed 9 March 2023).

Deserti, A. and Rizzo, F. (2020) 'Context dependency of social innovation: in search of new sustainability models', European Planning Studies, vol. 28, no. 5, pp. 864–880.

Di Vaio, A., Palladino, R., Pezzi, A. and Kalisz, D. E. (2021) 'The role of digital innovation in knowledge management systems: A systematic literature review', Journal of Business Research, vol. 123, pp. 220–231.

Dong, J. Q. and Götz, S. J. (2021) 'Project leaders as boundary spanners in open source software development: A resource dependence perspective', Information Systems Journal, vol. 31, no. 5, pp. 672–694.

Dufour, S., Lessard, D. and Chamberland, C. (2014) 'Facilitators and barriers to implementation of the AIDES initiative, a social innovation for participative assessment of children in need and for coordination of services', Evaluation and program planning, vol. 47, pp. 64–70.

Eichler, G. and Schwarz, E. (2019) 'What Sustainable Development Goals Do Social Innovations Address? A Systematic Review and Content Analysis of Social Innovation Literature', Sustainability, vol. 11, no. 2, pp. 1–18.

Fichman, R., Santos, B. D. and Zheng, Z. (2014) 'Digital Innovation as a Fundamental and Powerful Concept in the Information Systems Curriculum', Management Information Systems Quarterly, vol. 38, no. 2, pp. 329–353.

Fuchs, C. and Hess, T. (2018) 'Becoming Agile in the Digital Transformation: The Process of a Large-Scale Agile Transformation', Proceedings of the 39th International Conference on Information Systems (ICIS).

Gebken, L., Drews, P. and Schirmer, I. (2021) 'Stakeholder and Value Orientation in Digital Social Innovation: Designing a Digital Donation Concept to Support Homeless Neighbors', Proceedings of the 54th Hawaii International Conference on System Sciences (HICSS).

Geobey, S., Westley, F. R. and Weber, O. (2012) 'Enabling Social Innovation through Developmental Social Finance', Journal of Social Entrepreneurship, vol. 3, no. 2, pp. 151–165.

Grant, S. (2017) 'Social enterprise in New Zealand: an overview', Social Enterprise Journal, vol. 13, no. 4, pp. 410–426.

Gregor, S. (2006) 'The Nature of Theory in Information Systems', MIS Quarterly, vol. 30, no. 3, pp. 611–642.

Guandalini, I. (2022) 'Sustainability through digital transformation: A systematic literature review for research guidance', Journal of Business Research, vol. 148, pp. 456–471.

Guinan, P. J., Parise, S. and Langowitz, N. (2019) 'Creating an innovative digital project team: Levers to enable digital transformation', Business Horizons, vol. 62, no. 6, pp. 717–727.

Henriques, I. and Sadorsky, P. (1999) 'The Relationship between environmental commitment and managerial perceptions of stakeholder importance', Academy of Management Journal, vol. 42, no. 1, pp. 87–99.

Hsu, H.-Y., Liu, F.-H., Tsou, H.-T. and Chen, L.-J. (2019) 'Openness of technology adoption, top management support and service innovation: a social innovation perspective', Journal of Business & Industrial Marketing, vol. 34, no. 3, pp. 575–590.

Hund, A., Wagner, H.-T., Beimborn, D. and Weitzel, T. (2021) 'Digital innovation: Review and novel perspective', The Journal of Strategic Information Systems, vol. 30, no. 4, pp. 1–39.

Kayser, V., Nehrke, B. and Zubovic, D. (2018) 'Data Science as an Innovation Challenge: From Big Data to Value Proposition', Technology Innovation Management Review, vol. 8, no. 3, pp. 16–25.

Kohli, R. and Melville, N. P. (2019) 'Digital innovation: A review and synthesis', Information Systems Journal, vol. 29, no. 1, pp. 200–223.

Komatsu Cipriani, T. (2017) 'The emerging challenge of brand design and brand management in social innovations', The Design Journal, vol. 20, no. 1, 3536–3545.

Landis, J. R. and Koch, G. G. (1977) 'The Measurement of Observer Agreement for Categorical Data', Biometrics, vol. 33, no. 1, pp. 159–174.

Lettice, F. and Parekh, M. (2010) 'The social innovation process: themes, challenges and implications for practice', International Journal of Technology Management, vol. 51, no. 1, pp. 139–158.

Ludvig, A., Rogelja, T., Asamer-Handler, M., Weiss, G., Wilding, M. and Zivojinovic, I. (2020) 'Governance of Social Innovation in Forestry', Sustainability, vol. 12, no. 3, p. 1065.

Moriggi, A. (2020) 'Exploring enabling resources for place-based social entrepreneurship: a participatory study of Green Care practices in Finland', Sustainability Science, vol. 15, no. 2, pp. 437–453.

Muhos, M., Saarela, M., Foit, D. and Rasochova, L. (2019) 'Management priorities of digital health service start-ups in California', International Entrepreneurship and Management Journal, vol. 15, no. 1, pp. 43–62.

Nambisan, S., Lyytinen, K., Majchrzak, A. and Song, M. (2017) 'Digital Innovation Management: Reinventing Innovation Management Research in a Digital World', MIS Quarterly, vol. 41, no. 1, pp. 223–238.

Neumeier, S. (2017) 'Social innovation in rural development: identifying the key factors of success', The Geographical Journal, vol. 183, no. 1, pp. 34–46.

Newth, J. and Woods, C. (2014) 'Resistance to Social Entrepreneurship: How Context Shapes Innovation', Journal of Social Entrepreneurship, vol. 5, no. 2, pp. 192–213.

Oeij, P. R., van der Torre, W., Vaas, F. and Dhondt, S. (2019) 'Understanding social innovation as an innovation process: Applying the innovation journey model', Journal of Business Research, vol. 101, pp. 243–254.

Oganisjana, K., Laizāns, T. and Surikova, S. (2015) 'Factors influencing social innovation processes in Latvia: qualitative research perspective', Entrepreneurship and Sustainability Issues, vol. 3, no. 2, pp. 186–197.

Phills, J. A., Deiglmeier, K. and Miller. Dale T. (2008) 'Rediscovering Social Innovation', Stanford Social Innovation Review, vol. 6, no. 4, pp. 34–43.

Popov, E. V., Veretnnikova, A. Y. and Omonov, Z. K. (2016) 'Institutional Mechanism for Shaping Social Innovation', Economic and Social changes: Facts, Trends, Forecasts, vol. 47, no. 5, pp. 57–75.

Purtik, H. and Arenas, D. (2019) 'Embedding Social Innovation: Shaping Societal Norms and Behaviors Throughout the Innovation Process', Business & Society, vol. 58, no. 5, pp. 963–1002.

Qureshi, I., Pan, S. L. and Zheng, Y. (2021) 'Digital social innovation: An overview and research framework', Information Systems Journal, vol. 31, no. 5, pp. 647–671.

Ramilo, R. and Embi, M. R. (2014) 'Key determinants and barriers in digital innovation among small architectural organizations', Electronic Journal of Information Technology in Construction, vol. 19, pp. 188–209.

Ramilo, R., Embi, M. R. and Datta, S. (2015) 'Digital Innovation for Sustainable Design: Technological and Organizational Barriers', in SENVAR-INTA-AVAN Joint Conference.

Ribeiro, G. C., Oliveira, K. K. S. and Souza, R. A. C. (2021) 'DSI Strategy Canvas: Modelling the Digital Social Innovation Strategy', Journal of Social Entrepreneurship, pp. 1–29.

Rodrigo, L. and Palacios, M. (2021) 'What antecedent attitudes motivate actors to commit to the ecosystem of digital social innovation?', Technological Forecasting and Social Change, vol. 162, pp. 1–7.

Rosa, E. de (2017) 'Social innovation and ICT in social services: European experiences compared', Innovation: The European Journal of Social Science Research, vol. 30, no. 4, pp. 421–432.

Roundy, P. T. (2017) '"Doing good" while serving customers: Charting the social entrepreneurship and marketing interface', Journal of Research in Marketing and Entrepreneurship, vol. 19, no. 2, pp. 105–124.

Roundy, P. T. and Bonnal, M. (2017) 'The Singularity of Social Entrepreneurship: Untangling its Uniqueness and Market Function', The Journal of Entrepreneurship, vol. 26, no. 2, pp. 137–162.

Sammut, N., Spiteri, D., Sammut, J. P., Coppola, I., Lepre, R. and Lebrun, B. (2020) 'The Status of Sustainable Social Innovation in Malta', Sustainability, vol. 12, no. 10, pp. 1–10.

Schartinger, D., Rehfeld, D., Weber, M. and Rhomberg, W. (2020) 'Green social innovation – towards a typology', European Planning Studies, vol. 28, no. 5, pp. 1026–1045.

Scott, W. R. (2005) 'Institutional Theory: Contributing to a Theoretical Research Program', in Smith, K. G. and Hitt, M. A. (eds) Great Minds in Management: The Process of Theory, Oxford, United Kingdom, Oxford University Press.

Sharma, G. and Bansal, P. (2023) 'Partnering Up: Including Managers as Research Partners in Systematic Reviews', Organizational Research Methods, vol. 26, no. 2, pp. 262–291.

Solis-Navarrete, J. A., Bucio-Mendoza, S. and Paneque-Gálvez, J. (2021) 'What is not social innovation', Technological Forecasting and Social Change, vol. 173, pp. 1–9.

Solov'eva, T., Popov, A., Caro-Gonzalez, A. and Hua, L. (2018) 'Social Innovation in Spain, China and Russia: Key Aspects of Development', Economic and Social changes: Facts, Trends, Forecasts, vol. 11, no. 2, pp. 52–68.

Suseno, Y. and Abbott, L. (2021) 'Women entrepreneurs' digital social innovation: Linking gender, entrepreneurship, social innovation and information systems', Information Systems Journal, vol. 31, no. 5, pp. 717–744.

Tim, Y., Cui, L. and Sheng, Z. (2021) 'Digital resilience: How rural communities leapfrogged into sustainable development', Information Systems Journal, vol. 31, no. 2, pp. 323–345.

Tracey, P. and Stott, N. (2017) 'Social innovation: a window on alternative ways of organizing and innovating', Innovation, vol. 19, no. 1, pp. 51–60.

Vega, A. and Chiasson, M. (2019) 'A comprehensive framework to research digital innovation: The joint use of the systems of innovation and critical realism', The Journal of Strategic Information Systems, vol. 28, no. 3, pp. 242–256.

Vicente, P. N., Lucas, M., Carlos, V. and Bem-Haja, P. (2020) 'Higher education in a material world: Constraints to digital innovation in Portuguese universities and polytechnic institutes', Education and Information Technologies, vol. 25, no. 6, pp. 5815–5833.

Wade and Hulland (2004) 'Review: The Resource-Based View and Information Systems Research: Review, Extension, and Suggestions for Future Research', MIS Quarterly, vol. 28, no. 1, pp. 107–142.

Weber, E. P. and Khademian, A. M. (2008) 'Wicked Problems, Knowledge Challenges, and Collaborative Capacity Builders in Network Settings', Public Administration Review, vol. 68, no. 2, pp. 334–349.

Welthungerhilfe (2023) Child Growth Monitor [Online]. Available at https:www.childgrowthmonitor.org (Accessed 8 March 2023).

Westley, F., Antadze, N., Riddell, D. J., Robinson, K. and Geobey, S. (2014) 'Five Configurations for Scaling Up Social Innovation', The Journal of Applied Behavioral Science, vol. 50, no. 3, pp. 234–260.

Wolfswinkel, J. F., Furtmueller, E. and Wilderom, C. P. M. (2013) 'Using grounded theory as a method for rigorously reviewing literature', European Journal of Information Systems, vol. 22, no. 1, pp. 45–55.

Wood, S. (2012) 'Prone to Progress: Using Personality to Identify Supporters of Innovative Social Entrepreneurship', Journal of Public Policy & Marketing, vol. 31, no. 1, pp. 129–141.

Yoo, Y., Henfridsson, O. and Lyytinen, K. (2010) 'Research Commentary —The New Organizing Logic of Digital Innovation: An Agenda for Information Systems Research', Information Systems Research, vol. 21, no. 4, pp. 724–735.

Živojinović, I., Ludvig, A. and Hogl, K. (2019) 'Social Innovation to Sustain Rural Communities: Overcoming Institutional Challenges in Serbia', Sustainability, vol. 11, no. 24, pp. 1–27.

Automized Assessment for Professional Skills—A Systematic Literature Review and Future Research Avenues

Leonie Rebecca Freise and Ulrich Bretschneider

Abstract Globalization, technological progress, and demographic trends increasingly influence our labor markets. With changing labor markets and increasing digitalization, new competencies of workers are needed to meet demands. However, as a first step to developing these new skills, knowledge about the existing skills and their status quo is necessary. Here, automated skill assessment offers a crucial added value, as it can create a reliable and objective database. Based on a systematic investigation, our analysis shows, in four different areas, how skills and competencies in the automated assessment are (1) defined, (2) included as an element of analysis, (3) methodically recorded and processed, (4) which data source is used. In doing so, we offer insights into existing approaches to automated assessment of professional skills. We contribute to a better understanding of the design of automated skill assessment methods and provide perspectives on future research directions.

Keywords Data reliability · Automated skill assessment · Natural language processing · Literature review

1 Introduction

A growing amount of research studies predict that globalization, technological developments, and demographic trends will reshape our labor markets (OECD, 2018; Merchel et al. 2021). Bakhshi et al. (2017) argue that future skills will be favored not only by automation but by personnel shortages. These skills include interpersonal, higher-order cognitive, and system skills and will require transferable skills such as

L. R. Freise (✉) · U. Bretschneider
University of Kassel, Information Systems, Kassel, Germany
e-mail: leonie.freise@uni-kassel.de

U. Bretschneider
e-mail: bretschneider@uni-kassel.de

D. Beverungen et al. (eds.), *Conceptualizing Digital Responsibility for the Information Age*, Lecture Notes in Information Systems and Organisation 74,
https://doi.org/10.1007/978-3-031-80119-8_9

metacognition to perform tasks (World Economic Forum, 2018). To date, professional skill assessment relies on subjective evaluation from, e.g., supervisors, teammates, or task performance (Judrups et al. 2015; Petrov, 2020). This process requires substantial resources like working time from Human Resources (HR) (Gorlov et al. 2015) and lacks reliability and objectivity, i.e., no influence from others.

Although innovative HR methods exist to capture skills automatically, like natural language processing (NLP), a systematic overview of the opportunities for employers and employees is missing. Four main challenges comprise skill assessment (Rayón et al. 2014): a lack of scalability, the subjectivity of interpretation by evaluators, a difficulty finding latent skills behind activities, i.e., the operationalization of skills, and a lack of appropriate and applicable assessment methods. Accordingly, existing methods may not approach skill assessment with objectivity and reliability (Sander et al. 2020). As assessing the required skills for the 21st-century constitutes a challenge (Judrups et al. 2015), new approaches to support employees' skill development are discussed. Nevertheless, the diversity of new skills poses new demands on assessments, which need to capture more prosperous and complex skills (Rayón et al. 2014). Automated assessment is a potential solution to this problem. The increased availability of skill data enables technologies to capture and group skills and relate them to other processes like re- and upskilling. For example, NLP and algorithmic work improvement have been shown in labor market studies (Fareri et al. 2020). However, there is a lack of comprehensive reviews on applied automated skill assessment methods for professionals. Thus, this study aims to answer the research question: *RQ: What is the state-of-the-art regarding automized skill assessment of professionals, and what future research avenues can be identified?*

A systematic literature review following Webster and Watson (2002) and Vom Brocke et al. (2009) will be conducted to answer the research question. We aim to give an overview of automized skill assessment for employees in Information Systems (IS) research and related research like HR, Education, Management, and Organizational Behavior. The analysis focuses on skill definition, assessed skills, assessment approaches, data source, and results of the retrieved papers. We will summarize the most important findings and consolidate existing literature. This holistic literature review identifies research gaps, inconsistencies, and unresolved questions within the existing body of knowledge, thereby suggesting potential avenues for future research that will advance the scientific discourse on automated skill assessment.

2 Related Work

2.1 Definition of Professional Skills and Competencies

The conceptualization of skills and competencies has been subject to extensive research for nearly a century (e.g., Seashore, 1930). However, the definition remains unclear, mainly due to the difficulty delineating related concepts like competencies or abilities (Fareri et al. 2021). Weinert (1999) describes skills, knowledge, and abilities as part of competencies, while others argue that competencies and skills are hard to separate (Oates, 2002). The Cambridge Dictionary describes *skills* as the ability to complete a task as a result of practice (Cambridge Dictionary, 2022). This definition already outlines the demarcation problem of skills: the concept is defined by a similar concept (ability). *Competencies* are often described as integrating knowledge, skills, and abilities (Weinert, 1999; Markus et al. 2005). Despite ongoing discussions, a consensus has yet to be reached on the definition of competencies and the criteria that differentiate them from related concepts (Markus et al. 2005). Frameworks like the Organization for Economic Cooperation and Development (OECD) (2018) or Schüller et al. (2019) aim to provide a comprehensive overview of the existing terms building on Databases like O*NET (U.S. Department of Labor/Employment and Training Administration, 2022) or ESCO (European Commission, 2022) which provide thousands of entries. In summary, the skill and competency definition problem is not of missing data, but rather the conceptional basis is missing, hindering a common understanding.

The definition of hard skills is primarily common sense, while the conceptualization and delineation of soft skills remain unclear (Fareri et al. 2021). *Hard skills* are technical skills required to perform a task or job like programming (Hendarman & Cantner, 2018). On the contrary, there is a debate about whether soft skills are inherent or acquired. Some researchers consider *soft skills* as embedded personality traits (e.g., Deming & Kahn, 2018). Others see soft skills achievable through experience and knowledge (Mitchell et al. 2010; Robles, 2012). Recently, soft skills received much attention, and due to their relevance in today's workforce, they are often referred to as 21st-century skills (Trilling & Fadel, 2009; van Laar et al. 2017; OECD, 2018). Trilling and Fadel (2009) separate these skills for a digital and connected world into (1) learning and innovation skills enabling people to question facts critically and solve problems, (2) information, media, and technology skills referring to the competent use of information and communication technology (ICT), and (3) professional and life skills including cross-cultural skills, and flexibility. Similar, van Laar et al. (2017), who argue that 21st-century skills extend beyond digital skills and include ICT-related and non-ICT skills.

Professional requirements are evolving in response to changing job demands, with more than one-third of job ads asking for cognitive and social skills (Deming & Kahn, 2018). The shift towards more complex skills suggests rethinking professional skill requirements and their assessment (Autor et al. 2003), as current assessment methods focus on hard skills (van Laar et al. 2017). The practical implementation and accurate measurement pose challenges due to the complex and ambiguous nature of soft skills, compounded by their interdependencies. Considering this, a systematic and simultaneous approach to capturing diverse skills becomes indispensable, as emphasized by Unicef (2019). Given that individuals exhibit different skills (Rychen, 2016), it becomes necessary to address the distinct skills of employees during the assessment process. However, conventional face-to-face evaluations often encounter limitations regarding resource availability and personnel expertise within the work context. Consequently, the utilization of ICT for personalized assessments assumes paramount importance (CEDEFOP, 2017). As a contribution to an aggregate definition and delineation between these concepts, this paper captures the different perspectives on skills.

2.2 Automated Skill Assessment

Assessment is crucial in the corporate world. Its importance extends beyond recruitment and job suitability testing to the need for continuous learning and skills development. Therefore, the assessment includes evaluating, measuring, and reporting on individuals existing hard and soft skills and further development opportunities (Paiva et al. 2022). Assessment is at the heart of learning experiences and is crucial for shaping learners' understanding of the curriculum and their ability to progress (Hettiarachchi et al. 2015). In this context, individual skills can be assessed by questionnaires, years of experience (Pektor et al. 2019), or rating scales. Baartman et al. (2006) point out that the reliable assessment of skill acquisition is hindered as it is unclear which requirements need to be achieved. The question arises whether already established assessment criteria apply to the changed skill requirements or whether new methods or method combinations are necessary. The need for innovative professional skill assessment methods attracted the European Union's attention calling for standardized and ICT-based approaches (Redecker, 2013). Technology is vital in this process and adds value to assessment-related activities. In this regard, the digital assessment includes any web-based method that enables systematic inferences and assessments of skills, knowledge, and abilities (Guerrero-Roldán & Noguera, 2018). However, established non-digital methods are still based on subjective perception (Sander et al. 2020), and automated processes can prevent potential biases and discrimination (Gerogiannis et al. 2015).

Automated assessment tools have long been a research focus in computer science, particularly on programming skills. Some studies examine automatic approaches for programming skill assessment (Ala-Mutka, 2005; Souza et al. 2016). However, many lack a conceptual basis (Souza et al. 2016) or are already outdated (Ala-Mutka, 2005; Ihantola et al. 2010). Petrov (2020) presents a new attempt by selecting expert networks based on project results with algorithms. Similarly, Bohlouli et al. (2017) describe competency analysis in HR information systems and use mathematical and statistical software technologies to assess competencies in HR information systems. Their framework increases the efficiency of assigning specialists to projects and simplifies the hiring process. Part of the literature refers to data mining with CVs as data sources to extract skills, like Nikitinsky (2016), who investigates the possibility of improving talent and HR management with data mining. To sum up, there is a growing interest in exploring automated assessment, which extends beyond programming to holistic features like quality, behavior, security, and novel assessment methods (Paiva et al. 2022).

3 Research Approach

We followed a formal systematic literature review process by Vom Brocke et al. (2009) for searching and screening articles within relevant journals and conference proceedings of information systems, management studies, and education research. We used seven digital libraries, EBSCO Host, ACM Digital Library, AISeL, ScienceDirect, IEEE Xplore, ProQuest, and Web of Science, which include a substantial share of the relevant literature. The search queries were based upon key terms ((“assess *” OR “evaluat*” OR “test*”) AND (“skill*” OR “competenc*”) AND (“automat*” OR “algorithm*”)). The queries varied for the databases but were semantically equivalent. We included English articles published from 2000 to 2022 (August). The search revealed 7008 hints within the title, abstract, and keyword sections. We screened the titles and abstracts of these papers for relevance in alignment with our research question. After excluding duplicates and non-relevant publications, which did not address one of our research topics (i.e., automized assessment, algorithms for assessment, skills, competencies), we ended up with 125 publications. Next, papers dealing with automated skill assessment marginally, such as automatic feedback or grading, were removed. This led to 89 results. We then applied the inclusion criteria: (1) focus on the automatic assessment of professional skills/ competencies, (2) at least semi-automatic approach, (3) approach was evaluated with and designed for adults, either in university or work context, (4) professional skills or competencies as units of analysis, (5) focus on the automatic assessment of more than one skill or competency. This resulted in 22 studies. After conducting forward and backward searches using Google Scholar, five studies were added, resulting in 27 publications for in-depth analysis. Figure 1 outlines the paper selection process. Papers were examined using an explorative coding scheme (Mayring, 2015). We coded along pre-defined categories: (1) the conceptualization and definition of skills, competencies, and related terms, as research on these needs to be more apparent (Fareri et al. 2021). Further, we focused on (2) the examined skills used for assessment, to determine if automated methods primarily emphasize hard skills, as argued by van Laar et al. (2017) for conventional methods, or if the assessment methods align with the growing emphasis on soft skills. (3) The applied automatic assessment approach for these skills was analyzed. The reliable and up-to-date measurement of skills places increased demands on automated methods as these must be capable of both accurately measuring data and processing it (Paiva et al. 2022). (4) The data source was included. While CVs and resumes are a known source of data for skills (Guo et al. 2016; Chifu et al. 2017), this representation displays one point in time and thus has limited reliability (Ikegwu et al. 2022). The first author conducted analysis and coding, which were presented to the second author for validation. Any discrepancies were resolved through discussions to ensure the consistency and validity of the results.

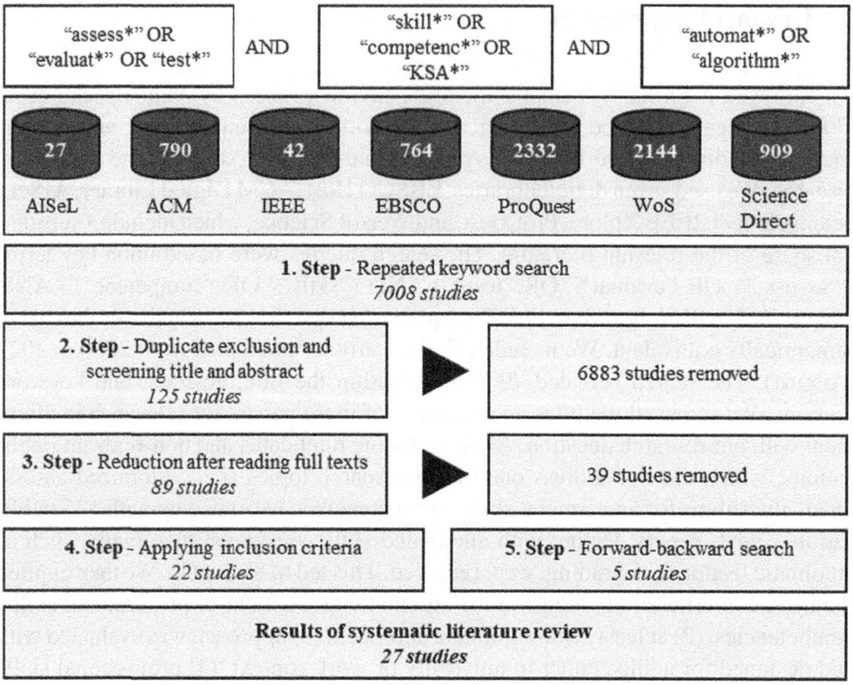

Fig. 1 Literature review process

4 Results

This section outlines how previous research described skills and competencies, which skills and competencies were covered and how the assessment methods were designed. Table 1 shows a concept matrix following Webster and Watson (2002) and outlines the papers' contribution to the specific categories.

The 27 included articles were published over the preceding eleven years (2011–2022), with 20 papers (71.4%) published after 2015 and four (14.8%) published in 2021 or 2022. This indicates the increasing importance and research interest. Most publications (19, 70.4%) are experimental studies on a method development and experimental evaluation. 40.7% (11) are conference papers, and 51.9% are journal articles (14). Based on journals, papers can be assigned to IS (7, 25.9%), AI and Algorithms (5, 18.5%), Education (4, 14.8%), Engineering (2, 7.4%), and Automatic Control (2, 7.4%). However, many categories include one paper, like Expert Systems or Mathematics.

Table 1 Conceptual matrix based on Webster and Watson (2002)

	Definition		Examined Concept			Automation Approach		Data source		
Unit of Analysis	Skill	Competency	Hard Skills	Soft Skills	Competencies	Extraction	Processing	Self-Assessment	Text	Behavior
Aguinaldo (2019)	x		x	x			x	x		
Bachtadze et al. (2019)		x			x		x			x
Barthakur et al. (2022)				x			x	x		
Cepero et al. (2015)				x		x	x			x
Chernyshov (2016)						x				x
Chifu et al. (2017)			x	x		x	x		x	
Colucci et al. (2011)		x			x		x		x	
Duchanoy et al. (2020)	x		x	x			x		x	
Dzwigol et al. (2020)		x			x		x		x	
Fahrenbach et al. (2020)					x		x		x	
Fareri et al. (2021)	x			x		x			x	
Fauzan (2018)		x	x	x			x	x		
Gerogiannis et al. (2015)			x				x			
Hoang et al. (2018)			x	x		x	x		x	
Judrups et al. (2015)		x			x	x				x
Konstantinidis et al. (2022)			x	x		x			x	

(continued)

Table 1 (continued)

	Definition		Examined Concept			Automation Approach		Data source		
Unit of Analysis	Skill	Competency	Hard Skills	Soft Skills	Competencies	Extraction	Processing	Self-Assessment	Text	Behavior
Leontyev et al. (2016)		x		x			x	x		
López et al. (2022)					x	x	x			
Lula et al. (2018)		x	x	x		x	x		x	
Nikitinsky (2016)		x			x	x	x		x	
Pektor et al. (2019)		x	x				x		x	
Petrov (2020)		x			x		x			x
Rayón et al. (2014)		x			x	x	x	x		
Shadskay et al. (2016)		x			x	x	x	x		
Zaouga et al. (2019)		x					x		x	
Zhang (2022)			x	x		x				x
Zhao et al. (2019)	x		x	x		x	x			x

4.1 *Definition of Skills and Competencies*

A notable finding is the lack of consensus on the definitions of skills and competencies. As Table 1 shows, 37% (10 papers) do not define one of these concepts. Some refer to skills as a concept with an apparent definition, like Cepero et al. (2015). In comparison, the definition is made over operationalization measures like Barthakur et al. (2022), who use course learning objectives to evaluate leadership development skills, or Chernyshov (2016), who assesses professional skills by group behavior. Further studies like Chifu et al. (2017) or Gerogiannis et al. (2015) focus on extracting information from texts, e.g., by NLP or fuzzy logic, rather than dealing with the question of what skill or competency is. Other papers use previous conceptualizations of skills like the ESCO database. However, they also lack a description of how skills are seen in the database (Hoang et al. 2018; Konstantinidis et al. 2022). Further studies neglect a definition (Long et al. 2003). López et al. (2022) define competencies as required by projects, e.g., documentation of requirements, without a clear delineation.

We distinguish between papers dealing with competency versus dealing with skills. Competency is the subject of interest in 13 papers (48.1%). These studies describe competency as a general term, including at least knowledge and skills (Bachtadze et al. 2019; Pektor et al. 2019; Petrov, 2020) or even motives (Fauzan, 2018), personal characteristics (Leontyev et al. 2016; Fauzan, 2018; Lula et al. 2018), self-concept values (Fauzan, 2018), attributes (Pektor et al. 2019), or expertise (Petrov, 2020). Dzwigol et al. (2020) define competencies as comprehensive, discrete, focused, congruent, and relevant. A shared characteristic is the inclusion of behavioral measures. However, we see a disagreement about behavior being an antecedent of competency or a result. On the one hand, Bachtadze et al. (2019) describe competency as "the ability to perform different patterns of behavior" (p.474), Lula et al. (2018) define competencies as accounting for a specific behavior, and Fauzan (2018) sees behavior as an operationalization of motives, and personal characteristics. On the other hand, Zaouga et al. (2019) describe behavior as part of competency. Accordingly, it remains unclear if behavior constitutes competencies in the first place or results from obtaining a competency.

Few studies provide a clear statement on the definition of skills. 15 papers name skills as a unit of analysis, and four define skills. Further, skills are seen as a unit of analysis in resumes or job postings (Zhao et al. 2019). The most explicit definition for skills is given by Duchanoy et al. (2020) as "acquired through professional experience and education, classified into industry knowledge, tools and technologies, interpersonal skills, and other skills." (p.5). The results demonstrate a significant gap between using skills as a concept for automated assessment methods and outlining what is involved in analyses. Fareri et al. (2021) are among the studies that address the difficulty of defining skills and establishing a conceptual basis for automated assessment, which is evident by stating that "the definition of the concept remains vague" (p.1).

4.2 Examined Skills Used for Assessment

Hard skills that are the primary object of assessment in papers of this literature review and include technical skills, e.g., being able to process and analyze data (Fauzan, 2018), and job-specific skills like IT, accounting, or logistic-related (Lula et al. 2018). Lula et al. (2018) thereby rely on the classification of Filipowicz (2014), which assigns skills to one of four competencies: social, personal, managerial, and professional. Soft skills are dominantly described (13, 48.1%) as the unit of analysis for automated assessment (e.g., Fauzan, 2018) compared to hard skills being analyzed in 11 (40.7%) papers and competencies being the unit of analysis in 10 (37%) papers. One can see that skills are often examined while no definition of skills is given (e.g., Gerogiannis et al. 2015; Chifu et al. 2017; Barthakur et al. 2022). Soft skills, like creative (Aguinaldo, 2019) or communication skills (Cepero et al. 2015; Aguinaldo, 2019), were considered. However, the granularity varies from rather broad terms like technical or managerial competencies (e.g., Dzwigol et al. 2020) over more concrete skills like communication (e.g., Aguinaldo, 2019) or problem-solving (e.g., Lula et al. 2018) to detailed ones like public speaking (e.g., Rasipuram & Jayagopi, 2020) or encoding emotions (Fareri et al. 2021). Examined soft skills include professionalism, loyalty, responsibility (Shadskay et al. 2016), and communication (e.g., Cepero et al. 2015; Fauzan, 2018). Leontyev et al. (2016) see activity competency as abilities for professional tasks, motivational-axiological competency as the readiness to show professional and personal competency, and integrative competency as the acquired general-cultural professional competency. Among the papers which are rather explorative in their methodology, Chernyshov (2016), Petrov (2020), Pektor et al. (2019), and Duchanoy et al. (2020) describe project-related skills. In comparison, Colucci et al. (2011) look for core competencies, Bachtadze et al. (2019) for team competencies, and Zhang (2022) takes employment skills into account. In comparison, Nikitinsky (2016) operationalizes competency by key terms for professional interest. Another group of papers relies on the conceptualization of known databases such as ESCO (Fareri et al. 2021; Konstantinidis et al. 2022) and O*NET or even providing their own taxonomies not described in detail (Chifu et al. 2017; Hoang et al. 2018; Zhao et al. 2019).

4.3 Applied Automatic Assessment Approach

Within this section, we differentiate between the data extraction method and the data processing, i.e., the method of how skills or competencies were extracted from the provided data and how they were processed afterward (e.g., clustering or classifying). Because of the focus of this literature review, we will not each algorithm or tool in detail.

(1) **Data extraction**: In the field of competency profiling, using automated solutions for data extraction is less common. 55.6% of papers (15) use an automatic

approach, while 13 (48.1%) use manual assessments like surveys or skill entries. Other studies, like Judrups et al. (2015), use a mix of automated and manually extracted data for competency profiling. Text mining methods are frequently employed among the papers that use automated approaches(e.g., Fahrenbach et al. 2020; Fareri et al. 2021; Konstantinidis et al. 2022). This involves extracting key terms from textual sources. One example is the named entity normalization to extract semantic entities (e.g., Hoang et al. 2018). NLP, namely the Latent Dirichlet Allocation (LDA), an algorithmic method, is used to identify semantic components from document texts like personnel profiles, CVs, or resumes (Lula et al. 2018). The LDA method acts as a filter, reducing information noise in the input data. Cepero et al. (2015) describe a system to extract human behaviors using a multi-modal analysis, which relies on pre-defined behavioral indicators to extract features of oral communication skills with technologies such as audio or face tracking systems. An end-to-end solution for the identification of skills is provided by Konstantinidis et al. (2022). They describe an unsupervised, i.e., without a human-annotated database, method for skill extraction. The method consists of a semantic similarity search based on text embeddings.

(2) **Data processing**: Algorithms for assessment are increasing, especially in the papers after 2015. For example, Aguinaldo (2019) applied a classification algorithm to the datasets to predict the outcome of a programming course. This classifying algorithm produced a decision list with rules such as a student with good communication skills will likely pass a class. Barthakur et al. (2022) use NLP and, first, manually code exemplar responses to extract linguistic features. Then they apply a random forest classifier algorithm to the training dataset. They created a system that can predict the reflection level of answers on leadership concepts. Hoang et al. (2018) use the named entity normalization system to develop a tagging system that examines the identified skills' correct meaning. These functions contribute to a skill taxonomy. Leontyev et al. (2016) use an algorithm as a qualimetric assessment approach to evaluate vocational training outcomes. Other approaches build on the extraction work of the LDA, and a classification model maps the retrieved components to specific classes of skills or competencies, such as managerial skills (Lula et al. 2018). Gerogiannis et al. (2015) take a slightly different approach and refer to a group-based fuzzy multi-criteria method. Liao et al. (2007) aim to evaluate and select professionals for software development tasks in line with the needed competencies and skills. López et al. (2022) combine a probabilistic Bayesian model with a trust graph for task grading. In comparison, Bachtadze et al. (2019) developed a model that is able to characterize skills, compare them to each other, calculate the cost of competence development, and determine the suitability of the individual's competence to task goals.

4.4 Data Sources

The data sources for automated assessments can be assigned into three groups. Firstly, traditional methods, i.e., not automated, such as questionnaires (Leontyev et al. 2016; Shadskay et al. 2016; Fauzan, 2018), self-or assessments (Leontyev et al. 2016; Shadskay et al. 2016) or a combination of both (e.g., Aguinaldo, 2019; Barthakur et al. 2022). The second group includes textual data such as personnel profiles (Colucci et al. 2011; Konstantinidis et al. 2022), like LinkedIn (Duchanoy et al. 2020; Fahrenbach et al. 2020), resumes or CVs (Chifu et al. 2017; Hoang et al. 2018; Zhao et al. 2019) or job advertisements (Lula et al. 2018; Pektor et al. 2019). The third group encompasses other sources, like behavioral data (Judrups et al. 2015), 360-degree evaluations, work performance data, and interviews. Studies like Petrov (2020) and Bachtadze et al. (2019) describe project data used for assessment. Dzwigol et al. (2020) use employee data such as experience in years, educational positions, and goal achievements. Rayón et al. (2014) use educational data inserted by students. Interestingly, Chernyshov (2016) uses eye-tracking data for attention behavior. López et al. (2022) simulated data from peer assessments. Cepero et al. (2015) utilized facial and pose recognition features to evaluate nonverbal communication elements in presentations.

5 Future Research Avenues

Assessing professional skills or competencies via automated measures is an important antecedent to equip professionals with the knowledge of their strengths and possible development paths. Further, it provides organizations with the needed reliability and objectivity to gain an overview of the skills of their employees. This systematic review aimed to investigate the state-of-the-art regarding automized skill assessment of employees in organizations. We analyzed extant research and provided an overview of four aspects of automated assessment: the general definition of skill and competency, the examined skills in the paper, the automated assessment method, and the data sources. The meaning of our results and significant implications for future research avenues are discussed below.

The reviewed papers exhibit a significant gap between claiming to analyze skills and defining what those skills are. Over one-third of the papers reviewed do not directly address the definition of skills or competencies for their automated assessment methods. Papers like Duchanoy et al. (2020) broadly group them into hard and soft skills but do not refer to inclusion or exclusion criteria. Nevertheless, without a precise definition, assessment relies on individual perception of what is seen as skills and what is written in CVs or resumes. Thus, a conceptual framework on skills in automatic assessment is needed to provide a reliable data basis. Using a design science research approach could answer how dimensions and characteristics of skills can be classified from an assessment-based perspective. The examined skills reflect a wide range of possible applications. The increased focus on soft skills confirms the increasing importance (Geisinger, 2016). The fact that communication is named often, sheds light on the fundamental importance of this skill also in relation to other skills like leadership (Keil et al. 2013) and strengthens the impression that skills are hierarchically structured and based on each other. Many papers do not specify which skills are part of their assessment, which could implicate that the presented methods may lack generalizability or that they assess behaviors that cannot be directly linked to specific skills. Among the methods used, most rely on NLP or an algorithmic method. These approaches enabled the development of automated assessment methods. However, the focus is still on skill data processing rather than extracting skills or competencies. This is perhaps due to the pre-existing processes in the field of skills assessment which still refer to questionnaires and self-evaluations such as psychometric tests and interviews (Hamza et al. 2021).

A recent increase in interest in automated skill assessment can be observed. Among the papers, we recognize a promising development toward a reliable assessment of skills. This will be ensured by a holistic assessment of professional skills from multiple sources rather than a view limited to one source like a CV or a recruiting questionnaire. Research streams are becoming more diversified. This is primarily due to the extension of the application contexts for automatic skill assessment. Whereas earlier publications concentrated on more easily quantifiable skills like programming, they now increasingly look at more elusive soft skills like empathy or problem-solving. However, this also requires a multi-source analysis since a single aspect cannot describe soft skills. The appropriate operationalization and underlying methodologies could be very different for each skill. Future research may consider combining soft skills with interdisciplinary approaches to extend the scope of automated skill assessment. A potential research inquiry is to explore the operationalization of soft skills, such as complex problem solving, for a dependable automated assessment database. Furthermore, soft skills are often still assessed by questionnaires and self-assessment measures, which are not automatically extracted from the original source. The emphasis on automatic processes lies in the data processing phases, specifically clustering, and classification. Apart from questionnaires, personnel profiles like LinkedIn are a convenient data source, but their reliability and objectivity are limited. Accordingly, methods to automatically retrieve data from multiple sources, like team or supervisor feedback, need to be explored.

Lastly, when exploring the application contexts for automized professional skill assessment, along with HR Processes like employee development, staffing processes within projects can be interesting. Like employee development decisions, staffing processes rely on subjective assessments (Sander et al. 2020) and require much working time from HR professionals (Gorlov et al. 2015). An automated process suggests possible development paths for employees or estimates which employees can work on what project (Furini et al. 2022).

6 Conclusion: Contribution to Theory and Practice

Accurate measurement of employee skills is crucial in the ever-changing world of work, necessitating an understanding of underlying concepts, methods, and designs. This systematic literature review provides an overview of automated assessment methods for professional skills, revealing that most methods rely on NLP mechanisms. However, defining and operationalizing skills fall behind, and critical reflection of the data basis is missing, which hinders the establishment of a reliable basis for automated skill assessment. Overall, the results provide a deeper insight into how skill assessment can be automated and which underlying definitions and conceptualizations are used. A substantial body of literature exists about assessing skills and competencies, with the participation of diverse academic disciplines lacking a comprehensive overview. Consequently, our scholarly contribution aims to undertake a systematic review and conceptualize the extant literature, bridging the existing gaps and providing a synthesized understanding. Furthermore, this review identifies potential avenues for future research exploration, enriching the academic discourse in this field. By answering the question *"What is the state-of-the-art regarding automized skill assessment of professionals and what future research avenues can be identified?"* we contribute to the literature by providing a concise knowledge base for future research by summarizing existing methods of automated skill assessment for professionals and providing guidance for practitioners on reliable assessment, which can empower employees to develop skills independently. By synthesizing diverse perspectives and critically analyzing existing literature, we derive insights and formulate potential research avenues that address research gaps, laying the groundwork for advancing knowledge in the field. Further, automated skill assessment presents practical advantages across diverse domains. It can enhance efficiency in HR or project staffing by significantly reducing the time and effort required to evaluate individuals' skills. Standardization can be achieved by implementing predefined criteria and algorithms, mitigating subjective biases by, e.g., recruiters, and ensuring greater reliability in skill evaluations. Scalability is facilitated, allowing for the simultaneous assessment of numerous individuals, which is particularly advantageous in educational institutions, recruitment processes, and corporate training programs. Moreover, automated skill assessment enables personalized feedback and recommendations tailored to individuals' performance, empowering targeted skill development plans that address specific strengths and weaknesses.

The following limitations should be noted. First, the selection and analysis process is based on the authors' subjective decisions, which can influence the results. Second, the systematic review attempted to cover skills in general, using a broad search strategy, but this search was limited to scientific databases. Accordingly, we cannot rule out the possibility of missing relevant papers. Third, we did not assess the methodological and overall quality of included articles, resulting in a less comprehensive review.

References

Aguinaldo, B.E. (2019) 21st Century Learning Skills Predictive Model Using PART Algorithm. In: Unknown (Ed.) *Proceedings of the 3rd International Conference on Machine Learning and Soft Computing - ICMLSC 2019, the 3rd International Conference,* 25–28 January, Da Lat, Viet Nam. ACM Press: New York, New York, USA, pp. 134–137.

Ala-Mutka, K.M. (2005) A Survey of Automated Assessment Approaches for Programming Assignments. *Computer Science Education,* 15(2), 83–102.

Autor, D.H., Levy, F. & Murnane, Richard, J. (2003) The skill content of recent technological change: An empirical exploration. *Quarterly journal of economics,* 118(4).

Baartman, L.K., Bastiaens, T.J., Kirschner, P.A. & van der Vleuten, C.P. (2006) The wheel of competency assessment: Presenting quality criteria for competency assessment programs. *Studies in Educational Evaluation,* 32(2), 153–170.

Bachtadze, N., Kulba, V., Nikulina, I., Zaikin, O. & Żylawski, A. (2019) Mathematical Model and Method of Analysis of the Personal and Group Competence to Complete the Project Task. *IFAC-PapersOnLine,* 52(13), 469–474.

Bakhshi, H., Downing, J.M., Osbrone, M.A. & Schneider, P. (2017) *The Future of Skills: Employment in 2030.* Pearson: London.

Barthakur, A., Kovanovic, V., Joksimovic, S., Zhang, Z., Richey, M. & Pardo, A. (2022) Measuring leadership development in workplace learning using automated assessments: Learning analytics and measurement theory approach. *British Journal of Educational Technology,* 53(6), 1842–1863.

Bohlouli, M., Mittas, N., Kakarontzas, G., Theodosiou, T., Angelis, L. & Fathi, M. (2017) Competence assessment as an expert system for human resource management: A mathematical approach. *Expert Systems with Applications,* 70, 83–102.

Cambridge Dictionary (2022) *skill.* Available from: https://dictionary.cambridge.org/dictionary/english/skill [Accessed 16 November 2022].

CEDEFOP (2017) *"European inventory on validation of non-formal and informal learning – 2016 update-: synthesis report,* Luxembourg. Available from: https://www.cedefop.europa.eu/files/4153_en.pdf [Accessed 28 September 2022].

Cepero, Á., Clapés, A. & Escalera, S. (2015) Automatic non-verbal communication skills analysis: A quantitative evaluation. *AI Communications,* 28(1), 87–101.

Chernyshov, K.R. (2016) Application of System Identification Techniques to Revealing Professional Skills of Teams of Human-Operators. *IFAC-PapersOnLine,* 49(32), 107–112.

Chifu, E., Chifu, V.R., Popa, I. & Salomie, I. (2017) A system for detecting professional skills from resumes written in natural language. In: *2017 13th IEEE International Conference on Intelligent Computer Communication and Processing (ICCP), 2017 13th IEEE International Conference on Intelligent Computer Communication and Processing (ICCP),* 7–9 September, Cluj-Napoca. IEEE, pp. 189–196.

Colucci, S., Tinelli, E., Di Sciascio, E. & Donini, F.M. (2011) Automating competence management through non-standard reasoning. *Engineering Applications of Artificial Intelligence,* 24(8), 1368–1384.

Deming, D. & Kahn, L.B. (2018) Skill requirements across firms and labor markets: Evidence from job postings for professionals. *Journal of Labor Economics,* 36(1).

Duchanoy, C.A., Moreno-Armendáriz, M.A., Calvo, H. & Hernández-Ramos, V.E. (2020) Career path level estimation and skill qualification feedback from textual descriptions. *Journal of Intelligent & Fuzzy Systems,* 39(2), 2409–2419.

Dzwigol, H., Dzwigol-Barosz, M., Miskiewicz, R. & Kwilinski, A. (2020) Manager competency assessment model in the conditions of industry 4.0. *Entrepreneurship and Sustainability Issues,* 7(4), 2630–2644.

European Commission (2022) *ESCO.* Available from: https://esco.ec.europa.eu/de [Accessed 28 September 2022].

Fahrenbach, F., Revoredo, K. & Santoro, F.M. (2020) Valuing prior learning: Designing an ICT artifact to assess professional competences through text mining. *European Journal of Training and Development*, 44(2/3), 209–235.

Fareri, S., Fantoni, G., Chiarello, F., Coli, E. & Binda, A. (2020) Estimating Industry 4.0 impact on job profiles and skills using text mining. *Computers in Industry*, 118, 103222.

Fareri, S., Melluso, N., Chiarello, F. & Fantoni, G. (2021) SkillNER: Mining and mapping soft skills from any text. *Expert Systems with Applications*, 184(1), 115544.

Fauzan, R. (2018) Model Performance Assessment Research Development Based on Competence using Rating Scales Method, 360 Degree and Algorithm Analytical Network Process at Telimek Lipi. *IOP Conference Series: Materials Science and Engineering*, 407, 12135.

Filipowicz, G. (2014) *Zarządzanie kompetencjami: perspektywa firmowa i osobista.* Wolters Kluwer.

Furini, M., Gaggi, O., Mirri, S., Montangero, M., Pelle, E. & Poggi, F. et al. (2022) Digital twins and artificial intelligence. *Communications of the ACM*, 65(4), 98–104.

Geisinger, K.F. (2016) 21st century skills: What are they and how do we assess them? *Applied Measurement in Education*, 29(4), 245–249.

Gerogiannis, V.C., Rapti, E., Karageorgos, A. & Fitsilis, P. (2015) A fuzzy linguistic approach for human resource evaluation and selection in software projects. In: *Proceedings of the 2015 International Conference on Industrial Engineering and Operations Management (IEOM), 2015 International Conference on Industrial Engineering and Operations Management (IEOM)*, 3–5 March, Dubai. IEEE.

Gorlov, S.M., Lazareva, N.V. & Fursov, V.A. (2015) Competence-Based Approach to the HR Management Using in Industrial Branch. *Asian Social Science*, 11(7).

Guerrero-Roldán, A.-E. & Noguera, I. (2018) A model for aligning assessment with competences and learning activities in online courses. *The Internet and Higher Education*, 38, 36–46.

Guo, S., Alamudun, F. & Hammond, T. (2016) RésuMatcher: A personalized résumé-job matching system. *Expert Systems with Applications*, 60, 169–182.

Hamza, P.A., Othman, B.J., Gardi, B., Sorguli, S., Aziz, H.M. & Ahmed, S.A. et al. (2021) Recruitment and selection: The relationship between recruitment and selection with organizational performance. *International Journal of Engineering, Business and Management*, 5(3).

Hendarman, A.F. & Cantner, U. (2018) Soft skills, hard skills, and individual innovativeness. *Eurasian Business Review*, 8(2), 139–169.

Hettiarachchi, E., Huertas, M.A. & Mor, E. (2015) E-assessment system for skill and knowledge assessment in computer engineering education. *International Journal of Engineering Education*, 31(2), 529–540.

Hoang, P., Mahoney, T., Javed, F. & McNair, M. (2018) Large-Scale Occupational Skills Normalization for Online Recruitment. *AI Magazine*, 39(1), 5–14.

Ihantola, P., Ahoniemi, T., Karavirta, V. & Sepälä, O. (2010) Review of Recent Systems for Automatic Assessment of Programming Assignments. In: Schulte, C. (Ed.) *Proceedings of the 10th Koli Calling International Conference on Computing Education Research, ACM*, New York, NY, pp. 86–93.

Ikegwu, A.C., Nweke, H.F., Anikwe, C.V., Alo, U.R. & Okonkwo, O.R. (2022) Big data analytics for data-driven industry: a review of data sources, tools, challenges, solutions, and research directions. *Cluster Computing*, 25(5), 3343–3387.

Judrups, J., Zandbergs, U. & Kazakovs, M. (2015) Competence based human resource development solution. *Engineering for Rural Development*, 14, 669–674.

Keil, M., Lee, H.K. & Deng, T. (2013) Understanding the most critical skills for managing IT projects: A Delphi study of IT project managers. *Information & Management*, 50(7), 398–414.

Konstantinidis, I., Maragoudakis, M., Magnisalis, I., Berberidis, C. & Peristeras, V. (2022) Knowledge-driven Unsupervised Skills Extraction for Graph-based Talent Matching. In: *Proceedings of the 12th Hellenic Conference on Artificial Intelligence, SETN 2022: 12th Hellenic Conference on Artificial Intelligence*, 07/09/2022 - 09/09/2022, Corfu Greece. ACM: New York, NY, USA.

Leontyev, V.V., Rebrina, F.G., Leontyeva, I.A. & Gafiyatullina, E.A. (2016) Evaluation of the Development of Professional Competence in Undergraduates: Methodical Aspects. *International Journal of Environmental and Science Education*, 11(14), 6592–6602.

Liao, X., Li, Y. & Lu, B. (2007) A model for selecting an ERP system based on linguistic information processing. *Information Systems*, 32(7), 1005–1017.

Long, S., Dowsing, R. & Craven, P. (2003) Knowledge-Based Systems for Marking Professional IT Skills Examinations. In: Macintosh, A. (Ed.) *Applications and Innovations in Intelligent Systems 10: Proceedings of ES2002, the Twenty-second SGAI International Conference on Knowledge Based Systems and Applied Artificial Intelligence*. Praxis: London, pp. 3–16.

López, A., Sabater-Mir, J. & Sierra, C. (2022) Probabilistic Models for Competence Assessment in Education. *Applied Sciences*, 12(5), 2368.

Lula, P., Oczkowska, R., Wiśniewska, S. & Wójcik, K. (2018) Ontology-based system for automatic analysis of job offers. In: *The 12th Professor Aleksander Zelias International Conference on Modelling and Forecasting of Socio-Economic Phenomena*, pp. 256–265.

Markus, L., Thomas, H.C. & Allpress, K. (2005) Confounded by competencies? An evaluation of the evolution and use of competency models. *New Zealand journal of psychology*, 34(2), 117.

Marrelli, A.F., Tondora, J. & Hoge, M.A. (2005) Strategies for developing competency models. *Administration and Policy in Mental Health and Mental Health Services Research*, 32(5), 533–561.

Mayring, P. (2015) Qualitative Inhaltsanalyse: Grundlagen und Techniken, 12., überarbeitete Auflage, Beltz Verlag. *Weinheim Basel*.

Merchel, R., Iqbal, T., Süße, T. & Knop, S. (2021) Digital Competencies and IT Skills as Employees' Resources to Cope with Digitalization Demands.

Mitchell, G.W., Skinner, L.B. & White, B.J. (2010) Essential soft skills for success in the twenty-first century workforce as perceived by business educators. *Delta Pi Epsilon Journal*, 52(1).

Nikitinsky, N. (2016) Improving talent management with automated competence assessment: Research summary. In: *Scientific-Practical Conference" Research and Development"*, pp. 73–82.

Oates, T. (2002) Key Competencies – Moving Toward Indicators and Assessments. In: Rychen, D., Salganik, L.H. & McLaughlin, M.E. (Eds.) *Contributions to the Second DeSeCo Symposium*, Geneva, Switzerland, pp. 169–201.

OECD (2018) *Future of Education and Skills 2030: Conceptual Learning Framework. 8th Informal Working Group (IWG) Meeting*. Paris, France.

Paiva, J.C., Leal, J.P. & Figueira, Á. (2022) Automated Assessment in Computer Science Education: A State-of-the-Art Review. *ACM Transactions on Computing Education*, 22(3), 1–40.

Pektor, O., Walek, B., Martinik, I. & Jaluvka, M. (2019) Hierarchical System for Evaluating Professional Competencies Using Takagi-Sugeno Rules. In: Silhavy, R. (Ed.) *Artificial Intelligence and Algorithms in Intelligent Systems*. Springer International Publishing: Cham, pp. 318–325.

Petrov, M. (2020) An Approach to Changing Competence Assessment for Human Resources in Expert Networks. *Future Internet*, 12(169), 1–10.

Rasipuram, S. & Jayagopi, D.B. (2020) Automatic multimodal assessment of soft skills in social interactions: a review. *Multimedia Tools and Applications*, 79(19-20), 13037–13060.

Rayón, A., Guenaga, M. & Núñez, A. (2014) Supporting Competency-Assessment through a Learning Analytics Approach Using Enriched Rubrics. In: García-Peñalvo, F.J. (Ed.) *Proceedings of the Second International Conference on Technological Ecosystems for Enhancing Multiculturality - TEEM '14, Proceedings of the Second International Conference on Technological Ecosystems for Enhancing Multiculturality - TEEM '14*, 1–3 October, Salamanca, Spain, pp. 291–298.

Redecker, C. (2013) The use of ICT for the assessment of key competences. *Joint Research Centre of the European Commission Scientific and Policy Report*.

Robles, M.M. (2012) Executive perceptions of the top 10 soft skills needed in today's workplace. *Business communication quarterly*, 75(4), 453–465.

Rychen, D. (2016) E2030 conceptual framework: key competencies for 2030 (DeSeCo 2.0).

Sander, G., van Dellen, B., Hartmann, I., Burger-Kloser, D. & Keller, N. (2020) Inclusive Leadership: How to deal with unconscious biases in human resources decisions. In: Tan, T.K., Gudić, M. & Flynn, P.M. (Eds.) *Struggles and successes in the pursuit of sustainable development.* Routledge: London, New York, pp. 45–54.

Schüller, K., Busch, P. & Hindinger, C. (2019) Future skills: ein framework für data literacy. *Hochschulforum Digitalisierung*, 46, 1–128.

Seashore, R.H. (1930) Individual differences in motor skills. *The Journal of General Psychology*, 3(1), 38–66.

Shadskay, A.S., Yudina, E.S., Latyshev, A.S., Malyshev, V.V. & Matsuta, V.V. (2016) Automated test system for evaluation of corporate and management staff competencies. In: *Proceedings of the 2016 Conference on Information Technologies in Science, Management, Social Sphere and Medicine, Information Technologies in Science, Management, Social Sphere and Medicine,* 23–26 May, Tomsk, Russia. Atlantis Press: Paris, France, pp. 393–396.

Souza, D.M., Felizardo, K.R. & Barbosa, E.F. (2016) A Systematic Literature Review of Assessment Tools for Programming Assignments. In: *2016 IEEE 29th International Conference on Software Engineering Education and Training (CSEET), 2016 IEEE 29th International Conference on Software Engineering Education and Training (CSEET),* 5–6 April, Dallas, TX, USA. IEEE, pp. 147–156.

Trilling, B. & Fadel, C. (2009) *21st century skills: Learning for life in our times.* Jossey-Bass: San Francisco, CA.

U.S. Department of Labor/Employment and Training Administration (2022) *Occupational Information Network (O*NET).* Available from: https://www.onetcenter.org/ [Accessed 28 September 2022].

Unicef (2019) Global framework on transferable skills. Available from: http://www.unicef.org/education [Accessed 28 September 2022].

van Laar, E., van Deursen, A.J., van Dijk, J.A. & Haan, J. de (2017) The relation between 21st-century skills and digital skills: A systematic literature review. *Computers in Human Behavior*, 72, 577–588.

Vom Brocke, J., Simons, A., Niehaves, B., Niehaves, B., Reimer, K. & Plattfaut, R. et al. (2009) Reconstructing the giant: On the importance of rigour in documenting the literature search process.

Webster, J. & Watson, R.T. (2002) Analyzing the Past to Prepare for the Future: Writing a Literature Review. *MIS Quarterly*, 26(2), 13–23.

Weinert, F.E. (1999) *Concepts of competence.* Contribution within the OECD project "Definition and Selection of Competencies: Theoretical and Conceptual Foundations (DeSeCo)", Neuchâtel, Switzerland.

World Economic Forum (2018) Towards a Reskilling Revolution: A Future of Jobs for All. Available from: https://www3.weforum.org/docs/WEF_FOW_Reskilling_Revolution.pdf [Accessed 29 September 2022].

Zaouga, W., Arfa Rabai, L.B. & Alalyani, W.R. (2019) Towards an Ontology Based-Approach for Human Resource Management. *Procedia Computer Science*, 151, 417–424.

Zhang, X. (2022) Development and Construction of Internet of Things Training Practice Platform for Employment Skills Assessment. *Journal of Sensors*, 2022.

Zhao, M., Javed, F., Jacob, F. & McNair, M. (2019) SKILL: A System for Skill Identification and Normalization. In: *Proceedings of the Twenty-Seventh Conference on Innovative Applications of Artificial Intelligence,* 2019, pp. 4012–4017.

The Type to Listen to the Machine? The Effect of Personality on the Use of AI Advice

Simon Asbach, Lorenz Graf-Vlachy, and Andreas Fügener

Abstract Personality is a key antecedent of individual differences in advice-taking from humans. We analyze whether and how personality also influences advice-taking from Artificial Intelligence (AI) systems, which are a promising source of advice to aid human decision-making. It is particularly important to understand advice-taking from AI systems because recent research shows that such systems are often used imperfectly. We consider the Big Five personality traits (extraversion, agreeableness, conscientiousness, neuroticism, and openness) as antecedents of the use of AI advice in a cross-sectional study with 595 participants. The results support our theoretical predictions that agreeableness and neuroticism are associated with an increased use of AI advice. Contrary to our predictions, openness seems associated with a decreased use of AI advice, whereas extraversion and conscientiousness do not seem to be related with the use of AI advice.

Keywords Personality · Big five model · Advice-taking · AI systems

1 Introduction

Research in psychology suggests that personality accounts for individual differences in humans' advice-taking behavior (e.g., Kausel et al. 2015; Schultze et al. 2018). While humans often solicit human advice for (difficult) decision-making, people differ in how much they use this advice. Personality traits can help to explain these

S. Asbach (✉) · L. Graf-Vlachy
Department of Business and Economics, TU Dortmund University, Dortmund, Germany
e-mail: simon.asbach@tu-dortmund.de

L. Graf-Vlachy
e-mail: lorenz.graf-vlachy@tu-dortmund.de

A. Fügener
Faculty of Management, Economics and Social Sciences, University of Cologne, Cologne, Germany
e-mail: andreas.fuegener@uni-koeln.de

D. Beverungen et al. (eds.), *Conceptualizing Digital Responsibility for the Information Age*, Lecture Notes in Information Systems and Organisation 74,
https://doi.org/10.1007/978-3-031-80119-8_10

differences as they account for users' idiosyncratic individual preferences and behaviors (Costa and McCrae, 1992a; 1992b; John et al. 2008; McCrae and John, 1992). For example, the personality trait agency, that is, the feeling of control over actions and their consequences, is associated with less advice-taking in quantitative estimation tasks (Schultze et al. 2018). Further, narcissism, that is, the belief in one's superior qualities, is also associated with less advice-taking in quantitative estimation tasks (Kausel et al. 2015). As first studies yielded promising results, researchers have called for more research to further understand the role of personality in advice-taking (Bonaccio and Dalal, 2006; Kausel et al. 2015; Schultze et al. 2018).

Personality also seems to play a critical role in the adoption and use of various types of Artificial Intelligence (AI) systems, such as robots and recommender systems (Esterwood et al. 2021a; Tkalcic and Chen, 2015). For example, research on human–robot interaction argues that a robot's personality should be similar to the user's personality to increase adoption rates (Esterwood et al. 2021b). Further, research demonstrates that people prefer to use AI-based music recommender systems if the AI system's recommendations match the personality of the user (e.g., focus on novelty of music; Wu et al. 2013). Due to the explanatory power of personality in the use of AI, such as robots and recommender systems, personality may also help to explain the use and enable the personalization of AI advice systems.

Such AI advice systems are a new and promising source of advice to aid human decision-making but are often used imperfectly by humans (Alvarado-Valencia and Barrero, 2014; Zhang et al. 2021). Due to the AI's ability to be trained on and in many cases to operate with large data sets, the AI's often superior accuracy to human judgment, and the AI's cost-effectiveness, AI advice is deployed in various decision-making domains, such as healthcare, business, military, and design (Buch et al. 2018; Nagar and Malone, 2011; Parasuraman et al. 2009; Zhang et al. 2021). Based on ethical considerations, humans usually only receive advice from an AI and remain responsible for the final decision (Zhang et al. 2020). Research argues that humans frequently fail to use AI (and other algorithmic) advice adequately (Alvarado-Valencia and Barrero, 2014; Dietvorst et al. 2015; Zhang et al. 2021). An example of imperfect use of AI advice is a crash of Google's autonomous car in 2015, which was the result of the driver underutilizing the AI system and manually applying the brakes leading to the car being hit from behind (Richtel and Dougherty, 2015).

Initial advances have been made to understand antecedents of the (imperfect) use of AI advice, but important questions remain. Recent literature points toward users' perceptions of AI, such as levels of trust, self-confidence, and confidence in the AI as antecedents of the (imperfect) use of AI advice (Bansal et al. 2019; Chong et al. 2022; Zhang et al. 2020). For example, people may show higher levels of trust and confidence in AI advice in objective domains, such as forecasting tasks, compared to subjective domains, such as deciding whether a joke is funny (Logg et al. 2019; Yeomans et al. 2019). Since research suggests increased trust and confidence in AI advice in objective domains, there remains the question of why people still tend to underutilize AI (and other algorithmic) advice in these domains (Alvarado-Valencia and Barrero, 2014; Dietvorst et al. 2015; Logg et al. 2019) and whether the extent of underutilization is the same across individuals.

Despite the fact that personality traits are an important antecedent of behavior in various fields, including decision-making processes (e.g., Ajzen, 2005; Lauriola and Levin, 2001; Riaz et al. 2012), only a few studies have tested the impact of user's personality traits on the use of AI advice in objective domains. Initial personality research argues that one of the Big Five personality traits, that is, conscientiousness, is related to people's use of smart algorithms for quantitative decision-making tasks (Man Tang et al. 2022). However, no research to our knowledge has tested the holistic effect of personality traits on use of AI advice in objective domains. This, however, could be crucial because understanding individual differences in the use of AI advice not only increases the understanding of imperfect use of AI advice between individuals but also lays the groundwork for a potential personalization to improve the use of AI advice. We address this issue in the current paper.

To understand important antecedents of imperfect use of AI advice in objective domains better and to test the potential value of AI advice personalization, we study the Big Five personality traits as antecedents of use of AI advice. We use the Big Five model as it is widely used and considered to comprehensively describe a person's personality structure (Costa and McCrae, 1992a; 1992b; Matthews et al. 2003; McCrae and Costa, 2008). Our work is based on a behavioral study. We collected data from 595 participants who performed a previously validated task that asks participants to forecast the demand for ten different products, before and after receiving advice from an AI (Lehmann et al. 2022). We measured the Big Five traits through the Big Five Inventory (BFI; John et al. 1991; 2008).

Our results partially support the idea that personality is related to the use of AI advice in objective domains. In line with our hypotheses, both agreeableness and neuroticism are associated with increased use of AI advice. Contrary to our hypotheses, however, openness is associated with less use of AI advice and extraversion as well as conscientiousness are not associated with use of AI advice. Despite some unexpected findings, the current paper provides crucial insights for AI-advice personalization to improve the use of these systems. Further implications as well as important limitations of the study are discussed.

2 Theoretical Background

2.1 Personality, Advice-Taking, and the Use of AI Advice

Extant research argues that personality is an important antecedent of both (i) people's use of human advice and (ii) their use of AI systems (e.g., Bonaccio and Dalal, 2006; Kausel et al. 2015; Park and Woo, 2022). On the first point, empirical research has run promising studies on personality as an antecedent of using advice from other humans, that is, advice-taking. Two of the most important personality traits in this regard seem to be agency and narcissism, which are both negatively associated with taking advice from other humans (Kausel et al. 2015; Schultze et al. 2018). As scholars agree on the importance of personality to understand antecedents of advice-taking, they call for more research in that area (Bonaccio and Dalal, 2006; Kausel et al. 2015; Schultze et al. 2018). On the second point, research suggests personality to also be an important antecedent of the use of AI and other computer systems, such as video games, virtual reality applications, recommender systems, robots, and many more (Esterwood, 2021a; Esterwood, 2021b; Johnson and Gardner, 2010; Tkalcic and Chen, 2015; Wallach et al. 2010). A recent meta-analysis of human personality and robot acceptance, for example, suggests that the personality traits extraversion, agreeableness, and openness predict robot acceptance (Esterwood, 2021a). As personality research has proven very helpful to understand advice-taking from humans and the use of AI systems, it stands to reason that it may also prove helpful regarding advice-taking from AI advice systems.

Despite its frequently superior accuracy compared to human judgment, people often use AI advice imperfectly – a phenomenon that puzzles researchers (Alvarado-Valencia and Barrero, 2014; Bansal et al. 2019; Zhang et al. 2021). Imperfect use of AI advice is especially surprising in objective domains, with concrete external standards. In these domains AI (and other algorithmic) advice has been found to be far superior to human judgment, but humans frequently underutilize AI (and other algorithmic) advice, resulting in unnecessarily inferior decisions (Alvarado-Valencia and Barrero, 2014; Dietvorst et al. 2015; Logg et al. 2019). Prior research suggests perceptions of the AI, such as a lack of trust, as causes of the problem (e.g., Bansal et al. 2019). However, the explanatory power of trust and the reasons for lack of trust are still debated (Chong et al. 2022; Zhang et al. 2020), leading various scholars to call for further research to improve the understanding of important antecedents of imperfect use of AI advice (Chong et al. 2022; Völkel et al. 2019; Zhang et al. 2020).

Notably, no extant research has performed a holistic test of personality as an antecedent of use of AI advice, which is surprising because scholars demonstrate that personality research is a potent way to understand and improve the use of both human advice and AI systems through personalization (e.g., Kausel et al. 2015; Park and Woo, 2022; Esterwood, 2021b). For example, a recent meta-analysis has found that robot acceptance is increased if a robot is programmed with a personality similar to the user's (e.g., measured by similarity between robot and user with regard to the Big Five personality traits; Esterwood, 2021b). We suggest transferring this idea to AI advice systems in objective domains, that is, studying the association between personality and use of AI advice in objective domains to understand important antecedents of use of AI advice and potentially pave the way for AI advice personalization.

2.2 Big Five Personality Traits

To operationalize personality, we use the Big Five model as it is the most established personality trait model in psychology and related fields (Matthews et al.

2003; McCrae and Costa, 1992). It was developed using a psycholexical approach and revealed five broad traits that are relatively stable across different situations (Asendorpf and Neyer, 2012; Costa and McCrae, 1992a; McCrae and John, 1992), namely extraversion, agreeableness, conscientiousness, neuroticism, and openness. The five traits are universal as they have been empirically shown to be equally valid for different sexes, races, cultures, and age groups (Ching et al. 2014). In the remainder of this section, we will discuss the nature of each of the five traits and their hypothesized associations with use of AI advice in objective domains.

Extraversion indicates the degree of engagement with the external world. Sub-facets of extraversion include friendliness, gregariousness, assertiveness, activity, and excitement-seeking. Thus, extraverted people can be described as outgoing, often feeling positive emotions, and seeking stimulating activities. In comparison, introverted people can be described as less outgoing, shy, and preferring to spend time alone (Gosling et al. 2003; Matthews et al. 2003; McCrae and John, 1992). In line with high levels of positive emotions in new situations, research suggests that extraverted people feel more comfortable interacting with autonomous machines (Syrdal et al. 2006). Similarly, a meta-analysis on robot acceptance supports the idea that extraversion is positively associated with robot acceptance (Esterwood et al. 2021a). Additionally, one central characteristic of extraversion is incentive motivation (Depue and Collins, 1999). Our study will incorporate monetary rewards for accurate quantitative estimates and the AI will be an aid to reach an optimal quantitative estimate. Thus, extraverted people should be more inclined to use the AI advice. Based on this rationale, we hypothesize:

Hypothesis 1 (H1): Extraversion will be positively related to use of AI advice.

Agreeableness indicates the degree of concern with cooperation and social harmony. Sub-facets of agreeableness include trust, morality, altruism, cooperation, modesty, and sympathy. Thus, agreeable people can be described as friendly, helpful, and understanding. In comparison, non-agreeable people can be described as less friendly, not very cooperative, and initiating disagreements (Gosling et al. 2003; Matthews et al. 2003; McCrae and John, 1992). Supporting findings on the high cooperative motivation, research shows that agreeable people show higher acceptance and utilization levels of robots (Esterwood et al. 2021a). Additionally, agreeable individuals are more likely to report perceived usefulness of a new technology (Devaraj et al. 2008). Lastly, a recent survey found that agreeable participants mostly display positive attitudes towards AI systems (Park and Woo, 2022), which may lead to increased use of AI advice. Based on this rationale, we hypothesize:

Hypothesis 2 (H2): Agreeableness will be positively related to use of AI advice.

Conscientiousness indicates the degree of control over human impulses. Sub-facets of conscientiousness include orderliness, reliability, achievement-striving, and self-discipline. Thus, conscientious people can be described as prudent, organized, and reliable. In comparison, non-conscientious people can be described as impulsive, unsystematic, and less reliable (Gosling et al. 2003; Matthews et al. 2003; McCrae and John, 1992). Regarding the use of AI advice, if conscientious people perceive an

AI as a very competent aid to achieve a mutual goal, this may satisfy their need for achievement, and they might be more tempted to use AI advice. However, research suggests that conscientious people benefit less from working with AI systems as their personality structure is not complementary to the nature of AI systems. Conscientious people are very orderly and like to stay in control of processes, which can be problematic if an AI system works at least partially as a black box (Man Tang et al. 2022). In particular, conscientious people prefer to stay in control and not use automation for complex tasks (Lin et al. 2020). Due to this preference for control over following black box systems and due to a rather complex quantitative task in our study, we hypothesize:

Hypothesis 3 (H3): Conscientiousness will be negatively related to use of AI advice.

Neuroticism, also often called emotional instability, indicates the degree to which a person experiences negative feelings. Sub-facets of neuroticism include anxiety, anger, depression, self-consciousness, and vulnerability. Neurotic people can be described as tense, often in a bad mood, and emotional. In comparison, non-neurotic people can be described as calm, free from a persistent bad mood, and emotionally stable (Gosling et al. 2003; Matthews et al. 2003; McCrae and John, 1992). The fact that neurotic people are anxious about new stimuli may lead to similar emotions when exposed to an AI with which people have never worked before. Further, neurotic people seem to experience higher stress when interacting with automation systems (Szalma and Taylor, 2011). However, recent research suggests that AI may fulfill neurotic people's need for warmth and that the use of a given AI system may satisfy the need for social relatedness (Park and Woo, 2022). Most importantly, neurotic people have a strong tendency to seek advice and support from external sources before making a decision, to decrease their high levels of uncertainty about a decision (Bayram and Aydemir-Dev, 2017; Ülgen et al. 2016). To summarize, the effect of initial negative emotions toward an AI on use of AI advice may be reversed by the feeling of relatedness and neurotic people's strong desire for external advice before making a decision. Based on this rationale, we hypothesize:

Hypothesis 4 (H4): Neuroticism will be positively related to use of AI advice.

Openness, also referred to as openness to experience, indicates the degree to which people are imaginative and creative. Sub-facets of openness include imagination, artistic interest, adventurousness, liberalism, and intellect. People high in openness can be described as individualistic, non-conforming, and aware of their feelings. In comparison, people low in openness can be described as down-to-earth, conventional, and less aware of their feelings (Gosling et al. 2003; Matthews et al. 2003; McCrae and John, 1992). Regarding the use of AI advice, research suggests that people high on openness tend to show increased interest in and increased use of new technological systems, such as robots for service tasks (Rossi et al. 2018; Svendsen et al. 2013). Additionally, a recent survey suggests that openness is associated with positive emotions and a higher functional attitude toward AI systems in general (Park and Woo, 2022). Based on this rationale, we hypothesize:

Hypothesis 5 (H5): Openness will be positively related to use of AI advice.

3 Methods

3.1 Participants and Procedure

We implemented the study in oTree (Chen et al. 2016) and collected data through CloudReseach and Amazon's Mechanical Turk (MTurk) in June 2022. Previous research has investigated online data collection extensively and has mostly concluded satisfactory data quality for behavioral studies (Eyal et al. 2021). Further, CloudResearch provided us with an approved list of participants allowing a higher-quality participant pool than alternative sample providers (formerly TurkPrime; see Litman and Robinson, 2020; Litman et al. 2017). Out of a total of 1,035 American workers, who agreed to participate, 595 completed the study with conclusive data (16 failed the initial attention checks, 333 failed the comprehension checks, 81 did not proceed until the end, and 10 needed to be omitted due to inconclusive data). On average, the 595 participants (322 males, 266 females, and 7 non-binary or with preference to keep their gender confidential) needed 15.8 min to complete our study.

We connected the study's forecasting task with a Judge Advisor System (JAS). The JAS is used to measure the extent to which a person assimilates advice (Gino, 2008; Logg et al. 2019; Sniezek and Buckley, 1995). The JAS in our study can be illustrated as follows. First, participants ("judges") made an initial forecast without external advice. Second, they received advice from an AI ("advisor"). Third, participants had the chance to change their initial forecast based on the AI advice and to provide their final forecast. The forecast is measured before and after receiving AI advice. The relative shift in the forecast then indicates the use of AI advice (Bonaccio and Dalal, 2006). Measuring the relative shift in the forecast allows us to use a continuous measure for the use of AI advice. Continuous measures capture more information than traditional categorical measures of use of advice, thus allowing stronger insights into people's AI-advice behavior. We use an ex ante perfect system as an advisor that provides advice leading to the highest expected outcome.

The procedure for participants follows the study of Lehmann et al. (2022) and is illustrated in Fig. 1. At the beginning of the study, participants read an introduction and completed attention checks. They also read instructions on the upcoming forecasting task including the following steps. They learned that they would make an initial judgment on a product forecast, receive advice, and then make their final decision. Participants then saw an example question and had to answer comprehension check questions correctly to proceed. Next, participants provided their initial demand forecasts. For each product, they saw the historical demand of ten time periods on a line chart and had to input an integer number for the demand in the upcoming period. Participants did not receive any additional information about the product at hand. We used line charts as research argues that they are the best presentation style when

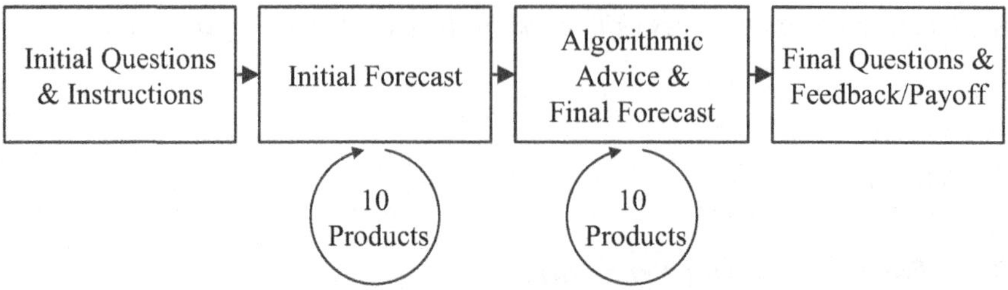

Fig. 1 Sequence of events in the study (adapted from Lehmann et al. 2022)

the characteristics of the demand data are unknown (Harvey and Bolger, 1996). As soon as participants finished the initial forecasts for all ten products, they proceeded to the final forecasts. For each of the ten products, they saw the same line chart as in the first round as well as their initial forecast, the AI advice, and a blank text field for their final forecast. Once participants finished the forecasting tasks, they proceeded to the final questions including the Big Five Inventory. Lastly, participants were debriefed and received feedback on their performance and their payoff. The payoff encompassed a base pay of \$1.50 and a performance-based bonus of up to \$1.00. We measured performance as the absolute percentage error (bounded by 0 and 1). The performance-based bonus for each product was computed as \$0.10 x (1 - absolute percentage error) as in Kremer et al. (2011).

Since our study was part of a larger data collection effort for related research projects, we manipulated the appearance of the AI in three ways: (1) no specific message in the control condition (e.g., "AI advice: 793"), (2) a message highlighting the AI's intent to achieve strong performance, (3) a message highlighting the AI's intent to avoid poor performance. A message (in condition (2) and (3)) was used to communicate the AI advice to the user and ideally increase the use of advice (e.g., "Updating your initial forecast by considering the AI advice can help you improve your performance and successfully achieve substantial gains. To improve your performance, the AI advises the number that can be seen below"). The AI advice did not include any additional details other than the number and a message, depending on the condition. In a first step of analysis, we consider the full sample across all three conditions. In an additional step of analysis, we consider whether the existence of the message (condition (2) and (3) versus no message (condition (1)) moderates the effects of personality on weight on advice.

3.2 Measures

Weight on Advice. The use of AI advice was measured by weight on advice (e.g., Bonaccio and Dalal, 2006). Weight on advice measures how much participants adjust their initial forecast towards the AI advice. More specifically, weight on advice is the difference between the initial and revised forecast divided by the difference between the initial forecast and the advice. Weight on advice of 0 occurs when a participant ignores advice completely and weight on advice of 1 occurs when a participant abandons their prior forecast to perfectly match the advice. We winsorize values less than zero to zero and greater than one to one to increase interpretability. This critical treatment of outliers is common and should be uncritical in the current study as the ratio of outliers being winsorized to all values is low, that is, 5.2% (e.g., Logg et al. 2019). For our analyses, we use the average weight on advice across all ten products.

Big Five Personality Traits. The Big Five personality traits were measured with the Big Five Inventory (BFI; John et al. 1991; 2008). The BFI comprises 44 items in total, which are rated on a five-point scale. Each item is categorized into one of the five personality dimensions. The score of an individual on a specific personality dimension is defined by the average score of the items that are categorized into this specific personality dimension (John et al. 1991; 2008). Evidence of both reliability and validity across different populations is reported in multiple studies (e.g., John et al. 2008).

4 Results

4.1 Summary

Our results yield partial support for the general hypothesis that personality—in the form of the traits agreeableness, neuroticism, and openness—is associated with use of AI advice. However, extraversion and conscientiousness do not show a significant association with use of AI advice. Further, the effect of personality on use of advice seems to depend on the presence of a message to communicate the advice. Unless specified otherwise, the analyses are based on the General Linear Model (GLM).

4.2 Confirmatory Analyses: Effect of Personality Across All Groups

The following regression analyses test the effect of the Big Five personality traits on use of AI advice while controlling for the regulatory focus of participants (measured using the 11-item Regulatory Focus Questionnaire; captured for use in a different research project; Grant and Higgins, 2003; Higgins et al. 2001) and type of message (no message versus the two types of messages).

Across all three conditions of the study, and in partial support of our predictions, some personality traits are related to the use of AI advice. More specifically, agreeableness (H2) and neuroticism (H4) both show a positive effect on use of advice,

Table 1 Summary of the regression analyses on the effect of Big Five traits on WOA across all treatment groups while controlling for the regulatory focus of participants and the type of message

Big five trait	*b*	*SE*	β	*t*	*p* > |*t*|
Extraversion	0.01	0.01	0.03	0.76	0.449
Agreeableness	0.07	0.01	0.20	4.87	< 0.001
Conscientiousness	– 0.02	0.01	– 0.05	– 1.04	0.300
Neuroticism	0.05	0.01	0.18	3.70	< 0.001
Openness	– 0.02	0.01	– 0.07	0.13	0.092

$b = 0.07$, $SE = 0.01$, $\beta = 0.20$, $t(7, 587) = 4.87$, $p < 0.001$, $\eta_p^2 = 0.04$, and $b = 0.05$, $SE = 0.01$, $\beta = 0.18$, $t(7, 587) = 3.70$, $p < 0.001$, $\eta_p^2 = 0.02$, respectively. The effect sizes of both effects based on partial eta squared (η_p^2) are rather small (Cohen, 1988). Counter to our predictions, openness (H5) shows a negative and small effect if the 10% significance level is adopted, $b = -0.02$, $SE = 0.01$, $\beta = -0.07$, $t(7, 587) = -1.69$, $p = 0.092$, $\eta_p^2 = 0.01$, and both extraversion (H1) and conscientiousness (H3) are not significantly related to use of advice, $p = 0.449$ and $p = 0.300$, respectively. Table 1 summarizes the aforementioned results.

4.3 Exploratory Analyses: Effect of Personality and Presence of a Message

Running separate regression analyses to account for different effects of message manipulation (condition (2) and (3)) versus no message manipulation (condition (1)), shows the following. If participants are shown a message on the AI's intent to communicate the AI advice (condition (2) and (3)), extraversion (if the 10% significance level is adopted), agreeableness, and neuroticism show a positive and small to medium effect on use of advice, $b = 0.02$, $SE = 0.01$, $\beta = 0.01$, $t(7, 361) = 1.69$, $p = 0.093$, $\eta_p^2 = 0.01$, $b = 0.10$, $SE = 0.02$, $\beta = 0.30$, $t(7, 361) = 5.50$, $p < 0.001$, $\eta_p^2 = 0.08$, and $b = 0.06$, $SE = 0.02$, $\beta = 0.25$, $t(7, 361) = 3.92$, $p < 0.001$, $\eta_p^2 = 0.04$, respectively. Further, openness shows a negative and small effect on use of advice, $b = -0.03$, $SE = 0.02$, $\beta = -0.10$, $t(7, 361) = -1.99$, $p = 0.047$, $\eta_p^2 = 0.01$. Lastly, conscientiousness shows a non-significant negative effect on use of advice, $b = -0.03$, $SE = 0.02$, $\beta = -0.09$, $t(7, 361) = -1.61$, $p = 0.108$, $\eta_p^2 = 0.01$. Table 2 summarizes the aforementioned results. If participants are not shown a message, no Big Five personality trait is significantly associated with use of AI advice. Running moderation analyses for each personality trait and the presence of a message on use of advice reveals that the effect of agreeableness is significantly moderated by the presence of a message, $b = -0.05$, $SE = 0.03$, $\beta = -0.39$, $t(9, 585) = 1.99$, $p = 0.047$, $\eta_p^2 = 0.01$. The moderation effects of the remaining Big Five traits and the presence of a message are non-significant.

Table 2 Summary of the regression analyses on the effect of Big Five traits on WOA across participants who received a message while controlling for the regulatory focus of participants and the type of message

Big five trait	*b*	*SE*	β	*t*	$p > \|t\|$
Extraversion	0.02	0.01	0.10	1.69	0.093
Agreeableness	0.10	0.02	0.30	5.50	< 0.001
Conscientiousness	– 0.03	0.02	– 0.09	– 1.61	0.108
Neuroticism	0.06	0.02	0.25	3.92	< 0.001
Openness	– 0.03	0.02	– 0.10	– 1.99	0.047

5 Discussion

The goal of the current paper was to build on extant personality research in the field of human advice and use of AI systems to understand antecedents of the imperfect use of AI advice in objective domains. Such understanding may enable future personalization of AI advice to improve the use of AI advice in objective domains. More specifically, our study uses data of 595 participants to test the association between the Big Five personality traits and the use of a forecasting AI advice system. In line with our predictions, agreeableness and neuroticism both show a positive effect on use of AI advice. Contrary to our predictions, however, openness exhibits a negative and smaller effect on use of AI advice than agreeableness and neuroticism. Further, both extraversion and conscientiousness do not show a significant relation to use of AI advice. Interestingly, in the presence of a specific message communicating the AI advice, extraversion also shows a significant but small association with use of AI advice.

These findings add to current literature in at least three different ways. First, scholars have called for more research to increase the understanding of use of AI systems (Chong et al. 2022; Völkel et al. 2019; Zhang et al. 2020). Specifically, personality research is underrepresented in the field of use of AI advice in objective domains. We answer this call by analyzing the Big Five personality traits, showing the promise of and opening the path for further personality research in this field. Second, we contribute to the discussion of imperfect use of AI advice. Our study shows that personality is an important antecedent of the use of AI advice and should not be neglected in further discussions of explanations for imperfect use of AI advice. Lastly, scholars have researched the role of personality in advice-taking from humans (Kausel et al. 2015; Schultze et al. 2018). The current paper provides first empirical evidence to compare the role of personality for human–human advice-taking to human-AI advice taking. Comparing the role of personality in both fields is important because it allows expanding personality theories through a new perspective, which will increase in importance as the importance of AI grows over the next years. In fact, the role of personality for human–human compared to human-AI advice-taking does not seem to be as straight forward as one might think, but there seem to be both similarities and differences that deserve consideration. On the similarities, for example, agentic and independent individuals are found to use advice from other humans less (Schultze et al. 2018). The current study points towards the same direction as emotionally stable people, who can generally be seen as more agentic, use AI advice less. On the differences, for example, the current study suggests that agreeableness is associated with more AI-advice taking. This finding lacks consistent support in the field of human–human advice-taking (Schultze et al. 2018). More research is needed to understand both similarities and differences of personality in the field of human–human versus human-AI advice taking.

The most important practical implication revolves around personalization of AI advice. Understanding a user's personality may enable practitioners to personalize AI systems to improve the use of such systems. In fact, practitioners could focus on the personality traits agreeableness and neuroticism as the current study suggests these traits to be more important for use of AI advice than the remaining Big Five traits. Considering the importance of agreeableness, for example, an AI could be built to increase motivation to use advice for people scoring low on agreeableness. People low on agreeableness usually share a tendency to initiate disagreements and carry doubts. To minimize disagreements and doubts, the AI could be equipped with a chat function enabling users to communicate their disagreements. The AI could then prepare arguments dealing with these disagreements to increase these users' motivation to use the AI advice. This is just a first idea around how results of the current study could stimulate future personalization of AI advice to improve the use of such systems. More research is needed to understand the robustness of AI advice personalization ideas resulting from the current study.

5.1 Limitations and Future Directions

Our paper's contributions should be considered in the context of some limitations that may stimulate promising future research. First, our results on personality traits as antecedents of use of AI advice are based on an ex ante perfect AI system. The association between a given personality trait and the use of AI advice might change if the AI system is not perfect but shows inferiority to humans in some dimensions. For example, agreeableness is positively associated with use of AI advice in our study. One of the main reasons is that agreeable people generally report higher usefulness of new technologies, such as AI systems (Devaraj et al. 2008). If an AI errs, perceived usefulness could fade as research has found that people are unforgiving towards erring AI (and other algorithmic) systems and lose trust in them quickly (Dietvorst et al, 2015). Thus, the positive association between agreeableness and use of AI systems might not hold in case of an imperfect system. Second, humans in our setting were not familiar with the forecasting AI deployed in our study. While this reflects many current real-world application contexts, there will be a growing number of experts using AI advisors constantly on their jobs. Consequently, the association of some personality traits with use of AI advice might change if working with an AI becomes more common. For example, the trait openness to experience may become less predictive of use of AI systems once the user has worked with the AI system over extended periods.

In terms of future directions, the current paper's unexpected findings may be explored further. Across all conditions, it was surprising to find a negative effect of openness on use of AI advice and no association between extraversion and conscientiousness and use of AI advice. Additionally, we did not expect the effects of some personality traits to become (marginally) significant once the users receive a specific message (versus no particular message about the intent of the AI). We suggest testing different mechanisms that may explain these unexpected findings. For example, the negative effect of openness across all groups seems to be driven by the message as openness shows no association with use of advice when there is no message ($p = 0.941$). This changes once a specific message is shown ($p = 0.047$). It might be that people high in openness are generally less interested in quantitative forecasting tasks as they look for more creative and stimulating tasks. They might thus feel indifferent about AI advice unless a specific message is displayed. In the latter case, they might then feel strongly against being influenced and act counter to the message to restore their individuality and creative mindset. Regarding extraversion, a specific message might strengthen the perception that the AI can help to reap a monetary reward in the study. Since extraverted people are reward oriented (Depue and Collins, 1999), a message may be convincing to extraverted people and lead to increased use of advice ($p = 0.454$ for no message and $p = 0.093$ when a message is shown). Taken together, the current paper sheds light on the effect of personality on use of AI advice in objective domains, paving the way for future research on this promising path.

References

Ajzen, I. (2005), *Attitudes, personality and behavior*. United Kingdom: McGraw–Hill.

Alvarado-Valencia, J. A. & Barrero, L. H. (2014), "Reliance, trust and heuristics in judgmental forecasting", *Computers in Human Behavior* **36**, 102-113.

Asendorpf, J. B. & Neyer, F. J. (2012), *Psychologie der Persönlichkeit*. Springer-Verlag.

Bansal, G., Nushi, B., Kamar, E., Lasecki, W. S., Weld, D. S. & Horvitz, E. (2019), "Beyond accuracy: the role of mental models in human-AI team performance", *Proceedings of the 7th AAAI Conference on Human Computation and Crowdsourcing*, 2–11.

Bayram, N. & Aydemir, M. (2017), "Decision-making styles and personality traits", *International Journal of Recent Advances in Organizational Behaviour and Decision Sciences* **3**(1), 905-915.

Bonaccio, S. & Dalal, R. S. (2006), "Advice-taking and decision-making: an integrative literature review, and implications for the organizational sciences", *Organizational Behavior and Human Decision Processes* **101**(2), 127-151.

Buch, V. H., Ahmed, I. & Maruthappu, M. (2018), "Artificial Intelligence in medicine: current trends and future possibilities", *British Journal of General Practice*, **68**(668), 143-144.

Ching, C. M., Church, A. T., Katigbak, M. S., Reyes, J. A. S., Tanaka-Matsumi, J., Takaoka, S., Zhang, H., Shen, J., Arias, R. M., Rincon, B. C. & Ortiz, F. A. (2014), "The manifestation of traits in everyday behavior and affect: a five-culture study", *Journal of Research in Personality* **48**, 1-16.

Chen, D. L., Schonger, M. & Wickens, C. (2016), "oTree – an open-source platform for laboratory, online, and field experiments", *Journal of Behavioral and Experimental Finance* **9**, 88–97.

Chong, L., Zhang, G., Goucher-Lambert, K., Kotovsky, K. & Cagan, J. (2022), "Human confidence in Artificial Intelligence and in themselves: the evolution and impact of confidence on adoption of AI advice", *Computers in Human Behavior* **127**, 107018.

Cohen, J. (1988), *Statistical power analysis for the behavioural sciences (2nd ed.)*. New York: Academic Press.

Costa, P. T. & McCrae, R. R., (1992a), "Four ways five factors are basic", *Personality and Individual Differences* **13**(6), 653-665.

Costa, P. T. & McCrae, R. R. (1992b), "The five-factor model of personality and its relevance to personality disorders", *Journal of Personality Disorders* **6**(4), 343-359.

Depue, R. A. & Collins, P. F. (1999), "Neurobiology of the structure of personality: dopamine, facilitation of incentive motivation, and extraversion", *Behavioral and Brain Sciences* **22**(3), 491-517.

Devaraj, S., Easley, R. F. & Crant, J. M. (2008), "Research note – how does personality matter? Relating the Five-Factor model to technology acceptance and use", *Information Systems Research* **19**(1), 93-105.

Dietvorst, B. J., Simmons, J. P. & Massey, C. (2015), "Algorithm aversion: people erroneously avoid algorithms after seeing them err", *Journal of Experimental Psychology: General* **144**(1), 114-126.

Esterwood, C., Essenmacher, K., Yang, H., Zeng, F. & Robert, L. P. (2021a), "A meta-analysis of human personality and robot acceptance in human-robot interaction", *Proceedings of the 2021 CHI Conference on Human Factors in Computing Systems*, 1–18.

Esterwood, C., Essenmacher, K., Yang, H., Zeng, F. & Robert, L. P. (2021b), "Birds of a feather flock together: but do humans and robots? A meta-analysis of human and robot personality matching", *Proceedings of the 30th IEEE International Conference on Robot & Human Interactive Communication (RO-MAN)*, 343–348.

Eyal, P., David, R., Andrew, G., Zak, E. & Ekaterina, D. (2021), "Data quality of platforms and panels for online behavioral research", *Behavior Research Methods* **54**, 1643-1662.

Gino, F. (2008), "Do we listen to advice just because we paid for it? The impact of advice cost on its use", *Organizational Behavior and Human Decision Processes* **107**(2), 234-245.

Gosling, S. D., Rentfrow, P. J. & Swann Jr, W. B. (2003), "A very brief measure of the Big Five personality domains", *Journal of Research in Personality* **37**(6), 504-528.

Grant, H. & Higgins, E. T. (2003), "Optimism, promotion pride, and prevention pride as predictors of quality of life", *Personality and Social Psychology Bulletin* **29**(12), 1521-1532.

Harvey, N. & Bolger, F. (1996), "Graphs versus tables: effects of data presentation format on judgmental forecasting", *International Journal of Forecasting* **12**(1), 119-137.

Higgins, E. T., Friedman, R. S., Harlow, R. E., Idson, L.C., Ayduk, O. N. & Taylor, A. (2001), "Achievement orientations from subjective histories of success: promotion pride versus prevention pride", *European Journal of Social Psychology* **31**(1), 3-23.

John, O. P., Donahue, E. M. & Kentle, R. L. (1991), *The Big Five Inventory – versions 4a and 54*. Berkeley, CA: University of California, Institute of Personality and Social Research.

John, O. P., Naumann, L. P. & Soto, C. J. (2008), "Paradigm shift to the integrative Big Five trait taxonomy: history, measurement, and conceptual issues", *in* John, O. P., Robins, R. W., and Pervin, L. A. (eds.) *Handbook of personality: Theory and research,* 114-158. New York, NY: Guilford Press.

Johnson, D. & Gardner, J. (2010), "Personality, motivation and video games", *Proceedings of the 22nd Conference of the Computer-Human Interaction Special Interest Group of Australia on Computer-Human Interaction*, 276–279.

Kausel, E. E., Culbertson, S. S., Leiva, P. I., Slaughter, J. E. & Jackson, A. T. (2015), "Too arrogant for their own good? Why and when narcissists dismiss advice", *Organizational Behavior and Human Decision Processes* **131**, 33-50.

Kremer, M., Moritz, B. & Siemsen, E. (2011), "Demand forecasting behavior: system neglect and change detection", *Management Science* **57**(10), 1827-1843.

Lauriola, M. & Levin, I. P. (2001), "Personality traits and risky decision-making in a controlled experimental task: an exploratory study", *Personality and Individual Differences* **31**(2), 215-226.

Lehmann, C. A., Haubitz, C. B., Fügener, A. & Thonemann, U. W. (2022), "The risk of algorithm transparency: how algorithm complexity drives the effects on the use of advice", *Production and Operations Management* **31**(9), 3419– 3434.

Lin, J., Matthews, G., Wohleber, R. W., Funke, G. J., Calhoun, G. L., Ruff, H. A., Szalma, J. & Chiu, P. (2020), "Overload and automation-dependence in a multi-UAS simulation: task demand and individual difference factors", *Journal of Experimental Psychology: Applied* **26**(2), 218-235.

Litman, L. & Robinson, J. (2020), *Conducting online research on Amazon Mechanical Turk and beyond.* Sage Publications.

Litman, L., Robinson, J. & Abberbock, T. (2017), "*TurkPrime. com: a versatile crowdsour-cing data acquisition platform for the behavioral sciences*", Behavior Research Methods **49**(2), 433–442.

Logg, J. M., Minson, J. A. & Moore, D. A. (2019), "Algorithm appreciation: people prefer algorithmic to human judgment", *Organizational Behavior and Human Decision Processes* **151**, 90-103.

Man Tang, P., Koopman, J., McClean, S. T., Zhang, J. H., Li, C. H., De Cremer, D., Lu, Y. & Ng, C. T. S. (2022), "When conscientious employees meet intelligent machines: an integrative approach inspired by complementarity theory and role theory", *Academy of Management Journal* **65**(3), 1019-1054.

Matthews, G., Deary, I. J. & Whiteman, M. C. (2003), *Personality traits.* Cambridge: Cambridge University Press.

McCrae, R. R. & Costa, P. T. (2008), "The Five-Factor theory of personality", *in* John, O. P., Robins, R. W., and Pervin, L. A. (eds.) *Handbook of personality: Theory and research*, 159–181. The Guilford Press.

McCrae, R. R. & John, O. P. (1992), "An introduction to the Five-Factor model and its applications", *Journal of Personality* **60**(2), 175-215.

Nagar, Y. & Malone, T. (2011), "Making business predictions by combining human and machine intelligence in prediction markets", *Proceedings of the 2011 International Conference on Information Systems (ICIS).*

Parasuraman, R., Cosenzo, K. A. & De Visser, E. (2009), "Adaptive automation for human supervision of multiple uninhabited vehicles: effects on change detection, situation awareness, and mental workload", *Military Psychology* **21**(2), 270-297.

Park, J. & Woo, S. E. (2022), "Who likes Artificial Intelligence? Personality predictors of attitudes toward Artificial Intelligence", *The Journal of Psychology* **156**(1), 68-94.

Riaz, M. N., Riaz, M. A. & Batool, N. (2012), "Personality types as predictors of decision-making styles", *Journal of Behavioural Sciences* **22**(2), 99-114.

Richtel, M. & Dougherty, C., (2015), *Google's driverless cars run into problem: cars with drivers.* URL: https://www.nytimes.com/2015/09/02/technology/personaltech/google-says-its-not-the-driverless-cars-fault-its-other-drivers.html. Accessed: 12.01.2023.

Rossi, S., Santangelo, G., Staffa, M., Varrasi, S., Conti, D. & Di Nuovo, A. (2018), "Psychometric evaluation supported by a social robot: personality factors and technology acceptance", *Proceedings of the 27th IEEE International Symposium on Robot and Human Interactive Communication (RO-MAN)*, 802–807.

Szalma, J. L. & Taylor, G. S. (2011), "Individual differences in response to automation: the Five-Factor model of personality", *Journal of Experimental Psychology: Applied* **17**(2), 71-96.

Schultze, T., Gerlach, T. M. & Rittich, J. C. (2018), "Some people heed advice less than others: agency (but not communion) predicts advice-taking", *Journal of Behavioral Decision Making* **31**(3), 430-445.

Sniezek, J. A. & Buckley, T. (1995), "Cueing and cognitive conflict in judge-advisor decision making", *Organizational Behavior and Human Decision Processes* **62**(2), 159-174.

Svendsen, G. B., Johnsen, J. A. K., Almås-Sørensen, L. & Vittersø, J. (2013), "Personality and technology acceptance: the influence of personality factors on the core constructs of the Technology Acceptance Model", *Behaviour & Information Technology* **32**(4), 323-334.

Syrdal, D. S., Dautenhahn, K., Woods, S., Walters, M. L. & Koay, K. L. (2006), "Doing the right thing wrong – personality and tolerance to uncomfortable robot approaches", Proceedings of the *15th IEEE International Symposium on Robot and Human Interactive Communication,* 183–188.

Tkalcic, M. & Chen, L. (2015), "Personality and recommender systems", *in* Ricci, F., Rokach, L., & Shapira, B. (eds.) *Recommender systems handbook*, 715-739. Boston, MA: Springer.

Ülgen, B., Sağlam, M. & Tuğsal, T. (2016), "Managers' personality traits over management styles and decision-making styles", *International Journal of Commerce and Finance* **2**(1), 125-136.

Völkel, S. T., Schödel, R., Buschek, D., Stachl, C., Au, Q., Bischl, B., Bühner, M. & Hussmann, H., (2019), "Opportunities and challenges of utilizing personality traits for personalization in HCI", *in* Augstein, M., Herder E., and Wörndl W. (eds.) *Personalized Human–Computer Interaction*, 31-69, Oldenburg: De Gruyter.

Wallach, H. S., Safir, M. P. & Samana, R. (2010), "Personality variables and presence", *Virtual Reality* **14**(1), 3-13.

Wu, W., Chen, L. & He, L. (2013), "Using personality to adjust diversity in recommender systems", *Proceedings of the 24th ACM Conference on Hypertext and Social Media*, 225–229.

Yeomans, M., Shah, A., Mullainathan, S. & Kleinberg, J. (2019), "Making sense of recommendations", *Journal of Behavioral Decision Making* **32**(4), 403-414.

Zhang, G., Raina, A., Cagan, J. & McComb, C. (2021), "A cautionary tale about the impact of AI on human design teams", *Design Studies* **72**, 1-23.

Zhang, Y., Liao, Q. V. & Bellamy, R. K., (2020), "Effect of confidence and explanation on accuracy and trust calibration in AI-assisted decision making", *Proceedings of the 2020 Conference on Fairness, Accountability, and Transparency*, 295–305.

The Sound of Progress: Investigating the Representation of Artificial Intelligence in Music

Leonardo Banh and Gero Strobel

Abstract The role of artificial intelligence in daily life is constantly advancing and has become an important topic of discussion. With music and its lyrics being a vehicle to express topics of society, this paper investigates how artificial intelligence is perceived by musicians and reflected in their songs. By analyzing the lyrics of over 1200 songs over three decades, this work applies sentiment analysis to extract polarities and emotions. The results provide insights into how musicians view and reflect the impact of artificial intelligence on society and how this is reflected in their song texts. The findings show an increase in songs mentioning artificial intelligence-related terms, with a trend of more songs implying negativity, such as anger. However, minor increases in positive emotions indicate musicians' ambivalent views on hopes and fear of artificial intelligence.

Keywords Artificial intelligence · Sentiment analysis · Music · Lyrics

1 Introduction

Artificial intelligence (AI) is rapidly advancing and becoming a prevalent part of daily life. From personal assistants, such as Siri and Alexa, to self-driving cars and medical diagnoses, AI impacts nearly every industry (Enholm et al. 2022). Generative AI tools like image generators (e.g., DALL-E) or chatbots (e.g., ChatGPT) are widely accessible and impress users with their capabilities (Pavlik, 2023). As AI continues to expand in private and professional sectors, the use of the technology raises important questions about its implications on society. Researchers are dealing with AI's impact on businesses and management (Berente et al. 2021), explainable AI (Barredo Arrieta

L. Banh (✉) · G. Strobel
Research Group for Information Systems and Software Engineering, University of Duisburg-Essen, Essen, Germany
e-mail: leonardo.banh@uni-due.de

G. Strobel
e-mail: gero.strobel@uni-due.de

D. Beverungen et al. (eds.), *Conceptualizing Digital Responsibility for the Information Age*, Lecture Notes in Information Systems and Organisation 74,
https://doi.org/10.1007/978-3-031-80119-8_11

et al. 2020; Bauer et al. 2021), ethics (Bostrom & Yudkowsky, 2018; Jobin et al. 2019), or legal aspects (Smuha, 2021). However, examining society's perception of AI and its attitude toward its widespread use is also essential. Understanding how technology impacts individuals fosters the formulation of adequate strategies to promote the design of better information systems, leading to wider acceptance and greater purpose for the users (Graf-Vlachy et al. 2018; Venkatesh et al. 2003).

The increasing role of AI in our world is also reflected by artists and their songs, exploring themes of technology, automation, as well as the future. Music as a form of self-expression is a pillar of human culture and has been widely used in history (Bennett, 2022). Popular song texts often embed political statements, stress human concerns of the time, or relate to specific historical events (Cooper, 1991; Pettijohn & Sacco, 2009). For instance, the song "We are the World" addresses the famine conditions in Africa, while the German song "99 Luftballons" thematizes the Cold War.

Therefore, analyzing music and its lyrics provides a vehicle to uncover topics of society and the inherent attitudes of musicians towards these topics. The analysis can also expose trends and form the foundation for future decisions and developments. With this research, we aim to provide a deeper understanding of how musicians respond to AI advancements and how popular music shapes the opinions on technology and its role in our lives. Besides music being a mirror of society, the attitudes of songs also influence music listeners (Jang & Lee, 2014). Thereby, the positive and negative views of musicians impact their listeners, justifying the analysis of lyrics to understand how society perceives AI. Prior research investigating society's perception on AI via newspaper and social media analysis showed ambivalent opinions (Fast & Horvitz, 2016; Gao et al. 2020). Against this backdrop, this paper seeks to investigate how AI is impacting daily life and how these developments are reflected in music, specifically focusing on the research question:

How is artificial intelligence perceived by musicians and reflected in their songs?

To address the research question, we analyzed the lyrics of 1221 songs from 30 years that referenced AI and related topics, such as machine learning, deep learning (DL), or deepfakes (Westerlund, 2019). We conducted a sentiment analysis as a natural language approach to foster a deeper understanding of the musicians' feelings and attitudes. Consequently, we analyzed the sentiments for changes in polarities and emotions over time to detect trends in musicians' perception of AI.

The study provides valuable insights into how AI impacts society and how society thinks about technology, guiding future efforts in dealing with AI, educating the public, and demystifying the technology. The remainder of this paper is structured as follows: First, we unfold related literature on the role of music in society and how research examines the perception of AI. Second, we describe our research method of analyzing how AI is perceived in music. Third, we present our preliminary analysis results from the systematic lyrics review to uncover trends. And forth, we conclude our research, discuss limitations, and give an outlook to future work.

2 Role of Music and Perception of AI

Music is a powerful tool for addressing humanity's hopes, fears, and anxieties. Throughout history, popular music has reflected the zeitgeist, capturing the mood and concerns of a particular time and place (Bennett, 2022). From protest songs to love ballads, music can reach people on an emotional level and express ideas and feelings that may be difficult to articulate in other forms. Usually, these songs have lyrics that complement the tune and instrumentals to provide another form of expression (Pettijohn & Sacco, 2009). Prior research shows topic changes reflected in music lyrics and their social and economic implications. For instance, researchers studied the expression of politics in music (Gosa, 2017), music's influence on political orientations (Fox & Williams, 1974), and the manifestation of social changes regarding gender identities or substance abuse (Christenson et al. 2012; Hall et al. 2012; Jang & Lee, 2014).

Related work on the change of perception of AI has shown that the discussion increased in the past years, with positive and negative directions (Cave & Dihal, 2019; Fast & Horvitz, 2016). For instance, the analysis of newspaper articles showed that the overall opinion is more optimistic than pessimistic (Fast & Horvitz, 2016). Though, related concerns such as fear of losing control or ethical fears have also grown. Moreover, social media content analysis on public perception of AI in medical care revealed that most people held positive attitudes but were concerned about the immaturity of AI technology and the lack of trust and humanistic care when human doctors were replaced (Gao et al. 2020). The distrust and fear towards AI technology could be due to factors such as the emergence of malicious deepfakes or no interest in science and technology (Albarrán Lozano et al. 2021; Romero & Young, 2022). However, focusing on newspaper and social media outlets as the primary data source can be subject to potential moderation or biases (Duarte et al. 2018).

3 Research Method

To analyze how musicians perceive AI, we base our research on a systematic lyric review to identify and mine opinions as well as trends in popular music song texts. We adapted the framework of a systematic literature review (Brocke et al. 2009) to produce a rigorous and reproducible outcome. We performed five searches with AI-related search strings, each in three lyrics databases (genius.com, songsear.ch, and lyrics.com), with initially 2472 hits in February 2023. After removing the duplicates, we additionally applied quality criteria by screening the results manually for irrelevant songs, i.e., non-musical texts, instrumental versions, and the use of keywords in a different context. Lastly, we excluded titles without access to full-text lyrics and removed outliers, resulting in a final set of 1221 songs over 30 years, from 1993 to 2023 (91% in English).

Based on the dataset, we conducted sentiment analyses to extract opinions and emotions (Abbasi & Chen, 2008; Storey & Park, 2022). Sentiment analysis is used for text classification to investigate the effect of sentiments on individuals, e.g., how headline and article sentiments influence the behavior of clicking and sharing on social media (Oh et al. 2022) or the effects of sentiments in public news articles or social media on to the finance market (Khan et al. 2022; Wang et al. 2018; Wilksch & Abramova, 2022). Adapting the work of Napier and Shamir (2018), we conducted a quantitative sentiment analysis to identify trends in the sentiments of AI-related music lyrics. We focused on the polarity, i.e., positive, neutral, or negative, as well as the emotions, i.e., anger, disgust, enjoyment, fear, neutral, sadness, and surprise (Ekman, 1992). For the automatic sentiment analysis, lexicon-based and machine learning approaches have been state-of-the-art, with the latter achieving better performances in natural language processing tasks (Medhat et al. 2014; Pipalia et al. 2020). Therefore, we employed transformer-based text classification models trained for sentiment analysis and emotion detection (Barbieri et al. 2020, 2021; Hartmann, 2022). Moreover, we applied simple linear regressions to analyze the link between the song sentiments and their release year to reveal trends over time. To provide a comparative baseline of sentiments, we also analyzed the sentiments of the Billboard Hot 100 record charts (i.e., 3000 songs from 1993–2023), a standard music industry ranking in the US regarding popular songs of a year (Napier & Shamir, 2018).

4 Preliminary Results

In total, we identified 1221 songs that had AI-related lyrics, i.e., mentioned the terms "A.I.," "artificial intelligence," "deep learning," "deepfake," and "machine learning." Fig. 1 shows the number of songs released over the years, distinguished by the search term. It can be noticed that the number of songs is increasing, with the first releases starting to appear after 2000 when the Internet and large training datasets became available (Russell & Norvig, 2016). Moreover, Internet and social media access fuel the information exchange and discussions about socially relevant topics (Bouvier & Machin, 2018). A sharp increase is evident from 2010 onwards. This change goes in hand with advancing developments in computational power and DL research, resulting in new use cases for AI (Kaynak, 2021). For instance, AI-based voice assistants emerged in publicly available smartphones and smart home devices in 2011 and 2014, respectively (Amazon, 2014; Apple, 2011). The latest advancements in the field of AI have appeared since 2017 and 2020 under the keywords "deep learning" and "deepfake," respectively. With research starting to focus on DL and artificial neural networks, e.g., Google's AlphaGo system beating a human champion player (Haenlein & Kaplan, 2019) or deepfakes reaching authentic capabilities to imposter celebrities and politicians (Westerlund, 2019), the trend in AI-related songs matches with scientific advancements that were also discussed by the media in public.

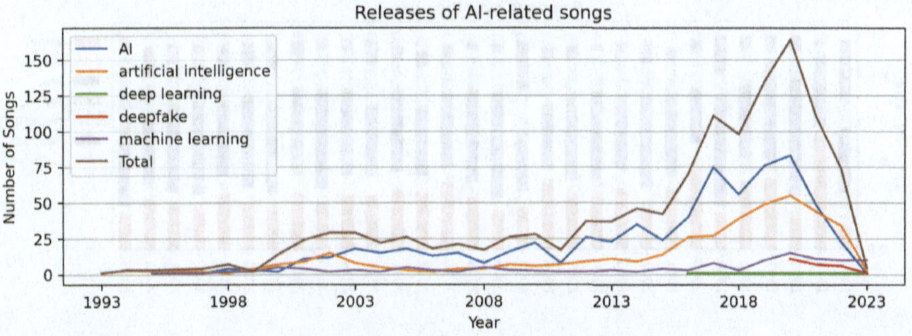

Fig. 1 Number of AI-related songs released over the years per search term

For the sentiment analysis, we used transformer-based language models that were fine-tuned to classify English and multilingual texts into sentiments to extract the polarity of the songs (Barbieri et al. 2020, 2021). We determined the sentiment sentence-wise and calculated the mean value for each song, resulting in values between 0 and 1 for each polarity. Cumulatively, the distribution of sentiments is relatively even, being overall 31.9% positive, 36% neutral, and 32.1% negative. Unpacking the individual polarities, we grouped our data by release year. The data shows a growing trend for songs with negative sentiments, while positive and neutral songs are getting less over the years. To analyze the link between the polarity of songs and their release year, we applied linear regression models. The regression trend line indicates sentiment changes over time, underlining a relationship between the release year and the sentiments (Napier & Shamir, 2018). Figure 2 shows the averaged polarity sentiments of our analyzed set with their respective regression line (solid) and the Billboard Hot 100 sentiments as a baseline (dashed). The slopes of the regression lines indicate a trend toward more negative sentiments and a decrease in neutral sentiments. The negative sentiments had the strongest linear relationship ($R^2 = 0.141$, $p < 0.001$), compared to positive sentiments ($R^2 = 0.102$, $p < 0.001$) and neutral sentiments ($R^2 = 0.025$, $p < 0.001$).

Diving deeper into the emotional tones embedded in the songs, we applied another text classification model that was fine-tuned to retrieve emotion sentiments on all English language songs (Hartmann, 2022). An overview of the emotion sentiment distribution is depicted in Fig. 3. Overall, the most prevalent emotion detected was

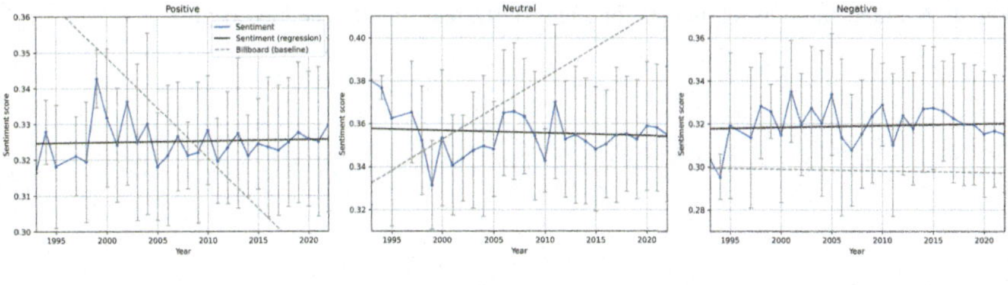

Fig. 2 Average polarity sentiments for positive (left), neutral (middle), and negative (right)

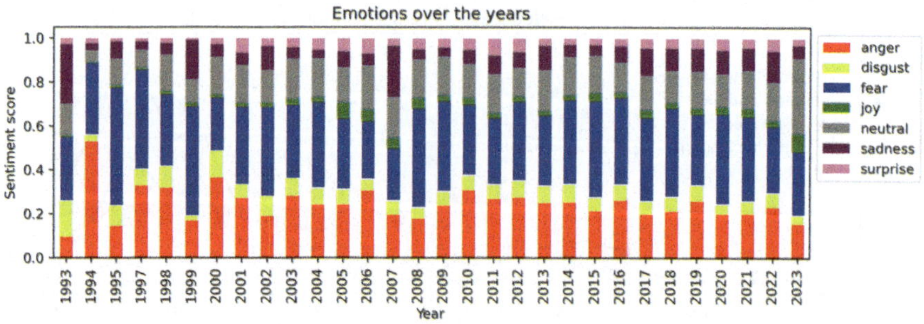

Fig. 3 Average emotion sentiments over the years

fear (36.5%), followed by anger (23.3%), neutral (16.5%), sadness (9.2%), disgust (7.0%), surprise (4.5%), and joy (2.9%).

For detecting trends regarding individual emotions, we applied another linear regression. Figure 4 shows the average sentiment scores for anger, fear, and joy. The high values of angry and afraid sentiments, compared to the Billboard baseline, suggest a prevalent negativity towards AI while an increasing trend of joy also indicate positivity. The mixture of emotions reflects the torn opinions of musician's perception towards AI. For instance, in "Plug In" by Bastille, AI is seen ambiguous with privacy doubts ("*A.I. [as] the messiah [learns] all my kinks and desires*"). On the other hand, Grimes' view in her song "We Appreciate Power" toward AI tends to be more positive ("*But AI will reward us when it reigns*") while in "Protocol" by Ophidian Memory AI is portrayed as something fearful taking over one's brain and consciousness ("*Cerebral cortex left paper thin; Artificial intelligence takes its place*"). Interestingly, these examples show that AI is portrayed as a person-being with its own goals and noticeable consequences for society.

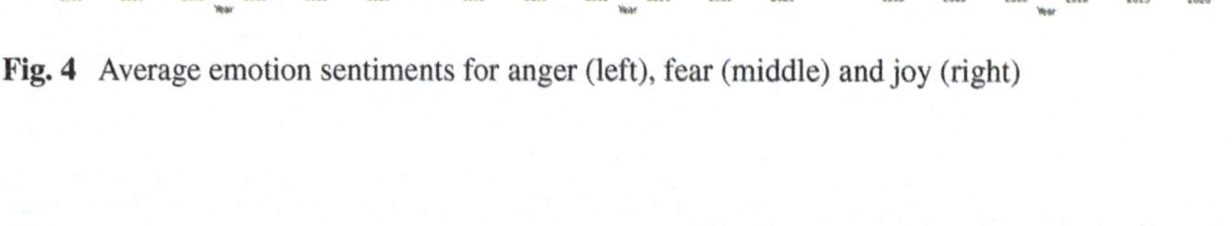

Fig. 4 Average emotion sentiments for anger (left), fear (middle) and joy (right)

5 Conclusion

This research provides a first look into musicians' perception of AI, based on a systematic lyrics search and a sentiment analysis of 1221 AI-related songs. The analysis shows that songs mentioning AI-related terms have increased over the years and tend to imply negative sentiments, especially fear and anger. Moreover, the results indicate a trend towards negativity with growing anger emotions. However, our results also show that the perception of AI varies in songs, with other emotions, such as joy, increasing as well. As the release dates of our analyzed songs correspond to developments in AI, our systematic lyrics search captured musicians' inherent sentiments and emotions towards AI and related technologies. Despite the ambivalent attitudes, these songs still paint a narrative for their listeners, creating assumptions and expectations against which AI technologies are assessed (Cave & Dihal, 2019). Nonetheless, lyrics represent a very specific subgroup of information because of musicians' self-selection into making music and with each song being consumed differently by a certain audience.

Future research will expand the explorative approach of this work. A broader lyrics search will be conducted to capture more relevant songs that do not explicitly mention AI. Analyzing other songs of the musicians considered and taking data about the musicians' demography and music genre into account can provide deeper insights into trends and patterns, e.g., by studying complementary topics via topic modeling techniques. Interviewing musicians to assess their thoughts in writing songs about AI contribute to a broader understanding. Evaluating our findings with music listeners against discrepancies in perception (e.g., through the lens of communication theories) can further confirm whether the lyrics' sentiments are reflective of the listeners' perceptions. In accordance with this year's conference theme, we call for measures to take "digital responsibility" and demystify AI technology by educating society about the possibilities and actual state of AI.

References

Abbasi, A., & Chen, H. (2008). CyberGate: A Design Framework and System for Text Analysis of Computer-Mediated Communication. *MIS Quarterly*, **32**(4), 811. https://doi.org/10.2307/25148873

Albarrán Lozano, I., Molina, J. M., & Gijón, C. (2021). Perception of Artificial Intelligence in Spain. *Telematics and Informatics*, **63**, 101672. https://doi.org/10.1016/j.tele.2021.101672

Amazon. (2014). *Introducing Amazon Echo. Always ready, connected, and fast. Just ask.* https://twitter.com/amazon/status/530410423397257216. Accessed: 22.02.2023.

Apple. (2011). *Apple Launches iPhone 4S, iOS 5 & iCloud* [Press release]. https://www.apple.com/newsroom/2011/10/04Apple-Launches-iPhone-4S-iOS-5-iCloud/. Accessed: 21.02.2023.

Barbieri, F., Anke, L. E., & Camacho-Collados, J. (2021). *XLM-T: Multilingual Language Models in Twitter for Sentiment Analysis and Beyond.* https://doi.org/10.48550/arXiv.2104.12250

Barbieri, F., Camacho-Collados, J., Anke, L. E., & Neves, L. (2020). TweetEval: Unified Benchmark and Comparative Evaluation for Tweet Classification. In T. Cohn, Y. He, & Y. Liu (Eds.), *Findings of the Association for Computational Linguistics: EMNLP 2020* (pp. 1644–1650). Association for Computational Linguistics. https://doi.org/10.18653/v1/2020.findings-emnlp.148

Barredo Arrieta, A., Díaz-Rodríguez, N., Del Ser, J., Bennetot, A., Tabik, S., Barbado, A., Garcia, S., Gil-Lopez, S., Molina, D., Benjamins, R., Chatila, R., & Herrera, F. (2020). Explainable Artificial Intelligence (XAI): Concepts, taxonomies, opportunities and challenges toward responsible AI. *Information Fusion*, **58**, 82–115. https://doi.org/10.1016/j.inffus.2019.12.012

Bauer, K., Hinz, O., van der Aalst, W., & Weinhardt, C. (2021). Expl(AI)n It to Me – Explainable AI and Information Systems Research. *Business & Information Systems Engineering*, **63**(2), 79–82. https://doi.org/10.1007/s12599-021-00683-2

Bennett, A. (2022). *Popular Music Heritage*. Springer International Publishing. https://doi.org/10.1007/978-3-031-08296-2

Berente, N., Gu, B., Recker, J., & Santhanam, R. (2021). Special Issue Editor's Comments: Managing Artificial Intelligence. *MIS Quarterly*, **45**(3), 1433–1450. https://doi.org/10.25300/MISQ/2021/16274

Bostrom, N., & Yudkowsky, E. (2018). The Ethics of Artificial Intelligence. In R. V. Yampolskiy (Ed.), *Artificial Intelligence Safety and Security* (pp. 57–69). Chapman and Hall/CRC. https://doi.org/10.1201/9781351251389-4

Bouvier, G., & Machin, D. (2018). Critical Discourse Analysis and the challenges and opportunities of social media. *Review of Communication*, **18**(3), 178–192. https://doi.org/10.1080/15358593.2018.1479881

Brocke, J. v., Simons, A., Niehaves, B., Reimer, K., Plattfaut, R., & Cleven, A. (2009). RECONSTRUCTING THE GIANT: ON THE IMPORTANCE OF RIGOUR IN DOCUMENTING THE LITERATURE SEARCH PROCESS. *ECIS 2009 Proceedings*.

Cave, S., & Dihal, K. (2019). Hopes and fears for intelligent machines in fiction and reality. *Nature Machine Intelligence*, **1**(2), 74–78. https://doi.org/10.1038/s42256-019-0020-9

Christenson, P., Roberts, D. F., & Bjork, N. (2012). Booze, drugs, and pop music: Trends in substance portrayals in the billboard top 100-1968-2008. *Substance Use & Misuse*, **47**(2), 121–129. https://doi.org/10.3109/10826084.2012.637433

Cooper, B. L. (1991). Lyrical Commentaries Learning from Popular Music. *Music Educators Journal*, **77**(8), 56–59. https://doi.org/10.2307/3398155

Duarte, N., Llanso, E., & Loup, A. (2018). Mixed Messages? The Limits of Automated Social Media Content Analysis. In S. A. Friedler & C. Wilson (Eds.), *Proceedings of Machine Learning Research, Proceedings of the 1st Conference on Fairness, Accountability and Transparency* (p. 106). PMLR.

Ekman, P. (1992). An argument for basic emotions. *Cognition and Emotion*, **6**(3-4), 169–200. https://doi.org/10.1080/02699939208411068

Enholm, I. M., Papagiannidis, E., Mikalef, P., & Krogstie, J. (2022). Artificial Intelligence and Business Value: a Literature Review. *Information Systems Frontiers*, **24**(5), 1709–1734. https://doi.org/10.1007/s10796-021-10186-w

Fast, E., & Horvitz, E. (2016). *Long-Term Trends in the Public Perception of Artificial Intelligence*. https://doi.org/10.48550/arXiv.1609.04904

Fox, W. S., & Williams, J. D. (1974). Political Orientation and Music Preferences Among College Students. *Public Opinion Quarterly*, **38**(3), 352. https://doi.org/10.1086/268171

Gao, S., He, L., Chen, Y., Li, D., & Lai, K. (2020). Public Perception of Artificial Intelligence in Medical Care: Content Analysis of Social Media. *Journal of Medical Internet Research*, **22**(7), e16649. https://doi.org/10.2196/16649

Gosa, T. L. (2017). Hip hop, authenticity, and styleshifting in the 2016 presidential election. *Journal of Popular Music Studies*, **29**(3), e12236. https://doi.org/10.1111/jpms.12236

Graf-Vlachy, L., Buhtz, K., & König, A. (2018). Social influence in technology adoption: taking stock and moving forward. *Management Review Quarterly*, **68**(1), 37–76. https://doi.org/10.1007/s11301-017-0133-3

Haenlein, M., & Kaplan, A. (2019). A Brief History of Artificial Intelligence: On the Past, Present, and Future of Artificial Intelligence. *California Management Review*, **61**(4), 5–14. https://doi.org/10.1177/0008125619864925

Hall, C. P., West, J. H., & Hill, S. (2012). Sexualization in Lyrics of Popular Music from 1959 to 2009: Implications for Sexuality Educators. *Sexuality & Culture*, **16**(2), 103–117. https://doi.org/10.1007/s12119-011-9103-4

Hartmann, J. (2022). *Emotion English DistilRoBERTa-base*. https://huggingface.co/j-hartmann/emotion-english-distilroberta-base. Accessed: 14.02.2023.

Jang, S. M., & Lee, H. (2014). When Pop Music Meets a Political Issue: Examining How "Born This Way" Influences Attitudes Toward Gays and Gay Rights Policies. *Journal of Broadcasting & Electronic Media*, **58**(1), 114–130. https://doi.org/10.1080/08838151.2013.875023

Jobin, A., Ienca, M., & Vayena, E. (2019). The global landscape of AI ethics guidelines. *Nature Machine Intelligence*, **1**(9), 389–399. https://doi.org/10.1038/s42256-019-0088-2

Kaynak, O. (2021). The golden age of Artificial Intelligence. *Discover Artificial Intelligence*, **1**(1). https://doi.org/10.1007/s44163-021-00009-x

Khan, W., Ghazanfar, M. A., Azam, M. A., Karami, A., Alyoubi, K. H., & Alfakeeh, A. S. (2022). Stock market prediction using machine learning classifiers and social media, news. *Journal of Ambient Intelligence and Humanized Computing*, **13**(7), 3433–3456. https://doi.org/10.1007/s12652-020-01839-w

Medhat, W., Hassan, A., & Korashy, H. (2014). Sentiment analysis algorithms and applications: A survey. *Ain Shams Engineering Journal*, **5**(4), 1093–1113. https://doi.org/10.1016/j.asej.2014.04.011

Napier, K., & Shamir, L. (2018). Quantitative Sentiment Analysis of Lyrics in Popular Music. *Journal of Popular Music Studies*, **30**(4), 161–176. https://doi.org/10.1525/jpms.2018.300411

Oh, H., Goh, K.-Y., & Phan, T. Q. (2022). Are You What You Tweet? The Impact of Sentiment on Digital News Consumption and Social Media Sharing. *Information Systems Research*, Article isre.2022.1112. https://doi.org/10.1287/isre.2022.1112

Pavlik, J. V. (2023). Collaborating With ChatGPT: Considering the Implications of Generative Artificial Intelligence for Journalism and Media Education. *Journalism & Mass Communication Educator*, 107769582211495. https://doi.org/10.1177/10776958221149577

Pettijohn, T. F., & Sacco, D. F. (2009). The Language of Lyrics. *Journal of Language and Social Psychology*, **28**(3), 297–311. https://doi.org/10.1177/0261927X09335259

Pipalia, K., Bhadja, R., & Shukla, M. (2020). Comparative Analysis of Different Transformer Based Architectures Used in Sentiment Analysis. In *2020 9th International Conference System Modeling and Advancement in Research Trends (SMART)* (pp. 411–415). IEEE. https://doi.org/10.1109/SMART50582.2020.9337081

Romero, R. A., & Young, S. D. (2022). Public perceptions and implementation considerations on the use of artificial intelligence in health. *Journal of Evaluation in Clinical Practice*, **28**(1), 75–78. https://doi.org/10.1111/jep.13580

Russell, S. J., & Norvig, P. (2016). *Artificial intelligence: A modern approach* (Third edition, Global edition). *Always learning*. Pearson.

Smuha, N. A. (2021). From a 'race to AI' to a 'race to AI regulation': regulatory competition for artificial intelligence. *Law, Innovation and Technology*, **13**(1), 57–84. https://doi.org/10.1080/17579961.2021.1898300

Storey, V. C., & Park, E. H. (2022). An Ontology of Emotion Process to Support Sentiment Analysis. *Journal of the Association for Information Systems*, **23**(4), 999–1036. https://doi.org/10.17705/1jais.00749

Venkatesh, Morris, & Davis (2003). User Acceptance of Information Technology: Toward a Unified View. *MIS Quarterly*, **27**(3), 425. https://doi.org/10.2307/30036540

Wang, Z., Ho, S.-B., & Lin, Z. (2018). Stock Market Prediction Analysis by Incorporating Social and News Opinion and Sentiment. In *2018 IEEE International Conference on Data Mining Workshops (ICDMW)* (pp. 1375–1380). IEEE. https://doi.org/10.1109/ICDMW.2018.00195

Westerlund, M. (2019). The Emergence of Deepfake Technology: A Review. *Technology Innovation Management Review*, **9**(11), 39–52. https://doi.org/10.22215/timreview/1282
Wilksch, M., & Abramova, O. (2022). The Predictive Power of Social Media Sentiment for Short-Term Stock Movements. *Wirtschaftsinformatik 2022 Proceedings*.

Human–Computer Interaction and Social Online Behavior

The Broken Leg of Algorithm Appreciation: An Experimental Study on the Effect of Unobserved Variables on Advice Utilization

Dirk Leffrang

Abstract Despite the widespread use of machine learning algorithms, their effectiveness is limited by a phenomenon known as algorithm aversion. Recent research concluded that unobserved variables can cause algorithm aversion. However, the impact of an unobserved variable on algorithm aversion remains unclear. Previous studies focused on situations where humans had more variables available than algorithms. We extend this research by conducting an online experiment with 94 participants, systematically varying the number of observable variables to the advisor and the advisor type. Surprisingly, our results did not confirm that an unobserved variable had a negative effect on advice-taking. Instead, we found a positive impact in an algorithm appreciation scenario. This study provides new insights into the paradoxical behavior in which people weigh advice more despite having fewer variables, as they correct for the advisor's errors. Practitioners should consider this behavior when designing algorithms and account for user correction behavior.

Keywords Algorithm aversion · Data · Decision-making · Advice-taking · Human–computer interaction

1 Introduction

Algorithms are playing an ever-growing role in a wide range of decision-making processes, from the workplace to our personal lives (Maedche et al. 2019). Algorithm-powered systems offer valuable support thanks to their unparalleled ability to process large amounts of data. Not least because of this property, algorithms have been outperforming human experts in terms of accuracy for decades (see Grove et al. 2000). While algorithms have the potential to offer many benefits, sometimes their use is met with skepticism and distrust compared to human advisors. This phenomenon, known as algorithm aversion, has been studied in various contexts (Jussupow et al. 2020).

D. Leffrang (✉)
Paderborn University, Paderborn, Germany
e-mail: dirk.leffrang@uni-paderborn.de

D. Beverungen et al. (eds.), *Conceptualizing Digital Responsibility for the Information Age*, Lecture Notes in Information Systems and Organisation 74,
https://doi.org/10.1007/978-3-031-80119-8_12

For example, people prefer human advice to algorithmic advice when predicting the success of students (Dietvorst et al. 2015). However, inconclusive results exist as the opposite observation was made as well, termed algorithm appreciation (Logg et al. 2019).

One possible explanation for algorithm aversion is that algorithms may not take unique circumstances into account (Longoni et al. 2019). The "broken leg" scenario, proposed by Mehl (1954), illustrates how algorithms can overlook unique characteristics. While an algorithm may be good at predicting the probability of an event, it may fail to account for unobserved variables, such as a broken leg. In contrast, a human expert who is aware of the broken leg can use this information to make a more informed decision.

In summary, algorithms' strengths lie in processing large amounts of data. Weaknesses arise when the algorithm suffers from unobserved variable bias. Based on these two considerations, the broken leg scenario appears to be unfair to the algorithm as the human expert had more observed variables. Therefore, we pose the research question: *What is the impact of an unobserved variable on algorithm appreciation?*

We address our research question by systematically varying (1) human versus algorithm advisors and (2) unobserved versus observed variables. We conducted an online experiment with 94 participants. To measure the weight participants gave to the received advice, we used the Judge-Advisor System (JAS) framework, which we will explain later in the paper (Bonaccio & Dalal 2006; Logg et al. 2019). Surprisingly, our findings contradicted the idea that an unobserved variable would lead to less weight on advice. Participants gave more weight to the advice. Varying advisor types, we found algorithm appreciation. We found no significant interaction between these effects.

This study extends previous research by providing empirical evidence that algorithms lacking an unobserved variable can lead to less advice-taking compared to a human advisor who observes that variable. The findings highlight how people weigh advice more heavily even when they have an unobserved variable. This paradoxical behavior may be due to people correcting for the advisor's errors. To address this paradoxical behavior, practitioners may need to design algorithms that account for their user's correction behavior or provide more transparent explanations.

2 Related Work and Hypothesis Development

2.1 Related Work

The Judge-Advisor System (JAS) is a framework for assessing how much people integrate advice from external sources into their own decision-making. A judge—whether a decision maker in a real-life scenario or a participant in an experiment—faces a prediction task and makes an initial prediction. Afterward, she may consult an advisor, for example, an algorithm or a human expert. The judge forms her final prediction by combining the initial prediction with the advisor's prediction, which is discounted and weighted depending on factors such as the advisor's characteristics (Bonaccio & Dalal 2006).

There is an ongoing debate on whether people generally have an aversion to or appreciation for algorithms. One of the factors related to algorithm aversion is the decision context. Research has observed that algorithm aversion tends to be lower in more objective tasks (Castelo et al. 2019). People view actions that benefit others as more significant for their own personal development than actions that are motivated by financial gain. As a result, they place a greater value on exhibiting empathy and independence when making decisions in situations where others are the primary beneficiaries (Heßler et al. 2022). In our study, we focus on objective tasks to minimize any unintended correlations with the decision maker's personal characteristics.

2.2 *Hypothesis Development*

Similar to current research on algorithm aversion, research in psychology has examined the effectiveness of human clinical judgment versus algorithmic approaches. In this context, Meehl's "broken leg" scenario is a thought experiment highlighting the limitations of relying solely on algorithmic approaches to make a prediction, such as predicting the probability of a person going to the cinema (Meehl 1954). The human expert had more information about the broken leg than the algorithm in this scenario.

However, algorithmic approaches generally outperformed humans by 10% in terms of accuracy, according to a meta-review of Grove et al. (2000). The only systematic factor that can give humans an advantage over algorithmic approaches is having access to more data, as highlighted by the authors. Building on these insights from psychological research, we wanted to reproduce the anecdotal scenario of Meehl (1954):

Hypothesis 1 In an objective prediction task, people will use the advice of an algorithm less when it suffers from an unobserved variable than the advice of a human expert who observes it.

Meehl (1954) varies two factors simultaneously. Table 1 shows two situations that the scenario does not address. First, it is unclear whether an unobserved variable such as the broken leg would hinder advice-taking from the algorithm as much as it benefited the human expert. Second, it remains unclear whether advice from a human expert would be preferable if she suffered from the same unobserved variable.

People exhibited algorithm aversion when the algorithmic advisor was imperfect (Dietvorst et al. 2015). Although subsequent studies failed to establish a general pattern of aversion, Prahl & Van Swol (2017) did find evidence of algorithm aversion after receiving bad advice. However, after non-significant differences directly after bad advice, Leffrang et al. (2023) reported increasing algorithm appreciation over

Table 1 Potential outcomes in the broken leg scenario of Meehl (1954)

	Unobserved variable	Observed variable
Algorithm	yes	?
Human	?	yes

time. In another study, participants only exhibited aversion if they had previously seen the advisor's prediction performance (Berger et al. 2021).

Overall, research found algorithm appreciation in multiple contexts (e.g., Dijkstra et al. 1998; Logg et al. 2019). Human reliance on automation can also lead to a bias known as automation bias (Goddard et al. 2012). In light of these findings, algorithm aversion appears to be more prevalent in temporal or subjective settings. Therefore, we propose:

Hypothesis 2 In an objective prediction task, people will use the advice of an algorithm more than the advice of a human expert.

In a prior study, participants could choose four of five variables as input data for an algorithm. The participants' choice of input variables did not significantly affect algorithm aversion (Jung & Seiter 2021). However, participants had no choice about the number of observable variables and could not choose for the human condition. Incomplete information can lead to suboptimal decision-making, as demonstrated in Akerlof's (1970) study on market signaling. In the broken leg scenario, the author considered human experts superior to formal methods when they had more information (Meehl 1954). Given that more variables theoretically enable better predictions, we propose independent of the advisor type:

Hypothesis 3 In an objective prediction task, people will use the advice of an advisor less when the advisor suffers from an unobserved variable than the advice of an advisor who observes it.

Einhorn (1986) discusses the implications of deterministic and probabilistic worldviews for prediction. In a deterministic world, everything is causal and every event can be perfectly predicted. In contrast, a probabilistic world contains random errors that can prevent perfect predictions. Humans have a tendency to reinterpret the past in a way that reflects a deterministic worldview. However, if individuals rely on this reinterpretation to predict the future, they may encounter inconsistencies between their predictions and reality due to the probabilistic nature of events. Models behind algorithms are simplified representations of reality as they are limited by their input data. Instead of assuming perfect predictability, algorithms aim to minimize errors by taking a probabilistic approach, according to the author.

Algorithm aversion arises from people's tendencies to overlook the probabilistic nature of predictions and overestimate the human ability to make deterministic predictions based on intuition and experience (Highhouse 2008). For example, people may resist medical algorithms out of fear that the algorithms might overlook their unique characteristics (Longoni et al. 2019). Human advisors may receive more credibility than algorithms when an unobserved variable is present because the advisors can compensate for the missing information using their intuition and experience. Since its invention, machine learning has built on the idea of enhancing its performance through data and experience in an inductive manner (Mitchell 1997). Empirically, demonstrating the algorithm's ability to improve its prediction performance could mitigate algorithm aversion (Berger et al. 2021). Based on the idea that algorithmic performance improves with more variables, we hypothesize:

Hypothesis 4 The effect of advisor type on advice-taking is greater for an advisor when the advisor suffers from an unobserved variable compared to an advisor who observes it.

3 Research Design

To test our hypotheses, we conducted a reward-based online experiment. We preregistered the experiment before we ran it[1]. While incentivization may not always improve performance, previous studies suggest it can enhance performance in prediction tasks (Camerer & Hogarth 1999). This is why incentivized experiments are frequently utilized for algorithm aversion investigations (see Burton et al. 2020).

Due to uncertainty about the training data for the algorithm, we opted not to use the broken leg scenario. Instead, we chose to use a typical objective task that has been used in previous research, namely the staffing of a call center (e.g., Berger et al. 2021).

3.1 Procedure

Participants accessed the instructions for the experiment through an online survey tool (LimeSurvey). They had to imagine themselves as a manager in a call center, assigned the responsibility of managing staff. The call center had recently gained a new client, and as a result, it was necessary to make regular estimates of the number of incoming calls. This was crucial for the call center to make informed decisions about staffing. Figure 1 shows the procedure of the experiment. The task assigned to participants was to predict the number of calls for a specific day by following these steps:

1. We presented them with data for a particular day and asked them to make a prediction for that day's incoming calls.
2. After submitting their prediction, we displayed an advisor's estimate for the same day using past data. They then had the possibility to revise their initial forecast.

[1] Note that we reworded the research question and hypotheses to provide a better reading flow, but did not change their meaning https://aspredicted.org/QZS_8R9.

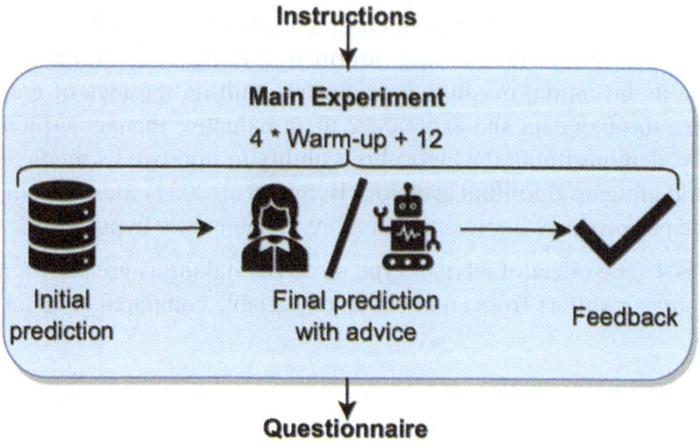

Fig. 1 Procedure of the experiment

3. Finally, we informed them of the actual number of phone calls.

As per our instructions, the number of calls on a specific day is primarily influenced by six variables:

- Quarter of the year (Q1 to Q4)
- Day of the month (1 to 31)
- Day of the week (Monday to Friday)
- Running of a promotion campaign (yes or no)
- Recent sales (above or below average)
- Recent website traffic (above or below average)

Berger et al. (2021) described the generation process behind the data in detail. Multiplying the factors for these six variables with a random influence determined the number of incoming calls. As in the experiment of Berger et al. (2021), we did not provide exact effect sizes of the variables. Instead, we showed visualizations displaying the effect sizes in comparison to an average day. For instance, the call center received an average amount of calls when there was no promotion and 20% more calls when there was a promotion. Participants also learned that the average daily call volume is 5000. We excluded the first four tasks as warm-up exercises from the subsequent data analysis.

3.2 Conditions and Participants

We employed a 2 × 2 within-subjects design with four conditions, varying in two factors:

1. Human versus algorithm

*You now have the possibility to adjust your initial estimate.

The estimate of the expert was: 3674

What is your estimate for the number of calls on the specified day?

Unfortunately, the expert was lacking the variable 'running a promotion campaign' when making this prediction.

Average number of calls	Quarter of the year	Day of the month	Day of the week	Running a promotion campaign	Recent sales	Recent website traffic
5000	Q1	8	Wednesday	yes	-5%	-10%

Fig. 2 Screenshot of the human condition with unobserved variable

2. Unobserved versus observed variable

The only distinction in the first factor was the origin of the advice provided. We informed the treatment group that the advice came from "an algorithm", while the control group received advice from "an expert". However, the actual advice given to both groups was the same.

Importantly, we informed participants in the unobserved variable condition that the advisor did not have the variable "promotion" when making predictions. Figure 2 shows an example of the stimuli in the experiment.

The experiment took place between February 2nd and February 13th. We offered an online experiment to third-year bachelor's students in a business informatics course at a medium-sized, IT-focused university in Europe. Participants got a bonus point for their final exam when they passed all attention checks and had a mean absolute percentage error (MAPE) below 0.1. They learned about these restrictions before the experiment and participation was voluntary. We excluded data from participants who failed to answer all of our questions, failed attention checks, consistently provided the same answers, or completed the tasks too quickly (i.e., less than 90 s for all tasks) or too slowly (i.e., more than two standard deviations above the mean participation time). We determined the necessary sample size for detecting a medium effect using G*Power (Faul et al. 2007), and the result was a minimum sample size of approximately 50. The test was a repeated measure, within factors test with Cohen's $f = 0.25$ (p. 355, Cohen 1988), indicating a medium effect size ($\alpha = 0.1$, power: 0.9, 1 group, 2 measurements).

3.3 *Model Specification*

In our experiment, we utilized the JAS paradigm and measured the Weight of Advice (WOA) as the dependent variable for each subject-task combination. WOA indicates the degree to which participants adopt either human or algorithmic advice (see Bonaccio & Dalal 2006):

$$WOA = \frac{|final\ prediction - intial\ prediction|}{|advisor's\ prediction - initial\ prediction|} \tag{1}$$

A value of zero indicates no adoption of the advice, while a value of one corresponds to full advice adoption. Based on earlier studies on algorithm appreciation (e.g., Logg et al. 2019), we performed Winsorization on any WOA values that were above 1 or below 0.

To analyze our data, we employed a linear mixed-effects model with varying intercepts for condition, participant, and task. Our dependent variable was WOA, and we defined each of the twelve prediction days as tasks. A combination of participant and task defined a task. We randomized the order of conditions for each participant.

A dummy variable indicated whether the participant was in the algorithm (Algorithm = 1) or human (Algorithm = 0) condition. Another dummy variable indicated whether the advisor had the promotion as an unobserved variable (Unobserved variable = 1). It resulted in the following generic model specification:

$$Y_i = \beta + \gamma_{algorithm[i]} + \delta_{unobservedvariable[i]} + \zeta_{participant[i]} + \eta_{task[i]} + \epsilon_i$$

4 Results

4.1 Model-Free Evidence

We obtained predictions from 145 people. After applying the exclusion criteria and dropping the warm-up tasks as mentioned above, 94 participants remained with 1128 predictions. Figure 3 displays the WOA by condition. There are no obvious differences between the algorithmic and human conditions. Surprisingly, the distributions indicate higher levels of WOA for the conditions where there was an unobserved variable. It appears that participants weighted the advice more if the advisor suffered from an unobserved variable.

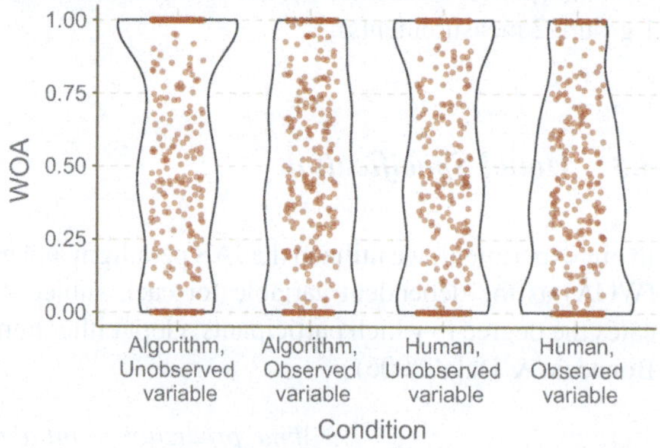

Fig. 3 Violin plots for WOA values by condition

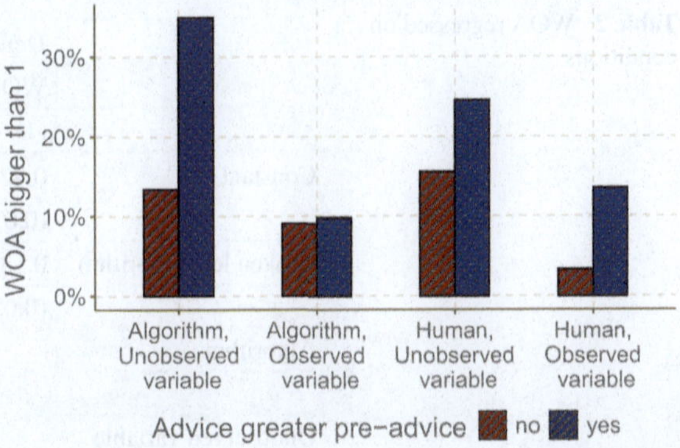

Fig. 4 Overshooting plot for WOA values by condition

Especially in the unobserved variable conditions, WOA took the value one which indicates potential overshooting due to the Winsorization. Overshooting happens for example when the participant's initial prediction was 80 and the advice was 100, but the final decision is 120. In this case, WOA takes a value greater than 1. However, Winsorization limits WOA to the value of 1. Figure 4 shows the fraction of overshooting by condition and by WOA values being bigger than 1. Notably, when the advice was greater than the pre-advice prediction of the participant in the algorithm, unobserved variable condition, 34.9% of the final predictions overshooted the advice. For the human, unobserved variable condition, 24.6% of the final predictions overshooted the advice. In 67.1% of all predictions, the participants' initial estimate was smaller than the advisor's predictions.

4.2 Estimation Results

Our first hypothesis claimed that in an objective prediction task, people will use the advice of an algorithm that lacks an unobserved variable less than the advice of a human expert who observes it. In order to test this hypothesis, we generated a subset for the two conditions presented in Table 1 in the Hypothesis Development (indicated by the label "yes"). We introduced a new variable "Broken leg algorithm", which took the value one if algorithm = 1 and unobserved variable = 1. The variable took the value zero if both were zero.

To test our hypothesis, we regressed WOA on the experimental condition described above, with participant and task differences taken into account as controls. We omitted observations that had undefined WOA differences (due to division by zero). Table 2 model (1) shows the results regarding our first hypothesis.

Surprisingly, the findings indicate that we cannot support our first hypothesis. On the contrary, the results suggested that for algorithms with an unobserved variable, there was about 13.6%-point more weight of advice compared to human advisors who observe that variable. This result was statistically significant ($p < 0.01$) and

Table 2 WOA regressed on conditions

	Dependent variable:		
	WOA		
	(1)	(2)	(3)
Constant	0.422***	0.420***	0.421***
	(0.035)	(0.032)	(0.033)
Broken leg Algorithm	0.136***		
	(0.024)		
Algorithm		0.047***	0.046*
		(0.017)	(0.025)
Unobserved variable		0.089***	0.088***
		(0.017)	(0.025)
Algorithm:			0.002
Unobserved variable			(0.036)
Participant?	✓	✓	✓
Task?	✓	✓	✓
Observations	564	1128	1128
Log likelihood	− 167.373	− 297.528	− 299.936
Akaike Inf. Crit	344.746	607.055	613.872
Bayesian Inf. Crit	366.422	637.225	649.070

Note * $p < 0.1$; ** $p < 0.05$; *** $p < 0.01$

appeared to be economically meaningful with regard to an average WOA of 0.559 across all conditions.

Our second hypothesis stated that people will use the advice of an algorithm more than the advice of a human expert. Just like for the previous hypothesis, we controlled for participant and task differences in model (2). The results implied that algorithms increase the weight of advice by 4.7%-points in comparison to humans ($p < 0.01$). Hence, we find support for our second hypothesis.

Our third hypothesis stated that people will use the advice of an advisor that lacks an unobserved variable less than the advice of an advisor that observes it. In contrast to our hypothesis, the coefficient in model (2) was positive and significant ($p < 0.01$). The results indicated that an unobserved variable increases the weight of advice by 8.9%-points. Therefore, we cannot support our initial hypothesis.

Our fourth hypothesis stated that the effect of advisor type on advice-taking is greater for an advisor who lacks an unobserved variable compared to an advisor who observes it.

To test this hypothesis, we created model (3) which also examines the interaction effect of the algorithm and an unobserved variable. Our results did not provide sufficient evidence for an interaction effect, as they did not reveal significant differences regarding the interaction term (Algorithm:Unobserved variable, $p > 0.10$). Thus, we do not find support for our last hypothesis.

The models had an intra-class correlation (ICC) of 0.27, 0.30, and 0.30 for the Participant variable. For the Task variable, the ICC was 0.06, 0.04, and 0.04. The ICC for Task (less than 0.05) suggests that it could be excluded. Doing so only led to minimal changes to the coefficients of interest, and the p-value for the coefficient of algorithm in model (3) was significant at the 5% level.

5 Discussion

In this paper, we examined the impact of an unobserved variable on algorithm aversion. We conducted an incentivized online experiment in a call center setting to address our research question. Surprisingly, we were unable to generalize the insights of the broken leg thought experiment to empirical advice-taking in a repeated measures design. Our results suggest an underlying effect of unobserved variables leading to more advice-taking.

We can confirm algorithm appreciation for an objective prediction task. Prior research argued that algorithm aversion is more likely for subjective tasks (Castelo et al. 2019). Algorithm appreciation is not necessarily a cognitive bias as algorithms have been outperforming humans for several decades (e.g., Grove et al. 2000). However, we gave imperfect advice and did not observe algorithm aversion as in prior studies (e.g., Dietvorst et al. 2015).

In a similar setting, researchers observed different levels of algorithm aversion and appreciation depending on the familiarity with the algorithm (Berger et al. 2021). In contrast to this study, we measured WOA at different time points. There can be temporal fluctuations in algorithm appreciation depending on the prediction performance (Prahl & Van Swol 2017). Therefore, we controlled for task-level differences between the time points. In the long run, we can confirm a general algorithm appreciation for objective tasks (Leffrang et al. 2023).

We cannot confirm that people use the advice of an advisor less when the advisor suffered from an unobserved variable. On the contrary, our results imply that people weighted the advice stronger if the advisor suffered from an unobserved variable. We did not observe a significant interaction effect of advisor type and unobserved variables. The ability to choose input variables for an algorithm had no significant impact on advice-taking in prior research (Jung & Seiter 2021). We extend this observation by identifying the number of observable variables as a relevant factor.

One possible explanation for our results could be that people corrected for the mistake the advisor made because of the unobserved variable. As highlighted in Fig. 4 in the model-free evidence, there was more overshooting in the unobserved variable condition compared to the observed variable condition when the advice was greater than the pre-advice prediction.

Participants knew that promotions increase the number of calls by approximately 20%. This is particularly noteworthy considering that 67.1% of the initial predictions fell below the advisors' predictions.

Instead of discounting the quality of the advice, people corrected the advisor's mistake. Paradoxically, correcting for an unobserved variable could lead to a greater weight being assigned to the advice compared to when the variable is observed.

To illustrate the logical nature of this paradoxical behavior, let's consider a simplified example. Imagine a scenario where a judge initially predicts the number of calls to be 80, while an advisor predicts 100. If participants were to assign equal weight to both predictions (see Logg et al. 2019), the final prediction would be 90, resulting in a WOA of 0.5. However, if the judge presumed that the advisor was unaware of a variable that would increase the prediction by 20%, the corrected prediction from the advisor would be 120. In such a scenario, giving equal weight to the judge's initial prediction and the corrected advisor's prediction would result in a final prediction of 100. As the advisor's actual estimate remains at 100, WOA increases from 0.5 to 1. Consequently, knowledge about unobserved variables can amplify the weighting of advice.

In Mehl's thought experiment about estimating the probability of going to a cinema, a judge would have been able to correct the algorithm's error if she had the information that the leg was broken. Since we gave the same numerical advice in our experiment across all four conditions, such a correction was unnecessary.

Observing a previously unobserved variable but leaving the performance unchanged might explain differences to Mehl's thought experiment in the case of a repeated measure design. In Mehl's application case, the algorithm predicted that the person would go to the cinema. However, the human expert predicted that the person would not go to the movies because of the broken leg. If the person goes to the movies despite the broken leg, then it will be rational to trust the algorithm next week, since the additional information from the human expert did not add any value.

We cannot confirm an interaction between the type of advisor and an unobserved variable. For our fourth hypothesis, we hypothesized that observing a previously unobserved variable would lead to a more deterministic worldview (see Einhorn 1986; Highhouse 2008). Future research can investigate to what extent multiple variables lead to such an effect.

This study adds to the current discussion on algorithm aversion versus appreciation by highlighting the importance of data. In light of the ongoing discourse surrounding the impact of AI systems operating as black boxes (Maedche et al. 2019), our research emphasizes data as an essential property of the decision-making process. Input data into algorithms can have an impact on decision-making even though the exact function of the algorithms is not explained (Wachter et al. 2018). However, more variables do not necessarily lead to more advice being taken. People can correct mistakes they think the advisor is making.

Practitioners need to consider these dynamics when designing effective advice-giving systems. Incorporating human imperfections into recommender systems can increase overall productivity (Sun et al. 2021). An unobserved variable, while keeping the performance constant can increase advice-taking. With this knowledge, practitioners can prevent human behavior from turning a feature into a bug.

6 Limitations and Outlook

It is important to note that our findings were based on a single experimental study. Although our power analysis suggested that our sample size is sufficient, we acknowledge the need for future research. To address this limitation, future research should conduct additional experiments and expand our sample size in order to enhance the robustness and generalizability of our conclusions.

We did not alter performance to vary only one factor between the conditions. In a real-world setting, the performance in the unobserved variable conditions will probably be lower if the advisor does not perform overfitting. Also, participants knew the approximate effect size of the unobserved variable, which is not always possible. Future work can vary the performance of the advisors and the effect size as additional degrees of freedom.

This research focused on objective tasks. More subjective contexts may trigger desires in the forms of empathy and autonomy (Heßler et al. 2022). Researchers can investigate whether there is an interaction between unobserved variables and application context.

Within-subjects designs bear the risk of carry-over effects. We chose this design to make it easier for participants to notice the difference between the unobserved and observed variable conditions. Future work can examine the experimental setup in a between-subjects design.

Current research frequently utilizes WOA as the dependent variable. However, potential analyses should take into account the limitations of WOA, such as overshooting, as indicated by Bonaccio & Dalal (2006). We utilized Winsorization to deal with overshooting. Future research can examine other measures of advice-taking.

We plan to investigate other properties of data such as the amount of data points and adding multiple variables to advisors. If we understand algorithms and their interaction with data better, we can also improve human–computer interaction.

References

Akerlof, G. A., 1970, "The market for "lemons": Quality uncertainty and the market mechanism", *The Quarterly Journal of Economics*, **84**(3), 488–500.

Berger, B., Adam, M., Rühr, A. & Benlian, A., 2021, "Watch me improve - Algorithm aversion and demonstrating the ability to learn", *Business and Information Systems Engineering*, **63**(1), 55–68.

Bonaccio, S. & Dalal, R. S., 2006, "Advice taking and decision-making: An integrative literature review, and implications for the organizational sciences", *Organizational Behavior and Human Decision Processes*, **101**(2), 127–151.

Burton, J. W., Stein, M.-K. & Jensen, T. B., 2020, "A systematic review of algorithm aversion in augmented decision making", *Journal of Behavioral Decision Making*, **33**(2), 220–239.

Camerer, C. F. & Hogarth, R. M., 1999, "The effects of financial incentives in experiments: A review and capital-labor-production framework", *Journal of Risk and Uncertainty*, **19**(1–3), 7–42.

Castelo, N., Bos, M. W. & Lehmann, D. R., 2019, "Task-dependent algorithm aversion", *Journal of Marketing Research*, **56**(5), 809–825.

Cohen, J., 1988, *Statistical power analysis for the behavioral sciences*, Lawrence Erlbaum Associates, Hillsdale, NJ, USA.

Dietvorst, B. J., Simmons, J. P. & Massey, C., 2015, "Algorithm aversion: People erroneously avoid algorithms after seeing them err.", *Journal of Experimental Psychology: General*, **144**(1), 114–126.

Dijkstra, J. J., Liebrand, W. B. G. & Timminga, E., 1998, "Persuasiveness of expert systems", *Behaviour and Information Technology*, **17**(3), 155–163.

Einhorn, H. J., 1986, "Accepting error to make less error", *Journal of Personality Assessment*, **50**(3), 387–395.

Faul, F., Erdfelder, E., Lang, A.-G. & Buchner, A., 2007, "G*Power 3: A flexible statistical power analysis program for the social, behavioral, and biomedical sciences", *Behavior Research Methods*, **39**(2), 175–191.

Goddard, K., Roudsari, A. & Wyatt, J. C., 2012, "Automation bias: A systematic review of frequency, effect mediators, and mitigators", *Journal of the American Medical Informatics Association*, **19**(1), 121–127.

Grove, W. M., Zald, D. H., Lebow, B. S., Snitz, B. E. & Nelson, C., 2000, "Clinical versus mechanical prediction: A meta-analysis", *Psychological Assessment*, **12**(1), 19–30.

Heßler, P. O., Pfeiffer, J. & Hafenbrädl, S., 2022, "When self-humanization leads to algorithm aversion: What users want from decision support systems on prosocial microlending platforms", *Business and Information Systems Engineering*, **64**(3), 275–292.

Highhouse, S., 2008, "Stubborn reliance on intuition and subjectivity in employee selection", *Industrial and Organizational Psychology*, **1**(3), 333–342.

Jung, M. & Seiter, M., 2021, "Towards a better understanding on mitigating algorithm aversion in forecasting: An experimental study", *Journal of Management Control*, **32**(4), 495–516.

Jussupow, E., Benbasat, I. & Heinzl, A., 2020, *Why are we averse towards algorithms? A comprehensive literature review on algorithm aversion*, in 'Proceedings of the European Conference on Information Systems', An Online AIS Conference, pp. 1–16.

Leffrang, D., Bösch, K. & Müller, O., 2023, *Do people recover from algorithm aversion? An experimental study of algorithm aversion over time*, in 'Proceedings of the Hawaii International Conference on System Sciences', Lahaina, HI, USA , pp. 4016–4025.

Logg, J. M., Minson, J. A., Moore, D. A. & States, U., 2019, "Algorithm appreciation: People prefer algorithmic to human judgment", *Organizational Behavior and Human Decision Processes*, **151**, 90–103.

Longoni, C., Bonezzi, A. & Morewedge, C. K., 2019, "Resistance to medical artificial intelligence", *Journal of Consumer Research*, **46**(4), 629–650.

Maedche, A., Legner, C., Benlian, A., Berger, B., Gimpel, H., Hess, T., Hinz, O., Morana, S. & Söllner, M., 2019, "AI-based digital assistants: Opportunities, threats, and research perspectives", *Business and Information Systems Engineering*, **61**(4), 535–544.

Meehl, P. E., 1954, *Clinical versus statistical prediction: A theoretical analysis and a review of the evidence.*, University of Minnesota Press, Minneapolis.

Mitchell, T., 1997, *Machine Learning*, McGraw-Hill Science/Engineering/Math.

Prahl, A. & Van Swol, L., 2017, "Understanding algorithm aversion: When is advice from automation discounted?", *Journal of Forecasting*, **36**(6), 691–702.

Sun, J., Zhang, D., Hu, H. & Van Mieghem, J. A., 2021, "Predicting human discretion to adjust algorithmic prescription: A large-scale field experiment in warehouse operations", *Management Science*, **68**(2), 846–865.

Wachter, S., Mittelstadt, B. & Russell, C., 2018, "Counterfactual explanations without opening the black box: Automated decisions and the GDPR", *Harvard Journal of Law & Technology*, **31**(2), 1–52.

A State of the Art Overview on Biosignal-Based User-Adaptive Video Conferencing Systems

Julia Seitz, Chiara Krisam, and Ivo Benke

Abstract Video conferencing systems are widely used in times of distributed teams since they support flexible work arrangements. However, they have negative impacts on users, such as lacking eye gaze or zoom fatigue. Adaptive interventions in video conferences based on user behavior provide interesting solutions to overcome these challenges, for example, by alerting users when looking tired. Specifically, biosignals measured by sensors like microphones or eye-trackers are a promising basis for adaptive interventions. To provide an overview of current biosignal-based user-adaptive video conferencing systems, we conducted a systematic literature review and identified 24 publications. We summarize existing knowledge in a morphological box and outline further research directions. Thereby, a focus on biooptical signals is visible. Current adaptations target audience feedback, expression understanding and eye gaze mostly by image and representation modifications. In future, we recommend including further biosignals and addressing more diverse problems by investigating adaptation capabilities of further software elements.

Keywords Video conferencing system · Adaptation · Systematic literature review

1 Introduction

In recent years, we see an increase in the use of video conferencing systems (VCS) when humans want to collaborate and interact across physical distances. For example, the use of VCS for corporate communication arose from approximately 50% in 2018,

J. Seitz (✉) · C. Krisam · I. Benke
Institute of Information Systems and Marketing, Karlsruhe Institute of Technology, Karlsruhe, Germany
e-mail: julia.seitz@kit.edu

C. Krisam
e-mail: chiara.krisam@kit.edu

I. Benke
e-mail: ivo.benke@kit.edu

D. Beverungen et al. (eds.), *Conceptualizing Digital Responsibility for the Information Age*, Lecture Notes in Information Systems and Organisation 74,
https://doi.org/10.1007/978-3-031-80119-8_13

to 72% in 2022 (Bitkom 2022) and managers predict to more frequently use VCS beyond the pandemic (Skillscouter 2022). However, there exist multiple challenges with VCS for productivity and well-being, such as lacking eye contact, lacking joint attention, reduced audience feedback, or fatigue due to prolonged, frequent meetings (Fauville et al. 2021; Kelly 2020; Karl et al. 2021). Despite several decades of research on video-mediated communication, to date, these problems are not yet solved in practice and research. Research has carved out a potential reason: the fact that individual VCS users differ from each other by individual characteristics, needs, and behavior (Döring et al. 2022; Valkenburg & Peter 2013). Moreover, the situations in which such problems arise are dynamic and not static. For example, they depend not only on the user's characteristics but also on the context and timing in the meeting. Therefore, it is challenging to design a VCS that fits all users and provides holistic support in all situations.

However, we increasingly see suggestions from research and practice, that the interface of the system should be able to react to problematic situations in video conferences and change the presentation of participants (Kaptelinin 2023, Pexip 2023, Seitz 2022, Abramova et al. 2021). One example might be to display personal status information such as the emotion or the stress level of VCS participants. As another example, one may show the presenter how attentive his audience is to allow the presenter to include breaks meaningfully or change the way of presentation when the audience is tired or bored (Sun et al. 2019; Kaptelinin 2023). Or, the other way around, the audience could be informed which part of a slide the presenter is currently gazing at to follow the presentation more closely (Langner et al. 2022). Besides, information about individual users may be useful to document fatiguing effects after a long day of meetings, and issue break recommendations or modify software elements that may increase fatigue, such as the self-view (Epstein 2020; Seitz et al. 2022) .

One approach to designing VCS is by making them user-adaptive and biosignal-based. Adaptive systems are systems that are able to change their behavior to meet the needs of users (Feigh et al. 2012). Thereby, this system class is comparable to established systems in information systems that are adaptable to the user, such as websites making use of adaptations based on behavioral data or user group characteristics (Reinecke & Bernstein 2013, White & Morris 2007).

User-adaptive systems require the continuous collection of information about the users. One key input source therefore are biosignals, especially in NeuroIS (Riedl & Léger 2016; Hettinger et al. 2003). Biosignals are defined by Schultz et al. (2013) as autonomous signals produced by living organisms and can be measured energetically using sensors. In VCS, we believe that biosignals may provide meaningful information, as the main input and output channels of the meetings are audio and video signals, which provide a broad range of verbal and non-verbal biosignals. In contrast to more traditional information systems, behavioral log and click data is less frequent available. Therefore, to collect biosignals, various types of sensors can be employed. This may cover existing cameras and microphones used in video conferences or established sensors such as eye-tracking or electroencephalography devices. Moreover, new wearable devices, may be beneficial to collect biosignals such as the heart rate when users are working in a mobile setup (Knierim et al. 2022; Zheng et al. 2014). Despite their enormous potential, however, to the best of our knowledge, there is no structured overview of biosignal-based user-adaptive VCS. We thus aim to answer the following question:

What is the state of the art of biosignal-based user-adaptive video conferencing systems (VCS) and what are future research directions?

To answer this research question, we conducted a structured literature review and analyzed 24 publications. We contribute with a conceptual framework for user-adaptive VCS based on existing definitions, we review and classify existing research, and we propose future research directions.

2 Conceptual Foundations

We aim to identify research that uses biosignals to design user-adaptive systems, particularly VCS. This interplay between human and technology is reflected in physiological computing. Subsequently, we describe the core concepts biosignals and user adaptation.

2.1 Biosignals

According to Schultz et al. (2013), a biosignal is an autonomous signal produced by an organism and measurable through sensors. Biosignals can be distinguished according to their physical properties in different categories: bioacoustic, biochemical, bioelectric, biomagnetic, biokinematic, biooptical, and biothermal (Telaar et al. 2014; Schultz et al. 2013). Sensors for the measurement of these signals differ between these types and also among the particular human signals. Depending on the sensor used for measurement, signals can belong to different categories. Most important in video conferencing are biooptical and bioacoustic signals. Biooptical signals are captured by a camera such as the movement of the eyes measured via eye-tracking or facial expressions extracted from video feeds. According to Schultz et al. (2013), biokinematic signals include signals such as blood pressure (BP) or pulse rate (PR). Also motion of the extremities or facial expressions (if measured via kinematic sensors) can be listed in this category (Telaar et al. 2014; Schultz et al. 2013). Bioacoustic signals cover signals that emanate from the voice. Furthermore, electrical signals are measured by detecting the potential difference between two electrodes, including signals from the peripheral nervous system such as electrodermal activity (EDA) or electrocardiograms (ECG), or from the central nervous system such as brain activity from electroencephalography (EEG).

Based on these signals, the biocybernetic loop describes the process which is underlying physiological computing and NeuroIS (Fairclough 2017; Pope et al.

1995). The biocybernetic loop is an iterative feedback loop that follows three steps: collection, analysis, and translation (Fairclough 2011). During the first step "collection" the signals are accumulated. Depending on the type of signals different measurement methods and sensors, like ECG or eye-tracking, can be applied. In the step "analysis" the signals are processed and artifacts can be identified. Fairclough (2017) mentions for instance the mapping of signals to emotional states. These artifacts can be utilized in the technology in the third step "translation". One example is the use of artifacts as commands in a brain-computer interface (BCI) to control the technology (Zander & Kothe 2011). Since the model represents a loop, following this step, a new iteration can be initiated.

2.2 *Adaptive Systems*

The term adaptation was shaped primarily by the field of biology and describes the adjustment of an organism to react to changes in its environment. However, the terminology "adaptive system" is also present in the Information Systems (IS) and Human–Computer Interaction (HCI) community. Feigh et al. define adaptive systems as "the technological component of joint human machine systems that can change their behavior to meet the changing needs of their users, often without explicit instructions from their users" (Feigh et al. 2012, p. 1009). The definition implies that the user can partially contribute to the adaptation. This differs from other definitions of adaptive systems, which describe adaptive systems more narrowly (see e.g., Benyon & Murray (1993)). On top, the paper includes a taxonomy for adaptations, which states that even small adaptations such as the highlighting of information already represents an adaptation.

Considering our use case of VCS, it is interesting to already look at such small adaptations as they might be helpful for users to receive direct feedback on their biosignals. For example, it might be helpful for users if the system recognizes when they are not attentive and provides feedback on the inattentiveness. In this case, the system itself would not have to change, but only support in alerting user behavior. Besides, users could change something in the system themselves after the system made a suggestion. For example, a recommendation to show or hide specific speakers could be helpful to highlight the person who is currently speaking. In this case, there is no direct adaptation by the system itself, but by the user.

In order to cover as many use cases as possible, we will use a very broad definition of adaptive systems in this paper. Based on the biocybernetic loop, we therefore define different types of adaptation mechanisms (see Fig. 1). Adaptation mechanism is used as an umbrella term for all actions along the biocybernetic loop where an adaption of the interface or functionality of the system takes place based on the biosignals of the users. In the case of VCS, it is important to mention that the adaptation mechanisms for the user are not necessarily based on the user's own biosignals. Rather, the signals of the interlocutor or a group of interlocutors are used for the modification of the system. Feedback is the simplest form of an adaptation mechanism. Here, biosignals

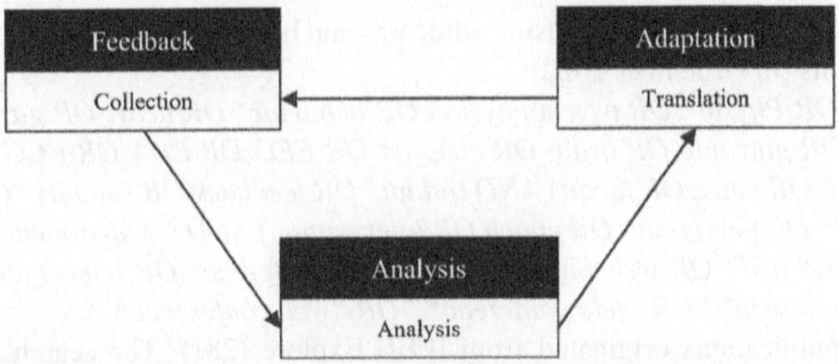

Fig. 1 Adaptation mechanisms (black) based on biocybernetic loop (white)

are collected, processed, and reflected back to the user in a form that the user can understand. During the analysis, the biosignals are subjected to an intermediate step. As in the biocybernetic loop, human states may be identified and reported to the user. During adaptation, in the ongoing also called deep adaptation, a modification of the system is automatically carried out based on the biosignals.

3 Research Method

3.1 Systematic Literature Review

To answer the research question we adopted the approach for systematic literature reviews by Webster & Watson (2002). The identification of the relevant literature involved three steps: First, a search string was utilized to identify literature in relevant databases. In the next step, the literature was screened using previously defined criteria, first on the basis of title and abstract and then on the basis of the full text. In the third step, the remaining literature was subjected to a forward and backward search. We performed the initial search on the three databases IEEE Explore, ACM Digital Library and AIS e-Library which are well established in the HCI, IS and computer science communities. We included only literature in English language, published in a peer-reviewed outlet after the year 2000 in our search.

The search string for the keyword search is based on the three components biosignals, VCS and adaptation mechanisms. Through testing different variations of search strings, several insights were gained on the keywords needed for the string. We noticed that some publications did not mention the term "biosignal" itself, although they were relevant for us. To avoid missing these publications, common biosignals were included in the search string. We also wanted to include systems that provide feedback, either directly or after analyzing the signals. Therefore, in addition, keywords describing feedback systems were included in the search string. Words were iteratively tested and added to the search string based on the results of the search. The final search string, using wildcards and boolean operators, identified 367 publications (in December 2022):

(Bio OR Physio* OR psychophysio* OR behavior* OR heart OR gaze OR eye OR skin OR galvanic OR brain OR electro* OR EEG OR EDA OR ECG OR GSR OR speech OR voice OR facial) AND (adapt* OR feedback OR support* OR aware OR sensit* OR personali* OR coach OR intervention) AND ("video-mediated" OR "video mediated" OR webconferenc* OR videoconferenc* OR teleconferenc* OR "video conferenc*" OR "tele conferenc*" OR "web conference*")*

Most publications originated from IEEE Explore (281). The search on ACM returned 78 publications, while the search on AISeL returned only eight publications. Afterward, we filtered the retrieved literature based on the following exclusion criteria (C):

C1 The article studies systems that work with biosignals as input.

C2 The article studies video conferencing systems (VCS).

C3 The article studies systems that give feedback on or adapt based on biosignals.

We applied the exclusion criteria to title and abstract of the publication set and after applying C1, 51 publications remained. After applying C2, 37, and after C3, 32 publications remained. Using the full texts as a basis, another 13 publications were sorted out. Next, we performed a forward and a backward search. This identified another five relevant papers, so that the final literature selection consisted of 24 publications.

3.2 Conceptual Framework of Analysis

To analyze the identified studies, we derived a conceptual framework of analysis based on the key concepts of this review. The classes used for the concept matrix correspond to the three concepts that were considered in this review: biosignals (1), VCS (2), and adaptation mechanisms (3). Based on this separation, subclasses were identified top-down from literature and bottom-up using inductive reasoning based on the identified literature (Nickerson et al. 2013). We used an iterative process involving the first and second author and derived subclasses and categories for each subclass. In a first step, the second author screened all publications and coded them in detail with regard to biosignals, VCS, and adaptation mechanism named in the publication. Afterward, we aimed to identify the most distinguishable elements in our publication set by discussing the differences of the papers and drawing on subclasses used in comparable publications (e.g., Loewe & Nadj (2020)). Subsequently, the second author mapped all publications to the aggregated categories based on the codes and the first and second author again verified the correct assignment of the publication to each category.

For **biosignals**, the categories defined by Schultz et al. (2013) were considered as subclasses. In our paper, we only report the signal categories that have been collected at least once. For the class of biosignals, we followed Schultz et al. (2013)

and used the categories biokinematic, biooptical, bioelectric, biothermal, and bioacoustic signals. For the class of **video conferencing systems (VCS)**, we observed the use of avatars (2.1) replacing the original video of the meeting partner. Similarly, we categorized whether systems used a three-dimensional (3D) or VR setting (2.2) instead of a two-dimensional (2D) image. For **adaptation mechanisms**, we differentiate the subclasses adaptation mechanism type, the direction, the target state, the representation, and the use of AI. For the subclass adaptation mechanism type (3.1) we identified the categories feedback, analysis, and deep adaptation. Deep adaptation refers to the adaptation in the biocybernetic loop, *deep adaptation* in our framework. The second subclass describes the direction of the adaptation, either whether the adaptation mechanism is applied for both parties (bidirectional) or one party (one directional) (3.2). Third, we distinguish between the target states (3.3) of the adaptation mechanism as an equivalent of the goal the adaptation aims to achieve. The following topics were identified: eye-contact and attention support, emotion and expression understanding, cognitive user state understanding, support for meeting performance, feedback on the audience and technical support for better immersion. Closely related to the target state and the aforementioned type of adaptation, the representation of the adaptation mechanism was examined (3.4). Finally, the intention of the use of artificial intelligence (AI) was classified (3.5). Following the types of adaptation mechanisms in 3.1, we distinguish the use of AI to gather the signals, to perform the analysis, or as actual deep adaptation technique of the representation.

4 Results

In the following, we first provide descriptive results on the publications and afterward describe the conceptual analysis. Therefore, we use the morphological box derived from our conceptual framework depicted in Fig. 2 and name exemplary publications for each category. A detailed categorization of all publications is visible here: https://osf.io/m72ny/?view_only=5dcb02caa9914c37887a32426b868acf.

4.1 Descriptive Results

Most articles (79%) were published in the last ten years (since 2012), with most papers published in 2018 and 2022, with respectively four and three publications. 18 articles were published in conference proceedings (75%) and six in journals (25%). All but one paper focus on the artifact development, e.g., the development of an user-adaptive VCS. Furthermore, 22 papers describe the evaluation. In 10 of the 22 papers, a proof of concept test was performed. This involved analyzing existing data to test the feasibility of the prototype. The remaining 13 papers involved a user study in a laboratory. In six cases, 10–19 participants were involved, in five cases there were 20–40 participants and in two cases the study involved more than 100 participants.

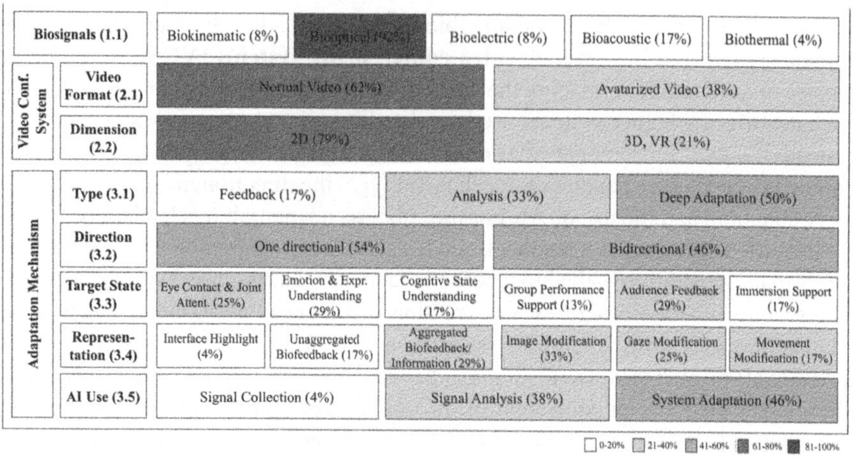

Fig. 2 Conceptual Framework (Percentage: share of publications addressing the category)

A between-subject design was used in five cases, and a within-subjects design in the other eight cases. The data collection was carried out by observing the participants in seven cases, and by self-reported measures in 12 cases. A combination of both methods was used in six cases. In all cases, the participants were actual users of the (prospective) systems.

4.2 Conceptual Results

Biosignals Except for two publications (Baig & GholamHosseini 2013, Tan et al. 2014), biooptical signals were involved in all publications (92%). Thereby, most frequently, facial expressions were analyzed (58%, e.g., Carter et al. (2016), Li et al. (2015)). Here, the camera image was mostly analyzed with the help of an AI (e.g., Menychtas et al. (2019), Murali et al. (2021)). In just under half of the studies, eye gaze was measured (42%, e.g., Carter et al. (2016), Otsuki et al. (2018)). In most cases, eye movements were recorded with a standard camera and analyzed later (7 publications, e.g., Pai et al. (2021), Schwartz et al. (2020)). Special eye-tracking devices were employed in three cases (Otsuki et al. 2018; Rae et al. 2011; Roberts et al. 2009). Head gestures were input signal in seven cases (29%, e.g., Murali et al. (2021)). As biokinematic signals, blood pressure and pulse rate were measured (8%, Baig & GholamHosseini (2013), Tan et al. (2014)). Bioelectric signals were recorded in two cases (8%). Thereby, EDA data (Tan et al. 2014) helped meeting participants assess the condition of their communication partner or an ECG (Baig & GholamHosseini 2013) was administered to track the patient's condition. Bioacoustic signals were measured in four cases (17%, e.g., Carter et al. (2016)). Similar to facial expressions, the voice was recorded with standard microphones, processed, and then analyzed, sometimes with the help of an AI (Rojas et al. 2022; Taguchi et al. 2018). In almost half of the studies, only a single kind of signal was recorded (46%, e.g., Li et al. (2015), Takemae et al. (2005)). Almost as often, two different kinds of signals were in use (33%, e.g., Murali et al. (2021), Song et al. (2018)). Among these, prominent combinations involved two different biooptical signals or voice input in addition to a biooptical signal (Rojas et al. 2022; Samrose 2018; Taguchi et al. 2018). Six publications involved three or more kinds of signals (e.g., Carter et al. (2016), Rae et al. (2011)).

Video Conferencing System Video Format: There were nine publications (38%) where the image of the person was not displayed directly (e.g., Carter et al. (2016), Nakazato et al. (2014)). Instead, a form of **avatar** (2.1) was displayed that was adapted to the person and their facial expression. Three cases can be distinguished. In the first case, the video of the person was taken and their facial expression was *mapped* to a previously defined avatar (Oh et al. 2016). In the second case, the actual image of the person was *abstracted*. A filter was applied to the image so that the video of the person would appear in a cartoon character style (Carter et al. 2016). In the third case, the face of a person is *reproduced* and placed on an avatar in a 3D environment (e.g., Rae et al. (2011), Roberts et al. (2009)). Often, the facial expression had to be reproduced because the subjects were wearing VR glasses (Schwartz et al. 2020; Song et al. 2018). Besides, in one system instead of facial expressions, an abstract representation of a human indicating its physiological measurements, such as pulsing a heart, was displayed next to the video of a person (Tan et al. 2014).

Dimension: In five publications (21%), the environment for the VCS was 3D (2.2, e.g., Rae et al. (2011), Roberts et al. (2009)). All other publications used 2D software.

Adaptation Mechanisms Type: Four systems only gave direct feedback on the biosignals (17%, Otsuki et al. (2018)). Thereby the signals were first summarized in a way that they could be understood by the users. Eight systems analyzed the biosignals in more detail before presenting the results to the users (34%, e.g., Li et al. (2015), Menychtas et al. (2019)). In most cases, facial expressions were used to determine the state of the conversation participants, however, with varying degrees of representation as visible below. A deep adaptation took place in 12 publications (50%, e.g., Carter et al. (2016), Oh et al. (2016)). Here, most systems performed modifications of image, gaze or movement as visible below. In half of the systems, the adaptation took place implicitly (e.g., Nakazato et al. (2014)). This means that the other meeting participants are unaware that an adaptation took place. For example, it is not apparent whether a person's smile was enhanced (Carter et al. 2016) or whether the eye gaze was adapted (Yang & Zhang 2004). Thereby, these implicit adaptations are predominantly present throughout the whole meeting and remain constant modifications of a specific feature.

Direction: Adaptation for every meeting participant took place in several systems bidirectionally (3.2, 46%, e.g., Murali et al. (2021), Oh et al. (2016)). Systems with one directional adaptations were used in online classes (Sartika et al. 2022; Sun et al. 2019) and in therapeutic settings to ease reading facial expressions or the identification of a patient's cognitive or emotional state (Carter et al. 2016; Baig & GholamHosseini 2013). In these publications, a clear distinction between the group that benefits from the adaptation and the group whose signals are used for the adaptation is visible. No systems were investigated that displayed the information only to the user whose signals were collected (e.g., notification of inattentiveness).

Target: A prominent adaptation target (3.3) of the publications is to positively influence the attention of the participants (25%, e.g., Schwartz et al. (2020), Takemae et al. (2004)). Here, systems in which eye contact or eye gaze support play a role are especially common (e.g., Otsuki et al. (2018), Roberts et al. (2009)). Further, publications that focus on the emotional state of the participants and aim to ease emotion and expression understanding are popular (29%, e.g., Rojas et al. (2022), Tan et al. (2014)) and nearly always use facial expressions. Another prominent target was encountering the problem of lacking audience feedback, for example by providing feedback on the presence of the audience (29%, e.g., Murali et al. (2021)). Besides, several publications aim to increase the understanding of the participant's cognitive states, especially the states of other participants (17%, e.g., Pai et al. (2021)). Besides, group performance, such as creativity, is supported by image modifications as well (13%, e.g., Li et al. (2015)). Some authors set the target as the mere feedback of the analysis of the audience (29%, e.g., Murali et al. (2021), Pai et al. (2021)). Finally, there are publications that aim to provide adaptations that support immersion (17%, e.g., Rae et al. (2011), Song et al. (2018)). Nearly all of these studies want to transfer the meeting into a 3D environment.

Representation: Closely related to feedback as the adaptation type, two times, established physiological signals such as PR were displayed in form of unaggregated feedback (17%, Baig & GholamHosseini (2013), Tan et al. (2014)). Additionally, in this category, two applications included signals related to the eyes and displayed the blink rate (Pai et al. 2021) or the eye movement (Otsuki et al. 2018). Moving beyond unaggregated feedback towards analysis, the representation of the user states varied. At the lowest level, in one system, only the interface element was highlighted according to the prevailing emotion (4%, Rojas et al. (2022)). As aggregated biofeedback information (29%), percentages indicated which emotion the person was currently feeling (Menychtas et al. 2019) or systems employed in a classroom setting showed the aggregated states of the students (e.g., percentage of students who are in flow, Sartika et al. (2022), Sun et al. (2019)). Moving beyond analysis towards adaptation, three prominent forms of modifications can be identified. First, systems modified the image or depiction of the person. In one system, the system adaptively changed which person to spotlight, i.e., whose video was displayed prominently by analyzing facial expressions (Murali et al. 2021). Besides, in the remaining cases, the image of the person's facial expression was adapted (e.g., Carter et al. (2016), Oh et al. (2016)). Besides, six systems adapted the eye gaze of the participants, mostly to create eye contact between the participants (e.g., Rae et al. (2011), Roberts et al. (2009)). The movements of the participants, including the head orientation, were adapted in four publications (e.g., (Song et al. 2018, Tewele et al. 2015)) The source data indicates that some systems modified more than one subject. Thus, five systems adapted two elements (e.g., Schwartz et al. (2020), Zhang et al. (2022)), and in one case three elements were undergoing adaptation (Song et al. 2018).

Artificial intelligence: AI (3.5) was applied in almost all systems (20 publications, 83%). One publication specifically describes that a CNN was used to measure the signal (Pai et al. 2021). In this case, the blinking of the eyes is detected. It should be noted that it cannot be ruled out that AI was also used during this step in other studies without explicitly describing it. In nine cases, AI was used to analyze the state of participants, for example, to determine their emotional status based on facial expressions or to measure attention in an online classroom (38%, e.g., Li et al. (2015), Menychtas et al. (2019)). In 11 publications, AI was used to perform an adaptation of the system (46%, e.g., Taguchi et al. (2018)). This included, for example, adjusting eye gaze (Yang & Zhang 2004) to establish eye contact or increasing the smiles of participants (Carter et al. 2016).

5 Discussion

In this work, we provide a systematic literature review including 24 publications on biosignal-based user-adaptive VCS. We categorized our findings in a conceptual framework derived in a top-down and bottom-up approach.

We believe that there are already some opportunities to incorporate biosignals into VCS in practice. The concept developed can provide a basis for practitioners to see how adaptive their systems already are and what existing researched approaches could be implemented to address known issues such as generating eye contact. For inexperienced companies, it can be especially interesting to implement less invasive methods, such as displaying feedback based on devices that are already available. More experienced companies can use the framework to develop new VCS features targeting the future research directions. Building on this practical experience, research can gain field-based insights into how users actually perceive those implementations. In the following, we discuss our review's findings by identifying future research directions, shown in Table 1.

Table 1 Current and future research directions

Area	Research focus (current)	Research direction (future)
Biosignal	Biooptical, Unimodal	Bioelectrical, Multimodal
Adaptation target	Eye gaze, Emotions, Audience feedback	Complex user states, Further problems of video meetings
Adaptation representation	One interface element (Image of participant)	Multiple interface elements, newly developed features
Evaluation method	Small scale user studies, proof of concept	Large scale, longitudinal, field studies

Integrate biosignals beyond biooptical signals: One striking aspect in current research is the primary focus on biooptical signals. Primarily, facial expressions and eye movements were used as input signals. This is most likely because video is recorded anyway and users do not require additional hardware to measure these signals. Incorporating eye gaze can also be easily implemented in the future with novel webcam eye tracking, for example to create artificial eye contact. Therefore, the analysis of video is a practical basis for adaptation. Related to this, we identify future research subdirections. First, we encourage scholars to investigate the use of bioacoustic signals as they are again collected in any way. Second, we recommend the use of wearable sensors which ease the measurement of physiological data provided as bioelectrical, biothermal or biokinematic signals. Building on findings from NeuroIS and passive brain-computer interfaces (BCI), such signals can provide information that video and audio signals are not able to convey as easily, such as detailed information about user's affective or cognitive states (Riedl & Léger 2016). On top, as data privacy is an important issue in signal collection and processing, making use of signals that do not analyze voice data or image data may be of special interest, especially in meetings where sensitive information is shared (i.e., therapy, confidential business meetings). Third, we hint to using these signals as an additional input signal and thereby overcome the problem of many-to-many relationships between signal patterns and user states (Brouwer et al. 2015).

Address more complex target states and problems beyond eye gaze, expression understanding, and audience feedback: The target of adaptation in most cases was to influence the attention of participants by supporting eye contact, ease emotion and expression understanding and provide audience feedback. All of these are frequently mentioned problems in research (Karl et al. 2021). However, the identified problems in VCS are not limited to this and the landscape of cognitive and affective user states that arise within a meeting are manifold and not only limited to attention and emotions per se. For example, boredom and the aforementioned fatigue are two common but not yet specifically observed phenomena (Döring et al. 2022, Peper et al. 2021). Also, turntaking is a common problem in video meetings (Seuren et al. 2021). Thus, we encourage researchers to focus on these more complex user states and engage in identifying if existing applications can already impact these user states as well or whether new systems need to be created for them.

Explore adaptation capabilities of 2D and 3D VCS beyond avatars and image modification and introduce advanced adaptation representations: Of particular interest was the number of modified elements and the representation of the adaptation. Overall, the identified types of adaptation mechanisms were always very specific to single elements. Even though half of the systems belong to the deepest level of adaptation mechanisms, "deep adaptation", the adaptation is represented only by modifying mostly only one aspect of the video element. For example, in 2D, multiple publications augmented video feeds with avatars as a first step towards 3D environments, such as Mozilla Hubs. Gaze and image modifications were thereby performed by using biosignals to mitigate lacking eye contact or enrich facial expressions. This is expected since the video element is a very prominent element of the

VCS. Also, using an avatar instead of one's own picture can bring advantages, such as increased privacy (Higgins & McDonnell 2021). In addition, mostly a bidirectional adaptation was used. Thus, the change was visible to the other meeting participants, and in some cases also to the user itself. One directional adaptations were again only visible to the other party. We argue that this results in various underexplored research areas. First, continuing to enrich video elements and avatars with the combined use of biosignals and AI to open up the possibility of reproducing facial expressions or eye gaze for avatars. This can increase the appeal of these environments and should be investigated further. Second, even though sometimes extra elements are added to the standard video as the display of the other participant's user state, the majority of the VCS described do not adapt other VCS features. Thus, future research should also investigate the adaptation capabilities of currently underexplored features (e.g., chat, shared spaces). Third, one directional adaptations only visible for the user whose input is processed are not investigated in our literature sample. As motivated in the introduction, we see potential to support users in overcoming displeasing user states (e.g., nervousness, fatigue) arising in video meetings by adapting the software based on such states, as done in other adaptive systems (Loewe & Nadj 2020).

Conduct large scale studies, field studies, and comparison studies: In terms of evaluation, we identify a strong focus on laboratory studies showing that even small changes in the picture can have a positive influence. As Fairclough (2009) points out, the real-world conditions do differ to laboratory settings, due to uncontrolled extraneous variables. Since scholars aim to introduce such adaptive systems in real-world settings, we argue that more extensive studies including field studies or longitudinal studies should be carried out in future to get real-world user feedback and achieve external validity (Mitchell & Jolley 2013). Besides, studies focus on adapting a single element and exploring its effect isolatedly so far. It would therefore be interesting to see whether a combination of several adaptations could bring advantages (e.g., increased user experience). In addition, inspired by the idea of meta-studies, it is interesting to compare the proposed techniques to identify the most promising one (Gurevitch et al. 2018).

Despite conducting the review rigorously, our results come with limitations. We acknowledge the risk of missing relevant publications due to our search strategy. We selected ACM and AIS as the major databases in IS and added IEEE as a more technical source. We propose including further databases, like Scopus or PubMed, in future to obtain more comprehensive results. Furthermore, the conceptualization is founded in literature but also includes categories derived in a bottom-up approach. We note that especially these subclasses are subject to bias from our review set and due to only involving two authors. We aimed to address these limitations by employing an iterative, structured process and transparent reporting.

6 Conclusion

Our article provides a state-of-the-art overview of VCS with feedback and adaptation via biosignals structured along a conceptual framework based on the biocybernetic loop (Fairclough 2011) and identified 24 publications in a systematic search. We found that most systems are limited to the adaptation of a single element. In the vast majority of cases, this involved the modification of the user's representation (gaze, image, motion). We were also able to show that in most systems the analysis of the video elements like facial expressions and eye gaze was used as input. Besides, we observed that the adaptation target mainly covered the topics eye gaze, audience feedback, and expression understanding. Furthermore, our work provides a basis for further research by outlining four research directions. We encourage researchers to develop new systems that address unsolved problems in VCS or work with biosignals beyond biooptical signals.

Acknowledgements Funded by the Deutsche Forschungsgemeinschaft (DFG, German Research Foundation)—GRK2739/1—Project Nr. 447089431—Research Training Group: KD2School—Designing Adaptive Systems for Economic Decisions.

References

Abramova, O., Gladkaya, M. & Krasnova, H. (2021), An unusual encounter with oneself: exploring the impact of self-view on online meeting outcomes, in '42nd International Conference on Information Systems', pp. 1–17.

Baig, M. M. & GholamHosseini, H. (2013), A remote monitoring system with early diagnosis of hypertension and hypotension, in '2013 IEEE Point-of-Care Healthcare Technologies (PHT)', IEEE, pp. 34–37.

Benyon, D. & Murray, D. (1993), 'Adaptive systems: from intelligent tutoring to autonomous agents', *Knowledge-Based Systems* **6**(4), 197–219.

Bitkom (2022), 'Wie häufig kommen die folgenden Kanäle für die interne und externe Kommunikation zum Einsatz?', *Statista* . Accessed: 2023-03-04.

Brouwer, A. M., Zander, T. O., van Erp, J. B., Korteling, J. E. & Bronkhorst, A. W. (2015), 'Using neurophysiological signals that reflect cognitive or affective state: Six recommendations to avoid common pitfalls', *Frontiers in Neuroscience* **9**(APR).

Carter, E. J., Hyde, J., Williams, D. L. & Hodgins, J. K. (2016), Investigating the influence of avatar facial characteristics on the social behaviors of children with autism, *in* 'Proceedings of the 2016 CHI conference on human factors in computing systems', pp. 140–151.

Döring, N., Moor, K. D., Fiedler, M., Schoenenberg, K. & Raake, A. (2022), 'Videoconference Fatigue: A Conceptual Analysis', *International Journal of Environmental Research and Public Health* **19**(4), 2061 - 2081.

Epstein, H.-A. B. (2020), 'Virtual meeting fatigue', *Journal of Hospital Librarianship* **20**(4), 356–360.

Fairclough, S. H. (2009), 'Fundamentals of physiological computing', *Interacting with Computers* **21**(1-2), 133–145.

Fairclough, S. H. (2011), 'Physiological computing: interfacing with the human nervous system', Sensing Emotions: The impact of context on experience measurements pp. 1– 20.

Fairclough, S. H. (2017), Physiological computing and intelligent adaptation, *in* 'Emotions and affect in human factors and human-computer interaction', Elsevier, pp. 539– 556.

Fauville, G., Luo, M., Muller Queiroz, A. C., Bailenson, J. N. & Hancock, J. (2021), 'Nonverbal Mechanisms Predict Zoom Fatigue and Explain Why Women Experience Higher Levels than Men', *SSRN Electronic Journal* .

Feigh, K. M., Dorneich, M. C. & Hayes, C. C. (2012), 'Toward a characterization of adaptive systems: A framework for researchers and system designers', *Human factors* **54**(6), 1008–1024.

Gurevitch, J., Koricheva, J., Nakagawa, S. & Stewart, G. (2018), 'Meta-analysis and the science of research synthesis', *Nature 2018* **555**(7695), 175–182.

Hettinger, L. J., Branco, P., Encarnacao, L. M. & Bonato, P. (2003), 'Neuroadaptive Technologies: Applying Neuroergonomics to the Design of Advanced Interfaces', *Theoretical issues in ergonomics* sciences **4**(1-2), 220–237.

Higgins, D. & McDonnell, R. (2021), A preliminary investigation of avatar use in videoconferencing, in '2021 IEEE Conference on Virtual Reality and 3D User Interfaces Abstracts and Workshops (VRW)', IEEE, pp. 540–541.

Kaptelinin, V. (2023), 'Interaction Design Solutions for Online Meetings', *Interactions* **30**(2), 42–46.

Karl, K. A., Peluchette, J. V. & Aghakhani, N. (2021), 'Virtual Work Meetings During the COVID-19 Pandemic: The Good, Bad, and Ugly:', *Small Group Research* **53**(3), 343–365.

Kelly, H. (2020), 'The most maddening part about working from home: Video conferences', The Washington Post . Accessed: 2023–03–04.

Knierim, M. T., Schemmer, M. & Bauer, N. (2022), 'A simplified design of a ceegrid ear-electrode adapter for the openbci biosensing platform', *HardwareX* 12, e00357.

Langner, M., Toreini, P. & Maedche, A. (2022), EyeMeet: A Joint Attention Support System for Remote Meetings, *in* 'CHI Conference on Human Factors in Computing Systems Extended Abstracts', ACM, New York, NY, USA, pp. 1–7.

Li, R., Curhan, J. & Hoque, M. E. (2015), Predicting video-conferencing conversation outcomes based on modeling facial expression synchronization, *in* '2015 11th IEEE International Conference and Workshops on Automatic Face and Gesture Recognition (FG)', Vol. 1, IEEE, pp. 1–6.

Loewe, N. & Nadj, M. (2020), Physio-adaptive systems-a state-of-the-art review and future research directions., *in* 'ECIS'.

Menychtas, A., Galliakis, M., Tsanakas, P. & Maglogiannis, I. (2019), Real-time integration of emotion analysis into homecare platforms, *in* '2019 41st Annual International Conference of the IEEE Engineering in Medicine and Biology Society (EMBC)', IEEE, pp. 3468–3471.

Mitchell, M. & Jolley, J. (2013), *Research design explained*, 8 edn, Wadsworth Publishing, Belmont, California.

Murali, P., Hernandez, J., McDuff, D., Rowan, K., Suh, J. & Czerwinski, M. (2021), Affectivespotlight: Facilitating the communication of affective responses from audience members during online presentations, *in* 'Proceedings of the 2021 CHI Conference on Human Factors in Computing Systems', pp. 1–13.

Nakazato, N., Yoshida, S., Sakurai, S., Narumi, T., Tanikawa, T. & Hirose, M. (2014), Smart face: enhancing creativity during video conferences using real-time facial deformation, *in* 'Proceedings of the 17th ACM conference on Computer supported cooperative work & social computing', pp. 75–83.

Nickerson, R. C., Varshney, U. & Muntermann, J. (2013), 'A method for taxonomy development and its application in information systems', *European Journal of Information Systems* **22**(3), 336–359.

Oh, S. Y., Bailenson, J., Krämer, N. & Li, B. (2016), 'Let the avatar brighten your smile: Effects of enhancing facial expressions in virtual environments', *PloS one* **11**(9), e0161794.

Otsuki, M., Maruyama, K., Kuzuoka, H. & Suzuki, Y. (2018), Effects of enhanced gaze presentation on gaze leading in remote collaborative physical tasks, *in* 'Proceedings of the 2018 CHI Conference on Human Factors in Computing Systems', pp. 1–11.

Pai, R., Dubey, A. & Mangaonkar, N. (2021), Real time eye monitoring system using cnn for drowsiness and attentiveness system, *in* '2021 Asian Conference on Innovation in Technology (ASIANCON)', IEEE, pp. 1–4.

Peper, E., Wilson, V., Martin, M., Rosegard, E. & Harvey, R. (2021), 'Avoid Zoom Fatigue, Be Present and Learn', NeuroRegulation 8(1), 47–56.

Pexip (2023), 'PEXIP'. URL: https://www.pexip.com/features/adaptive-composition

Pope, A. T., Bogart, E. H. & Bartolome, D. S. (1995), 'Biocybernetic system evaluates indices of operator engagement in automated task', *Biological psychology* **40**(1- 2), 187–195.

Rae, J. P., Steptoe, W. & Roberts, D. J. (2011), Some implications of eye gaze behavior and perception for the design of immersive telecommunication systems, *in* '2011 IEEE/ACM 15th International Symposium on Distributed Simulation and Real Time Applications', IEEE, pp. 108–114.

Reinecke, K. & Bernstein, A. (2013), 'Knowing What a User Likes: A Design Science Approach to Interfaces that Automatically Adapt to Culture', *MIS Quarterly* **37**(2), 427–453.

Riedl, R. & Léger, P.-M. (2016), 'Fundamentals of neurois', *Studies in neuroscience, psychology and behavioral economics* p. 127.

Roberts, D., Wolff, R., Rae, J., Steed, A., Aspin, R., McIntyre, M., Pena, A., Oyekoya, O. &Steptoe, W. (2009), Communicating eye-gaze across a distance: Comparing an eyegaze enabled immersive collaborative virtual environment, aligned video conferencing, and being together, *in* '2009 IEEE Virtual Reality Conference', IEEE, pp. 135–142.

Rojas, C., Zuccarelli, E., Chin, A., Patekar, G., Esquivel, D. & Maes, P. (2022), Towards enhancing empathy through emotion augmented remote communication, *in* 'CHI Conference on Human Factors in Computing Systems Extended Abstracts', pp. 1–9.

Samrose, S. (2018), Automated collaboration coach for video-conferencing based group discussions, *in* 'Proceedings of the 2018 ACM International Joint Conference and 2018 International Symposium on Pervasive and Ubiquitous Computing and Wearable Computers', pp. 510–515.

Sartika, N., Sukmana, Y., Eliviani, R. & Awaludin, R. (2022), Smart online class monitoring service design, *in* '2022 8th International Conference on Wireless and Telematics (ICWT)', IEEE, pp. 1–7.

Schultz, T., Amma, C., Heger, D., Putze, F. & Wand, M. (2013), 'Human-Machine Interfaces based on Biosignals', *Automatisierungstechnik* **61**(11), 760–769.

Schwartz, G., Wei, S.-E., Wang, T.-L., Lombardi, S., Simon, T., Saragih, J. & Sheikh, Y. (2020), 'The eyes have it: An integrated eye and face model for photorealistic facial animation', *ACM Transactions on Graphics (TOG)* **39**(4), 91–1.

Seitz, J. (2022), Designing user-adaptive video meeting systems, *in* 'Proceedings of 20th European Conference on Computer-Supported Cooperative Work', European Society for Socially Embedded Technologies (EUSSET).

Seitz, J., Benke, I. & Madche, A. (2022), 'Fatigued by yourself? towards understanding the impact of self-view designs in virtual meeting software', *SIGHCI 2022, HCI/MIS Workshop 2022 - The 21st Annual Pre-ICIS Workshop on HCI Research in MIS, Copenhagen, Denmark*

Seuren, L. M., Wherton, J., Greenhalgh, T. & Shaw, S. E. (2021), 'Whose turn is it anyway? Latency and the organization of turn-taking in video-mediated interaction', *Journal of Pragmatics* **172**, 63–78.

Skillscouter (2022), 'Video Conferencing Statistics'. **URL**: https://skillscouter.com/video-conferencing-statistics

Song, G., Cai, J., Cham, T.-J., Zheng, J., Zhang, J. & Fuchs, H. (2018), Real-time 3d face-eye performance capture of a person wearing vr headset, *in* 'Proceedings of the 26th ACM international conference on Multimedia', pp. 923–931.

Sun, W., Li, Y., Tian, F., Fan, X. & Wang, H. (2019), 'How presenters perceive and react to audience flow prediction in-situ: An explorative study of live online lectures', *Proceedings of the ACM on Human-Computer Interaction* **3**(CSCW), 1–19.

Taguchi, W., Nihei, F., Takase, Y., Nakano, Y. I., Fukasawa, S. & Akatsu, H. (2018), Effects of face and voice deformation on participant emotion in video-mediated communication, *in* 'Proceedings of the 20th International Conference on Multimodal Interaction: Adjunct', pp. 1–5.

Takemae, Y., Otsuka, K. & Mukawa, N. (2004), An analysis of speakers' gaze behavior for automatic addressee identification in multiparty conversation and its application to video editing, *in* 'RO-MAN 2004. 13th IEEE International Workshop on Robot and Human Interactive Communication (IEEE Catalog No. 04TH8759)', IEEE, pp. 581– 586.

Takemae, Y., Otsuka, K. & Yamato, J. (2005), Automatic video editing system using stereo-based head tracking for multiparty conversation, *in* 'CHI'05 extended abstracts on Human factors in computing systems', pp. 1817–1820.

Tan, C. S. S., Luyten, K., Van Den Bergh, J., Schöning, J. & Coninx, K. (2014), 'The role of physiological cues during remote collaboration', *Presence: Teleoperators and Virtual Environments* **23**(1), 90–107.

Telaar, D., Wand, M., Gehrig, D., Putze, F., Amma, C., Heger, D., Vu, N. T., Erhardt, M., Schlippe, T., Janke, M. et al. (2014), Biokit—real-time decoder for biosignal processing, *in* 'Fifteenth Annual Conference of the International Speech Communication Association'.

Tewele, M. K., Yousefi, S. & Milrad, M. (2015), Supporting video conference communication using a vision-based human facial synthesis approach, *in* '2015 SAI Intelligent Systems Conference (IntelliSys)', IEEE, pp. 807–812.

Valkenburg, P. M. & Peter, J. (2013), 'The Differential Susceptibility to Media Effects Model', *Journal of Communication* **63**(2), 221–243.

Webster, J. & Watson, R. T. (2002), 'Analyzing the past to prepare for the future: Writing a literature review', *MIS quarterly* pp. xiii–xxiii.

White, R. W. & Morris, D. (2007), Investigating the querying and browsing behavior of advanced search engine users, *in* 'Proceedings of the 30th Annual International ACM SIGIR Conference on Research and Development in Information Retrieval', SIGIR '07, Association for Computing Machinery, New York, NY, USA, p. 255–262.

Yang, R. & Zhang, Z. (2004), 'Eye gaze correction with stereovision for videoteleconferencing', *IEEE Transactions on Pattern Analysis and Machine Intelligence* **26**(7), 956–960.

Zander, T. O. & Kothe, C. (2011), 'Towards passive brain-computer interfaces: Applying brain-computer interface technology to human-machine systems in general', *Journal of Neural Engineering* **8**(2).

Zhang, Y., Yang, J., Liu, Z., Wang, R., Chen, G., Tong, X. & Guo, B. (2022), 'Virtualcube: An immersive 3d video communication system', *IEEE Transactions on Visualization and Computer Graphics* **28**(5), 2146–2156.

Zheng, Y.-L., Ding, X.-R., Poon, C. C. Y., Lo, B. P. L., Zhang, H., Zhou, X.-L., Yang, G.-Z., Zhao, N. & Zhang, Y.-T. (2014), 'Unobtrusive Sensing and Wearable Devices for Health Informatics', *IEEE Transactions on Biomedical Engineering* **61**(5), 1538– 1554.

What is the Minimum to Trust AI?—A Requirement Analysis for (Generative) AI-Based Texts

Christoph Tomitza, Myriam Schaschek, Lisa Straub, and Axel Winkelmann

Abstract The generative Artificial Intelligence (genAI) innovation enables new potentials for end-users, affecting youth and the inexperienced. Nevertheless, as an innovative technology, genAI risks generating misinformation that is not recognizable as such. The extraordinary AI outputs can result in increased trustworthiness. An end-user assessment system is necessary to expose the unfounded reliance on erroneous responses. This paper identifies requirements for an assessment system to prevent end-users from overestimating trust in generated texts. Thus, we conducted requirements engineering based on a literature review and two international surveys. The results confirmed the requirements which enable human protection, human support, and content veracity in dealing with genAI. Overestimated trust is rooted in miscalibration; clarity about genAI and its provider is essential to solving this phenomenon, and there is a demand for human verifications. Consequently, our findings provide evidence for the significance of future IS research on human-centered genAI trust solutions.

Keywords Human-centered · Generative AI · Trust · Requirements · ChatGPT

C. Tomitza (✉) · M. Schaschek · L. Straub · A. Winkelmann
Julius-Maximilians-Universität Würzburg, Würzburg, Germany
e-mail: Christoph.Tomitza@uni-wuerzburg.de

M. Schaschek
e-mail: Myriam.Schaschek@uni-wuerzburg.de

L. Straub
e-mail: Lisa.Straub@uni-wuerzburg.de

A. Winkelmann
e-mail: Axel.Winkelmann@uni-wuerzburg.de

D. Beverungen et al. (eds.), *Conceptualizing Digital Responsibility for the Information Age*, Lecture Notes in Information Systems and Organisation 74,
https://doi.org/10.1007/978-3-031-80119-8_14

1 Introduction

"As an AI language model, I strive to provide accurate and reliable information to the best of my abilities. However, since I am a machine learning algorithm, there is always a possibility that errors or inaccuracies can occur in my responses." (OpenAI 2023a). This is a generative Artificial Intelligence (genAI) system's response to the query of whether one can trust its output. Although the genAI's statement is valid, novice genAI end-users are neither enlightened nor confronted with this fact (Ng et al. 2021). Recent advances in genAI technologies present unique value and precede new research directions while posing challenges for society (Kshetri et al. 2023). Its generative nature distinguishes it from other Artificial Intelligence (AI) types. In particular, genAI's ability to produce multiple and divergent outputs for a given input allows them to mimic human behavior in an exploratory way fostering adoption and diffusion (Weisz et al. 2023). Unlike other AI models, genAI technology merges end-user and technology and creates ease of access in everyday life. The acceleration of genAI capabilities accompanied by public access to pre-trained models enable inexperienced users to co-creation with AI (Muller et al. 2022).

Alongside the advancement in Natural Language Generation (NLG), the integration of large language models fine-tuned with human feedback unlocked the generation of intelligent chat bots with remarkable abilities (Bai et al. 2022). A recent widespread solution is ChatGPT, provided by Open AI, which produces sophisticated responses to question prompts mostly indistinguishable to responses provided by human experts (Bai et al. 2022). In parallel to its rapid global adoption, attention raised towards its limitations and ethical reservations regarding its outputs misuse or abuse (Kshetri et al. 2023). Concerning novice end-users, AI-generated text poses a potential risk for spreading misinformation, as its complexity challenges the content provenance and veracity (Fielding 2019; Ali et al. 2021a, b).

In this context, researchers discovered that NLG models are prone to produce content unfaithful to its source input, which is referred to as hallucination (JiZiwei et al. 2023). In addition, end-users tend to evaluate sources primarily on superficial criteria, such as the website design or the availability of illustrations, which are elements that can be easily falsified or manipulated (Griesbaum 2022). In the case of AI-generated texts, end-users can neither see the corresponding input source nor verify how credible the information is. Accordingly, well-known methods such as the CRAAP test for verifying information sources are only applicable to a limited extent (Griesbaum 2022; Ali et al. 2021a, b). Therefore, it is even more drastic that NLG models hallucinate content veracity and trustworthiness for the end-user. The following conversation with a ChatGPT bot illustrates a hallucination example and the consequences of misinformation (Fig. 1).

In Germany, it is not allowed to camp wildly - it usually even corresponds to an administrative offense that can be punished with a fine (Hawlitschek et al. 2017). Therefore, the answer given was incorrect. Yet, it is even more problematic that the output is connected to a fake source misleading the end-user's trust. Due to the

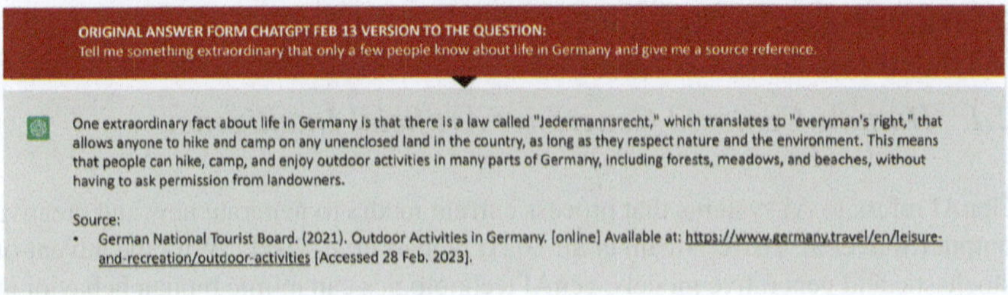

Fig. 1 Chat GPT Conversation (OpenAI 2023b)

probabilistic and generative nature of NLG models, outputs are prone to generative variability and inputs to pre-trained models can correspond to multiple outputs (Macneil et al. 2022; Dale 2021). Accordingly, compared to source citation in human-generated texts, it might not display the content provenance. At the current state, the end-user interface of publicly available genAI models do not inform end-users regarding the uncertainty of output. Especially, AI-novices with limited AI literacy might overestimate the trustworthiness of the system and are misled to spread misinformation (Long & Magerko 2020). This backdrop served as motivation to investigate the following research question:

What are the requirements to prevent end-users from overestimating trust in AI-generated texts?

To address our research question, we develop requirements for designing compliant genAI models that anticipate end-users' vulnerability. In doing so, we ground our results in scholarly literature and rely on two complementary survey studies to refine the determined requirements. In light of our findings, we discuss solution proposals to support future end-users in assessing the content veracity and trustworthiness independent of the educational level and AI literacy.

This paper is structured as follows: Sect. 2 provides a theoretical background on human-centered genAI and highlights preliminary work. Section 3 outlines the details of our research design. Subsequently, Sects. 4 and 5 present the derived requirements and supplementary survey results. In Sect. 6, we discuss our findings and derive implications. Finally, we conclude the paper with an outlook on future research avenues.

2 Theoretical Background

2.1 Human-Centered Generative Artificial Intelligence

GenAI refers to AI systems that process current media to generate new and creative output (Sbai et al. 2018; Nigam et al. 2021; Nobari et al. 2021). With the advent of stochastic and generative models, genAI technologies can mimic human behavior to the point where they no longer act as decision-makers but rather as end-user support (Seeber et al. 2020; Zhou et al. 2020). Accordingly, the role of AI is shifting from problemsolving to problem-finding (Seeber et al. 2020). Ignited by the public accessibility of new models, AI-based text generation has reinforced interest in human-centered AI research (Muller et al. 2022). In parallel, research attention shifts toward the method of text generation using intelligent chat bots (Radford et al. 2018) that has the distinct feature of co-creating outputs with end-user interaction (Lund & Ting 2023; King 2023).

Cutting-edge NLG models generate conversational responses to question prompts for everyday scenarios (Bai et al. 2022). While they can enhance productivity by generating outputs almost indistinguishable from human content (Lehmann et al. 2022), it is essential to understand and acknowledge its limitations to prevent end-users from overrated trust in AI-generated texts. Given its probabilistic nature, potential concerns from misuse and abuse can lead to reputation or legal issues, infringement on intellectual property, loss of privacy, or the dissemination of false information (e.g., Kshetri et al. 2023). Beyond those threats, ethical issues, such as bias, arise in the context of genAI as a black-box algorithm (e.g., Jovanovi´c & Campbell 2022, Muller et al. 2022).

Hence, it is essential to explore the end-users' perception of AI-generated text and their trust in the generated outputs. Few studies examined the impact of writing with AI (Lehmann et al. 2022) or empirically investigated the societal implications of AI-generated text and revealed that transparency in the use of AI can backfire (Longoni et al. 2022). Other studies have focused on ethical aspects of ChatGPT from the perspective of how it behaves concerning ethically dubious questions (e.g., Dantas 2023; Hasselbalch 2022). Still, open questions persist on how to prevent end-users from harmful decision-making. In this vein, we explore the end-user requirements of NLG models to enable the creation of human-centered genAI systems that promote more responsible usage.

2.2 Preliminary Work and Research Gap

Human-AI Collaboration. The first and most prominent focal point centers on the intersection between AI and end-users. With the emergence of large language models fine-tuned with human participation (Bai et al. 2022), applications in everyday life range from auto-generating text (Lehmann et al. 2022) to code completion (Weisz et al. 2023). The impact of AI assistance has been extensively researched in recent years, with mixed results about whether AI improves work performance or outcome quality (Weisz et al. 2021). With the rise of genAI as a conversational agent that co-creates solutions with end-users, AI's function evolves from decision support to assistance in activities involving the creation of an artifact (Weisz et al. 2022, Zdanowska & Taylor 2022). Research topics include how and what AI can generate and how can and should end-users contribute to the process and quality of outcomes (Muller et al. 2022).

Transparency and Ethics. As AI applications become more prevalent in everyday life, they raise ethical and societal concerns. In response, governments provided principles and regulations to guide organizations developing AI (Smuha 2019). In this light, several recent publications investigate concepts, such as trustworthiness (e.g., Thiebes et al. 2021), explainability (e.g., Meske et al. 2020; Liao & Varshney 2021), fairness (e.g., Lee et al. 2020, Datta et al. 2021), or responsibility (Blodgett et al. 2022; Arrieta et al. 2020), to develop methods under the umbrella term of AI ethics (Shneiderman 2020). A prevalent theme in the literature investigates system trust and trustworthiness as a contractual phenomenon based on the functionalities an AI system aspires to offer the end-user (Vianello et al. 2022).

Falsehood and Misinformation. Even dedicated researchers have been taken aback by the ability of AI-based chat bots to increase linguistic fidelity (Gašević et al. 2023). With the emergence of genAI models, AI is now being used in schools, universities, and research, and the human role shifts to creators and consumers (Ali et al. 2021a, b). Concurrently, chat bots are criticized for creating "cogent waffle" (Vincent 2022), i.e., producing grammatically correct nonsense, and social media networks even accelerate the spread of misinformation. In light of genAI and media bias, the issue of artificial hallucination, defined as machines producing seemingly realistic output that does not match real-world facts, has emerged as a severe issue (Alkaissi & McFarlane 2023, JiZiwei et al. 2023). In this context, mitigating harm includes understanding the technical systems that create deep fakes, how AI can lead to misinformation, and what trustworthy sources are (Ali et al. 2021a, b). Since young people are sensitive to misleading media, the research efforts on media and AI literacy in education amplify (Laupichler et al. 2022). Multiple studies emphasize the relevance of AI and media literacy in public. However, they also highlight the need for policymakers and AI development organizations to inform end-users to prevent harm (Ali et al. 2021a, b).

Ethical concerns about AI-based conversational agents have amplified on another level. While high-stakes issues are often relevant in discussions about AI decision-making (Wanner et al. 2020), various genAI models are publicly available and therefore have broader ethical and societal implications (Kshetri et al. 2023; Lund & Ting 2023). The research on designing compliant genAI models for text generation to mitigate potential harm is still in its infancy (e.g., Sun et al. 2022; Weisz et al. 2023). To date, scant attention has been paid to human-centered requirements to prevent end-users from overestimating trust in AI-generated texts.

3 Research and Survey Design

In order to define requirements that should be considered in society, we followed a four-stage research design and included a double iteration cycle with two surveys (Fig. 2).

Stage 1: We executed a structured literature review (vom Brocke et al. 2009) to inform our results with prior design knowledge (vom Brocke et al. 2020) on human-centered NLG models regarding end-user trust. For that, we determined the databases relevant to our research problem: AIS eLibrary, ACM, IEEE, Science Direct, and Web of Science. Then, we searched databases using the keywords: (*responsible* OR ethical OR *explainable* OR *trust* OR *human-centered*) AND ("*generative* AI" OR "*generative artificial intelligence*"). Subsequently, we limited the identified search results to relevant publications addressing our research question by performing a title and abstract analysis followed by a full-text analysis. Due to the manageability and timeliness of the search results, we did not define further inclusion or exclusion criteria. After a forward and backward search, we finally identified n = 46 relevant publications that target genAI and related challenges. Within this area of investigation, one can distinguish three general focal points: (i) human-AI collaboration (n = 12), (ii) transparency and ethics (n = 19), and (iii) falsehood and misinformation (n = 9) (see Sect. 2.2).

Stage 2: After identifying existing concepts, we focused on deriving the requirements. All authors subsequently reread the literature and performed data coding, mainly focusing on the crucial aspects for setting up requirements. We reconciled the coding results in a workshop and cross-checked the findings to define the requirements. Then, we clustered requirements into dimensions for better clarity and structuring. Through multiple iterations, we adjusted the dimensions and requirements to ensure that all key findings were incorporated and appropriately aligned.

Stage 3 and 4: To verify the established requirements, we conducted two surveys in February 2023. The first survey aimed to align the requirements based on the participants' answers, and the second survey evaluated the refined requirements. Additionally, we conducted a qualitative analysis of the survey results and included

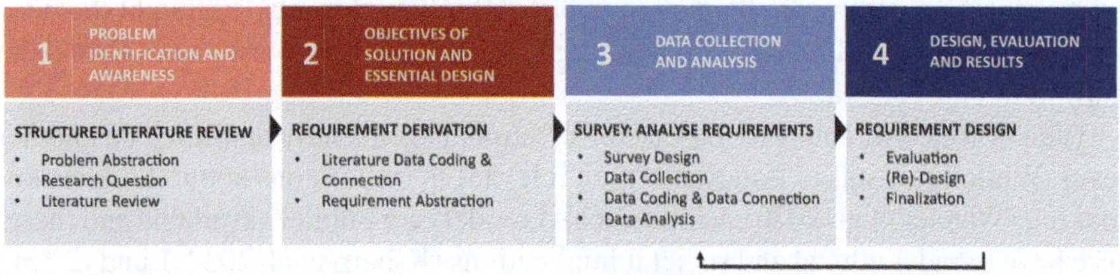

Fig. 2 Research design

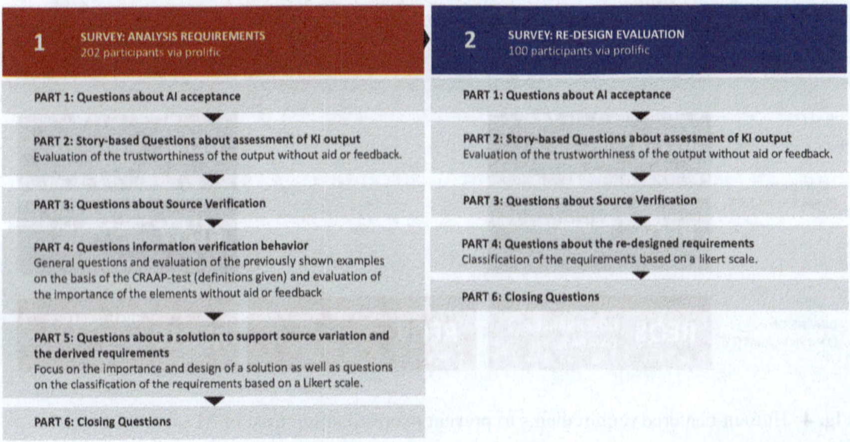

Fig. 3 Main sequence and structure of the two survey studies

the participants' explanations for their decisions and feedback to inform the requirements. In both studies, participants went through a story-based questionnaire about the impact of new text-generation systems (Fig. 3).

We conducted an explanatory cross-sectional survey with quantitative and qualitative elements (Pinsonneault & Kraemer 1993). In detail, the questionnaire included Likert items with five response options and written descriptors accompanied with open question to allow for participant feedback. We implemented both studies using the prolific.co platform[1] with monetary incentive. Regarding the survey participants, we prioritized a divers and transnational main target group with balanced gender and targeted residents of industrialized countries, such as Canada, United States, and European countries. Participants range in age from 18 to 62, and most of our participants are in the 21–30 age group. In general, we targeted potential adult end-users of genAI systems who did not necessarily have prior experience. To ensure a survey that genAI novices could complete, we developed a questionnaire based on a story representing the use of a genAI chat bot. See Tomitza et al. (2023) for more details on the surveys and the corresponding demographics of participants.

4 Human-Centered Requirements to Prevent End-Users from Overestimating Trust in AI-Generated Texts

In the subsequent Section, we present the synthesis of literature and survey data in light of three dimensions established through data coding and analysis. The dimensions classify requirements according to their focus and impact on future envisioned artifacts to mitigate harm. They divide into: (i) harm protection, (ii) human support,

[1] https://www.prolific.co/

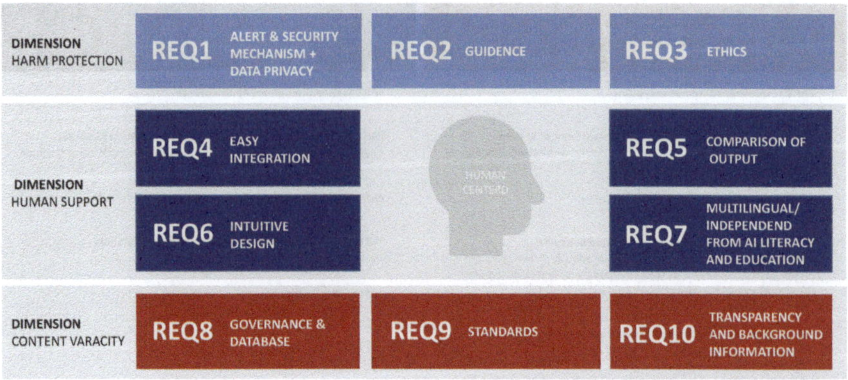

Fig. 4 Human-centered requirements to prevent overestimating trust in AI-generated texts

and (iii) content veracity. Figure 4 depicts the final requirements and associated dimensions. In the preceding subsections, we present the requirements in more detail.

Harm Protection. Several GenAI studies emphasize the importance of harm protection in relation to genAI outputs (According to several (Weisz et al. 2023; Longoni et al. 2022). Accordingly, we see the following requirements from the end-user perspective.

(REQ1) *Integrate alerts and security mechanisms to assess misinformation, detect deep fakes, and maintain personal data protection.* This statement involves data provided by end-users and data they disclose. Therefore, end-users must be aware of erroneous information and insufficient or inappropriate sources (Alkaissi & McFarlane 2023; Ali et al. 2021a, b). In addition, they need privacy protections for their personal data while dealing with genAI systems (Carlini et al. 2021).

(REQ2) *Create helpful guidance for users and educate them about the limitations and potential dangers of using it concerning the veracity and transparency of sources.* To prevent end-users from being misled, it is essential to guide inexperienced or young people in the use of genAI and confront them with the potential risk (Wolf 2019; Laupichler et al. 2022; Ali et al. 2021a, b). So they can learn to evaluate model outputs critically, and fake news should be recognizable easily as such.

(REQ3) *Consider & assure ethics (e.g., discrimination, fairness) and prevent ethically questionable rule-based corrections in favor of freedom of opinion.* The solution should recognize and declare ethically objectionable statements, discrimination, and fairness violations as such (Vianello et al. 2022, Lee et al. 2020, Weisz et al. 2023). However, a solution has not to practice discrimination by certifying sources of certain minorities as untrustworthy. Furthermore, the solution has not to correct automatically unethical statements in favor of freedom of speech.

Human Support. The following requirements regarding human support considers solution elements that concern handling. The aim is to avoid creating approaches that overburden the end-user.

(***REQ4***) *Ensure easy integration with existing information sources and simple use even for the information providers.* For a corresponding solution to gain the most significant possible acceptance by providers, it must be possible to integrate it effortlessly.

(***REQ5***) *Enable comparability of given information/outputs and ensure transferability /development of the solution to other information sources independent of AI.* The support structure has to enable a comparison of different outputs from one or different models or sources (Dhanorkar et al. 2021). Therefore, when not developed individually for one application (e.g., Chat GPT), the solution provides significant added value.

(***REQ6***) *Ensure a user-centered, contemporary, intuitive, and inclusive design that enables a ranking of outputs independently.* A high degree of usability enables higher stakes in terms of acceptance. The solution should be intuitive without requiring training time and incorporate desired functionality (Wolf 2019, Zdanowska & Taylor 2022).

(***REQ7***) *Consider multilingualism and education levels and create comprehensibility of solution regardless of AI competency /AI education level.* The developers of a solution should guarantee ease of use and build a simple and comprehensible support tool that considers sources from different countries and is understandable regardless of age and AI literacy (Laupichler et al. 2022; Ali et al. 2021a, b).

Content Veracity. The last dimension concerns content veracity. Negative influences on the output should be made transparent to the user. The synthesis led to the following requirements.

(***REQ8***) *Establish governance to ensure that the database grounds only on reliable sources or point out if not.* The solution must ensure that the provider only can use reliable databases or sources for their model development (Alkaissi & McFarlane 2023). The database is decisive for what is ultimately output to the end-user (Alkaissi & McFarlane 2023). Model and database have a crucial influence on the output, it is essential to create appropriate indications and clear approaches to devise more clarity of reliability.

(***REQ9***) *Create a contemporary standard and guarantee the solution's neutrality, comprehensibility, trustworthiness, and explainability.* Achieving a neutral, insusceptible, and contemporary standard that ensures the trustworthiness of genAI models is necessary. Furthermore, especially from an end-user perspective, an independent authority must verify and represent these.

(***REQ10***) *Demonstrate transparency (e.g., composition, accuracy, AI influence, content quality) by providing background information and support to cross-check.* End-users perceive AI models as black-boxes due to their untraceable complexity

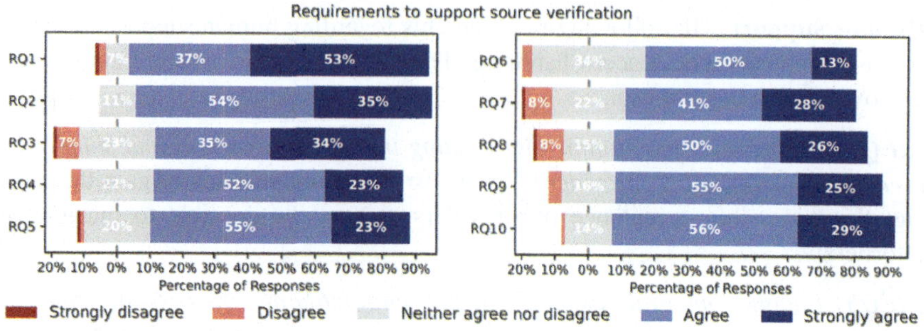

Fig. 5 Results of the second study regarding requirements

(Herm et al. 2023), which influences trustworthiness. Therefore, output accuracy and sources must be indicated to the end-users to extend trust (Dhanorkar et al. 2021). It is essential to display AI involvement and background information (Alkaissi & McFarlane 2023). For reliable results, systems must check responses before displaying them to the end-user, and afterward, guidance for manual evaluation is necessary (Wolf 2019).

We evaluated the requirements during our survey and the results depicted in Fig. 5 show that more than 63% of participants agreed to each requirement. The participants' agreement on requirements is equally distributed, but RQ1 outperforms the others, and RQ6 reached the lowest agreement.

5 Supplementary Study Results

The shown requirements provide a first basis for other developments of proper solutions. In our study, it became clear that over-reliance can be triggered simply through grammatically correct statements. To introduce the participants to the study, we asked them to put themselves in the role of planning a trip, showed three statements from ChatGPT, and asked them to rate their confidence in the statements (Fig. 6).

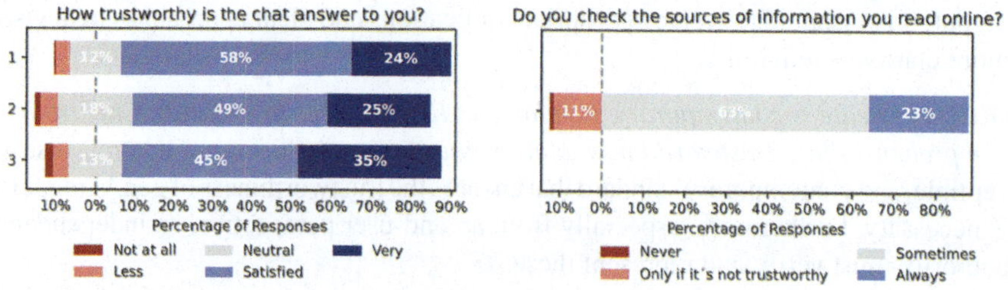

Fig. 6 Results of the first survey Part 2 (left) and 3 (right)

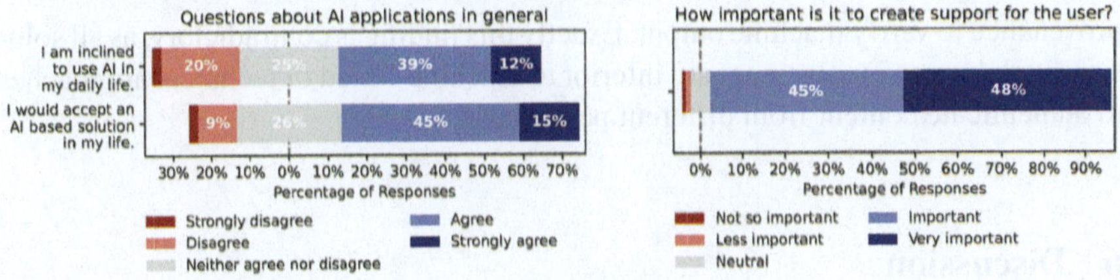

Fig. 7 Results of the first survey Part 1 (left) and 5 (right)

The statements shown in Part 2 of the survey were structured as follows: (1) Included possible travel locations, (2) featured a hallucination and incorrect source regarding camping in Germany, and (3) questioned the reliability of the previous statement while providing a detailed answer with additional incorrect source citations. Moreover, we allowed for participant feedback to justify the decision. The most striking finding that we observed reinforced trust by participants when gen AI used (incorrect) source citations. Participants ranked the responses trustworthy if they contained more detail or real-world examples. To increase trust, expanding the number of sources was sufficient. In line with previous studies, artificial hallucinations can cause absolute misdirection by simulating legal content, creating fake documented evidence, and making untrue fake reputations on non-existent websites that imitate credibility (Alkaissi & McFarlane 2023).

Although it is possible to create fraudulent sureness in generated texts by citing sources, these do not have to be correct sources, which we could see from the free text information in which participants indicated that they clicked on links that did not work and still trusted the response. The phenomenon that end-users ignore even aspects that are not true was also evident in the study from Bauer et al. (2023). Another result from the research indicates that most participants only sometimes check every piece of online information, as illustrated in Fig. 6. In connection with the aspect that participants were inclined to use AI in everyday life (Fig. 7), we see a need for action here.

While the results on the system´s output trustworthiness unveil an over-reliance bias, a closer look at the participants´ responses reveals a contradiction between trust in using the system and a general distrust of technical systems. After answering the questionnaire on system output and requirements, participants gave us feedback on how they envisage a trustworthy AI system. Despite the propelling results on system trust during usage, the solution suggestions reveal a high preference for human involvement and support. Examples are a real-time chat function, a contact button, expert committees to verify content, CRAAP test guidance, or supervision of AI by human experts. One participant that preferred human verification stated: "[*I want to h*]*ave a contactable human willing to provide more evidence to prove the AI's authenticity*". On a higher level of abstraction, we crystallized the paradox of the human need for human verification, namely the desire for human-made content provenance to verify machine output. Exactly this finding is contradictory, as all solutions with human involvement are inferior to machine-based or technical approaches to authenticate content from different perspectives.

6 Discussion

"AI puts everything in front of you. What's there not to believe?". Overall, this excerpt from a participant's response reflects the major insights of our studies. Moreover, it shows above all why harm protection, support for people, and content truthfulness are necessary and why addressing them through our established requirements is important.

Trust Miscalibration. Recent research confirms that a solid database and a well-trained model are essential for meaningful output. Furthermore, both factors show improvement through human-assisted uncovering and monitoring hallucinations (Alkaissi & McFarlane 2023), consistent with the participants' feedback. We advocate banning citations based on probability models, and developers must include specific rules for genAI systems in the source codes. Based on the study results, this has a significant and highly positive effect on protecting end-users from overestimating trust. Furthermore, a voluntary continuation of this approach prevents future legal regulations for AI developments, which were otherwise also seen by the survey participants as an instrument for protecting end-users. Instead of relying on legal regulations, many participants propose implementing trust grading systems (e.g., classification labels, trust charts, or raking systems). Further possible solutions included a web widget, a verification platform, color-coding, or the output of keywords for self-research. After all, it is evident that more research is required to develop adequate measures to prevent trust miscalibration.

Human Verification. Studies on end-user trust and trustworthiness of AI systems assume that AI providers and consumers should agree on contracts transparently and show that contracts might differ between the contexts of use and individual preferences (Vianello et al. 2022; Jacovi et al. 2021). In line with this, other studies demonstrate the need for explainable AI solutions to support end-user trust (Mohseni et al. 2021). In the context of our findings, we suggest further investigating the relationship between over-reliance on system output and explainability to mitigate misinformation. However, we want to highlight that this topic is even more complex as the role of the end-user and AI is shifting in the light of generative AI as a conversational agent. Thus, previous findings on AI as decision support might not be directly transferable to the new situation. Furthermore, both factors show improvement through human-assisted evaluation (Alkaissi & McFarlane 2023), which aligns with our participants' feedback.

Clarity. If the derived requirements were implemented in an end-user assessment system, clarity could be achieved on two levels. Firstly, it would foster media or AI literacy, and secondly, it would increase trust in the provider-consumer relationship. To increase media and AI literacy, there is a need for awareness and a better understanding of technical systems based on genAI (Wolf 2019). A solution that supports end-users dealing with chatGPT could increase media and AI literacy by giving the end-user information about algorithms, context, and outputs. A genAI system should not have handwritten rules or algorithms to avoid misinformation and to respect the freedom of opinion. Having unrestricted end-user support is essential during the interpretation phase of AI output. It is crucial for the end-users to realize how to comprehend the output in a supervised environment and evaluate their confidence level (Kshetri et al. 2023). Especially for younger people solutions with protective mechanisms are relevant, as growing up with the new technologies makes them less suspicious. Accordingly, they are more vulnerable to misleading information (Ali et al. 2021a, b).

To increase the trustworthiness in the provider-consumer relationship, the end-user needs background information about the system (Liao et al. 2020). Our study findings display that the background information should contain also insights about the property of AI, creators of AI, sponsors, funding, and the database. The provider can offer the consumer a FAQ solution with the necessary information. It should be standardized for all providers to increase transparency and trust. Providers should be transparent with consumers about the possibility of uncertain outputs and explain potential risks beforehand. This could prevent any disappointment or breach of trust in the future.

Limitations. Our study demonstrates that humans miscalibrate trust in AI-generated text induced by artificial hallucinations and we derive requirements to mitigate the harm caused. However, our findings must be understood relative to their context. The story-based questionnaire with Likert-type and open questions enabled quantitative and qualitative data analysis. Although we tried to mitigate bias in data collection by balancing out gender and sampling nationalities, we observed an uneven distribution in ethnicity. We conducted our survey using prolific.co platform that might not represent a cross-section of the entire society. Thus, we cannot formally rule out the presence of any bias. While our survey could benefit from a larger sample size, due to the received positive feedback and results, we are that the findings are representative and sound.

7 Conclusion and Outlook

GenAI enables new potential for society. Capabilities, such as the support in creating articles or the joint production of music, will increase (Kshetri et al. 2023). Thus, genAI bears risks for end-users, such as misinformation (Rudolph et al. 2023).

Our research identifies requirements to prevent end-users from overestimation trust in AI-generated texts. We conducted a literature review and two studies to develop and evaluate human-centered requirements. Our results contain ten requirements that indicate what a solution needs to support end-users by interpreting and dealing with text genAI. In addition, we abstracted three dimensions for developing such supporting systems. Furthermore, we observed that end-users trust the answers from genAI highly. If the chat bot provides references, the trustworthiness increase, regardless of the source's quality or the answer's content. Another observation is that participants desire to contact human support to verify the statements in case of issues or ambiguities.

With our results, we want to increase the awareness of IS research to investigate the trustworthiness of genAI and develop dedicated support to consider unintended consequences. Future work is required to transform the requirements into design principles and to implement prototypical solutions, such as a source-varifying label or a standardized FAQ. Likewise, there is a need to expand research intensity in trust and genAI and investigate the effects on end-users. In this context, it is interesting to look at the implications for platforms and deduce how the AI trust factor affects customer perception. Overall, long-term studies could be initiated. In addition, we see the current research regarding the influences of genAI on the end-user as expandable to reduce potential dangers and to promote the technology's further development. We want to contribute to the further evolution of technology and consciously point out the risk to enable the development of necessary solutions.

Acknowledgements This work has been developed in the project pipeAI (DIK0143/02) and is partly funded by the Bavarian Ministry of Economic Affairs, Regional Development and Energy within the R&D program "Informations-und Kommunikationstechnologie" managed by the VDI/VDE-IT. The authors are responsible for the content of this publication.

References

Ali , S., DiPaola, D., Lee, I., Sindato, V., Kim, G., Blumofe, R. & Breazeal, C. (2021), 'Children as creators, thinkers and citizens in an ai-driven future', Computers and Education: Artificial Intelligence 2.

Ali, S., DiPaola, D., Lee, I., Hong, J. & Breazeal, C. (2021), Exploring generative models with middle school students, in 'Conference on Human Factors in Computing Systems - Proceedings', Association for Computing Machinery.

Alkaissi, H. & McFarlane, S. I. (2023), 'Artificial hallucinations in chatgpt: Implications in scientific writing.', Cureus 15.

Arrieta, A. B., Díaz-Rodríguez, N., Ser, J. D., Bennetot, A., Tabik, S., Barbado, A., Garcia, S., Gil-Lopez, S., Molina, D., Benjamins, R., Chatila, R. & Herrera, F. (2020), 'Explainable artificial intelligence (xai): Concepts, taxonomies, opportunities and challenges toward responsible ai', Information Fusion 58, 82–115.

Bai, Y., Jones, A., Ndousse, K., Askell, A., Chen, A., DasSarma, N., Drain, D., Fort, S., Ganguli, D., Henighan, T. et al. (2022), 'Training a helpful and harmless assistant with reinforcement learning from human feedback', aXiv preprint arXiv:2204.05862 .

Bauer, K., von Zahn, M. & Hinz, O. (2023), 'Expl(AI)ned: The impact of explainable artificial intelligence on users' information processing', Inf. Syst. Res. .

Blodgett, S. L., Liao, Q. V., Olteanu, A., Mihalcea, R., Muller, M., Scheuerman, M. K., Tan, C. & Yang, Q. (2022), 'Responsible Language Technologies: Foreseeing and Mitigating Harms', Conference Human Factors in Computing Systems - Proceedings .

Carlini, N., Tramer, F., Wallace, E., Jagielski, M., Herbert-Voss, A., Lee, K., Roberts, A., Brown, T. B., Song, D., Erlingsson, U. et al. (2021), Extracting training data from large language models., in 'USENIX Security Symposium', Vol. 6.

Dale, R. (2021), 'Gpt-3: What's it good for?', Natural Language Engineering 27(1), 113– 118.

Dantas, A. C. (2023), 'Ethics in chatgpt and other ai's'. URL: https://medium.com/@adilmarcoelhodantas/ethics-in-chatgpt-and-other-ais-ee31ce8e9f09

Datta, P., Whitmore, M. & Nwankpa, J. K. (2021), 'A Perfect Storm', Digital Threats: Research and Practice 2(2).

Dhanorkar, S., Wolf, C. T., Qian, K., Xu, A., Popa, L. & Li, Y. (2021), 'Who needs to know what, when?: Broadening the Explainable AI (XAI) Design Space by Looking at Explanations across the AI Lifecycle', DIS 2021 - Proceedings of the 2021 ACM Designing Interactive Systems Conference: Nowhere and Everywhere pp. 1591–1602.

Fielding, J. A. (2019), 'Rethinking craap: Getting students thinking like fact-checkers in evaluating web sources', College & Research Libraries News 80(11), 620.

Gaševi´c, D., Siemens, G. & Sadiq, S. (2023), 'Empowering learners for the age of artificial intelligence', Computers and Education: Artificial Intelligence p. 100130.

Griesbaum, J. (2022), Informationskompetenz, Springer Berlin Heidelberg, pp. 67–98.

Hasselbalch, G. (2022), 'Testing chatgpt's ethical readiness'.**URL:** https://dataethics.eu/testing-chatgpts-ethical-readiness/

Hawlitschek, F., Kranz, T. T., Elsner, D., Fritz, F., Mense, C., Müller, M. B. & Straub, T. (2017), 'Sharewood-forest–a peer-to-peer sharing economy platform for wild camping sites in germany', HOHENHEIM DISCUSSION PAPERS IN BUSINESS, ECONOMICS AND SOCIAL SCIENCES p. 265.

Herm, L.-V., Heinrich, K., Wanner, J. & Janiesch, C. (2023), 'Stop ordering machine learning algorithms by their explainability! a user-centered investigation of performance and explainability', International Journal of Information Management 69, 102538.

Jacovi, A., Marasovi´c, A., Miller, T. & Goldberg, Y. (2021), 'Formalizing trust in artificial intelligence: Prerequisites, causes and goals of human trust in ai', FAccT2021 - Proceedings of the 2021 ACM Conference on Fairness, Accountability, and Transparency pp. 624–635.

JiZiwei, LeeNayeon, FrieskeRita, YuTiezheng, SuDan, XuYan, IshiiEtsuko, Jin, B., MadottoAndrea & FungPascale (2023), 'Survey of hallucination in natural language generation', ACM Computing Surveys 55.

Jovanovi´c, M. & Campbell, M. (2022), 'Generative Artificial Intelligence: Trends and Prospects', Computer 55(10), 107–112.

King, M. R. (2023), 'The Future of AI in Medicine: A Perspective from a Chatbot', Annals of Biomedical Engineering 51(2), 291–295.

Kshetri, N., Hughes, L., Jeyaraj, A., Kar, A. K., Dwivedi, Y. K., Slade, E. L. & Wright, R. (2023), 'Multidisciplinary perspectives on opportunities, challenges and implications of generative conversational ai for research, practice and policy', International Journal of Information Management forthcoming.

Laupichler, M. C., Aster, A., Schirch, J. & Raupach, T. (2022), 'Artificial intelligence literacy in higher and adult education: A scoping literature review', Computers and Education: Artificial Intelligence 3, 100101.

Lee, M. K., Grgi´c-Hlaˇca, N., Tschantz, M. C., Binns, R., Weller, A., Carney, M. & Inkpen, K. (2020), 'Human-centered approaches to fair and responsible AI', Conference on Human Factors in Computing Systems - Proceedings .

Lehmann, F., Markert, N., Dang, H. & Buschek, D. (2022), 'Suggestion Lists vs. Continuous Generation: Interaction Design for Writing with Generative Models on Mobile Devices Affect Text Length, Wording and Perceived Authorship', ACM International Conference Proceeding Series pp. 192–208.

Liao, Q. V., Gruen, D. & Miller, S. (2020), 'Questioning the AI: Informing Design Practices for Explainable AI User Experiences', Conference on Human Factors in Computing Systems - Proceedings pp. 1–15.

Liao, Q. V. & Varshney, K. R. (2021), 'Human-Centered Explainable AI (XAI): From Algorithms to User Experiences'.

Long, D. & Magerko, B. (2020), What is ai literacy? competencies and design considerations, in 'Proceedings of the 2020 CHI Conference on Human Factors in Computing Systems', CHI '20, Association for Computing Machinery, New York, NY, USA, p. 1–16.

Longoni, C., Fradkin, A., Cian, L. & Pennycook, G. (2022), 'News from Generative Artificial Intelligence Is Believed Less', ACM International Conference Proceeding Series 22, 97–106.

Lund, B. & Ting, W. (2023), 'Chatting about ChatGPT: How May AI and GPT Impact Academia and Libraries?', SSRN Electronic Journal .

Macneil, S., Tran, A., Mogil, D., Bernstein, S., Ross, E. & Huang, Z. (2022), 'Generating diverse code explanations using the gpt-3 large language model', Proceedings of the 2022 ACM Conference on International Computing Education Research - Volume 2 2, 3.

Meske, C., Bunde, E., Schneider, J. & Gersch, M. (2020), 'Explainable artificial intelligence: Objectives, stakeholders, and future research opportunities', https://doi.org/10.1080/10580530.2020.1849465 39, 53–63.

Mohseni, S., Zarei, N. & Ragan, E. D. (2021), 'A multidisciplinary survey and framework for design and evaluation of explainable ai systems', ACM Transactions on Interactive Intelligent Systems (TiiS) 11.

Muller, M., Chilton, L. B., Kantosalo, A., Maher, M. L., Martin, C. P. & Walsh, G. (2022), 'GenAICHI: Generative AI and HCI', Conference on Human Factors in Computing Systems - Proceedings .

Ng, D. T. K., Leung, J. K. L., Chu, S. K. W. & Qiao, M. S. (2021), 'Conceptualizing AI literacy: An exploratory review', Computers and Education: Artificial Intelligence 2, 100041.

Nigam, A., Pollice, R., Krenn, M., Gomes, G. D. P. & Aspuru-Guzik, A. (2021), 'Beyond generative models: superfast traversal, optimization, novelty, exploration and discovery (stoned) algorithm for molecules using selfies', Chemical Science 12, 7079–7090.

Nobari, A. H., Rashad, M. F. & Ahmed, F. (2021), 'Creativegan: Editing generative adversarial networks for creative design synthesis', Proceedings of the ASME Design Engineering Technical Conference 3A-2021.

OpenAI (2023a), 'Chatgpt feb 13 version'.

OpenAI (2023b), 'Chatgpt feb 13 version'.

Pinsonneault, A. & Kraemer, K. (1993), 'Survey research methodology in management information systems: an assessment', Journal of management information systems 10(2), 75–105.

Radford, A., Narasimhan, K., Salimans, T., Sutskever, I. et al. (2018), 'Improving language understanding by generative pre-training'.

Rudolph, J., Tan, S. & Tan, S. (2023), 'Chatgpt: Bullshit spewer or the end of traditional assessments in higher education?', Journal of Applied Learning and Teaching 6(1).

Sbai, O., Elhoseiny, M., Bordes, A., LeCun, Y. & Couprie, C. (2018), 'Design: Design inspiration from generative networks', Lecture Notes in Computer Science (including subseries Lecture Notes in Artificial Intelligence and Lecture Notes in Bioinformatics) 11131 LNCS, 37–44.

Seeber, I., Bittner, E., Briggs, R. O., de Vreede, T., de Vreede, G. J., Elkins, A., Maier, R., Merz, A. B., Oeste-Reiß, S., Randrup, N., Schwabe, G. & Söllner, M. (2020), 'Machines as teammates: A research agenda on ai in team collaboration', Information & Management 57, 103174.

Shneiderman, B. (2020), 'Bridging the Gap Between Ethics and Practice', ACM Transactions on Interactive Intelligent Systems (TiiS) 10(4).

Smuha, N. A. (2019), 'The eu approach to ethics guidelines for trustworthy artificial intelligence', Computer Law Review International 20(4), 97–106.

Sun, J., Liao, Q. V., Muller, M., Agarwal, M., Houde, S., Talamadupula, K. & Weisz, J. D. (2022), 'Investigating Explainability of Generative AI for Code through Scenario-based Design', International Conference on Intelligent User Interfaces, Proceedings IUI 22, 212–228.

Thiebes, S., Lins, S. & Sunyaev, A. (2021), 'Trustworthy artificial intelligence', Electronic Markets 31, 447–464.

Tomitza, C., Schaschek, M., Straub, L. & Winkelmann, A. (2023), 'Supplementary material for "what is the minimum to trust ai? - a requirement analysis for (generative) ai-based texts"'. **URL:** https://b2share.eudat.eu/records/5109b4ee67894844a419c20e6522dbbe

Vianello, A., Laine, S. & Tuomi, E. (2022), 'Improving Trustworthiness of AI Solutions: A Qualitative Approach to Support Ethically-Grounded AI Design', https://doi.org/10.1080/10447318.2022.2095478 .

Vincent, J. (2022), 'Openai's new chatbot can explain code and write sitcom scripts but is still easily tricked'. **URL:** https://www.theverge.com/23488017/openai-chatbot-chatgpt-ai-examples-web-demo

vom Brocke, J., Simons, A., Niehaves, B., Riemer, K., Plattfaut, R. & Cleven, A. (2009), Reconstructing the giant: On the importance of rigour in documenting the literature search process, in 'European Conference on Information Systems', pp. 2206–2217.

vom Brocke, J., Winter, R., Hevner, A. & Maedche, A. (2020), 'Special issue editorial–accumulation and evolution of design knowledge in design science research: a journey through time and space', Journal of the Association for Information Systems 21(3), 9.

Wanner, J., Herm, L.-V., Heinrich, K., Janiesch, C. & Zschech, P. (2020), White, grey, black: Effects of xai augmentation on the confidence in ai-based decision support systems., in 'Proceedings of Forty-First International Conference on Information Systems'.

Weisz, J. D., Maher, M. L., Strobelt, H., Chilton, L. B., Bau, D. & Geyer, W. (2022), 'HAI-GEN 2022: 3rd Workshop on Human-AI Co-Creation with Generative Models', International Conference on Intelligent User Interfaces, Proceedings IUI pp. 4–6.

Weisz, J. D., Muller, M., He, J. & Houde, S. (2023), 'Toward General Design Principles for Generative AI Applications'.

Weisz, J. D., Muller, M., Houde, S., Richards, J., Ross, S. I., Martinez, F., Agarwal, M. & Talamadupula, K. (2021), 'Perfection Not Required? Human-AI Partnerships in Code Translation', International Conference on Intelligent User Interfaces, Proceedings IUI pp. 402–412.

Wolf, C. T. (2019), 'Explainability scenarios: Towards scenario-based XAI design', International Conference on Intelligent User Interfaces, Proceedings IUI Part F1476, 252–257.

Zdanowska, S. & Taylor, A. S. (2022), 'A study of UX practitioners roles in designing real-world, enterprise ML systems', Conference on Human Factors in Computing Systems - Proceedings .

Zhou, Y., Koyama, Y., Goto, M. & Igarashi, T. (2020), 'Generative Melody Composition with Human-in-the-Loop Bayesian Optimization'.

Exploring Digital Social Norms Nudges in E-Grocery: Typical Consumer Testimonials with a Warm Glow

Phillip Gottschewski-Meyer, Nicole Lüddemann, Marvin Auf der Landwehr, and Christoph von Viebahn

Abstract Digitization offers several possibilities to alter consumer decisions to support social concerns. The objective of this study is to examine the impact of personalized digital social norm nudges on consumer decisions enriched with the theory of warm glow on e-grocery buying decisions with the aim of supporting social projects. Specific pro-social behaviors targeted were supporting fair payment of the producers of grocery goods, social inclusion projects and initiatives against poverty by deciding for a specific choice option. A between-subjects experiment was performed with the help of a questionnaire using a mock-up mobile grocery store to measure product choices. Results showed that claims supporting pro-social initiatives have a significant impact on buying decisions. Perceived product recommendation influenced our model positively, while we had a negative price impact. The study suggests that warm glow theory and enriched social norm nudges are effective tools for behavior change towards social initiatives.

Keywords Digital nudging · Social justice · Warm glow · E-grocery

P. Gottschewski-Meyer (✉) · N. Lüddemann · M. A. der Landwehr · C. von Viebahn
Faculty IV—Business and Informatics, Hochschule Hannover, Hannover, Germany
e-mail: phillip-oliver.gottschewski@hs-hannover.de

N. Lüddemann
e-mail: nicole-anika.lueddemann@hs-hannover.de

M. A. der Landwehr
e-mail: marvin.auf-der-landwehr@hs-hannover.de

C. von Viebahn
e-mail: christoph-von.viebahn@hs-hannover.de

D. Beverungen et al. (eds.), *Conceptualizing Digital Responsibility for the Information Age*, Lecture Notes in Information Systems and Organisation 74,
https://doi.org/10.1007/978-3-031-80119-8_15

1 Introduction

The rise of digital technologies and their presence in daily life is steadily evolving. Consumers are increasingly utilizing digital technologies for daily tasks, such as e-grocery shopping, in order to save both time and effort, *"like travel, transportation and in-store shopping time, as well as physical convenience"* (Gottschewski et al. 2022, pp. 1–2). Such everyday decisions on which grocery articles to buy can make a decisive contribution towards a more social, economic and ecologic sustainable world (Camilleri et al. 2019; Ganglmair-Wooliscroft and Wooliscroft 2022). Along with the digitization of retail and grocery shopping as well as various other domains the opportunities for information systems (IS) research to contribute to the reduction of (digital) inequalities have expanded (Vassilakopoulou and Hustad 2021). Its importance is very well known and already addressed in the research community, as *"sustainability constitutes the most important long-term problem that the world faces"* (Watson et al. 2021, p. 496). Yet, despite the evolving need for corporate social responsibility initiatives from both societal and regulative perspectives (Porter and Kramer 2006), social concerns such as social justice, social inclusion, social equity and alike are currently underrepresented in IS research (Schoormann and Kutzner 2020).

Grocery shopping, a routine task performed regularly, often requires minimal cognitive effort and relies on the use of heuristics (Ganglmair-Wooliscroft and Wooliscroft 2022). So, the possibility to alter decisions towards the better (i.e., a more socially equal world) by exploiting these heuristics is given. A promising concept to foster behaviors aimed at the welfare of society is the concept of digital nudging (Collier and Johnson 2021; Henkel et al. 2019), which is defined as "*any aspect of the choice environment that alters behaviour in a predictable way*" (Thaler and Sunstein 2009, p. 6). Digital Nudges (DN) can improve decision making in the digital hemisphere towards the individual or public welfare (Sunstein 2014; Weinmann et al. 2016). When implemented with a specific goal (Mirsch et al. 2017), various digital nudging concepts (DNC) each exploiting human heuristics to be effective have worked well in commercial areas (Dennis et al. 2020; Lehner et al. 2016), and especially in the context of online grocery shopping (Auf der Landwehr et al. 2021; Gottschewski et al. 2022). From a theoretical perspective, the concept of social norms (SN) may prove to be a promising approach in e-grocery to encourage more pro-social choices. SN have a decisive advantage over other concepts to alter behavior towards societal welfare, namely they can change collective attitudes, bring awareness about urgent societal issues (i.e., supporting social projects) and thus, increase social pressure to act socially acceptable or desirable (Andrighetto and Vriens 2022). Hence, SN can create peer effects, influencing the behavior of individuals within a group (Ajilore et al. 2014; Burke 2008). SN also might counter the diminishing effect of DN over time as it changes attitudes rather than short term behavior (Babar et al. 2023; e.g., Sunstein 2016). Also, Engler et al. (2019) argue that behavior is primarily related to in-group favoritism, a concept involving social comparison to distinguish between the preferred in-group towards the not preferred out-group. Thus, in-group favoritism could lead to positive reinforcement of the SN effect (i.e., injunctive norms). Though, in contrast to other DNCs, the efficacy of digital SN nudges has been found to be inconclusive and may be attributed to variations in the implementation of the SN nudge concept across studies. SN interventions were either unsuccessful (Auf der Landwehr et al. 2021; Katner and Jianu 2019) or partially successful (Stuber et al. 2022) indicating a socially accepted product via a claim (e.g., "*Bestseller*"). Yet, if used as a social comparison nudge, SN interventions were successfully implemented and changed buying behavior (DiCosola III and Neff 2020). Thus, we seek to investigate on the effect of peer group specific digital SN nudges on consumer behavior.

More recently, it has been recognized that "*warm glow*" is also a theory worth exploring to foster behavior related to social concerns (Iweala et al. 2019). Warm Glow (WG) is defined as positive emotional experience after the act of helping (Hörisch and Tenner 2020). In recent studies, WG was also investigated on in the e-grocery context, using pro-social and pro-environmental claims successfully (Iweala et al., 2019) or fostering recurring organic grocery purchases (Cahyasita et al. 2021). WG works because humans *"derive psychological benefits from […] altruistic actions"* (Cahyasita et al. 2021, p. 904) in feeling a "*warm glow*". Since it has been shown in various contexts that enriching DN interventions with other concepts has been found to have decent impacts on nudge effectivity (Jesse and Jannach 2021; Zimmermann and Renaud 2021), we seek to enrich the concept of peer group specific digital SN nudges with the theory of WG in one intervention to examine the effects on consumer decisions. Consequently, investigating on (a) peer group specific SN nudges in e-grocery (b) in combination with the theory of WG (c) to enhance effectivity of fostering consumer decisions that support social projects deserves examination and constitutes a research gap this study seeks to fill. Therefore, and following the calls for further research in IS on both social concerns (Schoormann and Kutzner 2020) and combinatorial nudges (Gottschewski et al. 2022) we opt to investigate on the following research questions (RQ):

> ***RQ1:*** *Does the implementation of digital social norm nudges, modeled on typical consumer testimonials, influence purchasing decisions in the context of e-grocery?*
> ***RQ2:*** *How does incorporating the warm glow concept affect the effectiveness of digital social norm nudges on pro-social grocery selection decisions?*

To answer our RQ, we conducted a randomized between subject experiment with the help of a questionnaire using a mock-up mobile grocery store testing SN interventions through peer group relevant testimonials (Friedman et al. 1976) and the influence of the WG theory on these interventions to foster pro-social behavior comparing against a control group without any intervention. Conducting online experiments in IS is an underused, yet, in the context of behavioral research particularly fruitful methodology and thus, we follow the call of Fink (2022) to expand the body of research in this area. This paper proceeds as follows: firstly, we shed light on the theoretical background of DN, the concept of SN and its relation to WG theory. Secondly, we outline our hypotheses and explain our research model. Then, we describe our experimental design. Afterwards we are testing our hypotheses. Subsequently, we present and discuss our results and highlight certain limitations of this study. Finally, we provide conclusions and ideas for future research to expand upon the findings of this paper.

2 Theoretical Background

2.1 Digital Social Norms Nudges in E-Grocery

IS can support to counter social concerns via a multitude of tools, concepts and methods (Vassilakopoulou and Hustad 2021), including digital nudges, which can refer to several concepts, such as the concept of social norms. Evolution has shown that humans adapt to the behavior of their social environment. People imitate behavioral patterns and want to do what is social and ethical, i.e., in accordance with good manners (van Vugt et al. 2014). Moreover, individuals exhibit a tendency to affirm socially desirable actions and behaviors while denying socially undesirable ones (Chung and Monroe 2003). Thus, SN can influence behavior by either demonstrating or suggesting that it is generally accepted to behave according to a target state (Lehner et al. 2016). As a means of persuasion in decision-making, SN are effective because people memorize that others have acted specifically in the same situation (Sunstein 2014).

Recent studies have explored DN in various application fields following the concept of SN. For example, Loschelder et al. (2019) proved the effectiveness of SN nudges in promoting the adoption of sustainable coffee to-go cups or Bauer et al. (2019) used SN to support suicide prevention. However, whilst research has identified several use-cases in which digital SN nudges are effective, only few studies have been conducted successfully within the area of e-grocery. Demarque et al. (2015) have used social influence in a virtual grocery shop and found these as effective to foster pro-environmental shopping behavior. Despite these findings, Auf der Landwehr et al. (2021) have found SN to be inappropriate to foster more eco-sustainable delivery slot selections. Richter et al. (2018) investigated on behavior when buying seafood online using descriptive SN and found sales dropping in a multitude of studies. Berger et al. (2020) also could not find any influence of digital SN nudges in their e-grocery experiment. Further studies also used textual claims indicating a peer group to follow (e.g. "*other customers also bought*") but failed in altering product choices (Bunten et al. 2021; Jansen et al. 2021).

However, there are also studies which have been successfully implemented SN interventions, such as DiCosola III and Neff (2020), investigating on SN to foster more healthy e-grocery choices. Studies using personalized SN in e-grocery following the concept of DN are scarce. For example, Bauw et al. (2022) showed positive effects using descriptive norms and personalized feedback. In summary, one could conclude it depends on how SN nudges are used in e-grocery to alter decisions for the good of society successfully. For our study, we use personalized typical consumer testimonials (TCT) as a special form of SN theory, that indicates social approval of product choices. Testimonials are peripherical cues and work best when a source–receiver similarity is given (Martin et al. 2008). Moreover, consumers feel the social presence of the testimonial which can reinforce the effect of the TCT (Elgaaied-Gambier et al. 2018), as it *"increases the accessibility of words that are applicable to social desirability"* (He et al. 2012, p. 303). Friedman et al. (1976) identified three types of endorsers, including the typical consumer who is described as an ordinary person with no special knowledge about the product beyond what can be gained through normal use. Typical consumer endorsers *"are most effective for products ranking low in risk"* (Dean and Biswas 2001, p. 43), such as grocery products. Also, TCTs are used to indicate positive transformative effects of the use of the product recommended (Schimmelpfennig 2019). Studies suggest that testimonials are more effective when the testimonial appears to be within the same in-group (e.g., age group or gender, cf. Gupta and George 2013) which can impact behavior as it is based on group identity (White et al. 2019).

2.2 *Warm Glow Theory to Foster Pro-Social Consumer Behavior*

Warm glow theory is an emerging topic of interest for promoting sustainable consumption and behavior (Mahasuweerachai and Suttikun 2022). The theory describes a positive emotional experience after engaging in actions that promote positive societal or environmental outcomes (Hartmann et al. 2017; Hörisch and Tenner 2020), perceived as a personal benefit and a feeling of a "warm glow" (Andreoni 1989; Taufik et al. 2015). The feeling itself arises from an activation of neurons which are similar to receiving a payment (i.e., activation of the mesolimbic pathway, cf. Harbaugh et al. 2007). Thus, consumers can be nudged into more pro-social behavior patterns if a WG reward is possible.

The application areas of the WG theory to promote socially beneficial outcomes are manifold. Halvorsen (2008) investigated on the willingness to recycle and found both, SN and WG, as inseparable factors that both increase recycling activities of households. Hartmann et al. (2017) were able to find WG as a decisive factor for pro-environmental behavior within the area of green electricity. Several studies utilized WG theory to enhance the effectivity of activities of charitable donations (e.g., Hörisch and Tenner 2020; Scharf 2014). Allison et al. (2013) examined how WG influences microloan funding of investors to support developing countries. Pro-social spending was found to have a positive effect on the mood, making a person even happier than spending the money for oneself (Dunn et al. 2014). In the context of e-grocery shopping, Iweala et al. (2019) were investigating on the effect of WG on food choices, finding pro-social (ethical) claims to be more effective as pro-environmental claims. Cahyasita et al. (2021) found a positive correlation between WG and the attitude to consume organic food repeatedly. Finally, Jia and Linden (2020) were investigating on green warm-glow within the context of food retailing and were able to predict pro-environmental decisions. Thus, we consider using WG theory to be a promising theory for behavioral change and seek to expand the existing body of knowledge in this regard. However, within the research area of DN, research including the theory of WG to promote socially beneficial outcomes is scarce. Reinholdsson et al. (2022) investigated on more eco-sustainable hamburger choices, but no effect of an informational nudge intervention using WG theory was found. Hence, investigating on the interplay between SN and WG theory to alter consumer decisions towards more pro-social behavior patterns is a subject worth exploring on, since SN offer serious advantages over other concepts of digital nudging to overcome the challenge of the need to act more digital and social responsible (Herden et al. 2021). Thus, we seek to shed light on the efficacy of a combination of SN and WG theory in one intervention using TCTs enriched with the theory of WG.

3 Hypotheses

SN can alter attitudes, raise awareness of societal issues, and increase social pressure for desirable behavior (Andrighetto and Vriens 2022). Moreover, the impact of SN on one person has the ability to impact the attitudes of numerous others (Ajilore et al. 2014; Burke 2008). In this study, we examine on a special form of SN, the TCT. According to Dean and Biswas (2001), TCT is suited best for products which are associated with a low risk. Grocery goods usually do not have a high price, nor do they have any associated risk when buying. Thus, interventions feature higher likeliness to be effective in this context. Also, the social presence of a testimonial should impact the efficacy of the message transported with the TCT (He et al. 2012). Also, we opt to use different testimonial messages, such as positive product reviews, transformative effects of buying the related product or a direct product recommendation. While positive product reviews and product recommendations are known for their effects on buying behavior (e.g., Wang et al. 2019), they also suggest a socially accepted product (Cialdini and Goldstein 2004) that directly addresses consumers. Suggesting transformative effects of products are used in marketing successfully (e.g., pharmaceuticals, cf. Schimmelpfennig 2019). Also, in-group favoritism could lead to a reinforcement of the SN effect (Engler et al. 2019), which is triggered by the peer group relevant testimonial in our study. Hence, we expect a high effectivity of the intervention and hypothesize:

> ***H1:*** *The presence of peer group relevant TCT interventions indicating a positive product review increases sales compared to the absence of an intervention*

***H2:** The presence of peer group relevant TCT interventions indicating a transformative effect of the purchase increases sales compared to the absence of an intervention.*
***H3:** The presence of peer group relevant TCT interventions indicating a product recommendation increases sales compared to the absence of an intervention.*

Enriching DN following the concept of SN with the theory of WG to foster purchase decisions which supports pro-social projects can enhance effectivity of DN interventions. Providing the opportunity to receive a WG reward from deciding for low-risk grocery goods can effectively nudge consumers towards adopting more pro-social behavior patterns (Liao et al. 2020). Communicating the intention behind an action that contributes to positive societal or environmental outcomes may enhance individuals' perception of attaining a WG (Bronnmann et al. 2021). In line with Schoormann and Kutzner (2020), we chose three social purposes (social inclusion, social justice, social equity) to be included in the message of the TCT. Additionally, combining or enriching DN interventions with other theories and concepts have shown better effectivity than single interventions in various other studies (Jesse and Jannach 2021; Zimmermann and Renaud 2021). Furthermore, providing the possibility to support projects related to social purposes triggers the need to act socially desirable (Chung and Monroe 2003), which is reinforced by the presence of the in-group testimonial (He et al. 2012).

***H4:** The presence of peer group relevant TCT interventions indicating a positive product review and supporting social inclusion projects increases sales compared to the absence of an intervention.*
***H5:** The presence of peer group relevant TCT interventions indicating a transformative effect of the purchase and supporting social justice projects increases sales compared to the absence of an intervention.*
***H6:** The Presence of Peer Group Relevant TCT Interventions Indicating Product Recommendation and Supporting Social Equity Projects Increases Sales Compared to the Absence of an Intervention*

To test above hypotheses, we will conduct an online experiment, which we will present in the next chapter. Our research model is depicted in Fig. 1.

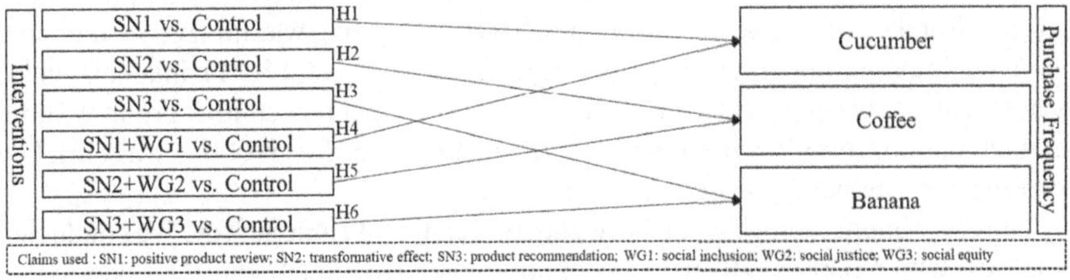

Fig. 1 Research model

4 Method

To answer our research questions and to conduct our experiment we developed a mobile grocery store mock-up using the platform Uizard. We opt for a design similar to the mobile webpage of a German grocery retail chain, in which three choice options per screen and product category were shown. The environment was designed including typical optical features of popular mobile webpages, such as a wish list, profile page and alike (cf. Fig. 2). Three common grocery categories were to be bought (coffee, bananas, cucumbers). We deliberately choose bananas and cucumbers as rather low involvement products and coffee as a high involvement product (Kuenzel and Musters 2007) to mix between cheaper and more expensive products. Within the product category, we opt for a price tolerance of ± 8% (92%/100%/108%) of the respective market price in January 2023 and decided to choose the most expensive products per category to be nudged to circumvent any price-induced effects on the decision (Hartmann-Boyce et al. 2018). To avoid brand affinity of the participants, we only chose generic no name products (cucumber, banana) or manipulated existing brand designs within one color spectrum (i.e., rust-brown for coffee). Furthermore, to avoid effects by sorting the products we mixed the nudge position between the products so that neither the nudged nor the cheapest product was at the same position within the three screens every participant had to go through. We created customer testimonials in a two-step approach. First, we designed our nudge interventions by following the DN design guidelines by Mirsch et al. (2018), namely by defining the nudge context and goal, the respective theory behind, specifically the digital nudge concept SN including the enrichment factor WG, TCT theory and social concern aspects to be covered within the interventions. Afterwards we created different textual claims as well as designs and aligned on the final selection within the research group in a common workshop. The TCT was then designed in the following manner: we randomly selected AI-generated pictures of average looking people per peer group to avoid any similarity with celebrities created by generative adversarial networks from the webpage thispersondoesnotexist.com. Generative adversarial networks are AI algorithms which generate infinite streams of photorealistic human faces, each of which is unique and never existed before (Karras et al. 2019). To cover all peer groups in our experiment, we chose to structure the interventions by age (18–29, 30–39, 40–49, 50–64, 65–99) and gender (male, female) and selected one picture per age group and gender to be the testimonial. Every age group was nudged by the same claim per intervention group (IG) (independent variables, cf. Fig. 1), independent of gender. Hence, we applied two IGs (SN, SN + WG) and one control group without an intervention. Both IGs used the same SN claim, the SN + WG IGs was enriched with the corresponding WG claim (cf. Fig. 2).

The experiment took place in the academic version of LimeSurvey. We conducted a pre-test with 5 participants using a cognitive-pretesting method (cf. Koskey 2016) to validate the survey and ensure participants understanding. Comments were incorporated into the survey as applicable. The final survey was done via a crowdsourcing platform (i.e., *Clickworker*) and participants were paid a small participation reward.

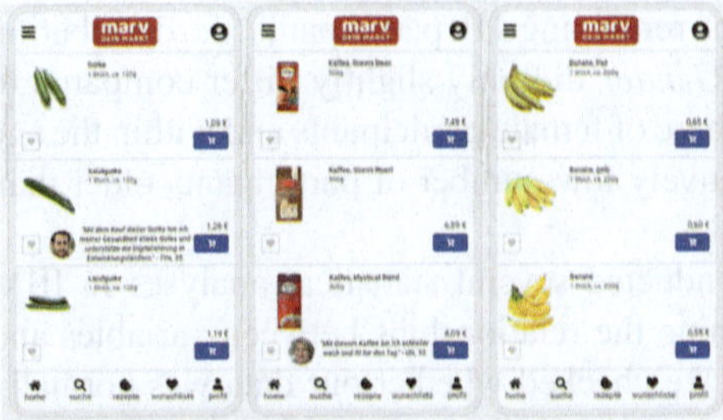

Product	Picture	SNx	SNxWGx	x
		"By buying this cucumber, I am doing something good for my health." - Eve, 19	*"By buying this cucumber, I am doing something good for my health and supporting digitalisation in developing countries." - Eve, 19*	1
		"This coffee makes me wake up faster and fit for the day." - Pia, 23	*"This coffee makes me wake up faster, fit for the day and 10% goes to projects against poverty in the country of production. Great!" - Pia, 23*	2
		"As an energy supplier, the perfect choice for a successful day!" - Kim, 26	*"As an energy supplier, the perfect choice for a successful day! Buying guarantees fair payment to the producer, great!" - Kim, 26*	3

SN1: positive product review; SN2: transformative effect; SN3: product recommendation; WG1: social inclusion; WG2: social justice; WG3: social equity; x=number of claim

Fig. 2 Choice environment (from left to right: SN1 + WG1 male 30–39, SN2 female 50–64, control) and TCT claims per intervention (translated to English, female 18–29 TCT)

Thoughtful use of crowdsourcing platforms expands participant diversity, capturing a wider range of demographics (education level, income, etc.) compared to traditional pools of university students, relatives, and friends (Mason and Suri 2012). When starting the experiment, participants were confronted with an initial screen which was explaining the reason and the topic of the experiment including a disclaimer for data protection. After entering the survey, a number between 1 and 3 was created not visible to the participants to allocate the user randomly to the IG (1 SN, 2 SN + WG, 3 Control). Then, the survey was divided in three sections. To ensure a high quality of the answers provided by the crowd workers, we first asked for the user identification number of the participants (to identify abusive users), age and gender. In the second section the participants were first informed about the shopping task and confronted with the mobile environment in which they ought to choose their product of choice per product category in three different screens. Selections were saved per participant to be able to evaluate the purchase frequency (dependent variable) later on. Afterwards, a manipulation check question (*"Did you recognize a product recommendation?"*) to ensure participants recognized the manipulation of the independent variable as intended and an attention check question were asked, along with a question for the reasons for the selection (multiple choice) as well as the general attitude towards social equity on a 5-point Likert-scale. After collecting data on the participant's online purchase frequency per time period, the experiment ended with a concluding message.

5 Results

5.1 Descriptive Statistics

Out of a total of 556 participants we had to exclude 137 due to either failed attention checks (25), failed manipulation checks (97) or not finishing the study (15). Although especially high for the manipulation checks (17.4%), exclusion rates are in line with other (digital nudging) experiments (e.g., Mager and Kranz 2021; Schär 2021; Schär et al. 2022; Terres et al. 2019). Within the remaining 419 participants, the distribution of the independent variables *Age* and *Gender* did only slightly differ compared to the German population, with a higher share of female participants and within the age group of 30–39 years as well as a relatively low number of participants older than 65 years (cf. further statistics in Table 1).

To evaluate our experiment, we conducted several statistical analyses in IBM SPSS Statistics 28.0.0.0 (190) to examine the relationships between variables and test for significant differences. Firstly, we checked whether our data was normally distributed using Kolmogorov-Smirnova (using Lilliefors significance correction) and Shapiro–Wilk tests, with the result that the data was not normally distributed. The homogeneity of the variances was further checked with Levene's test, which showed that no equality of variances could be assumed ($p < 0.05$). To correct for variance heterogeneity we performed a Welch ANOVA, which showed that the purchase frequency of the single items (SPF) differed statistically significant for the different interventions (cf. Table 1). Thus, we were able to continue with our statistical analysis.

Table 1 Selective descriptive statistics and Welch ANOVA

Selective descriptive statistics					
Controls	Mean	StD	Min	Max	N
Age group*	2.42	1.098	1	5	419
Gender**	0.42	0.499	0	2	419
Dependant variables—purchase frequencies					
SPF cucumber	0.17	0.378	0	1	419
SPF coffee	0.11	0.319	0	1	419
SPF banana	0.17	0.378	0	1	419
Independent variables—intervention groups					
SN	0.23	0.526	0	3	120
SN WG	0.80	1.021	0	3	135
Control	0.35	0.613	0	3	164
Welch ANOVA					
Dependant variables—purchase frequencies	Statistic***	dll	dt2	P	
SPF cucumber	6.656	2	271.7	0.002	
SPF coffee	6.814	2	261.7	0.001	
SPF banana	19.946	2	252.5	< 0.001	

* Gender was dummy coded (0 male, 1 female, 2 diverse)
** Age group was coded 1 = 18–29; 2 = 30–39; 3 = 40–49; 4 = 50–64; 5 = 65–99
*** Asymptotically F-distributed

5.2 Planned Contrast Analysis and Regression Analysis

To test our hypotheses, we performed a planned contrast analysis for not equal variances to investigate on the specific differences between the three IGs (cf. Table 2). Contrast 1 compared SN1-3 against control (H1-3), while contrast 2 compared SN + WG1-3 against control (H4-6). Results showed that contrast 1 has a significant effect for the intervention SN1 on the product cucumber. Contrast value reveals a negative impact. Thus, the intervention was backfiring and SPF was worse than control (contrast value (CV) = – 0.106; $p = 0.008$), so we reject H1. We further have to reject H2 and H3, showing no significant effect against control for the interventions on coffee (SN2: CV = – 0.021; $p = 0.488$) and banana (SN3: CV = 0.004; $p =$ 0.902). Contrast 2 was found to be non-significant for the product cucumber and intervention SN1 + WG1 (CV = 0.040; $p = 0.394$), but significant for both of the other interventions SN2 + WG2 on coffee (CV = 0.128; $p = 0.002$) and SN3 + WG3 on banana (CV = 0.284; $p > 0.001$), thus accepting H5 and H6 (cf. Table 2). To control for influences of the product type on the effect of the SN interventions we additionally tested rather unfamiliar organic products in a follow up study, with no significant differences ($p > 0.05$) against non-organic products.

Additionally, we performed three binomial logistic regression analyses per each product to examine the relationships between the different variables and to identify significant predictors and their effect on the related SPF. With N = 419 and a maximum of 11 predictors in our study the minimal sample size was exceeded to perform the analysis (Burmeister and Aitken 2012). We used the Box-Tidwell procedure to test linearity (Box and Tidwell 1962) and determined that all variables exhibited a linear correlation using Bonferroni correction ($\alpha = 0.004$). Multicollinearity did not have a confounding effect in the analysis, since the correlations between predictor variables were below $r < 0.60$. We removed outliers (cucumber: 0, coffee 1, banana 4) from the analysis because lever values were above the cut-off value of 0.2 according to Huber (1981) and their corresponding Cook distances were excessively high (Cook 1977). Overall models were statistically significant for all three products (cucumber $\chi^2(22) = 92.839$ p < 0.001; coffee $\chi^2(22) = 102.304$, $p < 0.001$; banana $\chi^2(22) = 152.254$, $p < 0.001$). Variance explanation was acceptable (cucumber $R^2 =$ 0.331) or good (coffee $R^2 = 0.430$) or even very good (banana $R2 = 0.520$) using

Table 2 Planned contrast analysis

SPF	Contrast	Contrast name	Contrast value	Std.-error	T	df	p
Cucumber	1	SN1 – Control	– 0.106	0.040	– 2.657	281.7	0.008**
Cucumber	2	SN1 + WG1 – Control	0.041	0.048	0.854	277.3	0.394
Coffee	1	SN2 – Control	– 0.021	0.030	– 0.694	273.8	0.488
Coffee	2	SN2 + WG2 – Control	0.128	0.041	3.131	225.0	0.002**
Banana	1	SN3 – Control	0.004	0.033	0.123	253.0	0.902
Banana	2	SN3 + WG3 – Control	0.284	0.047	6.085	201.4	< 0.001***

* indicates significance at 95%, ** at 99%, *** at 99.9% level

Nagelkerkes *R*2 (Backhaus et al. 2021). Goodness-of-fit using Hosmer–Lemeshow-test indicated a good model fit for all three analyses (cucumber $\chi^2(8) = 5.768$, $p > 0.05$; coffee $\chi^2(8) = 8.914$; $p > 0.05$; banana $\chi^2(8) = 3.738$, $p > 0.05$). Decision reason *price* contributed significantly negatively in predicting all of the three SPFs (cucumber and coffee at 99.9%, banana at 99% level) and *product recommendation* significantly positively at 99.9% for all three products. SPF of banana was also significant at 99.9% level for the purchase reason *gut feeling* and at 95% significant for decision reason *appealing product. SPF for cucumber was* as well found as negatively significant at 95% for *gender (female).* A detailed overview about the model coefficients and odds ratios is depicted in Table 3.

6 Implications, Limitations and Conclusion

The aim of this study was to investigate on peer group specific SN nudges using TCTs in the context of e-grocery. We further enriched the intervention with the theory of WG and measured its effects on consumer decisions. Our research model argued that the usage of these interventions will significantly increase purchase frequency against the control group. We found that especially the SN interventions were not successful, with SN1 (and SN2, though not significantly) even resulting in a backfire effect (Bicchieri and Dimant 2022), so the intervention decreased the SPF compared to control. SN interventions indicating a positive product review seem to provoke counter reactions by the participants, leading to a lower purchase rate than in the control group without an intervention. We believe that the intervention was not able to overcome the moderate price difference of 8%, especially for the higher price product coffee, since price was shown as a negative factor (B = − 1.905). We estimate that a higher price sensitivity due to the current high inflation rate and the ongoing energy crisis in Europe might have led to a more price sensitive choice behavior within the IG for SN. Although we opt to select equally looking product pictures, we cannot rule out a difference in *product appeal* between the choice options for the product banana, as found by the regression analyses. Also, altruistic actions, such as the act of supporting a purpose with the reward of a WG, work in the fast, intuitive cognitive system (Karlan and Wood 2017), similar to digital SN nudges (Vlaev et al. 2016), thus we believe *gut feeling* had an influence on the SPF for banana. Unexpectedly, we could not find any significant effect on the SPF of the product cucumber, which tried to trigger support for the digitization of emerging countries (SN1 + WG1). Since the single SN intervention was backfiring, we assume that the SN intervention was decreasing the overall effectiveness. Another possibility could be either that the understanding of the necessity of digitalization in emerging countries is low (Sunstein 2016), since it is not directly supporting people (i.e., digital participation, access to information, improved quality of life, cf. Schoormann and Kutzner 2020) or that participants may not perceive the project as a valuable contribution, as other priorities take precedence. Also, the relationship between effort (spending 8–16% more on a product) and benefit (reward in form of a WG) could be a possible reason

Table 3 Results of binary logistic regression

Dependant variable	SPF cucumber			SPF coffee			SPF banana		
Control variables	B	P	Exp(B)	B	P	Exp(B)	B	P	Exp(B)
Gender(l)	– 0.683	*0.039**	0.505	0.080	*0.841*	1.084	-0.578	*0.135*	0.560
Gut Feeling(l)	0.371	*0.251*	1.450	0.439	*0.275*	1.551	1.321	< *0.001****	3.750
Appealing Product(l)	0.566	*0.096*	1.761	0.480	*0.249*	1.616	0.791	*0.048**	2.207
Price(l)	– 1.487	< *0.001****	0.226	-1.919	< *0.001****	0.147	-1.046	*0.006***	0.351
Product recommendation(l)	2.429	< *0.001****	11.348	2.634	< *0.001****	13.925	3.137	< *0.001****	23.031

* indicates significance at 95%, ** at 99%, *** at 99.9% level; sig. variables only

for the participants not to choose the product (apart from the general reason *price* as found by regression analyses). Both other interventions related to social justice (SN2 + WG2) and social equity (SN3 + WG3) significantly increased consumers purchase frequency of the related products compared to the control group. Additionally, decision reason *product recommendation* had a highly significant statistical impact on the SPF of all products, which underlines the effectiveness of the interventions. Thus, the key contribution of this work is the finding that hybrid or enriched nudging concepts lead to a higher effectivity in terms of altering purchase behavior supporting societal beneficial outcomes. The enriched interventions have used the same testimonials as well as claims and were only enriched by additional information about a purposeful contribution towards projects supporting social projects triggered by the WG reward. This shows a certain willingness to spend more money for more value (i.e., contributing to societal good to receive a WG reward). A possible WG reward seemed to be a valuable reason for our participants to choose the most expensive product in the choice environment. Also, our results provide empirical support for the efficacy of WG theory to foster support for social projects and are congruent with the finding of other studies (e.g., Iweala et al. 2019; Mahasuweerachai and Suttikun 2022). Our research finds the usage of SN DNs in the context of e-grocery shopping as non-effective or even counter-productive, confirming results of other studies (e.g., Auf der Landwehr et al. 2021; Berger et al. 2020). Also, consistent with other studies (Jesse and Jannach 2021; Zimmermann and Renaud 2021), we showed that enriched DN can make a valuable contribution to more effective DN interventions.

However, our study was subject to several limitations. First, our participants were influenced by the prices used in the choice environment. Accordingly, we assume that income could be a variable for further studies to consider. Moreover, we suppose that the necessity to work as a crowd worker could indicate a lower than average household income, thus, controlling for the influence of available income could bring valuable insights of price effects on the support of pro-social purposes. Second, as we applied distinct product claims and choice options for each intervention group, we cannot entirely isolate the influence of the WG theory on the intervention's efficacy. Variations in buying behavior may not solely arise due to the nudge but also due to differences in the product features or appeal. Third, since we used a research panel in German-speaking countries only, we opt to choose mainly white, European looking people as testimonials. To investigate further in this context, testimonials could be tested which are more diverse in regards to outer appearance or gender, indicating belonging to a group which should be socially supported. Fourth, our experiment was conducted through a questionnaire that presented a mock-up mobile grocery store, and participants did not engage in actual grocery shopping. Conducting a field study in a real grocery store would likely yield more valid results. Therefore, research should involve companies to investigate on such initiatives that aim to elucidate the efficacy of enriched DN in real-world settings.

This study makes several contributions to the existing body of research. Firstly, we confirmed the non-effectiveness of SN interventions in e-grocery although personalized and using the concept of social presence in our intervention, consistent with other results in this context. Secondly, we examined a previously unexplored SN variant (typical consumer testimonial) in the context of digital nudges. Thirdly, we successfully enriched digital nudges following the concept of SN with the theory of WG with the goal to support projects related to pro-social purposes and hope, that our findings can help scholars as well as policy makers to foster more pro-social behavior. Yet, more research is needed to extend the knowledge in the area of DN fostering pro-social behavior, as the social aspect of sustainability still remains under researched but the imperative to enhance social equality on this planet remains an essential concern.

References

Ajilore, O., Amialchuk, A., Xiong, W. and Ye, X. (2014) 'Uncovering peer effects mechanisms with weight outcomes using spatial econometrics', *The Social Science Journal*, vol. 51, no. 4, pp. 645–651.

Allison, T. H., McKenny, A. F. and Short, J. C. (2013) 'The effect of entrepreneurial rhetoric on microlending investment: An examination of the warm-glow effect', *Journal of Business Venturing*, vol. 28, no. 6, pp. 690–707.

Andreoni, J. (1989) 'Giving with Impure Altruism: Applications to Charity and Ricardian Equivalence', *Journal of Political Economy*, vol. 97, no. 6, pp. 1447–1458.

Andrighetto, G. and Vriens, E. (2022) 'A research agenda for the study of social norm change', *Philosophical transactions. Series A, Mathematical, physical, and engineering sciences*, vol. 380, no. 2227, pp. 1–13.

Auf der Landwehr, M., Trott, M. and von Viebahn, C. (2021) 'Consumers Choice? Fostering Sustainability in Grocery Deliveries Through Digital Nudging', *ECIS 2021 Research Papers*.

Babar, Y., Curley, S., Ke, Z., de Liu and Sheffler, Z. (2023) 'The Effects of Digitally Delivered Nudges in a Corporate Wellness Program', *Journal of the Association for Information Systems*, vol. 24, no. 1, pp. 136–160.

Backhaus, K., Erichson, B., Gensler, S., Weiber, R. and Weiber, T. (2021) *Multivariate Analysemethoden*, Wiesbaden, Springer Fachmedien Wiesbaden.

Bauer, B. W., Tucker, R. P. and Capron, D. W. (2019) 'A Nudge in a New Direction: Integrating Behavioral Economic Strategies Into Suicide Prevention Work', *Clinical Psychological Science*, vol. 7, no. 3, pp. 612–620.

Bauw, M. de, La Revilla, L. S. de, Poppe, V., Matthys, C. and Vranken, L. (2022) 'Digital nudges to stimulate healthy and pro-environmental food choices in E-groceries', *Appetite*, vol. 172, p. 105971.

Berger, M., Müller, C. and Nüske, N. (2020) 'Digital Nudging in Online Grocery Stores: Towards Ecologically Sustainable Nutrition', *Proceedings of the 41st International Conference on Information Systems (ICIS)*. Hyderabad, India.

Bicchieri, C. and Dimant, E. (2022) 'Nudging with care: the risks and benefits of social information', *Public Choice*, vol. 191, pp. 443–464.

Box, G. E. and Tidwell, P. W. (1962) 'Transformation of the Independent Variables', *Technometrics*, vol. 4, no. 4, pp. 531–550.

Bronnmann, J., Stoeven, M. T., Quaas, M. and Asche, F. (2021) 'Measuring Motivations for Choosing Ecolabeled Seafood: Environmental Concerns and Warm Glow', *Land Economics*, vol. 97, no. 3, pp. 641–654.

Bunten, A., Porter, L., Sanders, J. G., Sallis, A., Payne Riches, S., van Schaik, P., González-Iraizoz, M., Chadborn, T. and Forwood, S. (2021) 'A randomised experiment of health, cost and social norm message frames to encourage acceptance of swaps in a simulation online supermarket', *PloS one*, vol. 16, no. 2, 1-16.

Burke, M. A. (2008) 'Social Multipliers', in *The New Palgrave Dictionary of Economics*, London, Palgrave Macmillan, pp. 1–7.

Burmeister, E. and Aitken, L. M. (2012) 'Sample size: how many is enough?', *Australian critical care : official journal of the Confederation of Australian Critical Care Nurses*, vol. 25, no. 4, pp. 271–274.

Cahyasita, D., Irham and Jamhari (2021) 'Intention to re-consume organic food: Sensory attributes, egoistic motive, and warm glow in the extended TPB', *AIMS Agriculture and Food*, vol. 6, no. 4, pp. 891–919.

Camilleri, A. R., Larrick, R. P., Hossain, S. and Patino-Echeverri, D. (2019) 'Consumers underestimate the emissions associated with food but are aided by labels', *Nature Climate Change*, vol. 9, no. 1, pp. 53–58.

Chung, J. and Monroe, G. S. (2003) 'Exploring Social Desirability Bias', *Journal of Business Ethics*, vol. 44, no. 4, pp. 291–302.

Cialdini, R. B. and Goldstein, N. J. (2004) 'Social influence: compliance and conformity', *Annual review of psychology*, vol. 55, pp. 591–621.

Collier, C. A. and Johnson, N. (2021) 'Nudging Charity: How Digital Nudges Influence Online Prosocial Behaviors', *Proceedings of the Twenty-Seventh Americas Conference on Information Systems (AMCIS)*. Montreal.

Cook, R.D. (1977) 'Detection of Influential Observation in Linear Regression', *Technometrics*, vol. 19, no. 1, p. 15. https://doi.org/10.2307/1268249

Dean, D. H. and Biswas, A. (2001) 'Third-Party Organization Endorsement of Products: An Advertising Cue Affecting Consumer Prepurchase Evaluation of Goods and Services', *Journal of Advertising*, vol. 30, no. 4, pp. 41–57.

Demarque, C., Charalambides, L., Hilton, D. J. and Waroquier, L. (2015) 'Nudging sustainable consumption: The use of descriptive norms to promote a minority behavior in a realistic online shopping environment', *Journal of Environmental Psychology*, vol. 43, pp. 166–174.

Dennis, A. R., Yuan, L., Feng, X., Webb, E. and Hsieh, C. J. (2020) 'Digital Nudging: Numeric and Semantic Priming in E-Commerce', *Journal of Management Information Systems*, vol. 37, no. 1, pp. 39–65.

DiCosola III, B. M. and Neff, G. (2020) 'Using Social Comparisons to Facilitate Healthier Choices in Online Grocery Shopping Contexts', *Extended Abstracts of the 2020 CHI Conference on Human Factors in Computing Systems*. Honolulu HI USA. New York, NY, USA, ACM, pp. 1–8.

Dunn, E. W., Aknin, L. B. and Norton, M. I. (2014) 'Prosocial Spending and Happiness', *Current Directions in Psychological Science*, vol. 23, no. 1, pp. 41–47. https://doi.org/10.1177/0963721413512503

Elgaaied-Gambier, L., Monnot, E. and Reniou, F. (2018) 'Using descriptive norm appeals effectively to promote green behavior', *Journal of Business Research*, vol. 82, pp. 179–191.

Engler, J.-O., Abson, D. J. and Wehrden, H. von (2019) 'Navigating cognition biases in the search of sustainability', *Ambio*, vol. 48, no. 6, pp. 605–618.

Fink, L. (2022) 'Why and How Online Experiments Can Benefit Information Systems Research', *Journal of the Association for Information Systems*, vol. 23, no. 6, pp. 1333–1346.

Friedman, H. H., Termini, S. and Washington, R. (1976) 'The Effectiveness of Advertisements Utilizing Four Types of Endorsers', *Journal of Advertising*, vol. 5, no. 3, pp. 22–24.

Ganglmair-Wooliscroft, A. and Wooliscroft, B. (2022) 'A hierarchy of sustainable grocery shopping behaviours: Using Rasch modelling to explore adoption groups', *Journal of Consumer Behaviour*.

Gottschewski, P. O., Auf der Landwehr, M., von Viebahn, C. and Staritz, J. (2022) 'Decreasing Shopping Duration by Altering Choice Environments? An Empirical Investigation of Individual and Hybrid Nudges in the Context of e-Grocery', *Wirtschaftsinformatik 2022 Proceedings*.

Gupta, M. and George, J. F. (2013) 'The Effects of Fictitious Customer Testimonials across Different Cultures', *AMCIS 2013 Proceedings*. Chicago.

Halvorsen, B. (2008) 'Effects of Norms and Opportunity Cost of Time on Household Recycling', *Land Economics*, vol. 84, no. 3, pp. 501–516.

Harbaugh, W. T., Mayr, U. and Burghart, D. R. (2007) 'Neural responses to taxation and voluntary giving reveal motives for charitable donations', *Science (New York, N.Y.)*, vol. 316, no. 5831, pp. 1622–1625.

Hartmann, P., Eisend, M., Apaolaza, V. and D'Souza, C. (2017) 'Warm glow vs. altruistic values: How important is intrinsic emotional reward in proenvironmental behavior?' *Journal of Environmental Psychology*, vol. 52, pp. 43–55.

Hartmann-Boyce, J., Bianchi, F., Piernas, C., Payne Riches, S., Frie, K., Nourse, R. and Jebb, S. A. (2018) 'Grocery store interventions to change food purchasing behaviors: a systematic review of randomized controlled trials', *The American journal of clinical nutrition*, vol. 107, no. 6, pp. 1004–1016.

He, Y., Chen, Q. and Alden, D. L. (2012) 'Consumption in the public eye: The influence of social presence on service experience' *Journal of Business Research*, vol. 65, no. 3, pp. 302–310.

Henkel, C., Seidler, A.-R., Kranz, J. and Fiedler, M. (2019) 'How to nudge pro-environmental behaviour: an experimental study', *ECIS 2019 Proceedings*. Stockholm, Association for Information Systems.

Herden, C. J., Alliu, E., Cakici, A., Cormier, T., Deguelle, C., Gambhir, S., Griffiths, C., Gupta, S., Kamani, S. R., Kiratli, Y.-S., Kispataki, M., Lange, G., Moles de Matos, L., Tripero Moreno, L., Betancourt Nunez, H. A., Pilla, V., Raj, B., Roe, J., Skoda, M., Song, Y., Ummadi, P. K. and Edinger-Schons, L. M. (2021) '"Corporate Digital Responsibility"', *Sustainability Management Forum | NachhaltigkeitsManagementForum*, vol. 29, no. 1, pp. 13–29.

Hörisch, J. and Tenner, I. (2020) 'How environmental and social orientations influence the funding success of investment-based crowdfunding: The mediating role of the number of funders and the average funding amount', *Technological Forecasting and Social Change*, vol. 161, pp. 1–11.

Huber, P.J. (1981) Robust Statistics. Hoboken, NJ, USA: John Wiley & Sons, Inc.

Iweala, S., Spiller, A. and Meyerding, S. (2019) 'Buy good, feel good? The influence of the warm glow of giving on the evaluation of food items with ethical claims in the U.K. and Germany', *Journal of Cleaner Production*, vol. 215, pp. 315–328.

Jansen, L., van Kleef, E. and van Loo, E. J. (2021) 'The use of food swaps to encourage healthier online food choices: a randomized controlled trial', *The international journal of behavioral nutrition and physical activity*, vol. 18, no. 1, p. 156.

Jesse, M. and Jannach, D. (2021) 'Explorations in Digital Nudging for Online Food Choices', *PACIS 2021 Proceedings*.

Jia, L. and Linden, S. (2020) 'Green but not altruistic warm-glow predicts conservation behavior', *Conservation Science and Practice*, vol. 2, no. 7, pp. 1–7.

Karlan, D. and Wood, D. H. (2017) 'The effect of effectiveness: Donor response to aid effectiveness in a direct mail fundraising experiment', *Journal of Behavioral and Experimental Economics*, vol. 66, pp. 1–8.

Karras, T., Laine, S., Aittala, M., Hellsten, J., Lehtinen, J. and Aila, T. (2019) *Analyzing and Improving the Image Quality of StyleGAN*.

Katner, K. and Jianu, R. (2019) 'The Effectiveness of Nudging in Commercial Settings and Impact on User Trust', *Extended Abstracts of the 2019 CHI Conference on Human Factors in Computing Systems*. Glasgow Scotland UK. New York, NY, USA, ACM, pp. 1–6.

Koskey, K. L. K. (2016) 'Using the Cognitive Pretesting Method to Gain Insight Into Participants' Experiences', *International Journal of Qualitative Methods*, vol. 15, no. 1, 1-13.

Kuenzel, J. and Musters, P. (2007) 'Social interaction and low involvement products', *Journal of Business Research*, vol. 60, no. 8, pp. 876–883.

Lehner, M., Mont, O. and Heiskanen, E. (2016) 'Nudging – A promising tool for sustainable consumption behaviour?' *Journal of Cleaner Production*, vol. 134, pp. 166–177.

Liao, Y.-K., Wu, W.-Y. and Pham, T.-T. (2020) 'Examining the Moderating Effects of Green Marketing and Green Psychological Benefits on Customers' Green Attitude, Value and Purchase Intention', *Sustainability*, vol. 12, no. 18, pp. 1–19.

Loschelder, D. D., Siepelmeyer, H., Fischer, D. and Rubel, J. A. (2019) 'Dynamic norms drive sustainable consumption: Norm-based nudging helps café customers to avoid disposable to-go-cups', *Journal of Economic Psychology*, vol. 75, Part A, pp. 1–23.

Mager, S. and Kranz, J. (2021) 'On the Effectiveness of Overt and Covert Interventions in Influencing Cookie Consent: Field Experimental Evidence', *ICIS 2021 Proceedings*.

Mahasuweerachai, P. and Suttikun, C. (2022) 'The Effect of Green Self-Identity on Perceived Image, Warm Glow and Willingness to Purchase: A New Generation's Perspective towards Eco-Friendly Restaurants', *Sustainability*, vol. 14, no. 17, pp. 1–13.

Martin, B. A., Wentzel, D. and Tomczak, T. (2008) 'Effects of Susceptibility to Normative Influence and Type of Testimonial on Attitudes Toward Print Advertising', *Journal of Advertising*, vol. 37, no. 1, pp. 29–43.

Mason, W. and Suri, S. (2012) 'Conducting behavioral research on Amazon's Mechanical Turk', *Behavior research methods*, vol. 44, no. 1, pp. 1–23.

Mirsch, T., Lehrer, C. and Jung, R. (2017) 'Digital Nudging: Altering User Behavior in Digital Environments', *Proceedings of the 13th International Conference on Wirtschaftsinformatik (WI 2017)*. St.Gallen. St.Gallen, pp. 634–648.

Mirsch, T., Lehrer, C. and and Jung, R. (2018) 'Making Digital Nudging Applicable: The Digital Nudge Design Method', *ICIS 2018 Proceedings*.

Porter, M. E. and Kramer, M. R. (2006) 'Strategy and society', *Harvard Business Review*, vol. 84, no. 12, pp. 78–93.

Reinholdsson, T., Hedesström, M., Ejelöv, E., Hansla, A., Bergquist, M., Svenfelt, Å. and Nilsson, A. (2022) 'Nudging green food: The effects of a hedonic cue, menu position, a warm-glow cue, and a descriptive norm', *Journal of Consumer Behaviour*.

Richter, I., Thøgersen, J. and Klöckner, C. (2018) 'A Social Norms Intervention Going Wrong: Boomerang Effects from Descriptive Norms Information', *Sustainability*, vol. 10, no. 8, pp. 1–20.

Schär, A. (2021) 'Social Pressure on Heavy Thinkers? The Influence of Need for Cognition on Pre-Purchase Social Norm Nudges', A*MCIS 2021 Proceedings, 27th annual Americas Conference on Information Systems (AMCIS)*, Online.

Schär, A., Dalmus, C. and Stanoevska-Slabeva, K. (2022) 'Nudging in the Pre-purchase Phase: On the Effectiveness of Social Norm Nudges, Previous TikTok Usage and Potential Interactions', *AMCIS 2022 Proceedings*.

Scharf, K. (2014) 'Impure prosocial motivation in charity provision: Warm-glow charities and implications for public funding', *Journal of Public Economics*, vol. 114, pp. 50–57.

Schimmelpfennig, C. (2019) 'The Use of Different Endorser Types in Advertising: A Content Analysis of Magazine Advertisements', *Journal of Global Marketing*, vol. 32, no. 3, pp. 139–153.

Schoormann, T. and Kutzner, K. (2020) 'Towards Understanding Social Sustainability: An Information Systems Research-Perspective', *ICIS 2020 Proceedings*. India.

Stuber, J. M., Lakerveld, J., Kievitsbosch, L. W., Mackenbach, J. D. and Beulens, J. W. J. (2022) 'Nudging customers towards healthier food and beverage purchases in a real-life online supermarket: a multi-arm randomized controlled trial', *BMC medicine*, vol. 20, no. 1, p. 10.

Sunstein, C. R. (2014) 'Nudging: A Very Short Guide', *Journal of Consumer Policy*, vol. 37, no. 4, pp. 583–588.

Sunstein, C. R. (2016) 'Nudges That Fail', *SSRN Electronic Journal*.

Taufik, D., Bolderdijk, J.W. and Steg, L. (2015) 'Acting Green Elicits a Literal Warm Glow', *Nature Climate Change*, vol. 5, no. 1, pp. 37–40. https://doi.org/10.1038/nclimate2449

Terres, P. et al. (2019) 'DIGITAL NUDGES FOR USER ONBOARDING: TURNING VISITORS INTO USERS', ECIS 2019 Proceedings. Association for Information Systems, Association for Information Systems, Stockholm.

Thaler, R. H. and Sunstein, C. R. (2009) *Nudge: Improving decisions about health, wealth and happiness*, London, Penguin Books.

van Vugt, M., Griskevicius, V. and Schultz, P. W. (2014) 'Naturally Green: Harnessing Stone Age Psychological Biases to Foster Environmental Behavior', *Social Issues and Policy Review*, vol. 8, no. 1, pp. 1–32.

Vassilakopoulou, P. and Hustad, E. (2021) 'Bridging Digital Divides: a Literature Review and Research Agenda for Information Systems Research', *Information systems frontiers : a journal of research and innovation*, pp. 1–15.

Vlaev, I., King, D., Dolan, P. and Darzi, A. (2016) 'The Theory and Practice of "Nudging": Changing Health Behaviors', *Public Administration Review*, vol. 76, no. 4, pp. 550–561.

Wang, W., Li, F. and Yi, Z. (2019) 'Scores vs. stars: A regression discontinuity study of online consumer reviews', *Information & Management*, vol. 56, no. 3, pp. 418–428.

Watson, R. T., Elliot, S., Corbett, J., Farkas, D., Feizabadi, A., Gupta, A., Iyer, L., Sen, S., Sharda, R., Shin, N., Thapa, D. and Webster, J. (2021) 'How the AIS can Improve its Contributions to the UN's Sustainability Development Goals: Towards A Framework for Scaling Collaborations and Evaluating Impact', *Communications of the Association for Information Systems*, vol. 48, no. 1, pp. 476–502.

Weinmann, M., Schneider, C. and vom Brocke, J. (2016) 'Digital Nudging', *Business & Information Systems Engineering*, vol. 58, no. 6, pp. 433–436.

White, K., Habib, R. and Hardisty, D. J. (2019) 'How to SHIFT Consumer Behaviors to be More Sustainable: A Literature Review and Guiding Framework', *Journal of Marketing*, vol. 83, no. 3, pp. 22–49.

Zimmermann, V. and Renaud, K. (2021) 'The Nudge Puzzle', *ACM Transactions on Computer-Human Interaction*, vol. 28, no. 1, pp. 1–45.

Can a Button Change Your Purchase?—The Effect of the Accessibility of Consumer Reviews on Consumers' Online Purchase Decisions

Andrea Wrabel, Alexander Kupfer, and Steffen Zimmermann

Abstract This study investigates whether the accessibility of consumer reviews matters for consumers' purchase decisions. Current research does not provide guidance on how to access consumer reviews to improve consumers' decision-making. Moreover, there is no consensus on the actual implementation of the access (i.e., immediate access or explicit access by clicking) to consumer reviews on existing online shopping websites. Building on the anchoring-and-adjustment model of belief updating and using an experimental approach, we find that requiring participants to explicitly access consumer reviews (by clicking on a button) significantly improves their purchase decisions: When choosing between products of different quality, they better align their perceived product values with the actual product quality. As a result, they are more likely to purchase the high-quality product. These findings provide important insights for e-commerce retailers and policy makers, as they offer guidance on how consumer reviews should be accessible to support consumers' decision-making.

Keywords Consumer reviews · Review accessibility · Online purchase decision

A. Wrabel (✉) · S. Zimmermann
Institute of Business Analytics, Ulm University, Ulm, Germany
e-mail: andrea.wrabel@uni-ulm.de

S. Zimmermann
e-mail: steffen.zimmermann@uni-ulm.de

A. Kupfer
Department of Information Systems, Production and Logistics Management, and Research Area Digital Science Center (DiSC), University of Innsbruck, Innsbruck, Austria
e-mail: alexander.kupfer@uibk.ac.at

D. Beverungen et al. (eds.), *Conceptualizing Digital Responsibility for the Information Age*, Lecture Notes in Information Systems and Organisation 74,
https://doi.org/10.1007/978-3-031-80119-8_16

1 Introduction

When making online purchase decisions, consumers are required to actively inform themselves about the quality of a product, as they typically have no prior experience with it. To learn about a product and its quality, however, consumers do not have to rely solely on information provided by the producer. Instead, they can use independent, more reliable, peer-generated information in the form of consumer reviews (Hajli et al. 2014).

Consumer reviews are part of most online shopping websites, but the design of the corresponding online review systems can vary. Such variations are known to influence consumers' perception of consumer reviews and consequently their decision-making process when shopping online (Gutt et al. 2019). On online shopping websites, there seems to be a consensus on the immediate display—and thus accessibility—of aggregated review information (e.g., average rating) while the display and accessibility of consumer reviews themselves vary considerably. On Amazon, consumer reviews are displayed on the same page as the product information and are therefore immediately accessible. Other online shopping websites such as BestBuy or Zalando require customers to click on a link or button to access and see consumer reviews. Moreover, research to date also does not provide guidance on how to implement the access to consumer reviews on websites. To our knowledge, there is no study that investigates how the accessibility of consumer reviews influences consumers' decision-making process. We therefore state the following research question to address this gap:

RQ: *How does the accessibility of consumer reviews on online shopping websites affect consumers' purchase decisions?*

We address this question by conducting a between-subject experiment in which consumers choose between two products of different quality. The quality of the products is described in consumer reviews. Thus, participants that put more weight to consumer reviews make better purchase decisions. To investigate the effect of the accessibility of consumer reviews, we apply the following treatment variation: consumer reviews are either immediately accessible together with product information or only accessible by explicitly clicking on a button. Based on the analysis of our experimental study, we find that the accessibility of consumer reviews significantly affects consumers' purchase decisions via perceived product value as mediating variable. In particular, we find that our participants' perceived product value is better aligned with actual product quality when consumer reviews are only accessible by explicitly clicking on a button. As a result, consumers are more likely to purchase the high-quality product instead of the low-quality product.

Our study contributes to research on the design of online review systems. In contrast to existing studies that mostly focus on the presentation within the set of consumer reviews, we investigate the effect of the accessibility of (the entire set of) consumer reviews. Thus, we contribute to the understanding of a design aspect that has merely been addressed although it substantially varies across online shopping websites. Our findings provide important insights for e-commerce retailers and policy makers alike regarding consumers' evaluation of product quality (using consumer reviews) during their purchase decision.

2 Related Literature

Over the past years, consumer reviews have become one of the most important features on online shopping websites and now represent an important determinant for online purchase decisions (see e.g., Floyd et al, 2014; Babić Rosario et al. 2016, 2020; Gutt et al. 2019 for comprehensive overviews). In addition, online shopping websites often prominently display aggregated review information (i.e., average rating, rating distribution, volume). Besides the well-studied effects of aggregated review information (e.g., Chevalier and Mayzlin 2006; Floyd et al. 2014), several studies also document that the consumer reviews themselves and their respective textual comments influence consumers' purchase decisions (Hu et al. 2014; Lei et al. 2022; Liu et al. 2019; van Helversen et al. 2018; Ziegele and Weber 2015). By observing that individual consumer reviews play a vital role for consumers, the latter studies actually "challenge the commonly accepted assumption of average ratings being the primary driver of consumers' purchase decisions" (Lei et al. 2022, p. 2393).

Furthermore, consumers are affected by the way consumer reviews are presented (Gutt et al. 2019). However, we identify that most studies investigate the presentation within the set of consumer reviews. They document that the presentation and composition of subsets (e.g., Jabr and Rahman 2022; Kupfer et al. 2020) or the ordering of consumer reviews (e.g., Alzate et al. 2021; Huang et al. 2014; Kaushik et al. 2018; Liu et al. 2019; Sparks and Browning 2011; Zhou and Guo 2017) affect consumer behavior in terms of purchase intention and helpfulness votes. In contrast to the presentation within the set of consumer reviews, the way the entire set of consumer reviews is being accessed is, however, mostly unstudied. We are—to the best of our knowledge—only aware of a study by Camilleri (2020) who investigates whether it matters at what time aggregated review information is accessed. The author observes that consumers rely more on aggregated review information when it is presented after general product information.

Although Camilleri's (2020) study comes close to the understudied question on the effect of the accessibility of review information on a website, the findings cannot be transferred to our context: First, review information simply appears after other product information in Camilleri (2020). In our study, we examine the more common practice that review information is only accessible by explicitly clicking on a button. Second, we focus on the consumer reviews themselves rather than aggregated review information. As outlined above, research highlights the importance of consumer reviews due to their additional information content. We address this research gap by using an experimental setting that requires participants to examine consumer reviews.

3 Theoretical Background and Hypotheses Development

We build on the anchoring-and-adjustment model of belief updating by Hogarth and Einhorn (1992) to develop our hypotheses on the effect of the accessibility of consumer reviews on consumers' purchase decisions. This model is based on the idea that individuals first form an initial belief (*anchor*) which is subsequently adjusted due to the influence of succeeding pieces of information. Throughout the decision-making process, individuals may use one of the following strategies to process succeeding pieces of information and adjust their beliefs: a *step-by-step* or *end-of-sequence* strategy. When applying a *step-by-step* strategy, individuals adjust their beliefs after processing each piece of information. This strategy is induced whenever individuals have to express their belief after each piece of information and typically leads to recency effects (i.e., individuals put more emphasis on more recently processed information). The *end-of-sequence* strategy, on the other hand, implies that individuals only adjust their beliefs after processing all information which typically results in primacy effects (i.e., individuals put more emphasis on earlier information).[1] Finally, when individuals have to express their belief only once after receiving all information, their prevalent strategy depends on the complexity of information and tasks.

Translated to the context of making online purchase decisions, this means that consumers can as well apply different strategies to process succeeding information and adjust their beliefs about products. Further, we expect different strategies to be prevalent depending on the accessibility of consumer reviews: If consumer reviews are only accessible by clicking on a button and therefore appear in a second step, we expect that consumers implicitly evaluate the first received information (for themselves) to decide if they indeed want to access consumer reviews. Thus, a *step-by-step strategy* is more likely induced (even if they are not explicitly asked to express their beliefs)—implying the sole presence of recency effects. If consumer reviews are immediately accessible together with further information (e.g., product features), we expect that consumers apply either a *step-by-step strategy* or *end-of-sequence strategy* (implying that either primacy or recency effects are present). Relatedly, Camilleri (2020) found consumers to rely more on aggregated review information when presented after general product information (i.e., stronger recency effects) compared to when presented together. This supports our expectation of a stronger recency effect when consumers are required to explicitly access consumer reviews compared to when they immediately access them together with other information.

Stronger recency effects imply that consumers put more emphasis on the information seen most recently (i.e., consumer reviews). As consumer reviews help to reduce information asymmetries (Manes and Tchetchik 2018; Park and Lee 2009), consumers that put more emphasis on them can better learn about the quality of a product. While positive comments in consumer reviews typically indicate that a

---

[1] This observation holds for basic information and simple tasks (Hogarth and Einhorn 1992). We expect this to be the case for typical online shopping situations, as nowadays consumers are familiar with purchasing a product online and also with consumer reviews.

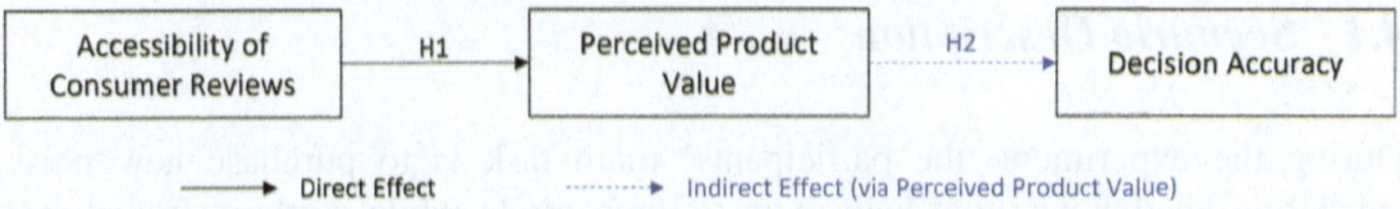

Fig. 1 Research model

product is of high quality and lead consumers to more favorably evaluate a product, negative comments indicate a low quality leading to a less favorable evaluation (e.g., Hu et al. 2014; Huang and Chen 2006; Lei et al. 2022; Liu et al. 2019; Ziegele and Weber 2015). Hence, consumers that positively (negatively) evaluate a product consequently perceive the value of a product as higher (lower). In other words, consumers putting more emphasis on consumer reviews (due to explicitly accessing them) are expected to better align their perceived product value with the actual product quality. Accordingly, we state our first hypothesis as follows:

H1: *Compared to immediately accessing consumer reviews, requiring consumers to explicitly access consumer reviews increases (decreases) the perceived product value of a high-quality (low-quality) product.*

If consumers perceive a product to be of high (low) value, they are more likely to purchase (discard) the product. Thus, if consumers' perceived product value is better aligned with the actual product quality, they are expected to rather purchase a high-quality than a low-quality product. Thus, consumers exhibit a high decision accuracy by choosing a high-quality product. As a direct consequence of H1, we expect that consumers that put more emphasis on consumer reviews when explicitly accessing them exhibit a higher decision accuracy. Accordingly, we hypothesize:

H2: *Compared to immediately accessing consumer reviews, requiring consumers to explicitly access consumer reviews indirectly increases decision accuracy via perceived product value.*

Figure 1 shows the corresponding research model and summarizes our hypotheses: We expect the accessibility of consumer reviews to directly affect perceived product value (i.e., H1) which serves as a mediator for consumers' decision accuracy (i.e., H2).

4 Research Methodology and Experimental Design

To test our hypotheses, we conduct a scenario-based online experiment with a between-subject design which we describe in the following section.

4.1 Scenario Description

During the experiment, the participants' main task is to purchase new noise-cancelling headphones that help them to concentrate while working from home. For this purpose, we implemented a scenario in which participants are forwarded to a fictive online shopping website offering two different headphones.

At first glance (i.e., without reading consumer reviews), both headphones appear to be similar. In particular, they have the same price and look, offer the same features, and exhibit the same aggregated review information (i.e., average rating, rating distribution, volume). The textual comments of the consumer reviews indicate, however, that one of the headphones is of higher quality than the other: The consumer reviews for the low-quality headphones highlight issues with the battery, microphone, and multi-device connectivity while these features work properly for the high-quality headphones. As the aggregated review information, however, are the same for both headphones, the quality differences can only be discovered by reading the consumer reviews.Overall, we show nine consumer reviews (six 5-star reviews, two 4-star reviews and one 3-star review) for each of the two headphones. While five consumer reviews are equivalent in their textual content and sentiment for both headphones, four of them indicate quality differences. The wording of the textual reviews was inspired by real consumer reviews on headphones from Amazon. To avoid a potential bias due to the order of the consumer reviews, we randomize their order.[2]

To proceed with the experiment, participants are asked to purchase one of the offered headphones by clicking on the respective "Purchase" button. A pop-up window was displayed when participants clicked on the "Purchase" button that asks them to confirm their decision. This helps us to ensure that participants do not accidently click on the "Purchase" button. To avoid a potential order bias due to product placement, the order of the two headphones (left/right) shown on the online shopping website is randomized.

4.2 Treatment Variation

To examine the effect of the accessibility of consumer reviews, we create two experimental groups: In the first group, consumer reviews are immediately accessible together with product information (control group). In the second group (treatment group), only product information is displayed when participants are forwarded to the online shopping website. Consumer reviews are only accessible by explicitly clicking on the respective "Read Reviews" button. Figure 2 shows an excerpt from

[2] As both products obtain the same aggregated review information, we also need to include low-rated reviews for the high-quality headphones. These, however, focus on rather subjective side aspects which are not linked to product quality itself (i.e., color of hard case, amount of packaging material). For a detailed description of the consumer reviews, we refer to the supplementary material available on the following OSF repository: 10.17605/OSF.IO/7KD3E.

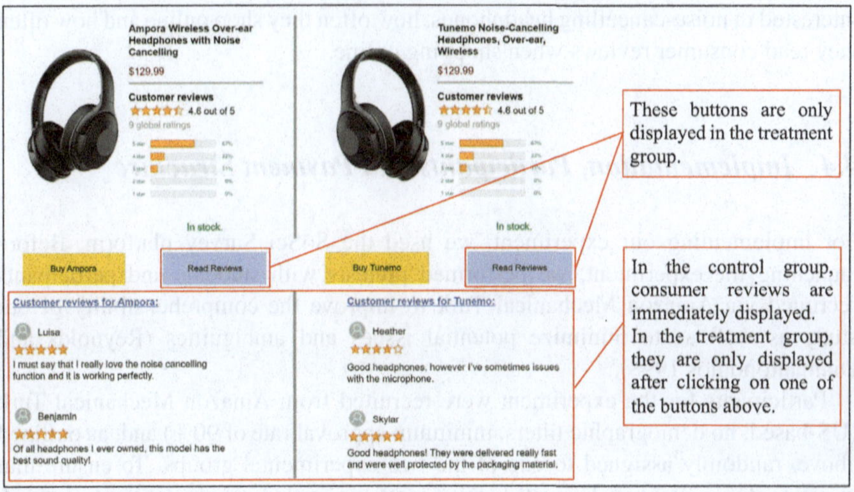

Fig. 2 Excerpt of the online shopping website

the online shopping website. Note that after clicking on the "Read Reviews" button, participants in the treatment group have the same website view as participants in the control group. Participants in the treatment group, however, also have the possibility to directly purchase without clicking on the "Read Reviews" button and therefore without accessing and seeing consumer reviews.

4.3 *Variables*

As outlined in Sect. 3, we expect the accessibility of consumer reviews to affect consumers' purchase decisions. By letting participants choose between two headphones of different quality, we can directly measure decision accuracy which represents our dependent variable. We define decision accuracy (*Accuracy*) as a binary variable being one (zero) if participants choose the high-quality (low-quality) headphones.

After choosing between the headphones, we ask participants to state their willingness-to-pay for each of the two headphones. As the absolute willingness-to-pay might be participant-specific, we calculate the relative difference between the willingness-to-pay for both headphones as follows: $\Delta_{WTP} = \frac{WTP_{HQ} - WTP_{LQ}}{WTP_{LQ}}$, where WTP_{HQ} (WTP_{LQ}) represents the willingness-to-pay for the high-quality (low-quality) headphones. A higher Δ_{WTP} implies that the values of both headphones are perceived as more different.

At the end of the experiment, we ask participants about their demographics (i.e., age, gender, education, and income) as well as their familiarity with the topic in the scenario. In particular, we ask them whether they own, plan to buy or are not interested in noise-cancelling headphones, how often they shop online and how often they read consumer reviews when shopping online.

4.4 Implementation, Participants and Payment Structure

For implementing our experiment, we used the SoSci Survey platform. Before launching the experiment, we performed pretests with students and participants recruited via Amazon Mechanical Turk to improve the comprehensibility of our study as well as to minimize potential issues and ambiguities (Reynolds and Diamantopoulos 1998).

Participants for the experiment were recruited from Amazon Mechanical Turk (US-based, no demographic filters, minimum approval rate of 90%) and, as outlined above, randomly assigned to one of the two experimental groups. To ensure that participants are attentive during the experiment, we implemented two attention check questions after participants stated their willingness-to-pay for both headphones. In particular, we asked participants based on true/false answer options about the price of the headphones and whether the headphones have a noise-cancelling feature. Note that these questions can be answered without reading the consumer reviews as otherwise, our final sample would suffer from self-selection.

All participants receive a base payment of $0.10 for completing the experiment. Participants who correctly answered the attention check questions, receive additional $0.50. To ensure that participants have an incentive to make meaningful decisions during the experiment, only participants who choose to purchase the high-quality headphones receive a bonus payment of $0.50. On the instruction page of the experiment, we informed participants that their final payment ranges from $0.10 up to $1.10 and that it depends on their decisions during the experiment. Assuming that participants pay full attention to the experiment (i.e., they buy the high-quality headphones), their compensation would be equivalent to $8.25 per hour when calculating with our expected time of 8 min to finish the experiment. On average, fully attentive participants needed about 6.30 min to complete the experiment and since they bought the high-quality headphones received $1.10 resulting in an average hourly wage of $10.48.

5 Analysis and Results

In total, we recruited 767 participants for our experiment. 596 of them correctly answered the attention check questions. We checked the data for outliers and dropped 18 participants in total that made a very quick purchase decision (i.e., 7 s or less) or entered abnormal high or nonnumerical values for their willingness-to-pay. Our final dataset hence comprises 578 participants with 335 (243) participants belonging to the treatment (control) group. To check whether sample randomization was appropriate, we tested the control variables for differences between treatment and control group using a nonparametric Wilcoxon rank-sum test. None of the control variables except for *Education* did significantly differ between the groups. Thus, we examined *Education* by applying a Chi-square test to check for differences in the answer distributions between the groups and did not find a significant difference. Hence, we conclude that our sample randomization is appropriate.[3]

5.1 Main Results

To get a first impression of the effects of the accessibility of consumer reviews on our main variables Δ_{WTP} and *Accuracy*, we present the summary statistics in Panel A of Table 1. For the treatment group, in which participants are required to explicitly access consumer reviews, we observe a larger difference in the perceived values of both headphones. In more detail, participants of the treatment group perceive the value of the high-quality headphones as approx. 24% higher compared to the low-quality headphones while participants of the control group only perceive it as 17% higher. We also observe a higher decision accuracy for the treatment group (85.7%) compared to the control group (82.7%).

To examine the statistical significance of the effect of the accessibility of consumer reviews on the perceived product value (i.e., H1), we estimate an ordinary least squares (OLS) model using heteroskedasticity-consistent robust standard errors with Δ_{WTP} as dependent variable and a treatment dummy (*Treat*) as independent variable. *Treat* is defined as a binary variable being one (zero) if participants are assigned to the treatment (control) group. The result of this exercise is shown in Panel B of Table 1. The coefficient represents the difference in Δ_{WTP} between the experimental groups and is statistically significant ($p < 0.05$). For robustness, we re-estimated the model including control variables which confirms our observation (not tabulated). Thus, requiring participants to explicitly access consumer reviews indeed increases the difference in the perceived product values. Hence, we find support for H1.

To test whether the accessibility of consumer reviews affects decision accuracy via perceived product value (i.e., H2), we apply a mediation analysis using the PROCESS macro (Model 4) for R (Hayes 2022). As suggested by Hayes (2022), we assess the statistical significance of indirect effects via a bootstrapping procedure. We base standard errors and 95% confidence intervals for the indirect effect on 5000 bias-corrected bootstrapping resamples. Results for the direct (first row) and indirect effect (second row) of the mediation analysis are shown in Panel C of Table 1. First, there is—as expected—no significant direct effect (i.e., *Treat* $\rightarrow$ *Accuracy*). Second, we observe a positive and statistically significant indirect effect (i.e., *Treat* $\rightarrow \Delta_{WTP} \rightarrow$ *Accuracy*). Hence, we observe a full mediation

[3] For a more detailed presentation of these results, we refer to the complete summary statistics included in the supplementary material.

Table 1 Main results

Panel A. Summary statistics

	Treatment Group (n = 335)				Control group (n = 243)				Diff in means
	Mean	SD	Min	Max	Mean	SD	Min	Max	
Δ_{WTP}	23.9%	40.4%	-50%	288.9%	17.4%	28.8%	– 34.6%	180.0%	6.5%
Accuracy	85.7%	35.1%	0	1	82.7%	37.9%	0	1	3.0%

Panel B. Effect on perceived product value

	Effect	SE
Treat → Δ_{WTP}	0.065**	0.029

Panel C. Effect on decision accuracy

	Effect	SE	LLCI	ULCI
Treat → *Accuracy*	0.045	0.269	−0.483	0.572
Treat → Δ_{WTP} → *Accuracy*	**0.840**	**0.435**	**0.108**	**1.820**

Notes Statistical significance is based on a Wilcoxon rank-sum test (Δ_{WTP}) and Chi-square test (Accuracy) in Panel A. Panel B shows the results of an ordinary least squares regression with heteroskedasticity-consistent robust standard errors (SE). For Panel A and Panel B, *** denotes $p < 0.01$, ** denotes $p < 0.05$ and * denotes $p < 0.010$, respectively. Panel C shows the results of a mediation analysis with 95% confidence intervals. Confidence intervals (LLCI/ULCI = Lower/Upper Limit of Confidence Interval) of indirect effects in Panel C are based on 5000 bootstrapping resamples and effects are presented in log-odds metrics because of the binary dependent variable (Accuracy). In Panel C, significant effects ($p < 0.05$) are indicated in bold of the effect of the accessibility of consumer reviews on decision accuracy. For robustness, we re-estimated the mediation analysis including control variables and the indirect effect remains significant for 90% confidence intervals (not tabulated). Therefore, requiring participants to explicitly access consumer reviews results in a higher decision accuracy. Hence, we can confirm H2 as well.

5.2 *Additional Insights*

The findings in the previous section supports both hypotheses suggesting that requiring consumers to explicitly access consumer reviews improves purchase decisions. However, our experimental design can result in the fact that some of our participants do not explicitly access consumer reviews and therefore not see consumer reviews at all. We therefore provide additional insights on this aspect.

First, 58 participants (approx. 17%) of the treatment group did not access and therefore not even see consumer reviews, although they had an incentive to do so due to the incentive-compatible payment structure of our experiment. Using participants' demographics, we can examine the determinants of whether a participant explicitly accesses consumer reviews or not.[4] For this purpose, we run a logit regression with *Accessed* as dependent variable, being one if participants explicitly access consumer reviews and zero otherwise, and participants' characteristics (i.e., our control variables) as independent variables. We observe that participants who infrequently purchase online ($p < 0.1$) or infrequently read reviews ($p < 0.01$) are most likely to not explicitly access consumer reviews. All remaining participant characteristics (i.e., age, gender, education, income, headphone usage) do not affect the likelihood to explicitly access consumer reviews.

Second, these 58 participants that did not access and therefore not see consumer reviews, could only randomly choose between the two headphones. In other words, they are not able to correctly evaluate product quality. This is actually the case and we find the average Δ_{WTP} of those participants to not be significantly different from zero ($p > 0.1$) and the *Accuracy* to not be significantly different from 50% ($p > 0.1$).

Third, when excluding those 58 participants, the positive effect of explicitly accessing the consumer reviews (treatment group) compared to immediately accessing them (control group) is—by definition—substantially stronger. In fact, we observe higher mean values for the treatment group ($\Delta_{WTP} = 28.0\%$, $Accuracy = 91.3\%$) compared to the main results. This also has consequences for the statistical tests: For re-estimating the OLS model from Sect. 5.1 with the reduced sample, the coefficient increases considerable ($\beta = 0.106, p < 0.01$). Similarly, the mediation analysis also indicates a substantially larger treatment effect being significant for 99% confidence intervals. Thus, we can conclude that the positive impact of those

[4] For this analysis, only participants of the treatment group are considered, as the participants of the control group did not have to explicitly access consumer reviews.

participants that accessed consumer reviews substantially outweighs the effects of the participants that did not access them.[5]

6 Discussion and Conclusion

Our study emphasizes that the accessibility of consumer reviews matters for consumers' purchase decisions. When consumer reviews are only accessible by explicitly clicking on a button, participants' perceived product value is better aligned with the actual product quality compared to the control group where consumer reviews are immediately accessible (i.e., H1). This, in turn, increases the likelihood to purchase the high-quality product rather than the low-quality product (i.e., H2). In other words, it positively impacts decision accuracy via perceived product value as a mediating variable. Importantly, this conclusion is based on the entire sample of the treatment group which also includes participants that did not access consumer reviews. Nonetheless, the positive effect of those participants that decided to explicitly access the consumer reviews outweighs the effect of those participants that did not access consumer reviews and that made, by definition, the worst decisions. To sum up, even though both experimental groups received the same overall information and the payment structure for participants was incentive-compatible, requiring them to explicitly access consumer reviews improves their purchase decisions.

6.1 *Theoretical Contribution*

This study adds to the understanding of how the design of online review systems affects consumer's purchase decisions. While many existing studies focus on the presentation within the set of consumer reviews, we are the first—to the best of our knowledge—to provide evidence on the accessibility of (the entire set of) consumer reviews. Guided by the anchoring-and-adjustment model of belief updating by Hogarth and Einhorn (1992), we observe consumers to put more emphasis on consumer reviews, if they are only accessible by clicking on a button indicating a (stronger) recency effect compared to immediately accessible consumer reviews. This may be due to a more likely induced *step-by-step strategy* of information processing and belief updating. In this context, we extend the findings by Camilleri (2020) as he neither investigated consumer reviews themselves nor that they are

[5] Note that for this comparison, individuals that are likely to ignore reviews are already excluded in the treatment group (by not clicking on the button) but not in the control group. Hence, this comparison might disadvantage the control group as it could still include participants that do not read consumer reviews although they are immediately accessible. To approximate this potential self-selection for the entire sample, we generally exclude those participants that are likely to not click on the button (i.e., those who infrequently purchase online or infrequently read reviews) and re-run the analyses. With the reduced sample, our findings remain unchanged.

only accessible by explicitly clicking on a button. Hence, we contribute by providing additional evidence that the anchoring-and-adjustment model of belief updating is also applicable for the accessibility of consumer reviews.

6.2 Limitations and Future Research

Overall, our study has certain limitations which however might serve as starting points for future research. First, we provided study participants with an artificial online shopping situation. Even though we designed an incentive-compatible payment structure implying that participants' decisions had real monetary consequences for them, decisions in a real online shopping situation might be different. This might particularly be true for very expensive products or services as they are related to a substantial financial loss in case that the purchased product is of low quality. While A/B-testing might be a potential solution to test our hypotheses in the field, it might come with other issues (e.g., existing customers being confused by a new design). Second, we only hypothesize that participants in the treatment group are more likely to apply the *step-by-step strategy*. Even though our findings are strongly supported by the anchoring-and-adjustment model of belief updating, future research might apply more fine-grained measurements like, for example, eye-tracking approaches. This might add further knowledge on how the accessibility of consumer reviews affects the way consumers process peer-generated information to evaluate product alternatives when making an online purchase decision. In addition, an eye-tracking approach could help to capture whether participants are reading consumer reviews at all and, if so, how intensely. This might be particularly worthwhile to deepen the understanding of the participants' behavior in the control group as the consumer reviews are immediately accessible. Finally, we only tested our hypotheses based on study participants that were using desktop devices. Given the recent research that highlights substantial differences between desktop and mobile usage due to different presentation of information (Fink and Papismedov 2022), it remains unclear if our findings can directly be transferred to users with mobile devices. Therefore, future research might perform a similar study focusing on the difference between the presentation on desktop and mobile devices.

6.3 Practical Implications

Our results guide e-commerce retailers' decisions on how to implement the access to consumer reviews. If e-commerce retailers want their customers to be well-informed about a product's quality, they should require them to explicitly access consumer reviews (e.g., by clicking on a link or button), as this will more likely induce a *step-by-step strategy* for processing information resulting in stronger recency effects. While being well-informed about a product's quality not only increases consumer satisfaction (i.e., by choosing a high-quality product), it also saves e-commerce retailers' money and reduces carbon dioxide emissions due to fewer product returns. On the other hand, our findings also indicate that e-commerce retailers could implement the access to consumer reviews in a way that consumers' attention is drawn away from them. Especially e-commerce retailers offering low-quality products might apply such a strategy. Policy makers should be aware of this potential misconduct and could require providers of online review systems to support consumers in processing peer-generated information. This could imply, for instance, that consumer reviews must be accessible in a similar way across e-commerce retailers. Finally, our observation that one type of consumer is likely to neglect consumer reviews can also be transferred to other settings with information asymmetries (e.g., reading reviews for a bank account, doctor, hiking paths, etc.). Those who neglect information from consumer reviews are likely to make bad decisions in different situations in life when information asymmetries are present. Hence, policy makers should have an incentive to make inexperienced consumers aware of consumer reviews as an important means to reduce information asymmetries.

Acknowledgements We thank the Austrian Science Fund (FWF): P32874-G for funding this research.

References

Alzate, M., Arce-Urriza, M. & Cebollada, J. (2021), 'Online Reviews and Product Sales: The Role of Review Visibility', *Journal of Theoretical and Applied Electronic Commerce Research* **16**(4), 638–669.

Babić Rosario, A., Sotgiu, F., Valck, K. de & Bijmolt, T. H. (2016), 'The Effect of Electronic Word of Mouth on Sales: A Meta-Analytic Review of Platform, Product, and Metric Factors', *Journal of Marketing Research* **53**(3), 297–318.

Babić Rosario, A., Valck, K. de & Sotgiu, F. (2020), 'Conceptualizing the electronic word-of-mouth process: What we know and need to know about eWOM creation, exposure, and evaluation', *Journal of the Academy of Marketing Science* **48**, 422–448.

Camilleri, A. R. (2020), 'The importance of online reviews depends on when they are presented', *Decision Support Systems* **133**, 113307.

Chevalier, J. A. & Mayzlin, D. (2006), 'The Effect of Word of Mouth on Sales: Online Book Reviews', *Journal of Marketing Research* **43**(3), 345–354.

Fink, L. & Papismedov, D. (2022), 'On the Same Page? What Users Benefit from a Desktop View on Mobile Devices', *Information Systems Research*.

Floyd, K., Freling, R., Alhoqail, S., Cho, H. Y. & Freling, T. (2014), 'How Online Product Reviews Affect Retail Sales: A Meta-analysis', *Journal of Retailing* **90**(2), 217–232.

Gutt, D., Neumann, J., Zimmermann, S., Kundisch, D. & Chen, J. (2019), 'Design of review systems—A strategic instrument to shape online reviewing behavior and economic outcomes', *Journal of Strategic Information Systems* **28**(2), 104–117.

Hajli, N., Lin, X., Featherman, M. & Wang, Y. (2014), 'Social Word of Mouth: How Trust Develops in the Market', *International Journal of Market Research* **56**(5), 673–689.

Hayes A. F (2022), *Introduction to Mediation, Moderation, and Conditional Process Analysis: A Regression-Based Approach.* Guilford Press.

Hogarth, R. M. & Einhorn, H. J. (1992), 'Order effects in belief updating: The belief-adjustment model', *Cognitive Psychology* **24**(1), 1–55.

Hu, N., Koh, N. S. & Reddy, S. K. (2014), 'Ratings lead you to the product, reviews help you clinch it? The mediating role of online review sentiments on product sales', *Decision Support Systems* **57**, 42–53.

Huang, J.-H. & Chen, Y.-F. (2006), 'Herding in online product choice', *Psychology and Marketing* **23**(5), 413–428.

Huang, L., Tan, C.-H., Ke, W. & Wei, K.-K. (2014), 'Do we order product review information display? How?' *Information & Management* **51**(7), 883–894.

Jabr, W. & Rahman, M. S. (2022), 'Online Reviews and the Information Overload: The Role of Selective, Parsimonious and Concordant Top Reviews and their Valence', *MIS Quarterly* **46**(3), 1517–1550.

Kaushik, K., Mishra, R., Rana, N. P. & Dwivedi, Y. K. (2018), 'Exploring reviews and review sequences on e-commerce platform: A study of helpful reviews on Amazon.in', *Journal of Retailing and Consumer Services* **45**, 21–32.

Kupfer, A., Maier, R., Zimmermann, S. & Thiele, J. J. (2020), 'Do Featured Consumer Reviews Matter?', *International Conference on Information Systems 2020 Proceedings.*

Lei, Z., Yin, D., Mitra, S. & Zhang, H. (2022), 'Swayed by the reviews: Disentangling the effects of average ratings and individual reviews in online word-of-mouth', *Production and Operations Management* **31**(6), 2393–2411.

Liu, X., Lee, D. & Srinivasan, K. (2019), 'Large-Scale Cross-Category Analysis of Consumer Review Content on Sales Conversion Leveraging Deep Learning', *Journal of Marketing Research* **56**(6), 918–943.

Manes, E. & Tchetchik, A. (2018), 'The role of electronic word of mouth in reducing information asymmetry: An empirical investigation of online hotel booking', *Journal of Business Research* **85**, 185–196.

Park, C. & Lee, T. M. (2009), 'Information direction, website reputation and eWOM effect: A moderating role of product type', *Journal of Business Research* **62**(1), 61–67.

Reynolds, N. & Diamantopoulos, A. (1998), 'The effect of pretest method on error detection rates', *European Journal of Marketing* **32**(5/6), 480–498.

Sparks, B. A. & Browning, V. (2011), 'The impact of online reviews on hotel booking intentions and perception of trust', *Tourism Management* **32**(6), 1310–1323.

van Helversen, B., Abramczuk, K., Kopeć, W. & Nielek, R. (2018), 'Influence of consumer reviews on online purchasing decisions in older and younger adults', *Decision Support Systems* **113**, 1–10.

Zhou, S. & Guo, B. (2017), 'The order effect on online review helpfulness: A social influence perspective', *Decision Support Systems* **93**, 77–87.

Ziegele, M. & Weber, M. (2015), 'Example, please! Comparing the effects of single customer reviews and aggregate review scores on online shoppers' product evaluations', *Journal of Consumer Behaviour* **14**(2), 103–114.

[illegible] The Future of [illegible]

[illegible]

[illegible]

[illegible]

[illegible]

[illegible]

[illegible]

[illegible]

[illegible]

[illegible]

Park, [illegible] compare [illegible] reputation and [illegible]

[illegible] The [illegible] effect [illegible]

Stanko, [illegible]

van Herpen, E., [illegible] Influence of [illegible] on [illegible] purchasing [illegible]

Zhou, S., & Guo, B. (2017). The order effect on online review helpfulness: A social influence perspective. *Decision Support Systems, 93*, 77–87.

Zucchini, M., [illegible] comparing the effect of simple [illegible]

Seizing the Potential of Algorithms: The Power of Personalized Persuasive Messages on the Use of Algorithmic Advice

Simon Asbach, Lorenz Graf-Vlachy, and Andreas Fügener

Abstract Recommendations of algorithms are frequently superior to human judgment, but humans often fail to seize the full potential of algorithms. Research has made initial advances to increase the use of algorithmic advice, but achieved levels remain far from optimal. However, research has not yet considered user personality traits to develop interventions to increase the use of algorithms. We propose to communicate the algorithmic advice via a persuasive message that fits the user's regulatory focus, i.e., the tendency towards promotion- versus prevention focus, to create regulatory fit. To test our hypotheses, we conduct an experiment with a forecasting task and 605 participants. Results support a positive effect of a persuasive message on the use of algorithmic advice. Further, results do not support a regulatory fit effect. Our article adds to theory and practice by developing and empirically testing novel interventions to increase the use of algorithms. Next research steps are discussed.

Keywords Use of algorithmic advice · Personalized advice · Regulatory fit · Behavioral experiment

S. Asbach (✉) · L. Graf-Vlachy
Department of Business and Economics, TU Dortmund University, Dortmund, Germany
e-mail: simon.asbach@tu-dortmund.de

L. Graf-Vlachy
e-mail: lorenz.graf-vlachy@tu-dortmund.de

A. Fügener
Faculty of Management, Economics and Social Sciences, University of Cologne, Cologne, Germany
e-mail: andreas.fuegener@uni-koeln.de

D. Beverungen et al. (eds.), *Conceptualizing Digital Responsibility for the Information Age*, Lecture Notes in Information Systems and Organisation 74,
https://doi.org/10.1007/978-3-031-80119-8_17

1 Introduction

Throughout history, humans have relied on human advice for (difficult) decision-making. At least partially thanks to the rise of "big data", a new source of advice is available to humans: algorithms. Algorithmic advice refers to the result of scripts of mathematical calculations (Logg et al. 2019) and has already become an essential ingredient in many professional and private decision-making processes, such as in headhunting, matchmaking, movie recommendations, styling, and financial advising (e.g., Siri, Google Search, LinkedIn, Tinder, Bumble, Netflix, Pandora, Club W, and Betterment) to name just a few examples (e.g., Gorwa et al. 2020; Lockey et al. 2021; Logg et al. 2019). This success of algorithms can be explained by a combination of superior accuracy and cost-effectiveness compared to human judgment (e.g., Logg et al. 2019; Silver 2012).

Despite the advantages of algorithmic advice, humans often fail to seize the full potential of algorithms. Even when faced with a superior algorithm, i.e., an algorithm that should generally be followed in 100% of the cases, humans usually only follow its advice about 30–50% of the time (e.g., Logg et al. 2019). Research on the reasons for this phenomenon is still ongoing, with egocentrism, overconfidence in one's judgment, and lack of trust being among the most frequently discussed ones (Logg et al. 2019). It should be recognized that underutilization may also be a carry-over effect from other situations in which a particular individual has correctly overridden a faulty algorithmic advice and trusted their own intuitions instead. In general, underutilization of algorithmic advice is especially problematic in objective domains with concrete, external standards of accuracy, such as forecasting tasks, since algorithmic advice usually surpasses human judgment in these domains (Dawes et al. 1989).

Initial advances have been made to increase humans' use of algorithmic advice, but they have found limited success. For example, research has shown that increasing the transparency of a complex algorithm increases the use of its advice only slightly from 49 to 56% (even when 100% would have been optimal), while increasing the transparency of a simple algorithm can even decrease the use of algorithmic advice (Lehmann et al. 2022). Further research investigated imperfect algorithms and found that people are more willing to use such an algorithm if they can adjust its output (Dietvorst et al. 2018). To our knowledge, no study has found a way to increase the use of advice from superior algorithms, i.e., systems that should generally be followed in all cases, to levels above 60%. Note that we focus on contexts in which the user does not receive feedback on the quality of the last algorithmic advice, which the user can use to inform their following decision, i.e., we focus on algorithms without performance feedback.

However, research has not yet considered the user's personality to study concrete interventions that increase humans' use of advice from superior algorithms, which is surprising because personality influences people's behavior to a large extent (e.g., Ajzen 2005). More specifically, personality traits describe tendencies to behave in a certain way (e.g., Ajzen 2005) and are mostly neglected when it comes to increasing the use of algorithmic advice. In fact, what initial research has done is generally link one specific personality trait, i.e., conscientiousness, to how well people use and benefit from algorithms (Man Tang et al. 2022). Given that personality traits thus appear to influence how well people use an algorithm, we conjecture that one might be able to tailor algorithmic advice to the user's personality traits to increase its use. Alas, with only few recent studies empirically testing the effect of algorithmic advice on actual behavior at all (e.g., Lehmann et al. 2022), there appears to be no extant research on increasing the use of algorithmic advice that considers user's personality traits when designing a message to communicate algorithmic advice. We address this gap in our current paper.

To increase the use of algorithmic advice, we propose (i) to communicate algorithmic advice via a persuasive message and (ii) to tailor the persuasive message to the user's regulatory focus orientation, i.e., tailor the message to an important personality trait to create regulatory fit. On the first point, if a persuasive message presents the algorithm as a high-quality advisor with a practical purpose, the user might experience elevated trust in the algorithm. Trust in various algorithm-based systems is a central antecedent for their acceptance and use (Choung et al. 2022; Shin 2020b; 2021). On the second point, research in personality psychology has established the construct of chronic regulatory focus as an important personality trait. Specifically, humans show a chronic tendency towards one of two separate regulatory focus orientations: promotion, with a focus on attaining progress or prevention, with a focus on maintaining the status-quo (Higgins 1997; 1998). If there is a match between the regulatory focus of the person and the message, this will create regulatory fit (Cesario et al. 2004; Higgins et al. 2003). Prior research suggests that regulatory fit can increase the persuasiveness of messages as participants "feel right" about following the message (Cesario et al. 2004; Cesario and Higgins 2008; Koenig et al. 2009). For example, a persuasive message that focuses on attaining progress, i.e., promotion focus, leads to a healthier nutrition behavior for promotion-oriented participants compared to prevention-oriented participants (Spiegel et al. 2004).

We test our research ideas by conducting a behavioral experiment, an emerging and promising method in information systems research (Gupta et al. 2018). To test the use of algorithmic advice we collected data from 605 participants who performed a previously validated task that asks participants to forecast the demand for ten different products, before and after receiving advice from an algorithm (Lehmann et al. 2020). The presentation of the algorithmic advice to the user differed across three experimental conditions: (1) control condition without a persuasive message, (2) experimental condition with a persuasive message representing regulatory fit, and (3) experimental condition with a persuasive message representing non-fit. Beyond measuring the use of algorithmic advice, we also measured participants' chronic regulatory focus, persuasiveness of the message, and trust in the algorithm.

Our results both partially support our hypotheses and include promising unexpected findings, allowing us to contribute novel insights on increasing the use of algorithmic advice for theory and practice. Specifically, our results support the hypothesis that administering a persuasive message leads to increased use of algorithmic advice. This main effect is mediated by trust in the algorithm. However, we find no support for the idea that a message representing regulatory fit (versus a message representing non-fit) increases the use of algorithmic advice. Further, we find that a message representing prevention orientation generally leads to increased use of algorithmic advice compared to a message representing promotion orientation. Next, we suggest exploring the current paper's unexpected findings further.

2 Theoretical Background

2.1 Use of Algorithmic Advice

While algorithmic advice frequently surpasses human judgment, humans often follow their own or another human's judgment instead (e.g., Grove et al. 2000; Dietvorst et al. 2015; De Baets and Harvey 2020). Algorithmic advice can be especially helpful in contexts with concrete, external standards of accuracy, such as forecasting tasks. Accurate forecasting is critical in professional and private domains, such as demand forecasting for organizations (Kremer et al. 2011; Lawrence et al. 2006) or traffic forecasting for travelers (Lana et al. 2018). Yet, decision-makers tend to misjudge the utility of algorithmic advice, and often end up making poor decisions. Researchers have even coined the term "algorithm aversion" to describe the decrease in the use of algorithmic versus human advice once participants see them make the same mistake (Dietvorst et al. 2015). After seeing an algorithm err, participants are averse to algorithms even if the algorithm generally outperforms humans. Further, especially domain-experts seem to reject helpful algorithmic advice more often even though they judge the accuracy of algorithmic advice better compared to non-experts (Allen and Choudhury 2022).

While the literature has mostly sought to explain why people use algorithms less than would be optimal, only initial advances have been made to develop concrete interventions to increase the use of algorithmic advice. Explanations for why algorithms may be used too little mainly cover five areas, namely (i) the level of previous algorithmic mistakes (Dietvorst et al. 2015), (ii) the level of domain experience (Allen and Choudhury 2022), (iii) the decision-making domain of the algorithm (subjective versus objective context; Logg et al. 2019), (iv) the perceived quality of the algorithm (Yu et al. 2019), and (v) the opacity or the lack of transparency of a given AI result (Lebovitz et al. 2022; Lehmann et al. 2022). Research in all five areas mostly focuses on perceptions of the algorithm, such as trust, perceived accuracy, or appreciation. However, only a few recent studies empirically test interventions to increase the use of algorithmic advice (e.g., Lehmann et al. 2022). Research is especially rare in the field of superior algorithms without receiving direct feedback on the algorithm's performance. Indeed, no research has found concrete interventions to increase the use of superior algorithmic advice to levels above 60% (Lehmann et al. 2022; Logg et al. 2019). We address this issue in the current paper.

We consider two potentially powerful factors to increase the use of algorithmic advice: first, the communication of algorithmic advice and second, the user's personality. On the first point, persuasive messages can increase the chances of people acting in a desired way. For example, persuasive messages of an Artificial Intelligence (AI) system can reduce a patient's unhealthy diet (Dragoni et al. 2020). On the second point, as personality, and more specifically, personality traits, are important determinants of people's behavior in general (e.g., Ajzen 2005), it seems reasonable to assume that personality traits also play a critical role for the use of algorithms. In fact, initial research postulates that conscientious people work less well with algorithms compared to non-conscientious people (Man Tang et al. 2022). More specifically, personality traits are important in advice-taking from humans. For example, the personality trait narcissism, i.e., the belief in one's superior qualities, is associated with less advice-taking (Kausel et al. 2015). Due to the importance of persuasive messaging and personality traits for following AI systems, using algorithms, and advice-taking, these factors likely also matter for the use of algorithmic advice. However, research has not yet considered these two factors to increase the use of algorithmic advice in objective domains. We attempt to address this gap.

2.2 *Persuasive Message*

The presence of a persuasive message to communicate algorithmic advice to the user versus a lack thereof should lead to higher use of algorithmic advice via elevated trust in the algorithm. Trust seems to play a central role in the acceptance and use of algorithmic systems in general, which can be seen by the fact that trust has been researched in a great variety of applications of algorithms, including algorithmic journalism (Shin 2022), healthcare (Lee and Rich 2021), hiring and work evaluations (Lee 2018), and algorithm-based forecasting (Dietvorst et al. 2015; 2018; Logg et al. 2019). We propose that a persuasive message increases trust in the algorithm through two ways. First, the perceived accuracy of an algorithm if the message presents the algorithmic advice as high-quality. Second, the message may elevate perceived reliability if the algorithm is presented with a practical purpose to the user, i.e., to achieve good performance or to avoid poor performance. We expect trust to be increased as multiple studies have reported perceived accuracy and reliability as important antecedents of elevated levels of trust in algorithmic systems (e.g., Glikson and Wolley 2020; Lockey et al. 2021; Shin 2020a; Shin and Park 2019). Further, we expect elevated trust to increase the use of algorithmic advice as various studies propose trust to be a central antecedent for the acceptance and use of various algorithmic systems (e.g., Choung et al. 2022; Shin 2020b; 2021; Söllner et al. 2016). This rationale leads to two hypotheses:

Hypothesis 1 (H1): The presence of a persuasive message will increase the use of algorithmic advice versus the control condition without a persuasive message.
Hypothesis 2 (H2): H1 will be mediated by trust in the algorithm.

2.3 Regulatory Fit

To adjust the algorithm to the user's personality, we propose tailoring the persuasive message to the user's regulatory focus. Regulatory focus theory postulates promotion and prevention orientation as two separate motivational orientations (Higgins 1997; 1998; 2016). Promotion-oriented individuals aim at progress, moving from their current state, "0", to a better " + 1" state. They focus on goal pursuit in terms of hopes, aspirations, and accomplishments. In contrast, prevention-oriented individuals aim at maintaining a satisfactory status quo, "0", ensuring against "– 1" losses. They focus on goal pursuit in terms of duties, obligations, and attaining security. Individuals usually show a chronic tendency towards either promotion or prevention orientation (Higgins 1997; 1998; 2016). Further, regulatory focus theory proposes different goal pursuit strategies for promotion versus prevention orientation, namely eagerness versus vigilance. Promotion-oriented individuals prefer using eager strategies ensuring gains (ways to advance) and ensuring against non-gains (not closing off possible advancements). In contrast, prevention-oriented individuals prefer using vigilant strategies ensuring non-losses (being careful) and ensuring against losses (avoiding mistakes; Higgins 1997; 1998; 2016).

Pairing a participant's promotion focus with an eager goal attainment strategy via a persuasive message (e.g., "To improve your performance, you can use algorithmic advice") and a participant's prevention focus with a vigilant goal attainment strategy (e.g., "To avoid poor performance, you can use algorithmic advice") would create regulatory fit. The reverse pairing would create non-fit (Cesario et al. 2004; Higgins et al. 2003). Regulatory fit of a persuasive message leads to "feeling right" which increases the positivity toward the focal item (Cesario et al. 2004; Cesario and Higgins 2008; Koenig et al. 2009). Multiple studies have found support for the increased persuasiveness of a message representing regulatory fit versus one representing non-fit, such as increasing the level of healthy food intake or increasing the physical exercise level of participants (for a review, see Avnet and Higgins 2021). Not surprisingly, regulatory fit is also associated with elevated levels of trust (e.g., Thongpapanl et al. 2018; Vaughn et al. 2010). Further, trust should lead to increased use of algorithmic advice as discussed in the rationale for hypothesis 2. This rationale leads to two hypotheses:

Hypothesis 3 (H3): A persuasive message representing regulatory fit will increase the use of algorithmic advice versus a message representing non-fit.

Hypothesis 4 (H4): H3 will be mediated by trust in the algorithm.

3 Methods

3.1 Participants and Procedure

The experiment was programmed in oTree (Chen et al. 2016) and launched on Amazon's Mechanical Turk in June 2022, via CloudResearch. We used CloudResearch as its approved participants list provides a higher-quality pool than other convenience sample providers (formerly TurkPrime; see Litman and Robinson 2020; Litman et al. 2017). Due to limited research to draw effect sizes from, we expected a small to medium effect size of d = 0.25 for both main effects (Cohen 1992). A priori power analysis with G*Power 3.1 (Faul et al. 2009) resulted in a required sample size of 597 participants to achieve 80% power (with $\alpha = 0.05$). Out of a total of 1035 workers who agreed to participate, 605 completed the experiment (16 failed the initial attention checks, 333 failed the comprehension checks, and 81 did not proceed until the end). The average participant needed 15.8 min to finish the experiment.

Our experiment used a forecasting task with a Judge Advisor System (JAS), which is used to measure the extent to which people assimilate advice (Gino 2008; Logg et al. 2019; Sniezek and Buckley 1995). First, participants ("judges") made an initial demand forecast without external advice. Second, they received advice from an algorithm ("advisor"). Third, they could update their initial forecast and provide their final forecast. The forecast was measured before and after receiving the advice, and the relative shift in the forecast indicates the use of advice (Bonaccio and Dalal 2006). We used an ex ante perfect system as an advisor that provides advice leading to the highest expected outcome.

Figure 1 illustrates the experiment's process, which follows the procedure of Lehmann et al. (2022). Participants first read a short introduction, answered attention checks, and filled out a regulatory focus questionnaire (Higgins et al. 2001). They also read instructions on the upcoming forecasting task including the information that they would make an initial judgment on a product forecast, receive advice, and then make their final decision. Participants were also shown an example question and had to answer the comprehension check questions on the forecasting task correctly to proceed. Next, participants provided their initial demand forecasts. For each product, they were shown the historical demand of ten time periods on a line chart and had to input an integer number for the demand in period 11. We chose line charts as they are perceived to be the best presentation style when the characteristics of the demand data are unknown (Harvey and Bolger 1996). Once participants finished the initial forecasts for ten products, they proceeded to the final forecast. For each product, they saw the same line chart as in the first round as well as their initial forecast, the algorithmic advice, and a blank text field for their final forecast. After finishing the forecasting task, participants completed final questions, e.g., on the persuasiveness of the messages and their trust in the algorithm. In the end, participants were debriefed and received feedback on their performance and their payoff. The payoff comprised a base pay of $1.50 and a performance-based bonus of up to $1.00. Performance was

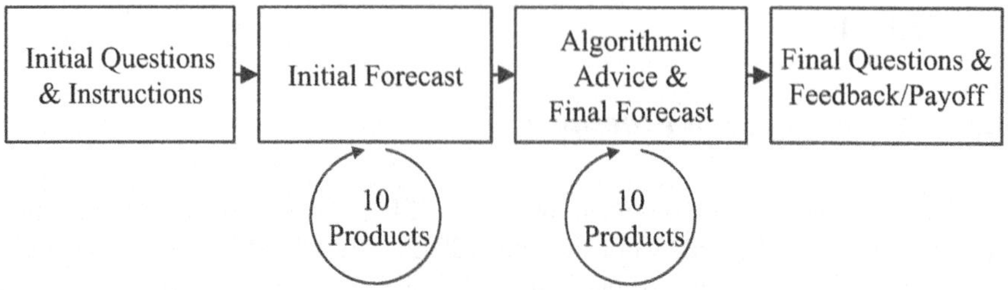

Fig. 1 Sequence of events in the experiment (adapted from Lehmann et al. 2022)

measured as the absolute percentage error (bounded by 0 and 1), and the performance-based bonus for each product was computed as \$0.10 × (1—absolute percentage error) as in Kremer et al. (2011).

3.2 *Treatment Manipulation*

We manipulated the appearance of the algorithm in three ways to test our hypotheses: (1) no persuasive message in the control condition, (2) a persuasive message representing regulatory fit, (3) a persuasive message representing non-fit. The persuasive message was the same within one condition across all ten products. The wording of the messages was based on previous research representing either an eager (for promotion-oriented people in the fit condition or for prevention-oriented people in the non-fit condition) or a vigilant (for prevention-oriented people in the fit condition or for promotion-oriented people in the non-fit condition) strategy (for a review of examples, see Avnet and Higgins 2021). Further, the message referred to the algorithm as an "AI". An example of a promotion-oriented message reads "Updating your initial forecast by considering the AI advice can help you improve your performance and successfully achieve substantial gains. To improve your performance, the AI advises the number that can be seen below". An example of a prevention-oriented message reads "Deviating from the AI advice can risk worsening your performance and you might fail to secure the best performance. To avoid poor performance, the AI advises the number that can be seen below."

3.3 *Measures*

Chronic Regulatory Focus of Participants. Chronic regulatory focus was measured with the 11-item Regulatory Focus Questionnaire, which uses a five-point scale (Grant and Higgins 2003; Higgins et al. 2001). Items measure the history of success and failure with promotion- and prevention-related strategies. The measure for chronic regulatory focus is generated by subtracting the mean rating of prevention-related items from the mean rating of promotion-related items. Evidence of both reliability and validity is reported in Higgins et al. (2001). An example item reads, "Compared to most people, are you typically unable to get what you want out of life (1 = "never or seldom" to 5 = "very often")?" (Higgins et al. 2001).

Weight on Advice. The use of algorithmic advice was measured by weight on advice (WOA; e.g., Bonaccio and Dalal 2006). WOA measures how much participants adjust their initial forecast towards the algorithmic advice. More specifically, WOA is the difference between the initial and revised forecast divided by the difference between the initial forecast and the advice. WOA of zero occurs when participants ignore advice completely and WOA of one occurs when participants abandon their prior forecast to perfectly match the advice. We winsorize values less than zero or greater than one to increase interpretability (e.g., Logg et al. 2019). We will use the average WOA across all products.

Persuasiveness and Trust. We measured persuasiveness to understand whether the messages indeed generated the desired effect. In line with previous research (Cesario et al. 2004; Koenig et al. 2009), participants rated how persuasive, convincing, compelling, influential, effective, and coherent the messages were. Items were rated on a seven-point scale. The scale showed satisfactory reliability ($\alpha = 0.94$).

Trust in the algorithm was operationalized through one item and rated on a seven-point scale. We did not expect reliability or validity issues. First, a relatively large sample of 605 participants should reduce concerns over random measurement error, i.e., unreliability. Second, the used item has high face-validity, which was confirmed by other researchers we consulted in the design process of our measure.

4 Results

4.1 Summary

Our results support the hypothesis that administering a message versus administering no message leads to higher use of algorithmic advice. This main effect was mediated by trust in the algorithm. However, our results did not support the notion that a message representing regulatory fit versus a message representing non-fit leads to higher use of algorithmic advice: $M_{Control} = 0.52$, $M_{Regulatory\ fit} = 0.66$, $M_{Non\text{-}fit} = 0.71$. The following analyses are based on 595 participants as we had to omit data of 10 participants due to their lack of a clearly identifiable chronic regulatory focus, i.e., they scored 0 on the RFQ scale (Higgins et al. 2001). Unless specified otherwise, the analyses are based on the General Linear Model (GLM).

4.2 Confirmatory Analyses

Perceived Persuasiveness of Messages. The messages proved to be broadly persuasive. On the seven-point scale, participants in the regulatory fit condition rated the persuasiveness at $M = 5.43$ ($SD = 1.17$) and at $M = 5.44$ ($SD = 1.22$) in the non-fit condition. The difference between the groups was not significant ($F(1, 367) = 0.01$, $p = 0.935$).

Effect of a Persuasive Message. As expected, participants showed significantly higher WOA when they received a persuasive message ($M = 0.69$, $SD = 0.24$) compared to a lack thereof ($M = 0.52$, $SD = 0.23$), $F(1, 593) = 73.32$, $p < 0.001$.

Further, trust mediates the positive relationship between the presence of a message versus the lack thereof on WOA. Bootstrapping analysis via PROCESS (Hayes 2009; 2017; Zhao et al. 2010) reveals a significant indirect effect, $IE = 0.04$, $SE = 0.01$, 95% CI [0.02, 0.06]. Figure 2 illustrates the mediation.

Effect of Regulatory Fit. Contrary to our predictions, persuasive messages in the fit condition are related to significantly lower WOA ($M = 0.66$, $SD = 0.24$) compared to the non-fit condition ($M = 0.71$, $SD = 0.25$), $F(1, 367) = 4.51$, $p = 0.034$ (see Fig. 3). Further, participants did not show different levels of trust in the fit—($M = 4.56$, $SD = 1.56$) versus the non-fit condition ($M = 4.63$, $SD = 1.65$), $F(1, 367) = 0.16$, $p = 0.686$.

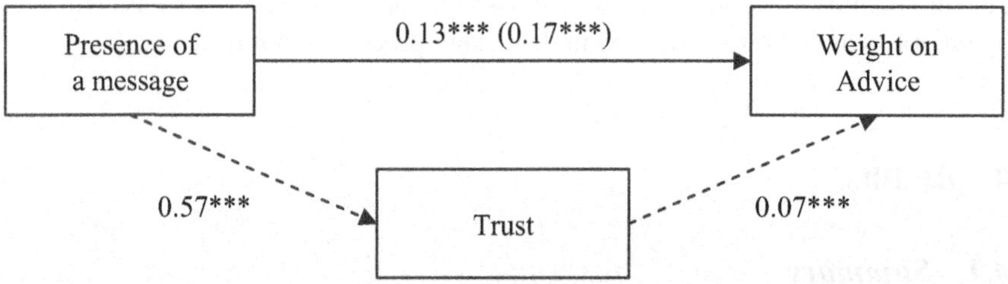

Fig. 2 Beta coefficients for total, direct, and indirect effects. $^{*}p < 0.1$. $^{**}p < 0.01$. $^{***}p < 0.001$

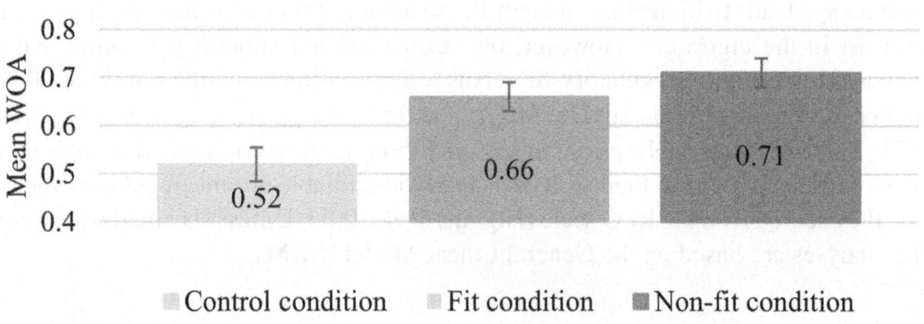

Fig. 3 Mean WOA per experimental condition with 95% confidence intervals

Effect of a Promotion—Versus Prevention-Oriented Message. Running separate analyses of variance shows that for prevention-oriented people, a prevention-oriented message (fit) is related to similar levels of WOA compared to a promotion-oriented message (non-fit), $M = 0.71$ ($SD = 0.25$) and $M = 0.67$ ($SD = 0.24$), respectively ($F(1, 160) = 1.31$, $p = 0.254$). However, for promotion-oriented people, a prevention-oriented message (non-fit) is related to higher levels of WOA compared to a promotion-oriented message (fit), $M = 0.76$ ($SD = 0.24$) and $M = 0.63$ ($SD = 0.23$), respectively ($F(1, 205) = 16.11$, $p < 0.001$). The interaction effect of regulatory focus of participants and regulatory focus of the message on WOA is marginally significant, $p = 0.087$ (Fig. 4 illustrates the simple slopes of the interaction effect). Hence, elevated WOA in the non-fit compared to the fit condition can mainly be explained by a positive effect of a prevention-oriented message on the WOA of promotion-oriented people. Across groups, a prevention-oriented message yields stronger effects on WOA ($M = 0.74$, $SD = 0.25$) than a promotion-oriented message ($M = 0.65$, $SD = 0.24$) and no message ($M = 0.52$, $SD = 0.23$), respectively ($F(2, 592) = 44.84$, $p < 0.001$). Figure 5 illustrates this effect.

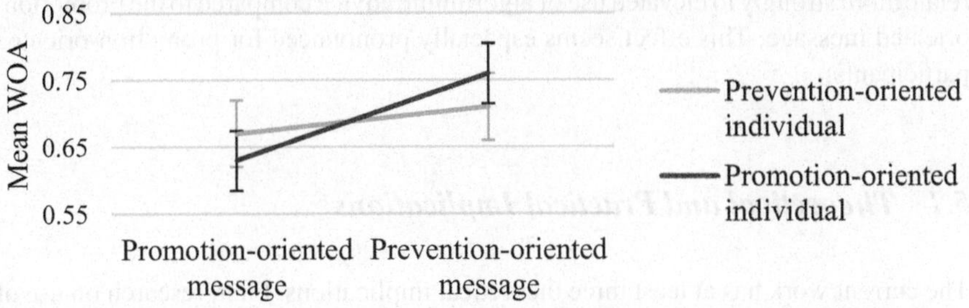

Fig. 4 Mean WOA per type of individual and type of message with 95% confidence intervals

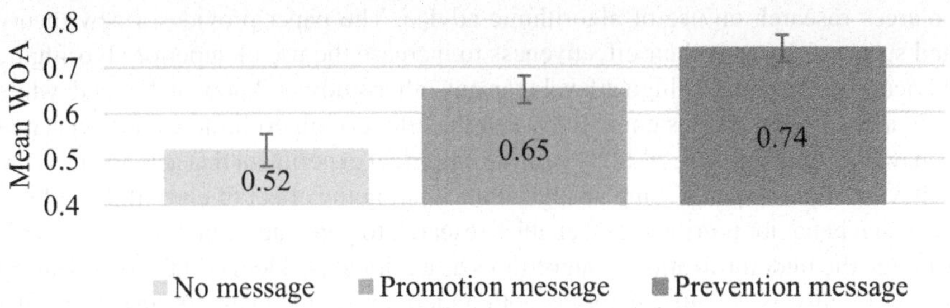

Fig. 5 Mean WOA per type of message with 95% confidence intervals

5 Discussion

Despite the frequently superior accuracy and cost-effectiveness of algorithmic advice compared to human judgment, humans often underutilize algorithms and fail to seize their full potential (Dietvorst et al. 2015; 2018; Logg et al. 2019; Meehl 1954). Research in the field of information systems has not yet found effective solutions and the underutilization of algorithms poses a critical problem for practitioners (Haak 2017; Harrell 2016). Our study proposes and tests ways to increase the use of superior algorithmic advice without performance feedback. In line with our predictions, the presence of a persuasive message regarding algorithmic advice seems to increase the use of algorithmic advice from 51 to 69% on average. As previous studies in the same setting usually measure use of algorithmic advice of up to 56% (Lehmann et al. 2022; Logg et al. 2019), our study's effect seems substantial. Further, results support our hypothesis that considerable parts of the main effect can be explained by trust in the algorithm. Contrary to our predictions, however, creating regulatory fit via a persuasive message versus non-fit does not seem to relate to increased use of algorithmic advice. Also, interestingly, the prevention-oriented message appears to relate more strongly to elevated use of algorithmic advice compared to the promotion-oriented message. This effect seems especially pronounced for promotion-oriented participants.

5.1 *Theoretical and Practical Implications*

The current work has at least three theoretical implications. First, research on use of algorithms has recognized the underutilization of algorithmic advice (Dietvorst et al. 2015; 2018; Logg et al. 2019; Meehl 1954), but has not theorized and tested powerful interventions to fight the problem effectively. The current study reduces this gap and enlarges research on use of algorithmic advice. The paper provides a new theory and successfully tests their effectiveness to increase the use of superior algorithmic advice to a substantially higher level than any other study we know of. Second, while only a few recent studies empirically test the effect of algorithmic advice on actual behavior (Lehmann et al. 2022), we run an empirical experiment that actually tests the behavior of participants using an algorithm. Testing the effect of algorithmic advice on actual behavior is critical as it enables research to generate value for practitioners, who see the underutilization of algorithms as a critical problem (Haak 2017; Harrell 2016). Finally, personality theory is both underrepresented in and promising for the information systems literature. We thus contribute by introducing regulatory focus, an established concept from personality psychology, to research on algorithmic advice in information systems.

Our findings contribute to practice by providing an empirically tested idea to improve the outcome of important decision processes. Superior algorithms are especially valuable in domains with concrete, external standards of accuracy, such as forecasting tasks (Dawes et al. 1989). Due to their potential value, the importance of algorithms has already increased in practice (Fildes and Petropolous 2015). However, most companies combine algorithmic advice with human judgment and frequently humans make the final call (e.g., Fildes and Petropoulos 2015; Khosrowabadi et al. 2022; Perera et al. 2019), often leading to algorithms being ultimately undervalued (Dietvorst et al. 2015; Logg et al. 2019). Our paper suggests persuasive messages as a concrete and highly effective mitigation to this problem.

5.2 *Future Directions*

In terms of future directions, the current paper's unexpected findings may be explored further. First, regulatory fit of a persuasive message does not result in increased use of algorithmic advice compared to non-fit. Second, a prevention-oriented message results in increased use of algorithmic advice compared to a promotion-oriented message. The reason for a lack of the regulatory fit effect may be due to the strength of the prevention-oriented message. In fact, we observe a positive but non-significant fit effect for prevention-oriented people, whereas we observe a negative fit effect on the use of algorithmic advice for promotion-oriented people. While trust in the algorithm does not explain the strength of the prevention-oriented message, it might be that the wording of the prevention- versus the promotion-oriented message suggests higher quality of the algorithm, which prior research has already linked to the use of algorithms (Yu et al. 2019). Another idea for an explanation of the participants' strong reaction to the prevention-oriented message might center on loss aversion. The threat of losing a monetary reward in an experiment might loom larger than the opportunity of gaining a monetary reward (Kahneman and Tversky 1979). Lastly, while we used the well-respected Regulatory Focus Questionnaire (Higgins et al. 2001), it should be acknowledged that inaccurate measurement of regulatory focus would lead to inaccurate application of regulatory fit and thus, an inaccurate effect of regulatory fit. In summary, the current paper provides a successful intervention to seize the potential of algorithmic advice, entails important theoretical and practical implications, and stimulates future research to continue this promising path.

References

Ajzen, I. (2005), *Attitudes, personality and behavior*. United Kingdom: McGraw-Hill.

Allen, R., & Choudhury, P. (2022), "Algorithm-augmented work and domain experience: The countervailing forces of ability and aversion", *Organization Science* **33**(1), 149–169.

Avnet, T. & Higgins, E. T. (2021), "Regulatory fit and non-fit: how they work & what they do", *Columbia Business School Research Paper Forthcoming*.

Bonaccio, S. & Dalal, R. S. (2006), "Advice-taking and decision-making: an integrative literature review, and implications for the organizational sciences", *Organizational Behavior and Human Decision Processes* **101**(2), 127–151.

Cesario, J. & Higgins, E. T. (2008), "Making message recipients "feel right" how nonverbal cues can increase persuasion", *Psychological Science* **19**(5), 415–420.
Cesario, J., Grant, H. & Higgins, E. T. (2004), "Regulatory fit and persuasion: transfer from "feeling right"", *Journal of Personality and Social Psychology* **86**(3), 388–404.
Chen, D. L., Schonger, M. & Wickens, C. (2016), "oTree—an open-source platform for laboratory, online, and field experiments", *Journal of Behavioral and Experimental Finance* **9**, 88–97.
Choung, H., David, P. & Ross, A. (2022), "Trust in AI and its role in the acceptance of AI technologies", *International Journal of Human–Computer Interaction*, 1–13.
Cohen, J. (1992), "A power primer", *Psychological Bulletin* **112**(1), 155–159.
Dawes, R. M., Faust, D. & Meehl, P. E. (1989), "Clinical versus actuarial judgment", *Science* **243**(4899), 1668–1674.
De Baets, S. & Harvey, N. (2020), "Using judgment to select and adjust forecasts from statistical models", *European Journal of Operational Research* **284**(3), 882–895.
Dietvorst, B. J., Simmons, J. P. & Massey, C. (2015), "Algorithm aversion: people erroneously avoid algorithms after seeing them err", *Journal of Experimental Psychology: General* **144**(1), 114–126.
Dietvorst, B. J., Simmons, J. P. & Massey, C. (2018), "Overcoming algorithm aversion: people will use imperfect algorithms if they can (even slightly) modify them", *Management Science* **64**(3), 1155–1170.
Dragoni, M., Donadello, I. & Eccher, C. (2020), "Explainable AI meets persuasiveness: translating reasoning results into behavioral change advice", *Artificial Intelligence in Medicine* **105**, 101840.
Faul, F., Erdfelder, E., Buchner, A. & Lang, A. G. (2009), "Statistical power analyses using G* Power 3.1: tests for correlation and regression analyses", *Behavior Research Methods* **41**(4), 1149–1160.
Fildes, R. & Petropoulos, F. (2015), "Improving forecast quality in practice", *Foresight: The International Journal of Applied Forecasting* **36**, 5–12.
Gino, F. (2008), "Do we listen to advice just because we paid for it? The impact of advice cost on its use", *Organizational Behavior and Human Decision Processes* **107**(2), 234–245.
Glikson, E. & Woolley, A. W. (2020), "Human trust in artificial intelligence: review of empirical research", *Academy of Management Annals* **14**(2), 627–660.
Gorwa, R., Binns, R. & Katzenbach, C. (2020), "Algorithmic content moderation: technical and political challenges in the automation of platform governance", *Big Data & Society* **7**(1), 1–15.
Grant, H. & Higgins, E. T. (2003), "Optimism, promotion pride, and prevention pride as predictors of quality of life", *Personality and Social Psychology Bulletin* **29**(12), 1521–1532.
Grove, W. M., Zald, D. H., Lebow, B. S., Snitz, B. E. & Nelson, C. (2000), "Clinical versus mechanical prediction: a meta-analysis", *Psychological Assessment* **12**(1), 19–30.
Gupta, A., Kannan, K. & Sanyal, P. (2018), "Economic experiments in information systems", *MIS Quarterly* **42**(2), 595–606.
Haak, T. (2017), *Algorithm aversion and HR-Tech.* URL: https://hrtrendinstitute.com/2017/02/13/algorithm-aversion-hr-trends-2017-5/. Accessed: 20.12.2022.
Harrell, E. (2016), "Managers shouldn't fear algorithm-based decision making", *Harvard Business Review*, 1–5.
Harvey, N. & Bolger, F. (1996), "Graphs versus tables: effects of data presentation format on judgmental forecasting", *International Journal of Forecasting* **12**(1), 119–137.
Hayes, A. F. (2009), "Beyond Baron and Kenny: statistical mediation analysis in the new millennium", *Communication Monographs* **76**(4), 408–420.
Hayes, A. F. (2017), *Introduction to mediation, moderation, and conditional process analysis: a regression-based approach.* Guilford publications.
Higgins, E. T., Friedman, R. S., Harlow, R. E., Idson, L.C., Ayduk, O. N. & Taylor, A. (2001), "Achievement orientations from subjective histories of success: promotion pride versus prevention pride", *European Journal of Social Psychology* **31**(1), 3–23.
Higgins, E. T., Idson, L. C., Freitas, A. L., Spiegel, S. & Molden, D.C. (2003), "Transfer of value from fit", *Journal of Personality and Social Psychology* **84**(6), 1140–1153.

Higgins, E. T. (1997), "Beyond pleasure and pain", *American Psychologist* **52**(12), 1280–1300.

Higgins, E. T. (1998), "Promotion and prevention: regulatory focus as a motivational principle", *in* Zanna, M. P. (ed.) *Advances in Experimental Social Psychology,* 30, 1–46. New York: Academic Press.

Higgins, E. T. (2016), "Promotion and prevention motivations", *in* Sternberg, R. J., Fiske, S. T., and Foss, D. J. (eds.) *Scientists making a difference: one hundred eminent behavioral and brain scientists talk about their most important contributions*, 301–305. Cambridge: University Press.

Kahneman, D. & Tversky, A. (1979), "Prospect Theory: an analysis of decision under risk", *Econometrica* **47**(2), 263–291.

Kausel, E. E., Culbertson, S. S., Leiva, P. I., Slaughter, J. E. & Jackson, A. T. (2015), "Too arrogant for their own good? Why and when narcissists dismiss advice", *Organizational Behavior and Human Decision Processes* **131**, 33–50.

Khosrowabadi, N., Hoberg, K. & Imdahl, C. (2022), "Evaluating human behaviour in response to AI recommendations for judgmental forecasting", *European Journal of Operational Research* **303**(3), 1151–1167.

Koenig, A. M., Cesario, J., Molden, D. C., Kosloff, S. & Higgins, E. T. (2009), "Incidental experiences of regulatory fit and the processing of persuasive appeals", *Personality and Social Psychology Bulletin* **35**(10), 1342–1355.

Kremer, M., Moritz, B. & Siemsen, E. (2011), "Demand forecasting behavior: system neglect and change detection", *Management Science* **57**(10), 1827–1843.

Lana, I., Del Ser, J., Velez, M. & Vlahogianni, E. I. (2018), "Road traffic forecasting: recent advances and new challenges", *IEEE Intelligent Transportation Systems Magazine* **10**(2), 93–109.

Lawrence, M., Goodwin, P., O'Connor, M. & Önkal, D. (2006), "Judgmental forecasting: a review of progress over the last 25 years", *International Journal of Forecasting* **22**(3), 493–518.

Lebovitz, S., Lifshitz-Assaf, H. & Levina, N. (2022), "To engage or not to engage with AI for critical judgments: How professionals deal with opacity when using AI for medical diagnosis", *Organization Science* **33**(1), 126–148.

Lee, M. K. & Rich, K. (2021), "Who is included in human perceptions of AI? Trust and perceived fairness around healthcare AI and cultural mistrust", *Proceedings of the 2021 Conference on Human Factors in Computing Systems,* 1–14.

Lee, M. K. (2018), "Understanding perception of algorithmic decisions: fairness, trust, and emotion in response to algorithmic management", *Big Data & Society* **5**(1), 1–16.

Lehmann, C. A., Haubitz, C. B., Fügener, A. & Thonemann, U. W. (2020), "Keep it mystic? The effects of algorithm transparency on the use of advice", *Proceedings of the 41st International Conference on Information Systems (ICIS),* 1–9.

Lehmann, C. A., Haubitz, C. B., Fügener, A. & Thonemann, U. W. (2022), "The risk of algorithm transparency: how algorithm complexity drives the effects on the use of advice", *Production and Operations Management* **31**(9), 3419–3434.

Litman, L. & Robinson, J. (2020), *Conducting online research on Amazon Mechanical Turk and beyond*. Sage Publications.

Litman, L., Robinson, J. & Abberbock, T. (2017), "TurkPrime. com: a versatile crowdsourcing data acquisition platform for the behavioral sciences", *Behavior Research Methods* **49**(2), 433–442.

Lockey, S., Gillespie, N., Holm, D. & Someh, I. A. (2021), "A review of trust in artificial intelligence: challenges, vulnerabilities and future directions", *Proceedings of the 54th Hawaii International Conference on System Science (HICSS),* 5463–5472.

Logg, J. M., Minson, J. A. & Moore, D. A. (2019), "Algorithm appreciation: people prefer algorithmic to human judgment", *Organizational Behavior and Human Decision Processes* **151**, 90–103.

Man Tang, P., Koopman, J., McClean, S. T., Zhang, J. H., Li, C. H., De Cremer, D., Lu, Y. & Ng, C. T. S. (2022), "When conscientious employees meet intelligent machines: an integrative approach inspired by complementarity theory and role theory", *Academy of Management Journal* **65**(3), 1019–1054.

Meehl, P. E. (1954), *Clinical versus statistical prediction: a theoretical analysis and a review of the evidence*. Minneapolis: University of Minnesota Press.

Perera, H. N., Hurley, J., Fahimnia, B. & Reisi, M. (2019), "The human factor in supply chain forecasting: a systematic review", *European Journal of Operational Research* **274**(2), 574–600.

Shin, D. & Park, Y.J. (2019), "Role of fairness, accountability, and transparency in algorithmic affordance", *Computers in Human Behavior* **98**, 277–284.

Shin, D. (2020a), "User perceptions of algorithmic decisions in the personalized AI system: perceptual evaluation of fairness, accountability, transparency, and explainability", *Journal of Broadcasting & Electronic Media* **64**(4), 541–565.

Shin, D. (2020b), "How do users interact with algorithm recommender systems? The interaction of users, algorithms, and performance", *Computers in Human Behavior* **109**, 1–10.

Shin, D. (2021), "The effects of explainability and causability on perception, trust, and acceptance: implications for explainable AI", *International Journal of Human-Computer Studies* **146**, 1–10.

Shin, D. (2022), "Expanding the role of trust in the experience of algorithmic journalism: user sensemaking of algorithmic heuristics in Korean users", *Journalism Practice* **16**(6), 1168–1191.

Silver, N. (2012), *The signal and the noise: the art and science of prediction*. United Kingdom: Penguin.

Sniezek, J. A. & Buckley, T. (1995), "Cueing and cognitive conflict in judge-advisor decision making", *Organizational Behavior and Human Decision Processes* **62**(2), 159–174.

Söllner, M., Hoffmann, A. & Leimeister, J. M. (2016), "Why different trust relationships matter for information systems users", *European Journal of Information Systems* **25**(3), 274–287.

Spiegel, S., Grant-Pillow, H. & Higgins, E. T. (2004), "How regulatory fit enhances motivational strength during goal pursuit", *European Journal of Social Psychology* **34**(1), 39–54.

Thongpapanl, N., Ashraf, A. R., Lapa, L. & Venkatesh, V. (2018), "Differential effects of customers' regulatory fit on trust, perceived value, and m-commerce use among developing and developed countries", *Journal of International Marketing* **26**(3), 22–44.

Vaughn, L. A., Harkness, A. R. & Clark, E. K. (2010), "The effect of incidental experiences of regulatory fit on trust", *Personal Relationships* **17**(1), 57–69.

Yu, K., Berkovsky, S., Taib, R., Zhou, J. & Chen, F. (2019), "Do I trust my machine teammate? an investigation from perception to decision", *Proceedings of the 24th International Conference on Intelligent User Interfaces*, 460–468.

Zhao, X., Lynch Jr, J. G. & Chen, Q. (2010), "Reconsidering Baron and Kenny: myths and truths about mediation analysis", *Journal of Consumer Research* **37**(2), 197–206.

How to Convey Resilience: Towards a Taxonomy for Conversational Agent Breakdown Recovery Strategies

Shengjia Feng

Abstract Conversational agents (CAs) have permeated our everyday lives in the past decade. Yet, the CAs we encounter today are far from perfect as they are still prone to breakdowns. Studies have shown that breakdowns have an immense impact on the user-CA relationship, user satisfaction, and retention. Therefore, it is important to investigate how to react and recover from breakdowns appropriately so that failures do not impair the CA experience lastingly. Examples for recovery strategies are the assumption of the most likely user intent (CA self-repair) or to ask for clarification (user-repair). In this paper, we iteratively develop a taxonomy to classify breakdown recovery strategies based on studies from scholarly literature and experiements with productive CA instances, and identify the current best practices described using our taxonomy. We aim to synthesize, structure and further the knowledge on breakdown handling and to provide a common language to describe recovery strategies.

Keywords Conversational agents · Resilience · Breakdown · Recovery strategies

1 Introduction

Conversational agents (CAs) went through one of the most impressive evolutions of all technological advancements. With the launch of the ChatGPT, the power of Artificial Intelligence (AI) seems infinite and tangible for everyone. Although business use cases for GPT conversational agents are yet to be explored (Chui et al. 2022), they can already be experienced in the form of personal assistants in mobile devices or as virtual customer service agents on websites. Users have high expectations as CAs oftentimes converse in a natural, human-like way. Yet, we observe limitations in their capabilities: While CAs previously often struggled with understanding or serving user inquiries (Luger and Sellen 2016), CAs based on large language models

S. Feng (✉)
Technical University Darmstadt, Software and Digital Business, Darmstadt, Germany
e-mail: shengjia.feng@gast.tu-darmstadt.de

D. Beverungen et al. (eds.), *Conceptualizing Digital Responsibility for the Information Age*, Lecture Notes in Information Systems and Organisation 74,
https://doi.org/10.1007/978-3-031-80119-8_18

give very persuasive answers with no factual grounding, a phenomenon called 'hallucination.' Studies show that when user encounter breakdowns in their interaction with a CA, it can lead to anger (Han et al. 2021), user dissatisfaction (Akhtar et al. 2019), and long-lasting negative adversions (Luger and Sellen 2016). In fact, Li et al. (2020a) found that nearly half of the users who abandoned a CA long-term only faced one breakdown. For CAs in productive use, breakdowns can cause severe Public Relations issues for the company (Prahl and Goh 2021). Hence, it is crucial to consciously develop and select repairment and recovery strategies to mitigate breakdown effects.

In this work, we aim to establish a comprehensive understanding of the design space and provide a framework to accurately describe recovery strategies. This common framework is needed to efficiently organize the design space and to identify designs that are yet to be explored in research and practice. Our research question is as follows:

RQ: What are the dimensions and characteristics of a taxonomy that comprehensively and accurately classifies a CA recovery strategy?

The purpose of this work is trifold: First, we develop a framework to describe CA recovery strategies based on research studies and productive instances of CAs. In a second step, we extract recurring patterns in the CAs investigated during taxonomy development. Lastly, we identify starting points for further studies. Following the call to further investigate CA design (Rapp et al. 2021), we aim to extend the existing knowledge and provide guidance on how to deal with unwanted CA failure.

2 Related Work

A CA is "*a software program that interacts with users using natural language*" (Shawar and Atwell 2007, p. 31) in a way as if a human was on the other side. CAs have had various roles throughout its long history: As a psychologist ('ELIZA'; Weizenbaum 1966), counsellor (Benyon et al. 2013), virtual buddy (Fitzpatrick et al. 2017; Inkster et al. 2018), in teaching roles (Baylor and Kim 2005; Ogan et al. 2012), and as a personal assistant (Klopfenstein et al. 2017). Today, CAs are at a developmental stage that they can support at the workplace (Feng and Buxmann 2020; Meyer von Wolff 2020) and workers may even consider them as collaborators rather than a tool (Bittner et al. 2019; Seeber et al. 2020). With the feasibility to train large language models, many new possibilities open up with its generative and conversational power.

But CAs can encounter breakdowns during interactions. A popular breakdown is Microsoft's *Tay* going rogue after only few hours of operation (Wakefield 2016). Although Tay's breakdown can be attributed to abusive users, the creators should foresee such critical interactions (Suárez-Gonzalo et al. 2019; Wolf et al. 2017). Amershi et al. (2019) proposed the category 'when wrong' for their design guidelines on Human-AI interaction, indicating that breakdowns are a normal stage of interaction to be considered. A breakdown, therefore, is a situation that does not contribute to the CA's value delivery and is most likely an exceptional state in the conversation, but should not be one that is unplanned for. However, neither the CA nor the user has to be aware of the breakdown, for instance, when ChatGPT hallucinates and the user cannot validate the statements due to lacking domain knowledge himself. In this work, we focus on cases where the CA does know its breakdown, since that is the prerequisite to trigger a recovery strategy to mitigate the negative effects of the situation.

Upon breakdown, the conversation needs to recover from the exceptional state in order to progress. This calls for a recovery strategy that decides on the next action. We can generally divide recovery strategies in two main categories: The system-repairs and the user-repairs. For a system-repair, the prerequisite is for the system to recognize its breakdown without user indication, e.g., by learning to recognize breakdowns using techniques like Machine Learning (Almansor and Hussain 2021; Kontogiorgos et al. 2020; Reinkemeier and Gnewuch 2022). A system-repair with no user involvement means that the system resolves the issue by assuming and executing the 'best next action' (e.g., Ashktorab et al. 2019) or by proceeding the conversation with the 'best intent' (e.g., Dippold 2023). User-repairs involve the user to different degrees to assist the CA and resolve the breakdown together. This can be conducted via asking questions to clarify a cryptic message (Müller et al. 2021) or providing options to proceed in the form of utterance templates or buttons (Benner et al. 2021). Furthermore, the perceived effect and the appropriateness of breakdown recovery strategies are influenced by many other factors, such as apologeticness (Song et al. 2023; Zhang et al. 2023a), usage of special language elements like Emojis (Liu et al., 2023; Wang et al. 2023), other anthropomorphic features (Seeger and Heinzl 2021), and timing of breakdown and recovery measures (Huang and Dootson 2022; Kim et al. 2023).

3 Methodology and Taxonomy Development

Based on Nickerson et al. (2012), a taxonomy T consists of n dimensions $D_i (1 \leq i \leq n)$. Each dimension D_i is a set of $k_i (i \geq 2)$ characteristics $C_{ij} (1 \leq j \leq k_i)$. In the taxonomy, the characteristics in the same dimension should be mutually exclusive and all dimensions collectively exhaustive, i.e., each object under consideration has exactly one characteristic C_{ij} of each dimension D_i. We follow the taxonomy development method proposed by Nickerson et al. (2012) to develop the taxonomy, therefore, the steps described in the following refer to their procedure.

Step 1: Determine meta-characteristic. We aim for a high-level design guide for CA creators on how to recover from a CA breakdown. Therefore, our meta-characteristic is 'recovery strategies for CA breakdowns.' Note that we treat breakdowns as single, standalone incidents. Different strategies can be applied by CA for multiple breakdowns, although consistency has shown to elevate usability (Li et al. 2020b).

Step 2: Determine ending conditions. After each iteration the taxonomy needs to be assessed regarding objective and subjective ending conditions. For our taxonomy development, we use all conditions as proposed by Nickerson et al. (2012, p. 9).

3.1 Iteration 1

Step 3: Conceptual-to-empirical. For the first iteration, we choose the conceptual-to-empirical approach to include work that can set a first basis that can be validated and extended in further iterations. Ashktorab et al. (2019) already provides a variety of recovery strategies that form the first dimensions of our taxonomy. This paper was selected as the authors already performed studies to investigate users' perceptions of the strategies which we can take into consideration for the second goal of this paper, which is to provide a best practice guideline to practitioners. The strategies provided also reflect common strategies one encounter in productive CAs.

Step 4c: Conceptualize new characteristics and dimensions of objects. Based on Ashktorab et al. (2019), we define three dimensions: 'Acknowledgment' indicates if the CA explicitly acknowledges the breakdown towards the user. The second dimension is the type of 'Explanation' to the user: the CA can provide what it understood (positive), what it did not understand (negative), or no explanation. The third dimension is the 'Coping Strategy Type:' the CA can cope on system-side, assist the user to repair, or rely on the user to handle the breakdown.

Step 5c: Examine objects for these characteristics and dimensions. For this iteration the objects can be directly taken from the studies by Ashktorab et al. (2019) as the dimensions are derived from their investigations. In their study, they investigated different customer service CAs in the fields of shopping, banking, and travel.

Step 6c: Create taxonomy. The taxonomy T_1 resulting from this first iteration is as follows: $T_1 = \{$Acknowledgment (Acknowledging, No acknowledgment), Explanation (Positive Explanation, Negative Explanation, No Explanation), Strategy Type (System-repair, Assisted User-repair, User-repair)$\}$.

Step 7: Ending Conditions met? Since this is the first iteration, the objective ending conditions are naturally not fulfilled. We consider T_1 fulfilling all subjective conditions except for comprehensiveness. Due to the small number of objects examined in this iteration, we cannot claim this attribute yet.

3.2 Iteration 2

Step 3: Empirical-to-conceptual. In the second iteration, our goal is to identify more objects from literature. Our approach is similar to a systematic literature review (SLR;

Kitchenham 2004; Webster and Watson 2002): We perform searches in the relevant databases AISeL, the ACM DL, ScienceDirect and IEEExplore. The latest search was performed in June 2023 with the search term *("conversational agent" OR "chatbot") AND ("breakdown" OR "repair" OR "resilience" OR "coping" or "recovery")*. We include all publications of 2017 or later as research interest significantly increased in this timeframe (Feng and Buxmann 2020; Rapp et al. 2021). This way, we can include a representative number of papers while limiting the effort as we do not aim to perform an exhaustive SLR. Where possible, only 'research articles' or 'peer-reviewed' publications are included. We scan the search results for original studies focusing on CA breakdowns and recovery strategies in three steps: We review the title, then the abstract and lastly, the full-text. We include publications about non-text-based agents if concepts were tested that are applicable to text-based CAs. Our process is depicted in Fig. 1 and yielded a total of 22 papers in the final set (duplicates removed).

Step 4e: Identify subset of objects. The final set of 22 papers includes 45 recovery strategies in total and is listed in Table 2 with the recovery strategies investigated classified based on the final taxonomy. When there are multiple strategies presented in one publication, each row refers to one strategy.

Step 5e: Identify common characteristics and group objects. Among the recovery strategies of the objects investigated in this iteration, we observe that there are different levels of acknowledgment. Many recovery strategies make use of anthropomorphism in the form of an apology to improve the CA's likeability and to retain trust in the user-CA relationship (e.g., Law et al. 2022; Mahmood et al. 2022; Song et al. 2023; Zhang et al. 2023b). We observe that button options are often used to continue with limited functional range (e.g., Ashktorab et al. 2019; Law et al. 2022; Li et al. 2020a). This aligns with findings that user expectations need to be managed to prevent (further) breakdowns (Luger and Sellen 2016). In addition to providing an explanation, we identify different types of explanations: the user's utterance was not understood correctly ("Unfortunately, I do not understand your request." from Diederich et al. 2020, p. 8) or the intent was not recognized ("Did you mean? need *help* *thank you* clinic's *location* *None* of these" from Dippold 2023, p. 27).

Step 6e: Group characteristics into dimensions to create taxonomy. Based on our observations, we extended 'Acknowledgment' with the apologetic acknowledgment.

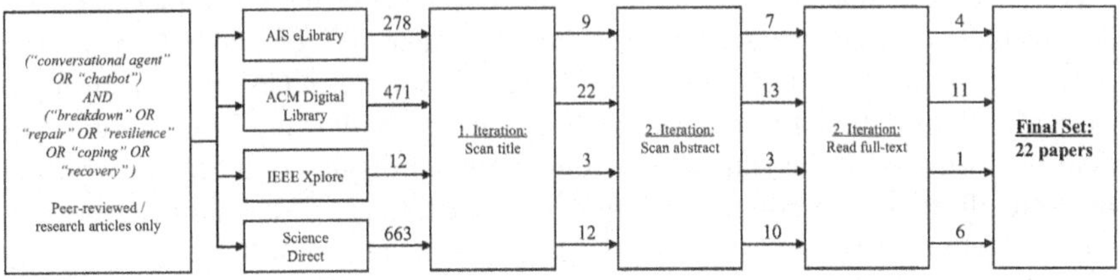

Fig. 1 Overview of the literature review process

We refine the assisted user-repair to differentiate between the 'open' assistance and the assistance with functional limitation. Lastly, we add a new dimension to account for the explanation type. The taxonomy T_2 is as follows: $T_2 = \{$Acknowledgment (Apologetic, Neutral, None), Explanation (Positive, Negative, None), Type of Explanation (Utterance-based, Intent-based, None), Strategy Type (System-repair, Limited Assisted User-Repair, Assisted User-repair, User-repair)$\}$.

Step 7: Ending Conditions met? Due to the addition and modification of dimensions, the objective ending conditions are not met. For the subjective ending conditions, this taxonomy is concise, extendible and explanatory and robust. However, we need at least one more iteration to prove comprehensiveness.

3.3 *Iteration 3*

Step 3: Empirical-to-conceptual. In our third iteration, we investigate CAs in productive use. In order to examine their recovery strategies, we need to provoke breakdowns first. For that, we develop a testing scheme to systematically evaluate based on different breakdown causes identified in Sect. 2. We define three utterances per breakdown cause, twelve in total. The complete testing scheme is provided in Table 1. Each utterance is entered in a new conversation session to avoid side effects from consecutive breakdowns. We search for CAs on landing pages as well as on 'Customer Service' and 'Contact' pages, since CAs are most often available on these pages and most likely allow for free text input (i.e., not a hard-wired decision tree logic), so the same testing scheme can be applied to all CAs tested. Hence, CAs in this iteration are mainly focusing on customer service management. In the utterances, placeholders are used for subjects to select appropriate in-scope and out-of-scope products. For example, asking for 'van' on an automotive company's website would be in-scope, but asking about a 'banana' is out-of-scope, whereas the opposite would be valid for a grocery store.

Step 4e: Identify new subset of objects. For our tests, we include publicy accessible CAs based on the following criteria: It is not only an interface to chat with a human, understands English, allows free text input, and is available for multiple conversations. Since CAs are oftentimes used to automate low-effort processes, CAs mostly used by larger companies with a high number of reoccurring (customer) requests. This leads to our strategy to scan the websites of Fortune 500 companies fron different industries for suitable chatbot instances. Despite a variety of CAs used in customer service, only few allow for free text input, many CAs built using low-code development platforms are more similar to a conversational display of a decision tree and therefore eliminate the possibility to provoke breakdowns. We examined five CAs from companies in the industries retail, automotive retail, consulting, transportation and information technology.

Table 1 CA testing scheme—overview of utterances

Trigger	Utterance	Description
Language/Vocabulary	*Können Sie mir nähere Informationen zu Ihren Produkten zusenden?*	Unknown language (German)
	Pouvez-vous m'envoyer des informations détaillées sur vos produits?	Unknown language (French)
	Send me information you're products	Language errors
Out-of-scope	*What is the weather like today?*	Off-topic request
	Please turn off the lights in the living room	Off-topic request
	Why does my [product] make weird noises?	Very specific request
Multiple in-scope intents	*I bought a [product] last week, but there is something wrong with it and I would like to return it. How is the process?*	Multiple intents: complaint, return process
	I have an account, but forgot my credentials. Now I want to change my address	Multiple intents: restore credentials, change address
	I ordered [product] but I need to change the billing address. If that is not possible, I will need to cancel my order	Multiple intents with if-condition: change address, cancel order
Low semantic value	*Hello*	Utterances with no/low semantic value
	Thank you	
	Lol	

Step 5e: Identify common characteristics and group objects. In our tests, we identify a new exerted type of acknowledgement: Unapologetic, but with willingness to help ("*I might be able to help…*"). Another characteristic we noticed is the transparent communication of the limits of the its capabilities. This constitutes a type of explanation that is neither evidence- nor example-based. Lastly, we found that almost all of the CAs offer the option to transfer to a human associate.

Step 6e: Group characteristics into dimensions to create taxonomy. In this iteration, we add two characteristics, the 'exerted' acknowledgement and the 'capability-based' type of explanation. In addition, we add the dimension 'delegation to human,' to cover the human back-up solution. The taxonomy after this iteration is therefore as follows: $T_3 = \{$Acknowledgment (Apologetic, Exerted, Neutral, None), Explanation (Positive, Negative, None), Type of Explanation (Utterance-based, Intent-based, Capability-Based, None), Strategy Type (System-repair, Limited Assist. User-Repair, Assist. User-repair, User-repair), Delegation to Human (Yes, No)$\}$.

Table 2 Final taxonomy and classification of all objects examined

Conversational agent	ACK				REA				EXP			REP				DH	
	Apologetic	Exerted	Neutral	None	Utterance	Intent	Capability	None	Positive	Negative	None	System	Lim. Ass. User	Ass. User	User	Yes	No
Count	23	4	21	12	12	9	6	33	10	7	43	10	12	13	25	9	51
Ashktorab et al. (2019)				X				X			X	X					X
			X					X			X				X		X
			X			X			X				X				X
			X			X			X				X				X
	X							X			X	X				X	
			X		X				X					X			X
	X				X					X				X			X
Beneteau et al. (2019)				X				X			X	X					X
	X							X			X				X		X
			X			X			X				X				X
Cheng et al. (2018)				X				X			X				X		X
Cuadra et al. (2021)	X							X			X				X		X
Diederich et al. (2020)			X		X						X				X		X
	X				X						X				X		X
Dippold (2023)				X				X			X	X					X
			X			X			X				X				X
	X				X					X					X		X

(continued)

Table 2 (continued)

Conversational agent	ACK				REA				EXP			REP				DH	
	Apologetic	Exerted	Neutral	None	Utterance	Intent	Capability	None	Positive	Negative	None	System	Lim. Ass. User	Ass. User	User	Yes	No
			X		X				X					X			X
	X						X			X				X		X	
Do et al. (2023)	X						X		X				X				X
Han et al. (2021)			X		X						X				X		X
			X		X						X		X				X
Huang and Dootson (2022)			X					X			X				X	X	
Khurana et al. (2021)			X					X			X			X			X
	X					X				X				X			X
Law et al. (2022)	X							X			X			X			X
	X							X			X				X		X
			X					X			X			X			X
			X					X			X				X		X
Li et al. (2020a)	X					X					X				X		X
Li et al. (2020b)			X			X			X				X				X

(continued)

Table 2 (continued)

Conversational agent	ACK				REA				EXP			REP				DH	
	Apologetic	Exerted	Neutral	None	Utterance	Intent	Capability	None	Positive	Negative	None	System	Lim. Ass. User	Ass. User	User	Yes	No
Liu et al. (2023)	X				X						X				X		X
	X						X				X				X		X
Mahmood et al. (2022)	X				X					X					X		X
Müller et al. (2021)				X	X				X				X				X
				X	X						X				X		X
Poser et al. (2021)	X					X				X					X	X	
Seeger and Heinzl (2021)			X					X			X		X				X
	X							X			X				X		X
Song et al. (2023)	X							X			X				X		X
		X						X			X				X		X
Wu et al. (2021)			X					X			X			X			X
Zargham et al. (2022)				X				X			X	X					X
Zhang et al. (2023b)	X							X			X				X		X
				X				X			X				X		X
Retail company	X							X			X				X		X

(continued)

Table 2 (continued)

Conversational agent	ACK				REA				EXP			REP				DH	
	Apologetic	Exerted	Neutral	None	Utterance	Intent	Capability	None	Positive	Negative	None	System	Lim. Ass. User	Ass. User	User	Yes	No
		X				X			X				X			X	
		X						X			X	X				X	
Transportation company		X						X			X				X		X
			X					X			X				X		X
	X						X			X				X			X
				X				X			X	X					X
Consulting company				X				X			X		X				X
	X						X				X			X			X
Automotive retail company			X				X				X		X			X	
				X				X			X	X					X
IT company			X					X			X			X			X
				X				X			X	X					X
			X					X			X	X				X	
	X							X			X			X		X	

Legend (Dimensions): *ACK:* Acknowledgment, *EXP:* Explanation, *REA:* Reason, *REP:* Repair, *DH:* Delegation to human

Step 7: Ending Conditions met? The objective ending conditions are not met as we added new characteristics and a dimension. After this iteration, we consider this taxonomy to be comprehensible as it now covers both research and practice instances. Nonetheless, we need at least one more iteration due to the objective ending conditions.

3.4 Iteration 4

Step 3: Conceptual-to-Empirical. We take this approach since we have now examined various objects and have a deeper knowledge of the recovery strategies.

Step 4c: Conceptualize new characteristics and dimensions of objects. To clarify the dimensions 'explanation' and 'type of explanation,' we rename the latter to 'reason.' Respectively, the characteristics are modified to match the naming. The 'strategy type' dimension is renamed to 'repair.' Lastly, we reorder the dimensions to reflect the chronological order of occurrence during a breakdown.

Step 5c: Examine objects for these characteristics and dimensions. We examined all objects from the previous iterations and they all fit in the new taxonomy.

Step 6c: Create taxonomy. The taxonomy is as follows: $T_4 = \{$Acknowledgment (Apologetic, Exerted, Neutral, None), Reason (Utterance, Intent, Capability, None), Explanation (Positive, Negative, None), Repair (System-repair, Limited Assist. User-Repair, Assist. User-repair, User-repair), Delegation to Human (Yes, No)$\}$.

Step 7: Ending Conditions met? Since we only renamed/reordered, the objective ending conditions are met. As the subjective ending conditions were already met after the last iteration, the development process ends here.

4 Taxonomy

Our final taxonomy consists of five dimensions with two to four characteristics each. In this section, we present the dimensions and characteristics in more detail. A classification of all objects from the development process is provided in Table 2 where each row represents one recovery strategy identified in the source.

Acknowledgment (ACK). The dimension 'acknowledgment' covers how the CA communicates the breakdown towards the user. If the CA acknowledges the breakdown, it can be done in different tones, such as being apologetic (Lee et al. 2010; Mahmood et al. 2022) or neutral (Law et al. 2022). Apologetic acknowledgments usually start with "*I'm sorry*" and have a friendly tone in the remainder of the response. In productive CAs, we often encountered the 'exerted' tone which conveys the CA's willingness to help in a friendly, but unapologetic tone. An exerted tone also includes any efforts from the CA to maintain a human-like, trustful relationship with the user (Song et al. 2023). The choice of acknowledgment can express different levels of anthropomorphism and convey a certain the CA personality.

Reason (REA). The dimension 'reason' classifies the breakdown reason that is communicated to the user. Therefore, it is a high-level classification rather than a breakdown of all possible failures to make the taxonomy explanatory. *Utterance* includes all breakdowns that are triggered because the utterance from the user could not be parsed because of reasons like a foreign language or unknown vocabulary. *Intent* covers breakdowns that happen when an utterance cannot be assigned to an intent with sufficient confidence. It can also happen that an intent was matched with a high confidence which is not in-scope of the CA, so the reason for the breakdown is the *capability*. This happens in goal-oriented CA (e.g., customer service) built on general purpose frameworks that contain a predefined set of unused intents or when a CA is not performing its designated tasks correctly. The communicated reason does not need to match the real reason for the breakdown to conceal quality issues that might have other negative effects. For instance, the CA can communicate that the intent is out of scope (capability) although the issue is that the user has entered an utterance in a non-supported language.

Explanation (EXP). The CA can optionally add an explanation on why the breakdown occurred. A positive explanation explains what the it *has* understood, a negative explanation shows why it was *not* able to understand the user input utterance. Explanation means that the reason of failure needs to be elaborated in a way that is helpful to the user. For instance, "*I am sorry that I was not able to understand your question*" (Law et al. 2022, p. 5) does not qualify as an explanation, but "*I couldn't recognize the Predict Trend Function*" (Khurana et al. 2021, p. 3) does.

Repair (REP). The repair dimension classifies recovery strategies based on the type of their repair mechanism. That is, how the CA recovers after a breakdown. We differentiate between a system-repair, a limited assisted user-repair, an assisted user-repair, and the complete user-repair. A *system-repair* is a repair mechanism that does not involve the user in the process. For instance, the CA assumes the best matching intent despite a low confidence and executes consequential actions without user involvement or confirmation. The *limited assisted user-repair* has a low involvement of the user by limiting the functional range. Examples are providing options that are most likely to match the user's intent or asking the user to confirm an intent. In these cases, the options provided by the CA are the only way moving forward in the conversation, the user is not allowed to 'change the topic.' Hence, it is a 'limited' assisted user-repair. *Assisted user-repair*, in contrast, allows for the user to repair the breakdown more freely with the assistance of the CA in the form of hints, examples, and other guidance. The user can rephrase or correct the understanding with no limitations in functionality. The assistance for the user-repair can be transported in the form of an explanation of the breakdown, an example utterance, or other information that helps the user to repair. *User-repair* includes all recovery strategies that rely on the user to repair the breakdown. That is, the CA does not perform any valuable action, and does not propose any way to help the user achieve their intents. Yet, the CA can restart or continue the conversation in a way that the user has the opportunity to send a different utterance.

Delegation to Human (DH). Some CAs are backed by a human associate who can takeover upon breakdown. This dimension indicates whether the recovery strategies includes handing over the request to a human (*yes/no*). The handover does not need to be automatic, but can also be offered as one of the options to the user.

5 Discussion

5.1 Findings and Recurring Recovery Strategies

The most part of the recovery strategies (48/60) prescribe to admit a breakdown and interact with the user to resolve the issue instead of making assumptions. However, only a third of the strategies include apologetic behavior (23/60) although a CA has anthropomorphic traits by its conversational nature. We observe a discrepancy between research and practice regarding the explanation of the breakdown. While half of the strategies in research (23/45) provide reasons and a third even detailed explanations (15/45), we rarely encounter this in productive CAs (4/15 and 2/15, respectively). As productive CAs tend not to explain the breakdown, it is intransparent to the user what exactly failed, providing no assistance to for the user to repair. Productive CAs often refer to a human as a fallback solution, while in research, they are rarely examined. Our tests reveal that the productive CAs often cannot perform other tasks outside the purpose the were built for, thus have very limited functional ranges that are tailored to specific customer support queries. Regardless, most of the productive CA are still capable of handling utterances with low semantic value and smalltalk.

The most prevalent three patterns we observe among the recovery strategies in the CAs examined are rather 'simple:' With seven mentions, one of the highest recurring is the 'ignore the breakdown and move on' strategy. This means that the CA simply ignores that a breakdown has occurred, does not provide any kind of acknowledgment or even explanation towards the user, and performs the next action that it considers as the best suitable for this case. This pattern reoccurred in both literature (Ashktorab et al. 2019; Beneteau et al. 2019; Dippold 2023; Zargham et al. 2022) and in the productive instances. For the productive CAs, we cannot know for sure if the breakdown was actively detected or if the action was performed with no special mitigation strategy. Tied in occurrence with the ignorance strategy is the recovery strategy to 'apologize and let the user fix it.' The CA does acknowledge the breakdown, but provides no further explanation or assistance. The user is left to resolve the issue on their own, e.g. by rephrasing their request. This recovery strategy was mostly prevalent in literature with six out of seven times (e.g., Beneteau et al. 2019, Cuadra et al. 2021; Law et al. 2022). Third ranks the recovery strategy to 'neutrally acknowledge the breakdown counterquestion/narrow down the space.' Examples for this recovery strategy is the introduction of buttons for the user to specify their request, or to ask a specific counterquestion ("Do you mean …?"). This recovery strategy was only found in literature (e.g., Ashktorab et al. 2019; Dippold 2023; Li et al. 2020b).

5.2 *Implications for Research and Practice*

We developed a taxonomy for recovery strategies based on CAs in productive use and studies in literature. A taxonomy provides a common language to describe recovery strategies and helps to identify research gaps, which we will discuss in the following.

Based on the prevalence of studies on the effect of anthropomorphism in research (Diederich et al. 2021; Seeger and Heinzl 2021; Zhang et al. 2023b), it is surprising that for breakdown recovery, the usage of apologetic behavior is that low. This can be in line with the observation that a chatbot's apology is not perceived as a sincere apology (Zhang et al. 2023a) and therefore omitted for efficiency reasons.

While the recovery strategies in this taxonomy focus on single breakdowns, the repair may not be successful, and lead to subsequent breakdowns. Based on previous findings, three consecutive breakdowns can already lead to users abandoning the CA (Li et al. 2020a). However, the combination of different recovery strategies for consecutive breakdowns have not yet been tested to our knowledge. This raises the question: Which recovery strategy *pattern* is the most effective to counteract the impact of breakdowns? Additionally, what impact does the choice of recovery strategies have on the relationship between the CA and the user? We suspect that, similar to human–human interaction, the answers to the questions have many influencing factors, including the CA personality, the user personality, and the purpose of the CA. Human-like communication has shown to increase the perceived enjoyment (de Sá Siqueira et al. 2023), so it is probable that anthropomorphism can help in mitigating breakdowns.

Before the background of the recovery strategies grounding our taxonomy, we can observe a discrepancy in the strategies investigated in literature and in productive CAs, as described in Sect. 5.1. This calls for the question to investigate if the recovery strategies tested in theory and in experimental setups are not feasible or suitable for real-world use cases, or if external influencing factors participate in the design decision that do not exist or are not replicable in research experiment settings.

During the development of our taxonomy, we discover clear potentials in productive CA. As current CAs provide little transparency on the reason of a breakdown, it is not clear to the user what had caused it. However, as research as shown, users prefer to have evidence of why the CA was not able to process their request appropriately (Ashktorab et al. 2019). Therefore, we call for more transparency in productive CA.

Although automation is one of the reasons for a CA, the CAs' authority to perform tasks needs to be carefully chosen. Executing the 'best matching action' despite low confidence on the intent recognition without user confirmation can lead to negative consequences like users giving up (Luger and Sellen 2016). It is crucial to choose the appropriate recovery strategy not only when a breakdown occurs, but to also adjust timings of potential breakdown points. A breakdown at a later stage as well as a handover to a human processor can lead to user aggression (Huang and Dootson 2022; Kim et al. 2023). We recommend to make more use of explicit user confirmations, which can be tedious due to the extra conversation turn, but are perceived as polite and meaningful by the user (Ashktorab et al. 2019). A superfluous repair attempt when there is nothing to repair may put the CA capabilities in question. However, the "*positive impact of self-repair in the wake of an error outweighs the negative impact of overcorrection.*" (Cuadra et al. 2021, p. 27).

6 Limitations and Outlook

Although we included recovery strategies that originate in research with voice-based and/or embodied CAs, we only considered properties that are applicable to text-based CAs. It is clear that the taxonomy can be extended to include different modalities contained in the recovery, such as gestures (Mori et al. 2021) and physical design (Kontogiorgos et al. 2020). However, our taxonomy can be applied and is extensible as per the qualitative requirement so further dimensions can be added as needed. This can be investigated in future research in the context of robotic service agents. Second limitation of this work is that in the literature review underlying this taxonomy development, we only include studies that focus on breakdown recovery. Due to the large body of knowledge around CAs in general, it is probable that there are many more studies that contain recovery strategies not yet included in this taxonomy which can be examined for potential future development of this taxonomy. Lastly, we have only examined a small number of productive CAs due to the reasons given in Sect. 3.3. With the emergence of business use cases for large language models, there will be further evaluation needed to update and extend this taxonomy including more CAs in productive use, with a particular focus on new types of CAs like ChatGPT.

References

Akhtar, M., Neidhardt, J. & Werthner, H. (2019), 'The Potential of Conversational agents: Analysis of Conversational agent Conversations,' *in* IEEE Conference on Business Informatics, pp. 397–404.

Almansor, E. H. & Hussain, F. K. (2021), 'Fuzzy Prediction Model to Measure Chatbot Quality of Service,' *in* Proceedings of the 2021 IEEE International Conference on Fuzzy Systems.

Amershi, S., Weld, D., Vorvoreanu, M., Fourney, A., Nushi, B., Collisson, P., Suh, J., Iqbal, S., Bennett, P. N., Inkpen, K., Teevan, J., Kikin-Gil, R. & Horvitz, E. (2019), 'Guidelines for Human-AI Interaction,' *in* CHI Conference on Human Factors in Computing Systems.

Ashktorab, Z., Jain, M., Liao, Q.V. & Weisz, J.D. (2019), 'Resilient Conversational agents: Repair Strategy Preferences for Conversational Breakdowns,' *in* CHI Human Factors in Computing Systems, no. 254.

Baylor, A. L. & Kim, Y. (2005), 'Simulating Instructional Roles Through Pedagogical Agents,' *International Journal of Artificial Intelligence in Education* 15(2), pp. 95–115.

Beneteau, E., Richards, O. K., Zhang, M., Kientz, J. A., Yip, J. & Hiniker, A. (2019), 'Communication Breakdowns Between Families and Alexa,' *in* CHI Conference on Human Factors in Computing Systems.

Benner, D., Elshan, E., Schöbel, S. & Jansen, A. (2021), 'What Do You Mean? A Review on Recovery Strategies to Overcome Conversational Breakdowns of Conversational Agents,' *in* Proceedings of the 2021 International Conference on Information Systems, no. 13.

Benyon, D., Gambäck, B., Hansen, P., Mival, O. & Webb, N. (2013), 'How Was Your Day? Evaluating a Conversational Companion,' *IEEE Transactions on Affective Computing* 4(3), pp. 299–311.

Bittner, E. A. C., Oeste-Reiß, S. & Leimeister, J. M. (2019), 'Where is the Bot in Our Team? Toward a Taxonomy of Design Option Combinations for Conversational Agents in Collaborative Work,' *in* Hawaii International Conference on System Sciences, pp. 284–293.

Cheng, Y., Yen, K, Chen, Y., Chen, S. & Hiniker, A. (2018), 'Why Doesn't It Work? Voice-Driven Interfaces and Young Children's Communication Repair Strategies,' *in* Proceedings of the 17th ACM Conference on Interaction Design and Children, pp. 337–348.

Chui, M., Roberts, R. & Yee, L. (2022), 'Generative AI is Here: How Tools Like ChatGPT Could Change Your Business,' *Quantum Black AI by McKinsey*.

Cuadra, A., Li, S., Lee, H., Cho, J. & Ju, W. (2021), 'My Bad! Repairing Intelligent Voice Assistant Errors Improves Interaction,' *Proceedings of the ACM Human-Computer Interaction* 5(CSCW1).

de Sá Siqueria, M. A., Müller, B. C. N. & Bosse, T. (2023), 'When Do We Accept Mistakes From Conversational agents? The Impact of Human-Like Communication on User Experience in Conversational agents That Make Mistakes,' *International Journal of Human-Computer Interaction*.

Diederich, S., Lembcke, T.-B., Brendel, A. B. & Kolbe, L. M. (2020), 'Not Human After All: Exploring the Impact of Response Failure on User Perception of Anthropomorphic Conversational Service Agents,' *in* Proceedings of the 2020 European Conference on Information Systems, no. 110.

Diederich, S., Lembcke, T.-B., Brendel, A. B. & Kolbe, L. M. (2021), 'Understanding the Impact that Response Failure Has on How Users Perceive Anthropomorphic Conversational Service Agents: Insights From an Online Experiment,' *AIS Transactions on Human-Computer Interaction* 13(1), pp. 82–103.

Dippold, D. (2023), '"Can I Have the Scan on Tuesday?" User Repair in Interaction with a Task-Oriented Chatbot and the Question of Communication Skills for AI,' *Journal of Pragmatics* 204, pp. 21–32.

Do, H. J., Kong, H.-K., Tetali, P., Lee, J. & Bailey, B. P. (2023), 'To Err is AI: Imperfect Interventions and Repair in a Conversational Agent Facilitating Group Chat Discussions,' *ACM Human-Computer Interaction* 7(CSCW1), no. 99.

Feng, S. & Buxmann, P. (2020), 'My Virtual Colleague: A State-of-the-Art Analysis of Conversational Agents for the Workplace,' *in* Hawaii International Conference on System Sciences, pp. 156–165.

Fitzpatrick, K. K., Darcy, A. & Vierhile, M. (2017), 'Delivering Cognitive Behavior Therapy to Young Adults With Symptoms of Depression and Anxiety Using a Fully Automated Conversational Agent (Woebot): A Randomized Controlled Trial,' *JMIR Mental Health* 4(2), e19.

Han, E., Yin, D. & Zhang, H. (2021), 'Interruptions During a Service Encounter: Dealing with Imperfect Chatbots,' *in* Proceedings of the 2021 International Conference on Information Systems.

Huang, Y.-S. S. & Dootson, P. (2022), 'Conversational agents and Service Failure: When Does it Lead to Customer Aggression,' *Journal of Retailing and Consumer Services* 68, no. 103044.

Inkster, B., Sarda, S. & Subramanian, V. (2018), 'An Empathy-Driven, Conversational Artificial Intelligence Agent (Wysa) for Digital Mental Well-Being: Real-World Data Evaluation Mixed-Methods Study,' *JMIR mHealth and uHealth* 6(11), no. e12106.

Khurana, A., Alamzadeh, P. & Chilana, P. K. (2021), 'ChatrEx: Designing Explainable Conversational agent Interfaces for Enhancing Usefulness, Transparency, and Trust,' *in* IEEE Symposium on Visual Languages and Human-Centric Computing.

Kim, A., Yang, M. & Zhang, J. (2023), 'When Algorithms Err: Differential Impact of Early vs. Late Errors on Users' Reliance on Algorithms,' *ACM Transactions on Computer-Human Interaction* 30, no. 14.

Kitchenham, B. (2004), *Procedures for Performing Systematic Reviews*. Keele University.

Klopfenstein, L. C., Delpriori, S., Malatini, S. & Boglioli, A. (2017), 'The Rise of Bots: A Survey of Conversational Interfaces, Patterns, and Paradigms,' *in* Designing Interactive Systems Conference, pp. 555–565.

Kontogiorgos, D., Pereira, A., Sahindal, B., van Waveren, S. & Gustafson, J. (2020), 'Behavourial Responses to Robot Conversational Failures,' *in* Proceedings of the 2020 ACM/IEEE International Conference on Human-Robot Interaction, pp. 53–62.

Law, E. L.-C., Følstad, A. & van As, N. (2022), 'Effects of Humanlikeness and Conversational Breakdown on Trust in Conversational agents for Customer Service,' *in* NordiCHI Nordic Conference on Human-Computer Interaction.

Lee, M. K., Kiesler, S., Forlizzi, J., Srinivasa, S. & Rybski, P. (2010), 'Gracefully Mitigating Breakdowns in Robotic Services,' *in* ACM/IEEE International Conference on Human-Robot Interaction (HRI).

Li, C.-H., Ye, S.-F., Chang, T.-J., Tsai M.-H., Chen, K. & Chang, Y.-J. (2020a), 'A Conversation Analysis of Non-Progress and Coping Strategies with a Banking Task-Oriented Conversational agent,' *in* CHI Conference on Human Factors in Computing Systems, no. 82.

Li, T. J.-J., Chen, J., Xia, H., Mitchel, T. M. & Myers, B.A. (2020b), 'Multi-Modal Repairs of Conversational Breakdowns in Task-Oriented Dialogs,' *in* ACM Symposium on User Interface Software and Technology, pp. 1094–1107.

Liu, D., Lv, Y. & Huang, W. (2023), 'How Do Consumers React to Chatbots' Humorous Emojis in Service Failures,' *Technoloy in Society* 73, no. 102244.

Luger, E. & Sellen, A. (2016), '"Like Having a Really bad PA": The Gulf between User Expectation and Experience of Conversational Agents,' *in* CHI Conference on Human Factors in Computing Systems, pp. 5286–5297.

Mahmood, A., Fung, J. W., Won, I. & Huang, C.-M. (2022), 'Owning Mistakes Sincerely: Strategies for Mitigating AI Errors,' *in* CHI Conference on Human Factors in Computing Systems.

Meyer von Wolff, R., Hobert, S., Masuch, K. & Schumann, M. (2020), 'Conversational agents at Digital Workplaces – A Grounded-Theory Approach for Surveying Application Areas and Objectives,' *Pacific Asia Journal of the Association for Information Systems* 12(2), pp. 64–102.

Mori, T., Jokinen, K. & Den, Y. (2021), 'On the Use of Gestures in Dialogue Breakdown Detection,' *in* Proceedings of the 24th Conference on the Oriental COCOSDA Internation Committee for the Coordination and Standardisation of Speech Databases and Assessment Techniques.

Müller, R., Paul, D. & Li, Y. (2021), 'Reformulation of Symptom Decsriptions in Dialogue Systems for Fault Diagnosis: How to Ask for Clarification,' *International Journal of Human-Computer Studies* 145, no. 102516.

Nickerson, R. C., Varshney, U. & Muntermann, J. (2012), 'A Method for Taxonomy Development and its Application in Information Systems,' *European Journal of Information Systems* 22, pp. 336–359.

Ogan, A., Finkelstein, S., Mayfield, E., D'Adamo, C., Matsuda, N. & Cassell, J. (2012), '"Oh, dear Stacy!" Social Interaction, Elaboration, and Learning with Teachable Agents,' *in* CHI Conference on Human Factors in Computing Systems.

Poser, M., Singh, S. & Bittner, E. A. C. (2021), 'Hybrid Service Recovery: Design for Seamless Inquiry Handovers Between Conversational Agents and Human Service Agents,' in *Proceedings of the 54th Hawaii Conference on System Sciences*, pp. 1181–1190.

Prahl, A & Goh, W. W. P. (2021), '"Rogue Machines" and Crisis Communication: When AI Fails, How Do Companies Publicly Respond?' *Public Relations Review* 47(4), no. 102077.

Rapp, A., Curti, L. & Boldi, A. (2021), 'The Human Side of Human-Conversational agent Interaction: A Systematic Literature Review of Ten Years of Research on Text-Based Conversational agents,' *International Journal of Human-Computer Studies* 151, no. 102630.

Reinkemeier, F. & Gnewuch, U. (2022), 'Designing Effective Conversational Repair Strategies for Conversational agents,' *in* European Conference on Information Systems.

Seeber, I., Bittner, E., Briggs, R. O., de Vreede, T., de Vreede, G.-J., Elkins, A., Maier, R., Merz, A. B., Oeste-Reiß, S., Randrup, N., Schwabe, G. & Söllner, M. (2020), 'Machines as Teammates: A Research Agenda on AI in Team Collaboration,' *Information & Management* 57(2), no. 103174.

Seeger, A.-M. & Heinzl, A. (2021), 'Chatbots Often Fail! Can Anthropomorphic Design Mitigate Trust Loss in Conversational Agents for Customer Service?' *in* Proceedings of the 2021 European Conference on Information Systems, no. 12.

Shawar, B. A. & Atwell, E. (2007), 'Conversational agents: Are They Really Useful?,' *LDV-Forum* 22(1), pp. 31–50.

Song, M., Zhang, H., Xing, X. & Duan, Y. (2023), 'Appreciation vs. Apology: Research on the Influence Mechanism of Chatbot Service Recovery Based on Politeness Theory,' *Journal of Retailing and Consumer Services* 73, no. 103323.

Suárez-Gonzalo, S., Mas-Manchón, L. & Guerrero-Solé, F. (2019), 'Tay is You. The Attribution of Responsibility in the Algorithmic Culture,' *Observatorio* 13(2), pp. 1–14.

Wakefield, J. (2016), 'Microsoft conversational agent is taught to swear on Twitter,' *BBC*. URL: https://www.bbc.com/news/technology-35890188/ (visited on November 08, 2022).

Wang, K.-Y., Chih, W.-H. & Honora, A. (2023), 'How Emoji Use in Apology Messages Influences Customers' Responses in Online Service Recoveries: The Moderating Role of Communication Style,' *International Journal of Information Management* 69, no. 102618.

Webster, J. & Watson, R.T. (2002), 'Analyzing the Past to Prepare for the Future: Writing a Literature Review,' *Management Information Systems Quarterly* 26(2), pp. xiii–xxiii.

Weizenbaum, J. (1966), 'ELIZA – A Computer Program for the Study of Natural Language Communication Between Man and Machine,' *Computational Linguistics* 9(1), pp. 36–45.

Wolf, M. J., Miller, K. W. & Grodzinsky, F. S. (2017), 'Why We Should Have Seen That Coming: Comments on Microsoft's Tay "Experiment," and Wider Implications,' *The ORBIT Journal* 1(2), pp. 1–12.

Wu, M.-H., Yeh, S. F., Chang, X. & Chang, Y.-J. (2021), 'Exploring User's Preferences for Conversational agent's Guidance Type and Timing,' *in* ACM Conference On Computer-Supported Cooperative Work and Social Computing, pp. 191–194.

Zargham, N., Pfau, J., Schnackenberg, Z. & Malaka, R. (2022), '"I Didn't Catch That, But I'll Try My Best': Anticipatory Error Handling in a Voice Controlled Game,' *in* Proceedings of the 2022 CHI Conference on Human Factors in Computing Systems, no. 153.

Zhang, J., Zhu, Y., Wu, J. & Yu-Buck, G. F. (2023a), 'A Natural Apology is Sincere: Understanding Artificial' Performance in Symbolic Recovery,' *International Journal of Hospitality Management* 108, no. 103387.

Zhang, X., Lee, S. K., Kim, W. & Hahn, S. (2023b), '"Sorry, it was my Fault": Repairing Trust in Human-Robot Interactions,' *International Journal of Human-Computer Studies* 175, no. 103031.

Towards a Taxonomy for Neighborhood Volunteering Management Platforms

Hans Betke, Michaelle Bosse, Fotini Tzavala-Reusch, Stephan Kuehnel, and Stefan Sackmann

Abstract The management and organization of volunteering in the social sector have been strongly influenced by technological progress over the last two decades. New proposals for IT-based volunteering management platforms that draw on many elements of social media are appearing with increasing frequency. In this article, we analyzed the current state of the art and use a methodological approach to develop a taxonomy for classifying existing and emerging developments in the field. The taxonomy is intended to assist practitioners in selecting appropriate systems for their respective purposes as well as support researchers in identifying research gaps. The resulting research artifact has undergone an initial evaluation and can support maintaining a better overview in a growing subject area.

Keywords Volunteer management · Information and communication system · Volunteer platform · Taxonomy · Social engagement

H. Betke (✉)
Fraunhofer Institute for Open Communication Systems, Fraunhofer Center for the Security of Socio-Technical Systems, Berlin, Germany
e-mail: hans.betke@fokus.fraunhofer.de

M. Bosse · F. Tzavala-Reusch · S. Kuehnel · S. Sackmann
Martin-Luther-University Halle-Wittenberg, Chair for Information Systems, Esp. Business Information Management, Halle (Saale), Germany
e-mail: michaelle.bosse@wiwi.uni-halle.de

F. Tzavala-Reusch
e-mail: fotini.tzavala@wiwi.uni-halle.de

S. Kuehnel
e-mail: stephan.kuehnel@wiwi.uni-halle.de

S. Sackmann
e-mail: stefan.sackmann@wiwi.uni-halle.de

D. Beverungen et al. (eds.), *Conceptualizing Digital Responsibility for the Information Age*, Lecture Notes in Information Systems and Organisation 74,
https://doi.org/10.1007/978-3-031-80119-8_19

1 Introduction

Civil volunteer support has become an important cornerstone of our society and can be found in many areas of our lives. Social commitment is practiced, e.g., in areas of sport, culture, teaching, refugee, or youth welfare by a steadily growing number of people (Simonson et al. 2021). In 2018, the World's Volunteerism Report of the United Nations Volunteers program (UNV 2018) identified more than one billion volunteers worldwide providing their workforce to face challenges in their home countries or international contexts.

The advent of mobile devices and social media has impacted volunteer help in many ways (Eimhjellen et al. 2018) and recent events like the COVID-19 pandemic further increased the relevance of digital solutions in volunteering (Lachance 2021). Information and communication technologies are increasingly being used in the mediation of those seeking and offering help in neighborhood assistance (Pereira et al. 2018). Whereas in the past advertisements were rather placed decentrally, e.g., on websites or offline on 'bulletin boards', today approaches are being discussed in research to bring the players together via social platforms (e.g. Kapsammer et al. 2021; Betke 2018).

There are two main use cases discussed in the literature regarding IT-assisted volunteer coordination. The first is approaches from the field of disaster management, which mostly aim at bringing together physical or digital spontaneous volunteers with the work of official first responders (e.g. Fuchs-Kittowski et al. 2018, Neubauer et al. 2013). These approaches are subject to the special conditions of a disaster situation and are not considered in this work. In contrast, the focus of this paper is on the second use case of volunteering in everyday situations. Approaches in this area often address voluntary help in the residential environment on topics such as education, helping the elderly, socializing, etc. (e.g. Akin et al. 2019; Neubauer et al. 2021). Currently, several approaches already exist, and many more research projects are underway.

To enable practitioners to better classify existing solutions and to support researchers in identifying research gaps, we started to develop a taxonomy for the classification of volunteer management systems for everyday life situations. In this paper, we present the current development status of the taxonomy, which was developed considering the method of Nickerson et al. (2013) and based on a structured literature review. Following iterations of the development process will also include the opinions and experiences of the affected user groups and practitioners.

In the next section, we provide insight into the methodological approach before presenting the taxonomy in the third chapter. The results of an initial evaluation indicate the usefulness of the taxonomy. The paper closes with a critical conclusion.

2 Methodological Approach

The first step of the taxonomy development method of Nickerson et al. (2013) is to define a meta-characteristic for the subsequent selection of dimensions. In our case, this is: "characteristics of IT platforms for the allocation of everyday volunteering and neighborhood assistance". Since the method is iterative, we must define objective and subjective ending conditions. We used the same ending conditions as suggested by Nickerson et al. (2013) and did not define any specific ones. The method offers a conceptual-to-empirical and an empirical-to-conceptual approach. As the research is still in progress, we only present the results of an initial iteration of the empirical-to-conceptual approach in this paper. All elements of the taxonomy were derived from objects of study, in our case volunteer platforms, which were discussed in the literature. The completed research will also include conceptual-to-empirical iterations, e.g., based on the knowledge of experts.

To identify the objects of investigation we conducted a literature analysis according to the method of vom Brocke et al. (2009). The following scientific databases where were searched: ACM Digital Library, IEEE Xplore, JSTOR, Science Direct, and SpringerLink. To identify as many relevant dimensions and characteristics as possible, the overarching search terms "civic engagement" and "volunteer management" were used. The search resulted in 2,730 hits in all searched databases. To refine the search of objects, only recent articles (publication date: 01/01/2016 and beyond) were considered. Since many of the publications found did not fall within the scope of our study, we defined exclusion criteria (EC) to filter out irrelevant articles. As already mentioned in the introduction, we excluded papers that address "disaster management" (EC1), as this falls outside the scope of our study. The same applies to the terms "e-government" (EC2) and "e-participation" (EC3), as they focus on government affairs. Due to the focus of our study on platforms, we also defined an inclusion criterion (IC) by including only those contributions that could clearly relate to IT platforms in the context of everyday volunteering and neighborhood assistance (IC1). Finally, there were 32 relevant works (objects of study) that could be used for taxonomy development (see Fig. 1).

Search string	„civic engagement" OR „volunteer management"				
Search fields	title & abstract				
Databases	ACM Digital Library	IEEE Xplore	JSTOR	Science Direct	SpringerLink
Database hits	167	61	875	716	911
Total hits	2730				
Hits after title selection	88	**Hits after abstract selection**	55		
Hits after fulltext selection (final hits)	32				

Fig. 1 Structured literature search process

3 An Initial Taxonomy for Neighborhood Volunteering Management Platforms

In this section, we present the taxonomy (Fig. 2) build from the abovementioned objects of study from the literature search and explain their 12 dimensions and 33 characteristics. For the purpose of clarity, the 12 identified dimensions have been assigned to four categories. At this stage, the taxonomy only includes non-exclusive characteristics. This is because our taxonomy is not to be interpreted from a dimension-oriented but from a platform-oriented point of view. From a dimension-oriented point of view, one could believe that, e.g., a communication type cannot be 1:1 and m:n at the same time. However, from a platform-oriented perspective, both communication types can be implemented and used. Please note that most dimensions and characteristics have been derived from more than one source, but for better legibility and clarity, we mostly list only one relevant reference at a time.

The category "System Design" describes the type of medium for which the platform is designed. The *application* dimension determines whether a platform provides its user interfaces as a mobile application (Angarita et al. 2019) for smartphones, tablets, smartwatches, etc., and/or as a desktop application for laptops, PC, etc. (Lindberg et al. 2019). In terms of the *user interface*, the literature discusses implementation in the form of social networks (similar to Twitter, and Facebook) or games, following the model of other massively multiplayer online games (Dumrewal et al. 2018; Lindberg et al. 2019).

The category "Tasks" comprises five dimensions. Regarding the *organization* of tasks, these can be commissioned centrally by a single organization (NGO, company, municipality) (e.g., garbage disposal in the neighborhood) or decentralized by individual users (e.g., an elderly person asks for shopping help) (Kapsammer et al. 2017). The *matching* addresses the allocation of tasks to a specific user. In the manual method, the user who has an intention to help must identify and select suitable tasks from the pool using filters (pull principle). Automatic matching uses an algorithm to match profiles and task data for the automatic assignment of a specific user to

Category	Dimension	Characteristics				
System design	application	mobile	desktop			
	user interface	social network	game			
Tasks	organization	central	decentral			
	matching	manual	semi-automatic	automatic		
	execution	online	physical			
	frequency	one-time	recurring			
	purpose	social	education	emergency		
Communication	feature	chat	comment	post	sharing	
	input	text	picture	video		
	type	1:1	1:n	m:n		
Reward system	game design elements	score	badges	leader-board	level-up	none
	incentives	monetary	non-monetary			

Fig. 2 Taxonomy for neighborhood volunteering management platforms

tasks (push principle) (Schönböck et al. 2016). The semi-automatic methods add a coordination supervisor to the process who assigns users to tasks aided by decision support functions (Mazlan et al. 2018). The *execution* dimension indicates whether the tasks are to be done physically (e.g., interpreting for a refugee during an official visit) or could also take place online (e.g., tutoring a student in mathematics via video chat). Online tasks are not tied to one location and can be done from anywhere (Chen 2017). In terms of *frequency*, we distinguish whether the volunteering is a one-time task (e.g., helping a neighbor carry up a heavy piece of furniture) or a recurring/ongoing task (e.g., doing weekly grocery shopping for a user) (Rehm et al. 2018). The purpose of the tasks and thus of the entire platform forms another dimension. Typical purposes can be social (Tong 2020) (e.g., the user seeks a conversation partner due to loneliness), educational (Silva et al. 2018) (e.g., find language tandem partners), or emergency-driven (Cerioli and Ribaudo 2019) (e.g., collective clean-up in the neighborhood after a storm).

In the category of "Communication", three dimensions are distinguished. Communication *features* for user interaction on volunteer platforms include chats (i.e., individual and group messages) and posts (in various media formats), which may also be commented on and shared with other users (Brandtzaeg et al. 2016). The *input* dimension describes the media formats that users can handle on the platform. These can be text (e.g., SMS, in-app chat, email), video (e.g., instruction videos as part of an online help service), or images (e.g., photos of trash lying around that needs to be cleaned up in the neighborhood) (Angarita et al. 2019). The *type* dimension refers to the number of people communicating with each other. The characteristic 1:1 means communication takes place exclusively between two users (e.g., in a private chat) (Mazlan et al. 2018), 1:n means the ability of one user to reach several other users (e.g., serial messaging or posting) (Schönböck et al. 2016). The n:m communication allows many users to communicate together at the same time (e.g., via group chat) (Mazlan et al. 2018).

The last category includes the reward systems that a platform offers to influence user motivation away from intrinsic factors. *Game design elements* can serve to maintain and build extrinsic motivation by awarding points and badges for completing tasks and challenges or interactions (Hassan and Hamari 2020). By earning points or badges, users can reach certain levels (and possibly unlock new features in the app) (Rehm et al. 2018). Leaderboards are a way to motivate by comparing with other users (Todtenhausen and Fuchs-Kittowski 2020). The last dimension *incentives* considers the presence of monetary reward systems (e.g., discounts on certain products or gifts from sponsors) on the platform (Tong 2020). Non-monetary incentives arise mainly from community recognition, such as simple gratitude from a user, or awards as part of Gamification (Brandtzaeg et al. 2016).

4 Evaluation

Following the notes on ex-ante evaluations by Pries-Heje et al. (2008), the 8 objective ending conditions were already considered as part of the first iteration. In addition, we conducted an expert survey using a questionnaire, in which we addressed two issues (Damarowsky et al. 2022): First, we wanted to determine if the experts believe that the subjective ending conditions (SEC) defined by Nickerson et al. (2013) were met. Second, perceived usefulness (PU) was assessed using the scale items proposed by Davis (1989). All items were adapted to the context of our study and are listed in Fig. 3.

The questionnaire was introduced with a brief description of the project as well as a possible scenario in the context of software development in which the taxonomy is used. In choosing the sample size, we followed the so-called "10 ± 2 rule" (Hwang and Salvendy 2010), which states that 8 to 12 respondents are sufficient for the evaluation of the usefulness of an artifact or technology. The questionnaire was completed by 8 people, all of whom had good technical understanding and knowledge related to volunteer coordination (4 basic knowledge, 4 extensive knowledge). Respondents rated the statements using a 7-point verbal-numerical Likert scale (1 = disagree, ..., 7 = agree).

The results of the evaluation are shown in Fig. 4. Despite a different scattering of the agreements to the individual SEC items, it is striking that they all have the same median m = 6. Based on this positive assessment, we consider the SEC of our initial taxonomy to be fulfilled. A more broadly spread picture emerges for the items of perceived usefulness. While PU2, PU3, and PU5 have a high median of m = 6, PU1 scores with a comparatively low median of m = 4. The median of m = 4 indicates a neutral attitude towards the "speed of use" of the taxonomy. Although one respondent consistently rated all statements with a value of 3, the median responses indicate an overall positive perception of the usefulness of the taxonomy, although there is room for improvement.

#	Scale items for subjective ending conditions (SEC)
SEC 1	The number of dimensions allows the taxonomy to be meaningful yet not cluttered or overwhelming.
SEC 2	The dimensions and characteristics allow sufficient differentiation between the objects of interest.
SEC 3	All objects or a (random) sample of objects within the area of interest can be classified.
SEC 4	A new dimension or a new characteristic of an existing can easily be added.
SEC 5	Dimensions and characteristics of objects are sufficiently explained.
#	**Scale items for perceived usefulness (PU)**
PU 1	The taxonomy enables me to accomplish tasks more quickly (e.g., fast detection of suitable matching methods).
PU 2	The taxonomy improves my job performance (e.g., identifying the most suitable platform characteristics).
PU 3	The taxonomy improves my productivity (e.g., better/simpler selection of most suitable platform characteristics).
PU 4	The taxonomy enhances my effectiveness on the job (e.g., identifying required or most relevant platform features).
PU 5	The taxonomy makes it easier to do my job (e.g., selecting the most suitable platform characteristics is facilitated).
PU 6	Overall, I find the taxonomy useful in my job.

Fig. 3 Items of the questionnaire

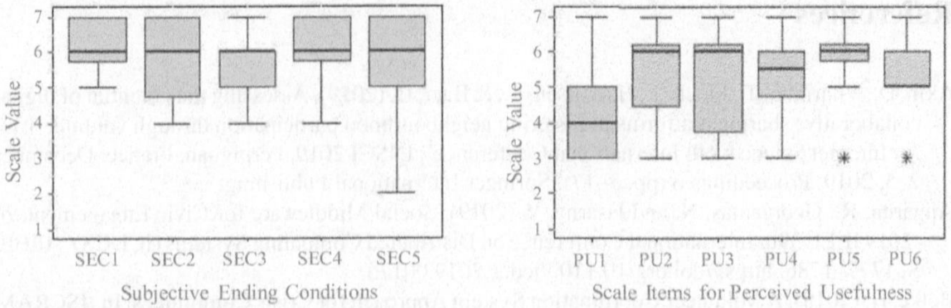

Fig. 4 Evaluation results

5 Conclusion

In this paper, we introduced an initial version of a taxonomy for the classification of neighborhood volunteering management platforms. The taxonomy was created based on the empirical-to-conceptual approach of Nickerson et al (2013) and includes 4 categories, 12 dimensions, and 33 characteristics. First evaluation results show that the taxonomy has the potential to become a useful tool for users and researchers in the field.

However, the results are also subject to limitations that need to be addressed in further research. One limitation is the subjectivity of the taxonomy resulting from the individual construction steps. Despite the methodological foundation, already the selection of suitable sources in the literature analysis, i.e., the selection of the objects of study, is already influenced by the authors' understanding of the topic and their expertise. This also applies to the derivation of suitable characteristics and dimensions, which could be influenced, e.g., by the authors' target visions. Furthermore, the relevant literature found is limited by the search terms and the databases used. However, since extensibility is one of the SEC considered when creating a taxonomy, the subsequent addition of further dimensions and characteristics is possible, so this limitation is not permanent. In conducting our evaluation, the sample size and respondent selection affect the results. To keep bias effects as low as possible in this setting, we at least surveyed a heterogeneous group of experts.

In the next step of this research, we want to improve the taxonomy in further iterations that follow the conceptual-to-empirical approach, incorporating interviews with practitioners and analysis of ready-to-use platforms, and then re-test for all ending conditions. Future research efforts may also aim to test the taxonomy with users of existing volunteer management systems to gain insights into their experiences and perspectives, providing additional information on existing approaches. This would create a tool in which practitioners could directly identify approaches suitable for their purposes and provide researchers with the existing best-practices.

References

Akin, D., Vilarinho, T., Floch, J., Halvorsen, T., & Baer, D. (2019), Assessing the potential of digital collaborative sharing platforms in fostering neighbourhood participation through volunteerism. *In* 'Internet Science: 6th International Conference', INSCI 2019, Perpignan, France, December 2–5, 2019, Proceedings 6 (pp. 3–17). Springer International Publishing.

Angarita, R., Georgantas, N. and Issarny, V. (2019): Social Middleware for Civic Engagement. *In* '2019 IEEE 39th International Conference on Distributed Computing Systems (ICDCS)': IEEE, S. 1777–1786. https://doi.org/10.1109/icdcs.2019.00176.

Betke, H. (2018), A Volunteer Coordination System Approach for Crisis Committees. In 'ISCRAM - Proceedings of the 15th International Conference on Information Systems for Crisis Response and Management', Rochester, NY, USA, May 20–23, 2018. ISCRAM Association.

Brandtzaeg, P. B, Haugstveit, I. M, Lüders, M. and Følstad, A. (2016), How Should Organizations Adapt to Youth Civic Engagement in Social Media? A Lead User Approach. In *Interact. Comput* **28** (5), S. 664–679. Taylor & Francis, Inc., Philadelphia. https://doi.org/10.1093/iwc/iwv041.

Cerioli, M. and Ribaudo, M. (2019), Civic participation powered by ethereum: a proposal. *In* 'Companion Proceedings of the 3rd International Conference on the Art, Science, and Engineering of Programming (Programming '19)'. Association for Computing Machinery, New York, NY, USA, Article 15, 1–6. https://doi.org/10.1145/3328433.3328449

Chen, J. (2017), Can online social networks foster young adults' civic engagement? In: *Telematics and Informatics* **34** (5), S. 487–497. https://doi.org/10.1016/j.tele.2016.09.013.

Damarowsky, J., Kühnel, S., Seyffarth, T., Sackmann, S. (2022), Augmented Reality-Systeme zur Unterstützung der Workflow-Ausführung – Entwicklung und praktische Anwendung einer Taxonomie. *HMD* **59**, 54–77, https://doi.org/10.1365/s40702-021-00831-y

Davis, F. D. (1989). Perceived usefulness, perceived ease of use, and user acceptance of information technology. *MIS Quarterly*, vol. 13, no. 3, pp. 319–340.

Dumrewal, A., Basu, A., Atreja, S., Mohapatra, P., Aggarwal, P, and Dasgupta, G. B. (2018), CitiCafe: Conversation-Based Intelligent Platform for Citizen Engagement, S. 180–189. https://doi.org/10.1145/3152494.3152511.

Eimhjellen, I., Steen-Johnsen, K., Folkestad, B., & Ødegård, G. (2018), Changing patterns of volunteering and participation. In *Scandinavian civil society and social transformations: The case of Norway*, 25–65. https://doi.org/10.1007/978-3-319-77264-6

Fuchs-Kittowski, F., Jendreck, M., Meissen, U., Rösler, M., Lukau, E., Pfennigschmidt, S., and Hardt, M. (2018), ENSURE-Integration of volunteers in disaster management. *In* 'Environmental Software Systems. Computer Science for Environmental Protection: 12th IFIP WG 5.11 International Symposium', ISESS 2017, Zadar, Croatia, May 10-12, 2017, Proceedings (pp. 247–262). Cham: Springer International Publishing.

Hassan, L. and Hamari, J. (2020), Gameful civic engagement: A review of the literature on gamification of e-participation. In *Government Information Quarterly* **37** (3), S. 1–21. https://doi.org/10.1016/j.giq.2020.101461.

Hwang, W. and Salvendy, G. (2010), Number of people required for usability evaluation, in *Communications of the ACM*, 53, 5, 130–133.

Kapsammer, E., Kimmerstorfer, E., Pröll, B., Retschitzegger, W., Schwinger, W., Schönböck, J., Dürk, N., Rossi, G., and Gordillo, Silvia (2017), iVOLUNTEER. A Digital Ecosystem for Life-long Volunteering. *In* 'Proceedings of the 19th International Conference on Information Integration and Web-based Applications & Services. iiWAS2017: The 19th International Conference on Information Integration and Web-based Applications & Services'. Salzburg Austria, 04 12 2017 06 12 2017. Association for Computing Machinery- Digital Library. New York, NY: ACM (ACM Digital Library), S. 366–372. https://doi.org/10.1145/3151759.3151801.

Kapsammer, E., Pröll, B., Retschitzegger, W., Schwinger, W., Weißenbek, M., Schönböck, J., and Pührerfellner, M. (2021), iVOLUNTEER—A Platform for Digitization and Exploitation of

Lifelong Volunteer Engagement. In 'Enterprise Information Systems: 22nd International Conference, ICEIS 2020', Virtual Event, May 5–7, 2020, Revised Selected Papers (pp. 386-411). Cham: Springer International Publishing.

Lachance, E. L. (2021), COVID-19 and its impact on volunteering: Moving towards virtual volunteering. In *Leisure Sciences*, **43**(1–2), 104-110.

Lindberg, R.S.N., Maushagen, J. and De Troyer, O. (2019), Combining a Gamified Civic Engagement Platform with a Digital Game in a Loosely Way to Increase Retention. *In* 'Proceedings of the 21st International Conference on Information Integration and Web-based Applications & Services'. Edited by Eric Pardede, Ivan Luiz Salvadori, Matthias Steinbauer, Ismail Khalil und Gabriele Anderst-Kotsis. iiWAS2019: The 21st International Conference on Information Integration and Web-based Applications & Services. Munich Germany, 02 12 2019 04 12 2019. New York, NY, United States: Association for Computing Machinery (ACM Digital Library), S. 679–683. https://doi.org/10.1145/3366030.3366117.

Mazlan, N., Ahmad, S. S. S., Kamalrudin, M., Zaki Abu Bakar, A. (2018), Volunteer selection based on crowdsourcing approach. In *J Ambient Intell Human Comput* **9** (3), S. 743–753. https://doi.org/10.1007/s12652-017-0490-8.

Neubauer N, Daum C, Miguel-Cruz A, Liu L (2021) Mobile alert app to engage community volunteers to help locate missing persons with dementia. In *PLOS ONE* **16** (7): e0254952. https://doi.org/10.1371/journal.pone.0254952

Neubauer, G., Nowak, A., Jager, B., Kloyber, C., Flachberger, C., Foitik, G., & Schimak, G. (2013), Crowdtasking–a new concept for volunteer management in disaster relief. In *Environmental Software Systems*. 10th IFIP WG 5.11 International Symposium, ISESS 2013, Neusiedl am See, Austria, October 9-11, 2013. Proceedings 10 (pp. 345-356). Springer Berlin Heidelberg.

Nickerson, R. C., Varshney, U. and Muntermann, J. (2013), A method for taxonomy development and its application in information systems, In *European Journal of Information Systems* **22** 3, 336-359.

Pereira, G. V., Parycek, P., Falco, E., Kleinhans, R. (2018), Smart Governance in the Context of Smart Cities: A Literature Review. In *Information Polity*, 23, n **2**, pp.143–162. Special issue on Evidence-based Government: Secure, Transparent and Responsible Digital Governance.

Pries-Heje, J., Baskerville, R., Venable, J. R. (2008), Strategies for Design Science Research Evaluation. ECIS 2008 Proceedings. 87.

Rehm, S., Foth, M. and Mitchell, P. (2018), DoGood: examining gamification civic engagement, and collective intelligence. In *AI & Soc 33* 1**,** S. 27–37. Springer Verlag. https://doi.org/10.1007/s00146-017-0711-x.

Schönböck, J., Raab, M., Altmann, J., Kapsammer, E., Kusel, A., Pröll, B., Retschitzegger, W. and Schwinger, W. (2016), A Survey on Volunteer Management Systems. In 'Proceedings of the 49th Annual Hawaii International Conference on System Sciences'. 5–8 January 2016, Kauai, Hawaii. 2016 49th Hawaii International Conference on System Sciences (HICSS). Koloa, HI, USA, 1/5/2016 - 1/8/2016. Piscataway, NJ: IEEE, S. 767– 776. https://doi.org/10.1109/HICSS.2016.100.

Silva, F., Proença, T. and Ferreira, M. R. (2018), Volunteers' perspective on online volunteering—a qualitative approach. In *Int Rev Public Nonprofit Mark* **15** *(4)*, S.531 552. https://doi.org/10.1007/s12208-018-0212-8.

Simonson, J., Kelle, N., Kausmann, C., Karnick, N., Arriagada, C., Hagen, C., Hameister, N., Huxhold, O., Tesch-Römer, C. (2021). Volunteering in Germany: Key findings of the Fifth German Survey on Volunteering (FWS 2019). Bundesministerium für Familie, Senioren, Frauen und Jugend, Berlin. https://nbn-resolving.org/urn:nbn:de:0168-ssoar-74767-6

Todtenhausen, L., Fuchs-Kittowski, and F. (2020), Gamification for Mobile Crowdsourcing Applications: An Example from Flood Protection. In *Advances and New Trends in Environmental Informatics. ICT for Sustainable Solutions*. ed. Rüdiger Schaldach in cooperation with Karl-Heinz Simon, Jens Weismüller und Volker Wohlgemuth. Cham: Springer International Publishing AG (Progress in IS Ser), S. 37–53. https://doi.org/10.1007/978-3-030-30862-9_3.

Tong, K. (2020), Healthcare Volunteers' Significant Impact on Primary Care: Experiences and Challenges from the Perspective of a Non-government Organisation. In *Primary Care Revisited. Interdisciplinary Perspectives for a New Era* **1st** ed. 2020. Singapore: Springer Singapore; Imprint Springer (Springer eBook Collection), S. 253–276. https://doi.org/10.1007/978-981-15-2521-6_16.

United Nations Volunteers program (2018), The thread that binds: Volunteerism and community resilience—2018 State of the World's Volunteerism Report. Accessed in: https://unv-swvr2018.org/files/51692_UNV_SWVR_2018_WEB.pdf

vom Brocke, J., Simons, A., Niehaves, B., Niehaves, B., Reimer, K., Plattfaut, R. and Cleven, A (2009) Reconstructing the giant: On the importance of rigour in documenting the literature search process, *ECIS 2009 Proceedings*.

Revealing the Voices of Resistance: A Q-Methodology Study on Platform Workers in the Gig Economy

Matthias Weber, Ulrich Remus, Manfred Geiger, and Alexander de Jong

Abstract While algorithmic management generates several benefits for platform companies, it emanates several issues for workers, which they perceive as threats triggering different forms of resistance behaviors. Although recent studies identify these issues and resistance behaviors, the perspective of the actual subject of resistance, i.e., the gig worker or group of gig workers with resistant behaviors, is yet not well understood. By adopting a Q-methodology mixed-method approach this study tries to identify resistance types of gig workers, explore their characteristics and similarities, and therefore give a voice to the subject of resistance. Based on 21 threats and 14 resistance behaviors, identified in a literature review, we develop a Q-set containing 35 statements, which will be used for data collection with the goal of revealing the richness of the resistance phenomenon in the context of work in the gig economy.

Keywords Algorithmic management · Resistance · Q-Methodology

M. Weber (✉) · U. Remus · A. de Jong
Department of Information Systems, Production and Logistics Management, University of Innsbruck, Innsbruck, Austria
e-mail: matthias.j.weber@uibk.ac.at

U. Remus
e-mail: ulrich.remus@uibk.ac.at

A. de Jong
e-mail: alexander.de-jong@uibk.ac.at

M. Geiger
IU Internationale Hochschule GmbH, Munich, Germany
e-mail: manfred.geiger@iu.org

D. Beverungen et al. (eds.), *Conceptualizing Digital Responsibility for the Information Age*, Lecture Notes in Information Systems and Organisation 74,
https://doi.org/10.1007/978-3-031-80119-8_20

1 Introduction

The platform business model is becoming one of the most dynamic features in the global economy, as it is predicted that by 2025, one-third of labor transactions will be conducted through digital platforms (Cini 2022; Masiero 2021; Standing 2021; Wong 2022). This evolution has been made possible by rapid advances in algorithmic technology and the resulting increasing incorporation of algorithms into organizational processes, reducing the need for human decision-making in management (Baptista et al. 2020; Cini 2022). In the scientific discourse, this use of algorithmic technology in a management context is referred to as algorithmic management (AM). It is defined as a system of oversight, governance, and control practices based on algorithms that are making and executing automated decisions, which affect the work process, and consequently limit human involvement and oversight of the work process (Bucher et al. 2021; Duggan et al. 2020; Lee et al. 2015; Möhlmann and Zalmanson 2017). Although AM practices are currently used primarily in the gig economy, which encompasses short-term, on-demand, and typically small task-based (the "gigs") labor, they will be adopted in other economic sectors soon (Standing 2021; Tan et al. 2021).

While AM generates several strategic benefits for platform companies prior work also points to causing work environment tensions which negatively impact platform workers (Park and Ryoo 2023; Kellogg et al. 2020; Gal et al. 2020; Rosenblat and Stark 2016). These negative impacts can affect workers' well-being and health (Jhaver et al. 2018; Wood et al. 2019; Zhang et al. 2022). As a result from this algorithmic unfairness (Schulze et al. 2022) and its effects on workers' health, recent studies found that workers begin to develop resistance behaviors as a reaction to being managed by algorithms (Anwar and Graham 2020; Ferrari and Graham 2021; Tassinari and Maccarrone 2020; Woodcock 2021).

Even though previous research has done a first step in identifying resistance behaviors, the findings often overlook the workers themselves, as the prevailing consensus is that AM is something workers as a whole are exposed to, which overlooks the individual characteristics of workers or groups of workers that resist this type of management (Bucher et al. 2021). But understanding resistance demands attention to the subject of resistance, which refers to an individual actor (Marakas and Hornik 1996) or a group of actors (Markus 1983), in our case the worker or the group of workers with similar resistance perspectives and behaviors (Lapointe and Rivard 2005). Therefore, to better understand the subject of resistance, we propose the following research question:

What are the types of workers that resist algorithmic management practices?

Answering this question is of high importance for two main reasons. First, identifying the resistance types of gig workers complements the current deductive theorization of resistance behaviors by inductively exploring the characteristics and similarities of resistant gig workers. Second, this research explores the actual subject of resistance and therefore contributes by setting the needed groundwork upon which future theories can be built. This is important because to use a theory meaningfully to describe, analyze, or explain, the theoretical model should take into account the richness and subjectivity of the phenomenon under study, such as the characteristics of resistant individuals or groups (Doty and Glick 1994; Gregor 2006). It also lays the groundwork for practical, legal and social action.

2 Theoretical Background and Literature Review

2.1 *Resistance to Algorithmic Management*

Resistance as a theoretical concept is one of the important pillars of this study. It is a complex and multifaceted concept and is influenced by many research streams and disciplines, including sociology, political science, psychology, and change management. We follow the conceptualization of resistance by Hollander and Einwohner (2004) who define resistance based on four core dimensions: action, opposition, recognition, and intent. Lapointe and Rivard (2005) adapted these dimensions to an information system (IS) context and defined five components of resistance to information technology implementation: behaviors, object, subject, threats, and initial conditions. Thus, user resistance can be defined as a user's adverse behavior or reaction (Hirschheim and Newman 1988) to perceived threats that are related to an object of resistance, which could be a system (Marakas and Hornik 1996) or the implementation of information technology (Joshi 1991). If we now transfer this understanding of resistance to our research context, AM represents a system to remotely manage workers, based on data collection and surveillance of workers to enable automated decision-making and therefore functions as the object of resistance (Mateescu and Nguyen 2019). Since workers are the subject of resistance, we define resistance to AM, in line with Lapointe and Rivard (2005), as workers' adversely intended behavioral actions in response to perceived threats emanating from AM as the object of resistance. As we are interested in the subject of resistance, we need to identify and then understand what workers might perceive as threats and what their adverse behavioral responses to these threats are.

Identifying Perceived Threats and Resistance Behaviors. We conducted a literature review to identify threats emanating from AM and resistance behaviors. We further categorized the perceived threats based on the resistance determinants framework by Klaus and Blanton (2010). A summary of the results can be found in Table 1.

Table 1 Literature review on perceived threats and resistance behaviors

Category	Perceived threats	Sources
Individual issues	Uncertainty, distrust, anxiety, sleep deprivation, isolation, frustration, burnout, loss of control, stress, powerlessness	Eslami et al. (2019), Jhaver et al. (2018), Wood et al. (2019), Zhang et al. (2022), Cheng and Foley (2019), Weber et al. (2022), Jabagi et al. (2019), Bartel et al. (2019), Jarrahi et al. (2020), Möhlmann and Zalmanson (2017)
System issues	Opacity, complexity, adaptiveness, fallibility, restriction	Möhlmann et al. (2021), Pregenzer et al. (2021b), Rani et al. (2021), Burrell (2016), Eslami et al. (2019), Weber et al. (2022), Schulze et al. (2022), Kellogg et al. (2020)
Organizational issues	Limited support, surveillance, data sovereignty, information asymmetry, payment, shadow employer	Veen et al. (2020), Rosenblat et al. (2014), Zuboff (2019), Rosenblat and Stark (2016), Calo and Rosenblat (2017), Bucher et al. (2021), Rani et al. (2021)
Resistance behavior	**Sources**	
Coping	Sariraei et al. (2022)	
Vanishing	Bucher et al. (2021)	
Denying	Pregenzer et al. (2021a)	
Mocking	Pregenzer et al. (2021b)	
Sensemaking	Möhlmann et al. (2022)	
Empowering	Yu et al. (2022)	
Complaining	Jiang et al. (2021), Pregenzer et al. (2021a)	
Gaming	Bambauer and Zarsky (2018), Petre et al. (2019)	
Circumventing	Jarrahi and Sutherland (2019)	
Manipulating	Cameron and Rahman (2022)	
Collectivizing	Pregenzer et al. (2021b)	
Organizing	Martin et al. (2014)	
Striking	Vandaele (2022), Kellogg et al. (2020)	
Quitting	Jiang et al. (2021)	

3 Methodology

Based on the nature of the research question and the intended contribution, the adoption of a methodological approach that is capable of revealing the richness of the resistance phenomenon in the context of gig work is needed. This approach is found in the mixed-method approach of Q-methodology (Stephenson 1986), which offers a rigorous and systematic way of capturing human subjectivity by measuring a person's viewpoints, opinions, and attitudes (Brown 1993). Unlike conventional survey-based research designs that aim to gather data based on a predetermined set of variables, this approach attempt to capture a diverse range of individual perspectives, opinions, and attitudes (Stephenson 1986). This is accomplished by presenting respondents with self-referencing statements and instructing them to categorize them according to specific sorting instructions (Brown 1993). Although still rather uncommon in IS research it is well-suited for researching user or group attitudes (Thomas and Watson 2002) and there is a hand full of Q-methodology studies in high-ranked IS journals (Klaus et al. 2010; Mettler et al. 2017; Mettler and Wulf 2019; Tractinsky and Jarvenpaa 1995).

A Q-methodology study includes four steps: defining the concourse by collecting a wide range of perspectives on the topic, representing a set of statements referred to as the Q-set, letting study participants rank the Q-set statements concerning how much they agree or disagree with them (Q-sorting), and analyzing and interpreting the sorting by applying statistical factor analysis (Brown 1993; Mettler et al. 2017). Since each statement is sorted in relation to all others in any given Q-sort, a Q-factor analysis correlates individual viewpoints into factors that represent the individual's subjective view on the topic (Brown 1980; Klaus et al. 2010). Unlike survey studies, which are based on the assumption that each measurement is made independently of all others and therefore use by-variable factor analysis to report a composite average opinion, Q-methodology inverts this approach by conducting a by-person factor analysis (Watts and Stenner 2012; Klaus et al. 2010). As a result, each revealed factor will potentially identify a group of persons instead of a group of variables (Watts and Stenner 2012). This makes it a mixed-method approach as it stands at the intersection of qualitative and quantitative research because it includes the quantitative analysis lacking in most qualitative methods (Stephenson 1986), yet it also includes the rich concourse of the participants, a feature generally found in grounded theory methods (Klaus et al. 2010).

3.1 Q-set Development and Study Design

The aim of Q-set design is to generate a set of items, in our case, written statements about the issues emanating from AM in the form of perceived threats and descriptions of resistance behavior, that provide good coverage in relation to the research question (Watts and Stenner 2012; Stephenson 1952). We followed what Watts and Stenner (2012) refer to as a structured Q-set development by first defining the concourse through the above theorization of resistance to AM and then beginning the sampling process by breaking down the topic into a series of issues with AM, resulting in perceived threats and resistance behaviors, identified based on the literature reviews above. We identified 21 threats that workers perceive as potentially adverse and may trigger a resistance response, of which we identified 14 forms. Based on this, we developed an initial Q-set with two alternative statements per threat and two alternative statements for each identified resistance behavior, resulting in an initial Q-set of 70 statements. This put the Q-set on the upper end of the recommended range for statements, which is between 40 and 80 (Smith et al. 1995; Curt 1994). We then refined and reduced the initial Q-set through a pilot process (Watts and

Stenner 2012) that included the screening of the Q-set by the co-authors, and other researchers, which were experts on the subject or Q-methodology experts. This led to the final Q-set, which included a refined statement for each threat and resistance behavior, resulting in 35 statements. Due to space restrictions, we are only able to show the part of the Q-set presented in Table 2. The complete Q-set can be provided by the authors upon request.

To design the study and setup the online Q-Sort we used *EQ Web Sort* (Banasick 2023a). For the study design we followed the recommendation of Watts and Stenner (2012) and let participants first categorize the statements in three ranking categories (disagree, neutral, agree) followed by the main sorting for which we use a fixed-choice nine-point (− 4 to + 4) normal distribution, recommended for Q-sets with 40 items or less (Brown 1980). This range and slope was chosen in regards to the complex nature of the topic resulting in a steeper kurtosis and ultimately less decisions and more range for sorting (Watts and Stenner 2012). Post-sorting consists of asking participants the reasons and meaning for ranking the respective items in the most disagree/agree position followed by demographic questions and specific questions (name of the platform, duration of working there, percentage of monthly net income generated) which will help to compare emerging factors. For the main P-set, as the sample of participants is called in Q-methodology, we apply a strategic sampling strategy, since each participant becomes a variable the goal is to obtain a representative sample of gig workers (Watts and Stenner 2012; Klaus et al. 2010). To draw a strategic sample, which represents gig workers sufficiently, we follow the classification of

Table 2 Exemplary Q-set statements

Perceived threat	Statements
Sleep deprivation	I experience sleep deprivation because of the algorithm's expectation of being always available to work
Isolation	It's hard to build relationships with other gig workers because the algorithm creates an isolating work environment
Frustration	It's frustrating to not know what factors are influencing my work assignments
Complexity	The complexity of the platform's rules are hard for me to understand
Adaptiveness	I feel like the algorithm is constantly adapting my working conditions without me being able to control it
Opacity	Due to the opacity of the algorithm, it's difficult for me to understand how I'm being evaluated and managed
Resistance behavior	**Statement**
Coping	I have developed coping mechanisms to handle work-related stress
Vanishing	I know how to avoid being monitored by the algorithm
Mocking	I sarcastically mock the decisions of the algorithm
Empowering	I see myself as an independent contractor rather than an employee, which gives me a sense of empowerment
Manipulating	I manipulate the algorithm to give me an advantage

gig work by Duggan et al. (2020) and focus on workers working in crowd-work (e.g. Upwork, Fiverr) and app-work (e.g. Uber, Lieferando), as these sectors are characterized by high use of AM. Q-methodology is favorable to studies with smaller but well-selected samples, as it aims to establish the existence of certain viewpoints and thus to understand, explain and compare them to one another (Brown 1980; Watts and Stenner 2012). For sample size, we aim for fewer participants than the number of statements (Watts and Stenner 2012).

4 Outlook and Next Steps

Before the main data collection a pilot test will be conducted with the final measurement instrument using a small sample to obtain participant feedback and optimize the instrument as needed (Klaus et al. 2010). For the data analysis we will be using *Ken-Q Analysis* (Banasick 2023b). In terms of results, we intend to identify worker resistance types or groups with distinct characteristics and behaviors. Identifying such groups can contribute significantly to understanding gig workers as a whole, whose needs currently tend to go unrecognized. Furthermore, with Q-methodology as a mixed-method approach, the results could benefit future quantitative research by isolating effects or influences based on resistant worker groups but also future qualitative research by focusing on social or collective dynamics within certain groups. Additionally, our results could also have practical implications and could help to shape legal framework conditions for workers and platforms.

Acknowledgements This research was funded in whole, or in part, by the Austrian Science Fund (FWF): P 35031-GBL. For the purpose of open access, the author has applied a CC BY public copyright license to any Author Accepted Manuscript version arising from this submission.

References

Anwar, M. A. & Graham, M. (2020). Hidden transcripts of the gig economy: labour agency and the new art of resistance among African gig workers. *Environment and Planning A: Economy and Space,* 52, 1269–1291.

Bambauer, J. & Zarsky, T. (2018). The algorithm game. *Notre Dame L. Rev.,* 94, 1.

Banasick, S. (2023a). *EQ Web Sort* [Online]. Available: https://github.com/shawnbanasick/eq-web-sort [Accessed 23.03.2023].

Banasick, S. (2023b). *Ken-Q Analysis* [Online]. Available: https://shawnbanasick.github.io/ken-q-analysis/ [Accessed 09.05.2023].

Baptista, J., Stein, M.-K., Klein, S., Watson-Manheim, M. B. & Lee, J. (2020). Digital work and organisational transformation: Emergent digital/human work configurations in modern organisations. Elsevier.

Bartel, E., MacEachen, E., Reid-Musson, E., Meyer, S. B., Saunders, R., Bigelow, P., Kosny, A. & Varatharajan, S. (2019). Stressful by design: Exploring health risks of ride-share work. *Journal of Transport & Health,* 14, 100571.

Brown, S. R. (1980). *Political subjectivity: Applications of Q methodology in political science*, Yale University Press.

Brown, S. R. (1993). A primer on Q methodology. *Operant subjectivity,* 16, 91–138.

Bucher, E. L., Schou, P. K. & Waldkirch, M. (2021). Pacifying the algorithm–Anticipatory compliance in the face of algorithmic management in the gig economy. *Organization,* 28, 44–67.

Burrell, J. (2016). How the machine 'thinks': Understanding opacity in machine learning algorithms. *Big data & society,* 3, 2053951715622512.

Calo, R. & Rosenblat, A. (2017). The taking economy: Uber, information, and power. *Colum. L. Rev.,* 117, 1623.

Cameron, L. D. & Rahman, H. (2022). Expanding the locus of resistance: Understanding the co-constitution of control and resistance in the gig economy. *Organization Science,* 33, 38–58.

Cheng, M. & Foley, C. (2019). Algorithmic management: The case of Airbnb. *International Journal of Hospitality Management,* 83, 33–36.

Cini, L. (2022). Resisting algorithmic control: Understanding the rise and variety of platform worker mobilisations. *New Technology, Work and Employment.*

Curt, B. C. (1994). *Textuality and tectonics: Troubling social and psychological science*, Open University Press.

Doty, D. H. & Glick, W. H. (1994). Typologies as a unique form of theory building: Toward improved understanding and modeling. *Academy of management review,* 19, 230–251.

Duggan, J., Sherman, U., Carbery, R. & McDonnell, A. (2020). Algorithmic management and app-work in the gig economy: A research agenda for employment relations and HRM. *Human Resource Management Journal,* 30, 114–132.

Eslami, M., Vaccaro, K., Lee, M. K., Elazari Bar On, A., Gilbert, E. & Karahalios, K. User attitudes towards algorithmic opacity and transparency in online reviewing platforms. Proceedings of the 2019 CHI Conference on Human Factors in Computing Systems, 2019. 1–14.

Ferrari, F. & Graham, M. (2021). Fissures in algorithmic power: Platforms, code, and contestation. *Cultural Studies,* 35, 814–832.

Gal, U., Jensen, T. B. & Stein, M.-K. (2020). Breaking the vicious cycle of algorithmic management: A virtue ethics approach to people analytics. *Information and Organization,* 30, 100301.

Gregor, S. (2006). The nature of theory in information systems. *MIS quarterly*, 611–642.

Hirschheim, R. & Newman, M. (1988). Information systems and user resistance: theory and practice. *The Computer Journal,* 31, 398–408.

Hollander, J. A. & Einwohner, R. L. Conceptualizing resistance. Sociological forum, 2004. Springer, 533–554.

Jabagi, N., Croteau, A.-M., Audebrand, L. K. & Marsan, J. (2019). Gig-workers' motivation: thinking beyond carrots and sticks. *Journal of Managerial Psychology.*

Jarrahi, M. H. & Sutherland, W. Algorithmic management and algorithmic competencies: Understanding and appropriating algorithms in gig work. International Conference on Information, 2019. Springer, 578–589.

Jarrahi, M. H., Sutherland, W., Nelson, S. B. & Sawyer, S. (2020). Platformic management, boundary resources for gig work, and worker autonomy. *Computer supported cooperative work (CSCW),* 29, 153–189.

Jhaver, S., Karpfen, Y. & Antin, J. Algorithmic anxiety and coping strategies of Airbnb hosts. Proceedings of the 2018 CHI Conference on Human Factors in Computing Systems, 2018. 1–12.

Jiang, J., Adam, M. & Benlian, A. (2021). Algoactivistic Practices in Ridesharing-A Topic Modeling & Grounded Theory Approach.

Joshi, K. (1991). A model of users' perspective on change: the case of information systems technology implementation. *MIS quarterly*, 229–242.

Kellogg, K. C., Valentine, M. A. & Christin, A. (2020). Algorithms at work: The new contested terrain of control. *Academy of Management Annals,* 14, 366–410.

Klaus, T. & Blanton, J. E. (2010). User resistance determinants and the psychological contract in enterprise system implementations. *European Journal of Information Systems,* 19, 625–636.

Klaus, T., Wingreen, S. C. & Blanton, J. E. (2010). Resistant groups in enterprise system implementations: a Q-methodology examination. *Journal of Information Technology,* 25, 91–106.

Lapointe, L. & Rivard, S. (2005). A multilevel model of resistance to information technology implementation. *MIS quarterly*, 461–491.

Lee, M. K., Kusbit, D., Metsky, E. & Dabbish, L. Working with machines: The impact of algorithmic and data-driven management on human workers. Proceedings of the 33rd annual ACM conference on human factors in computing systems, 2015. 1603–1612.

Marakas, G. M. & Hornik, S. (1996). Passive resistance misuse: overt support and covert recalcitrance in IS implementation. *European Journal of Information Systems,* 5, 208–219.

Markus, M. L. (1983). Power, politics, and MIS implementation. *Communications of the ACM,* 26, 430–444.

Martin, D., Hanrahan, B. V., O'neill, J. & Gupta, N. Being a turker. Proceedings of the 17th ACM conference on Computer supported cooperative work & social computing, 2014. 224–235.

Masiero, S. Digital platform workers under COVID-19: A subaltern perspective. Proceedings of the 54th Hawaii International Conference on System Sciences, 2021. 6349.

Mateescu, A. & Nguyen, A. (2019). Algorithmic management in the workplace. *Data & Society,* 8, 1030332.

Mettler, T. & Wulf, J. (2019). Physiolytics at the workplace: Affordances and constraints of wearables use from an employee's perspective. *Information Systems Journal,* 29, 245–273.

Mettler, T., Sprenger, M. & Winter, R. (2017). Service robots in hospitals: new perspectives on niche evolution and technology affordances. *European Journal of Information Systems,* 26, 451–468.

Möhlmann, M. & Zalmanson, L. (2017). Hands on the wheel: Navigating algorithmic management and Uber drivers'. *38th ICIS Proceedings.*

Möhlmann, M., Zalmanson, L., Henfridsson, O. & Gregory, R. (2021). Algorithmic management of work on online labor platforms: When matching meets control. *MIS Quarterly.*

Möhlmann, M., de Lima Salge, C. A. & Marabelli, M. (2022). Algorithm Sensemaking: How Platform Workers Make Sense of Algorithmic Management. *Journal of the Association for Information Systems.*

Park, S. & Ryoo, S. (2023). How Does Algorithm Control Affect Platform Workers' Responses? Algorithm as a Digital Taylorism. *Journal of Theoretical and Applied Electronic Commerce Research,* 18, 273–288.

Petre, C., Duffy, B. E. & Hund, E. (2019). "Gaming the system": Platform paternalism and the politics of algorithmic visibility. *Social Media+ Society,* 5, 2056305119879995.

Pregenzer, M., Remus, U. & Wiener, M. (2021a). Algorithms in the Driver's Seat: Explaining Workers' Reactions to Algorithmic Control. *ECIS.*

Pregenzer, M., Wieser, F., Santiago Walser, R. & Remus, U. (2021b). Obscure Oversight: Opacity Drives Sensemaking and Resistance Behavior in Algorithmic Management. *ICIS.*

Rani, U., Kumar Dhir, R., Furrer, M., Gőbel, N., Moraiti, A. & Cooney, S. (2021). *World employment and social outlook: the role of digital labour platforms in transforming the world of work,* International Labour Organisation.

Rosenblat, A. & Stark, L. (2016). Algorithmic labor and information asymmetries: A case study of Uber's drivers. *International journal of communication,* 10, 27.

Rosenblat, A., Kneese, T. & Boyd, D. (2014). Workplace surveillance. *Open Society Foundations' Future of Work Commissioned Research Papers.*

Sariraei, S. A., Chênevert, D. & Vandenberghe, C. (2022). What Is on Your Gig Radar? Toward a Hierarchical Structure of Coping. *International Journal of Environmental Research and Public Health,* 19, 14219.

Schulze, L., Trenz, M., Cai, Z. & Tan, C.-W. (2022). Algorithmic Unfairness on Digital Labor Platforms: How Algorithmic Management Practices Disadvantage Workers.

Smith, J. A., Langenhove, L. V. & Harre, R. (1995). Rethinking methods in psychology. *Rethinking Methods in Psychology*, 1–224.

Standing, G. (2021). *The corruption of capitalism: Why rentiers thrive and work does not pay*, Biteback Publishing.
Stephenson, W. (1952). Q-methodology and the projective techniques. *Journal of Clinical Psychology,* 8, 219–229.
Stephenson, W. (1986). Protoconcursus: The concourse theory of communication. *Operant Subjectivity,* 9, 37–58.
Tan, Z. M., Aggarwal, N., Cowls, J., Morley, J., Taddeo, M. & Floridi, L. (2021). The ethical debate about the gig economy: A review and critical analysis. *Technology in Society,* 65, 101594.
Tassinari, A. & Maccarrone, V. (2020). Riders on the storm: Workplace solidarity among gig economy couriers in Italy and the UK. *Work, Employment and Society,* 34, 35–54.
Thomas, D. M. & Watson, R. T. (2002). Q-sorting and MIS research: A primer. *Communications of the Association for information Systems,* 8, 9.
Tractinsky, N. & Jarvenpaa, S. L. (1995). Information systems design decisions in a global versus domestic context. *Mis Quarterly*, 507–534.
Vandaele, K. (2022). Vulnerable food delivery platforms under pressure: protesting couriers seeking "algorithmic justice" and alternatives. *Forthcoming in Routledge Handbook of the Gig Economy, edited by I. Ness, New York, Routledge.*
Veen, A., Barratt, T. & Goods, C. (2020). Platform-capital's 'app-etite'for control: A labour process analysis of food-delivery work in Australia. *Work, Employment and Society,* 34, 388–406.
Watts, S. & Stenner, P. (2012). Doing Q Methodological Research: Theory, Method and Interpretation. Sage Publications.
Weber, M., Remus, U. & Pregenzer, M. (2022). A New Era of Control: Understanding Algorithmic Control in the Gig Economy. *ICIS*.
Wong, S. I. (2022). Job Crafting Can Help Digital Gig Workers Build Resilience. *Harvard Business Review.* https://hbr.org/2022/01/job-crafting-can-help-digital-gig-workers-build-resilience.
Wood, A. J., Graham, M., Lehdonvirta, V. & Hjorth, I. (2019). Good gig, bad gig: autonomy and algorithmic control in the global gig economy. *Work, Employment and Society,* 33, 56–75.
Woodcock, J. (2021). *The fight against platform capitalism: an inquiry into the global struggles of the gig economy*, University of Westminster Press.
Yu, Z., Treré, E. & Bonini, T. (2022). The emergence of algorithmic solidarity: unveiling mutual aid practices and resistance among Chinese delivery workers. *Media International Australia,* 183, 107–123.
Zhang, A., Boltz, A., Wang, C.-W. & Lee, M. K. Algorithmic Management Reimagined For Workers and By Workers: Centering Worker Well-Being in Gig Work. Proceedings of ACM CHI, 2022.
Zuboff, S. Surveillance capitalism and the challenge of collective action. New labor forum, 2019. SAGE Publications Sage CA: Los Angeles, CA, 10–29.

Advances in Theory, Methods and Philosophy

How Explainable AI Methods Support Data-Driven Decision-Making

Dominik Stoffels, Susanne Grabl, Thomas Fischer, and Marina Fiedler

Abstract Explainable AI (XAI) holds great potential to reveal the patterns in black-box AI models and to support data-driven decision-making. We apply four post-hoc explanatory methods to demonstrate the explanatory capabilities of these methods for data-driven decision-making using the illustrative example of unwanted job turnover and human resource management (HRM) support. We show that XAI can be a useful aid in data-driven decision-making, but also highlight potential drawbacks and limitations of which users in research and practice should be aware.

Keywords Explainable AI · Machine learning · Data-driven decision-making

1 Introduction

Data-driven decision-making is becoming increasingly important in information systems (IS) research and in practice. Artificial intelligence (AI) uses data and predictive models to make decisions (Fernández-Loría et al. 2022) that will, for example, increase efficiency in organizations. Machine learning (ML) is a subdivision of AI which uses algorithms to discover patterns in complex datasets to make predictions

D. Stoffels (✉) · S. Grabl · T. Fischer · M. Fiedler
University of Passau, Passau, Germany
e-mail: stoffe11@ads.uni-passau.de

S. Grabl
e-mail: susanne.grabl@uni-passau.de

T. Fischer
e-mail: thomas.fischer@fh-steyr.at

M. Fiedler
e-mail: marina.fiedler@uni-passau.de

T. Fischer
University of Applied Sciences Upper Austria, Steyr, Austria

D. Beverungen et al. (eds.), *Conceptualizing Digital Responsibility for the Information Age*, Lecture Notes in Information Systems and Organisation 74,
https://doi.org/10.1007/978-3-031-80119-8_21

based on the learned patterns (Hong et al. 2007; Jordan and Mitchell 2015; Brynjolfsson and Mitchell 2017; Sturm et al. 2021; Yang et al. 2022). For example, ML is used to predict cancer in patients based on x-ray scans (Kourou et al. 2015), to assess user engagement on social media (Shin et al. 2020), or to predict employee performance or turnover for human resource management (HRM) in an organizational context (Yuan et al. 2021).

One category of ML algorithms on which we want to focus is supervised ML algorithms (as opposed to unsupervised ML and reinforcement learning, Benbya et al. 2021). In supervised ML algorithms the available data consists of labeled examples (i.e., each data point contains features and an associated class—a label). The goal of supervised learning algorithms is for them to learn a function that maps feature vectors (inputs) to labels (outputs) as accurately as possible (Hastie et al. 2009). Using various features, ML models can learn and generalize patterns in the data to predict the label without knowing other correlations in this context. With knowledge of the labels, ML models can monitor their learning and reduce prediction error. In doing so, an AI system can use the ML model to make decisions based on the model's prediction. The trade-off for the high predictive accuracy of the models is limited interpretability. Therefore, a more complex model can lead to higher predictive accuracy, but also reduce interpretability (Shrestha et al. 2021). This particularly applies to black-box ML models. From a theoretical and practical perspective, these models are superior in minimizing prediction error (Goldstein et al. 2015), but the more complex the model, the less interpretable it is. For example, simple ML models such as decision trees provide a high degree of transparency; human users can understand every decision because they can directly visualize and understand decision trees. A random forest, however, which can basically consist of up to ten thousand decision trees, cannot be visualized or represented in such a way that human users can interpret it (Stoffels et al. 2022).

Since AI systems are integrated into all types of decision-making processes, an ever more urgent debate is taking place in academia about the extent to which people who develop AI or are affected by an AI-enabled decision can understand how the resulting decision mechanism works and why it arrives at a particular decision (Yang et al. 2022). Consequently, we need more interpretable approaches (Mitchell et al. 2001; Avrahami et al. 2022), referred to as explainable AI (XAI) methods (Guidotti et al. 2018; Barredo Arrieta et al. 2020; Hamm et al. 2021). Importantly, these methods not only aim to explain one particular decision (Fernández-Loría et al. 2022); they also attempt to derive actions.

XAI has become increasingly important in IS research, having already been used methodologically (Choudhury et al. 2021; Fernández-Loría et al. 2022) and empirically (Senoner et al. 2022). However, current IS research does not address the various capabilities of different XAI methods for data-driven decision-making. To address this gap, we trained seven ML models and, building on these models, we compare four different XAI methods, local model-agnostic methods, global model-agnostic methods, and counterfactual explanations. In doing so, we examine the following research questions:

Which methods are applicable to which type of decision-making? Are the explanations between the methods explicit, or can different explanations emerge?

To demonstrate the different capabilities of XAI for data-driven decision-making in an understandable way, we illustratively use organizational data to predict and explain unwanted job turnover and analyze how XAI can benefit data-driven decision-making in human resource management (HRM).

2 Research Background

Data-Driven Decision-Making. One of the most popular application areas for AI in organizations is in decision-making where it offers many potential benefits on a strategic level (e.g., product quality improvement, improved understanding of customer needs, or more accurate organizational resources planning, Borges et al. 2021). Through their ability to learn from additional datapoints over time, AI systems can create knowledge that assists humans in their decision-making or they could even be applied to automate tasks and act autonomously (Shrestha et al. 2021; van den Broek et al. 2021; Shollo et al. 2022). These capabilities have been advocated as an important addition to IS theorizing (Berente et al. 2019; Miranda et al. 2022). Further, AI proponents have argued that how AI is used in practice to create working theories could be an important future avenue for creating grand theories in IS (Tremblay et al. 2021).

A particular obstacle to human interaction with AI, in practice as well as in theorizing, is the opacity of certain ML algorithms (Müller et al. 2016; Faraj et al. 2018; Berente et al. 2021). It can be difficult for professionals to make use of the knowledge created by AI systems if they cannot follow the logic that was applied to arrive at a certain result (e.g., Lebovitz et al. 2022). Various approaches, such as envelopment (Asatiani et al. 2021), have been presented to circumvent this issue. XAI could be a more direct approach to deal with the opacity of algorithmic decision-making (Gunning et al. 2019).

A promising application for XAI and data-driven decision-making could be in HRM and employee retention, given the scarcity of high-skilled employees in these contexts (Oswald et al. 2020). Unwanted employee turnover affects organizations on multiple levels, as it is expensive, ties up resources, and causes low business performance (Chowdhury et al. 2022). Hence, practitioners and scholars are trying to predict and understand unwanted employee turnover as accurately as possible (Farrell and Rusbult 1981; Zhao et al. 2018; Oswald et al. 2020; Choudhury et al. 2021; Wang and Zhi 2021; Yuan et al. 2021; Avrahami et al. 2022). ML and XAI have great potential to predict and reveal the reasons for unwanted job turnover in organizations and promise powerful support for data-driven decision-making in HRM to keep valued employees in the organization (Oswald et al. 2020; Chowdhury et al. 2022).

Explainable AI (XAI) and Black Box Models. Previous research has shown that XAI can promote trust among users of black-box AI systems (Barredo Arrieta et al. 2020; Hamm et al. 2021). Black-box AI refers to the comprehensibility of AI models and systems. As the underlying models become more complex, AI systems seem to be a black-box (Meske et al. 2022). Thus, with growing complexity, a trade-off between explainability and model performance emerges, which significantly influences individuals and organizations (Alt 2018). Therefore, to promote the adoption of AI systems, Hamm et al. (2021) assume that XAI methods should be a part of AI implementations. In addition, they emphasize the importance of XAI for organizations and developers to meet regulatory requirements that improve the AI system.

Overview of XAI Methods. There are multiple XAI methods which can provide powerful support in explaining AI systems' decisions, and which enable us to grasp the underlying patterns (Molnar 2020). So-called *model-agnostic* XAI methods have the advantage that they can be used independently on the ML model and, therefore, count as the counterpart of *model-specific* XAI methods. Consequently, these methods have attracted a great deal of interest in the IS literature (Choudhury et al. 2021; Chowdhury et al. 2022; Fernández-Loría et al. 2022; Senoner et al. 2022). XAI methods can also be categorized based on the range of cases they aim to explain, into *local* (i.e., single case) and *global* (i.e., all cases in a dataset) methods (Barredo Arrieta et al. 2020). Local methods can provide explanations for single predictions (i.e., for a specific employee) (Molnar 2020). In cases of employee retention, these methods show the characteristics, such as salary, which have the greatest influence on the model decision (i.e., they indicate the main characteristics that determine employees' resignation). Yet, this only gives the reasons for the turnover of individual employees, which can vary greatly. In comparison, global methods show the influence of the characteristics in general (i.e., which affect many or all employees) (Molnar 2020; Stoffels et al. 2022). Some XAI methods also show how a single feature influences the model outcome, so that researchers achieve fine-grained insight into the interactive pattern between the specific feature and the model outcome (Goldstein et al. 2015; Choudhury et al. 2021). While these XAI methods only show a trend of the pattern between the features and the actual prediction, counterfactual explanations can provide a quantitative explanation (Fernández-Loría et al. 2022).

Counterfactual explanations provide a practical extension to local and global methods, as they offer a means for deciding on a course of action that will change an outcome variable's value. While local and global methods commonly provide us with an overview of the importance of given features in a prediction, counterfactuals offer us a combination of features and the extent of change that needs to be implemented for the outcome to change. This can be important in practice, as high feature importance for a prediction does not necessarily affect the model's decision (Fernández-Loría et al. 2022).

Implementations of XAI Methods. Current IS research mainly uses post-hoc XAI methods, such as shapley additive explanation values (SHAP) (Fernández-Loría et al. 2022; Senoner et al. 2022), local interpretable model-agnostic explanations (LIME) (Chowdhury et al. 2022), partial dependence plots (PDP) (Mehdiyev and Fettke 2020;

Choudhury et al. 2021), or counterfactual explanations (Fernández-Loría et al. 2022) implemented using e.g., diverse counterfactual explanations (DiCE) (Mothilal et al. 2020).

SHAP is technically a local model-agnostic method based on a game-theoretic approach (Lundberg and Lee 2017), but it can also provide global explanations (Molnar 2020). Senoner et al. (2022) use SHAP to reveal learned patterns between complex manufacturing process data and achieved quality. In contrast, Fernández-Loría et al. (2022) are very critical of this use of SHAP. They show that SHAP has limited informative value and also that features with high feature importance according to SHAP can actually have no influence on the models' decisions. Thereby, they emphasize the use of counterfactual explanations. Counterfactual explanations offer the advantage of not showing features ' relative influence on the prediction; instead, they show how much a feature value must vary to change the model's actual prediction (Mothilal et al. 2020).

Another XAI method is partial dependence plots (PDP), which can show the impact a feature has on the model output (Mehdiyev and Fettke 2020; Kamath and Liu 2021). For example, the PDP shows how a single feature (e.g., employee salary) is related to the impact of termination. Thus, PDP is one of the global model-agnostic methods (Molnar 2020). Choudhury et al. (2021) emphasize the value of PDP in gaining deep insight into models. They use it in a methodological context to explain the difference in predictive accuracy between a simpler model (decision tree) and a more complex model (random forest). In this context, PDP show that the complex model learned more fine-grained patterns than the simpler model.

In contrast, LIME (Ribeiro et al. 2016) can show the influence of each feature on a single prediction, for example a single employee. Chowdhury et al. (2022) use this local model-agnostic method to show the potential of XAI in the context of turnover. They imply the use of XAI to gain HRM users' trust in AI systems and to improve data-driven decision-making. In contrast, John-Mathews (2021) views these types of post-hoc explanations more critically. Using LIME illustratively, he concludes that post-hoc explanations lead to misleading or partial information about the learned pattern. In addition, Stoffels et al. (2022) reveal empirically, that different patterns can arise using models of the same quality.

DiCe are an implementation that give counterfactual explanations, which answer the "what if" questions. Thus, DiCe can provide examples that are impactful enough to change the model's prediction (Mothilal et al. 2020). Besides DiCe there is a range of other implementations that can generate counterfactual explanations (Guidotti 2022). Mothilal et al. (2020) show that the explanations of DiCe do not match those of SHAP and LIME. Further, Fernández-Loría et al. (2022) found that counterfactual explanations provide more appropriate explanations than the other methods, although the potential disadvantage of the Rashomon effect is stated.

While the use of ML models to leverage XAI is already increasingly common in IS research, and thus in the data-driven decision-making literature (Bertsimas and Kallus 2020; de Bruijn et al. 2022; Elgendy et al. 2022), the learned models remain under-investigated, thus requiring a deeper investigation. Also, there are no studies that comprehensively consider and critically reflect on the use of different

XAI methods and their implications for data-driven decision-making in the context of unwanted job turnover and HRM support.

3 Data and Methods

We base our illustration of XAI in HRM on the publicly available dataset "IBM HR Analytics Employee Attrition and Performance" (Subhash 2017), a synthetic dataset created by IBM that contains 35 metric and nominal features with administrative data, performance data, job satisfaction data, and data on individual characteristics (e.g., age and gender) of 1470 fictitious employees (Subhash 2017). Our goal in illustratively using different XAI methods has been to predict turnover (0 = no turnover, 1 = turnover) based on these characteristics and to make the prediction interpretable to define measures for HRM. In the chosen dataset, 16% of the employees had resigned. The width of the features' skewness ranged from -0.55 ("*YearsSinceLastPromotion*") to 1.98 ("*WorkLifeBalance*"). We translated the ordinal variable "education" into years of education ("*YearsEducation*"). As this was a synthetic data set, there were no data quality issues or missing values.

Since it was not clear a priori which ML model would provide the best performance, a sample of models had to be selected (Choudhury et al. 2021). We applied seven different ML models: linear regression (LR) (Hosmer et al. 2013), k-nearest neighbors (KNN) (Cover and Hart 1967), random forest (Breiman 2001a), c-support vector classification (SVM) (Cortes and Vapnik 1995), decision tree (DT) (Breiman et al. 1984), gradient boosting classifier (GB) (Friedman 2002), and adaboost classifier (AdaBoost) (Freund and Schapire 1997). Notably, we also included ML models that are not considered black-boxes (e.g., LR, DT and KNN), to showcase their performance in comparison to black-box models. For all models we used the default hyperparameters, which are set in the "scikit-learn" library (scikit-learn 2023).

We used min–max scaling for numeric features to ensure the same range of values (Nayak et al. 2014). In addition, we used one-hot coding for nominal features (Hancock and Khoshgoftaar 2020). To evaluate performance, we used a training-test split of 80/20, thus we used 80% as training data and 20% as test data (Hastie et al. 2009; Berrar 2018) and the F1 score. The F1 score is the harmonic mean of precision (how many of the positive predictions are actually positive) and recall (the ratio of all positive cases that the model was able to identify correctly) (Choudhury et al. 2021). The F1 score's advantage over accuracy is that unbalanced classes are considered. Usually more employees stay in the organization than leave it, so the dataset is unbalanced. Accuracy only takes into account how many predictions are correct. Thus, if we assume that 99% of employees do not quit and only 1% of employees resign, assigning all employees to stay in the organization would already yield a prediction accuracy of 99%, even though the model learned nothing (Choudhury et al. 2021). Therefore, we chose the ML model with the highest F1 score for the further analysis with XAI. If other models had a non-significantly worse F1 score, we included these models due to their comparable predictive ability.

We applied LIME (Ribeiro et al. 2016), SHAP (Lundberg and Lee 2017), PDP (Kamath and Liu 2021), and DiCE (Mothilal et al. 2020) to analyze the learned pattern of the best performing ML model. For SHAP we used the Kernel Explainer, because it is usable for all ML models. The more accurate Tree Explainer is only usable for tree models (Lundberg et al. 2020). Additionally, for the global explanations, we created a subsample containing only instances with employees who had resigned. Further, we checked whether the results had been influenced from seen to unseen instances. If multiple ML models achieved a comparable F1 score, we analyzed all models using these XAI methods to determine whether the different models had learned the same patterns (Breiman 2001b; Stoffels et al. 2022).

4 Results

As usual in ML approaches, we first attempted to find an accurate predictive model for our dataset. We analyzed the F1 score the selected ML models reached, as summarized in Table 1. AdaBoost performed slightly better than GB and RF in reaching an F1 score of 85.2%. In contrast, the other models (i.e., LR, KNN, SVM, DT) performed significantly worse. SVM achieved an F1 score of only 59.8%. Subsequently, we chose the models with the highest F1 scores to analyze the models more deeply using the selected XAI methods. Since the GB (84.8%) and RF (83.4%) scores were comparable to AdaBoost's, we also checked these models using the XAI methods.

In the following two sections, we highlight contributions that can be derived for data-driven decision-making from the use of XAI—based on the example of HRM.

4.1 Individualized Decision-Making (Local Methods)

Local model-agnostic methods can explain a single prediction, in this context the model's prediction of an individual employee's turnover. As Chowdhury et al. (2022) mentioned, this method can be used in different ways, including consideration of trust and understanding of the model, diagnosing the model and its performance, and determining why certain employees are likely to leave the organization. In particular, these methods can be used to define countermeasures for the individual employee. We chose three employees and analyzed their possible reasons for leaving the organization using SHAP.

Table 1 Average F1 scores of the trained ML models

Model	LR	KNN	RF	SVM	DT	GB	AdaBoost
F1 (%)	74.4	66.7	83.4	59.8	75.4	84.8	85.2

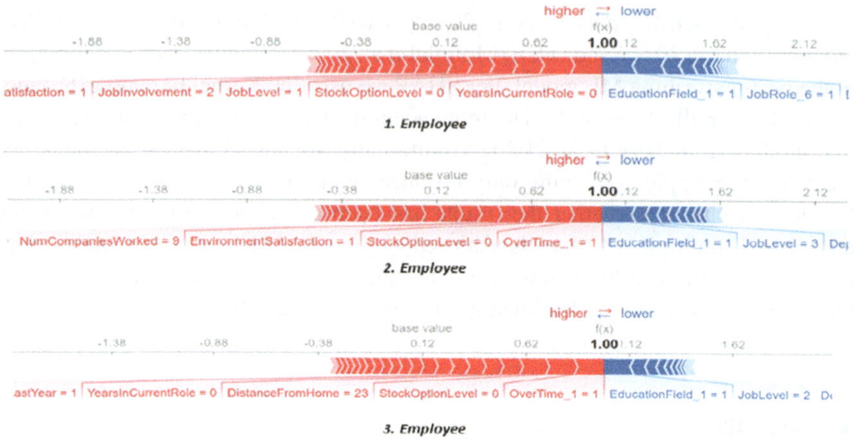

Fig. 1 SHAP force plots of single instances (i.e., employees)

Figure 1 shows the SHAP force plots of three employees. The features colored red indicate that they contribute to the model's prediction of turnover, while the blue features contribute to the model's prediction of no turnover. If the model predicts turnover (model output = 1), the red colored features have a greater impact on the model prediction and lead to the final model decision for turnover. Therefore, HRM can use this information to determine which features and with which relative feature values lead to turnover.

While for all three employees the lack of stock options (*StockOptionLevel*) was a reason to leave the organization, the other reasons for each differed considerably. For example, for the second and third employee, overtime (*OverTime_1*) was the main reason, while for the first employee it was the short time in the current role (*YearsInCurrentRole* = 0).

4.2 Global Decision-Making (Global Methods)

In contrast to local model-agnostic methods, global model-agnostic methods can indicate multiple predictions or, alternatively, the particular influence of single features on the models' predictions (Molnar 2020). In Fig. 2, the SHAP summary plot ranks the influence of the features of all employees, as well as of all employees who resigned, for the Adaboost model.

The features that had the greatest influence on the model decision are shown in descending order. We see that in some cases the important features are different compared to those Fig. 1 shows for single instances. Still, we retain a high level of information, as we are provided with not only a ranking of features or an overall effect score, but also with an overview of the effects for each included instance, summarized in a distribution plot (Lundberg et al. 2020). The main influencing factor is found

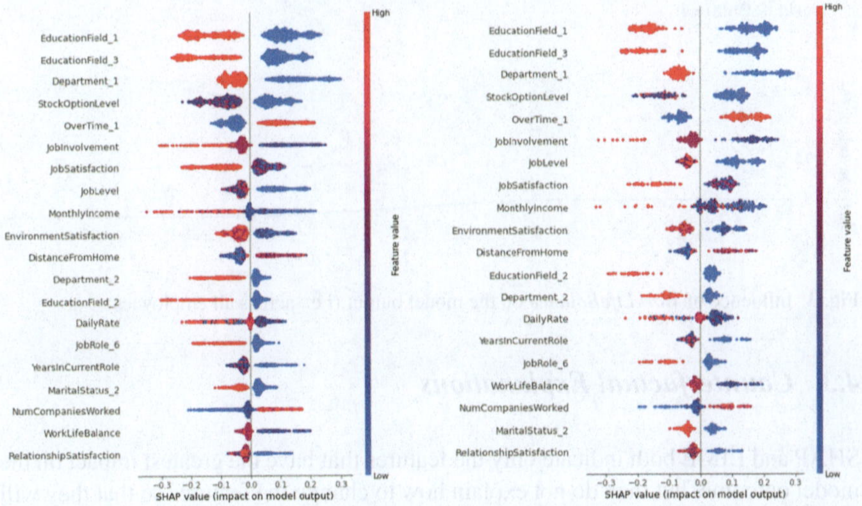

Fig. 2 SHAP summary plot of all employees (left) and only employees who had resigned (right)

to be the employee's education (*EducationField_1*, *EducationField_3*), while the already discussed features of *OverTime_1* and *StockOptionLevel* are also amongst the most important features. Besides, SHAP shows that the most important features (up to the 6th) have not changed in the subgroup of resigned employees. Colors are used to indicate the current value of the feature. Thus, high feature values are shown with red, while low feature values are shown with blue. For example, a high monthly income (*MonthlyIncome*) in comparison to other employees is red, while a low income is marked in blue. This can be used by HRM to identify the main reasons for unwanted turnover in the organization and could serve as a basis for defining data-driven global HRM strategies. Thus, in our example a rise in the stock options and measures to reduce overtime should be in focus, as these are identified among the most important characteristics.

SHAP, as well as other global model-agnostic methods such as PDP, can additionally visualize a single feature's influence on model output across (all) employees (Molnar 2020; Choudhury et al. 2021). This is illustrated in Fig. 3. As expected, the probability of leaving the organization decreases as work-life balance (*WorkLifeBalance*) increases. The curve could help HRM to determine an optimal value for work-life balance. As the plot shows, the impact on the model result decreases significantly if the *WorkLifeBalance* level, which is marked in red, is between 2 to 3. Thus, further increasing the *WorkLifeBalance* has little impact on the model decision, and probably a similar impact on the employee. With this help, HRM can identify on a more fine-grained basis, the extent to which certain features (i.e., employee circumstances) should be changed to reduce turnover in the organization. We see this as an important complement to local explanations and simple feature importance rankings (Choudhury et al., 2021), since the progression can highlight broader relationships.

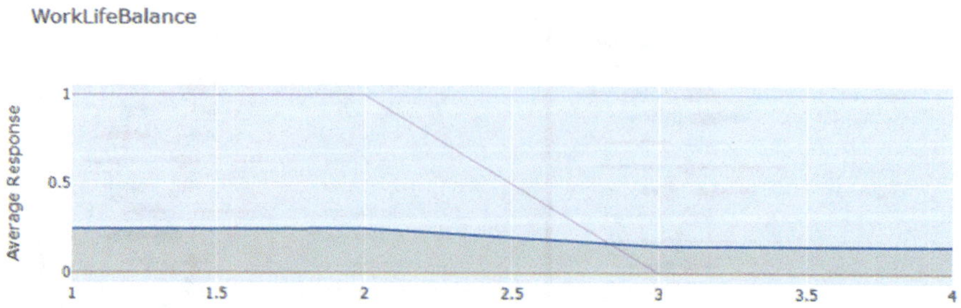

Fig. 3 Influence of *WorkLifeBalance* on the model output (i.e., across all employees)

4.3 Counterfactual Explanations

SHAP and LIME both indicate only the features that have the greatest impact on the model outcome, but they do not explain how to change the features so that they will actually change the model's or employee's decision. For example, these methods do not show how much more the salary should increase to change the employee's decision about leaving the organization (Fernández-Loría et al. 2022). Further, PDP only show the average influence of a single feature on the model outcome, but the method does not provide an answer to whether an increase in a detected threshold is sufficient to change the prediction as well.

Therefore, the use of counterfactual explanations is suggested (Fernández-Loría et al. 2022), which we adopt in using DiCE (Mothilal et al. 2020). We use the functionality of the DiCE implementation to consider only characteristics that HRM can change directly or indirectly, such as raising the salary (*MonthlyIncome*) or addressing the distance from home issue (*DistanceFromHome*) (e.g., by providing a second home).

In the first row, Fig. 4 shows each characteristic's values for the selected employee who left the organization. We then determined five different counterfactual explanations that actually changed the model decision to remain in the organization. We added the change in the feature value for each explanation in the next five rows. DiCE gives HRM five different options for changing the model's decision, and probably also that of the employee in question. For example, a change in JobLevel (e.g., level 1–2) would not change the decision in this the model (i.e., of the employee) from turnover to no turnover. With the exception of the fourth explanation, a significant increase in salary (between 848 and 2317) would be required to change the decision.

We see several advantages of using counterfactual explanations: First, HRM can decide which characteristics they can easily target to avoid unwanted turnover. Second, counterfactual explanations provide different courses of action as there is (in most cases) not just one way of changing the prediction. Finally, the model gives a precise value of the characteristics required to change the prediction, thus directing HRM toward a very specific action. Compared to the other presented XAI methods, no further interpretation is required to define actions, because SHAP and LIME give only the relative importance of each characteristic. Hence, a further HRM analysis

	Features							
	Monthly Income	Job Satisfication	StockOption Level	WorkLife Balance	OverTime	DistanceFrom Home	Job Involvement	JobLevel
Turnover	1261	2	0	4	0	8	2	1
DiCE - No Turnover (New feature value)	2109	2	0	3	0	8	4	1
	3578	1	0	4	0	8	4	1
	2572	2	1	3	0	8	3	1
	1009	4	0	4	0	1	4	1
	2996	1	0	4	0	1	3	1
DiCE - No Turnover (Feature value difference)	848	0	0	-1	0	0	2	0
	2317	-1	0	0	0	0	2	0
	1311	0	1	-1	0	0	1	0
	-252	2	0	0	0	-7	2	0
	1735	-1	0	0	0	-7	1	0

Fig. 4 Counterfactual explanations for a single instance (i.e., an employee)

is necessary to define a specific action such as offering a concrete salary increase. If, however, the focus is not on the formulation of measures but on the analysis of the reasons for turnover, counterfactual explanations require more investigation, as they do not directly provide a visualization of the most important influencing characteristics.

5 Discussion

We have demonstrated the use of different XAI methods to analyze organizational data and to develop explanations of turnover and related actions for HRM. Thereby, we show that data-driven actions require different XAI methods for different objectives. Global model-agnostic methods provide a global view of the model decision and the overall main influencing factors of the model. This insight can provide important data-driven support for general strategies in an organization. Local model-agnostic methods are useful for creating actions suited to individual instances, such as single employees. Nevertheless, we must address the limitations of these methods, thereby also offering potential for future research.

Different XAI Methods, Different Explanations. Global and local model-agnostic methods do not explain the model's prediction in the same way, or put differently, they provide significantly different explanations. Therefore, the patterns disclosed by the different methods are not robust and lead to different explanations and interpretations.

This leads to a major problem with the post-hoc explanations presented. While the ML model's performance can be evaluated using, for example, the F1 score for decisions on whether the model is sufficient to use, there is no actual test or metric for evaluating XAI methods. Therefore, we cannot accurately measure the error or evaluate which method would provide the correct explanations. If different methods provide different explanations and ultimately suggest different actions, this, of course, poses a significant problem for HRM or data-driven decision-making.

We have illustrated this issue by comparing the LIME and SHAP local model-agnostic methods. We find that the local explanations of LIME and SHAP are significantly different for the same employees. Table 2 illustrates two employees and the local explanations of LIME and SHAP. The two cases show significant differences in the effects the features have on the model decision. While we acknowledge that nominal features and one-hot coding can lead to confounding outcomes in XAI methods (as with *EducationField* features), other features, especially numeric features, should be closely ranked in their impact on model decision.

Therefore, users of XAI methods in practice as well as in research should be aware that these methods provide only approximate explanations and can lead to different explanations and interpretations depending on the chosen method. We suggest using at least two different methods to assess the extent to which we can trust the results. Again, counterfactual explanations have the advantage that these explanations at least change the model's actual decision (Fernández-Loría et al. 2022), which the other methods cannot achieve.

Different ML Models, Different Explanations. Not only can different XAI methods lead to different explanations, but different models of comparable quality analyzed with the same XAI method can also yield different explanations. We illustrate this issue in Fig. 5, which shows the top five features in the SHAP summary plots of AdaBoost, GB, as well as RF. While the features shown here are partly similar and show small shifts (e.g., *StockOptionLevel*), there are also cases were completely different features are among the most important ones, such as *MaritalStatus_1* in the RF model.

Table 2 LIME and SHAP for local explanations of two instances (i.e., employees)

Employee	Top three features (LIME vs. SHAP)	
First illustrative employee	EducationField_3	EducationField_1
	EducationField_1	YearsInCurrentRole
	EducationField_4	StockOptionLevel
Second illustrative employee	EducationField_3	OverTime_1
	EducationField_1	EducationField_1
	StockOptionLevel	StockOptionLevel

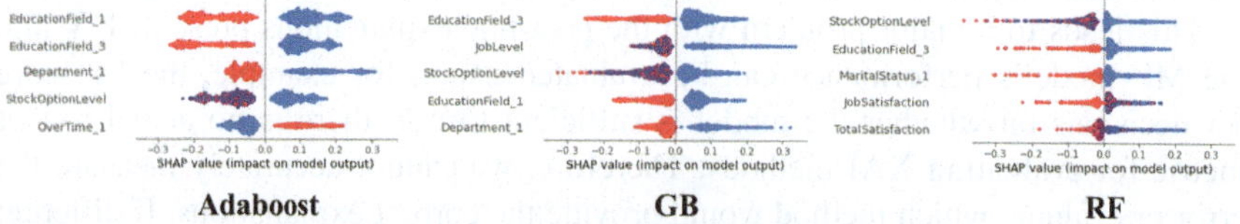

Fig. 5 Comparison of SHAP summary plots (all employees)

Therefore, we should be aware of the possible effects of the *Rashomon Effect* (Breiman 2001b) and its implications for data-driven decision-making. We recommend the following procedure as suggested in Stoffels et al. (2022): If several models have the same quality (e.g., F1 score), then all models should be examined with XAI methods. Thereafter, there are two possibilities: either there is no Rashomon Effect (i.e., the models have learned the same patterns), or the learned patterns significantly disagree. The first case requires no further action, because the models have learned robust patterns and increased our confidence in those patterns. However, in the second case, we should critically reflect on these models and the database. Thus, further analysis of the models to determine the possible cause of the discrepancy is required, as this would ensure meaningful decisions in the context of data-driven decision-making.

Implications and Future Work. Given the two main shortcomings of local and global methods we have demonstrated, we see the high potential of counterfactual explanations for data-driven decision-making in practice. They are not as inconsistent as the other methods because they ensure that the explanations actually change the models' decisions. Thus, they provide not only a relative indication of which characteristics are important, but also a necessary quantitative change in those characteristics to receive a specific action toward data-driven decision-making. We have to acknowledge, however, that using counterfactual explanations requires a high degree of domain knowledge in order for them to be useful because they provide several alternatives that need to be carefully weighed against one another (Mithas et al. 2022). In addition, counterfactuals are subject to some of the drawbacks of ML and XAI, such as the Rashomon effect; therefore, those individuals choosing which specific decision alternatives to consider, need transparency and clear criteria (Artelt and Hammer 2019).

Besides the potential limitations of XAI methods we compared in this study, we also need to mention some research limitations, since they offer potential for further investigation. First, we used synthetic data. Yet, to reveal further strengths and weaknesses of XAI methods it could be worthwhile to repeat the comparison portrayed in this study using multiple sets of real data. Second, we used only a selected set of ML algorithms and XAI method implementations, which could feasibly be extended in future research using additional methods (see e.g., Barredo Arrieta et al. 2020). The algorithms and methods could also be supplemented by further methods that are becoming increasingly popular, such as supervised clustering used to identify characteristic groups of employees (Cooper et al. 2021).

References

Alt, R. (2018), 'Electronic Markets and Current General Research', *Electronic Markets* **28**(2), 123–128.

Artelt, A. & Hammer, B. (2019), 'On the Computation of Counterfactual—A Survey', *arXiv preprint*, http://arxiv.org/abs/1911.07749.

Asatiani, A., Malo, P., Nagbøl, P. R., Penttinen, E., Rinta-Kahila, T. & Salovaara, A. (2021), 'Sociotechnical Envelopment of Artificial Intelligence: An Approach to Organizational Deployment of Inscrutable Artificial Intelligence Systems', *Journal of the Association for Information Systems* **22**(2), 325–352.

Avrahami, D., Pessach, D., Singer, G. & Ben-Gal, H. C. (2022), 'A Human Resources Analytics and Machine-Learning Examination of Turnover: Implications for Theory and Practice', *International Journal of Manpower* **43**(6), 1405–1424.

Barredo Arrieta, A., Díaz-Rodríguez, N., Del Ser, J. et al. (2020), 'Explainable Artificial Intelligence (XAI): Concepts, Taxonomies, Opportunities and Challenges Toward Responsible AI', *Information Fusion* **58**, 82–115.

Benbya, H., Pachidi, S. & Jarvenpaa, S. L. (2021), 'Special Issue Editorial: Artificial intelligence in Organizations: Implications for Information Systems Research', *Journal of the Association for Information Systems* **22**(2), 281–303.

Berente, N., Seidel, S. & Safadi, H. (2019), 'Research Commentary - Data-Driven Computationally Intensive Theory Development', *Information Systems Research* **30**(1), 50–64.

Berente, N., Gu, B., Recker, J. & Santhanam, R. (2021), 'Managing Artificial Intelligence', *MIS Quarterly* **45**(3), 1433–1450.

Berrar, D. (2018), 'Cross-Validation', *Encyclopedia of Bioinformatics and Computational Biology: ABC of Bioinformatics* **1**(3), 542–545.

Bertsimas, D. & Kallus, N. (2020), 'From Predictive to Prescriptive Analytics', *Management Science* **66**(3), 1025–1044.

Borges, A. F. S., Laurindo, F. J. B., Spínola, M. M., Gonçalves, R. F. & Mattos, C. A. (2021), 'The Strategic Use of Artificial Intelligence in the Digital Era: Systematic Literature Review and Future Research Directions', *International Journal of Information Management* **57**, 102225.

Breiman, L., Friedman, J. H., Olshen, R. A. & Stone, C. J. (1984), *Classification and regression trees*. Taylor & Francis.

Breiman, L. (2001a), 'Random Forests', *Machine Learning* **45**, 5–32.

Breiman, L. (2001b), 'Statistical Modeling: The two Cultures', *Statistical Science* **16**(3), 199–215.

Brynjolfsson, E. & Mitchell, T. (2017), 'What can Machine Learning do? Workforce Implications', *Science* **358**(6370), 1530–1534.

Choudhury, P., Allen, R. T. & Endres, M. G. (2021), 'Machine Learning for Pattern Discovery in Management Research', *Strategic Management Journal* **42**(1), 30–57.

Chowdhury, S., Joel-Edgar, S., Kumar Dey, P., Bhattacharya, S. & Kharlamov, A. (2022), 'Embedding Transparency in Artificial Intelligence Machine Learning Models: Managerial Implications on Predicting and Explaining Employee Turnover', *The International Journal of Human Resource Management Preprint*.

Cooper, A., Doyle, O. & Bourke, A. (2021), "Supervised Clustering for Subgroup Discovery: An Application to COVID-19 Symptomatology", *in* 'Machine Learning and Principles and Practice of Knowledge Discovery in Databases', Springer, pp. 408–422.

Cortes, C. & Vapnik, V. (1995), 'Support-Vector Networks', *Machine Learning* **20**(3), 273–297.

Cover, T. & Hart, P. (1967), 'Nearest Neighbor Pattern Classification', *IEEE transactions on information theory* **13**(1).

de Bruijn, H., Warnier, M. & Janssen, M. (2022), 'The Perils and Pitfalls of Explainable AI: Strategies for Explaining Algorithmic Decision-Making', *Government Information Quarterly* **39**(2), 101666.

Elgendy, N., Elragal, A. & Päivärinta, T. (2022), 'DECAS: A Modern Data-Driven Decision Theory for Big Data and Analytics', *Journal of Decision Systems* **31**(4), 337–373.

Faraj, S., Pachidi, S. & Sayegh, K. (2018), 'Working and Organizing in the Age of the Learning Algorithm', *Information and Organization* **28**(1), 62–70.

Farrell, D. & Rusbult, C. E. (1981) ,'Exchange Variables as Predictors of Job Satisfaction, Job Commitment, and Turnover: The Impact of Rewards, Costs, Alternatives, and Investments', *Organizational Behavior and Human Performance* **28**(1), 78–95.

Fernández-Loría, C., Provost, F. & Han, X. (2022), 'Explaining Data-Driven Decisions made by AI Systems: The Counterfactual Approach', *MIS Quarterly* **46**(3), 1635–1660.

Freund, Y. & Schapire, R. E. (1997), 'A Decision-Theoretic Generalization of On-Line Learning and an Application to Boosting', *Journal of Computer and System Sciences* **55**(1), 119–139.

Friedman, J. H. (2002), 'Stochastic Gradient Boosting', *Computational Statistics and Data Analysis* **38**(4), 367–378.

Goldstein, A., Kapelner, A., Bleich, J. & Pitkin, E. (2015), 'Peeking Inside the Black Box: Visualizing Statistical Learning With Plots of Individual Conditional Expectation', *Journal of Computational and Graphical Statistics* **24**(1), 44–65.

Guidotti, R., Monreale, A., Ruggieri, S., Turini, F. et al. (2018), 'A Survey of Methods for Explaining Black Box Models', *ACM Computing Surveys* **51**(5).

Guidotti, R. (2022), 'Counterfactual Explanations and How to Find Them: Literature Review and Benchmarking', *Data Mining and Knowledge Discovery.*

Gunning, D., Stefik, M., Choi, J., Miller, T. et al. (2019), 'XAI-Explainable Artificial Intelligence', *Science Robotics* **4**(37), 4–6.

Hamm, P., Wittmann, H. & Klesel, M. (2021), Explain it to Me and I will Use it: A proposal on the Impact of Explainable AI on Use Behavior, *in* 'ICIS 2021 Proceedings'.

Hancock, J. T. & Khoshgoftaar, T. M. (2020), 'Survey on categorical data for neural networks', *Journal of Big Data* **7**(1), 1–41.

Hastie, T., Tibshirani, R. & Friedman, J. (2009), *The Elements of Statistical Learning.* Springer Science+Business Media.

Hong, W.-C., Wei, S.-Y. & Chen, Y.-F. (2007), 'A Comparative Test of Two Employee Turnover Prediction Models', *International Journal of Management* **24**(2), 216–229.

Hosmer, D. W., Lemeshow, S. & Sturdivant, R. X. (2013), *Applied Logistic Regression.* 3rd edn. Wiley.

John-Mathews, J.-M. (2021), Critical Empirical Study on Black-box Explanations in AI, *in* 'ICIS 2021 Proceedings'.

Jordan, M. I. & Mitchell, T. M. (2015), 'Machine Learning: Trends, Perspectives, and Prospects', *Science* **349**(6245), 255–260.

Kamath, U. & Liu, J. (2021) *Explainable Artificial Intelligence: An Introduction to Interpretable Machine Learning.* Springer.

Kourou, K., Exarchos, T. P., Exarchos, K. P., Karamouzis, M. V. & Fotiadis, D. I. (2015), 'Machine Learning Applications in Cancer Prognosis and Prediction', *Computational and Structural Biotechnology Journal* **13**, 8–17.

Lebovitz, S., Lifshitz-Assaf, H. & Levina, N. (2022), 'To Engage or Not to Engage with AI for Critical Judgments: How Professionals Deal with Opacity When Using AI for Medical Diagnosis', *Organization Science* **33**(1), 126–148.

Lundberg, S. M. & Lee, S. I. (2017), A Unified Approach to Interpreting Model Predictions, *in* '31st Conference on Neural Information Processing Systems (NIPS)'.

Lundberg, S. M., Erion, G., Chen, H., DeGrave, A. et al. (2020), 'From Local Explanations to Global Understanding with Explainable AI for Trees', *Nature Machine Intelligence* **2**(1), 56–67.

Mehdiyev, N. & Fettke, P. (2020), Prescriptive Process Analytics with Deep Learning and Explainable Artificial Intelligence, *in* 'European Conference on Information Systems Proceedings'.

Meske, C., Bunde, E., Schneider, J. & Gersch, M. (2022), 'Explainable Artificial Intelligence: Objectives, Stakeholders, and Future Research Opportunities', *Information Systems Management* **39**(1), 53–63.

Miranda, S., Berente, N., Seidel, S., Safadi, H. & Burton-Jones, A. (2022), 'Computationally Intensive Theory Construction: A Primer for Authors and Reviewers', *MIS Quarterly* **46**(2), iii–xviii.

Mitchell, T. R., Holtom, B. C., Lee, T. W. & Erez, M. (2001), 'Why people stay: Using job embeddedness to predict voluntary turnover', *Academy of Management Journal* **44**(6), 1102–1121.

Mithas, S., Xue, L., Huang, N. & Burton-Jones, A. (2022), 'Editor's comments: Causality meets diversity in information systems research', *MIS Quarterly* **46**(3), iii–xviii.

Molnar, C. (2020), *Interpretable Machine Learning*. Leanpub.

Mothilal, R. K., Sharma, A. & Tan, C. (2020), Explaining Machine Learning Classifiers through Diverse Counterfactual Explanation, *in* 'Proceedings of the 2020 Conference on Fairness, Accountability, and Transparency (FAT 2020)', pp. 607–617.

Müller, O., Junglas, I., vom Brocke, J. & Debortoli, S. (2016), 'Utilizing Big Data Analytics for Information Systems Research: Challenges, Promises and Guidelines', *European Journal of Information Systems* **25**, 289–302.

Nayak, S. C., Misra, B. & Behera, H. S. (2014), 'Impact of Data Normalization on Stock Index Forecasting', *International Journal of Computer Information Systems and Industrial Management Applications* **6**, 257–269.

Oswald, F. L., Behrend, T. S., Putka, D. J. & Sinar, E. (2020), 'Big Data in Industrial-Organizational Psychology and Human Resource Management: Forward Progress for Organizational Research and Practice', *Annual Review of Organizational Psychology and Organizational Behavior* **7**, 505–533.

Ribeiro, M. T., Singh, S. & Guestrin, C. (2016), "Why Should I Trust You?" Explaining the Predictions of Any Classifier, *in* 'Proceedings of the 22nd ACM SIGKDD International Conference on Knowledge Discovery and Data Mining'.

scikit-learn (2023), scikit-learn. Machine learning in Python, https://scikit-learn.org/stable/index.html. Accessed: 06.06.2023.

Senoner, J., Netland, T. & Feuerriegel, S. (2022), 'Using explainable artificial intelligence to improve process quality: Evidence from semiconductor manufacturing', *Management Science* **68**(8), 5557–6354.

Shin, D., He, S., Lee, G. M., Whinston, A. B. et al. (2020), 'Enhancing Social Media Analysis with Visual Data Analytics: A Deep Learning Approach', *MIS Quarterly* **44**(4), 1459–1492. doi:

Shollo, A., Hopf, K., Thiess, T. & Müller, O. (2022), 'Shifting ML Value Creation Mechanisms: A Process Model of ML Value Creation', *Journal of Strategic Information Systems* **31**(3), 101734.

Shrestha, Y. R., Fang He, V., Puranam, P. & von Krogh, G. (2021), 'Algorithm Supported Induction for Building Theory: How Can We Use Prediction Models to Theorize?', *Organization Science* **32**(3), 856–880.

Stoffels, D., Faltermaier, S., Strunk, K. S. & Fiedler, M. (2022), Opening the black-box of AI: Challenging Pattern Robustness and Improving Theorizing through Explainable AI Methods, *in* 'ICIS 2022 Proceedings'.

Sturm, T., Gerlach, J., Pumplun, L., Mesbah, N. et al. (2021), 'Coordinating Human and Machine Learning for Effective Organizational Learning', *MIS Quarterly* **45**(3), 1581–1602.

Subhash, P. (2017), IBM HR Analytics Employee Attrition & Performance, Kaggle - Database, https://www.kaggle.com/datasets/pavansubhasht/ibm-hr-analytics-attrition-dataset. Accessed: 02.11.2022.

Tremblay, M. C., Kohli, R. & Forsgren, N. (2021), 'Theories in Flux: Reimagining Theory Building in the Age of Machine Learning', *MIS Quarterly* **45**(1), 455–459.

van den Broek, E., Sergeeva, A. & Huysman, M. (2021), 'When the Machine Meets the Expert: An Ethnography of Developing AI for Hiring', *MIS Quarterly* **45**(3), 1557–1580.

Wang, X. & Zhi, J. (2021), 'A machine learning-based analytical framework for employee turnover prediction', *Journal of Management Analytics* **8**(3), 351–370.

Yang, G., Ye, Q. & Xia, J. (2022), 'Unbox the Black-Box for the Medical Explainable AI via Multi-Modal and Multi-Centre Data Fusion: A Mini-Review, two Showcases and Beyond', *Information Fusion* **77**, 29–52.

Yuan, S., Kroon, B. & Kramer, A. (2021), 'Building Prediction Models with Grouped Data: A Case Study on the Prediction of Turnover Intention', *Human Resource Management Journal*.

Zhao, Y., Hryniewicki, M. K., Cheng, F., Fu, B. & Zhu, X. (2018), "Employee Turnover Prediction with Machine Learning: A Reliable Approach", *in* 'Proceedings of the 2018 Intelligent Systems Conference (IntelliSys) Volume 2'. Springer International Publishing, pp. 737–758.

How Best to Hunt a Mammoth—Toward Automated Knowledge Extraction from Graphical Research Models

Sebastian Huettemann, Roland M. Mueller, Kai R. Larsen, Barbara Dinter, and Joshua Campos Chiny

Abstract In the Information Systems (IS) discipline, central contributions of research projects are often represented in graphical research models, clearly illustrating constructs and their relationships. Although thousands of such representations exist, methods for extracting this source of knowledge are still in an early stage. We present a method for (1) extracting graphical research models from articles, (2) generating synthetic training data for (3) performing object detection with a neural network, and (4) a graph reconstruction algorithm to (5) storing results into a designated research model format. We trained YOLOv7 on 20,000 generated diagrams and evaluated its performance on 100 manually reconstructed diagrams from the Senior Scholars' Basket. The results for extracting graphical research models show a F1-score of 0.82 for nodes, 0.72 for links, and an accuracy of 0.72 for labels, indicating the applicability for supporting the population of knowledge repositories contributing to knowledge synthesis.

Keywords Knowledge extraction · Graphical research models · Object detection · Theory repositories · Knowledge synthesis

---

S. Huettemann (✉) · R. M. Mueller · J. C. Chiny
Berlin School of Economics and Law, Berlin, Germany
e-mail: sebastian.huettemann@hwr-berlin.de

R. M. Mueller
e-mail: roland.mueller@hwr-berlin.de

J. C. Chiny
e-mail: chiny.jc@gmail.com

K. R. Larsen
University of Colorado, Boulder, USA
e-mail: kai.larsen@colorado.edu

B. Dinter
Chemnitz University of Technology, Chemnitz, Germany
e-mail: barbara.dinter@wirtschaft.tu-chemnitz.de

D. Beverungen et al. (eds.), *Conceptualizing Digital Responsibility for the Information Age*, Lecture Notes in Information Systems and Organisation 74,
https://doi.org/10.1007/978-3-031-80119-8_22

1 Introduction

Long before humans started to write letters, they painted pictures. Research suggests that some of the paintings in one of the most outstanding testaments of early human culture—the Lascaux Cave—depict hunting strategies that were used for education purposes and thereby knowledge sharing (Groeneveld 2016; Maier et al. 2021). Such hunting strategies could be seen as early forms of theories depicting relationships between causes and effects: ten hunters, six spears, four axes, and setting a proper trap lead to a first surprised, then angry, and eventually dead mammoth.

Long after humans started to write letters, they still paint pictures. In a way, performing research in IS today is similar to hunting a mammoth ten thousand years ago—with slight differences regarding the research focus. Instead of trying to identify theories about relationships between deadly instruments and hunting success, today's researchers try to identify theories about relationships between Information Technology and human behavior.

However, even after hundreds of thousands of years, we still share a central challenge with our ancestors: synthesizing our knowledge. For early humans, the only way to extend their knowledge might have been by exchanging information with hunters from different tribes, most likely by inspecting their neighbors' cave paintings. Fortunately, today's theories are no longer carved in stone but into paper and digital media. Unfortunately, the amount of available articles has grown to an immense body of knowledge that expands continuously and fast (Bornmann et al. 2021). This can lead to a range of unwanted side effects, such as information overload and knowledge fragmentation where conventional approaches to literature reviews tend to miss relevant articles (Larsen et al. 2019).

There have been attempts to create theory repositories in the form of databases to support researchers in synthesizing information from constructs, their definitions, and semantic relations (Mueller 2015; Dann et al. 2019; Li et al. 2020). However, populating such databases is a major undertaking as automated methods for knowledge extraction are still in an early phase (Scharfenberger et al. 2021). Most existing approaches (Li and Larsen 2011; Mueller and Huettemann 2018; Mueller and Abdullaev 2019) use natural language processing (NLP) for exclusively analyzing the text of papers. In addition to text, illustrating and reporting research findings in the form of diagrams evolved into well-accepted practice and is at the core of many successful research articles. In the IS discipline, graphical research models are widely used, providing an overview of factors or theoretical constructs in empirical settings, experiments, and surveys (Palvia et al. 2006; Recker 2013; Kiessling et al. 2020).

Technical progress in the development of object detection algorithms based on deep learning technologies made it possible to extract information from graphical research models. A stream of research contributes to the population and maintenance of theory repositories in IS by aiming to automatically detect constructs, path coefficients, and items from research diagrams and structural equation models (Auer et al. 2013; Scharfenberger et al. 2021; Schoelch et al. 2022).

Some of the current limitations however include low variation in training data which might impede generalizability and challenges in inferring the relationships between individual elements in diagrams. We aim to contribute towards developing methods for knowledge extraction from graphical research models, and ask the following research question: *How can we improve the extraction of knowledge from graphical research models in scientific articles to support the population of theory repositories?*

In this article, we propose a method for (1) classifying and extracting graphical research models from scientific articles, (2) creating synthetic training data, (3) performing object classification, (4) re-constructing detected graph structures, and (5) persisting findings into a meta-model. We focus on the analysis of graphical research models (Palvia et al. 2006; Recker 2013; Kiessling et al. 2020) whereas other types of diagrams, e.g., process models, reference frameworks, or organigrammes, have their own characteristics where for instance the shape of objects indicates special meaning. The proposed method could inform future work in other areas but would need to be modified towards interpreting the specific semantics of other types of diagrams.

2 Theoretical Background

2.1 *Knowledge Extraction and Analysis from Text*

Text mining and other NLP techniques have been the predominant means to extract and analyze knowledge from scientific articles. Li and Larsen (2011) presented a system for extracting constructs from IS papers. Larsen and Bong (2016) proposed a method for construct detection that surpassed latent semantic analysis. Li et al. (2020) presented a framework for extracting constructs and relationships from text. Mueller and Huettemann (2018) presented the tool CauseMiner to extract constructs and their interrelations from hypotheses and propositions in research articles. Mueller and Abdullaev (2019) presented DeepCause which extends CauseMiner by using a deep learning architecture for causal extraction.

However, these approaches share the challenge of locating, identifying, and extracting relevant information bits in the form of constructs and their interrelations from full-text scientific articles which can lead to ambiguous results.

2.2 *Knowledge Extraction and Analysis from Diagrams*

A number of studies aimed to extract figures from research articles. Clark and Divvala (2016) presented the algorithm PDFFigures 2.0 for extracting figures and tables. Their algorithm locates figures by reasoning about empty regions in text and identifying captions. Siegel et al. (2018) developed a deep neural model for detecting figures in PDF documents called DeepFigures. They approached the task of image classification and object detection by applying an OverFeat detection architecture to image embedding's. Their model detects bounding boxes for figures in PDF documents and was deployed in the academic search engine Semantic Scholar to extract figures from articles. Genz and Funk (2020) used convolutional neural networks (CNN) for the detection of structural equation models by converting pages of scientific papers to images.

Auer et al. (2013) presented an optical graph recognition approach attempting to perform the task of interpreting extracted figures. Their method was based on traditional image processing techniques, recognizing edges and their attachments to vertices. Attempts to detect objects and their interrelations in offline hand-drawn diagrams (Schaefer and Stuckenschmidt 2019; Fang et al. 2022) utilized more sophisticated technologies, such as Recurrent-CNNs.

Closely related to this article, Scharffenerger et al. (2021) focused on identifying and extracting knowledge from structural equation models in research articles. They identified and extracted figures from PDF articles via Recurrent-CNNs to detect constructs, path coefficients, and items via YOLOv4 (Bochkovskiy et al. 2020), a neural network for object detection. They used a rather small training dataset with 534 images and achieved good results.

Schoelch et al. (2022) developed an approach that included the automated recreation of graphs, preserving information about the interrelations between objects. They created a synthetic dataset consisting of 12,000 diagrams to train YOLOv5 (Jocher et al. 2022). They performed object detection, text recognition per EasyOCR (EasyOCR 2023), and graph reconstruction by applying a set of heuristics to analyze the predicted bounding box information. For evaluating the performance on real diagrams, they manually labeled 24 diagrams from DISKNET (Dann et al. 2019). Their results indicate an accurate detection of nodes, but a less accurate detection of edges with a direction.

Previous approaches mentioned several limitations that might be addressed by future work. Scharffenberger et al. (2021) neither mapped text to bounding boxes nor path coefficients to edges. We also found that they omitted the detection of edges. Schoelch et al. (2022) mentioned problems in the detection and analysis of edges as well. In addition, they were not able to detect arrowheads and reported limitations in generating synthetic training data, such as low variation in nodes, arrow- and edge-types, and layouts that are often more randomly organized than human-structured diagrams. These aspects might decrease the generalizability of models trained on such input data.

With our approach, we aim to build on these limitations and suggestions for future work. We explore the usage of Graphviz to add more variety and structure to synthetic training data, and show that current versions of object detection algorithms are able to detect different types of nodes, arrows, and edges in synthetic as well as real-world diagrams. We further illustrate how to reconstruct a detected graph from bounding box information to infer relationships between nodes, and we compare and incorporate OCR technology to evaluate the extraction of text from nodes and edges.

3 Knowledge Extraction from Graphical Research Models

We aim to build on related work, applying state-of-the-art technologies to cover a complete workflow: from a corpus of research articles with diagrams to the extraction of constructs and their interrelations in a knowledge base. More than a case of incremental improvements in each task, this is about evaluating the potential of a whole pipeline of challenges. In such a setup, every error propagates through the pipeline rendering the final result as interpretable and useful, or not. Our proposed method consists of five steps. The complete flow from research articles to reconstructed diagrams is illustrated in Fig. 1. We describe each step in the following subsections.

3.1 Step 1: Image Detection and Classification from Research Articles

We analyzed 700 research articles published in the AIS Basket of eight (AIS 2021) in 2018 and 2019 and extracted all figures from these articles by using the tool PDFFigures 2 (Clark and Divvala 2016) resulting in a total of 922 images. We manually classified the images into two categories; those showing either graphical research models or the empirical results of a research model vs. all remaining figures.

We compared the performance of Naive Bayes, SVM, Random Forest, BERT, and SciBert by training them with only the captions and a combination of captions plus the text that was extracted from the figures themselves. We also implemented an Xception-model that was pre-trained on ImageNet and fine-tuned with the annotated images. In addition, we trained an ensemble classifier with the best-performing Naive Bayes, SVM, Random Forest, SciBERT, and Xception models. Eventually, we used

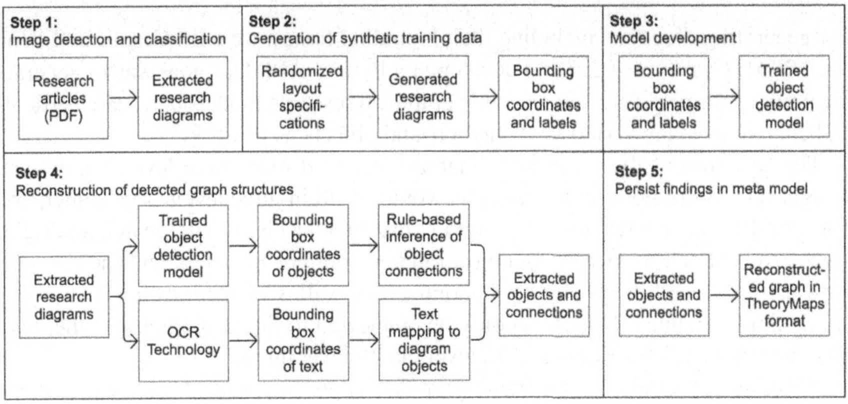

Fig. 1 Knowledge extraction from graphical research models

Table 1 Image classification results of top 5 models by macro F1-scores

Model	Data	Precision	Recall	Macro-F1
Stacking classifier	Fig + Cap + Text	0.93	0.91	0.92
SciBERT	Cap + Text	0.90	0.88	0.89
Ensemble Classifier	Fig + Cap + Text	0.92	0.85	0.88
SVM	Cap + Text	0.90	0.85	0.87
Xception	Fig	0.86	0.86	0.86
Dummy	N.A	0.37	0.50	0.43

the probabilities of the best-performing models to train a stacking classifier meta-model that outperformed all previous models. This classifier yielded an accuracy of 0.94 and a macro F1-score of 0.92.

All models that used text data performed better when the image text was also included in the dataset. We first did some general preprocessing on the data, including removing numbers, punctuation, multiple whitespaces, stop words, and short words, converting the text to lowercase, and applying lemmatization. We have also created a dummy classifier as a baseline which predicted the most frequent label for all the data. Table 1 shows detailed metrics of the top 5 best-performing models by macro F1-score.

For the evaluation, we used standard measures in NLP where precision is calculated as true positives / (true positives + false positives), recall is calculated as true positives/(true positives + false negatives), and F1-score is calculated as 2 * (precision * recall)/(precision + recall). Macro F1-scores provide an unweighted average of F1-scores for the individual classes (SciKit Learn 2023b; SciKit Learn 2023a).

3.2 *Step 2: Generation of Synthetic Training Data*

For generating diagrams including their bounding boxes, we used Graphviz (Ellson et al. 2004; Graphviz 2022) and developed a Python API. Our goal was to generate diagrams as training data that resemble graphical research models in research articles and contain as many variations in layouts and objects as possible.

The structure of the generated diagrams is based on a three-level hierarchical design. In a top-to-bottom diagram this would result in three levels: top, center, and bottom whereas, in a left-to-right diagram, the three levels are left, center, and right, respectively. Each level can contain a random number of nodes and the distance between nodes and levels can be randomized as well. Connections between nodes are randomly defined. Nodes can only be connected to the next level, i.e., there are no connections between nodes from level one to level three.

We defined four classes for training: nodes, edges, arrowheads, and edge labels. Figure 2 shows an example of a simple generated diagram where the respective bounding boxes for training are marked in orange. We defined bounding boxes for

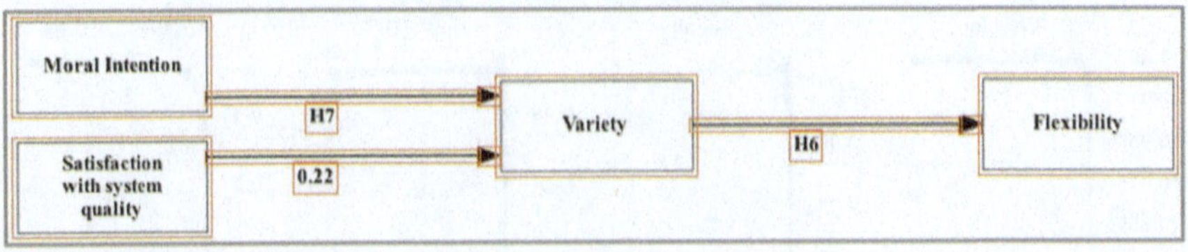

Fig. 2 Generated training data example with bounding boxes

Table 2 Diagram randomization examples

Attribute	Randomization options
Node-shape	Rectangle, ellipse, circle, only_text, rectangle_rounded_corners
Fonts	Arial, Helvetica, Times, Courier (normal, bold, italic)
Fontsize	8, 10, 12
Node-width	In inches: 1.3, 1.6, 2, 2.5
Node-height	In inches: 0.6, 0.8, 1, 1.3, 0.2
Graph-style	Right-left, left–right, top–bottom, bottom-top
Edge-type	Straight, curved, orthogonal
Edge-style	Solid, dashed, dotted, bold

all classes as rectangles. We further applied extensive randomization across generated diagrams. To illustrate the variety in synthetic training data, Table 2 contains selected examples of randomization options.

3.3 *Step 3: Model Development*

YOLO stands for "You Only Look Once" and denotes a series of object detection algorithms. Previous work used YOLOv4 (Scharfenberger et al. 2021) and YOLOv5 (Schoelch et al. 2022). In YOLOv6, improvements for detecting small objects were added (Olorunshola et al. 2023). YOLOv7 contained additional improvements regarding speed and accuracy and demonstrated a 13.7% increase in average precision compared to YOLOv6 (Wang et al. 2022).

We experimented with a pre-trained version of YOLOv7 (Wang et al. 2022) and performed fine-tuning by training the model with training sets of different sizes: 10,000, 20,000, 50,000, and 100,000. For each training set, we split the data into train, validation, and test sets with a ratio of 70/20/10. We did not find noticeable improvements in precision, recall, and mean average precision values when training a model with more than 20,000 images. One reason could be that the model internalized most of the possible layout structures given the selected randomization options.

We followed the guidelines for model development from the YOLOv5 documentation (Ultralytics 2022) and additionally included 1400 background images without

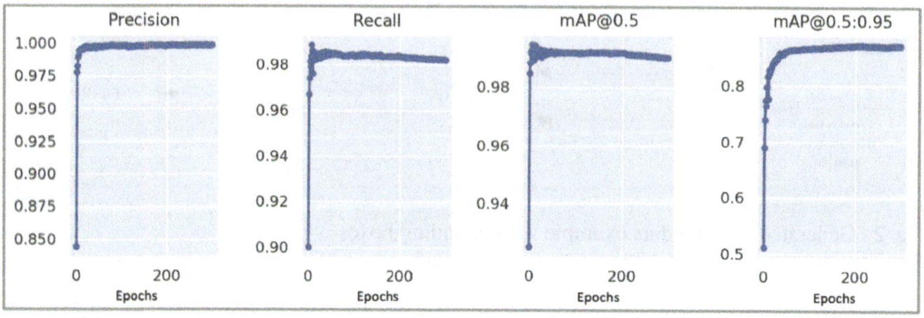

Fig. 3 Selected metrics from YOLOv7 results

any labels to the training and 300 background images to the validation set. Setting the confidence threshold to 0.5 provided the best results.

Figure 3 shows selected evaluation results from the final model, trained on 20,000 synthetically generated diagrams. Training the model for 300 epochs, resulted in a precision of 0.99, a recall of 0.98, a mean average precision for a confidence threshold of 0.5 (mAP@0.5) of 0.99, and a mean average precision averaged over different confidence thresholds from 0.5 to 0.9 (mAP@0.5:0.95) of 0.86.

3.4 *Step 4: Reconstruction of Detected Graph Structures*

We created an algorithm to reconstruct the interconnections between nodes from the detected bounding box coordinates. Figure 4 illustrates an example of a simple extracted diagram. Each element is detected as a bounding box including a designated label, e.g., *node*, *arrowhead*, *edge,* or *edge label*. We iterate through all edge objects and check for overlaps with nodes and arrowheads. Whenever we find an arrowhead, we check for a connection with another node. We analyze the position of an arrowhead on an edge to get the direction of the arrow. For detecting labels, we take the label that is closest to the center of an edge. If an edge is diagonal, we can use the position of the arrowhead to infer the position of the other end of the edge.

We performed several tests with optical character recognition technologies, such as EasyOCR (EasyOCR 2023) and Tesseract (Tesseract 2023). EasyOCR provided

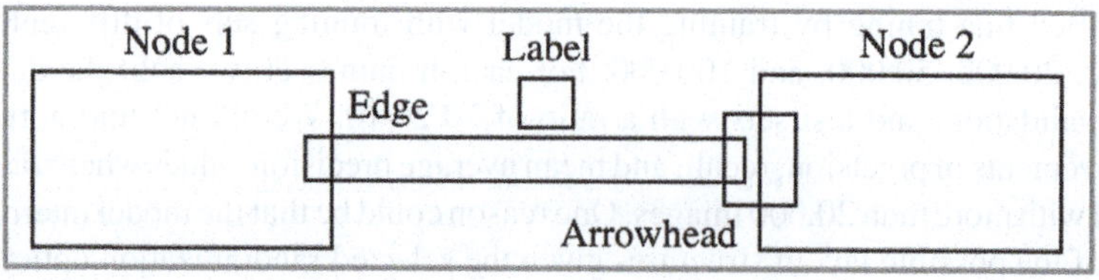

Fig. 4 Detected bounding boxes and classes

better performance than Tesseract but was still not able to capture all texts correctly. The detection of edge labels, such as "H1", "0.39", and "+", worked only in a small fraction of cases. We therefore decided to use PaddleOCR (Du et al. 2020) which outperformed the other technologies. PaddleOCR outputs bounding box information of detected texts from images. We mapped the detected texts from PaddleOCR with the positions of nodes, edges, and edge labels in the reconstructed diagram to infer semantic connections between constructs.

3.5 *Step 5: Persist Findings in Meta-Model*

We propose a meta-model for graphical research models building up on the meta-model of Mueller for analyzing inter-theory relationships (Mueller 2015). Figure 5 illustrates the meta model and its components.

Diagrams can be coded into a research model. Such a structure is able to capture objects and their interrelations from research diagrams. In our implementation, we assume that every node in a diagram contains a construct. A construct can alternatively act as a moderator or be part of a subset where multiple constructs are grouped. The extraction of moderating relationships and grouped nodes is however not yet supported. We interpret two connected nodes in a diagram as two connected constructs where their connection implies a causal direction. Such connections between constructs form a hypothesis where the source construct represents a cause and the target construct an effect. Based on coding research diagrams according to our meta-model, we store extracted information from diagrams in a structured YAML format allowing for querying information for subsequent analysis steps.

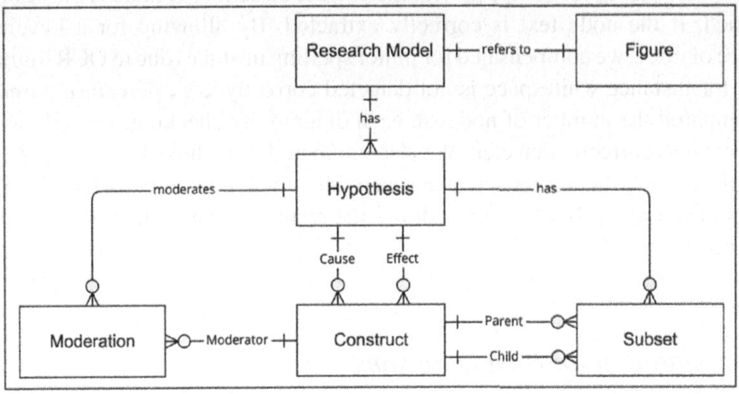

Fig. 5 A meta-model for graphical research models

Table 3 Evaluation on synthetic diagrams

Metric	Nodes	Links
Absolute count in ground truth	8949	7969
Absolute count in detection results	8949	7832
Precision	0.99	0.98
Recall	0.99	0.96
F1	0.99	0.97

4 Evaluation

4.1 Evaluation on Synthetic Diagrams

Our goal is to find out how well the proposed method is able to capture semantic relationships from research diagrams. We therefore generated 1000 diagrams with randomized layouts as illustrated in Table 2. For each diagram, we generated a YAML file containing a research model description that represents constructs and their interrelations serving as ground truth. We performed object detection on the generated diagrams and used our algorithm for graph reconstruction to infer relationships between detected constructs. This resulted in a second YAML file containing the detection result for each diagram.

We developed a routine to compare the ground truth against the detection results and adjusted common machine learning metrics (precision, recall, F1) to evaluate the graph reconstruction task. We define precision as the fraction of correctly extracted objects (which can be nodes or links) among all extracted objects. We define recall as the fraction of correctly extracted objects among all true objects. A link is correct if it connects the right two nodes with the correct direction. A node is only correctly identified, if the node text is correctly extracted. By allowing for a Levenshtein distance of three, we compensated for minor spelling mistakes due to OCR limitations where for instance whitespace is not detected correctly, e.g., *perceived easeof use*. We compared the number of nodes in each diagram by checking if a node with the same text was correctly detected. We also compared if the links between nodes were correctly set and whether related labels were identified. For correctly identified links, the label accuracy is 0.52. Table 3 shows the results of the evaluation for synthetic diagrams.

4.2 Evaluation on Real Diagrams

We extracted 573 graphical research models by performing image detection and classification (step 1) on research articles of the AIS Basket (AIS 2021). We manually classified the extracted models into suitable (n = 384) and not suitable (n = 189) for automated extraction. Not suitable models utilized layouts that contained elements

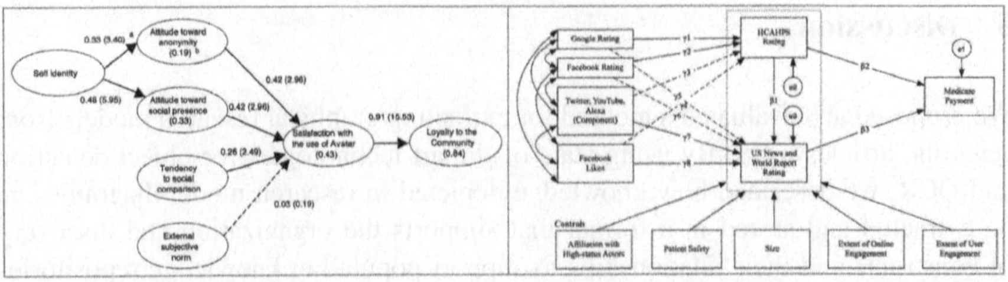

Fig. 6 Examples for supported (left) and not supported layouts (right). Left: Kim and Song (2004); right: Ivanov and Sharman (2018)

such as crossing edges that we did not include in our prototype. Although nodes in such models get detected correctly, the detection of correct links between nodes is not yet supported. From the 384 suitable models, we sampled 100 diagrams for manual evaluation. Figure 6 shows examples of supported and not supported layouts.

One of the authors and a master student in IS each translated 45 of the sampled diagrams into the proposed meta-model format (step 5) by manually creating YAML files. For calculating interrater reliability, both annotators annotated 10 diagrams and compared the results. We used the F1 score for measuring interrater reliability, due to the structure of the annotation task that does not allow us to use standard inter-annotator measures like Cohen's Kappa. The F1 score with a Levenshtein distance of three for nodes, links, moderations, and subsets, was 0.97, 0.92, 1.0, and 1.0, respectively. The resulting 100 manually recreated research diagrams form the gold standard.

We performed automated object detection and graph reconstruction on the extracted 100 diagrams resulting in the respective YAML files containing research models according to our meta-model. To compare the gold standard against the automatically detected research models, we used the same routine as for the evaluation of generated diagrams, including allowing for a Levenshtein distance of three to account for OCR limitations. The average accuracy of detected link labels is 0.72. Table 4 shows the results.

Table 4 Evaluation against manually annotated real diagrams

Metric	Nodes	Links
Absolute count in ground truth	664	581
Absolute count in detection results	583	526
Precision	0.88	0.76
Recall	0.8	0.7
F1	0.82	0.72

5 Discussion

We proposed and evaluated a method for extracting graphical research models from scientific articles in IS. By using state-of-the-art technologies for object detection and OCR, we described how knowledge depicted in research model diagrams can be extracted and stored in a format that supports the organization and discovery of constructs and their relationships to support populating knowledge repositories (Dann et al. 2019; Li et al. 2020) for the IS community.

With this approach, we have built up on the related works of Scharfenberger et al. (2021) and Schoelch et al. (2022) who developed similar approaches. In addition to the work of Scharfenberger et al. (2021), our method detects links between constructs and includes a graph reconstruction algorithm for the interpretation of detected bounding boxes. Thereby, we can associate constructs with each other and labels to edges enabling inference of causal directions. We further implemented OCR technology for text extraction to persist findings according to the proposed meta-model. In contrast to Schoelch et al. (2022), we integrated an object detection approach into a complete workflow proving its applicability in a scientific domain. We also advanced their approach by detecting the positions of arrowheads and training a neural network for object detection with a higher variety in node- and edge design. We further tested and implemented current technologies and introduced an algorithm for graph reconstruction, demonstrating that this approach works in a real-world scenario.

The results from the evaluation against 1000 synthetic diagrams indicate a very accurate performance in detecting constructs (F1 = 0.99) and links (F1 = 0.97) with limitations in assigning the correct labels (accuracy = 0.52) to links between nodes. The results from the evaluation against 100 manually reconstructed diagrams from scientific articles in IS show slightly lower results for the detection of constructs (F1 = 0.82), links (F1 = 0.72), and label assignments (accuracy = 0.72).

We reviewed the annotated images of the model to identify potential reasons for the differences between manual and synthetic evaluation results. Some of the differences most likely resulted from lower image resolution of real-world diagrams which led to incorrect OCR, bigger font size for labels which led to an increased accuracy score, and some not yet supported features such as grouped nodes and the detection of moderating relationships. We initially trained the model with diagrams that only included connections to nodes on adjacent levels as described in Sect. 3.2. We found that the model was capable of generalizing well to the real-world dataset as it correctly identified edges connecting nodes on various levels.

5.1 Limitations

There are different sources of errors relating to object detection accuracy, OCR accuracy, and graph reconstruction accuracy. We found that horizontal lines pose

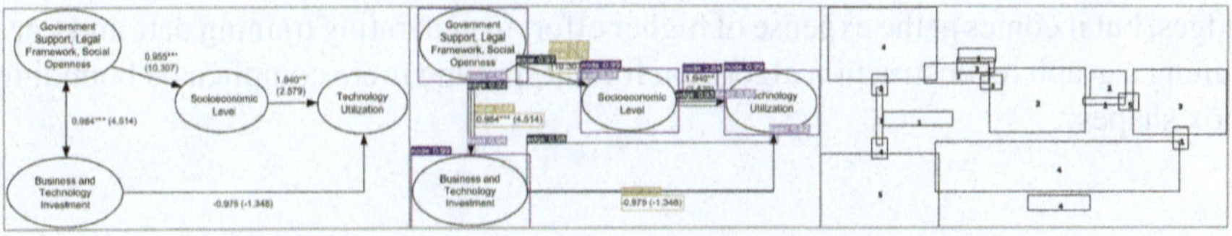

Fig. 7 From real diagram to object detection results to bounding box inference

a challenge to our trained object detection model. Missing such objects leads to follow-up errors as a connection between objects can not be inferred during graph reconstruction, resulting in missing links between constructs in our database. In addition, the detection of single-character edge labels, such as "+" or "−" poses a challenge for OCR. Both issues indicate problems in detecting objects with a low pixel density in very thin shapes. More extensive image preprocessing might help mitigate this shortcoming.

Our algorithm for graph reconstruction relies on interpreting labels and coordinates of bounding boxes. The main challenge is to infer the path of edges as diagonal edges are represented as rectangles. For our implementation, we based our inference on the pragmatic decision that every edge is interpreted as a straight edge. Based on this assumption, we can infer the path of an edge by analyzing the position of a connected arrowhead and thereby assign source and target nodes of a connection. Figure 7 illustrates this approach and also shows an example where a cornered edge is still interpreted correctly.

Although the approach works well in the majority of cases, it is not able to accurately detect paths of curved or cornered edges. This also impedes the accurate allocation of labels to edges. Using instance segmentation where instead of a bounding box the precise shape of an object is used for training a model could increase accuracy. However, it would also lead to additional complexity as these shapes contain much more detailed coordinates, leading to challenges in creating training data and in automatically reconstructing graphs to detect connections between objects.

5.2 Future Work

In order to accurately support the population of theory repositories allowing for analyzing constructs and their interrelations on a large scale, some challenges must be addressed to further improve the performance of this method. Our approach could be enhanced by extending the graph reconstruction algorithm to add detection capabilities for moderating relationships and grouped nodes. However, we think that the hardest challenge is the correct detection of edges in diagrams. Using instance segmentation to get the exact shape of an arrow might be a way towards more overall accuracy. Such an approach would also enable the correct assignment of labels to edges, but it comes at the expense of higher effort in generating training data and fine-tuning a graph reconstruction algorithm for interpreting more complicated bounding box shapes.

6 Conclusion

In this article we presented a method for automated knowledge extraction from graphical research models covering a workflow from research articles to persisting findings in a designated data format. We (1) classified and extracted research diagrams from scientific articles, (2) created synthetic training data of high variance, (3) performed object classification with state-of-the-art technologies, (4) reconstructed detected graph structures and (5) stored our findings into a meta-model for graphical research models. The performance in correctly extracting, interpreting, and reconstructing real-world diagrams shows good results for the detection and interpretation of constructs (F1 = 0.82), links (F1 = 0.72), and labels (0.72). Future developments could incorporate instance segmentation techniques to overcome limitations in edge interpretation and label assignment.

As an introductory note, we boldly claimed that performing research in IS today—where researchers need to manually analyze hundreds of articles to get an overview of the state of the art—is not too different from the prehistoric approaches of our early ancestors to research better hunting strategies by comparing and assessing cave paintings across their friendly neighbors' caves.

Naturally, we do not know if our ancestors eventually managed to find the best theory to hunt a mammoth but we presented a method that can support researchers today in collecting data from thousands of articles reducing the amount of necessary manual labor. We hope that in the not-too-distant future, the work from months and sometimes even years can be reduced to minutes enabling new kinds of analyses tapping into the collective knowledge of researchers in IS. Similar to cave paintings that informed ancient hunters, the semi-automated extraction and synthesis of research diagrams could support researchers in setting out to hunt their next big scientific discovery.

References

AIS (2021), Senior Scholars' Basket of Journals, https://aisnet.org/page/SeniorScholarBasket, Accessed: 15.11.2021.

Auer, C., Bachmaier, C., Brandenburg, F.J., Gleißner, A. & Reislhuber, J. (2013), 'Optical Graph Recognition', *Journal of Graph Algorithms and Applications* **17**(4), pp. 541–565.

Bochkovskiy, A., Wang, C.-Y. & Liao, H.-Y.M. (2020), YOLOv4: Optimal Speed and Accuracy of Object Detection, http://arxiv.org/abs/2004.10934, Accessed: 7.11.2022.

Bornmann, L., Haunschild, R. & Mutz, R. (2021), 'Growth rates of modern science: a latent piecewise growth curve approach to model publication numbers from established and new literature databases', *Humanities and Social Sciences Communications* **8**(1), pp. 1–15.

Clark, C. & Divvala, S. (2016), PDFFigures 2.0: Mining Figures from Research Papers, *in* 'Proceedings of the 16th ACM/IEEE-CS on Joint Conference on Digital Libraries' ACM, pp. 143–152.

Dann, D., Maedche, A., Teubner, T., Mueller, B. & Meske, C. (2019), DISKNET – A Platform for the Systematic Accumulation of Knowledge in IS Research, *in* 'Proceedings of the 40th International Conference on Information Systems (ICIS)', p. 11.

Du, Y., Li, C., Guo, R., Yin, X., Liu, W., Zhou, J., Bai, Y., Yu, Z., Yang, Y., Dang, Q. & Wang, H. (2020), PP-OCR: A Practical Ultra Lightweight OCR System, http://arxiv.org/abs/2009.09941, Accessed: 10.11.2022.

EasyOCR (2023), EasyOCR - Github Repository, https://github.com/JaidedAI/EasyOCR, Accessed: 9.3.2023.

Ellson, J., Gansner, E.R., Koutsofios, E., North, S.C. & Woodhull, G. (2004), Graphviz and Dynagraph—Static and Dynamic Graph Drawing Tools, *in* Jünger, M. & Mutzel, P. (eds.) 'Graph Drawing Software' Mathematics and Visualization, Springer Berlin Heidelberg, pp. 127–148.

Fang, J., Feng, Z. & Cai, B. (2022), 'DrawnNet: Offline Hand-Drawn Diagram Recognition Based on Keypoint Prediction of Aggregating Geometric Characteristics', *Entropy* **24**(3), p. 425.

Genz, T. & Funk, B. (2020), Using CNNs to Detect Graphical Representations of Structural Equation Models in IS Papers, *in* 'WI2020 Zentrale Tracks' GITO Verlag, pp. 115–120.

Graphviz (2022), Graphviz - An Open Source Graph Visualization Software, https://graphviz.org/, Accessed: 7.11.2022.

Groeneveld, E. (2016), World History Encyclopedia - Lascaux Cave, https://www.worldhistory.org/Lascaux_Cave/, Accessed: 22.9.2022.

Ivanov, A. & Sharman, R. (2018), 'Impact of User-Generated Internet Content on Hospital Reputational Dynamics', *Journal of Management Information Systems* **35**(4), pp. 1277–1300.

Jocher, G. et al. (2022), YOLOv5 - Relase Version 6.2, https://zenodo.org/record/7002879, Accessed: 7.11.2022.

Kiessling, S., Figl, K. & Miniukovich, A. (2020), Graphical Research Models in the Information Systems Discipline, *in* 'Proceedings of the 53rd Hawaii International Conference on System Sciences'.

Kim, Y.J. & Song, J. (2004), Unveiling User Characteristics in Virtual Communities and the Impact on E-Commerce, *in* 'Proceedings of the International Conference on Information Systems (ICIS)', p. 15.

Larsen, K.R. & Bong, C.H. (2016), 'A tool for addressing construct identity in literature reviews and meta-analyses', *MIS Quarterly* **40**(3), pp. 1–23.

Larsen, K.R., Hovorka, D.S., Dennis, A.R. & West, J.D. (2019), 'Understanding the Elephant: The Discourse Approach to Boundary Identification and Corpus Construction for Theory Review Articles', *Journal of the Association for Information Systems* , pp. 887–927.

SciKit Learn (2023a), Example of Precision-Recall metric to evaluate classifier output quality, https://scikit-learn/stable/auto_examples/model_selection/plot_precision_recall.html, Accessed: 10.3.2023.

SciKit Learn (2023b), SciKit Learn Metrics - sklearn.metrics.f1_score, https://scikit-learn/stable/modules/generated/sklearn.metrics.f1_score.html, Accessed: 5.3.2023.

Li, J. & Larsen, K.R. (2011), Establishing Nomological Networks for Behavioral Science: a Natural Language Processing Based Approach, *in* 'Proceedings of the International Conference on Information Systems (ICIS)'.

Li, J., Larsen, K. & Abbasi, A. (2020), 'TheoryOn: A Design Framework and System for Unlocking Behavioral Knowledge Through Ontology Learning', *MIS Quarterly* **44**(4), pp. 1733–1772.

Maier, G.J., Musholt, E.A. & Stava, L.J. (2021), 'Lascaux Cave, Part Four: Evidence of Hunting', *Journal of Transpersonal Psychology* **53**(1).

Mueller, R. & Abdullaev, S. (2019), DeepCause: Hypothesis Extraction from Information Systems Papers with Deep Learning for Theory Ontology Learning, *in* 'Hawaii International Conference on System Sciences (HICSS)'.

Mueller, R.M. & Huettemann, S. (2018), Extracting Causal Claims from Information Systems Papers with Natural Language Processing for Theory Ontology Learning, *in* 'Proceedings of the 51st Hawaii International Conference on System Sciences'.

Mueller, R.M. (2015), A Meta-Model for Inferring Inter-Theory Relationships of Causal Theories, *in* '48th Hawaii International Conference on System Science (HICSS)' IEEE, pp. 4908–4917.

Olorunshola, O.E., Irhebhude, M.E. & Evwiekpaefe, A.E. (2023), 'A Comparative Study of YOLOv5 and YOLOv7 Object Detection Algorithms', *Journal of Computing and Social Informatics* **2**(1), pp. 1–12.

Palvia, P., Midha, V. & Pinjani, P. (2006), 'Research Models in Information Systems', *Communications of the Association for Information Systems* **17**.

Recker, J. (2013), *Scientific Research in Information Systems*. Springer.

Schaefer, B. & Stuckenschmidt, H. (2019), Arrow R-CNN for Flowchart Recognition, *in* '2019 International Conference on Document Analysis and Recognition Workshops (ICDARW)' IEEE, pp. 7–13.

Scharfenberger, J., Funk, B. & Mueller, B. (2021), The Augmented Theorist - Toward Automated Knowledge Extraction from Conceptual Models, *in* 'International Conference on Information Systems (ICIS)'.

Schoelch, L., Steinhauser, J., Beichter, M., Seibold, C., Yang, K., Knäble, M., Schwarz, T., Mädche, A. & Stiefelhagen, R. (2022), Towards Automatic Parsing of Structured Visual Content through the Use of Synthetic Data, *in* '26th International Conference on Pattern Recognition (ICPR)'.

Siegel, N., Lourie, N., Power, R. & Ammar, W. (2018), Extracting Scientific Figures with Distantly Supervised Neural Networks, *in* 'Proceedings of the 18th ACM/IEEE on Joint Conference on Digital Libraries', pp. 223–232.

Tesseract (2023), Tesseract OCR - Github Repository, https://github.com/tesseract-ocr/tesseract, Accessed: 9.3.2023.

Ultralytics (2022), YOLOv5 Documentation - Tips for Best Training Results, https://docs.ultralytics.com/tutorials/training-tips-best-results/, Accessed: 9.11.2022.

Wang, C.-Y., Bochkovskiy, A. & Liao, H.-Y.M. (2022), YOLOv7: Trainable bag-of-freebies sets new state-of-the-art for real-time object detectors, http://arxiv.org/abs/2207.02696, Accessed: 7.11.2022.

Student Track

Digital Detox Research: An Analysis of Applied Methods and Implications for Future Studies

Nina Hager, Fabian J. Stangl, and René Riedl

Abstract The development and increasing use of technology worldwide can lead to potential negative consequences for individuals' well-being and productivity. To counteract negative consequences, both scientific research and practice have shown increasing interest in digital detox research, a rising phenomenon of abstinence and temporary or complete disengagement from digital technologies. To lay a foundation for future research, we conducted a systemic literature review with a focus on the methodological aspects of the existing empirical digital detox studies. Our literature search process revealed a total of 65 studies. Our analyses of this literature basis revealed five different research fields (communication, education, tourism, well-being and health, work environment), and we analyzed the empirical studies in these fields regarding applied research approach, research method, and sample size. This review provides methodological insights to advance the scientific inquiry on digital detox research, a relatively nascent, yet increasingly relevant research topic.

Keywords Digital Detox · Digital Detox Research Designs · Empirical Digital Detox Studies · Methodological Review

N. Hager · F. J. Stangl (✉) · R. Riedl
Digital Business Institute, School of Business and Management, University of Applied Sciences Upper Austria, Steyr, Austria
e-mail: fabian.stangl@fh-steyr.at

N. Hager
e-mail: nina.hager@fh-steyr.at

R. Riedl
e-mail: rene.riedl@fh-steyr.at

R. Riedl
Institute of Business Informatics—Information Engineering, Johannes Kepler University Linz, Linz, Austria

D. Beverungen et al. (eds.), *Conceptualizing Digital Responsibility for the Information Age*, Lecture Notes in Information Systems and Organisation 74,
https://doi.org/10.1007/978-3-031-80119-8_23

1 Introduction

Digital technologies are ubiquitous in today's business, management, and organizational context. The adoption and use of digital technologies enables numerous benefits. These include, among others, pervasive access to information, rapid communication, and increased productivity (Riedl et al. 2012). Businesses can also benefit in terms of effectiveness and efficiency (Melville et al. 2004) by continuously evaluating and adapting their business infrastructure to take advantage of improvements in digital technologies (Bharadwaj et al. 2013).

The overuse of digital technologies, however, also entails both psychological and physiological risks. A recent review, for example, examined the scientific literature on the risk of Facebook use (Stangl et al. 2023). The results indicated that excessive and uncontrolled use of Facebook, the most used social networking site in the world (Statista 2022), may be associated with various negative psychological (e.g., perceived depression) and physiological effects (e.g., human brain alteration). As another example, evidence indicates that technostress, also referred to as digital stress, also constitutes a serious issue in both economy and society in general (e.g., Tarafdar et al. 2010; Ayyagari et al. 2011; Riedl 2013).

The use and role of new digital technologies and rapid pace of technological change, however, brings increasing complexity and makes academic research necessary in many ways to ensure beneficial interaction between humans and technology. Constant interruptions during task performance (Chen and Karahanna 2018; Puranik et al. 2020; Stangl and Riedl 2023b, 2023c), continuous electronic performance monitoring (Smith et al. 1992; Aiello and Kolb 1995; Kalischko and Riedl 2020, 2021), unstable systems and long response times (Emurian 1991, 1993; Riedl et al. 2012, 2013; Anderson et al. 2016; Jenkins et al. 2016; Riedl and Fischer 2018; Kalischko et al. 2020) are just some of the triggers for worry, anxiety, and stress that individuals face in an increasingly digital world, which may referred to as the "dark side" of digital technologies (Tarafdar et al. 2013).

Also, an overuse of digital technologies can lead to higher stress levels and negative effects on performance and productivity (for a review, please see Fischer and Riedl 2017). For example, the radical adoption and extensive use of videoconferencing systems such as Microsoft Teams or Zoom can lead to stress-related depletion of physiological and cognitive resources as a consequence of prolonged and inappropriate use of videoconferencing tools, which is referred to as videoconferencing fatigue or Zoom fatigue (Bailenson 2021; Montag et al. 2022; Riedl 2022). Notably, well-being and health can have an influence on work performance and productivity (Riedl 2013; Pflügner et al. 2021). Additionally, long-term exposure to stress can have adverse effects on well-being and health (Riedl 2013), further exacerbating the impact on work performance.

To mitigate the negative consequences of the use and ubiquity of digital technologies, strategies are needed that both enhance well-being (Stephanidis et al. 2019) and enable to work effectively and efficiently (Tams et al. 2020; Baham et al. 2022). Due to the increasing use of digital technologies and acceleration of processes worldwide (Couffe and Michael 2017) and the resulting potential negative consequences (Mirbabaie et al. 2022), the phenomenon of abstinence and temporary disengagement from digital technologies, hereafter referred to as *digital detox*, has received growing interest in both scientific research and practice. Drawing on prior definitions by Mirbabaie et al. (2022) and Syvertsen and Enli (2020), and in line with previous research (Stangl and Riedl 2023a, 2024a), we define digital detox as the temporary or complete disengagement from digital technologies (e.g., abstaining temporarily from social media platforms such as Facebook, Instagram, or Snapchat), while also considering strategies to reduce exposure to digital technologies (e.g., taking regular breaks from computer work).

Note that temporarily abstaining from the use of digital technologies seems to be a promising strategy to mitigate the negative psychological and physiological effects that may be caused by excessive and uncontrolled use of digital technologies. Indeed, research has found that brief abstinence from Facebook can significantly increase perceived life satisfaction (Tromholt 2016) and also lowers cortisol levels as an indicator of physiological stress (Vanman et al. 2018). Similarly, reducing the daily time spent on Facebook can also significantly reduce perceived depressive symptoms while significantly increasing perceived life satisfaction (Brailovskaia et al. 2020). Research on digital detox could thus contribute to well-being and health, and to the preventive recovery of equanimity and balance when using digital technologies (Mirbabaie et al. 2022).

Following the call for more research to explore the phenomenon of digital detox by Mirbabaie et al. (2022), this review aims to analyze the methodological aspects of the existing empirical digital detox studies. Such a methodological review can advance a research topic by providing perspectives on appropriate research methods and insights into the appropriate use of different methods (Pinsonneault and Kraemer 1993; Chong and Reinders 2021). To the best of our knowledge, a systematic review on the methodological design of digital detox research does not exist. Hence, as a companion to the publication by Mirbabaie et al. (2022) on the first conceptualization of digital detox in the information systems discipline, we address the following research question: **How were the existing empirical digital detox studies methodologically designed?** More specifically, our analyses highlight aspects related to applied research approach, research method, and sample size of empirical digital detox studies.

The remainder of this paper is structured as follows. Section 2 describes the methodology of our review. Results are presented in Sect. 3. Section 4 follows with a discussion of the contributions and implications along with limitations of our study. Finally, in Sect. 5, we make concluding remarks.

2 Review Methodology

The starting point of our research was to obtain an initial comprehensive overview of the quantity of digital detox research and existing definitions. As Mirbabaie et al. (2022) noted, conceptualizations of digital detox are inconsistent and often vague. In our exploratory search process, we were indeed able to identify several synonyms for digital detox, including "digital abstinence" (Turel et al. 2018), "digital detoxing" (e.g., Wysocki 2019), "digital detoxification" (e.g., El-Khoury et al. 2021), "digital disconnection" (Schwarzenegger and Lohmeier 2021), "digital reversion" (e.g., Baumer et al. 2015), and "technology non-use" (e.g., Hesselberth 2018).

Note that due to the conceptual ambiguity in current digital detox research (Mirbabaie et al. 2022), we also had to iteratively expand our search term syntax and used specific search terms, namely "digital free tourism" (e.g., Cai and McKenna 2023), "offline tourism" (e.g., Syvertsen 2022), "unplugged tourism" (e.g., Pawłowska-Legwand and Matoga 2021), and "digital nudge" (e.g., Purohit et al. 2020) to capture the characteristics of the different research fields.

In our literature search process, however, we then considered variations and alternative terms to the identified synonyms of digital detox. As an example, we used "internet detox" or "online detox" as different terms for digital detox, which we have therefore asterisked to generalize the term for search when it can have multiple meanings (i.e., *detox* includes "digital detox(ing)", "internet detox(ing)", or "online detox(ing)" and other terms that include "detox"). Overall, the keywords derived from this exploratory search process provided a methodologically sound foundation for the search of empirical digital detox studies.[1] Additionally, this overview can serve as foundation for a common language for researchers and prevent the further proliferation of synonyms (Barki et al. 1988).

To determine the scope and range of existing empirical digital detox studies and the methodological designs addressed therein, we conducted a scoping review (Paré et al. 2015; Schryen et al. 2017; Schryen et al. 2020) and considered peer-reviewed journals and conference publications in German and English with no publication year restriction. Also, the review process was based on existing recommendations for conducting literature searches (Webster and Watson 2002; vom Brocke et al. 2009).

To be included in this review, we focused exclusively on peer-reviewed papers that empirically examined digital detox. The literature search process was conducted in eight literature databases. We searched ACM Digital Library, Association for Information Systems eLibrary, Emerald Group Publishing, EBSCO Information Services, IEEE Xplore, Science Direct, Scopus, and Web of Science with our keywords,

[1] Thus, for our literature search process, we used several synonyms for digital detox (Digital Abstinence, Digital Detoxification, Digital Detoxing, Digital Disconnection, Digital Reversion, Technology Non-Use), specific search terms to capture characteristics of the different research fields (Digital Free Tourism, Digital Nudge, Offline Tourism, Unplugged Tourism), and variations and alternative terms to the identified synonyms for digital detox (Internet Detox, Online Detox), where we asterisked the term 'digital detox' to generalize the term for search when it can have multiple meanings (Internet Detox*, Online Detox*).

ensuring a broad and valid consideration of empirical digital detox studies. After searching the databases, we screened all articles and removed duplicates and unrelated papers based on title and abstract, which left us 74 unique papers out of 325 papers originally found in the databases.

The remaining papers were then analyzed in-depth based on the full text to ensure that keywords were not superficial and that the article contained content relevant to our research goal (i.e., methodological design of empirical digital detox studies). During this process, we excluded, for example, the paper by Mirbabaie et al. (2022) because this work was conceptual and not empirical in nature. Following this filtering strategy, 48 unique papers remained for further analysis.

When reviewing a paper in full text, we also conducted a backward search (i.e., searching the references) and forward search (i.e., citation tracking) as final step to identify additional relevant literature, resulting in a total of 17 additional unique papers. As a consequence, the literature base of our analyses comprises 65 empirical digital detox studies published before and in June 2022, including 57 journal papers (88%) and 8 conference proceedings papers (12%).

3 Review Results

In this section, we present the main findings of our literature review. Our literature search process revealed a total of 65 empirical digital detox studies. Our analyses revealed five different research fields (communication, education, tourism, well-being and health, work environment), which are described below with respect to applied research approach, research method, and sample size of empirical digital detox studies. We will also describe one study in more detail as an example. Overall, our review shows that most empirical studies on digital detox used an experimental research approach (34%) as research approach, followed by a qualitative (32%) or a quantitative research approach (26%), and only a small proportion used a mixed-methods (5%) or multimethod research approach (3%).

3.1 Digital Detox Studies in the Research Field of Communication

Three empirical digital detox studies were found. These 3 studies included 2 studies with an experimental research approach and 1 study with a quantitative research approach. These digital detox studies have examined the effects of environmental intervention on social interactions (Cesareo et al. 2021), the effects of digital detox on communication capability (Anashkina et al. 2020), and the effects of digital technology use on communication load and the relationship with perceived stress and psychological stress (Reinecke et al. 2017).

Table 1 Digital detox studies in the research field of communication

Reference	Research method	Sample size
Anashkina et al. (2020)	Longitudinal quasi-experimental study	36
Cesareo et al. (2021)	Case–control experimental study	74
Reinecke et al. (2017)	Cross-sectional survey study	1557

As an example, the research by Anashkina et al. (2020) investigated whether digital detoxing can improve communication skills and promote responsible media use. Before the experiment began, diagnostic methods were used to determine the level of involvement in media communication activities. Thereby, the participants were divided into three groups according to their level of involvement: high, medium, and low. Participants then took part in the digital detox camp "Offliner," where they completely abstained from digital devices and technologies for two days. Instead, they had to practice interpersonal communication techniques or offline activities (e.g., public relations). In this way, communication potential and responsible use of digital media could be determined. Finally, the diagnostic procedures were performed again. All three groups were found to have developed positive communication skills and greater control over their use of digital technologies. The second group (i.e., group with average level of involvement in media communication activities) made the greatest progress. An overview of the methodological design of the three studies that examined digital detox in the research field of communication can be found in Table 1.

3.2 Digital Detox Studies in the Research Field of Education

Two empirical digital detox studies were found. These 2 studies included 1 study with an experimental research approach and 1 study with a quantitative research approach. These digital detox studies have examined the digital technology consumption behaviors (Wood and Muñoz 2021) and the effects of digital technologies on social interactions (Ugur and Koc 2015).

As an example, Ugur and Koc (2015) conducted a cross-sectional study to examine distraction by technology in the classroom. All 349 respondents reported owning a smartphone, with nearly 99% of them texting daily, and 98% also texting while waiting for class to start and using their smartphone intensively once or twice per class to engage with their smartphone. The smartphone is used during class to check the time or data (about 77%), use calculators (about 54%), check WhatsApp messages (about 60%), send messages (about 41%), surf the Internet (about 33%), or use Facebook (about 22%). According to the study, students are not willing to refrain from smartphone use without strict guidelines. These results also show that the need for

Table 2 Digital detox studies in the research field of education

References	Research method	Sample size
Ugur and Koc (2015)	Cross-sectional survey study	349
Wood and Muñoz (2021)	Experimental study with a time-series design	66

digital detox measures in education is increasing. An overview of the methodological design of the three studies that examined digital detox in the research field of education can be found in Table 2.

3.3 *Digital Detox Studies in the Research Field of Tourism*

Seventeen empirical digital detox studies were found. These 17 studies included 14 studies with a qualitative research approach, 2 studies with a mixed-methods research approach, and 1 study with a quantitative research approach. These digital detox studies have examined digital detox offerings (Amato et al. 2019; Pawłowska-Legwand and Matoga 2021; Schwarzenegger and Lohmeier 2021), motives, motivation or tensions for or during digital detox vacations (Pearce and Gretzel 2012; Paris et al. 2015; Dickinson et al. 2016; Fan et al. 2019; Egger et al. 2020; Díaz-Meneses and Estupinán-Ojeda 2022; Zhang and Zhang 2022; Hassan et al. 2022; Jiang and Balaji 2022; Syvertsen 2022; Cai and McKenna 2023), and the effects of digital detox vacation on the character (Karlsen 2020; Li et al. 2020).

As an example, Schwarzenegger and Lohmeier (2021) focused on analyzing digital detox offers by analyzing the online representation (i.e., websites and Instagram profiles) of tourism agencies, hotels, and other accommodation facilities. They also conducted nine interviews with executives in tourism marketing and hotel managers. The results allowed them to identify three main themes for promoting digital detox: (1) nature and authenticity, (2) (re)connecting with the self, finding balance, and (3) connecting with family/friends/locals. An overview of the methodological design of the seventeen studies that examined digital detox in the research field of tourism can be found in Table 3.

3.4 *Digital Detox Studies in the Research Field of Well-Being and Health*

Thirty-eight empirical digital detox studies were found. These 38 studies included 19 studies with an experimental research approach, 11 studies with a quantitative research approach, 6 studies with a qualitative research approach, 1 study with a multimethod research approach, and 1 study with a mixed-methods research approach. These digital detox studies have examined problematic digital technology

Table 3 Digital detox studies in the research field of tourism

References	Research method	Sample size
Amato et al. (2019)	Content analysis of accommodations	6
Cai and McKenna (2023)	Longitudinal auto ethnographic study	2
Díaz-Meneses and Estupinán-Ojeda (2022)	Cross-sectional survey study	346
Dickinson et al. (2016)	Content analysis of interviews	48
	Cross-sectional survey study	339
Egger et al. (2020)	Content analysis of interviews	17
Fan et al. (2019)	Content analysis of interviews	51
Floros et al. (2021)	Content analysis of interviews	17
Hassan et al. (2022)	Content analysis of interviews	20
Jiang and Balaji (2022)	Content analysis of interviews	20
	Cross-sectional survey study	460
	Cross-sectional survey study	368
Karlsen (2020)	Informal dialogues with participants	30
	Content analysis of interviews	4
Li et al. (2020)	Content analysis of interviews	65
Pawłowska-Legwand and Matoga (2021)	Content analysis of websites	270
Paris et al. (2015)	Content analysis of responses	25
Pearce and Gretzel (2012)	Content analysis of focus group discussions	37
Schwarzenegger and Lohmeier (2021)	Content analysis of online representations	N/A
	Content analysis of interviews	9
Syvertsen (2022)	Observations at offline sites	3
	Content analysis of dialogues	30
Zhang and Zhang (2022)	Content analysis of user-generated contents	22
	Content analysis of interviews	16

use (Sheldon, Abad and Hinsch 2011; Skierkowski and Wood 2012; Hinsch and Sheldon 2013; Turel and Cavagnaro 2019; Handa and Ahuja 2020; Fryman and Romine 2021; Keller et al. 2021; Phillips and Shipps 2022), reasons for digital detox (Helsper and Reisdorf 2013; Jorge 2019; Muench et al. 2020; Matthes et al. 2022), reasons for returning to social media reversion after digital detox (Baumer et al. 2015), the effects of digital detox on well-being during the COVID-19 pandemic (Liu et al. 2021), the effects of environmental intervention on digital technology use (Tromholt 2016; Stieger and Lewetz 2018; van Wezel et al. 2021; Olson et al. 2022), the effects of environmental intervention on social interactions (Sutton 2020), the effects of involuntary digital detox (Liao and Sundar 2022), the effects of self-tracking technologies (Ko et al. 2015; Kent 2020), the general effects of digital detox on well-being (Anrijs et al. 2018; Vanman, Baker and Tobin 2018; Eide et al. 2018; Hunt et al. 2018; Turel, Cavagnaro and Meshi 2018; Vally and D'Souza 2019; Wilcockson et al. 2019; Hanley et al. 2019; Brown and Kuss 2020; Fioravanti et al. 2020; El-Khoury et al. 2021; Hall et al. 2021; Mutsvairo et al. 2022) and performance (Dunican et al. 2017), and the perception of digital detox applications (Nguyen 2022).

As an example, Hunt et al. (2018) conducted an longitudinal experimental study with a with randomized controlled trial (RCT) design with 143 participants to examine social media use in relation to well-being. Smartphone use was continued regularly at the beginning of the experiment. After one week, subjects were randomly divided into an experimental group (limiting media use to ten minutes per day) and a control group (not limiting media use). The restriction of social media use led to a significant decrease in perceived loneliness and depression in the experimental group compared to the control group after three weeks. Also, participants were generally more aware of their social media consumption, which was due to digital detox. However, the results did not show no significant differences between the two groups in terms of fear of missing out, perceived anxiety, perceived self-esteem, perceived social support, and psychological well-being. An overview of the methodological design of the thirty-eight studies that examined digital detox in the research field of well-being and health can be found in Table 4.

3.5 *Digital Detox Studies in the Research Field of Work Environment*

Five empirical digital detox studies were found. These 5 studies included 3 studies with a quantitative research approach, 1 study with a qualitative research approach, and 1 study with a multimethod research approach. These digital detox studies have examined the effect of digital detox on work performance (Basu 2019; Umasankar et al. 2022) or on focused work performance (Karlsen and Ytre-Arne 2022) or during the COVID-19 pandemic (Schmitt, Breuer and Wulf 2021), as well as the effect of digital detox on perceived social connectedness of remote workers (Mirbabaie et al. 2020).

As an example, the research by Basu (2019) focused on the effects of digital detox on individuals' work performance. Indeed, there are some opportunities in the workplace to integrate digital detox. These include regular screen breaks, relaxing classes such as yoga, and technology-free meetings. A survey of 70 employees who had already undergone digital detox was used to test the hypothesis of whether digital detoxing affects individual worker performance. According to the study, digital detox leads to better work performance among employees. The participants also confirmed that digital detox helped them to identify more with their work and increase their

Table 4 Digital detox studies in the research field of well-being and health

References	Research method	Sample size
Anrijs et al. (2018)	Longitudinal quasi-experimental study	10
Baumer et al. (2015)	Longitudinal panel survey study	3539 (t_1)
	Content analysis of survey responses	3539 (t_1)
Brown and Kuss (2020)	Longitudinal quasi-experimental study	61
	Content analysis of survey responses	61
Dunican et al. (2017)	Longitudinal quasi-experimental study	18
Eide et al. (2018)	Longitudinal experimental study with RCT design	127
El-Khoury et al. (2021)	Cross-sectional survey study	68
Fioravanti et al. (2020)	Longitudinal experimental study with RCT design	80
Fryman and Romine (2021)	Cross-sectional survey study	159
Hall et al. (2021)	Longitudinal experimental study with RCT design	130
Handa and Ahuja (2020)	Cross-sectional survey study	240
Hanley et al. (2019)	Longitudinal experimental study with RCT design	78
Helsper and Reisdorf (2013)	Cross-sectional survey study	559
Hinsch and Sheldon (2013)	Longitudinal panel survey study	114
	Longitudinal panel survey study	104
Hunt et al. (2018)	Longitudinal experimental study with RCT design	143
Jorge (2019)	Content analysis of online contents	N/A
Keller et al. (2021)	Longitudinal experimental study with RCT design	232
Kent (2020)	Longitudinal ethnographic study	14
Ko et al. (2015)	Longitudinal quasi-experimental study	62
Liao and Sundar (2022)	Content analysis of online contents	223815
Liu et al. (2021)	Cross-sectional survey study	322
Matthes et al. (2022)	Cross-sectional survey study	453
	Longitudinal panel survey study	833 (t_1)
	Cross-sectional survey study	760
	Cross-sectional survey study	672
Muench et al. (2020)	Longitudinal panel survey study	120
Mutsvairo et al. (2022)	Content analysis of interviews	10
Nguyen (2022)	Cross-sectional survey study	263
Olson et al. (2022)	Longitudinal experimental study with interventional design	51

(continued)

Table 4 (continued)

References	Research method	Sample size
	Longitudinal experimental study with RCT design	70
Phillips and Shipps (2022)	Cross-sectional survey study	475
Sheldon et al. (2011)	Cross-sectional survey study	1002
	Cross-sectional survey study	96
	Longitudinal panel survey study	98 (t_1)
	Longitudinal panel survey study	78
Skierkowski and Wood (2012)	Longitudinal experimental study with RCT design	23
Stieger and Lewetz (2018)	Longitudinal experimental study with interventional design	152
Sutton (2020)	Longitudinal ethnographic study	~ 1000
Tromholt (2016)	Longitudinal experimental study with RCT design	888
Turel et al. (2018)	Longitudinal experimental study with RCT design	555
Turel and Cavagnaro (2019)	Longitudinal experimental study with RCT design	415
Vally and D'Souza (2019)	Longitudinal experimental study with RCT design	78
van Wezel et al. (2021)	Longitudinal experimental study with RCT design	76
Vanman et al. (2018)	Longitudinal experimental study with RCT design	123
Widdicks et al. (2022)	Content analysis of workshop discussions	13
Wilcockson et al. (2019)	Longitudinal experimental study with interventional design	36

motivation to work. An overview of the methodological design of the five studies that examined digital detox in the research field of work environment can be found in Table 5.

4 Review Discussion

The review results provide a valuable foundation for future research activities on digital detox research. Based on our results, in the following we describe contributions and implications along with limitations that could provide opportunities for future research on this relatively nascent and highly relevant research topic.

Table 5 Digital detox studies in the research field of work environment

References	Research method(s)	Sample size
Basu (2019)	Cross-sectional survey study	70
Karlsen and Ytre-Arne (2022)	Content analysis of interviews	22
Mirbabaie et al. (2020)	Experimental study with RCT design	36
	Content analysis of interviews	12
Schmitt et al. (2021)	Cross-sectional survey study	403
Umasankar et al.(2022)	Cross-sectional survey study	463

4.1 Implications and Contributions

We contribute to research by providing a perspective on the methodological design of empirical digital detox studies. Overall, our review shows that most empirical studies on digital detox used surveys (34%) as research method, followed by a content analysis (30%) or experiments (30%), and only a small proportion used ethnography (4%), informal dialogues (1%) or observations (1%). Notably, this distribution varied by research field. For example, in the research field "Tourism" content analyses (71%) are predominantly used, whereas in the research field "Well-Being and Health", experiments (44%) or surveys (40%) are predominantly used.

The sample sizes of empirical digital detox studies ranged from 2 to 223,815 (mean [±SD]: 3,051 ± 24,843; median 78). Notably, this distribution varied by research method. For example, the sample size for surveys ranged from 68 to 3,539 (mean [±SD]: 495 ± 734; median 293), while for experiments it ranged from 10 to 888 (mean [±SD]: 157 ± 209; median 78).

As main implication, our review revealed that research on digital detox constitutes a nurturing ground for the application of measurement pluralism rather than focusing on a particular research approach. Based on the analysis of applied research approaches, we can draw two major implications for empirical digital detox studies. *First*, one possible research approach could be qualitative research combined with elements and benefits of quantitative research approaches in a mixed-methods approach (Venkatesh et al. 2013, 2016). Indeed, the sequential collection and analysis of qualitative and quantitative data contribute to gaining deeper insights into the perception of digital detox and expanding our current knowledge. As an example, Dickinson et al. (2016) used a qualitative research approach to explore digital detox in depth in a tourism context before then examining it in quantitative research to understand patterns in a broader context.

Second, to extend previous research findings, research could also incorporate neurophysiological measures as part of a multimethod research approach (Brewer and Hunter 1989; Johnson et al. 2007) to complement self-report or behavioral measures in research designs to draw more definitive conclusions about effects (e.g., Léger et al. 2014). Indeed, neuroscientific and neurophysiological tools and measurements play a vital role in advancing various research fields (e.g., interruption science; Stangl and

Riedl 2024b) and could be used to better understand human cognition, emotions, and behavior, along with their consequences, in the context of the development, adoption, and use of digital technologies (Riedl et al. 2010, 2017, 2014; Dimoka et al. 2012; Riedl and Léger 2016) (for a detailed discussion of methods used in cognitive neuroscience, please see Senior et al. 2009; for an overview of neurophysiological tools with a discussion of the strengths and weaknesses of each measurement method per research setting, please see Riedl and Léger 2016, pp. 47–72).

Among other neurophysiological measurements, heart rate and heart rate variability, for example, can be used as physiological indicators of autonomic nervous system activity for various measurement purposes, such as arousal or perceived stress (Stangl and Riedl 2022b). In particular, advancing technology has enabled various methods to track and monitor physiological parameters, including smart clothing or other wearable devices, which could be used as a potential early warning system to detect stress in the workplace in real time (Stangl and Riedl 2022a, 2022c).

Notably, we also identified three studies (i.e., Dunican et al. 2017; Anrijs et al. 2018; Vanman et al. 2018) that used neurophysiological measurements in their research. For example, Vanman et al. Tobin (2018) measured participants' salivary cortisol, which is considered an objective indicator of stress (Rohleder et al. 2006; Pearlmutter et al. 2020). Hence, conducting studies with neuroscientific and neurophysiological measurements (e.g., salivary cortisol before and after digital detox intervention) seems promising to advance digital detox research (for a review on digital detoxing from a neurophysiological measurement perspective, please see Stangl and Riedl 2024a). Overall, a combination of different research approaches offers promising opportunities for future research to explore and systematically examine digital detox.

4.2 Limitations

Our work is not free of limitations. First, a limitation of our review is the language restriction, as we only included studies in German or English. Therefore, the results cannot be generalized and excluded studies in other languages. As an example, we identified a study in Turkish (Sunar et al. 2018), which we were unable to include in this review.

Second, the number of search terms and search strings used is another limitation. Due to the conceptual ambiguity in digital detox research (Mirbabaie et al. 2022), it is possible that some empirical research was overlooked and not included in the literature review. To the best of our knowledge, however, this review is the most comprehensive review of peer-reviewed empirical digital detox studies currently available, as other reviews were able to identify a much smaller number of studies despite the inclusion of non-peer-reviewed papers. For example, the review by Özdemir and Goktas (2021) identified 20 studies and the review by Radtke et al. (2022) identified 21 studies. Future research addressing the above limitations could therefore provide further insights into digital detox research.

5 Concluding Remarks

Digital detox seems promising to enable a conscious, temporary break from the digital world. Indeed, research has shown that various digital detox measures help to reduce stress, strengthen social bonds, and escape from the daily hustle. Especially in recent years, the number of scientific publications on digital detox has increased steadily. Therefore, to survey and analyze the previous research and the methodological design of the empirical digital detox studies, a systematic literature review was conducted, which also provides researchers with an important overview of the different methodological designs to investigate digital detox.

We conclude that research on digital detox is still in a relatively nascent stage. However, we expect an increasing number of further publications on this highly relevant research topic in the coming years. Hence, it will be rewarding to see what insights future research will reveal on digital detox.

Acknowledgements This research was funded by the Austrian Science Fund (FWF) as part of the project "Technostress in Organizations" (project number: P 30865) and by the Federal State of Upper Austria through the Austrian Research Promotion Agency (FFG) as part of the project "Interruption" at the University of Applied Sciences Upper Austria.

References

Aiello, J. R. and Kolb, K. J. (1995) 'Electronic performance monitoring and social context: Impact on productivity and stress', *Journal of Applied Psychology*, 80(3), pp. 339–353.

Amato, A., Rovai, M. and Andreoli, M. (2019) 'Digital detox tourism as a resource for the enhancement of cultural heritage. A development study for Certosa di Pisa in Calci (Tuscany)', in *Proceedings of the International Forum on World Heritage and Legacy Culture Creativity Contamination.*

Anashkina, N., Shmatko, M. and Tkachenko, O. (2020) 'Digital-detox technology for vocational guidance selection of applicants for media communications area', *Mediaobrazovanie*, 60(4), pp. 570–580.

Anderson, B. B. *et al.* (2016) 'How users perceive and respond to security messages: A NeuroIS research agenda and empirical study', *European Journal of Information Systems*, 25(4), pp. 364–390. https://doi.org/10.1057/ejis.2015.21.

Anrijs, S. *et al.* (2018) 'MobileDNA: Relating physiological stress measurements to smartphone usage to assess the effect of a digital detox', in Stephanidis, C. (ed.) *HCI International 2018—Posters' Extended Abstracts: 20th International Conference, HCI International 2018, Las Vegas, NV, USA, July 15–20, 2018, Proceedings, Part II*. CCIS. Cham: Springer, pp. 356–363. https://doi.org/10.1007/978-3-319-92279-9_48.

Ayyagari, R., Grover, V. and Purvis, R. (2011) 'Technostress: Technological antecedents and implications', *MIS Quarterly*, 35(4), pp. 831–858. https://doi.org/10.2307/41409963.

Baham, C. *et al.* (2022) 'Generational differences in handling technology interruptions: A qualitative study', *European Journal of Information Systems*, pp. 1–21. https://doi.org/10.1080/0960085X.2022.2070557.

Bailenson, J. N. (2021) 'Nonverbal overload: A theoretical argument for the causes of Zoom fatigue', *Technology, Mind, and Behavior*, 2(1). https://doi.org/10.1037/tmb0000030.

Barki, H., Rivard, S. and Talbot, J. (1988) 'An information systems keyword classification scheme', *MIS Quarterly*, 12(2), pp. 299–322. https://doi.org/10.2307/248855.

Basu, R. (2019) 'Impact of digital detox on individual performance of the employees', *International Journal of Research and Analytical Reviews*, 6(2), pp. 378–381.

Baumer, E. P. S. *et al.* (2015) 'Missing photos, suffering withdrawal, or finding freedom? How experiences of social media non-use influence the likelihood of reversion', *Social Media + Society*, 1(2), pp. 1–14. https://doi.org/10.1177/2056305115614851.

Bharadwaj, A. *et al.* (2013) 'Digital business strategy: Toward a next generation of insights', *MIS Quarterly*, 37(2), pp. 471–482. https://doi.org/10.25300/MISQ/2013/37:2.3.

Brailovskaia, J. *et al.* (2020) 'Less Facebook use—More well-being and a healthier lifestyle? An experimental intervention study', *Computers in Human Behavior*, 108, p. 106332. https://doi.org/10.1016/j.chb.2020.106332.

Brewer, J. and Hunter, A. (1989) *Multimethod research: A synthesis of styles*. Newbury Park: Sage Publications.

Brown, L. and Kuss, D. J. (2020) 'Fear of missing out, mental wellbeing, and social connectedness: A seven-day social media abstinence trial', *International Journal of Environmental Research and Public Health*, 17(12), p. 4566. https://doi.org/10.3390/ijerph17124566.

Cai, W. and McKenna, B. (2023) 'Power and resistance: Digital-free tourism in a connected world', *Journal of Travel Research*, 62(2), pp. 290–304. https://doi.org/10.1177/00472875211061208.

Cesareo, M. *et al.* (2021) 'The ubiquity of social reinforcement: A nudging exploratory study to reduce the overuse of smartphones in social contexts', *Cogent Psychology*. Edited by D. O'Connor, 8(1), p. 1880304. https://doi.org/10.1080/23311908.2021.1880304.

Chen, A. J. and Karahanna, E. (2018) 'Life interrupted: The effects of technology-mediated work interruptions on work and nonwork outcomes', *MIS Quarterly*, 42(4), pp. 1023–1042. https://doi.org/10.25300/MISQ/2018/13631.

Chong, S. W. and Reinders, H. (2021) 'A methodological review of qualitative research syntheses in CALL: The state-of-the-art', *System*, 103, p. 102646. https://doi.org/10.1016/j.system.2021.102646.

Couffe, C. and Michael, G. A. (2017) 'Failures due to interruptions or distractions: A review and a new framework', *The American Journal of Psychology*, 130(2), pp. 163–181. https://doi.org/10.5406/amerjpsyc.130.2.0163.

Díaz-Meneses, G. and Estupinán-Ojeda, M. (2022) 'The outbreak of digital detox motives and their public health implications for holiday destinations', *International Journal of Environmental Research and Public Health*, 19(3), p. 1548. https://doi.org/10.3390/ijerph19031548.

Dickinson, J. E., Hibbert, J. F. and Filimonau, V. (2016) 'Mobile technology and the tourist experience: (Dis)connection at the campsite', *Tourism Management*, 57, pp. 193–201. https://doi.org/10.1016/j.tourman.2016.06.005.

Dimoka, A. *et al.* (2012) 'On the use of neurophysiological tools in IS research: Developing a research agenda for NeuroIS', *MIS Quarterly*, 36(3), pp. 679–702. https://doi.org/10.2307/41703475.

Dunican, I. C. *et al.* (2017) 'The effects of the removal of electronic devices for 48 hours on sleep in elite judo athletes', *Journal of Strength and Conditioning Research*, 31(10), pp. 2832–2839. https://doi.org/10.1519/JSC.0000000000001697.

Egger, I., Lei, S. I. and Wassler, P. (2020) 'Digital free tourism—An exploratory study of tourist motivations', *Tourism Management*, 79, p. 104098. https://doi.org/10.1016/j.tourman.2020.104098.

Eide, T. A. *et al.* (2018) 'Smartphone restriction and its effect on subjective withdrawal related scores', *Frontiers in Psychology*, 9, p. 1444. https://doi.org/10.3389/fpsyg.2018.01444.

El-Khoury, J. *et al.* (2021) 'Characteristics of social media "detoxification" in university students', *Libyan Journal of Medicine*, 16(1), p. 1846861. https://doi.org/10.1080/19932820.2020.1846861.

Emurian, H. H. (1991) 'Physiological responses during data retrieval: Comparison of constant and variable system response times', *Computers in Human Behavior*, 7(4), pp. 291–310. https://doi.org/10.1016/0747-5632(91)90017-U.

Emurian, H. H. (1993) 'Cardiovascular and electromyograph effects of low and high density work on an interactive information system', *Computers in Human Behavior*, 9(4), pp. 353–370. https://doi.org/10.1016/0747-5632(93)90028-Q.

Fan, D. X. F., Buhalis, D. and Lin, B. (2019) 'A tourist typology of online and face-to-face social contact: Destination immersion and tourism encapsulation/decapsulation', *Annals of Tourism Research*, 78, p. 102757. https://doi.org/10.1016/j.annals.2019.102757.

Fioravanti, G., Prostamo, A. and Casale, S. (2020) 'Taking a short break from Instagram: The effects on subjective well-being', *Cyberpsychology, Behavior, and Social Networking*, 23(2), pp. 107–112. https://doi.org/10.1089/cyber.2019.0400.

Fischer, T. and Riedl, R. (2017) 'Technostress research: A nurturing ground for measurement pluralism?', *Communications of the Association for Information Systems*, 40(17), pp. 375–401. https://doi.org/10.17705/1CAIS.04017.

Floros, C. *et al.* (2021) 'Imagine being off-the-grid: Millennials' perceptions of digital-free travel', *Journal of Sustainable Tourism*, 29(5), pp. 751–766. https://doi.org/10.1080/09669582.2019.1675676.

Fryman, S. and Romine, W. (2021) 'Measuring smartphone dependency and exploration of consequences and comorbidities', *Computers in Human Behavior Reports*, 4, p. 100108. https://doi.org/10.1016/j.chbr.2021.100108.

Hall, J. A. *et al.* (2021) 'Experimentally manipulating social media abstinence: Results of a four-week diary study', *Media Psychology*, 24(2), pp. 259–275. https://doi.org/10.1080/15213269.2019.1688171.

Handa, M. and Ahuja, P. (2020) 'Disconnect to detox: A study of smartphone addiction among young adults in India', *Young Consumers*, 21(3), pp. 273–287. https://doi.org/10.1108/YC-12-2019-1077.

Hanley, S. M., Watt, S. E. and Coventry, W. (2019) 'Taking a break: The effect of taking a vacation from Facebook and Instagram on subjective well-being', *PLOS ONE*. Edited by J. Jankowski, 14(6), p. e0217743. https://doi.org/10.1371/journal.pone.0217743.

Hassan, T. H., Salem, A. E. and Saleh, M. I. (2022) 'Digital-free tourism holiday as a new approach for tourism well-being: Tourists' attributional approach', *International Journal of Environmental Research and Public Health*, 19(10), p. 5974. https://doi.org/10.3390/ijerph19105974.

Helsper, E. J. and Reisdorf, B. C. (2013) 'A quantitative examination of explanations for reasons for internet nonuse', *Cyberpsychology, Behavior, and Social Networking*, 16(2), pp. 94–99. https://doi.org/10.1089/cyber.2012.0257.

Hesselberth, P. (2018) 'Discourses on disconnectivity and the right to disconnect', *New Media & Society*, 20(5), pp. 1994–2010. https://doi.org/10.1177/1461444817711449.

Hinsch, C. and Sheldon, K. M. (2013) 'The impact of frequent social Internet consumption: Increased procrastination and lower life satisfaction', *Journal of Consumer Behaviour*, 12(6), pp. 496–505. https://doi.org/10.1002/cb.1453.

Hunt, M. G. *et al.* (2018) 'No more FOMO: Limiting social media decreases loneliness and depression', *Journal of Social and Clinical Psychology*, 37(10), pp. 751–768. https://doi.org/10.1521/jscp.2018.37.10.751.

Jenkins, J. L. *et al.* (2016) 'More harm than good? How messages that interrupt can make us vulnerable', *Information Systems Research*, 27(4), pp. 880–896. https://doi.org/10.1287/isre.2016.0644.

Jiang, Y. and Balaji, M. S. (2022) 'Getting unwired: What drives travellers to take a digital detox holiday?', *Tourism Recreation Research*, 47(5–6), pp. 453–469. https://doi.org/10.1080/02508281.2021.1889801.

Johnson, R. B., Onwuegbuzie, A. J. and Turner, L. A. (2007) 'Toward a definition of mixed methods research', *Journal of Mixed Methods Research*, 1(2), pp. 112–133. https://doi.org/10.1177/1558689806298224.

Jorge, A. (2019) 'Social media, interrupted: Users recounting temporary disconnection on Instagram', *Social Media + Society*, 5(4), pp. 1–19. https://doi.org/10.1177/2056305119881691.

Kalischko, T. and Riedl, R. (2020) 'Physiological measurement in the research field of electronic performance monitoring: Review and a call for NeuroIS studies', in Davis, F. D. et al. (eds) *Information Systems and Neuroscience: NeuroIS Retreat 2020*. LNISO. Cham: Springer, pp. 233–243. https://doi.org/10.1007/978-3-030-60073-0_27.

Kalischko, T. and Riedl, R. (2021) 'Electronic performance monitoring in the digital workplace: Conceptualization, review of effects and moderators, and future research opportunities', *Frontiers in Psychology*, 12, p. 633031. https://doi.org/10.3389/fpsyg.2021.633031.

Kalischko, T., Fischer, T. and Riedl, R. (2020) 'Techno-unreliability: A pilot study in the field', in Davis, F. D. et al. (eds) *Information Systems and Neuroscience: NeuroIS Retreat 2019*. LNISO. Cham: Springer, pp. 137–145. https://doi.org/10.1007/978-3-030-28144-1_15.

Karlsen, F. and Ytre-Arne, B. (2022) 'Intrusive media and knowledge work: How knowledge workers negotiate digital media norms in the pursuit of focused work', *Information, Communication & Society*, 25(15), pp. 2174–2189. https://doi.org/10.1080/1369118X.2021.1933561.

Karlsen, F. (2020) 'Digital detox camp: Values and motivations for engaging in digital disconnect', *Proceedings of the 21st Annual Conference of the Association of Internet Researchers*. https://doi.org/10.5210/spir.v2020i0.11244.

Keller, J. *et al.* (2021) 'A mobile intervention for self-efficacious and goal-directed smartphone use in the general population: Randomized controlled trial', *JMIR mHealth and uHealth*, 9(11), p. e26397. https://doi.org/10.2196/26397.

Kent, R. (2020) 'Self-tracking health over time: From the use of Instagram to perform optimal health to the protective shield of the digital detox', *Social Media + Society*, 6(3), pp. 1–14. https://doi.org/10.1177/2056305120940694.

Ko, M. *et al.* (2015) 'NUGU: A group-based intervention app for improving self-regulation of limiting smartphone use', in *Proceedings of the 18th ACM Conference on Computer Supported Cooperative Work & Social Computing*. New York, NY, USA: ACM, pp. 1235–1245. https://doi.org/10.1145/2675133.2675244.

Léger, P.-M. *et al.* (2014) 'Precision is in the eye of the beholder: Application of eye fixation-related potentials to information systems research', *Journal of the Association for Information Systems*, 15(10), pp. 651–678. https://doi.org/10.17705/1jais.00376.

Li, J., Pearce, P. L. and Oktadiana, H. (2020) 'Can digital-free tourism build character strengths?', *Annals of Tourism Research*, 85, p. 103037. https://doi.org/10.1016/j.annals.2020.103037.

Liao, M. and Sundar, S. S. (2022) '#facebookdown: Time to panic or detox? Understanding users' reactions to social media outage', in *Proceedings of the CHI Conference on Human Factors in Computing Systems*, pp. 1–8. https://doi.org/10.1145/3491101.3519674.

Liu, H. *et al.* (2021) 'COVID-19 information overload and generation Z's social media discontinuance intention during the pandemic lockdown', *Technological Forecasting and Social Change*, 166, p. 120600. https://doi.org/10.1016/j.techfore.2021.120600.

Matthes, J. *et al.* (2022) 'Reflective smartphone disengagement: Conceptualization, measurement, and validation', *Computers in Human Behavior*, 128, p. 107078. https://doi.org/10.1016/j.chb.2021.107078.

Melville, N., Kraemer, K. and Gurbaxani, V. (2004) 'Information technology and organizational performance: An integrative model of IT business value', *MIS Quarterly*, 28(2), pp. 283–322. https://doi.org/10.2307/25148636.

Mirbabaie, M., Stieglitz, S. and Marx, J. (2022) 'Digital detox', *Business & Information Systems Engineering*, 64(2), pp. 239–246. https://doi.org/10.1007/s12599-022-00747-x.

Mirbabaie, M. *et al.* (2020) 'Digital detox – Mitigating digital overuse in times of remote work and social isolation', in *Proceedings of the 31st Australasian Conference on Information Systems*.

Montag, C. *et al.* (2022) 'On the associations between videoconference fatigue, burnout and depression including personality associations', *Journal of Affective Disorders Reports*, 10, p. 100409. https://doi.org/10.1016/j.jadr.2022.100409.

Muench, C. *et al.* (2020) 'Time to log off: An analysis of factors influencing the willingness to participate in a long-term "Digital Detox" with the smartphone', in Stephanidis, C. and Antona, M. (eds) *HCI International 2020 - Posters: 22nd International Conference, HCII 2020, Copenhagen, Denmark, July 19–24, 2020, Proceedings, Part III*. CCIS. Cham: Springer, pp. 209–216. https://doi.org/10.1007/978-3-030-50732-9_28.

Mutsvairo, B., Ragnedda, M. and Mabvundwi, K. (2022) '"Our old pastor thinks the mobile phone is a source of evil." Capturing contested and conflicting insights on digital wellbeing and digital detoxing in an age of rapid mobile connectivity', *Media International Australia*, pp. 1–15. https://doi.org/10.1177/1329878X221090992.

Nguyen, V. T. (2022) 'The perceptions of social media users of digital detox apps considering personality traits', *Education and Information Technologies*, 27(7), pp. 9293–9316. https://doi.org/10.1007/s10639-022-11022-7.

Olson, J. A. *et al.* (2022) 'A nudge-based intervention to reduce problematic smartphone use: Randomised controlled trial', *International Journal of Mental Health and Addiction*. https://doi.org/10.1007/s11469-022-00826-w.

Özdemir, M. A. and Goktas, L. S. (2021) 'Research trends on digital detox holidays: A bibliometric analysis, 2012-2020', *Tourism & Management Studies*, 17(3), pp. 21–35. https://doi.org/10.18089/tms.2021.170302.

Paré, G. *et al.* (2015) 'Synthesizing information systems knowledge: A typology of literature reviews', *Information & Management*, 52(2), pp. 183–199. https://doi.org/10.1016/j.im.2014.08.008.

Paris, C. M. *et al.* (2015) 'Disconnected and unplugged: Experiences of technology induced anxieties and tensions while traveling', in Tussyadiah, I. and Inversini, A. (eds) *Information and Communication Technologies in Tourism 2015: Proceedings of the International Conference in Lugano, Switzerland, February 3–6, 2015*. Cham: Springer, pp. 803–816. https://doi.org/10.1007/978-3-319-14343-9_58.

Pawłowska-Legwand, A. and Matoga, Ł. (2021) 'Disconnect from the digital world to reconnect with the real life: An analysis of the potential for development of unplugged tourism on the example of Poland', *Tourism Planning & Development*, 18(6), pp. 649–672. https://doi.org/10.1080/21568316.2020.1842487.

Pearce, P. L. and Gretzel, U. (2012) 'Tourism in technology dead zones: Documenting experiential dimensions', *International Journal of Tourism Sciences*, 12(2), pp. 1–20. https://doi.org/10.1080/15980634.2012.11434656.

Pearlmutter, P. *et al.* (2020) 'Sweat and saliva cortisol response to stress and nutrition factors', *Scientific Reports*, 10(1), p. 19050. https://doi.org/10.1038/s41598-020-75871-3.

Pflügner, K. *et al.* (2021) 'Personality profiles that put users at risk of perceiving technostress: A qualitative comparative analysis with the Big Five personality traits', *Business & Information Systems Engineering*, 63(4), pp. 389–402. https://doi.org/10.1007/s12599-020-00668-7.

Phillips, B. and Shipps, B. (2022) 'Problematic technology use: The impact of personality and continued use', *The Journal of the Southern Association for Information Systems*, 9(1), pp. 38–63. https://doi.org/10.17705/3JSIS.00021.

Pinsonneault, A. and Kraemer, K. (1993) 'Survey research methodology in management information systems: An assessment', *Journal of Management Information Systems*, 10(2), pp. 75–105. https://doi.org/10.1080/07421222.1993.11518001.

Puranik, H., Koopman, J. and Vough, H. C. (2020) 'Pardon the interruption: An integrative review and future research agenda for research on work interruptions', *Journal of Management*, 46(6), pp. 806–842. https://doi.org/10.1177/0149206319887428.

Purohit, A. K., Barclay, L. and Holzer, A. (2020) 'Designing for digital detox: Making social media less addictive with digital nudges', in *Proceedings of the CHI Conference on Human Factors in Computing Systems*, pp. 1–9. https://doi.org/10.1145/3334480.3382810.

Radtke, T. *et al.* (2022) 'Digital detox: An effective solution in the smartphone era? A systematic literature review', *Mobile Media & Communication*, 10(2), pp. 190–215. https://doi.org/10.1177/20501579211028647.

Reinecke, L. *et al.* (2017) 'Digital stress over the life span: The effects of communication load and internet multitasking on perceived stress and psychological health impairments in a German probability sample', *Media Psychology*, 20(1), pp. 90–115. https://doi.org/10.1080/15213269.2015.1121832.

Riedl, R. and Fischer, T. (2018) 'System response time as a stressor in a digital world: Literature review and theoretical model', in Nah, F. F.-H. and Xiao, B. S. (eds) *HCI in Business, Government, and Organizations: 5th International Conference, HCIBGO 2018, Held as Part of HCI International 2018, Las Vegas, NV, USA, July 15–20, 2018, Proceedings*. LNISA. Cham: Springer, pp. 175–186. https://doi.org/10.1007/978-3-319-91716-0_14.

Riedl, R. and Léger, P.-M. (2016) *Fundamentals of NeuroIS: Information systems and the brain*. Heidelberg: Springer. https://doi.org/10.1007/978-3-662-45091-8.

Riedl, R. *et al.* (2010) 'On the foundations of NeuroIS: Reflections on the Gmunden Retreat 2009', *Communications of the Association for Information Systems*, 27(15), pp. 243–264. https://doi.org/10.17705/1CAIS.02715.

Riedl, R. *et al.* (2012) 'Technostress from a neurobiological perspective: System breakdown increases the stress hormone cortisol in computer users', *Business & Information Systems Engineering*, 4(2), pp. 61–69. https://doi.org/10.1007/s12599-012-0207-7.

Riedl, R. *et al.* (2013) 'Computer breakdown as a stress factor during task completion under time pressure: Identifying gender differences based on skin conductance', *Advances in Human-Computer Interaction*, 2013, p. 420169. https://doi.org/10.1155/2013/420169.

Riedl, R., Davis, F. D. and Hevner, A. R. (2014) 'Towards a NeuroIS research methodology: Intensifying the discussion on methods, tools, and measurement', *Journal of the Association for Information Systems*, 15(10), pp. I–XXXV. https://doi.org/10.17705/1jais.00377.

Riedl, R. et al. (2017) Neuroscience in information systems research: Applying knowledge of brain functionality without neuroscience tools. Cham: Springer. https://doi.org/10.1007/978-3-319-48755-7.

Riedl, R. (2013) 'On the biology of technostress: Literature review and research agenda', *ACM SIGMIS Database: The DATA BASE for Advances in Information Systems*, 44(1), pp. 18–55. https://doi.org/10.1145/2436239.2436242.

Riedl, R. (2022) 'On the stress potential of videoconferencing: Definition and root causes of Zoom fatigue', *Electronic Markets*, 32(1), pp. 153–177. https://doi.org/10.1007/s12525-021-00501-3.

Rohleder, N. *et al.* (2006) 'The psychosocial stress-induced increase in salivary alpha-amylase is independent of saliva flow rate', *Psychophysiology*, 43(6), pp. 645–652. https://doi.org/10.1111/j.1469-8986.2006.00457.x.

Schmitt, J. B., Breuer, J. and Wulf, T. (2021) 'From cognitive overload to digital detox: Psychological implications of telework during the COVID-19 pandemic', *Computers in Human Behavior*, 124, p. 106899. https://doi.org/10.1016/j.chb.2021.106899.

Schryen, G. *et al.* (2017) 'Literature reviews in IS research: What can be learnt from the past and other fields?', *Communications of the Association for Information Systems*, 41(30), pp. 759–774. https://doi.org/10.17705/1CAIS.04130.

Schryen, G. *et al.* (2020) 'A knowledge development perspective on literature reviews: Validation of a new typology in the IS field', *Communications of the Association for Information Systems*, 46(7), pp. 134–186. https://doi.org/10.17705/1CAIS.04607.

Schwarzenegger, C. and Lohmeier, C. (2021) 'Creating opportunities for temporary disconnection: How tourism professionals provide alternatives to being permanently online', *Convergence: The International Journal of Research into New Media Technologies*, 27(6), pp. 1631–1647. https://doi.org/10.1177/13548565211033385.

Senior, C., Russell, T. and Gazzaniga, M. S. (2009) *Methods in mind*. Cambridge: MIT Press.

Sheldon, K. M., Abad, N. and Hinsch, C. (2011) 'A two-process view of Facebook use and relatedness need-satisfaction: Disconnection drives use, and connection rewards it', *Journal of Personality and Social Psychology*, 100(4), pp. 766–775. https://doi.org/10.1037/a0022407.

Skierkowski, D. and Wood, R. M. (2012) 'To text or not to text? The importance of text messaging among college-aged youth', *Computers in Human Behavior*, 28(2), pp. 744–756. https://doi.org/10.1016/j.chb.2011.11.023.

Smith, M. J. *et al.* (1992) 'Employee stress and health complaints in jobs with and without electronic performance monitoring', *Applied Ergonomics*, 23(1), pp. 17–27. https://doi.org/10.1016/0003-6870(92)90006-H.

Stangl, F. J. and Riedl, R. (2022a) 'Measurement of heart rate and heart rate variability: A review of NeuroIS research with a focus on applied methods', in Davis, F. D. et al. (eds) *Information Systems and Neuroscience: NeuroIS Retreat 2022*. LNISO. Cham: Springer, pp. 269–283. https://doi.org/10.1007/978-3-031-13064-9_28.

Stangl, F. J. and Riedl, R. (2022b) 'Measurement of heart rate and heart rate variability in NeuroIS research: Review of empirical results', in Davis, F. D. et al. (eds) *Information Systems and Neuroscience: NeuroIS Retreat 2022*. LNISO. Cham: Springer, pp. 285–299. https://doi.org/10.1007/978-3-031-13064-9_29.

Stangl, F. J. and Riedl, R. (2022c) 'Measurement of heart rate and heart rate variability with wearable devices: A systematic review', in *Proceedings of the 17th International Conference on Wirtschaftsinformatik*.

Stangl, F. J. and Riedl, R. (2023a) 'Digital Detoxing als Maßnahme gegen digitalen Stress: Auf die Verwendung digitaler Technologien temporär verzichten', *Theologisch-praktische Quartalschrift*, 171(3), pp. 274–283.

Stangl, F. J. and Riedl, R. (2023b) 'Interruption science as a research field: Towards a taxonomy of interruptions as a foundation for the field', *Frontiers in Psychology*, 14, p. 1043426. https://doi.org/10.3389/fpsyg.2023.1043426.

Stangl, F. J. and Riedl, R. (2023c) 'Interruptions in the workplace: An exploratory study among digital business professionals', in Nah, F. F.-H. and Siau, K. (eds) *HCI in Business, Government and Organizations: 10th International Conference, HCIBGO 2023, Held as Part of the 25th HCI International Conference, HCII 2023, Copenhagen, Denmark, July 23–28, 2023, Proceedings, Part II*. LNCS. Cham: Springer, pp. 400–422. https://doi.org/10.1007/978-3-031-36049-7_29.

Stangl, F. J. and Riedl, R. (2024a) 'Neurophysiological measurements in the research field of digital detoxing: Review and implications for future research', in Davis, F. D. et al. (eds) *Information Systems and Neuroscience: NeuroIS Retreat 2023, Vienna, Austria*. LNISO. Cham: Springer, pp. 105–121. https://doi.org/10.1007/978-3-031-58396-4_10.

Stangl, F. J. and Riedl, R. (2024b) 'Neurophysiological measurements in the research field of interruption science: Insights into applied methods for different interruption types based on an umbrella review', in Davis, F. D. et al. (eds) *Information Systems and Neuroscience: NeuroIS Retreat 2023, Vienna, Austria*. LNISO. Cham: Springer, pp. 123–152. https://doi.org/10.1007/978-3-031-58396-4_11.

Stangl, F. J. *et al.* (2023) 'Negative psychological and physiological effects of social networking site use: The example of Facebook', *Frontiers in Psychology*, 14, p. 1141663. https://doi.org/10.3389/fpsyg.2023.1141663.

Statista (2022) *Most popular social networks worldwide as of January 2022, ranked by number of monthly active users (in millions)*. Available at: https://www.statista.com/statistics/272014/global-social-networks-ranked-by-number-of-users/ (Accessed: 11 February 2023).

Stephanidis, C. *et al.* (2019) 'Seven HCI grand challenges', *International Journal of Human–Computer Interaction*, 35(14), pp. 1229–1269. https://doi.org/10.1080/10447318.2019.1619259.

Stieger, S. and Lewetz, D. (2018) 'A week without using social media: Results from an ecological momentary intervention study using smartphones', *Cyberpsychology, Behavior, and Social Networking*, 21(10), pp. 618–624. https://doi.org/10.1089/cyber.2018.0070.

Sunar, H., Gökçe, F. and Cihangir, İ. S. (2018) 'A new approach to tourism: Digital restoration', in *Proceedings of the Conference on Innovation and Global Issues in Social Sciences*, pp. 318–330.

Sutton, T. (2020) 'Digital harm and addiction: An anthropological view', *Anthropology Today*, 36(1), pp. 17–22. https://doi.org/10.1111/1467-8322.12553.

Syvertsen, T. and Enli, G. (2020) 'Digital detox: Media resistance and the promise of authenticity', *Convergence: The International Journal of Research into New Media Technologies*, 26(5–6), pp. 1269–1283. https://doi.org/10.1177/1354856519847325.

Syvertsen, T. (2022) 'Offline tourism: Digital and screen ambivalence in Norwegian mountain huts with no internet access', *Scandinavian Journal of Hospitality and Tourism*, 22(3), pp. 195–209. https://doi.org/10.1080/15022250.2022.2070540.

Tams, S. *et al.* (2020) 'Worker stress in the age of mobile technology: The combined effects of perceived interruption overload and worker control', *Journal of Strategic Information Systems*, 29(1), p. 101595. https://doi.org/10.1016/j.jsis.2020.101595.

Tarafdar, M., Tu, Q. and Ragu-Nathan, T. S. (2010) 'Impact of technostress on end-user satisfaction and performance', *Journal of Management Information Systems*, 27(3), pp. 303–334. https://doi.org/10.2753/MIS0742-1222270311.

Tarafdar, M., Gupta, A. and Turel, O. (2013) 'The dark side of information technology use', *Information Systems Journal*, 23(3), pp. 269–275. https://doi.org/10.1111/isj.12015.

Tromholt, M. (2016) 'The Facebook experiment: Quitting Facebook leads to higher levels of well-being', *Cyberpsychology, Behavior, and Social Networking*, 19(11), pp. 661–666. https://doi.org/10.1089/cyber.2016.0259.

Turel, O. and Cavagnaro, D. R. (2019) 'Effect of abstinence from social media on time perception: Differences between low-and at-risk for social media "addiction" groups', *Psychiatric Quarterly*, 90(1), pp. 217–227. https://doi.org/10.1007/s11126-018-9614-3.

Turel, O., Cavagnaro, D. R. and Meshi, D. (2018) 'Short abstinence from online social networking sites reduces perceived stress, especially in excessive users', *Psychiatry Research*, 270, pp. 947–953. https://doi.org/10.1016/j.psychres.2018.11.017.

Ugur, N. G. and Koc, T. (2015) 'Time for digital detox: Misuse of mobile technology and phubbing', *Procedia—Social and Behavioral Sciences*, 195, pp. 1022–1031. https://doi.org/10.1016/j.sbspro.2015.06.491.

Umasankar, M. *et al.* (2022) 'Disconnect to reconnect: Employee wellbeing through digital detoxing', *Journal of Positive School Psychology*, 6(2), pp. 4463–4673.

Vally, Z. and D'Souza, C. G. (2019) 'Abstinence from social media use, subjective well-being, stress, and loneliness', *Perspectives in Psychiatric Care*, 55(4), pp. 752–759. https://doi.org/10.1111/ppc.12431.

van Wezel, M. M. C., Abrahamse, E. L. and Vanden Abeele, M. M. P. (2021) 'Does a 7-day restriction on the use of social media improve cognitive functioning and emotional well-being? Results from a randomized controlled trial', *Addictive Behaviors Reports*, 14, p. 100365. https://doi.org/10.1016/j.abrep.2021.100365.

Vanman, E. J., Baker, R. and Tobin, S. J. (2018) 'The burden of online friends: The effects of giving up Facebook on stress and well-being', *The Journal of Social Psychology*, 158(4), pp. 496–508. https://doi.org/10.1080/00224545.2018.1453467.

Venkatesh, V., Brown, S. A. and Bala, H. (2013) 'Bridging the qualitative-quantitative divide: Guidelines for conducting mixed methods research in information systems', *MIS Quarterly*, 37(1), pp. 21–54. https://doi.org/10.25300/MISQ/2013/37.1.02.

Venkatesh, V., Brown, S. A. and Sullivan, Y. (2016) 'Guidelines for conducting mixed-methods research: An extension and illustration', *Journal of the Association for Information Systems*, 17(7), pp. 435–494. https://doi.org/10.17705/1jais.00433.

vom Brocke, J. *et al.* (2009) 'Reconstructing the giant: On the importance of rigour in documenting the literature search process', in Newell, S. et al. (eds) *Proceedings of the 17th European Conference on Information Systems*, pp. 2206–2217.

Webster, J. and Watson, R. T. (2002) 'Analyzing the past to prepare for the future: Writing a literature review', *MIS Quarterly*, 26(2), pp. xiii–xxiii.

Widdicks, K. *et al.* (2022) 'Escaping unsustainable digital interactions: Toward "more meaningful" and "moderate" online experiences', *International Journal of Human-Computer Studies*, 165, p. 102853. https://doi.org/10.1016/j.ijhcs.2022.102853.

Wilcockson, T. D. W., Osborne, A. M. and Ellis, D. A. (2019) 'Digital detox: The effect of smartphone abstinence on mood, anxiety, and craving', *Addictive Behaviors*, 99, p. 106013. https://doi.org/10.1016/j.addbeh.2019.06.002.

Wood, N. T. and Muñoz, C. (2021) 'Unplugged: Digital detox enhances student learning', *Marketing Education Review*, 31(1), pp. 14–25. https://doi.org/10.1080/10528008.2020.1836973.

Wysocki, S. (2019) *The digital detox story*. Available at: https://www.digitaldetox.com/blog/the-digital-detox-story (Accessed: 11 February 2023).

Zhang, M. and Zhang, X. (2022) 'Between escape and return: Rethinking daily life and travel in selective unplugging', *Tourism Management*, 91, p. 104521. https://doi.org/10.1016/j.tourman.2022.104521.

Shopping in a Virtual Reality: A Stimulus-Organism-Response (S-O-R) Based Systematic Literature Review

Sophia Elsholz, Jakob J. Korbel, and Rüdiger Zarnekow

Abstract The virtual reality (VR) technology has become increasingly relevant in recent years due to the advantages that occur through the representation of the real within a virtual world. One promising application area of VR is virtual shopping, i.e., providing customers with the ability to visit virtual stores instead of purchasing products on 2D websites or brick-and-mortar stores. To gain insights into the opportunities of the technology in the realm of shopping, we emphasize and discuss the literature on the use of VR for shopping based on a systematic literature review, thereby deepening our understanding of virtual retail concepts and synthesizing the empirical evidence on the advantages of VR. For this purpose, we developed a stimulus-organism-response (S-O-R) based framework to summarize the key findings. The results comprise suggestions for VR shopping applications as well as possible future research avenues.

Keywords Virtual reality · VR · Retail · Shopping · SOR

1 Introduction

In recent years, the online sale of products, i.e., E-commerce, has become increasingly important, not least because of the COVID-19 pandemic. The lockdowns during the pandemic fostered the relevance of E-commerce, as brick-and-mortar stores had to close and find new ways to distribute their products (Nistor 2021). However, traditional online shops are associated with several disadvantages compared to shopping

S. Elsholz (✉) · J. J. Korbel · R. Zarnekow
Technische Universität Berlin, Chair of Information and Communication Management, Berlin, Germany
e-mail: s.elsholz@tu-berlin.de

J. J. Korbel
e-mail: jakob.j.korbel@tu-berlin.de

R. Zarnekow
e-mail: ruediger.zarnekow@tu-berlin.de

D. Beverungen et al. (eds.), *Conceptualizing Digital Responsibility for the Information Age*, Lecture Notes in Information Systems and Organisation 74,
https://doi.org/10.1007/978-3-031-80119-8_24

in brick-and-mortar stores, such as a higher perceived product risk (Lau and Lee 2019), since the products cannot be experienced physically. One promising technological approach that is supposed to address these disadvantages in online shopping is virtual reality (VR).

While the VR technology has been the subject of research for decades, the recent developments pertaining VR hardware allow to enroll the technology to end customers at a reasonable price and low entry barriers, making it usable for consumers—especially due to the efforts of the company Meta. Currently, VR devices are primarily used for gaming, watching movies, or exercising (National Research Group 2022), but there are many other areas where VR has a high potential, such as education (Radianti et al. 2020), tourism (Beck et al. 2019), and shopping (Xi and Hamari 2021). Shopping in a VR has several potential benefits: it does not only allow customers to feel presence in a store but is also safe and time-efficient since customers can shop from home (Hassanein and Head 2014). In addition, users can have a better experience than in traditional online shopping, can interact with objects and can try on clothing from home. Furthermore, they can also get a feeling on how certain furniture pieces could look in real life. Due to the availability of customer-friendly hardware today, these advantages are also recognized by the customers. According to PwC, 32% of the customers using VR purchase products after testing or browsing them via VR. Another 19% of users purchase luxury goods via their devices (PwC 2022).

The objective of this paper is to synthesize these advantages of VR for online retail by reviewing literature on shopping in VR environments. Therefore, we rely on the stimulus-organism-response (S-O-R) framework (Mehrabian and Russell 1974). The S-O-R framework offers a valuable theoretical lens through which to understand and analyze the effects of VR on online retail. This framework posits that stimuli from the environment (such as VR characteristics) influence the internal psychological processes of individuals (cognitive and affective outcomes), which, in turn, shape their behavioral responses (purchase intentions and decisions). By adopting this framework, we aim to unravel the intricate relationships between VR characteristics, psychological outcomes, and consumer behavior in the context of online shopping. Using this framework, we can systematically analyze how specific VR features and design elements influence consumers' perceptions, emotions, and subsequent purchase intentions. Understanding these relationships not only fills a current research gap but also provides valuable insights on how VR shopping applications can be designed to create the optimal environment for purchasers and maximize companies' revenues.

To achieve the research objectives, we analyzed 43 quantitative studies pertaining VR shopping based on systematic literature review. The methodological approach, i.e., literature selection and coding process, is described in Sect. 2, followed by a descriptive analysis. Afterwards, the studies are analyzed in Sect. 3, and discussed by introducing a unified graph which summarizes the relevant findings in Sect. 4.1. From this graph, we derive practical suggestions for VR shopping applications in 4.2 and a future research agenda for VR shopping in Sect. 4.3. Finally, the results of the study are summarized in Sect. 5.

2 Methodology

The methodology of this paper is based on the guidelines of Webster and Watson (Webster and Watson 2002) for executing systematic literature reviews. The proposed guidelines specify the study selection process and the means of data extraction. In this section, the search strategy and selection process are described, followed by a two-step process to develop categories for the literature reviewed.

2.1 Search Strategy

To ensure a comprehensive sample of research studies, the literature search processes were conducted in the two databases Web of Science and AISeL. For both databases, the identical search string was used: ("virtual reality" OR VR) AND (shop* OR retail* OR commerce OR business). The terms were searched in the title, abstract and keywords (Web of Science) and subject in the AISeL database, respectively.

2.2 Study Selection

The study selection process consisted of two phases as shown in Fig. 1. In the first phase, we conducted a preliminary search in the databases Web of Sience and AISeL ($n = 716$). A pre-screening of the initial sample set for duplicates, publications in languages other than English, and unavailable studies, resulted in the exclusion of 26 articles. In the second phase, the detailed screening, we excluded a further 647 studies due to the (1) document type, (2) year of publication, and (2) the scope of the studies. To ensure a high quality of the results, only (1) journal articles and conference proceedings were included in the study, leading to the exclusion of 55 publications (document type). In addition, although VR has been studied for decades, the first modern HMDs sold for commercial purposes were introduced in 2014 (Kushner 2014). Therefore, studies conducted before this year were excluded, resulting in the exclusion of 235 publications. However, the highest number of publications were excluded due to scope of this study (357) based on three exclusion criteria. The first criterion pertains studies whose content is beyond the thematic scope of this literature review (286), such as medical studies, educational studies or studies that used VR for shopping, but rather to verify concepts related to brick-and-mortar stores. Criterion two relates to the methodological approaches within the articles. Since this study aims on emphasizing measurable quantitative effects, publications that do not focus on quantitative research designs (44) were excluded from the sample set. The last criterion concerns studies that investigate other technologies than VR, for example augmented reality (AR) or desktop computer screens (27). After the screening process, the final set comprises 43 publications.

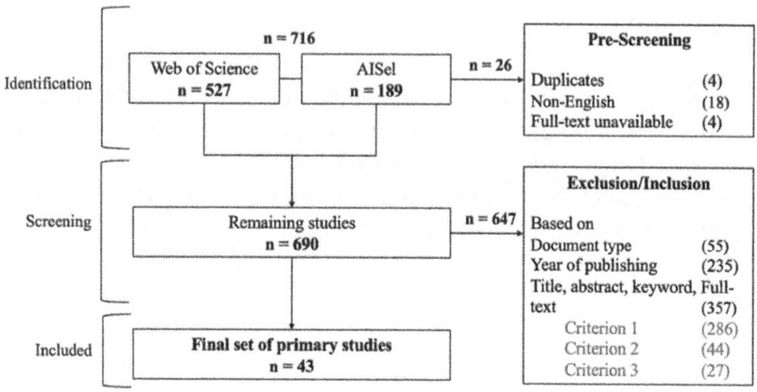

Fig. 1 Study search and selection process

2.3 *Data Extraction*

The aim of the data extraction process is to extract the most relevant information from the final set of studies. For this purpose, we created a table containing meta information about all articles. This table included authors, year of publishing, title and abstract among other things. After collecting meta information from the relevant articles, we started an iterative process to develop a classification system. In the first step, we created further columns to have a first overview over the investigated constructs in each article. The purpose of the second iteration was to refine and improve the category system by inspecting them more closely. The resulting categories follow the S-O-R framework (Mehrabian and Russel 1974), meaning that the categories represent specific instances of either stimulus (the input), organism (the process within humans) or response (the output). A modified version of S-O-R including VR specific aspects can be found in Sect. 4.3. In the next phase, we used the developed category system to describe the relationships between the concepts studied in the articles. This process consisted of four steps. In the first step, all variables, their influential connection, and the direction of their connection were visualized in a unified graph. We only considered concepts that were identified as significant in the research studies. Since the number of connections between the different factors and outcomes can be considered complex, we synthesized the findings into the previously developed categories and further abstracted the connections in step three. Finally, in a fourth step, we were able to derive the S-O-R based framework that assigns the categories to one of S-O-R's main categories.

2.4 *Descriptive Statistic*

In the following, we describe the included publications statistically in order to provide an overview on the year-wise distribution and publication outlets.

Year of publishing. As described in the methodology section, the literature review only includes studies more recent than 2014. However, the first publication in the sample is from 2017 (1). The number of publications increases after 2017, from 3 publications in 2018, to 10 in 2019, with a peak in 2020 (12 publications). The contributions slowly decline in 2021 (11). Since the selection of articles was performed in August 2022 the number of articles for 2022 is smaller than for previous years (6).

Publishing outlets. Table 1 shows the outlets in which the studies were published. The most encountered outlet is the "Journal of Business Research" (14%), followed by the "Journal of Retailing and Consumer Services" (7%). Five outlets published two papers each: "Applied Sciences", "Fashion and Textiles", "Food Research International", "Psychology and Marketing" and "Virtual Reality" (4.7% each). The remaining outlets only published one of the papers in the sample set.

3 Results

The result section synthetizes the findings of the literature in the identified and previously defined categories (1) products, (2) device and control, (3) theories, (4) general and application dependent VR characteristics, (5) psychological outcomes, and (6) behavioral outcomes.

Products. This category lists the most common types of products offered in the VR shopping environments. Most studies focus on selling clothing or shoes (31%) and groceries (31%). In case of the latter, the customers navigate through a virtual supermarket. The third most common product category are specific kinds of food or beverage, such as cereals (16%). Less considered products are furniture (9%), kitchen appliances (4%) or tools (2%).

Device and control. The experimental settings in the studies differ in terms of the used VR devices. The type of the device determines not only the quality of the graphics but also its usability, e.g., wired head-mounted displays (HMDs) provide a higher resolution while smartphone-based VR solutions are easier to use. Most of the studies (58%) use wired HMDs. They provide the best graphics quality due to being directly connected to a computer. From the remaining studies, the majority (33%) does not specify the device used. Smartphone-based HMDs were rarely used (7%) and only one study uses a wireless HMD that processes the application directly inside the device. The user input is mostly controlled by hand-held controllers (53%). In this category the subject holds two small wireless controllers, one in each hand.

Table 1 Publishers and corresponding studies

Venue/outlet	Studies	#	%
Journal of Business Research	Alzayat and Lee (2021), Cowan et al. (2021), Han et al. (2020), Meiflner et al. (2020), (Pizzi et al. (2020), van Berio et al. (2021)	6	14,0
Journal of Retailing and Consumer Services	Lombart et al. (2019), Schnack et al. (2021b), Schnack et al. (2021a)	3	7,0
Applied Sciences-Basel	Kim and Ha (2021), Moghaddasi et al. (2021)	2	4,7
Fashion and Textiles	Jang et al. (2019), Jin et al. (2021)	2	4,7
Food Research International	Schnack et al. (2019), Siegrist et al. (2019)	2	4,7
Psychology and Marketing	Hilkcn et al. (2022), Mishra et al. (2021)	2	4,7
Virtual Reality	Lau and Lee (2019), Su et al. (2020)	2	4,7
Behavior and Information Technology	Wu et al. (2019b)	1	2,3
Communication Research Reports	McCain et al. (2018)	1	2,3
Computers in Human Behavior	Lombart et al. (2020)	1	2,3
Electronics	Liu et al. (2020)	1	2,3
Foods	Jacobsen et al. (2022)	1	2,3
Frontiers in Psychology	Plechata et al. (2019)	1	2,3
Frontiers in Robotics and AI	Verhulst et al. (2018)	1	2,3
Heliyon	Moes and van Vliet (2017)	1	2,3
Human-centric Computing and Information Sciences	Wu et al. (2019a)	1	2,3
IEEE Access	Meirinhos et al. (2022)	1	2,3
Information Resources Management Journal	Hsu et al. (2020)	1	2,3
Information Systems Journal	Kinzinger et al. (2022)		2,3
Interacting with Computers	Pengnate et al. (2020)	1	2,3
International Journal of Advanced Computer Science and Applications	Dad et al. (2018)	1	2,3
Journal of Retail and Distribution Management	Xue et al. (2020)	1	2,3
Internet Research	Wang et al. (2019)	1	2,3
Journal of Consumer Behaviour	Schnack et al. (2020)	1	2,3
Journal of Interactive Marketing	Kang et al. (2020)	1	2,3
Journal of Management Information Systems	Peukert et al. (2019)	1	2,3

(continued)

Table 1 (continued)

Venue/outlet	Studies	#	%
Journal of Marketing Research	Luangrath et al. (2022)	1	2,3
Journal of Product St Brand Management	Naderi et al. (2020)	1	2,3
Journal of Research in Interactive Marketing	Kim et al. (2021)	1	2,3
Mobile Information Systems	Alkamey and Almakki (2022)	1	2,3
Multimedia Tools and Applications	Jang and Hsieh (2021)	1	2,3
		43	

39% of the studies do not specify the input device. Finally, only a minority of the applications were controlled by the hands of the users (5%).

Theories. The effects of VR technology can be explained by various theories. These theories can be categorized into consumer experience and acceptance theories, and cognitive theories. Prominent consumer experience and acceptance theories in the reviewed studies are the "Media Richness Theory" (20%), the "Technology Acceptance Model" (TAM) (20%) and the "Telepresence Theory" (13%). The Media Richness Theory states that the effectiveness of a communication method depends on the richness of information (Daft and Lengel 1986). Especially VR has the potential to provide information through different channels, such as auditive signals, but also information boxes or virtual salespersons. The Technology Acceptance Model describes how the customers' perceived ease of use and usefulness of the VR technology influence their acceptance of this new shopping possibility (Davis 1989). Lastly, the Telepresence Theory concerns technology which is intended to create a level of immersion and engagement that can evoke emotions and behaviors similar to those experienced in face-to-face interactions (Steuer 1992). For that purpose, HMDs are very suitable due to the high perceived immersion of the screens. Cognitive theories try to find explanations for human behavior by utilizing insights into processes occurring in the human brain. The most applied of those in the literature sample is the "Flow Theory" (16%). The Flow Theory suggests that an optimal experience occurs when the challenges and skills, in the case of this study a VR experience, are in balance, leading to a state of immersive concentration and enjoyment (Csikszentmihalyi 1990). The second most encountered theory is the "Theory of Reasoned Actions" (10%). The Theory of Reasoned Action can be applied to understand consumer behavior in VR shopping by examining the influence of attitudes, subjective norms, and perceived behavioral control on consumers' intentions (Ajzen and Fishbein 1980), e.g., in adopting and engaging with VR shopping experiences.

General and application dependent VR characteristics. General VR characteristics deal with aspects that are related to all applications that utilize VR. In comparison to shopping in a brick-and-mortar store or a traditional online store, VR has many advantages and new features. Although the technology is the subject of research for decades, there are multiple hardware components that need to be improved to generate the best experience. In contrast to traditional online stores, VR shopping allows for a higher degree of interactivity, which is the most examined phenomenon (21%). In the reviewed studies, interactivity also includes playfulness and responsiveness. The second highest focus in the studies are usability aspects of VR devices. This includes accessibility, difficulty, and efficiency (17%). The topic of usefulness has also been a major research aspect in terms of general VR characteristics (13%). Another commonly encountered topic dealt with the informational aspect of VR devices (12%) in terms of media richness, novelty and informativeness. Since a well working hardware is crucial for customer acceptance, several studies focusing on the hardware have been carried out (10%). For example, it was examined how the subjects rate the display, smoothness, or readability. Another focus is the environment (10%), which includes the atmosphere, vividness, and realism. Experiments show which parts of the VR experience the participants appreciate the most. The interaction between customer and system can occur in different ways. Some studies explore the influence of the input device, as well as how realistic the vicarious touch is perceived by the subjects (8%). Others include the body and how body ownership is perceived by customers (5%), the influence of movement on the experience (3%) and how subjects assess information security risks (2%). Different applications offer different ways to present products and stores. In addition, they differ in terms of design quality and additional features. The category of application dependent VR characteristics deals with all attributes that are determined by the application designers. Most of the studies explored different product features (42%). These include technical aspects like the graphical quality of the goods, but also other attributes like perceived product healthiness, attractiveness, or presentation type. The second most examined area is the store itself (21%). This includes general aesthetics and environment, as well as the ease of finding products. Some studies investigate the comfort (13%), as well as application functions, such as gestures (13%) or sounds (8%). Only a minority of studies examined the effect of avatars (4%) and personalization (4%).

Psychological outcomes. The psychological outcomes were divided into two categories: cognitive outcomes and affective outcomes. Cognitive outcomes aim to determine the effects of the stores on the human brain and the perception of the applications, which is strongly related to processes and states of the brain and the autonomic nervous system (Riedl and Léger 2016). The most explored outcome variables are aspects related to the perceived value (23%). Furthermore, several studies made experiments concerning recall and learning (23%). In addition, price-related aspects were an important research topic (16%). The fourth most encountered area in terms of cognitive outcomes is activation and attention (10%). Stimulated processes such as challenge and creative thinking are further examined topics (6%). Regarding affective outcomes, i.e., theories that explain feelings and emotions of humans, the presence is the most encountered topic (29%). Presence includes social presence, physical presence, and spatial presence. The second most examined affective outcomes concern positive emotions such as arousal, satisfaction, and pleasure (23%). The hedonic motivation is examined by a minor number of studies (10%) with the aim to examine how certain VR attributes influence the perceived joy. Since the customers' attitude determines whether they will use VR technology again in the future, a large part of the reviewed literature deals with attitude towards and using VR (9%). Other experiments address the experience (7%), brand attitude (7%) and activative feelings, such as entertainment or fun (6%). Only a small number of studies examined negative feelings, like worries or stress (3%).

Behavioral outcomes. Behavioral outcomes consist of purchase attributes and behavioral intentions and actions. Purchase attributes characterize the most important properties of the purchased products and time spent by customers on the purchase. Most of the studies focus on the total time spent in the virtual environment (26%) and the total price paid (22%). An important research aspect has been specific attributes of the bought products (22%), e.g., if the products were healthy or how high the private label share is. Some studies also investigated the total number of items bought (17%). Other research areas include the number of impulsive purchases (9%) and the shelf location of the chosen items (4%). Behavioral intentions and actions are influenced by the mental state of customers. The analyzed literature is mostly focused on the purchase intention and purchase decision (48%). This not only emphasizes the economic importance of VR shopping, but also the intention to adopt or reuse VR technology, for example for private purposes. The intention to adopt or reuse play an important role in many studies (16%). Some experiments investigated the interaction with the product, e.g., searching for more information (10%) or the general behavioral intention (10%). Lastly, articles examined the word-to-mouth intention, i.e., tell others about their experience (7%), and the intention to visit a virtual store in the future (3%).

4 Discussion

In this section, we discuss the results by synthesizing relevant constructs from the literature to derive a general framework for VR shopping based on the S-O-R-framework. Afterwards we draw on the relationships between the categories to develop practical suggestions for VR shopping applications and propose areas for potential future research.

4.1 General Framework for Shopping in VR

The S-O-R theory distinguishes between Stimulus, Organism, and Response (Mehrabian and Russel 1974): The Stimulus refers to the environmental factors or events that affect an individual's behavior or experience. It can be anything that can be perceived by the senses, such as visual or auditory stimuli. In the VR shopping context, VR characteristics belong to the category Stimulus. The Organism meditates between

Stimulus and Response and refers to the individual's affective and psychological outcomes in the context of VR shopping. The Response is therefore influenced by the Stimulus and Organism and refers to the observable and measurable behaviors or outcomes resulting from the interaction between the stimulus and the organism. Our VR shopping framework includes the Response subcategories behavioral intentions and purchase attributes.

Our general framework for shopping in VR assigns all examined constructs in the reviewed literature to the main S-O-R main categories, boundary conditions, or device/control. Figure 3 illustrates the significant relationships between the concepts/constructs and the number of studies that have validated a positive significance, represented by the line thickness. Concepts that contain a group of variables are bold and described below. In the graph, the concepts' input node are described by circles which are connected to other concepts to show a significant relationship. Examined variables that belong to the category of the Stimulus are general VR characteristics and application dependent characteristics such as usability, informativeness, interactivity and the environment. Those influence cognitive and affective psychological outcomes, such as attitudes, positive and negative feelings, or presence, which in turn influence the response, consisting of behavioral intentions and purchase attributes. Examples for that category include purchase intention, behavior, and the intention to reuse the technology. Within the main S-O-R categories, there are also variable groups influencing other variables of the same category. The boundary condition age affects the usability on the one hand and positive feelings on the other hand. Device and gestures are related to variables of each of the main categories. Figure 3 shows that the S-O-R framework is appropriate to understand how VR shopping applications have an impact on consumer's cognitive and effective outcome as well as their behavior. VR shopping applications can profit from these findings and use them for implementing more appealing stores and applications. Concrete suggestions derived from our findings are explained in the next section.

4.2 Practical Implications for VR Shopping Applications

The results from the literature review and the developed framework allow to derive five practical implications for VR shopping applications. We deduced the implications from the relationships between concepts/constructs that have been verified as significant at least more than two times in the reviewed studies. The recommendations are based on the S-O-R framework in Fig. 3, as highlighted in the texts. For example, three studies detect a positive relation between informativeness and purchase intention. Due to this positive relation, we derived the first suggestion to make use of the ability of VR to incorporate information in various ways in the stores. The five implications comprise:

1. *Include various product information in the store.* Shops should focus on how they can integrate various kinds of information (S) for the customers instead

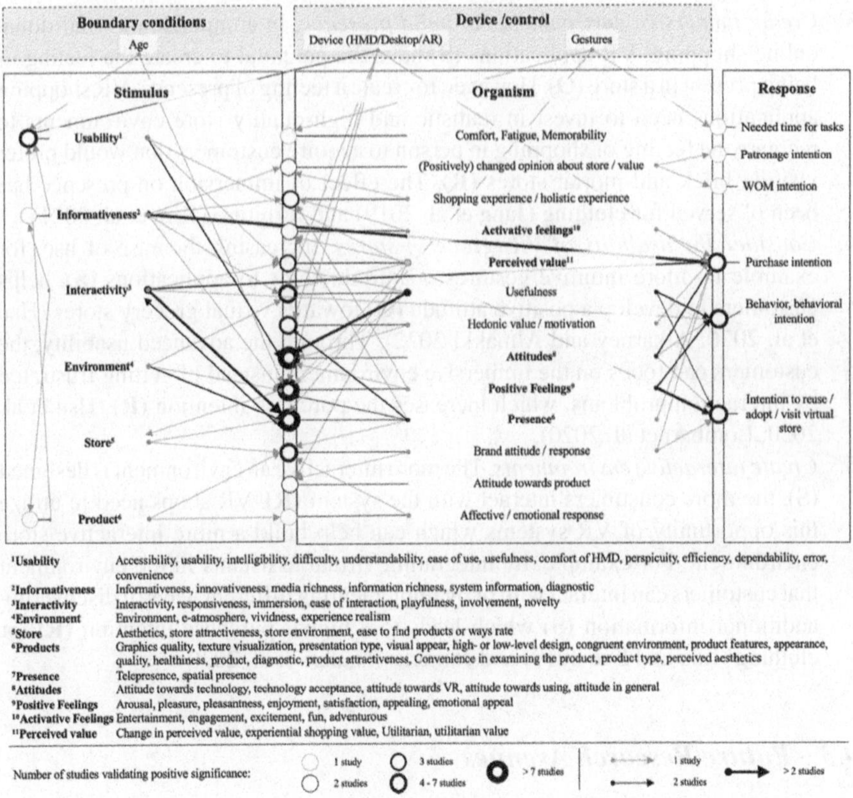

Fig. 3 The aggregation of the most relevant concepts shows how different categories for VR shopping are influenced by others based on significant relationships in the reviewed literature

of merely showing the products in VR. For example, shop owners can integrate information boards close to the products in the virtual shop. The positive effect on the purchase intention (**R**) has been verified for various product types: clothing (Moes and van Vliet 2017), groceries (Hsu et al. 2020) and furniture (Kang et al. 2020). Thus, additional information sources should be evaluated and integrated when designing VR shopping environments.

2. *Develop additional VR shops alongside traditional online stores*. Compared to other shopping possibilities like desktop or AR, VR (**S**) has the highest impact on positive feelings (**O**). For instance, enjoyment and pleasure when shopping for clothing (Jin et al. 2021; Liu et al. 2020) or an increased intention to adapt the technology when shopping for groceries (Alkarney and Almakki 2022) and tourism (Jang and Hsieh 2021). Also, the behavioral intention is influenced by more positive feelings for clothing (Dad et al. 2018) and furniture (Kim et al. 2021). Thus, online shop owners are advised to offer the possibility to shop in VR next to the traditional website or AR services to utilize these advantages.

3. *Create immersive environments to build presence.* In comparison to traditional online shopping, VR applications **(S)** have the potential to create the feeling of being present in a store **(O)**. However, to create a feeling of presence, VR shopping applications need to invest in realistic and high-quality store environments to recreate the feeling of shopping in person to acquire customers that would prefer visiting brick-and-mortar stores **(R)**. The effect of immersion on presence has been observed for clothing (Jang et al. 2019) and furniture (Kim et al. 2021).
4. *Consider the usability of VR (grocery) stores.* Increasing the ease of use, for example by more intuitive gestures or introductions to applications **(S)**, helps customers to develop a positive attitude **(O)** towards virtual grocery stores (Hsu et al. 2020; Alkarney and Almakki 2022). Through the advanced usability, the customers can focus on the immersive environment instead of getting frustrated by interaction problems, which increases the purchase intention **(R)** (Hsu et al. 2020; Lombart et al. 2020).
5. *Create interactive environments.* The more interactive an environment is designed **(S)**, the more consumers interact with the system **(R)**. VR shops need to utilize this opportunity of VR systems which can help build a more interactive store environment. For example, by integrating virtual assistants in the environment that customers can interact with or by implementing different ways of discovering additional information **(S)** which leads to a higher purchase intention **(R)** for clothing (Lau and Lee 2019) and cameras (Naderi et al. 2020).

4.3 Future Research Avenues

Apart from the practical implications, the results allow the identification of research gaps that have barely been addressed in current VR shopping research. To align the future research avenues with the findings in this study, the relation to the S-O-R framework in Fig. 3 is highlighted in every paragraph.

Target group analysis. Although part of the quantitative studies concerned the influence of age on the perception of VR, none of the publications investigated and determined different target groups for VR shopping. In contrast to traditional stores, VR allows to provide different shopping environments **(S)** to different kinds of customers and could thus directly be adjusted to the target audience. Since the environment has an indirect influence on purchase intention and intention to use/adopt **(R)**, potentially through the mediation of the users' internal reactions **(O)**, the relationship of environment and demographical aspects should be studied to exploit this benefit, e.g., explore specific VR shopping applications for demographic groups.

Comparison of wired and wireless HMDs. Only one study relied on wireless HMDs, i.e., the Oculus Quest (Kim and Ha 2021). The remaining studies used wired headsets or did not provide any information about the device in use **(S)**. However, it must be assumed that the type of HMD, wired or wireless, plays a major role for customers **(O, R)**. Advantages of wireless headsets are that customers can move freely in a room and without been hindered by a physical cable. On the other hand, wireless headsets include the necessary computational units, whereas wired headsets are connected to desktop computers that are more powerful and thus can provide a higher graphical quality.

Optimal shelf locations and structures. VR allows sellers to easily expand their shops. Compared to physical stores, they can expand their store by making simple adjustments without relocating the store or pay more rent **(S)**. In the past, only little research addressed the optimal shelf locations. It was observed that purchase rates increase with higher shelf levels for regular store shelves (Schnack et al. 2020). However, the optimal shelf size and space between shelves has not been studied as well as how to structure shelfs.

Explore the social experience in VR shopping. Another possible future research avenue could be social aspects of shopping in VR. These include social experiences **(O)** on the one hand and social effects **(R)** on the other hand. Social experiences can be interactive shops where customers have the possibility to talk to others, for example friends or salespeople, even though they can physically be in other parts of the world **(S)**. Such social effects only sparsely been addressed in the reviewed literature. Future studies could explore how shopping in VR is related to appreciation by others or even peer pressure **(O-R)**.

Negative feelings and outcomes related to VR shopping. Many of the reviewed studies focused on positive feelings such as enjoyment, pleasure, or arousal and on activative feelings, such as entertainment or engagement. Nevertheless, only a minority of the studies focus on negative feelings related to VR technology **(O)**. The only mentioning of negative feelings relate to stress and worries about fitting problems when buying clothing (Liu et al. 2020; Schnack et al. 2021b). Future research may focus on other negative feelings, such as fear or confusion, regret, shopping addiction, or frustration after shopping in a virtual world **(O-R)**.

5 Conclusion and Limitations

The aim of this study was to investigate and synthesize the evidence on the effects of VR shopping based on a systematic literature review and the S-O-R framework. For this purpose, we selected and analyzed 43 quantitative studies. In order to synthesize the publications, we classified the constructs and concepts, which showed positive significant relationships in the identified studies, into categories that have been developed in a two-step process. Subsequently, we constructed a unified graph based on S-O-R that highlights the positive relationships. Based on the unified graph, practical implications could be derived for relationships that were significant in at least two research studies. The practical implications comprise the importance of interactivity, presence, and usability in the development of VR shopping applications as well as the use of various information and the creation of VR shops alongside traditional online stores. In addition, the analysis of the publications led to the identification of five research gaps, i.e., future research avenues: the investigation of target groups, the influence of the hardware devices in use (wired, wireless), optimal shopping room design (e.g., shelf positioning), social aspects, and negative feelings and outcomes.

Apart from the practical and theoretical implications, the study has several limitations. First, the literature search was only carried out in two databases, which limits the number of accessible publications. In addition, the analyzed sample set contains no conference proceedings (excluded in the screening process). Second, no forward–backward search was performed in this study, thus additional relevant publications may not have been included in the sample set. The inclusion of additional databases and a forward–backward search may strengthen the results in this study. Third, limitations stem from the selected constructs/relationships for the practical implications. While we focus on the relationships with the highest number of validated positive significance, the remaining positive relationships have been neglected in this study. Thus, future research could focus on investigating the relationships that were validated twice or less in the reviewed studies in order to derive further theoretical and practical implications.

References

Ajzen, I. & Fishbein, M. (1980), Theory of reasoned action/theory of planned behavior, Social Psychology, 2007, 67–98.

Alkarney, W. & Almakki, R. (2022), Factors affecting the intention to use virtual stores: Perspectives of consumers in saudi arabia, Mobile Information Systems.

Alzayat, A. & Lee, S. H. M. (2021), Virtual products as an extension of my body: Exploring hedonic and utilitarian shopping value in a virtual reality retail environment, Journal of Business Research, 130:348–363.

Beck, J., Rainoldi,M. & Egger, R. (2019), Virtual reality in tourism: a state-of-the-art review, Tourism Review 74.3: 586–612.

Cowan, K., Spielmann, N., Horn, E. & Griffart, C. (2021), Perception is reality... how digital retail environments influence brand perceptions through presence, Journal of Business Research, 123:86–96.

Csikszentmihalyi, M. (1990), Flow: The psychology of optimal experience, New York: Harper & Row.

Dad, A. M., Rehman, A. A., Kear, A. & Davies, B. J. (2018), The effect of music on shoppers' shopping behaviour in virtual reality retail stores: mediation analysis, International journal of advanced computer science and applications, 9(1):135–145.

Daft, R.L. & Lengel, R. H. (1986), Organizational information requirements, media richness and structural design, Management Science, 32, 554–571.

Davis, F. D. (1989), Perceived usefulness, perceived ease of use, and user acceptance of information technology, MIS Quarterly, 319–340.

Han, S.-L., An, M., Han, J. J. & Lee, J. (2020), Telepresence, time distortion, and consumer traits of virtual reality shopping, Journal of Business Research, 118:311–320.

Hassanein, K. & Head, M. (2014), Social Presence For Online Shopping Success: A Review And Agenda For Future Research, WEI International Academic Conference Proceeding.

Hilken, T., Chylinski, M., Keeling, D. I., Heller, J., de Ruyter, K. & Mahr, D. (2022), How to strategically choose or combine augmented and virtual reality for improved online experiential retailing, Psychology & Marketing, 39(3):495–507.

Hsu, W.-C., Chen, P.-H. & Chen, C.-Y. (2020), An exploration of the impact of virtual reality interfaces on online shopping, Information Resources Management Journal (IRMJ), 33(2):19–39.

Jacobsen, L. F., Mossing Krogsgaard-Jensen, N. & Peschel, A. O. (2022), Shopping in reality or virtuality? a validation study of consumers' price memory in a virtual vs. physical supermarket, Foods, 11(14):2111.

Jang, Y.-T. & Hsieh, P.-S. (2021), Understanding consumer behavior in the multimedia context: incorporating gamification in vr-enhanced web system for tourism e-commerce, Multimedia Tools and Applications, 80(19):29339–29365.

Jang, J. Y., Hur, H. J. & Choo, H. J. (2019), How to evoke consumer approach intention toward vr stores? Sequential mediation through telepresence and experiential value, Fashion and Textiles, 6(1):1–16.

Jin, B., Kim, G., Moore, M. & Rothenberg, L. (2021), Consumer store experience through virtual reality: its effect on emotional states and perceived store attractiveness, Fashion and Textiles, 8(1):1–21.

Kang, H. J., Shin, J.-h. & Ponto, K. (2020), How 3d virtual reality stores can shape consumer purchase decisions: the roles of informativeness and playfulness, Journal of Interactive Marketing, 49:70–85.

Kim, J. & Ha, J. (2021), User experience in vr fashion product shopping: Focusing on tangible interactions, Applied Sciences, 11(13):6170.

Kim, J.-H., Kim, M., Park, M. & Yoo, J. (2021), How interactivity and vividness influence consumer virtual reality shopping experience: the mediating role of telepresence, Journal of Research in Interactive Marketing.

Kinzinger, A., Steiner, W., Tatzgern, M. & Vallaster, C. (2022), Comparing low sensory enabling (lse) and high sensory enabling (hse) virtual product presentation modes in e-commerce, Information Systems Journal.

Kushner, D. (2014), Virtual reality's moment, IEEE Spectrum 51.1: 34–37.

Lau, K. W. & Lee, P. Y. (2019), Shopping in virtual reality: a study on consumers' shopping experience in a stereoscopic virtual reality, Virtual Reality, 23(3):255–268.

Liu, Y., Liu, Y., Xu, S., Cheng, K., Masuko, S. & Tanaka, J. (2020), Comparing vr-and ar-based try-on systems using personalized avatars, Electronics, 9(11):1814.

Lombart, C., Millan, E., Normand, J.-M., Verhulst, A., Labbé- Pinlon, B. & Moreau, G. (2019), Consumer perceptions and purchase behavior toward imperfect fruits and vegetables in an immersive virtual reality grocery store, Journal of Retailing and Consumer Services, 48:28–40.

Lombart, C., Millan, E., Normand, J.-M., Verhulst, A., Labbé- Pinlon, B. & Moreau, G. (2020), Effects of physical, non-immersive virtual, and immersive virtual store environments on consumers' perceptions and purchase behavior, Computers in Human Behavior, 110:106374.

Luangrath, A. W., Peck, J., Hedgcock, W. & Xu, Y. (2022), Observing product touch: The vicarious haptic effect in digital marketing and virtual reality, Journal of Marketing Research, 59(2):306–326.

McCain, J., Ahn, S. J. & Campbell, W. K. (2018), Is desirability of the trait a boundary condition of the proteus effect? a pilot study, Communication Research Reports, 35(5):445–455.

Mehrabian, A. & Russell, J. (1974), An Approach to Environmental Psychology, MIT Press.

Meirinhos, G., Gonçalves, G., Melo, M. & Bessa, M. (2022), Using virtual reality to demonstrate and promote products: the effect of gender, product contextualization and presence on purchase intention and user satisfaction, IEEE Access.

Meißner, M., Pfeiffer, J., Peukert, C., Dietrich, H. & Pfeiffer, T. (2020), How virtual reality affects consumer choice, Journal of Business Research, 117:219–231.

Mishra, A., Shukla, A., Rana, N. P. & Dwivedi, Y. K. (2021), From "touch" to a "multisensory" experience: The impact of technology interface and product type on consumer responses, Psychology & Marketing, 38(3):385–396.

Moes, A. & van Vliet, H. (2017), The online appeal of the physical shop: How a physical store can benefit from a virtual representation, Heliyon, 3(6):e00336.

Moghaddasi, M., Marín-Morales, J., Khatri, J., Guixeres, J., Chicchi Giglioli, I. A. & Alcañiz, M. (2021), Recognition of customers' impulsivity from behavioral patterns in virtual reality, Applied Sciences, 11(10):4399.

Naderi, E., Naderi, I. & Balakrishnan, B. (2020), Product design matters, but is it enough? Consumers' responses to product design and environment congruence, Journal of Product & Brand Management.

National Research Group (2022), Beyond Reality. Is the long-awaited VR revolution finally on the horizon? https://assets.ctfassets.net/0o6s67aqvwnu/1zmWdgZfYLEEbdLS2DCtNi/0b5737 16bd56b0a4c09aede06b4325d9/Beyond_Reality_April_2022.pdf

Nistor, A. (2021), The Influence of the COVID-19 Pandemic on E-Commerce. Trends and Challenges before and after COVID-19, Revista Economica 73.3 (2021): 151–161.

Pengnate, S., Riggins, F. J. & Zhang, L. (2020), Understanding users' engagement and responses in 3d virtual reality: The influence of presence on user value, Interacting with Computers, 32(2):103–117.

Peukert, C., Pfeiffer, J., Meißner, M., Pfeiffer, T. & Weinhardt, C. (2019), Shopping in virtual reality stores: the influence of immersion on system adoption, Journal of Management Information Systems, 36(3):755–788.

Pizzi, G., Vannucci, V. & Aiello, G. (2020), Branding in the time of virtual reality: Are virtual store brand perceptions real? Journal of Business Research, 119:502–510.

Plechatá, A., Sahula, V. Fayette, D., & Fajnerová, I. (2019), Age-related differences with immersive and non-immersive virtual reality in memory assessment, Frontiers in Psychology, 10.

PwC (2022), Consumer respond to waves of disruption, Global Consumer Insights Pulse Survey. https://www.pwc.com/gx/en/consumer-markets/consumers-respond-to-waves-of-disruption/gcis-report-june-2022.pdf

Radianti, J., Majchrzak, T. A., Fromm, J. & Wohlgenannt, I. (2020), A systematic review of immersive virtual reality applications for higher education: Design elements, lessons learned, and research agenda, Computers & Education, 147:103778.

Riedl, R., & Léger, P. M. (2016), Tools in NeuroIS research: an overview. Fundamentals of NeuroIS: Information Systems and the Brain, 47–72.

Schnack, A., Wright, M. J. & Holdershaw, J. L. (2019), Immersive virtual reality technology in a three-dimensional virtual simulated store: Investigating telepresence and usability, Food Research International, 117:40–49.

Schnack, A., Wright, M. J. & Holdershaw, J. L. (2020), An exploratory investigation of shopper behaviour in an immersive virtual reality store, Journal of Consumer Behaviour, 19(2):182–195.

Schnack, A., Wright, M. J. & Elms, J. (2021a), Investigating the impact of shopper personality on behaviour in immersive virtual reality store environments, Journal of Retailing and Consumer Services, 61:102581.

Schnack, A., Wright, M. J. & Holdershaw, J. L. (2021b), Does the locomotion technique matter in an immersive virtual store environment?–comparing motion-tracked walking and instant teleportation, Journal of Retailing and Consumer Services, 58:102266.

Siegrist, M., Ung, C.-Y., Zank, M., Marinello, M., Kunz, A., Hartmann, C. & Menozzi, M. (2019), Consumers' food selection behaviors in three- dimensional (3d) virtual reality, Food research international, 117:50–59.

Steuer, J. (1992), Defining virtual reality: dimensions determining telepresence, Journal of Communication, Vol. 42 No. 4, pp. 73–93.

Su, K.-W., Chen, S.-C., Lin, P.-H. & Hsieh, C.-I. (2020), Evaluating the user interface and experience of vr in the electronic commerce environment: a hybrid approach, Virtual Reality, 24(2):241–254.

van Berlo, Z. M., van Reijmersdal, E. A., Smit, E. G. & van der Laan, L. N. (2021), Brands in virtual reality games: Affective processes within computer-mediated consumer experiences, Journal of Business Research, 122:458–465.

Verhulst, A., Normand, J.-M., Lombart, C., Sugimoto, M. & Moreau, G. (2018), Influence of being embodied in an obese virtual body on shopping behavior and products perception in vr, Frontiers in Robotics and AI, 5:113.

Wang, Y.-S., Yeh, C.-H., Wang, Y.-M., Tseng, T. H., Lin, H.-H., Lin, S. & Xie, M.-Q. (2019), Investigating online consumers' responses to product presentation modes: Does product type really matter? Internet Research.

Webster, J. & Watson, R. (2002), Analyzing the past to prepare for the future: Writing a literature review, MIS quarterly xiii-xxiii.

Wu, H., Luo, W., Pan, N., Nan, S., Deng, Y., Fu, S. & Yang, L. (2019a), Understanding freehand gestures: a study of freehand gestural interaction for immersive vr shopping applications, Human-centric Computing and Information Sciences, 9(1):1–26.

Wu, H., Wang, Y., Qiu, J., Liu, J. & Zhang, X. (2019b), User-defined gesture interaction for immersive vr shopping applications, Behaviour & Information Technology, 38(7):726–741.

Xi, N. & Hamari, J. (2021), Shopping in virtual reality: A literature review and future agenda, Journal of Business Research, 134:37–58.

Xue, L., Parker, C. J. & Hart, C. (2020), How to design fashion retail's virtual reality platforms, International Journal of Retail & Distribution Management, 48(10):1057–1076.

Applying Random Forests in Federated Learning: A Synthesis of Aggregation Techniques

Mattis Bodynek, Florian Leiser, Scott Thiebes, and Ali Sunyaev

Abstract Random forests (RFs) are a versatile choice for many machine learning applications. Despite their promising efficiency and simplicity, RFs are seldom used in collaborative scenarios like federated learning (FL). In FL, training data is scattered among a federation of clients. To train federated models, a central server aggregates inputs from all clients. For RFs as non-parametric models, coordinating the training phase and aggregating the global model is non-trivial. Design choices regarding the evaluation of candidate splits and the aggregation of decision trees prove to be context-specific. In this work, we identify aggregation techniques proposed in extant literature. The identified techniques are categorized across dimensions like training coordination, inference process, and privacy. We find an important distinction between synchronous and asynchronous techniques and evaluate the practical suitability of aggregation techniques by comparing advantages and drawbacks for prediction robustness and technical feasibility. Our results facilitate design choices of future federated RFs.

Keywords Random forest · Federated learning · Literature review

M. Bodynek (✉) · F. Leiser · S. Thiebes · A. Sunyaev
Karlsruhe Institute of Technology, Karlsruhe, Germany
e-mail: mattis.bodynek@student.kit.edu

F. Leiser
e-mail: florian.leiser@kit.edu

S. Thiebes
e-mail: scott.thiebes@kit.edu

A. Sunyaev
e-mail: sunyaev@kit.edu

D. Beverungen et al. (eds.), *Conceptualizing Digital Responsibility for the Information Age*, Lecture Notes in Information Systems and Organisation 74,
https://doi.org/10.1007/978-3-031-80119-8_25

1 Introduction

Across many data-heavy applications like healthcare or finance, machine learning (ML) applications are becoming increasingly relevant. Supervised ML applications require large amounts of training data, which is troublesome when that data is residing in siloed environments (Rieke et al. 2020). Collaborations could enrich the data sets and improve the predictions for all parties, but the exchange of sensitive data is often not possible due to strict privacy regulations or the protection of proprietary knowledge (Kairouz et al. 2021). Federated learning (FL) seeks to overcome these impediments by adapting ML techniques to multi-client environments. Federated ML models are trained collaboratively without violating data privacy requirements. In traditional FL, clients start by training parametric models like neural networks on locally available data sets. In each iteration, the local model updates are aggregated by a central server. The aggregated model is then made available to all participating clients (McMahan et al. 2017).

Studies suggest that the success of ML models in practice is determined by a range of factors surpassing quality measures established in research (Ishikawa and Yoshioka 2019). Factors like explainability and user-friendliness are critical for the long-term adoption of a model, especially in areas with high accountability standards (Varghese 2020). Neural networks are the most researched models in FL but dissatisfy some of these requirements (Paleyes et al. 2022). More explainable, less complex predictors like decision trees or regression models may suffer from inferior predictive performance (Bell et al. 2022). Random forests (RFs) can bridge this gap between explainability and predictive quality (Varghese 2020). RFs are supervised ML models built by compiling multiple decision trees in an ensemble and aggregating the outputs for predictions (Breiman 1996). They can process categorical and high-dimensional data with good predictive performance (Cutler et al. 2012), while facilitating the employment of explainability techniques (De Fazio et al. 2023). For a deep technical introduction into RFs, we suggest the review of Biau and Scornet (2016) as a starting point.

The unique balance between prediction quality and explainability (Varghese 2020) makes RFs appealing models for FL as well. However, the non-parametric nature of the underlying decision trees necessitates dedicated aggregation techniques for federated RFs (FRFs) (Li et al. 2021). A range of these techniques has been proposed so far. However, existing knowledge of different techniques may be inaccessible to potential users because authors use different terminology and focus on specific applications. By synthesizing the body of work on FRFs and characterizing existing techniques, we aim to guide researchers and practitioners in identifying relevant solutions. Thus, we ask the research question (RQ):

RQ: Which aggregation techniques for FL with RFs exist in research, and how do they compare with each other?

To answer our RQ, we review aggregation techniques for FRFs found in scientific literature. The identified techniques are structured by applying categorical mappings to make them more accessible to the reader. Subsequently, we evaluate the techniques based on developed criteria regarding their suitability in practice. Together, the literature review and subsequent evaluation contribute to an improved understanding of different aggregation techniques for RFs and non-parametric models in general. Our results serve as a basis for informed and thus more confident decisions on the design of the aggregation process, ultimately facilitating design choices for the application of non-parametric models in FL.

2 Background on Federated Learning

With the increasing interest in collaborative ML models, FL gained a lot of interest over the past years (Yang et al. 2019). In traditional FL, raw training data remains distributed at each client and is not exchanged across client boundaries, achieving strong data protection. A central server receives "focused updates intended for immediate aggregation [...] used to achieve the learning objective" (Kairouz et al. 2021). A fundamental question for the application of FRFs is the interconnection of data provisioning by local clients and the aggregation by a central server, which can be designed in numerous ways. To describe this central concept, we use the term *aggregation technique* as the combined strategy for data provisioning by technically or legally separated clients and the aggregation of this data into a shared model.

An important distinction of FL regards the participating clients. Cross-device FL is concerned with training a global model by leveraging inputs of many unreliable clients whose individual contribution is asymptotically insignificant (Kairouz et al. 2021). Cross-silo FL on the other hand describes federated systems which involve fewer but more powerful and reliable clients, such as data centers (Kairouz et al. 2021). FL can further be differentiated regarding the partitioning of training data. The most common scenario is horizontal FL, where clients share the same feature space but hold data on different samples. Conversely, in vertical FL, clients share the same samples but hold data on different feature sets. In practice, vertically partitioned data is most relevant in the context of cross-silo FL. Federated transfer learning constitutes situations where neither feature nor sample spaces align (Kairouz et al. 2021).

An emerging paradigm in FL is multi-task learning (Kairouz et al. 2021), where every local learning task is considered separately. This is especially relevant when data is not identically and independently distributed (IID). While IID assumptions are often violated globally, they may hold for subsets of client data. Under these conditions, multi-task FL can outperform global models (Kairouz et al. 2021).

Table 1 Settings for the conducted scoping study

Criterion	Detail
Language	English
Timeframe	01/2016–10/2022
Databases	IEEE Xplore, ACM Digital Library, Scopus, ProQuest
Source	Journals, Conferences, arXiv preprints
Status	Peer-reviewed or currently under review
Search area	Abstract only
Search terms	([“distributed” OR “federated” OR “incremental”] AND [“learning” OR “machine learning” or “ML”] OR FedML) AND (forest OR tree OR trees)

3 Review Methodology

To synthesize and assess the current state of research on FRFs, we conducted a scoping review. This method is well-suited for the exploration of research areas that have not been reviewed thoroughly yet (Mays et al. 2001). In particular, we followed the framework of Arksey & O'Malley (2005) to conduct the review.

3.1 Study Selection

Table 1 summarizes our search strategy, including search terms and inclusion criteria. Figure 1 visualizes the review process. The search yielded 293 unique records after removing duplicates (n = 159). In a first iteration, title and abstract of the records were screened and 234 manuscripts with no apparent relevance were excluded. The full texts of the remaining 59 records were retrieved and examined in more detail, where we excluded 38 publications due to insufficient eligibility. In the end, we charted 21 publications.

3.2 Data Charting

In addition to general metadata, we extracted information for six facets representing central characteristics of the identified aggregation techniques. These facets were determined through a targeted, exploratory analysis of the included publications. In this process, we prioritized categories with high discriminatory power. We developed an initial set of eight candidates, which we found to be relevant beyond the scope of FRFs. Two of these (namely, *explainability* and *problem domain*) were discarded, as they were not present in enough sources and thus did not provide sufficient insights

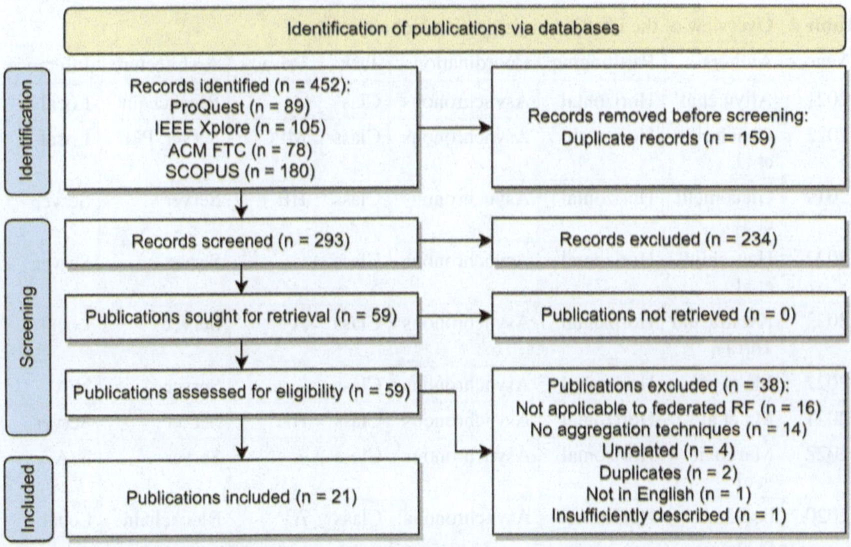

Fig. 1 Outline of the review process

into the differences between techniques within our sample. The remaining six facets are described below.

4 Review Results

An overview of the identified aggregation techniques and the evaluated mapping dimensions is displayed in Table 2. The overwhelming majority of the proposed systems apply cross-device FL. Clients are typically not only data sources but also influence the training phase and prediction process. Most studies investigate configurations between 2 and 100 clients (Hauschild et al. 2022, Liu et al. 2020), where each client resembles an institutional data domain. The work of Kalloori and Klingler (2022) even aims at "involving corporate companies instead of mobile devices in the federated learning process".

Partitioning. The first facet captures the partitioning of training data across clients. We differentiate between *horizontal*, *vertical* FL, and *federated transfer learning.*

Researchers have explored data partitioning for FRFs with a clear tendency toward horizontal FL. Aggregation techniques within vertical FL appear to be particularly homogeneous with respect to our mapping dimensions like privacy (83% apply HE) and inference (83% joint inference). Interestingly, we did not find any examples for federated transfer learning (FTL) in the reviewed work. The notion of transfer learning precedes FL and describes differences in domains, tasks, and distributions (Pan and Yang 2009), which is a broader mandate than the FL-specific definition by

Table 2 Overview of the identified aggregation techniques

Year	Authors	Partitioning	Coordination	Task	Privacy	Architecture	Inference
2021	Aliyu et al	Horizontal	Asynchronous	Class	–	Blockchain	Local
2022	Gencturk et al	Horizontal	Asynchronous	Class	MPC	Server, P2P	Local
2019	Giacomelli et al	Horizontal	Asynchronous	Class	HE	Server	Server
2022	Hauschild et al	Horizontal	Asynchronous	Class	–	Server	Server
2022	Kwatra and Torra	Horizontal	Asynchronous	Class	A	Server	Local
2022	Ma et al	Horizontal	Asynchronous	Class	–	Server	N/A
2021	Ma et al	Horizontal	Asynchronous	Class	HE	Server	Server
2022	Markovic et al	Horizontal	Asynchronous	Class	–	Server	N/A
2020	de Souza et al	Horizontal	Asynchronous	Class	A	Blockchain	Local
2021	Zhang et al	Horizontal	Asynchronous	Class	–	Server	Local
2021	Kwatra and Torra	Horizontal	Asynchronous	Class, Reg	–	Server	N/A
2022	Kalloori and Klingler	Horizontal	Synchronous	Class	DP	Server	Local
2022	Liu et al	Horizontal	Synchronous	Class	DP	MC	Local
2020b	Liu et al	Horizontal	Synchronous	Class, Reg	DP	Server	Local
2016	Guo et al	Horizontal	Synchronous	Reg	–	Server	Local
2022	Ge et al	Vertical	Synchronous	Class	–	Server	Joint
2021	Hou et al	Vertical	Synchronous	Class	HE	MC-Server	Joint
2021b	Liu et al	Vertical	Synchronous	Class	HE	MC-Server	N/A
2021	Liu et al	Vertical	Synchronous	Class, Reg	HE	Server	Joint
2020	Wu et al	Vertical	Synchronous	Class, Reg	HE, MPC, DP	MC	Joint
2022	Yao et al	Vertical	Synchronous	Class, Reg	HE	Server	Joint

Kairouz et al. (2021). Following the earlier notion, some have labeled personalized or multi-task FL as FTL (Saha and Ahmad 2021). We keep to the stricter definition, as it is more precise and does not overlap with the fields of horizontal and vertical FL.

Coordination. The second facet describes the coordination of the model training phase. We identified two architectural patterns, which we termed *asynchronous* and *synchronous* training, in consistency with other FL research (Zhang et al. 2020). The coordination of the model training phase determines the contents of the interaction between client and server. In asynchronous training of FRFs, clients build decision trees independently on their local data without model-specific communication. After finishing training, clients send their local models to the server, which aggregates the received data into a global RF. On the other hand, synchronous aggregation techniques collaboratively build decision trees across all clients under the coordination of an aggregation server. For each new node, clients provide information about the composition of their local data set. The server then finds and broadcasts the optimal split according to the provided data. With the globally selected split, nodes are expanded by recursively partitioning the local data at each client.

Across the 21 included publications, 11 employ asynchronous coordination, all within horizontal FL. The aggregating entity may apply a processing strategy to modify the composition of the federated model. The observed strategies fall into weighting, filtering, merging, or full compilation of all decision trees. Filtering reduces the size of the global RF by only considering a subset of local trees, either randomly (Hauschild et al. 2022) or performance-based (Markovic et al. 2022, Ma et al. 2021). Weighting techniques regulate the influence of each tree on the final prediction. Similar to filtering, we found different performance-based weighting methods (Gencturk et al. 2022, Ma et al. 2022). Lastly, merging techniques create decision trees by merging sets of local input trees. The identified approaches range from simple, node-wise selection rules (Kwatra and Torra 2022) to complex, transformation-based mechanisms (Kwatra and Torra 2021).

Ten of the reviewed sources instead employ synchronous training. In horizontal FL, each client holds a unique local data set with the respective labels. During training, clients provide summarized representations of the label distributions, so the central server can determine the global split (Guo et al. 2016, Kalloori and Klingler 2022). In systems relying on aggregating distribution data, clients communicate using histograms, which can be implemented for both classification (Kalloori and Klingler 2022) and regression tasks (Guo et al. 2016). A key property of histograms is the ability to merge adjacent bins. This enables a dynamic aggregation process, where the set of evaluated candidate splits is not explicitly defined at the time of aggregation. Alternatively, the server distributes a fixed set of split values to all clients (Liu et al. 2022, 2020). In this case, the results are aggregated directly, since all clients evaluate the same candidate splits.

In vertical FL, clients either have access to all or none of the labels. If label data is available to all clients, they can autonomously compute the locally optimal split (Ge et al. 2022). The server can then determine the globally optimal split by comparing all local results. However, most vertical synchronous techniques assume labels are proprietary data of a single entity. In this scenario, clients can only share preliminary data for candidate splits, for instance in the form of quantile statistics (Yao et al. 2022, Liu et al. 2021b). This data always has to be forwarded to the entity holding the labels.

Task. The reviewed work covers both classification (*class*) and regression (*reg*) tasks. The type of prediction task was determined either by explicit comments of the authors or by analyzing the proposed algorithms.

Only one publication focuses exclusively on regression tasks, whereas five approaches allow for both classification and regression. The most commonly mentioned prediction task is binary or multi-class classification with 15 identified sources.

Privacy. We identified four different privacy preservation techniques throughout training and prediction. Secure multi-party computation (*MPC*) allows for secure evaluation of a function based on private inputs of each client (Damgård et al. 2012). Homomorphic encryption (*HE*) transforms clients' inputs with homomorphic functions, scrambling the inputs but maintaining algebraic relations between them. Differential privacy (*DP*) introduces noise in models to mask a client's contribution (Kairouz et al. 2021). Lastly, anonymization (*A*) protects samples by removing or blurring any identifiable information. Out of all included publications, seven integrate HE schemes to secure their communication. Wu et al. (2020) employ HE to reduce communication overhead compared to solely relying on MPC. Their HE scheme supports addition, multiplication, and the dot product. Additionally, they employ an MPC protocol based on additive secret sharing for the secure comparison of the computed split impurities (Wu et al. 2020). Gencturk et al. (2022) propose a P2P network where MPC allows for anonymous computing of the performance of local models on other clients' data. Four approaches apply DP, including Kalloori and Klingler (2022), who use histograms with added noise to communicate distribution data to the server. Liu et al. (2020) propose a complex, multi-layer system for perturbing label information. Anonymization is employed in the form of *k*-anonymity (Kwatra & Torra 2022) and by excluding identifiable information from the aggregation process (de Souza et al. 2020).

Architecture. Different communication architectures of aggregation techniques are compared in our fifth facet. *Server* describes the traditional setting, where all clients have the same role within the system and communication is routed through a central server. In architectures with a main client (*MC*), all coordination is handled by one of the clients. It embodies the role of the server, but still participates in the training. *MC-Server* scenarios are relevant for vertical FL, where one client holds all label data. Communication is handled by an aggregation server, which additionally forwards all local partition data to this main client. Peer-to-peer (*P2P*) architectures enable communication protocols without a centralized server. Finally, blockchain-based systems (*blockchain*) rely on decentralized ledgers, where clients store retrieval information for locally trained models.

The traditional client–server architecture is the prevalent communication setup among the reviewed approaches. Only three techniques with asynchronous training implement blockchain-based (Aliyu et al. 2021, de Souza et al. 2020) or P2P (Gencturk et al. 2022) architectures. We found variations regarding the entity controlling the flow of information among synchronously trained techniques. Some approaches introduce a main client with additional responsibilities for the protocol (Hou et al. 2021, Wu et al. 2020).

Inference. Our sixth facet describes the provision of the global model along with the involved parties. Three types of prediction processes can be distinguished. First, each client may apply the global model independently in a local inference system (*local*). Each client, therefore, has access to the federated model and has full control over the prediction process. Server-side inference (*server*) is initiated by a prediction request, which is processed by the aggregation server. Access to the federated model is provided via an API or a web application. Lastly, joint inference (*joint*) requires both clients and server to become active to generate predictions. Hence, the global model does not reside at one entity but is distributed across multiple clients. This design requires consensus across all stakeholders on the usage of the federated model.

Most systems apply local inference, especially in horizontal FL. A simple approach is letting the server distribute the global RF to all authorized recipients after completing training (Kwatra and Torra 2022). Alternatively, each individual client decides which decision trees should be incorporated into their local ensemble. Hereof, Aliyu et al. (2021) let clients publish local models to a blockchain, from where authorized users can download the models for local usage. In synchronous training, participants can keep track of the collaboratively built trees during training (Liu et al. 2020), skipping the distribution step. Three approaches enable server-side inference, all applying asynchronous training. The global model may not be distributed due to privacy concerns, easier practical use, and monetized prediction processes. Joint inference between clients and server is only implemented in approaches with vertically partitioned data. The aggregation server only holds encrypted or referential information about the model (Liu et al. 2021). In addition to privacy protection, this can be employed to prohibit usage without the consent of all involved clients.

5 Evaluation

Within our study, we found that FRFs are typically applied in cross-silo environments. The nature of the clients eliminates many challenges associated with the cross-device setting prevalent in FL research, such as limited computational resources and unreliability of clients (Kairouz et al. 2021). Hence, cross-silo techniques should not be discussed in terms of cross-device requirements. We, therefore, developed evaluation criteria applicable to the cross-silo setting. As we set out to evaluate the suitability for a broad range of applications in practice, we limited our scope to domain-agnostic criteria. Hence, we settled on prediction robustness and technical feasibility. We excluded other interesting facets (e.g., explainability) since their implications remain largely independent of the applied techniques. The two selected dimensions allow us to draw generalizable conclusions regarding the practical suitability of aggregation techniques.

We focus on the differentiation between synchronous and asynchronous training phases, as our findings hint at the importance of this property. The simple, binary

Table 3 Main findings of the conducted comparison

Dimension	Synchronous training	Asynchronous training
Statistical heterogeneity	No performance loss compared to non-federated baseline	Prediction quality may degrade with imbalanced distributions and dataset sizes
Multi-task capabilities	Requires prior knowledge about the similarity of local datasets	Optimal composition of aggregated model(s) can be determined a posteriori
Communication overhead	May increase considerably with the size and complexity of the system	Highly parallelizable and scalable due to only a single communication phase
Adaptability necessitates	Rigid model structure necessitates complete retraining for updates	Client contributions are fully decoupled and hence dynamically modifiable

categorization directly applies to all reviewed techniques. Furthermore, it allows us to make assumptions about the data flow during training without losing generalizability of our results. Going forward, we first motivate and describe the developed criteria before presenting the results for synchronous and asynchronous training. An overview of the main findings can be found in Table 3. Importantly, our review did not identify asynchronous techniques within vertical FL. For the remainder of the evaluation, we will thus limit the scope to the horizontal setting.

5.1 Prediction Robustness

In FL, clients independently collect their own training data, which is never shared with other parties. Because data is collected differently across clients, the common assumption of IID data seldom holds in practice (Kairouz et al. 2021). In reality, the sizes of local data sets can differ substantially across clients. Additionally, not all local data sets may follow the same distribution. Robustness against statistical heterogeneity has been identified as a core challenge in FL (Li et al. 2020).

Across our sample, we saw two node expansion strategies for synchronous training. First, the server can directly compute their aggregated quality if all clients locally evaluate the same set of candidate splits (Liu et al. 2022, 2020). Second, clients may send distribution data summarizing their local sample to the server (Kalloori and Klingler 2022, Guo et al. 2016). The server then computes candidate splits after aggregating the local distributions. In terms of prediction robustness, the second strategy is preferable, since merging local distribution data reveals the structure of the global data set to the server, resulting in an optimal split which is agnostic to size disparities. Shifts in local distributions do not affect the global model either, as it is built on representations of the global distribution. Depending on the granularity of local distribution data, like the histogram bin size (Guo et al. 2016), the resulting model can be equivalent to one trained on the union of local data sets. This is also referred to as "lossless" (Chen et al. 2021) performance.

In asynchronous training, clients are fundamentally decoupled and candidate splits can only be evaluated on locally available data. Each local decision tree thus only incorporates information extracted from one data set. If size imbalances are unaccounted for in the aggregation process, the prediction output may be biased toward clients with larger data sets. Weighting the trees with respect to the size of the training data set can counter this effect, albeit not consistently across different configurations (Hauschild et al. 2022). On top of size imbalances, distribution heterogeneity can negatively impact the prediction quality of asynchronously trained models due to the lack of data exchange across client boundaries during training. This cannot be countered easily, as the introduction of inter-client knowledge would go against the asynchronous approach.

The creation of individualized models for all clients can elegantly circumvent the issue of statistical heterogeneity (Li et al. 2020). In this context, we found asynchronous training to be more suitable because each decision tree is based on the local distribution of a single client. The utility of the model can thus be maximized by letting clients decide the composition of the model for their local prediction task (de Souza et al. 2020). In synchronously trained FRFs, each tree is based on contributions from all clients. Multitask strategies are only practical if clients are known to have similar local distributions prior to training. Quantifying the similarity of local data sets a priori is possible (Liu et al. 2022) but adds further complication and is a potential source for data leakage. Synchronous aggregation techniques are hence less suitable for multi-task FL.

5.2 Technical Feasibility

The practical suitability of aggregation techniques also depends on their technical feasibility. For a start, communication efficiency can be a central bottleneck in FRFs, since the communication delay between clients and server makes up a large share of the total training time in cross-silo FL (Zhang et al. 2020). Furthermore, technical feasibility also entails the ability to adapt to dynamic environments (Ishikawa and Yoshioka 2019). This becomes especially relevant when requirements are insufficiently defined from the start or when recurring changes are anticipated (Ishikawa and Yoshioka 2019). An aggregation technique capable of dynamically reacting and adapting to systemic changes is more versatile and thus more likely to be applied in practice.

Synchronous coordination has a few drawbacks regarding technical feasibility. First, building a decision tree synchronously is communication-intensive. Clients first need to share their input data with the server, which then distributes the optimal split (Kalloori and Klingler 2022), resulting in at least two communication phases per node. Node expansion within the same tree layer can be parallelized. However, the server cannot expand a node until all clients have provided their data. The slowest client determines the processing speed for each node (Zhang et al. 2020). In asynchronous training, only one large communication phase is necessary to make local models available to the server. Since clients train independently, their contributions are fully decoupled. The communication overhead associated with asynchronous training hence does not grow problematically with the number of clients or the size of local models.

Each synchronously built decision tree is based on multiple local data sets. When new clients are introduced, or incremental updates are necessary, the global RF thus has to be completely retrained to incorporate new information. The cost–benefit relation of maintaining a synchronously trained model becomes less economical the more frequently a system is modified. Asynchronous FRFs on the other hand allow for continuous integration of new clients and facilitate the revocation of inputs. Moreover, they enable individualized updates to decision trees within the global RF, for instance when data is accumulated over time and models need to be continuously retrained. In case future system requirements are not fully understood from the start, the flexibility associated with asynchronous training ensures that the federated system remains adaptable.

Additionally, the impact of privacy preservation techniques on communication efficiency must also be considered. Encryption techniques in particular require a significant amount of computation and can dominate the processing time (Zhang et al. 2020). Since encryption has to be applied before sending local data, the cumulative overhead of encryption grows with the number of transmission phases and the amount of transmitted data. Summed up, the communication overhead for synchronous aggregation techniques is comparably high and can depend on a range of factors. The training complexity and the rigidity of the resulting FL model limit synchronous training to static environments.

6 Discussion

6.1 Principal Findings

In this study, we analyzed extant literature on the aggregation of RFs in FL. We identified 21 studies investigating FRFs. Therein, we found the majority of approaches to apply horizontal FL. Our results suggest that a key feature determining the properties of an aggregation technique is the coordination of the training phase. The choice regarding synchronous or asynchronous training determines the information flow between the involved parties. The behavior of the resulting system depends on whether the decision trees are built on local data of a single client per tree, or in a round-based process involving multiple clients. Thus, we compared synchronous and asynchronous approaches in terms of their prediction robustness and their technical feasibility.

Our results indicate that synchronously trained models can produce superior federated models in the presence of non-IID data, where local data sets are of unequal size or follow different underlying distributions. This is because the resulting global RF is structurally similar to its non-federated counterpart. The impact of size imbalances in asynchronous training can be mitigated by size-based weighting (Hauschild et al. 2022). Still, we found no other examples of size-based processing techniques. Additionally, the effects of distribution heterogeneity cannot be mitigated in asynchronous training because cross-client information is unavailable. The combined impact of size imbalances and distribution heterogeneity on asynchronous FRFs has not been investigated yet, but the prediction quality may degrade as well. However, building a global model in the presence of statistical heterogeneity may not align with the practical requirements. Individualized models tend to perform better here since they are tailored to the non-IID local distributions (Kairouz et al. 2021). For individualization approaches like multi-task FL, asynchronous training has an advantage due to the decoupled nature of the decision trees. Synchronous techniques are less applicable, as they produce decision trees with tightly interwoven client contributions. This can undermine the utility for individual stakeholders, a crucial factor for the success of a federated system (Huang et al. 2022). Regarding the technical feasibility, asynchronous training incurs far less communication overhead because the training process for individual clients is largely decoupled. This makes it the preferable option for environments that require scalability and adaptability. The global model allows for targeted, dynamic updates, which hints toward potential applications in incremental FL. Since each tree only depends on the input of a single client, their influence on the final prediction can easily be adjusted. In synchronous training, there may be scenarios where frequent retraining becomes uneconomical due to the complex training process. Additionally, there is a trade-off in synchronous training between performance and a more accurate representation of local data (Guo et al. 2016). Analogously, the cost of privacy-preservation techniques such as encryption comes into play, since the associated overhead increases with the frequency and size of data transmissions.

6.2 Implications

Our work yields several important implications for research and practice. For one, we provide a structured categorization of extant work on the aggregation of RFs in FL. With the rising interest in both RF and FL, their intersection becomes ever more relevant. By synthesizing and highlighting recent efforts in this intersection, we demonstrate the benefits of non-parametric approaches, ultimately contributing to the transition from inferior local models to federated systems. With the categorization of existing approaches, our work sets the stage for gaining deeper insights into the structural relationships between aggregation techniques. Our results show that the choice of synchronous or asynchronous training is an important driver of the robustness and applicability of FRFs. With this distinction, we complement the standard comparison from a data distribution perspective (horizontal vs. vertical) with a training coordination perspective (synchronous vs. asynchronous). This distinction allows for novel, model-agnostic insights into FL systems. Finally, the investigation into the practical suitability of aggregation techniques enables more knowledgeable design choices. Concretely, asynchronous coordination of the training phase tends to be more feasible in practical applications. This is due to its simplicity, superior efficiency, and the decoupled nature of client contributions. Nevertheless, the ability of synchronous FRF implementations to produce a potentially lossless global model may be a decisive trait under certain circumstances. Complex decisions often hinder the instantiation of ML systems. Our research facilitates the decision-making process and makes an informed application of FRFs more attainable. Our results are applicable across many disciplines.

6.3 Limitations and Future Research

FRFs are used across many domains, making it likely that we did not capture all relevant literature. However, our search covered a large share of extant work. We assumed cross-silo FL in the evaluation, since this is what most reviewed approaches focused on. Yet, some techniques can be applied in cross-device FL as well (Aliyu et al. 2021). Furthermore, our review found no aggregation techniques within vertical FL implementing asynchronous training. Since we focused on comparing synchronous and asynchronous coordination, we limited the evaluation to horizontal FL. Whether asynchronous training could be applied successfully in scenarios with vertically partitioned data is an open question. The evaluation speaks toward the practical applicability of techniques with asynchronous training. Our considerations for the prediction robustness in the presence of statistical heterogeneity are less conclusive and depend on assumptions about the underlying data. A quantitative investigation into the effects of statistical heterogeneity on synchronous and asynchronous training is the logical next step.

7 Conclusion

RFs are a popular choice for ML tasks because they are simple to use and reliably produce good results. Their application in FL environments, however, has thus far received limited attention. We conducted a comprehensive review on FRFs and synthesized aggregation techniques. Furthermore, we evaluated the identified aggregation techniques based on previously developed criteria to expose differences. Our results show that extant research generally assumes the cross-silo setting. As for the partitioning of local data, vertical FRFs have been explored less than horizontal FRFs. The most influential design choice for FRFs is the coordination of the model training phase since synchronous or asynchronous training have implications for the robustness of the resulting system against statistical heterogeneity and its applicability in dynamic, uncertain environments. We present implications for both future research on FL protocols and the practical application of FRFs. Future research can derive recommendations for suitable aggregation techniques from our findings. More research is necessary to better understand the characteristics of federated data sets and their implications on design choices for cross-silo FL. Going forward, we encourage further research into the decision for synchronous or asynchronous training, specifically in the form of quantitative studies.

References

Aliyu, I., Feliciano, M. C., van Engelenburg, S., Kim, D. O. & Lim, C. G. (2021), 'A blockchain-based federated forest for sdn-enabled in-vehicle network intrusion detection system', *IEEE Access* **9**, 102593–102608.

Arksey, H. & O'Malley, L. (2005), 'Scoping studies: towards a methodological framework', *International Journal of Social Research Methodology* **8**(1), 19–32.

Bell, A., Solano-Kamaiko, I., Nov, O. & Stoyanovich, J. (2022), It's just not that simple: An empirical study of the accuracy-explainability trade-off in machine learning for public policy, *in* '2022 ACM Conference on Fairness, Accountability, and Transparency', FAccT '22, Association for Computing Machinery, New York, NY, USA, p. 248–266.

Biau, G. & Scornet, E. (2016), 'A random forest guided tour', *Test* **25**, 197–227. Breiman, L. (1996), 'Bagging predictors', *Machine Learning* **24**(2), 123–140.

Chen, X., Zhou, S., Guan, B., Yang, K., Fao, H., Wang, H. & Wang, Y. (2021), Fed-eini: An efficient and interpretable inference framework for decision tree ensembles in vertical federated learning, *in* '2021 IEEE International Conference on Big Data (Big Data)', IEEE, pp. 1242–1248.

Cutler, A., Cutler, D. R. & Stevens, J. R. (2012), 'Random forests', *Ensemble machine learning: Methods and applications* pp. 157–175.

Damgård, I., Pastro, V., Smart, N. & Zakarias, S. (2012), Multiparty computation from somewhat homomorphic encryption, *in* R. Safavi-Naini, ed., 'Advances in cryptology—CRYPTO 2012', Lecture Notes in Computer Science, Springer, Berlin and Heidelberg, pp. 643–662.

De Fazio, R., Di Giovannantonio, R., Bellini, E. & Marrone, S. (2023), 'Explainabilty comparison between random forests and neural networks—case study of amino acid volume prediction', *Information* **14**(1), 21.

de Souza, L. A. C., Antonio F. Rebello, G., Camilo, G. F., Guimaraes, L. C. B. & Duarte, O. C. M. B. (2020), Dfedforest: Decentralized federated forest, *in* '2020 IEEE International Conference on Blockchain (Blockchain)', IEEE Computer Society, pp. 90–97.

Ge, N., Li, G., Zhang, L. & Liu, Y. (2022), 'Failure prediction in production line based on federated learning: an empirical study', *Journal of Intelligent Manufacturing* **33**(8), 2277–2294.

Gencturk, M., Sinaci, A. A. & Cicekli, N. K. (2022), 'Bofrf: A novel boosting-based federated random forest algorithm on horizontally partitioned data', *IEEE Access* **10**, 89835–89851.

Giacomelli, I., Jha, S., Kleiman, R., Page, D. & Yoon, K. (2019), 'Privacy-preserving collaborative prediction using random forests', *AMIA summits on translational science proceedings* **2019**, 248.

Guo, T., Kutzkov, K., Ahmed, M., Calbimonte, J.-P. & Aberer, K. (2016), Efficient distributed decision trees for robust regression, *in* 'Machine Learning and Knowledge Discovery in Databases: European Conference, ECML PKDD 2016, Riva del Garda, Italy, September 19–23, 2016, Proceedings, Part II 16', Springer, pp. 79–95.

Hauschild, A.-C., Lemanczyk, M., Matschinske, J., Frisch, T., Zolotareva, O., Holzinger, A., Baumbach, J. & Heider, D. (2022), 'Federated random forests can improve local performance of predictive models for various health care applications', *Bioinformatics* **38**(8), 2278–2286.

Hou, J., Su, M., Fu, A. & Yu, Y. (2021), 'Verifiable privacy-preserving scheme based on vertical federated random forest', *IEEE Internet of Things Journal* **9**(22), 22158– 22172.

Huang, C., Huang, J. & Liu, X. (2022), 'Cross-silo federated learning: Challenges and opportunities', *arXiv preprint*.

Ishikawa, F. & Yoshioka, N. (2019), How do engineers perceive difficulties in engineering of machine-learning systems?—questionnaire survey, *in* '2019 IEEE/ACM Joint 7th International Workshop on Conducting Empirical Studies in Industry (CESI) and 6th International Workshop on Software Engineering Research and Industrial Practice (SER&IP)', IEEE, pp. 2–9.

Kairouz, P., McMahan, H. B., Avent, B., Bellet, A., Bennis, M., Bhagoji, A. N., Bonawitz, K., Charles, Z., Cormode, G., Cummings, R. et al. (2021), 'Advances and open problems in federated learning', *Foundations and Trends in Machine Learning* **14**(1– 2), 1–210.

Kalloori, S. & Klingler, S. (2022), Cross-silo federated learning based decision trees, *in* J. Hong, M. Bures, J. W. Park & T. Cerny, eds, 'Proceedings of the 37th ACM/SIGAPP Symposium on Applied Computing', ACM, New York, NY, USA, pp. 1117–1124.

Kwatra, S. & Torra, V. (2021), A survey on tree aggregation, *in* '2021 IEEE International Conference on Fuzzy Systems (FUZZ-IEEE)', IEEE, pp. 1–6.

Kwatra, S. & Torra, V. (2022), A k-anonymised federated learning framework with decision trees, *in* 'Data Privacy Management, Cryptocurrencies and Blockchain Technology: ESORICS 2021 International Workshops, DPM 2021 and CBT 2021, Darmstadt, Germany, October 8, 2021, Revised Selected Papers', Springer, pp. 106–120.

Li, Q., Wen, Z., Wu, Z., Hu, S., Wang, N., Li, Y., Liu, X. & He, B. (2021), 'A survey on federated learning systems: Vision, hype and reality for data privacy and protection', *IEEE Transactions on Knowledge & Data Engineering* (01), 1–1.

Li, T., Sahu, A. K., Talwalkar, A. & Smith, V. (2020), 'Federated learning: Challenges, methods, and future directions', *IEEE Signal Processing Magazine* **37**(3), 50–60.

Liu, B., Tan, C., Wang, J., Zeng, T., Shan, H., Yao, H., Huang, H., Dai, P., Bo, L. & Chen, Y. (2021b), 'Fedlearn-algo: A flexible open-source privacy-preserving machine learning platform', *arXiv preprint*.

Liu, S., Wang, J. & Zhang, W. (2022), 'Federated personalized random forest for human activity recognition', *Mathematical biosciences and engineering : MBE* **19**(1), 953– 971.

Liu, Y., Chen, M., Zhang, W., Zhang, J. & Zheng, Y. (2020b), 'Federated extra-trees with privacy preserving', *arXiv preprint*.

Liu, Y., Ma, Z., Yang, Y., Liu, X., Ma, J. & Ren, K. (2021), 'Revfrf: Enabling crossdomain random forest training with revocable federated learning', *IEEE Transactions on Dependable and Secure Computing* **19**(6), 3671–3685.

Ma, X., Liao, L. X., Li, Z. & Chao, H.-C. (2022), 'Asynchronous federated learning for elephant flow detection in software defined networking systems', *Journal of Physics: Conference Series* **2216**(1), 012085.

Ma, Z., Ma, J., Miao, Y., Liu, X., Choo, K.-K. R. & Deng, R. H. (2021), 'Pocket diagnosis: Secure federated learning against poisoning attack in the cloud', *IEEE Transactions on Services Computing* **15**(6), 3429–3442.

Markovic, T., Leon, M., Buffoni, D. & Punnekkat, S. (2022), Random forest based on federated learning for intrusion detection, *in* 'Artificial Intelligence Applications and Innovations: 18th IFIP WG 12.5 International Conference, AIAI 2022, Hersonissos, Crete, Greece, June 17–20, 2022, Proceedings, Part I', Springer, pp. 132–144.

Mays, N., Roberts, E. & Popay, J. (2001), 'Synthesising research evidence'. McMahan, B., Moore, E., Ramage, D., Hampson, S. & Aguera y Arcas, B. (2017), 'Communication-efficient learning of deep networks from decentralized data', *Artificial Intelligence and Statistics* pp. 1273–1282.

Paleyes, A., Urma, R.-G. & Lawrence, N. D. (2022), 'Challenges in deploying machine learning: a survey of case studies', *ACM Computing Surveys* **55**(6), 1–29.

Pan, S. J. & Yang, Q. (2009), 'A survey on transfer learning', *IEEE Transactions on knowledge and data engineering* **22**(10), 1345–1359.

Rieke, N., Hancox, J., Li, W., Milletarì, F., Roth, H. R., Albarqouni, S., Bakas, S., Galtier, M. N., Landman, B. A., Maier-Hein, K., Ourselin, S., Sheller, M., Summers, R. M., Trask, A., Xu, D., Baust, M. & Cardoso, M. J. (2020), 'The future of digital health with federated learning', *NPJ digital medicine* **3**, 119.

Saha, S. & Ahmad, T. (2021), 'Federated transfer learning: Concept and applications', *Intelligenza Artificiale* **15**(1), 35–44.

Varghese, J. (2020), 'Artificial intelligence in medicine: chances and challenges for wide clinical adoption', *Visceral medicine* **36**(6), 443–449.

Wu, Y., Cai, S., Xiao, X., Chen, G. & Ooi, B. C. (2020), 'Privacy preserving vertical federated learning for tree-based models', *Proceedings of the VLDB Endowment* **13**(12), 2090–2103.

Yang, Q., Liu, Y., Chen, T. & Tong, Y. (2019), 'Federated machine learning', *ACM Transactions on Intelligent Systems and Technology* **10**(2), 1–19.

Yao, H., Wang, J., Dai, P., Bo, L. & Chen, Y. (2022), 'An efficient and robust system for vertically federated random forest', *arXiv preprint*.

Zhang, C., Li, S., Xia, J., Wang, W., Yan, F. & Liu, Y. (2020), Batchcrypt: Efficient homomorphic encryption for cross-silo federated learning, *in* '2020 USENIX annual technical conference (USENIX ATC 20)', pp. 493–506.

Zhang, H., Bosch, J., Olsson, H. H. & Koppisetty, A. C. (2021), Af-dndf: Asynchronous federated learning of deep neural decision forests, *in* '2021 47th Euromicro Conference on Software Engineering and Advanced Applications (SEAA)', IEEE, pp. 308–315.

Social Aspects in Organisational Cyber-Security Effectiveness—Of British Coal Mines, Resilience and Emergence

Tom F. Hofmann, Danielly de Paula, and Falk Uebernickel

Abstract Cyber-security, which plays a key role in all areas of the digital world, from the power grid to healthcare, is mainly addressed from an analytical, engineering perspective. This research looks at social factors impacting real-life cyber-security, and their possible effects, such as resilience and emergence. Semi-structured interviews were conducted with 20 participants from a broad range of international organisations. Their analysis shows that social factors are indeed relevant to cyber-security. Tension within social structures in organisations (e.g., employee-supervisor relationship, and peer pressure within teams) can signifi- cantly impact cyber-security effectiveness. The study concludes that cyber-security should be addressed through social-technical system design, in recognition of the fundamental interdependence of social and technical aspects. As a corollary, organisational cyber-security needs to be treated as a so-called wicked problem, for which a reductionist engineering approach is futile. The complexity and ambiguity of cyber-security's socio-technical challenges calls for adequate principles, ways of thinking and methods.

Keywords Socio-technical systems · Complex adaptive systems · Cyber-Security · Human-Centred design · Wicked problems

T. F. Hofmann (✉) · D. de Paula · F. Uebernickel
Hasso Plattner Institute, Chair for Design Thinking and Innovation Research, University of Potsdam, Potsdam, Germany
e-mail: tom@wicked.design

D. de Paula
e-mail: danielly.depaula@hpi.de

F. Uebernickel
e-mail: falk.uebernickel@hpi.de

D. Beverungen et al. (eds.), *Conceptualizing Digital Responsibility for the Information Age*, Lecture Notes in Information Systems and Organisation 74,
https://doi.org/10.1007/978-3-031-80119-8_26

1 Introduction

Digital technology provides a trove of new opportunities and advantages. Digitisation, and also cyber-security—the discipline of making the deployment of digital technology secure—are here to stay. Cyber-security has become an essential requirement, affecting business operations, research activities, and critical national infrastructures such as hospitals, power and utilities companies and the military. Cyber-security is commonly seen to be driven by technology and processes, to which people are expected to adapt through initiatives that promote training and awareness (Andress 2003). There is a general belief that cyber-security incidents are caused by deficiencies in people interacting with technology (Baxter and Sommerville 2011) and that improved technical understanding derived from training and improved awareness is the key to employee compliance (Ling et al. 2019).

Yet, despite all efforts at training employees, cyber-attacks based on social factors have remained very successful. The success of human-targeted tactics can be traced back more than 10 years, see for example reports from the FBI (Federal Bureau and of Investigation (FBI) 2011, 2020), Verizon (Verizon 2011, 2021) and Europol (European Union Agency for Law 2011, 2021). Recently, the challenge of ensuring employees' compliance with cyber- security policies has been investigated by IS scholars (Alec Cram et al. 2019, 2020). Research on social factors in cyber-security has increased in the past decade, mostly focusing on the individual, who is considered a risk factor (Streeter 2013) or weakest link (Caldwell 2012). A clear risk that stems from social aspects is the increasing usage of shadow-IT (Mallmann et al. 2018). The availability of easy-to- use technology, such as cloud services and smartphones, enables people to operate their own digital infrastructure, outside of organisational boundaries and without the knowledge and approval of IT-departments. This results in a broadened threat landscape and increased risks (Symantec 2018). While people seem to be aware of risks, they decide to ignore them in favour of achieving their goals (Györy et al. 2012). Recently, the importance of investigating the phenomenon through the lens of Socio-Technical Systems (STS) theory has gained some initial recognition. STS theory (Trist and Bamforth 1951) traces its origins back to 1949, where it described the role and interaction of technology and social aspects in British coal mines. As such, it has been linked to cyber-security mostly as a tool of analysis and as a framework to develop "better" controls. While STS theory helps assess the influence of such socio-technical factors, it does not provide insights into mechanisms and phenomena such as emergence. As a result, previous research has not given consideration to a number of other social factors, such as social relationships (Streeter 2013; Caldwell 2012). In recognition of this shortfall, the present study argues that a combination of STS and Complex Adaptive Systems (CAS) theory makes us better equipped to understand both social-technical interactions and underlying social mechanisms affecting employee compliance with cyber-security policies.

The aim of this study is to propose a conceptual model illustrating factors relevant to the design of cyber-security measures and susceptible to affect it. Accordingly, the research questions that guided this study are: What social factors are relevant to cyber- security, and how do they affect it (RQ1)? and What is the impact of knowledge and awareness training on employee compliance with cyber-security measures (RQ2)? In view of the complexity of the research questions, we adopted two different perspectives. First, we interviewed senior managers to obtain insights from operational knowledge. We then obtained insights from the organisational regulatory body. Considering that STS theory is not enough to understand how social factors affect cyber-security, we borrowed concepts from CAS theory. This paper contributes to theory by expanding the knowledge of socio-technical theory through the development of a hybrid model that combines elements from STS and CAS to explain socio-technical interactions and the underlying social mechanisms that affect employee compliance with cyber-security policies. From a managerial perspective, our study is a call for organisations to shift the view from a compliance paradigm to a more human-centric view when creating cyber-security policies.

2 Theoretical Background

We gathered relevant concepts, principles and theories from three main topics: cyber-security, STS and CAS.

2.1 Cyber-Security

The term cyber-security is somewhat ambiguous (Solms et al. 2013), and we therefore address the differences between ICT-, information- and cyber-security. Information and Communication Technology (ICT) security is concerned with the protection of technological assets, which store, process and transmit digital data. Accordingly, ICT-security is considered a subset of information-security since the security of all resources and processes dealing with information is an essential requirement. If this condition is not given, the information itself cannot be deemed secure. Information-security addresses the confidentiality, availability and integrity of information. Therein, the term information includes digital and analogue forms, whether it be for storage, processing or transport. Cyber-security addresses the safety of people, and even societies and nations from risks emerging through the usage of the cyber-space. Their interests—including assets that are not information-based—are to be protected. Examples are the usage of the cyber-space to commit crime, like fraud and extortion, or to threaten people's safety, as in stalking or harassment. In this study, we group ICT-, information- and cyber-security under the umbrella term cyber-security.

A major challenge faced by scholars and practitioners in the field of cyber-security is the growing number of cyber-attacks and data breaches in organisations. According to Dtex Systems, 50% of data breaches are a result from non-compliance with cyber-security policy, with an average cost of some $4 million per event (Dtex Systems 2018). Unsurprisingly, 40% of businesses reported not trusting their employees to appropriately use IT (Alec Cram et al. 2020). Indeed, the top three concerns of organisations related to employee non-compliance are: (1) inappropriate sharing of data via mobile devices; (2) physical loss of mobile devices, exposing organisations to risk; and 3) inappropriate IT resource use by employees (Alec Cram et al. 2020). People are seen as the weakest link in cyber-security, and IT executives implement compliance-inducing measures such as education campaigns to persuade employees and users to adopt safer behaviour (Alec Cram et al. 2020; McLaughlin and Gogan 2018). However, organisations do not have the resources to ensure that employees comply with cyber-security guidelines or to identify which measures are effective. There is even strong evidence that such compliance- inducing measures are ineffective and harmful (Alec Cram et al. 2019). Overall, the studies mentioned above highlight the need to move away from straightforward compliance-inducing measures and to understand how to design more effective strategies. Here, we borrowed concepts from STS and CAS theory to propose how cyber-security should be structured as a challenge in organisational (system) design, with a more human-centric view.

2.2 Socio-technical Theory—The Promises of Technology and British Coal Mines

Digital technology promises a vast increase in productivity and efficiency, similar to anticipations in post-WWII Great Britain. As new technology changed the way people worked (Trist and Bamforth 1951), the promise of increased productivity failed (Trist 1981; Pasmore et al. 2019). Managers and engineers enforcing the adoption of new technology by workers were not familiar with the working environment. Management saw the source of their problems in the workers' unwillingness to comply with directives about how to exploit the new technology. The local workforce insisted that the new technology could not be operated as directed by the engineers, because of extremely unpredictable underground conditions and resulting safety issues (Pasmore and Khalsa 1993). Yet, results in one mine, in which management chose the approach of closely collaborating with the workers, were extremely good (Pasmore et al. 2019). They were enabled to adapt new technology to fit their needs, through emergence (Trist and Bamforth 1951). The discovery of the positive effect of self-organising teams was considered to "contain dynamite" (Frans 1991) as it questioned hierarchical management, and the researchers were denied publication of their findings (Trist 1981). In cyber-security, we observe a similarly strong focus on hierar- chical structures, on top-down commands, on the assumption that technology will fix everything, and on the perception that problems result from people's unwillingness to adapt to technology and follow policies. STS theory was explicitly developed around the notion of *systems* (Trist 1981). A system can be defined as "sets of elements standing in interaction" (Bertalanffy et al. 1968), such as teams, organisations or societies. In STS theory, organisations consist of a multitude of elements in constant mutual interaction. Trist and Bamforth divided every organisational system into a social (sub-)system and a technical (sub-)system (Pasmore and Khalsa 1993). The social system includes people, but also their relationships, their professional and personal culture, the management methods in place, and any given experiences of work- ing in the organisation. The technical system as such includes technology, but also the policies regulating actual work. This insight is relevant because the current framework applied in cyber-security only considers (individual) people, processes and technology (PPT) (Andress 2003), ignoring the social context and its influence on people. Successful or unsuc- cessful system performance depends on the interactions of social and technical factors. Some of them are intentionally designed, relying on straightforward cause-and-effect relationships. Other interactions are of complex, unpredictable, often unintentional, or even undesirable, and non-linear in nature (Walker et al. 2008). People are not machines and cannot be programmed to behave like technical components—a fact few cyber-security researchers and practitioners appear to be aware of. While much work in cyber-security aims at achieving behavioural change, it appears to be remarkably ineffective (Bada et al. 2015). Furthermore, optimising just one system—be it only the social system, or only the technical one—will result in a sub-optimal performance of the overall system, i.e., of the organisation as a whole (Trist 1981; Walker et al. 2008; Fred Emery 1990). This holds also for modifications to social and technical systems, which increase the possibility and emergence of unforeseen, undesired and undesigned non-linear relationships (Walker et al. 2008). A corollary of this, and the most important objective in the design of STS (Walker et al. 2008), is the necessity of a *joint optimisation* of social and technical systems (Trist 1981; Fred Emery 1990). Research on STS should be conducted at three broad levels: the micro (primary work team), meso (organisation) and macro levels (societies) (Trist 1981). This is especially important because most studies on humans and cyber-security focus on the individual, rather than including social structures. Cyber-security is very much focused on technological advancements, while STS provides a holistic approach, considering social and technical factors and their interrelationships. This approach has been used to promote systems thinking in cyber-security, designing and supporting education (Zoto et al. 2018, 2019), addressing human and cultural factors (Corradini and Nardelli 2019). STS theory has also been used to develop conceptual models to analyse organisations in the context of cyber-security (Malatji et al. 2019) and corresponding risks (McEvoy and Kowalski 2019). Research showed the importance of STS design towards ef- fective cyber-security (Sadok et al. 2020), yet it lacked information on what social factors are involved and need to be considered. Considering the social factors research narrowed the view and focused on the individual (Østby et al. 2019). This led to the belief that knowledge and training are necessary to adapt people to technology. The research analysed mostly focuses on the individual, neglecting other social factors inside and outside the organisation. An important aspect of STS is the characteristic of complexity (Luzeaux 2011), which is also true for cyber-security (Pieters 2013). System phenomena—such as self-organisation, non-linear behaviour, resilience and emergence (Luzeaux 2011)—lead to tangible effects, like shadow-IT (Chua and Storey 2014), serving thousands of users (Symantec. 2018). Those features are inherent to CAS (Holland 2002). We therefore propose to consider STS as a type of CAS, applying a *system of systems* approach in analysing STS (Luzeaux 2011).

2.3 Complex Adaptive Systems

Complex adaptive systems are defined as "systems composed of interacting agents described in terms of rules. The agents adapt by changing their rules as experience accu- mulates" (Holland 1996). Scholars have formulated the theory of CAS in various ways, however, three components are consistently mentioned: *agents*, *interactions*, and an *environment* (Gell-Mann 1995). Agents are individuals actors within a CAS and represent a wide variety of entities such as humans, organisations, objects or concepts. They have the ability to perceive their environment, interact with other agents and the environment in many ways, which can result in complex and unpredictable emergent behaviour (i.e., emergence). Emergence is a bottom-up process that refers to "collective phenomena that are collaboratively created by individuals, yet are not reducible to individual action" (Keith Sawyer 2005). It is an inherent property of CAS, and enables complex systems to adapt, learn and change according to influences of their internal and/or external environment. As an irreducible property of an organisation, it can neither be fully understood nor predicted by examining the parts, such as people or technology, alone. Shadow-IT is irreducible, insofar as it had not existed as a recognised component of the organisation beforehand. Emergent properties often contribute to the resilience of a system. Resilience is the ability of a system (Luzeaux 2011) or an individual (Sawaragi 2020) to survive, adapt and learn when facing difficulties or changes in its environment. It is often related to specific risks, hazards, or periods of crisis (Gang et al. 2013), but also represents the capability to respond to a range of different, less severe, novel disturbances (Faulkner et al. 2018). Overall, CAS has been the subject of a number of studies that address how human actors self-organise in organisational contexts and what behaviours emerge (Nan and Yong 2014; Dong et al. 2022). These studies are part of the "third wave" of systems theory, which primarily seeks to characterise the properties and mechanisms of bottom-up processes (Nan 2011). However, as a relatively new stream of thought, CAS theory is still evolving on the topic of emergence in specific. This study extends the third-wave of systems theory through the development of a hybrid model that combines elements from CAS with STS to explain what social factors affect employee compliance with cyber-security measures. It extends current research on the concept of complexity and its impact on cyber security (Norman and Koehler 2017; Olagbemiro 2019; Slangen 2016).

3 Methodology

We present a qualitative social science study, based on two theories of organisational design, i.e., STS and CAS theories. This study aims to create a conceptual model that illustrates factors that are relevant to the design of cyber-security measures and susceptible to affect it. To achieve our research goal, we gathered data about operational knowledge from selected organisations and their cyber-security activities. Operational knowledge encompasses insights into the inner workings of an organisation, e.g., how decisions were made, what challenges appeared, what the response was and why (Kaiser 2014). The research of operational knowledge is based on concepts derived from the underlying frameworks of STS and CAS theory. The smallest unit of analysis, at the micro level, are the actual work groups—or teams—in the organisation. This is where conflicts or challenges between cyber-security and daily business possibly arise. As such, our study follows the original research design approach of Trist and Bamforth (Trist 1981; Walker et al. 2008). We selected two groups of participants, representing distinct levels within the organisation: senior managers and cyber-security experts.

3.1 Sampling Strategy and Research Setting

We used snowball sampling (Myers and Newman 2007) to purposefully select our participants on the basis of the following criteria. First, we targeted a wide range of key organisations from different types of industry sector, size and geographical location. For instance, we included multi-billion US$ financial companies, an international law firm, hospitals, a research institute and a country's military department. The geographical diversity ranges from local businesses in the SME category to international enterprises. It contains 3 SMEs, 1 intermediate enterprise and 10 large enterprises. Second, to gain insights from the perspective of a regulatory body, we targeted organisational-internal senior cyber-security experts (meso level), and to obtain operational knowledge (micro level), we targeted senior managers. The two perspectives allowed us to contrast views and experiences of those who plan and implement cyber-security measures with those who are affected by them as employees. Third, we systematically collected and analysed our empirical data until 'no new data appear[ed]' (Morse 1995) in line with our research approach (Klein and Myers 1999). Theoretical saturation was reached with a set of 20 senior experts from 14 leading organisations. An overview of our interviewee's background and their codes can be found in Table 1. The organisations were chosen to ensure a diverse cross-sector dataset, encompassing a variety of hierarchical and operational organisation models.

Table 1 Organisation and interviewee overview

Organisation	Interviewees/ID	Employees	Revenue/Budget (USD)	Area of operations
Armed forces	Dept. Head/B001	9–12k	70–100B	Europe
Research and education	Researcher/B002	–	–	Europe
Chemicals and process industry	Vice Pres. IT/B003 CISO/S001	15–18k	10-13B	Globally
Finance	Prog. Manager/ B004 Chief DLP Officer/S007	72–75k	18-21M	Globally
Finance	Software Eng./B007	48–51k	21–24B	Globally
Power and utilities	Head Consulting & Services/S010 Head of Comms./B010	–	–	Switzerland
Consulting	Cyber-Sec Advisor/ B008	135–140k	21–24M	Globally
Logistics and transport	Deputy Editor in Chief/B009 Sr. InfoSec Awareness/ S002	96–100k	10–13B	Globally
Globally	CIO/CISO/S003	6–9k	15–18B	Globally
Luxury goods Healthcare	CISO/S003	2–3k	210–240M	Europe
Municipality	Key Acc. Mgr./B005 CISO/S005	18–21k	9–12B	Switzerland
Law firm and legal counselling	CIO/S006	0.1–0.3k	30-33M	Europe
NGO	CISO/S008	6–9k	7–10B	Globally
Foundation	Head of Sec./S009 Prod. Marketing Mgr./B006	0.1–0.3k	30–33M	Switzerland

3.2 Data Collection

We followed well-established guidelines for qualitative research for data collection and analysis (Gioia et al. 2013), i.e., constant comparison, iterative conceptualisation, scaling up, and theoretical integration. We conducted a thorough literature review in 10 different databases: ACM Digital Library, Google Scholar, IEEE Xplore, JSTOR, SAGE Journal, SAGE Knowledge Science, Direct Scopus, Springer and Wiley Online Library. For each database, we designed a search query to combine cyber-security, socio-technical system theory and complex adaptive system theory terms. We reviewed and verified the results to (a) address social factors, beyond the individual, in the research and (b) mention a com- bination of STS and CAS in regards to explicitly explaining the internal mechanics and phenomena in an organisation (such as resilience and emergence). Our set of data sources build on semi-structured interviews that took place in 2021. To achieve two perspectives on the same phenomenon, we created two sets of questions as part of the construction of the interview guideline. The interview guideline was developed according to the under- lying theoretical-analytical categories of the two system theories (Bogner et al. 2002), STS and CAS. The questions for the senior managers aimed to understand the needs, challenges, and responses of their particular team concerning cyber-security measures, whereas the ques- tions for the cyber-security experts focused on how and why organisations established those measures. All interviews lasted around 60–90 min and were conducted online in either German, Swiss German or English, depending on the interviewee's preference. We developed the interview guide according to the underlying theoretical-analytical categories of the two system theories, STS and CAS. This theory-led approach allows a reciprocal examination of textual interpretation and theoretical knowledge in the phase of analysis (Bogner et al. 2002). From the 20 interviews, 17 were allowed to be recorded. The answers and comments from the three non-recorded interviews were directly paraphrased after the interview for later analysis. Considering that many participants were aware that their behaviour was non-compliant with the organisation's policies and the cyber-security experts were concerned about disclosing potential cyber risks to an outsider, a challenge during recruitment and when conducting the interviews was earning the participants' trust. The initial reluctance was mitigated after the interviewing author demonstrated professional business expertise in the field.

3.3 Data Analysis and Model Development

Our research analysis consisted of the three main phases of transcription, coding and network analysis of categories and themes (Saldaña 2013). In the first phase, 17 recorded interviews were fully transcribed, and prosodic and paraverbal utterance features were omitted. 3 interviews without recording were paraphrased during the interview and reviewed afterwards. In the second phase, the transcripts were coded to identify relevant material in the text. Coding was conducted in two main parts: (1) Deductive codes are derived from the pre-formulated, STS and CAS theory-based aspects of analysis. (2) An inductive coding cycle was used for a more detailed analysis of the text concerning the operational knowledge of the interviewee and its relationship to the study. It was also used to identify new and emerging patterns within the statements. The first author developed two corresponding codebooks. The codebooks and results were reviewed by the other authors. In the third phase, categories and themes were developed, based on a codes- to-theory model for qualitative inquiry (Saldaña 2013). A CAQDAS software was used to enable tool-based analysis and networking. Non-English interviews were carefully translated into English by the authors who have advanced English skills. We analysed the data through multiple rounds, balancing the discovery of new insights from the data with structures and principles derived from theoretical models and concepts from STS and CAS. The process led to the development of a hybrid model that extends studies on STS and cyber-security to include theoretical concepts from CAS. We incorporated social and technical subsystems of STS (including social factors and how they extend beyond organisational boundaries) and the CAS aspects of emergence and resilience, as identified in this study. The model was developed iteratively by the first author and reviewed by the other authors. It allows to analyse phenomena such as shadow-IT in a unique way, by enabling to identify internal and external social factors and the potential self-amplification of emergent behaviour.

4 Results

In this study, we identified various social factors capable of influencing and impacting organisational cyber-security, as predicted by STS theory. Furthermore, mechanisms has been observed leading to non-compliant behaviour, which are related to CAS theory. We developed a conceptual model to represent the results and the relationships between various elements and phenomena, shown in Fig. 1. The lower part is borrowed from STS theory (Bostrom and Heinen 1977), representing the organisation and their social and technical subsystems. Inside the organisation, the social subsystem consists of the individual people but also of their relationships, hierarchies and social structures. We extended this subsystem beyond organisational boundaries to represent external social factors between and transcending organisations. The lower right part represents the work and technical elements. The latter have been also extended beyond the organisation to represent and show how publicly available technology is integrated in emergent behaviour. The middle part depicts CAS phenomena—resilience and emergence—and their interaction with organisations. Solutions such as shadow-IT emerge from people's resilience in combination with available technologies. They can lead to positive feedback, as the workaround helps to get a job done, but also to negative one, e.g. when it violates compliance. Therefore, the model allows for a better understanding of the different social factors, e.g. peer pressure, their effects, e.g. fear and insecurity, and the impact through resilience and emergence in terms of information security policy design (Moody et al. 2018). The upper part represents the risks stemming from the emergent, non-compliant, behaviour.

4.1 Social Factors that Affect Cyber-Security

This research identified two groups of social factors, one related to the individual, and the other to relationships between people (RQ1). Motivation - both *intrinsic* and *extrinsic*—is a significant factor at the individual level, mentioned by 100% of interviewees. On an individual level, intrinsic and extrinsic motivation has shown to

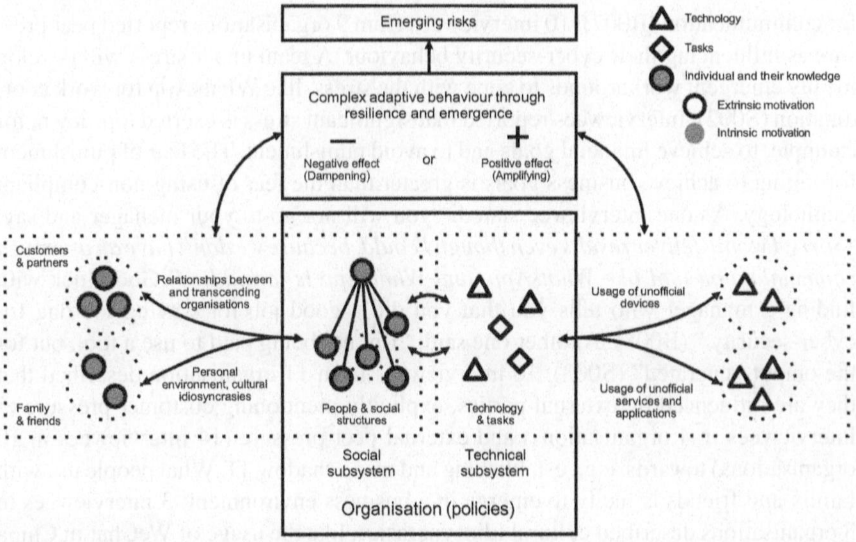

Fig. 1 Cyber-security in the context of STS and CAS

be a significant factor being mentioned by all interviewees. Intrinsically-motivated behaviours are generated by the sense of personal satisfaction that they bring. We identified three sub-factors: *autonomy*, *mastery* and *purpose*. Interviewees reported they want the freedom to design their workplace in order to achieve their goals, do good quality work and get the job done (S002). 16 out of 20 interviewees stated this is an important factor in regard to cyber-security compliance. This was particularly voiced in the healthcare domain, where employees seem to use shadow-IT frequently with justifications relating to mastery, such as "We save lives, we work with patients. [...] formalism and such comes second" (S005). We found that intrinsic factors are interrelated rather than separated, and can be influenced by extrinsic factors. Extrinsically-motivated behaviours are performed to receive (or avoid receiving) something from others based on three factors: *compensation*, *punishment* and *reward*. Financial incentives as part of a bonus plan (S006) or the fear of being punished for failed goals (B009) are examples of this.

Another strong social factor are *relationships*. They occur within organisations, but also extend beyond their boundaries. Inside organisations, influential relationships ap- pear horizontally in teams and peer groups, and vertically top-down between superiors and employees. External relationships occur between organisations, through customer pressure and peer dynamics, and transcending organisation, through the personal envi- ronment and cultural idiosyncrasies. 19 interviewees across 13 organisations reported that relationships contribute to non-compliant behaviour, while 12 interviewees in 10 organisations mentioned group dynamics, e.g., WhatsApp. Despite being non-compliant, it gets used because people need to circumvent technical and organisational restrictions; for example, using WhatsApp for communication (B007). 10 interviewees from 9 organisations reported peer pressure as influencing their cyber-security behaviour. A team under stress will develop locally emergent workarounds to cope with the stress, like WhatsApp for work coordination (S002). Interviewees reported that significant stress is exerted top-down, for example, to achieve financial goals and to avoid punishment. The fear of punishment for failing to achieve business goals is greater than the fear of using non-compliant technology. As one interviewee stated: "you will not go to your manager and say: "*Sorry, I won't deliver results even though I could, because we don't have an approved communication tool like WhatsApp, and WhatsApp is forbidden.*" Good luck with finding a manager who tells you that you did a good job for waving the flag for cyber-security." (B008). Another one said: "I'm not being paid to use a tool, but for the output generated" (S003). 16 interviewees from 11 organisation described that they are influenced by external parties, explicitly mentioning customer pressure (5 interviewees in 4 organisations) and external peer pressure (14 interviewees in 10 organisations) towards, e.g., establishing and using shadow-IT. What people use with family and friends is likely to emerge in a business environment. 3 interviewees in 3 organisations described cultural idiosyncrasies, like the usage of WeChat in China (S001).

4.2 Resilience, Emergence, and Risks

The effects of social factors lead to two CAS phenomena: *resilience* and *emergence*, see 2.3. People react to stress and disturbances through resilience, in the form of adaption and recovery, as was observed in 100% of the organisations. This led to emerging non- compliant behaviour, such as shadow-IT, which was observed in every organisation. Emergence is not a local, isolated phenomenon; it appears and manifests itself within and among teams, across all hierarchical levels of an organisation, from team leaders to middle and C-level management. Furthermore, it can extend beyond organisational boundaries, e.g., when working with clients and partners.

13 of the interviewed organisations have cyber-security policies and guidelines in place. Yet, 17 interviewees from 12 organisations confirmed that their organization was aware of shadow-IT or other workarounds. Interestingly, management did not enforce compliance with organisational guidelines, but rather—implicitly and willingly—condoned shadow-IT as an emergent solution for the sake of business. In one organisation, board members simply overruled policies in order to use actually prohibited tools like Zoom (S001). Others said they had to attend external events hosted on Zoom. As it was forbidden they switched to private devices (B003). The business interviewees and their colleagues were well aware of their risky behaviour, but consciously decided to ignore them, in favour of their business, team or personal goals. All 10 interviewed cyber-security experts were aware of the existence and usage of unofficial tools and services in their organisation. While they are without a doubt knowledgeable and capable of solving complicated—technical—problems, they struggle to address complex ones, like emergence. The interviews showed

that the different factors are interrelated, to different degrees. Extrinsic motivation turned out to be the most influential factor, encouraged by organisational design, e.g., through bonus structures. Superiors are widely motivated to achieve monetary gains—an extrinsic motivation—and oftentimes exert pressure onto on their teams to prioritise financial goals over compliance. If in addition a client demands the usage of non-compliant tools, such as Google Drive, employees will give in in order to not to endanger the project, and to satisfy their supervisor's demands.

This behaviour caused substantial risks. The three main contributions towards in- creasing organisational risks are: usage of unofficial devices; usage of unofficial ser- vices/applications; and uncontrollable use and handling of data. This results in three main risk categories: direct risks towards cyber-security controls; data privacy risks; and contractual (legal) risks. The most apparent risks are the ones related to cyber- security objects. The usage of non-compliant, unauthorised and unaudited solutions can compromise the confidentiality, availability and integrity of organisational information. Additional risks are partly a byproduct of emergent behaviour, such as violations of data privacy regulations, e.g., GDPR, or official secrets acts, which can lead to reputational and financial damage. Another risk is the potential violation of contractual agreements. Both can impact organisations, as well as the individual, resulting in legal sanctions for both parties, i.e., liability claims. Many interviewees confirmed that they and their colleagues are generally aware of possible risks.

4.3 *Knowledge and Awareness in Fostering Compliance*

Our study also explored the role and effect of knowledge and awareness, as they are popular controls in organisations and science. 12 out of 14 organisations conduct cyber- security training, including passive elements—such as blog posts and videos—and active elements—like e-learning and questionnaires. Generally, the assumption is that the problem is due to a lack of knowledge, and that people will adapt if they know more about cyber-security. The aim is to alter employee behaviour to match technical requirements. We found that this assumption is flawed, (RQ2). 15 out of 20 interviewees stated that employees in their organisations are (well) aware of potential cyber-security risks; however, in all 14 organisations unofficial or unauthorised tools and services (shadow-IT) were used. Here, we showed that non-compliant behaviour originates from conscious decisions due to conflicting goals and interests—based on intrinsic and extrinsic motivation—rather than from a lack of knowledge or awareness, and that organisational and socio-structural influences are neglected in organisations' measures addressing cyber-security.

5 Conclusion

This research confirms the value of systems thinking in cyber-security. It extends existing work in the area of STS and cyber-security (Baxter and Sommerville 2011) by identifying various social factors and their influence, from the individual to supervisor relationships and peer pressure. Those factors are significantly influenced by the organisation design - such as bonus systems or work culture. They even extend beyond organisational boundaries, including clients, partners, families and friends. As such, this study also confirms the approach to conduct STS research at the work group level, rather than the individual (Trist 1981).

It confirms the two main principles in STS design (Walker et al. 2008). Focusing on technical optimisations of cyber-security, while neglecting social factors, leads to unhealthy effects (Trist and Bamforth 1951; Pasmore et al. 2019). By applying CAS theory, we provide an explanation for "non-linear" and complex phenomena (Walker et al. 2008) resulting in effects such as shadow-IT. The notion of "humans as the weakest link" (Caldwell 2012) contradicts the findings of this study. The same is true for the assumption that awareness is key (Ling et al. 2019). Instead, it is a range of social factors (Pasmore and Khalsa 1993) that contribute to safe behaviour. As technology advanced from coal mines to cloud computing, the underlying principles of STS still apply.

The study included multi-national organisations, yet it might be beneficial to extend future research to interviews outside the EU region. Furthermore, a longitudinal study can provide further insights and confirm the findings through a quantitative approach. Future research could usefully explore the relevance of systems thinking in the field of cyber-security. A combined approach of STS and CAS theories also seems to be beneficial for understanding and designing better-performance cyber-security.

From a theoretical perspective, our study makes a timely and necessary contribution to the current debate about employees compliance with cyber-security policies. First, we expand the knowledge of STS theory to combine elements from CAS to explain the underlying social mechanisms affecting cyber-security. Then, we identified relevant factors from industry practices and integrated into the conceptual framework. Further- more, this paper contributes to practice by recommending policymakers to consider social aspects when designing cyber-security controls. Comprehending cyber-security as a problem which can be addressed by technology alone appears to be the real elephant in the room. Today's focus of cyber-security on technology and processes is necessary, but by no means sufficient. Given the complexity of STS and the effects of CAS, the authors suggest that organisational cyber-security is rather a wicked problem (Rittel and Webber 1973; Horst 1988) than a complicated one. Furthermore, solutions need to address human desirability, business viability, and technical feasibility (Trist et al. 1963). In this context, we recommend researchers and practitioners to look at the current body of knowledge on human-centred design (Paula et al. 2023; Gerken et al. 2022) and its potential in designing effective systems (Buchanan 1992).

References

Amanda Andress. *Surviving security: How to integrate people, process, and technology*. Auerbach Publications, 2nd edition, 2003–12–18. ISBN 978-0-429-21043-3. https://doi.org/10.1201/9780203501405.

Gordon Baxter and Ian Sommerville. Socio-technical systems: From design methods to systems engineering. *Interacting with Computers*, 23(1):4–17, 2011–01. https://doi.org/10.1016/j.intcom.2010.07.003.

Ling Li, Wu He, Li Xu, Ivan Ash, Mohd Anwar, and Xiaohong Yuan. Investigating the impact of cybersecurity policy awareness on employees' cybersecurity behavior. *International Journal of Information Management*, 45:13–24, 2019–04. https://doi.org/10.1016/j.ijinfomgt.2018.10.017.

Federal Bureau of Investigation (FBI). 2020 internet crime report, 2020. URL https://web.archive.org/web/20220422112606/https://www.ic3.gov/Media/PDF/AnnualReport/2020_IC3Report.pdf.

Federal Bureau of Investigation (FBI). 2011 internet crime report, 2011. URL https://web.archive.org/web/20220422112208/https://www.ic3.gov/Media/PDF/AnnualReport/2011_IC3Report.pdf.

Verizon. 2021 data breach investigations report (DBIR), 2021. URL https://web.archive.org/web/20220422122253/https://www.verizon.com/business/resources/reports/2021-data-breach-investigations-report.pdfx.

Verizon. 2011 data breach investigations report (DBIR), 2011. URL https://web.archive.org/web/20220122034248/http://www.wired.com/images_blogs/threatlevel/2011/04/Verizon-2011-DBIR_04-13-11.pdf.

European Union Agency for Law Enforcement Cooperation. Internet organised crime threat assessment (IOCTA) 2021, 2021. URL https://web.archive.org/web/20220422111850/https://www.europol.europa.eu/cms/sites/default/files/documents/internet_organised_crime_threat_assessment_iocta_2021.pdf.

European Union Agency for Law Enforcement Cooperation. Internet organised crime threat assessment (IOCTA) 2011, 2011. URL https://web.archive.org/web/20220422111842/https://www.europol.europa.eu/cms/sites/default/files/documents/octa2011.pdf.

W. Alec Cram, Jeffrey G. Proudfoot, and John D'Arcy. Maximizing employee compliance with cybersecurity policies. *MIS Quarterly Executive*, 19(3), 2020.

W. Alec Cram, John D'Arcy, and Jeffrey G. Proudfoot. Seeing the forest and the trees: A meta-analysis of the antecedents to information security policy compliance. *MIS Quarterly*, 43(2):525–554, 2019.

Devin C. Streeter. The effect of human error on modern security breaches. *Strategic Informer: Student Publication of the Strategic Intelligence Society*, 1(3):2, 2013.

Tracey Caldwell. Training—the weakest link. *Computer Fraud & Security*, 2012 (9):8–14, 2012–09. https://doi.org/10.1016/S1361-3723(12)70091-X.

Gabriela L. Mallmann, Antonio Carlos Gastaud Maçada, and Mírian Oliveira. The influence of shadow IT usage on knowledge sharing: An exploratory study with IT users. *Business Information Review*, 35(1):17–28, 2018–03. https://doi.org/10.1177/0266382118760143.

Symantec. 2018 Symantec shadow data report, 2018. URL https://web.archive.org/web/20220422115647/https://docs.broadcom.com/doc/2018-shadow-year-report-en.

Andreas Györy, Anne Cleven, Falk Uebernickel, and Walter Brenner. Exploring the shadows: IT governance approaches to user-driven innovation. In *European Conference on Information Systems*, page 13, 2012.

Eric L. Trist and Kevin W. Bamforth. Some social and psychological consequences of the longwall method of coal-getting: An examination of the psychological situation and defences of a work group in relation to the social structure and technological content of the work system. *Human Relations*, 4(1):3–38, 1951–02. https://doi.org/10.1177/001872675100400101.

Rossouw von Solms and Johan van Niekerk. From information security to cyber security. *Computers & Security*, 38:97–102, 2013–10. https://doi.org/10.1016/j.cose.2013.04.004.

Dtex Systems. The 2018 insider threat intelligence report. URL https://www.dtexsystems.com/resources/white-papers/2018-insider-threat-intelligence-report/.

Mark-David McLaughlin and Janis Gogan. Challenges and best practices in information security management. *MIS Quarterly Executive*, 17(3):12, 2018. URL https://aisel.aisnet.org/misqe/vol17/iss3/6.

Eric L. Trist. *The evolution of socio-technical systems: A conceptual frame-work and an action research program.* Ontario Ministry of Labour, Ontario Quality of Working Life Centre, 1981. ISBN 978-0-7743-6286-3. URL https://web.archive.org/web/20220422115915/https://trove.nla.gov.au/work/18802828.

William Pasmore, Stu Winby, Susan Albers Mohrman, and Rick Vanasse. Reflections: Sociotechnical systems design and organization change. *Journal of Change Management*, 19(2):67–85, 2019-04-03. ISSN 1469-7017, 1479–1811. https://doi.org/10.1080/14697017.2018.1553761.

William A. Pasmore and Gurudev S. Khalsa. The contributions of Eric Trist to the social engagement of social science. *Academy of Management Review*, 18(3): 546–569, 1993.

Frans M. van Eijnatten. An anthology of the socio-technical systems design (STSD) paradigm: From autonomous work groups to democratic dialogue and integral organizational renewal. 1991.

Ludwig von Bertalanffy, Wolfgang Hofkirchner, and David Rousseau. *General System Theory: Foundations, Development, Applications.* 1st edition, 1968.

Guy H. Walker, Neville A. Stanton, Paul M. Salmon, and Daniel P. Jenkins. A review of sociotechnical systems theory: A classic concept for new command and control paradigms. *Theoretical Issues in Ergonomics Science*, 9(6):479–499, 2008–11. https://doi.org/10.1080/14639220701635470.

Maria Bada, Angela M. Sasse, and Jason R. C. Nurse. Cyber security awareness campaigns: Why do they fail to change behaviour? page 15, 2015. https://doi.org/10.48550/arXiv.1901.02672.

Fred Emery. Characteristics of socio-technical systems. In Eric Trist, Hugh Murray, and Beulah Trist, editors, *The social engagement of social science, Volume 2*. University of Pennsylvania Press, 1993-01-31. ISBN 978-1-5128-1905-2. https://doi.org/10.9783/9781512819052-009.

Erjon Zoto, Mazaher Kianpour, Stewart James Kowalski, and Edgar Alonso Lopez- Rojas. A socio-technical systems approach to design and support systems thinking in cybersecurity and risk management education. *Complex Systems Informatics and Modeling Quarterly*, (18):65–75, 2019-04-30. https://doi.org/10.7250/csimq.2019-18.04.

Erjon Zoto, Stewart James Kowalski, Edgar Alonso Lopez Rojas, and Mazaher Kianpour. Using a socio-technical systems approach to design and support systems thinking in cyber security education. CEUR Workshop Proceedings, 2018. ISBN 1613-0073.

Isabella Corradini and Enrico Nardelli. Building organizational risk culture in cyber security: The role of human factors. In Tareq Z. Ahram and Denise Nicholson, editors, *Advances in human factors in cybersecurity*, volume 782 of *Advances in intelligent systems and computing*, pages 193–202. Springer International Publishing, 2019. ISBN 978-3-319-94781-5 978-3-319-94782-2. https://doi.org/10.1007/978-3-319-94782-2_19.

Masike Malatji, Sune Von Solms, and Annlizé Marnewick. Socio-technical systems cybersecurity framework. *Information and Computer Security*, 27(2):233–272, 2019-06-12. https://doi.org/10.1108/ICS-03-2018-0031.

Thomas Richard McEvoy and Stewart James Kowalski. Deriving cyber security risks from human and organizational factors—A socio-technical approach. *Complex systems informatics and modeling quarterly*, (18):47–64, 2019-04-30. https://doi.org/10.7250/csimq.2019-18.03.

Moufida Sadok, Christine Welch, and Peter Bednar. A socio-technical perspective to counter cyber-enabled industrial espionage. *Security Journal*, 33(1):27–42, 2020-03. https://doi.org/10.1057/s41284-019-00198-2.

Grethe Østby, Lars Berg, Mazaher Kianpour, Basel Katt, and Stewart James Kowalski. A socio-technical framework to improve cyber security training: A work in progress. CEUR Workshop Proceedings, 2019. ISBN 1613-0073.

Dominique Luzeaux, editor. *Complex systems and systems of systems engineering.* ISTE, 2011. ISBN 978-1-84821-253-4.

Wolter Pieters. Defining the weakest link; comparative security in complex systems of systems. In *2013 IEEE 5th International conference on cloud computing technology and science*, pages 39–44. IEEE, 2013-12. ISBN 978-0-7695-5095-4. https://doi.org/10.1109/CloudCom.2013.101.

Cecil Eng Huang Chua and Veda C. Storey. Central IT or shadow IT? Factors shaping users' decision to go rogue with IT. page 14, 2014.

John H. Holland. Complex adaptive systems and spontaneous emergence. In Al- berto Quadrio Curzio and Marco Fortis, editors, *Complexity and industrial clusters*, Contributions to economics, pages 25–34. Physica-Verlag HD, 2002. ISBN 978-3-7908-1471-2 978-3-642-50007-7. https://doi.org/10.1007/978-3-642-50007-7_3.

John H. Holland. *Hidden order: How adaptation builds complexity*. Addison Wesley Longman Publishing Co., Inc., 1996.

Murray Gell-Mann. *The quark and the jaguar: Adventures in the simple and the complex*. Macmillan, 1995.

R. Keith Sawyer. *Social emergence: Societies as complex systems*. Cambridge University Press, 2005.

Tetsuo Sawaragi. Design of resilient socio-technical systems by human- system co-creation. *Artificial Life and Robotics*, 25(2):219–232, 2020-05. https://doi.org/10.1007/s10015-020-005 98-3.

Gang Wu, Adriana Feder, Hagit Cohen, Joanna J. Kim, Solara Calderon, Dennis S. Charney, and Aleksander A. Mathé. Understanding resilience. *Frontiers in behavioral neuroscience*, 7:10, 2013

Lucy Faulkner, Katrina Brown, and Tara Quinn. Analyzing community resilience as an emergent property of dynamic social-ecological systems. *Ecology and Society*, 23(1), 2018. https://doi.org/10.5751/ES-09784-230124.

Ning Nan and Yong Lu. Harnessing the power of self-organization in an online community during organizational crisis. *MIS Quarterly*, 38(4):1135–1158, 2014.

Xueyan Dong, Xuan Xiong, Tienan Wang, and Jingjing Ge. Self-organization power: Exploring the synthesis process of self-organization in emergencies - a qualitative study based on COVID-19 epidemic lockdown in China. In *PACIS 2022 Proceedings. 292.*, 2022.

Ning Nan. Capturing bottom-up information technology use processes: A complex adaptive systems model. *MIS Quarterly*, pages 505–532, 2011.

Michael D. Norman and Matthew T. K. Koehler. Cyber defense as a complex adaptive system: A model-based approach to strategic policy design. In *Proceedings of the 2017 International Conference of The Computational Social Science Society of the Americas*, pages 1–1, 2017.

Albert Olagbemiro. Cyberspace as a complex adaptive system and the policy and operational implications for cyberwarfare. In *National Security: Breakthroughs in Research and Practice*, pages 250–264. IGI Global, 2019.

Rick Slangen. Understanding cyber-risk by investigating the behaviour of defender and threat agent organisations: Why a complex adaptive systems perspective con- tributes to further understanding cyber-risk. 2016.

Robert Kaiser. *Qualitative Experteninterviews*. Springer Fachmedien Wiesbaden, 2014. ISBN 978-3-658-02478-9 978-3-658-02479-6. https://doi.org/10.1007/978-3-658-02479-6.

Michael D. Myers and Michael Newman. The qualitative interview in is research: Examining the craft. *Information and organization*, 17(1):2–26, 2007.

Janice M. Morse. The significance of saturation, 1995.

Heinz K. Klein and Michael D. Myers. A set of principles for conducting and evaluating interpretive field studies in information systems. *MIS Quarterly*, pages 67–93, 1999.

Dennis A. Gioia, Kevin G. Corley, and Aimee L. Hamilton. Seeking qualitative rigor in inductive research: Notes on the Gioia methodology. *Organizational Research Methods*, 16(1):15–31, 2013–01. https://doi.org/10.1177/1094428112452151.

Alexander Bogner, Beate Littig, and Wolfgang Menz. *Das Experteninterview*. Springer, 2002. ISBN 3-531-14447-2. https://doi.org/10.1007/978-3-322-93270-9.

Johnny Saldaña. *The coding manual for qualitative researchers*. SAGE, 2nd edition, 2013. ISBN 978-1-4462-4736-5 978-1-4462-4737-2.

Robert P. Bostrom and J. Stephen Heinen. MIS problems and failures: A socio- technical perspective. Part I: The causes. *MIS Quarterly*, 1(3):17, 1977–09. https://doi.org/10.2307/248710.

Gregory D. Moody, Mikko Siponen, and Seppo Pahnila. Toward a unified model of information security policy compliance. *MIS Quarterly*, 42(1):285–312, 2018. https://doi.org/10.25300/MISQ/2018/13853.

Horst W. J. Rittel and Melvin M. Webber. Dilemmas in a general theory of planning. *Policy sciences*, 4(2):155–169, 1973.

Horst W. J. Rittel. *The reasoning of designers*. IGP, 1988.

Eric Trist, Gurth Higgin, Hugh Murray, and Alex Pollock. *Organizational choice: Capabilities of groups at the coal face under changing technologies: The loss, rediscovery & transformation of a work tradition*. Routledge, 1963. ISBN 0-203-43632-6.

Danielly de Paula, Carolin Marx, Ella Wolf, Christian Dremel, Kathryn Cormican, and Falk Uebernickel. A managerial mental model to drive innovation in the context of digital transformation. *Industry and innovation*, 30(1):42–66, 2023.

Stefanie Gerken, Falk Uebernickel, and Danielly de Paula. *Design thinking: a global study on implementation practices in organizations: Past-present-future*. Universitätsverlag Potsdam, 2022.

Richard Buchanan. Systems thinking and design thinking: The search for principles in the world we are making. *She Ji: The journal of design, economics, and innovation*, 5(2):85–104, 2019–22. https://doi.org/10.1016/j.sheji.2019.04.001.

Richard Buchanan. Wicked problems in design thinking. *Design issues*, 8(2):5, 1992–21. https://doi.org/10.2307/1511637.

Influencing Factors for the Adoption of Speech Assistance in Manufacturing

Philipp Klingner and Philipp Scharfe

Abstract In recent years, there has been a steady increase in the use of speech assistants in the private environment. Although such assistance systems would also be beneficial for manufacturing (for example, because workers have their hands free), speech assistants have not yet been widely used in the industrial environment. Against this background, we develop in this article a model with factors that influence the decision of industrial firms whether to adopt speech assistance for manufacturing. In order to do so, we rely on the Technology-Organization-Environment (TOE) framework and by interviewing 10 experts from firms that develop or use speech assistance solutions. Our model consists of 17 context factors that influence whether companies adopt speech assistance in manufacturing.

Keywords Speech assistance · Voice assistance · Manufacturing · Technology-organization-environment (TOE)

1 Introduction

Over the last years, there has been a rise in the usage of speech assistance in the fields of entertainment and smart home (Langen 2022). Applications such as Siri, Google Assistant and Cortana can now be found on all mobile devices. So-called smart speakers are increasingly being used in private households. According to a recent study, 21% of Germans own at least one smart speaker and half of all Germans already use speech-based assistance in their everyday lives (Herz et al. 2022). This shows that speech assistance is already wide applied in the private sector. Due to their intuitive and simple operation, these systems are mainly used to retrieve information or to control smart devices in the household (Ammari et al. 2019; Maedche et al. 2019).

P. Klingner · P. Scharfe (✉)
Chair of Business Information Systems, esp. Business Engineering, Technical University of Dresden, Dresden, Germany
e-mail: philipp.scharfe@tu-dresden.de

D. Beverungen et al. (eds.), *Conceptualizing Digital Responsibility for the Information Age*, Lecture Notes in Information Systems and Organisation 74,
https://doi.org/10.1007/978-3-031-80119-8_27

Despite this growing acceptance in the consumer sector, speech-based assistants are only applied to a limited extent in the manufacturing context. The only established industrial use case is pick-by-voice technology in logistics, in which an employee is guided to the corresponding goods via a headset and can call up speech-based information about them (Kalla and Seiter 2021). However, speech assistance would offer multiple advantages in the manufacturing domain. For example, speech as a form of interaction is more efficient than other forms because more information can be exchanged in less time. In addition, workers have their hands free and can move around freely, allowing parallel work to be carried out. This could lead to increased efficiency in maintenance processes or the control of technical equipment in production (Fischer et al. 2017; Langen 2022; Udoka 1991). Against this background, it is necessary to understand what factors lead to or hamper the decision of industrial firms to adopt speech assistance in their manufacturing processes.

Related literature already studied factors that influence the adoption of assistance systems (e.g., Meyer von Wolff et al. 2021; Rodriguez Cardona et al. 2019). However, these studies have a focus on digital workplaces or the insurance industry and it remains questionable if their findings can be generalized to assistance systems that primary interact via speech and that operate in manufacturing processes with their particularities (e.g., loud background noises). Therefore, these studies only provide limited understanding regarding factors that influence the adoption of speech assistance in manufacturing environments. Reacting to that, we want to answer the following research question: *What factors influence firms' decision whether to adopt speech assistance in manufacturing processes*?

To answer this research question, we conducted 10 interviews with industrial experts that develop or use speech assistance systems and identified 17 factors that influence the adoption of such systems in manufacturing (Döring and Bortz 2016). We structure these factors along the Technology-Organization-Environment (TOE) framework (Tornatzky and Fleischer 1990). The remainder of this study is structured in the following way: First, we describe the research background regarding speech assistance in manufacturing and the TOE-framework. After a brief description of our methodology, we then present our results and the 17 factors. We conclude by discussing our results and limitations.

2 Research Background

2.1 Speech Assistance in Manufacturing

Speech assistance can be described as "a core technology for human–machine interaction [that] provide access to product offerings, information, and services via natural language" (Langen 2022, S. 1). The interaction via natural language or speech has various advantages compared to the interaction via a Graphical User Interface (GUI).

Since people talk faster than they type, speech interactions have a shorter conversation time. In addition, speech interaction avoids navigation through often complex graphical menus. Keyboards (e.g., on a screen) for typing are often small and therefore difficult to use. This is particularly a problem in manufacturing, where workers often wear gloves. Moreover, keyboards for typing need the use of hands and visual attention. This leads to distractions and work interruptions. A conversation via speech avoids these mentioned problems (Fischer et al. 2017; Langen 2022; Udoka 1991).

The architecture of a speech assistance system consists of five key elements, which are passed through in a process. First, the acoustic front end (AFE, such as a microphone) records the spoken words. These words are then transformed into machine readable text by using a machine-learning trained Natural Language Understanding unit (NLU). As third component, the dialog manager (DM) handles the conversation with the user and generates the response. As fourth and fifth components, the text-to-speech (TTS) and audio playback (AP) units transform this response into natural speech and play it back to the user (Langen 2022).

Speech assistance can be applied in manufacturing for various scenarios. One scenario is the monitoring and control of industrial devices and machines (Langen 2022). For example, Loch et al. (2018) describe the scenario where a machine for cleaning beverage bottles is controlled via a speech assistance system. Another application scenario is the maintenance of manufacturing equipment and machines. For example, such an assistance solution can guide service technicians interactively by providing instructions, checklists, and wiki pages. Moreover, such a speech-based assistance system can also be used as a training tool (Langen 2022; Loch et al. 2018).

2.2 Technology-Organization-Environment (TOE) Framework

In literature few models have been proposed explaining the adoption of organizational technology on a firm level (Dwivedi et al. 2012). One of these models is the TOE framework, which describes that three groups of context factors (i.e., technological context, organizational context, and environmental context) explain the adoption of innovative technology (Dwivedi et al. 2012; Tornatzky and Fleischer 1990).

First, the *technological context* includes all the technologies and their characteristics that are relevant to the firm (i.e., those ones that are already used by the organization and those that are offered on the market but not currently in use). Second, the *organizational context* describes resources and characteristics of the company (including linking structures, intra-firm communication processes, the amount of slack resources, and the firm size). Third, the *environmental* context describes "the arena in which a firm conducts its business—its industry, competitors, the macroeconomic context, and the regulatory environment" (Dwivedi et al. 2012, S. 235). Moreover, these three groups of context factors interact with each other and influence the decision of whether to adopt a new technology.

Since we seek to explain what factors influence industrial organizations whether to adopt speech assistance in manufacturing processes, we see the TOE framework as an appropriate underlying framework for this research. Moreover, the TOE framework has been widely applied for similar research (e.g., Demlehner and Laumer 2020; Meyer von Wolff et al. 2021; Rodriguez Cardona et al. 2019).

3 Methodology

To identify the influencing factors on the adoption of speech assistance in manufacturing, we conducted interviews with industry experts following established methodological guidelines (Döring and Bortz 2016; Schultze and Avital 2011). In general, we applied a three-step approach.

First, we selected our interview partners. For this purpose, it is first necessary to define who can be considered as an expert for our interviews. We identified two groups of possible interview partners. One group includes employees of companies from the manufacturing sector that currently implement or already use speech assistance. The second group consists of the software developers who offer speech assistance solutions for the manufacturing environment. Moreover, another requirement was that our interview partners have multiple years of experience in the field of industrial speech assistance. In the first group (the users of speech assistance), we distinguished on the basis of roles between managers and shop floor workers. For the second group (the providers of speech assistance), we distinguished between the roles of sales representatives and software engineers. We tried to conduct interviews with both groups and each both roles in order to get a comprehensive overview of the relevant factors. In total, we conducted 10 interviews. Table 1 provides an overview of our interviewed companies, the interviewed employees and their roles.

Second, we conducted 10 semi-structured interviews remotely via a conference system between January and May 2022. The interviews lasted in average between 30 and 60 min. One longer interview took two hours. The structure of the interview questions followed the TOE framework. First, we asked for the factors included in the TOE framework (e.g., about the regulatory environment for the environmental context). Then, we continued with open question to identify more factors. We recorded the interviews and transcribed them.

Third, we relied on a structured approach to analyze the content of the interview transcripts. In particular, the first author developed codes (open coding) and assigned them to the three contexts described in the TOE framework. These codes were then the basis for the formulation and structuring of the identified factors (axial coding). Since we conducted our interviews in German, we translated the final coding and the factors into English. To improve the reliability of the coding, the second author checked the coding results.

Table 1 Overview of our interview partners

No	Function	Sector	Size	U/MA	U/SF	P/SA	P/SE
1	Engineer	Cert	SME		X		
2	CEO	Auto	SME	X			
3	Engineer	Aero	LE		X		
4	Senior AI Develop	ICT	LE				X
5	Project Manager	ICT	LE				X
6	Head of Sales	ICT	SME			X	
7	Sales Manager	ICT	SME			X	
8	Energy Manager	Auto	LE		X		
9	CEO	Auto	SME			X	
10	Project Manager	Auto	LE			X	

Abbreviations: (1) Groups and roles: *U/MA* User/Manager; *U/SF* User/Shop floor worker; *P/SA* Provider/Sales representative; *P/SE* Provider/Software engineer (2) (Firm) size: *SME* Small and medium-sized enterprise; *LE* large enterprise (3) Sector: *Aero*: Aerospace; *Auto*: Automotive; *Cert* Industrial certification, *ICT* Information and communication technology

4 Results

Our study identified 17 factors explaining whether firms adopt speech assistance for manufacturing. We structure these factors along the three dimensions of the TOE framework (see Fig. 1).

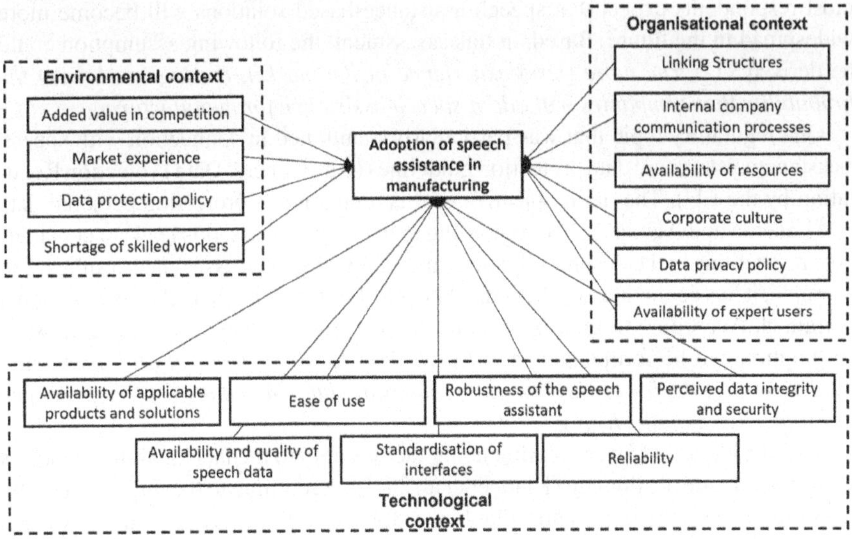

Fig. 1 Adoption of speech assistance in manufacturing processes

4.1 Environmental Context

A central reason for introducing new technologies is to generate added value in order to prevail in an intensely competitive environment (Phillips and Schirmer 2008). However, according to the interviewees, speech-based projects have a high initial expense and the benefit varies depending on the use case or is sometimes difficult to express in monetary profit before introducing the system. Overall, the interviewees expect a gain in efficiency, which is expressed, for example, through shorter throughput times or less downtime. In some use cases, even personnel can be saved or employees can be deployed in a more targeted manner. This is mainly due to the possibility of parallel work with the free hands and the increased mobility or independence of location. Overall, the expected added value in a competitive environment has a positive influence on the introduction of speech assistance, which is why the following assumption was made: *A1: The higher (lower) the expected added value in a competitive environment, the higher (lower) the probability that companies will adopt speech assistance for manufacturing.*

According to the interviewed experts has the availability of market experience an influence on the adoption of speech assistance. If there are more firms that already adopted speech assistance and/ or developed and implemented such solutions (e.g., consultants), the more firms can share their experience (Langen 2022; Wang 2022; Xu et al. 2021). This would lead to a better dissemination of this technology, as the following statement exemplifies: "*You already break down the barriers for each other with the customers if the introduction of speech assistance has already been considered [by others]*" (Expert 6). However, according to the respondents' assessment, there is currently limited experience on the market. Once this hurdle is overcome, most respondents expect that speech assistance-based solutions will become more widespread in the future. Based on this assessment, the following assumption could be derived: *A2: The more (less) experience in the market, the higher (lower) the probability that companies will adopt speech assistance for manufacturing.*

One regulatory topic that was particularly mentioned in connection with speech assistance systems are data protection guidelines (e.g., General Data Protection Regulation by the EU). The main objective of this regulation is protecting personal data (De Lacerda and Aguiar 2019). According to the interviewees, this leads to considerable restrictions in the design, selection, and usage of speech assistance systems. For example, it has an impact on where the data may be stored or where the speech model is trained. According to the impressions described in the interviews, the following assumption can be formulated: *A3: The stricter (looser) the legal data protection guidelines are, the lower (higher) the probability that companies will adopt speech assistance for manufacturing.*

The last identified external influencing factor refers to the lack of skilled workers in the manufacturing domain (Klapper et al. 2019). According to the interviewees, by using speech as an intuitive and suitable way for interaction, such assistance systems offer the possibility to collect domain-specific process knowledge and to use it for the training and instruction of new employees. If the system is intelligent enough, it can also be adapted to the employee's qualifications and experience. Accordingly, the following assumption can be made: *A3: The higher (lower) the shortage of skilled workers, the higher (lower) the probability that companies will adopt speech assistance for manufacturing.*

4.2 Technological Context

Another factor is the availability of necessary products and solutions (Dwivedi et al. 2012). This factor was considered important by almost all interviewees. They referred to multiple hardware and software solutions that are crucial for developing, implementing, and using speech assistance in manufacturing. These products and solutions can be single components (e.g., a microphone/ a speech-to-text software) or the whole system consisting of multiple components (e.g., the final software system that talks via speech with the user). Moreover, the interviewees mentioned that the performance of these relevant products and solutions increased within the last years, which has a positive effect on adopting speech assistance. Correspondingly, we formulated the following assumption: *A4: The higher (lower) the availability of applicable speech assistance products and solutions on the market, the higher (lower) the likelihood that companies will adopt such solutions for manufacturing.*

Speech data is the basis for training a language model that transforms spoken words into machine-readable text (Langen 2022). Accordingly, the availability and quality of speech data could be identified as a general influencing factors for the adoption of speech assistance. There are pre-trained language models (e.g., provided by Google) for the speech-to-text conversation. However, the interview partners highlighted that the language model must be adapted to the specific technical vocabulary in the desired manufacturing domain. Some data, such as end-user formulations, are not available in the pre-trained language model, but have to be worked out during the speech assistance development/ set-up (Runkler 2010; Wang et al. 2021). Overall, the following general assumption can be made: *A5: The higher (lower) the availability and quality of speech data, the higher (lower) the probability that companies will adopt speech assistance for manufacturing.*

Another influencing factor identified was the ease of use or user-friendliness of the speech assistance (Davis 1989). The core idea of all interviewees was that the use of speech assistance solution must be as simple as possible as the following statement shows "*ideally the speech assistant is so intuitive that [the manufacturing worker] does not have to learn much new*" (Expert 4). To reach this ease of use, the interviewees emphasized some design characteristics of the speech assistance solution. First, the speech assistance system should minimize waiting times. This means that the user does not want to wait long on the systems response to a speech input. Second, the correct structuring of the dialogues also leads to easier operation. Overall, suppose the processes and timings of the dialogue match the employee's working methods and the employee can enter the queries intuitively with the application-specific vocabulary. In that case, this ensures that the system integrates seamlessly and the employee hardly has to learn anything new. According to the respondents, this positively influences the acceptance of the systems, which leads to the following assumption: *A6: The easier (harder) it is to use speech assistants, the higher (lower) the probability that companies will adopt such solutions in manufacturing.*

On-site conditions pose a particular challenge in the industrial sector. In addition to the loud noise caused by technical equipment, the speech assistant system must also be able to deal with harsh physical conditions (e.g., wetness and dirt) (Fischer et al. 2017; Loch et al. 2018; Mayer and Pantförder 2014; Scharfe et al. 2022). Accordingly, not only the algorithms of the speech recognizer are in demand here, but also the selected hardware must be correspondingly robust. According to the interviewees, very specific headsets are used to deal with the mentioned environmental conditions. Modern microphone technology also supports the filtering of background noise and facilitates further processing by the software. In some cases, several microphones are used to better separate the interfering signal from the useful signal. Based on interviewees' statements, the following assumption can be derived: *A8: The more robust (vulnerable) the solutions are against harsh settings, the higher (lower) the probability that companies will adopt speech assistance for manufacturing.*

Another influencing factor is the standardization of interfaces (Stich et al. 2015). The interview partners highlighted that speech assistance systems are often connected via interfaces with other software systems in the manufacturing environment (e.g., machine control systems or manufacturing management systems). To enable limited efforts to connect the speech assistance system with these other systems the speech assistance one should have standardized interfaces. This leads us to the following assumption: *A9: The higher (lower) the degree of standardization of the interfaces of the systems to be connected, the higher (lower) the probability that companies will adopt speech assistance for manufacturing.*

According to the interviewees, a particular problem with speech-based data interaction solutions is the perceived integrity of the data. The following statement by Expert 4 sums up this observation well: "*The general fear of employees with speech assistants is that they will be bugged and that bosses will be able to track what they have done and when. This fear is actually unjustified due to data protection laws*". End users are therefore afraid of data misuse. From the point of view of the providers of such solutions, however, this is unjustified because the software prevents such use of the data due to legal regulations. According to the interviewees, appropriate transparency must be created to allay users' concerns. For this, employees using speech assistance must be informed about data storage and processing. Against the background of these observations, the following assumption was made: *A10: The better (worse) the perceived data integrity, the higher (lower) the probability that companies will adopt speech assistance for manufacturing.*

Another key factor from a technological perspective is the reliability of the speech assistance system (Loch et al. 2018). Our interview partners also confirmed this. The following statement of a speech assistance provider illustrates the importance: "*if I were to present [the product] and three values did not work [...] then it would be rejected immediately [by the customer], no matter what was good before [...] we must not have an error rate that is greater than 1.5 to 2%*" (Expert 6). Accordingly, not understanding or misunderstanding the speech input or a not understandable speech output can have fatal consequences, especially in industrial environments with high efficiency and safety demands (Loch et al. 2018). This leads to the following assumption: *A11: The higher (lower) the reliability, the higher (lower) the probability that companies will adopt speech assistance for manufacturing.*

4.3 Organizational Context

So-called 'linking structures' refer to interdepartmental structures (e.g., enabled by IT systems) within an organization and the information exchange they provide (Dwivedi et al. 2012). According to the interviewees, these structures make it possible for a (speech-based) assistant system to connect different departments. For example, by linking information from the production department with that from the warehouse department, employees can call up the availability of materials directly in the production process. Therefore, such linking structures lead to increased efficiency. Against this background, the following assumption was made: *A12: The better (worse) the linking structures in a company are, the higher (lower) the probability that this company will adopt speech assistance for manufacturing.*

Another influencing factor are the company's internal communication processes. It was pointed out that any new technology must be communicated well to the manufacturing employees. Therefore, the interviewees argued that a good communication strategy is necessary to reduce the obstacles and reservations towards speech-based solutions as a new technology. Overall, the following assumption can be made: *A13: The better the company's internal communication processes are, the higher (lower) the probability that this company will adopt speech assistance for manufacturing.*

The interview partners referred to various resources that are necessary for the adoption of speech assistance. In addition to the necessary capital, the availability of staff and time play an important role. Moreover, two respondents pointed to the necessary (IT) infrastructure as another resource (Langen 2022). Based on these findings, the following assumption can be made: *A14: The greater (smaller) the availability of an organization's resources, the higher (lower) the probability that this company will adopt speech assistance for manufacturing.*

Based on the interviews, corporate culture was also identified as another influencing factor. The interviewees pointed out that employees, especially management, must be open to innovative technologies (such as speech assistance). Overall, this leads to the following assumption: *A15: The more innovative (conservative) the corporate culture, the higher (lower) the probability that this company will adopt speech assistance in manufacturing.*

Another topic described in detail by our interview partners are company guideline restrictions through internal company regulations on data storage and transfer (Langen 2022). These guidelines either originate from the company management or are set by the works council. A frequently discussed point is the preference for on-premise solutions over cloud-based approaches. This makes implementation more expensive, as companies have to provide the necessary infrastructure themselves and update it regularly. Overall, these restrictions have a strong inhibiting effect and, in many cases, ensure that the adoption process stalls and existing solutions cannot be used. For this reason, the following assumption can be made: *A16: The stricter (looser) the companies data privacy policies are, the lower (higher) the probability that this company will introduce speech assistance in manufacturing.*

The last organisational influencing factor identified was the availability of expert users. According to the statements of our interview partners, an early involvement of expert users from manufacturing (e.g., those who know production processes and the used designations) is indispensable for a successful development and adaptation of the speech assistance solution to the needs of the user company. Special process knowledge is needed to create the dialogues. Through early feedback, special user needs and ways of working can be recognised and taken into account in the speech assistance system. As these expert users are involved in the company's daily business, it is often a challenge to involve them. However, their involvement increases the user-friendliness of the speech assistance system and the associated acceptance. Based on these findings, the following assumption can be made: *A17: The higher (lower) the availability of expert users, the higher (lower) the probability that this company will adopt speech assistance in manufacturing.*

5 Discussion

In our study, we identified 17 factors explaining whether firms adopt speech assistance in manufacturing processes and structure them along the three dimensions of the TOE framework. Our study contributes to practice and research.

For the field of research, we contribute to the literature that focuses on factors whether firms adopt (speech-based) assistance systems (e.g., Meyer von Wolff et al. 2021; Rodriguez Cardona et al. 2019). While some of the identified factors (e.g., added value in competition) were also identified in a similar way by these other studies, some factors (e.g., robustness) are rather unique for the specific application scenario of manufacturing. Moreover, we point to some general factors that are not manufacturing specific and have been highlighted only to a limited extent in the existing literature (e.g., perceived data integrity and security). This allows to develop general factors that are necessary for the adoption of (speech-based) assistance systems. Moreover, our 17 factors could be the focus of future research. For example, scholar could investigate how these factors (e.g., a corporate culture that supports the adoption of innovative technologies) can be implemented in companies. This would support the adoption of speech-based assistance systems. Generally, our interview partners rated the potential and possible added value of such assistance systems as high. Moreover, our study is also beneficial for practitioners. (Potential) users of speech assistance or their consultants could use our factors as assessment tool to decide whether speech assistance is a suitable solution for their manufacturing processes.

As any study, our research also has some limitations. First, we only rely on a limited number of interviews. We tried to minimize that limitation by interviewing partners who provide different perspectives (e.g., users and developers of such solutions). However, in the future our results could be verified at a larger scale (e.g., by conducting a survey in the manufacturing field). Second, we did not evaluate the strength of the different factors. Maybe some factors have a higher influence on the decision whether to adopt speech assistance. This could be another starting point of future research.

In conclusion, we hope that our study provides more insights to research and practice on whether to adopt speech assistance as an innovative technology in manufacturing processes.

References

Ammari, T., Kaye, J., Tsai, J. Y., & Bentley, F. (2019), 'Music, Search, and IoT: How People (Really) Use Voice Assistants', *ACM Transactions on Computer-Human Interaction* **26**(3), 1–28.

Davis, F. D. (1989), 'Perceived Usefulness, Perceived Ease of Use, and User Acceptance of Information Technology', *MIS Quarterly* 13(3), 319–340.

De Lacerda, A. R. T., & Aguiar, C. S. R. (2019), FLOSS FAQ chatbot project reuse: How to allow nonexperts to develop a chatbot, *in* 'Proceedings of the 15th International Symposium on Open Collaboration', ACM, pp. 1–8.

Demlehner, Q., & Laumer, S. (2020), Shall We Use It or Not? Explaining the Adoption of Artificial Intelligence for Car Manufacturing Purposes, *in* 'Proceedings of the Twenty-Eighth European Conference on Information Systems', AIS, pp. 1–16.

Döring, N., & Bortz, J. (2016), *Forschungsmethoden und Evaluation in den Sozial- und Humanwissenschaften.* Springer.

Dwivedi, Y. K., Wade, M. R. & Schneberger S. L. (2012), *Information Systems Theory.* Springer.

Fischer, J., Pantforder, D., & Vogel-Heuser, B. (2017), Improvement of maintenance through speech interaction in cyber-physical production systems, *in* 'Proceedings of the15th International Conference on Industrial Informatics (INDIN)', IEEE, pp. 290–295.

Herz, C., Metzen, M., & Mittendorf, D. (2022). Smart Speaker & Voice Studie 2021–2022. https://www.beyto.com/smart-speaker-voice-studie-2021-2022/. Accessed: 22.3.2023.

Kalla, M., & Seiter, M. (2021), "Einsatzszenarien digitaler Sprachassistenz-systeme im Dienstleistungsmanagement", *in* 'Künstliche Intelligenz im Dienstleistungsmanagement', Springer, pp. 155–183.

Klapper, J., Gelec, E., Pokorni, B., Hämmerle, M., & Rothenberger, M. (2019). Potenziale Digitaler Assistenzsysteme, https://publica.fraunhofer.de/entities/publication/71ea4a00-def9-4b7a-9596-9bf0bca489c6/details. Accessed 14.03.2023.

Langen, M. (2022), Speech Assistance: Use Cases in Industry, *in* 'Proceedings of the 28th International Conference on Engineering, Technology and Innovation (ICE/ITMC) & 31st International Association For Management of Technology (IAMOT)', IEEE, pp. 1–6.

Loch, F., Magerstedt, S., & Vogel-Heuser, B. (2018), Nutzerspezifische Assistenz in manuellen Prozeduren mit Hilfe von Sprachinteraktion, *in* '19. Leitkongress der Mess- und Automatisierungstechnik'.

Maedche, A., Legner, C., Benlian, A., Berger, B., Gimpel, H., Hess, T., Hinz, O., Morana, S., & Söllner, M. (2019), 'AI-Based Digital Assistants: Opportunities, Threats, and Research Perspectives', *Business & Information Systems Engineering* **61**(4), 535–544.

Mayer, F., & Pantförder, D. (2014), "Unterstützung des Menschen in Cyber-Physical-Production-Systems", *in* 'Industrie 4.0 in Produktion, Automatisierung und Logistik', Springer, pp. 481–491.

Meyer von Wolff, R., Hobert, S., & Schumann, M. (2021) Sorry, I Can't Understand You! – Influencing Factors and Challenges of Chatbots at Digital Workplaces, in '*Proceedings of the 16th International Conference on Wirtschaftsinformatik*'.

Phillips, J. J., & Schirmer. (2008), *Return on Investment in der Personalentwicklung*. Springer.

Rodriguez Cardona, D., Werth, O., Schönborn, S., & Breitner, M. H. (2019), A Mixed Methods Analysis of the Adoption and Diffusion of Chatbot Technology in the German Insurance Sector, *in* 'Proceedings of the Twenty-fifth Americas Conference on Information Systems', AIS, pp.1–10.

Runkler, T. A. (2010), *Data Mining*. Vieweg+Teubner.

Scharfe, P., Ludwig, H., Bley, K., Wiener, M., & Schmidt, T. (2022), Data-driven Failure Management: An Ontology-based Speech Recognition App for Failure Capturing in Manufacturing Processes, *in* 'Proceedings of the 19th Conference of the Italian Chapter of AIS (ItAIS) & the 14th Mediterranean Conference on Information Systems (MCIS)', pp. 1–15.

Schultze, U. & M. Avital (2011), 'Designing Interviews to Generate Rich Data for Information Systems Research', *Information and Organization* **21**(1), 1–16.

Stich, V., Jordan, F., Birkmeier, M., Oflazgil, K., Reschke, J., & Diews, A. (2015), "Big Data Technology for Resilient Failure Management in Production Systems", *in* 'Advances in Production Management Systems: Innovative Production Management Towards Sustainable Growth', Springer, pp. 447–454.

Tornatzky, L. G., & Fleischer, M. (1990), *The Processes of Technological Innovation*. Lexington Books.

Udoka, S. J. (1991), 'Automated data capture techniques: A prerequisite for effective integrated manufacturing systems', *Computers & Industrial Engineering* **21**(1–4), 217–221.

Wang, K., He, B., & Zhu, W.-P. (2021), CAUNet: Context-Aware U-Net for Speech Enhancement in Time Domain, *in* 'International Symposium on Circuits and Systems (ISCAS)', IEEE, pp.1–5.

Wang, L. (2022), 'A futuristic perspective on human-centric assembly', *Journal of Manufacturing Systems* **62**, 199–201.

Xu, X., Lu, Y., Vogel-Heuser, B., & Wang, L. (2021). 'Industry 4.0 and Industry 5.0—Inception, conception and perception', *Journal of Manufacturing Systems* **61**, 530–535.

Selecting Appropriate Process Models for IT Projects: Towards a Tool-Supported Decision Approach

Michael Dominic Harr and Sarah Seufert

Abstract The appropriate selection of suitable process models plays an important role for IT project success. To aid in decision-making, IT project management literature offers a plethora of decision models for selecting suitable process models, however, hybrid process models are often neglected and adoption in practice is low or non-existent. To address this challenge, we draw on contingency theory to develop and implement a tool-supported decision model for the selection and evaluation of appropriate process models for IT projects, thereby leveraging artificial intelligence and machine learning in the context of a self-enforcing network. Our model provides an objective tool to assess process model suitability. Results from a conducted online survey with project management experts indicate high validity. Therefore, we contribute to the field of IT project management by expanding AI-based decision models for selecting and evaluating process models through extending the range of covered models and implementing inherent weighting of criteria.

Keywords IT project management · Process models · Decision model · Self-enforcing network · Contingency theory

1 Introduction

In recent years, technological advances induced by ongoing digitization in a wide range of disciplines have also had an impact on information technology (IT) project management (Simion et al. 2018), leading to IT projects becoming increasingly complex in terms of their goals and scope (Alami 2016; Ribeiro et al. 2021). To cope with increasing levels of complexity, uncertainty, and volatile environments (Bianchi et al. 2020), a "logical construct (or architecture)" (Zachman 1987, p. 276),

M. D. Harr (✉) · S. Seufert
Faculty of Computer Science, University of Duisburg-Essen, Essen, Germany
e-mail: michael.harr@icb.uni-due.de

S. Seufert
e-mail: sarah.seufert@icb.uni-due.de

D. Beverungen et al. (eds.), *Conceptualizing Digital Responsibility for the Information Age*, Lecture Notes in Information Systems and Organisation 74,
https://doi.org/10.1007/978-3-031-80119-8_28

principles, methods, and an abstract procedure are required (Balzert 2009). Process models play a crucial role by providing tools and methods to structure the project teams' tasks (Broy and Kuhrmann 2021), thereby acting as a systematic blueprint for planning, realization, and monitoring of projects within a standardized framework (Fischer et al. 1998; Wieczorrek and Mertens 2011). Although there are arguments against the use of process models (e.g., neglecting the human factor in projects (Hardgrave et al. 2003)), literature "has traditionally viewed them as axiomatically appropriate to improving both, the process and product of systems development" (Fitzgerald 1998, p. 317). This is also reflected in the widespread use of a wide variety of process models in practice (Kuhrmann and Linssen 2014), whereby a paradigm shift towards agile approaches is gaining momentum in organizations to react more adequately to volatile and uncertain environments (e.g., Lee and Xia 2010; Cram and Newell 2016; Recker et al. 2017). Despite the frequent utilization of process models in practice, most IT projects fail in terms of adherence to timeframe, quality, or requirements (Fenech and De Raffaele 2013). According to a study by PricewaterhouseCoopers (2014), the average IT project overruns the budget by 27% with one out of six projects exceeding the budget by over 200% and the timeframe by more than 70% (Flyvbjerg and Budzier 2011). Noticeably high failure rates and studies, indicating that unsuitable process models are a major reason for failure imply, at least in part, deficient decisions on the selection and evaluation of process models in practice (MacCormack and Verganti 2003; Bianchi et al. 2020). Although no consensus exists on the effects of the appropriate process model selection on IT project success, some studies indicate that the use of suitable process models favors project success (e.g., The Standish Group 2010; Jorge-Martinez et al. 2022) while the use of unsuitable practices leads to poorer project management and overall satisfaction with project outcomes (Cooper 2007; Shenhar and Dvir 2007). Due to IT projects' unique environments and dynamic contexts leading to the absence of one-fits-all solutions (Howell et al. 2010), a plethora of decision models to assist in the selection of appropriate process models were developed in literature. However, adoption in organizations is slow or almost non-existent (Fitzgerald 1998; Albers 2021). Hence, Shapiro et al. (2007, p. 249) ascribe a recognized discrepancy referred to as "lost in translation" gap. Reasons can be identified both within the organizations themselves as well as in the shortcomings of existing decision models. On the one hand, due to resource constraints, selection is based on the advice of consultants seeking to sell their own approaches (Vavpotič et al. 2004). Further reasons are compliance with certificates (Klüver and Klüver 2015) or retention of the status quo (e.g., Samuelson and Zeckhauser 1988). On the other hand, existing decision models constitute, apart from a few exceptions (e.g., Klüver and Klüver 2015; Albers 2021), theoretical approaches without practical implementation, rendering their utilization within project organizations challenging.

Drawing on these observations, our research question is "*how can the decision-making capabilities of organizations be enhanced for the selection and evaluation of process models for IT projects*?"

To answer the research question, we develop and implement a tool-assisted decision model that leverages artificial intelligence (AI) and machine learning (ML) and extends existing AI-based decision models for the selection and evaluation of process models for IT projects by considering a wider range of covered process models and introducing a weighting of criteria.

The remainder of this paper is structured as follows: First, we provide a brief introduction to contingency theory, IT project management approaches, and related work regarding existing decision models. Then, we proceed with the description of the methodological approach followed by the development, implementation, and validation of our proposed AI-based decision model. Finally, we reflect on limitations and propose avenues for future research.

2 Conceptual Background and Related Work

2.1 Contingency Theory and Types of IT Projects

Contingency theory proposes that an organization's survivability and effectiveness depend on the fit to their context (Drazin and de Ven 1985; Howell et al. 2010). Hence, organizations are contingent on specific factors, which impact organizational characteristics under consideration (Wood 1979; Howell et al. 2010). Applied to IT project management, contingency theory criticizes "universalism" (Wood 1979, p. 335) and proposes that IT project management practices and projects "should be tailored to suit its context" (Howell et al. 2010, p. 257). Although project management literature predominantly "assume[d] that all projects are fundamentally similar" (Shenhar 2001, p. 394), recent research highlights the absence of one-fits-all solutions for IT projects; instead IT projects are dependent on their type and contingent characteristics for the selection of suitable process models and the successful execution of the IT project (Cockburn 2000; Cicmil and Hodgson 2006; Howell et al. 2010; Kabir and Rusu 2016; Lehmann 2016). Nevertheless, differences between project types are "commonly ignored" (Lehmann 2016, p. 2) in scientific publications. Taking into account the contingency theory, IT projects can be characterized depending on surrounding contingent factors inherent in contingency dimensions.

Howell et al. (2010) identified five contingency dimensions: uncertainty, complexity, criticality, urgency, and team empowerment. Uncertainty encompasses factors, both known and unknown, whose influence on the IT project is difficult to assess in advance (Alami 2016; Andersen 2016). The complexity of an IT project is regarded as the "degree of differentiation and interdependence of project elements" (Howell et al. 2010, p. 258). Criticality refers to the effects and consequences of unforeseeable events (Lindvall et al. 2002; Howell et al. 2010). Urgency refers to the magnitude to which time constraints (e.g., pace and time pressure) matter in project activities (Pearson 1990; Howell et al. 2010; Geraldi et al. 2011). The last contingency dimension deals with team capabilities in a broader sense, focusing on (internal) team-related factors (e.g., Cockburn 2000; Lindvall et al. 2002; Boehm and Turner 2003), as well as (external) organizational factors like the geographic distribution or the organizational culture (e.g., Boehm and Turner 2003; van Donk and Molloy 2008).

Drawing on contingent factors above and on existing definitions of IT projects in literature, an IT project can be defined as a non-routine and temporary endeavor that is contingent on environmental factors and deals with the creation of IT artifacts, which is usually undertaken in phases to achieve one or more defined objectives (Wallace 2015; BSI 2019; Hughes et al. 2019; Jayakody and Wijayanayake 2021).

2.2 *Approaches to IT Project Management*

IT project management is a complex endeavor in which the project manager is required to orchestrate several project aspects (e.g., project processes, stakeholders, or team members) simultaneously to achieve the project's objectives (Bakker 2010; PMI 2021; Bourdeau and Shuraida 2022). To date, IT project management is an evolving phenomenon that suffers from plurality and fragmentation (Atkinson 1999; Kolltveit et al. 2007; Turner et al. 2013). Hence, drawing on Alexander and Davis' (1991) hierarchy of process models, Fig. 1 delimitates ambiguous terms in IT project management.

Following the line of reasoning by Alexander and Davis (1991), the IT project management approach encompasses guiding principles and beliefs and presents an overarching and abstract outline of how a specific IT project is managed, designed, and governed (Iivari et al. 2000; Gemino et al. 2021). Prevailing literature distinguishes between traditional, agile, and hybrid IT project management approaches (Albers 2021; Azenha et al. 2021; Ciric et al. 2022; Lagstedt et al. 2022). The traditional approach to IT project management reflects a "transformation view of production" (Anantatmula 2021, p. 16), meaning that inputs into an IT project are transformed by strictly adhering to an initial project plan to fulfill the objectives (Špundak 2014; Ciric et al. 2022). The agile approach is based on the values of the agile manifesto (e.g., Beck et al. 2001; Fowler and Highsmith 2001) and differs from the traditional approach by providing more flexibility to change (Anantatmula 2021;

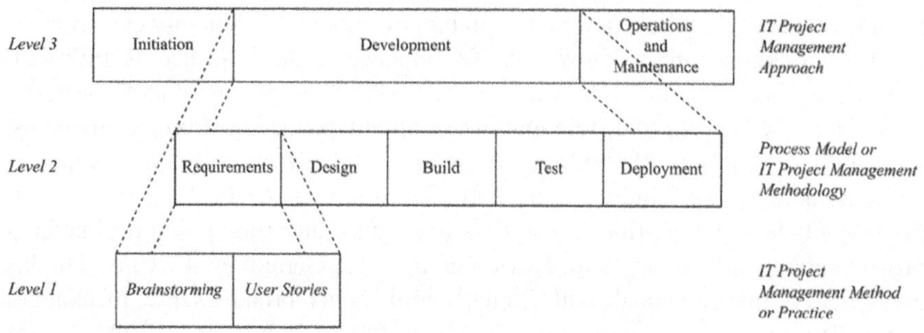

Fig. 1 Delimitation of ambiguous terms in IT project management

Gemino et al. 2021). The hybrid approach to IT project management is an emerging phenomenon that either combines traditional and agile approaches or traditional and agile practices into an overarching process model (Gemino et al. 2021; Lagstedt et al. 2022). Hybrid approaches thus tend to reflect a construction-based approach that can be tailored to individual needs by combining traditional and agile practices and methods (Jacobson et al. 2007; Tell et al. 2019).

Process models (e.g., Scrum, Waterfall, Kanban) represent a specific instance of an IT project management approach and are defined as organized sets of concepts, methods (or practices), guiding principles, beliefs, and multi-step procedures that can be tailored to specific requirements (Iivari et al. 2000; Gemino et al. 2021; Bakhirkin and Lukin 2022). They reduce the complexity of IT projects and thus increase the likelihood of IT project success (Terlizzi et al. 2016; Jayakody and Wijayanayake 2021; Bourdeau and Shuraida 2022).

IT project management practices constitute precise techniques or procedures to manage and execute a single phase of an IT project or a single aspect of a process model within an IT project (Gemino et al. 2021).

2.3 Decision Models for Selecting and Evaluating Process Models

The prevailing literature shows that the selection and evaluation of appropriate process models are complex and non-trivial tasks, inter alia due to a large number of available process models (e.g., Vavpotič et al. 2004; Kuhrmann and Linssen 2014), their possibilities to be combined or customized (e.g., Sommerville 2018; Albers 2021), and their suitability for organizations with different types of IT projects exhibiting various characteristics (Vavpotič et al. 2004; Klüver and Klüver 2015). In IT project management research, a range of decision models have already been established to facilitate the selection of suitable process models for IT projects (e.g., Zachman 1987; Alexander and Davis 1991; Noack and Schienmann 1999; Gräßle et al. 2010; Habermann 2013; Bakhtouchi and Rahmouni 2018; Albers 2021). However, a large proportion of the decision models simplify the selection and evaluation by differentiating between IT project management approaches (level 3), i.e., whether a traditional or an agile approach should be selected (e.g., Little 2005; Howell et al. 2010; Ahimbisibwe et al. 2017; Butler et al. 2020), or whether a hybrid approach should be constructed that combines traditional and agile practices and methods (e.g., Jacobson et al. 2007; Tell et al. 2019; Papadakis and Tsironis 2020). Several decision models have been established in the literature to discern and evaluate specific process models for IT projects on the second hierarchy level (e.g., Kettunen and Laanti 2005; Jain and Chandrasekaran 2009; Hicdurmaz 2012; Moyo et al. 2013; Dawson and Dawson 2014). However, existing approaches in literature either exclusively focus on a single domain (e.g., Vavpotič et al. 2004; Langer et al. 2010), take a specific perspective (e.g., Zachman 1987), only contrast a few selected

Table 1 Integrative decision models incorporating all approaches

Hierarchy	Author(s)
Level 3: IT project management approach	Wysocki (2019), Azenha et al. (2021), Ciric et al. (2022), Lagstedt et al. (2022)
Level 2: Process models	Klüver and Klüver (2015), Albers (2021)

process models (e.g., Fitsilis 2008; Gräßle et al. 2010), or they neglect to take into account emerging hybrid process models to a sufficient extent (Albers 2021). Therefore, literature lacks comprehensive decision models that encompass all approaches within their decision framework, since only a limited number of identified decision models meet this criterion, as outlined in Table 1.

While recent approaches by Klüver and Klüver (2015) and Albers (2021) address some of the mentioned shortcomings and leverage AI and ML in the context of a self-enforcing network (SEN), the model lacks inherent weighting of criteria and thus implicitly assumes that each characteristic is equally important for the selection of suitable process models.

3 Method

Drawing on principles of proper modeling and prescriptive decision theory (Schütte 1998; Laux et al. 2018), an enhanced decision model based on Albers' (2021) proposed model is developed, implemented, and validated ex-post in three stages.

First, the decision field is established by conducting a literature review regarding existing process models and considered criteria in IT project management research. Second, the decision model is then implemented in a SEN[1] developed by Klüver and Klüver (2015) since it has the advantage that, in contrast to established artificial neural networks, the knowledge within the weighted matrix is not generated arbitrarily, but comprehensibly based on known cognitive learning rules (Klüver and Klüver 2021). Third, to validate our enhanced decision model, we conducted an online survey with project management experts from German-speaking countries. In detail, invitations were sent to experts from an IT consulting company and a leading German automotive manufacturer. Eligible participants included project management experts who had successfully completed a recent IT project and held prominent roles within those IT projects (e.g., project manager). The experts were asked to characterize ex post a recent successfully executed IT project based on the questionnaire by Albers (2021). In line with Ciric et al. (2022) the questionnaire included a self-reporting (subjective) assessment of the process model, the IT project and its characteristics, and the success of the IT project, as perceived by the respondents. The assessment of

[1] The SEN is an artificial neural network based on unsupervised learning that encompasses three fundamental components: a semantic matrix ordering relations between process models and their criteria, a neural network, and a component for visualization (Klüver and Klüver 2015).

the characterized IT project's success is based on Shenhar and Dvir's (2007) proposed multidimensional framework for determining project success. In total, the online questionnaire consisted of 8 sections in which a total of 144 variables were queried. In total, 9 successfully completed IT projects were characterized by the experts and eligible for further validation. Finally, decision model validation consisted of inserting successful and ex-post characterized IT projects from respondents into the SEN as input vectors to then validate, whether the SEN would have suggested the same approach and/or process model that was actually adopted.

4 Decision Model for the Selection of Process Models

4.1 *Development of the Decision Model*

Based on identified process models in the context of a conducted literature review (see https://bit.ly/3Q79Fp8), the most frequently mentioned process models applicable to IT projects were included as alternatives in the decision field. In total, $n = 17$ process models are considered as alternatives within the decision field. Thus, a total of 6 (35.29%) traditional, 9 (52.94%) agile, and 2 (11.76%) standardized hybrid process models are considered alternatives (see https://bit.ly/44TPpvd). In contrast to Albers (2021), standards and overarching frameworks were loaded into the SEN but neglected in the evaluation. In addition, Albers (2021) declares ScrumBan as a hybrid process model, however, in the context of this paper it is by definition an agile process model, since two agile process models are combined and not a traditional and an agile process model.

Each process model is defined by one or more criteria, resulting in a tuple of attributes (i.e., vector) that characterizes the process model (Laux et al. 2018). Due to the fact that Albers' (2021) proposed decision model is the only one covering all identified contingency dimensions and due to the intention to enable a comparison between Albers' (2021) decision model and the decision model developed in the context of this paper, Albers (2021) criteria were adopted. In total, 15 project-specific (e.g., budget size, goal uncertainty), 37 project management-specific (e.g., change perception, contract relationship), 17 project team-specific (e.g., team location, team commitment), and 12 organizational evaluation criteria (e.g., management style, monetary incentives) are considered, which contain both subjective and objective evaluations (for a complete list see https://bit.ly/43sKUH6).

To evaluate the suitability of process models, Albers' (2021) carried out an empirical survey with experts from the German-speaking IT project management domain. By evaluating the process models through experts from the field, practice-relevant findings were thus identified, particularly with regard to the subjective criteria, which are based on actual experience and impressions from the field (Albers 2021). Therefore, we adopted Albers' (2021) survey results for input into the SEN.

4.2 Implementation of the Decision Model

Considered criteria, their coding within the SEN, the values obtained through Albers' (2021) expert survey, and the linguistic scores into which the obtained values were recoded were automatically loaded into the SEN as comma-separated values and displayed in the Attribute Editor.

The Attribute Editor has the following configuration options: For attributes, r_{def} represents the default value, $r_{\min}$ and $r_{\max}$ represent the respective minimum/ maximum value of the attribute, and $n_{\min}$ as well as $n_{\max}$ represent the left/right interval limits to which the attribute is normalized. The variable μ is defined as the standard deviation of the attribute and σ as the expected value of the variable. "Transformation" describes the procedure by which the variables are preprocessed, with normalization, strict normalization, and standardization available for selection (Klüver and Klüver 2021). The cue validity factor (*cvf*) is a numerical factor that can strengthen or weaken their importance (Albers 2021; Klüver and Klüver 2021). The variables $v_{\min}$ and $v_{\max}$ describe the minimum/maximum weight value of the semantic matrix for an attribute. To set up the semantic matrix using the raw data (i.e., v_{raw}), further following variables are defined: Let O be the set of objects, i.e., the process models, which have been evaluated through Albers' (2021) expert survey. Then, $O = \{o_1, o_2, \ldots, o_m\}$, where $m = \|O\|$ for $\forall m \in \mathbb{N}^+$. Furthermore, let A be the set of attributes with $A = \{a_1, a_2, \ldots, a_k\}$, where $k = A$ for $\forall k \in \mathbb{N}^+$. Let $F : A \to \{1.0, 1.5, 2.0\}$ be the application that associates to each attribute $a_k \in A$ a *cvf* for the attribute. In addition, let V bet the set of matrices with $V = \{v_{raw}, v_{norm}, v_{sm}\}$. Finally, let the raw semantic matrix v_{raw} be the matrix $(k \times m)$, expressing the level of affiliation of each attribute to each associated object (Klüver and Klüver 2021).

For normalization, a bipolar scale ranging from − 1 to 1 (i.e., interval [− 1;1]) is specified for coding the attributes. That is, for all attributes, $n_{\min} = -1$ and $n_{\max} = 1$ is defined. Proper normalization of the semantic matrix v_{raw} into v_{norm} is then done automatically by computing Eq. (1).

$$v_{norm} = \frac{v_{raw} - r_{\min}}{r_{\max} - r_{\min}} * (n_{\max} - n_{\min}) - n_{\min} \tag{1}$$

For the artificial neural network to be generated, the normalized semantic matrix must be transformed into the weight matrix (v_{sm}) by drawing on a learning rule (Albers 2021). In the weight matrix, weights are assigned to the associations between the objects and the attributes (Klüver and Klüver 2015). The weight of an attribute associated with an object w_{oa} is initially obtained by applying Eq. (2):

$$w_{oa} = c * v_{sm}, \tag{2}$$

where c represents the learning rate. A learning rate of $c = 0.1$ is selected, as this is sufficient in most cases (Klüver and Klüver 2021). The neural network can be easily reconstructed and retraced following the logic that a given weight value of a future time $w(t+1)$ can be determined from its value at the previous time adding a delta (Δw), as shown in Eq. (3).

$$w(t+1) = w(t) + \Delta w \tag{3}$$

The delta (Δw) is calculated by an adapted learning rule, which incorporates the *cvf's* into the computation of the weights. We incorporate the self-enforcing rule (SER) as the main learning rule, which is presented in Eq. (4).

$$\Delta w = c * v_{sm} * cvf_a \tag{4}$$

For the classification of the process models, attribute neurons related to the objects are activated externally. The activation function is then used to calculate the values of the terminal activations of the object neurons in the artificial neural network (Klüver and Klüver 2015, 2021). We chose the enforcing activation function (EAF) presented in Eq. (5) as it was explicitly developed for the SER by Klüver and Klüver (2015, 2021) and thus supports the self-enforcing dynamics of the artificial neural network.

$$a_j = \sum_{i=1}^{n} \frac{w_{ij} * a_i}{1 + |w_{ij} * a_i|} \tag{5}$$

In Eq. (5), a_j represents the activation value of the receiving neuron j, a_i represents the activation value of the sending neuron i, and w_{ij} represents the weight of the connection between i and j (Klüver and Klüver 2021).

Since criteria exist, which contribute more significantly to selecting a suitable process model than others, different *cvf's* were applied to the attributes based on identified literature and the agile manifesto (Fowler and Highsmith 2001) as shown in Table 2.

Table 2 Adapted Cvf's of important criteria

Criteria c_n	Attribute name	cvf_a	Author(s)
c_6	Novelty/Market uncertainty	2.0	Ratbe et al. (1999), Ahimbisibwe et al. (2017), Butler et al. (2020), Ciric et al. (2022)
c_{13}	(IT project) complexity	2.0	
c_{15}	(IT product) complexity	2.0	
c_{39}	Requirements volatility	2.0	
c_{38}	Time of requirements elicitation	1.5	Beck et al. (2001), Fowler and Highsmith (2001)
c_{44}	Stakeholder integration	1.5	
c_{59}	Team's hierarchical task organization	1.5	
c_{61}	Team communication culture	1.5	
c_{62}	Reflection on collaboration	1.5	
c_{64}	Willingness to learn and change	1.5	
c_{67}	Trust within the team	1.5	

All other attributes were assigned a $cvf = 1.0$. Listed authors have demonstrated the significance of these attributes for the decision to select a suitable IT project management approach, which is why the cvf was doubled, as this illustrates the high relevance of the attributes (Klüver and Klüver 2021). For attributes whose value has not been empirically validated but whose importance for the selection of agile process models is nonetheless relevant, a slightly increased cvf was set ($cvf = 1.5$) based on the agile manifesto (e.g., Beck et al. 2001; Fowler and Highsmith 2001).

Accordingly, by computing Eqs. (2)–(5) with the provided *cvf's* in Table 2, the final and weighted semantic matrix v_{sm} is created with a learning rate of $c = 0.1$ and one iteration.[2]

4.3 Retrospective Validation and Discussion

In total, 9 successfully completed IT projects were characterized by the respondents. A total of four (44.44%) traditional process models, four (44.44%) agile process models, and one (11.11%) hybrid process model were adopted. Regarding the IT projects that adopted traditional process models, Structured Systems Analysis and Design Method (SSADM) was used once and the waterfall model was used three times as the process model. In agile IT projects, Scrum was adopted three times and Feature-Driven Development (FDD) once. The IT project adopting a hybrid approach used Software Development Agile (SoDa) for this purpose. On average, all IT projects were perceived as successful by the respondents with traditional process models (82.01%) being marginally less successful than agile (85.73%) and hybrid (90.00%) ones. Regarding potential outliers, all characterized IT projects are relatively representative and comparable (79.11%) on average. Since the IT projects characterized by the respondents are both successful and comparable, the identified process models could be transferred into the SEN as input vectors. Before, however, the values of each of the criteria had to be recoded in a similar fashion as the values in Albers' (2021) expert survey. Hence, the obtained values were recoded into the linguistic scores for the input into the SEN. The decision model is considered to be valid if it proposes the same process model for an IT project that has adopted it. Validity is determined numerically by the values of the final activation of the neurons (i.e., provided rankings in the SEN), or else by the Euclidean distances. The validation is conducted following Alexander and Davis' (1991) hierarchy of process models at the 2nd and 3rd levels. The three best and the single best recommendation of the model are examined in each case, both from the ranking list and from the distance list. The validity percentage of the decision model is calculated for each level.[3]

---

[2] A thorough explanation of all constructs and transformations is beyond the scope of this paper. For further explanation, see Klüver & Klüver (2015, 2021) and Albers (2021).

[3] The following values always refer to the validity without the inclusion of the characterized IT project adopting SSADM, since there were no entries in the semantic matrix for this process model.

Regarding the suitability of the first proposed process model for each input vector, the decision model is 100% valid for the recommendation of a suitable approach to IT project management, which means that for each input vector, the decision model recommends a process model that belongs to the same overarching approach to IT project management. Considering the validity on the level of process models, the ranking still suggests 75% of the correct identical process models. Regarding the Euclidean distance, 62.5% of the first recommended process models are correct. Looking at the first three proposed process models, a similar picture emerges: regarding the IT project management approach, the decision model proposes a process model of the appropriate approach based on the rankings in 83.33% of the cases. In 91.67% of the cases, the decision model proposes a process model of the appropriate approach based on the Euclidean distance. For a total of 54.17% of each of the first three recommended process models, the correct process model was suggested based on the ranking or Euclidean distance. In summary, the developed decision model is 100% valid in determining the overarching approach to IT project management. Regarding specific process models, it is quite valid, as it first suggests a suitable process model for an input vector with a probability between 62.5 and 75%—depending on the selected metric.

In an equivalent manner, the validity of Albers' (2021) decision model was determined and compared to the results of our enhanced decision model. Overall, our decision model performs equally well or better in terms of recommending process models that can be assigned to the same IT project management approach as the process model of the input vector. With respect to the Euclidean distance, the developed decision model performs about 11.11% better than Albers' (2021) decision model. However, when considering the specific process model recommendation, the developed model performs ambivalent: if only the first recommendation of the decision models is considered, the decision model performs between 10.0 and 12.5% worse than Albers' (2021) decision model. If, on the other hand, the first three process model recommendations for each input vector are considered, it can be seen that the developed model performs equally well or up to 4.17% better than Albers' (2021) decision model.

Based on the Euclidean distances, the map visualization (Fig. 2) illustrates the similarities between the IT projects. It is apparent that the evaluation and assessment of the IT projects or process models occurred heterogeneously, as shown in their broad distribution. However, the IT projects characterized by the experts (highlighted in color) are predominantly assigned to the correct corresponding cluster: the three IT projects using Scrum are located within the agile cluster and the three IT projects using the waterfall model are located within the traditional cluster. SoDa—representing a hybrid process model—is located between the traditional and agile clusters, which illustrates the combination of agile and traditional practices. FDD—typically agile—can be classified as a hybrid approach based on the characterization, which reinforces the importance of adapting existing process models to constantly changing contextual factors (Henderson-Sellers and Ralyté 2010; Joslin and Müller 2014). This is in line with current research on situational method engineering (SME), which emphasizes that standardized or individually constructed process models must be adapted to changing environmental requirements and project characteristics, for IT projects to be accomplished successfully (Henderson-Sellers and Ralyté 2010; Gottschalk et al. 2021). Our AI-based decision model incorporates SME principles (e.g., Henderson-Sellers and Ralyté 2010; Gottschalk et al. 2021) by drawing on contingency theory to acknowledge situational factors (e.g., market uncertainty), organizational context (e.g., management style), and team capabilities (e.g., team diversity). By aligning with SME principles, our decision model can cater to the unique requirements of individual IT projects, therefore providing more nuanced recommendations and promoting better project outcomes. In addition, IT projects can be re-characterized at any time, for example, if an adaptation of the process model is necessary due to changing requirements. Thus, our decision model can be utilized for standardized traditional, agile, and hybrid process models as well as for constructed or customized process models, since it allows a classification and comparison between current and previous IT projects without the need for reference vectors.

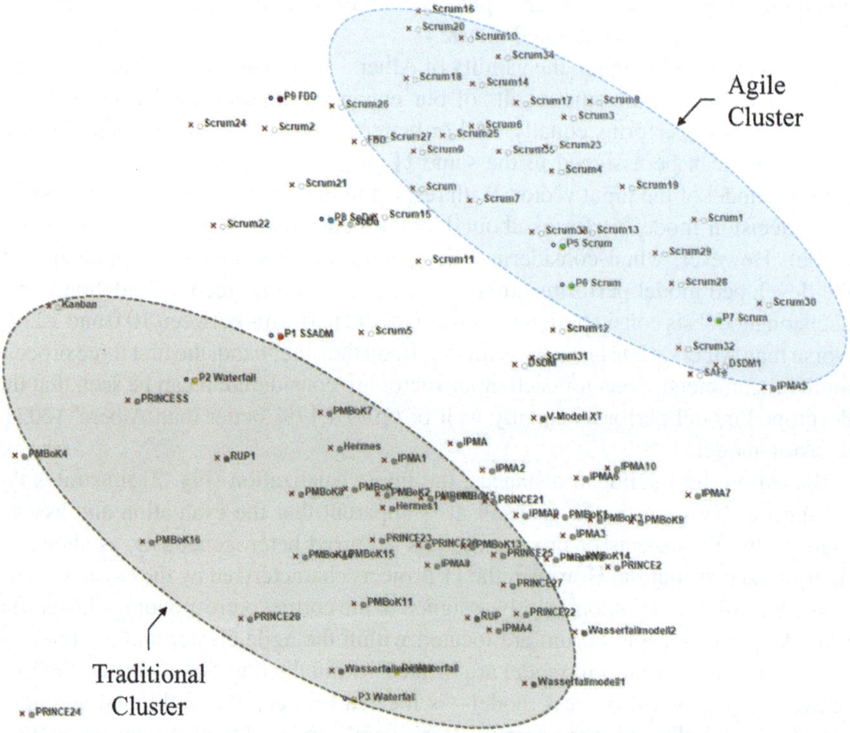

Fig. 2 Map visualization of input vectors in the SEN

5 Conclusion

We developed and implemented an AI-based and tool-supported decision model for the selection and evaluation of appropriate process models for IT projects. Building on preliminary work by Albers (2021), we developed an enhanced and practically evaluated decision model that can be easily implemented by organizations and that leverages AI and ML to support decision-makers in diverse contexts. Hence, we contribute to the ongoing dialogue on SME and contingency theory by proposing a novel decision model addressing the construction and adaption of process models due to changing contextual factors. Based on attributes identified in the literature that significantly influence the selection of process models, individual attribute weights were implemented, which led to higher overall activation of neurons, especially for the agile process models, thus facilitating a better overall decision. Hence, we contribute to the field of IT project management and SME by extending existing AI-based decision models by extending the range of considered process models and introducing a weighting of criteria.

The present paper is subject to several limitations and restrictions. With regard to the online questionnaire, its validity can be questioned, since the inherent constructs of the questionnaire were not validated and included self-reporting subjective answers. Due to this small sample (9 characterized IT projects), no comprehensive validation can be guaranteed and further research is required to assess the validity of the decision model. Since experts characterized successfully implemented IT projects in the online questionnaire, there is a further threat to validity in that successfully implemented IT projects may also have adopted inappropriate process models. However, it is implicitly assumed in the context of this research paper that successful IT projects have also properly adopted successful process models.

Future research could empirically validate our proposed decision model and adjust modifications that lead to better decision-making. In contrast to the retrospective characterization of IT projects, the validation could be done ex-ante, which would involve having the decision model propose a process model for an IT project, whose success would then be evaluated after completion. By analyzing case studies and real-world examples, future research should investigate the interplay between process model selection and its successful implementation, to support decision-makers towards better project outcomes.

References

Ahimbisibwe, A., Daellenbach, U. & Cavana, R.Y. (2017), 'Empirical comparison of traditional plan-based and agile methodologies: Critical success factors for outsourced software development projects from vendors' perspective', *Journal of Enterprise Information Management*, **30**(3), pp. 400–453.

Alami, A. (2016), 'Why do information technology projects fail?', *Procedia Computer Science*, **100**, pp. 62–71. https://doi.org/10.1016/j.procs.2016.09.124

Albers, C. (2021), 'Bewertung und Auswahl von Vorgehensmodellen im IT-Projektmanagement—Ein Ansatz für die Unternehmenspraxis', in J. Klüver and C. Klüver (eds.) *Neue Algorithmen für praktische Probleme*. Wiesbaden: Springer Fachmedien, pp. 21–38.

Alexander, L.C. & Davis, A.M. (1991), 'Criteria for selecting software process models', in *Proceedings of the Fifteenth Annual International Computer Software & Applications Conference*. Tokyo, Japan: IEEE Computer Society Press, pp. 521–528.

Anantatmula, V.S. (2021), 'Project Management Concepts', in A. Petrillo, F. De Felice, G. Lambert-Torres, and E.L. Bonaldi (eds.) *Operations Management - Emerging Trend in the Digital Era*. IntechOpen. https://doi.org/10.5772/intechopen.93766.

Andersen, E.S. (2016), 'Do project managers have different perspectives on project management?', *International Journal of Project Management*, **34**(1), pp. 58–65.

Atkinson, R. (1999), 'Project management: Cost, time and quality, two best guesses and a phenomenon, its time to accept other success criteria', *International Journal of Project Management*, **17**(6), pp. 337–342.

Azenha, F.C., Reis, D.A. & Fleury, A.L. (2021), 'The Role and Characteristics of Hybrid Approaches to Project Management in the Development of Technology-Based Products and Services', *Project Management Journal*, **52**(1), pp. 90–110.

Bakhirkin, M. V & Lukin, V.N. (2022), 'Agilefall—Modern Realities of IT Project Management', in M.N. Favorskaya, I.S. Nikitin, and N.S. Severina (eds.) *Advances in Theory and Practice of Computational Mechanics*. Singapore: Springer (Smart Innovation, Systems and Technologies), pp. 393–408.

Bakhtouchi, A. & Rahmouni, R. (2018), 'A tree decision based approach for selecting software development methodology', in *2018 International Conference on Smart Communications in Network Technologies, SaCoNeT 2018*. El Oued, Algeria: IEEE, pp. 211–216.

Bakker, R.M. (2010), 'Taking Stock of Temporary Organizational Forms: A Systematic Review and Research Agenda', *International Journal of Management Reviews*, **12**(4), pp. 466–486.

Balzert, H. (2009), 'Was ist Softwaretechnik?', in H. Balzert (ed.) *Lehrbuch der Softwaretechnik: Basiskonzepte und Requirements Engineering*. 3rd ed. Heidelberg: Spektrum Akademischer Verlag, pp. 17–22.

Beck, K., Beedle, M., van Bennekum, A., Cockburn, A., Cunningham, W., Fowler, M., Grenning, J., Highsmith, J., Hunt, A., Jeffries, R., Kern, J., Marick, B., Martin, R.C., Mellor, S., Schwaber, K., Sutherland, J. & Thomas, D. (2001), *Manifesto for agile software development*. https://agilemanifesto.org/iso/en/manifesto.html. Accessed: 05/10/2023.

Bianchi, M., Marzi, G. & Guerini, M. (2020), 'Agile, stage-gate and their combination: Exploring how they relate to performance in software development', *Journal of Business Research*, **110**, pp. 538–553.

Boehm, B. & Turner, R. (2003), 'Using risk to balance agile and plan- driven methods', *Computer*, **36**(6), pp. 57–66.

Bourdeau, S. & Shuraida, S. (2022), 'A Conceptual Definition of Information Technology Project Management: A Campaign-Driven Perspective', in *Proceedings of the 55th Hawaii International Conference on System Sciences*, pp. 7172–7181.

Broy, M. & Kuhrmann, M. (2021), 'Vorgehensmodelle in der Softwareentwicklung', in M. Broy and M. Kuhrmann (eds.) *Einführung in die Softwaretechnik*. Berlin, Heidelberg: Xpert.press. Springer Vieweg, pp. 83–124.

BSI (2019), 'BS 6079:2019+C1:2019'. BSI Standards Limited.

Butler, C.W., Vijayasarathy, L.R. & Roberts, N. (2020), 'Managing Software Development Projects for Success: Aligning Plan- and Agility-Based Approaches to Project Complexity and Project Dynamism', *Project Management Journal*, **51**(3), pp. 262–277.

Cicmil, S. & Hodgson, D. (2006), 'New Possibilities for Project Management Theory: A Critical Engagement', *Project Management Journal*, **37**(3), pp. 111–122.

Ciric, D., Lalic, B., Delić, M., Gracanin, D. & Stefanovic, D. (2022), 'How project management approach impact project success? From traditional to agile', *International Journal of Managing Projects in Business*, **15**(3), pp. 494–521.

Cockburn, A. (2000), 'Selecting a project's methodology', *IEEE Software*, **17**(4), pp. 64–71.

Cooper, R.G. (2007), 'Managing technology development projects', *IEEE Engineering Management Review*, **35**(1), pp. 67–67.https://doi.org/10.1109/EMR.2007.329141

Cram, W.A. & Newell, S. (2016), 'Mindful revolution or mindless trend? Examining agile development as a management fashion', *European Journal of Information Systems*, **25**(2), pp. 154–169.

Dawson, C. & Dawson, R. (2014), 'Software Development Process Models: A Technique for Evaluation and Decision-Making', *Knowledge and Process Management*, **21**(1), pp. 42–53.

Drazin, R. & de Ven, A.H. Van (1985), 'Alternative Forms of Fit in Contingency Theory', *Administrative Science Quarterly*, **30**(4), pp. 514–539.

Fenech, K. & De Raffaele, C. (2013), 'Overcoming ICT project failures - A practical perspective', in *2013 World Congress on Computer and Information Technology, WCCIT 2013*. Sousse, Tunisia: IEEE.

Fischer, T., Biskup, H. & Müller-Luschnat, G. (1998), 'Begriffliche Grundlagen für Vorgehensmodelle', in R. Kneuper, G. Müller-Luschnat, and A. Oberweis (eds.) *Vorgehensmodelle für die betriebliche Anwendungsentwicklung*. 1st ed. Wiesbaden: Vieweg+Teubner Verlag, pp. 13–31.

Fitsilis, P. (2008), 'Comparing PMBOK and agile project management software development processes', in T. Sobh (ed.) *Advances in Computer and Information Sciences and Engineering*. Dordrecht: Springer, pp. 378–383.

Fitzgerald, B. (1998), 'An empirical investigation into the adoption of systems development methodologies', *Information & Management*, **34**(6), pp. 317–328.

Flyvbjerg, B. & Budzier, A. (2011), 'Why your IT project may be riskier than you think', *Harvard Business Review*, **89**(9), pp. 23–25.

Fowler, M. & Highsmith, J. (2001), 'The Agile Manifesto', *Software Development*, **9**, pp. 28–32.

Gemino, A., Horner Reich, B. & Serrador, P.M. (2021), 'Agile, Traditional, and Hybrid Approaches to Project Success: Is Hybrid a Poor Second Choice?', *Project Management Journal*, **52**(2), pp. 161–175.

Geraldi, J., Maylor, H. & Williams, T. (2011), 'Now, let's make it really complex (complicated): A systematic review of the complexities of projects', *International Journal of Operations and Production Management*, **31**(9), pp. 966–990.

Gottschalk, S., Yigitbas, E., Nowosad, A. & Engels, G. (2021), 'Situation-Specific Business Model Development Methods for Mobile App Developers', in A. Augusto, A. Gill, S. Nurcan, I. Reinhartz-Berger, R. Schmidt, and J. Zdravkovic (eds.) *Enterprise, Business-Process and Information Systems Modeling. BPMDS EMMSAD 2021 2021. Lecture Notes in Business Information Processing, vol 421*. Springer, Cham, pp. 262–276. https://doi.org/10.1007/978-3-030-79186-5_17.

Gräßle, M., Thomas, O. & Dollmann, T. (2010), 'Vorgehensmodelle des Product-Service Systems Engineering', in O. Thomas, P. Loos, and M. Nüttgens (eds.) *Hybride Wertschöpfung*. Berlin, Heidelberg: Springer, pp. 82–129.

Habermann, F. (2013), 'Hybrides Projektmanagement — agile und klassische Vorgehensmodelle im Zusammenspiel', *HMD Praxis der Wirtschaftsinformatik*, **50**(5), pp. 93–102.

Hardgrave, B.C., Davis, F.D. & Riemenschneider, C.K. (2003), 'Investigating determinants of software developers' intentions to follow methodologies', *Journal of Management Information Systems*, **20**(1), pp. 123–151.

Henderson-Sellers, B. & Ralyté, J. (2010), 'Situational method engineering: State-of-the-art review', *Journal of Universal Computer Science*, **16**(3), pp. 424–478.

Hicdurmaz, M. (2012), 'A fuzzy multi criteria decision making approach to software life cycle model selection', *Proceedings of the 38th EUROMICRO Conference on Software Engineering and Advanced Applications, SEAA 2012*, pp. 384–391.

Howell, D., Windahl, C. & Seidel, R. (2010), 'A project contingency framework based on uncertainty and its consequences', *International Journal of Project Management*, **28**(3), pp. 256–264.

Hughes, B., Ireland, R., West, B., Smith, N. & Shepherd, D.I. (2019), *Project management for IT-related projects*. 3rd ed. Swindon, UK: BCS Learning and Development.

Iivari, J., Hirschheim, R. & Klein, H.K. (2000), 'A dynamic framework for classifying information systems development methodologies and approaches', *Journal of Management Information Systems*, **17**(3), pp. 179–218.

Jacobson, I., Ng, P.W. & Spence, I. (2007), 'Enough of Processes - Lets do Practices.', *The Journal of Object Technology*, **6**(6), p. 41. https://doi.org/10.5381/jot.2007.6.6.c5.

Jain, R. & Chandrasekaran, A. (2009), 'Rapid System Development (RSD) Methodologies: Proposing a Selection Framework', *Engineering Management Journal*, **21**(4), pp. 30–35.

Jayakody, J.A.V.M.K. & Wijayanayake, W.M.J.I. (2021), 'Challenges for adopting DevOps in information technology projects', in *2021 International Research Conference on Smart Computing and Systems Engineering (SCSE)*. IEEE, pp. 203–210. https://ieeexplore.ieee.org/document/9568348/.

Jorge-Martinez, D., Misra, S., Butt, S.A. & Ayeni, F. (2022), 'Estimation Techniques for Scrum: A Qualitative Systematic Study', in A. Abraham, A.M. Madureira, A. Kaklauskas, N. Ghandhi, A. Bajaj, A.K. Muda, D. Kriksciuniene, and J.C. Ferreira (eds.) *Innovations in Bio-Inspired Computing and Applications. IBICA 2021. Lecture Notes in Networks and Systems*. Springer, Cham, pp. 818–829. https://doi.org/10.1007/978-3-030-96299-9_77.

Joslin, R. & Müller, R. (2014), 'The impact of project methodologies on project success in different contexts', in *Project Management Institute Research and Education Conference*. Phoenix, Arizona: Project Management Institute.

Kabir, M. & Rusu, L. (2016), 'IT project development using capability maturity model', *Information Resources Management Journal*, **29**(4), pp. 35–48.

Kettunen, P. & Laanti, M. (2005), 'How to steer an embedded software project: tactics for selecting the software process model', *Information and Software Technology*, **47**(9), pp. 587–608.

Klüver, C. & Klüver, J. (2021), *Neue Algorithmen für praktische Probleme: Variationen zu künstlicher Intelligenz und künstlichem Leben*. 1st ed, *Neue Algorithmen für praktische Probleme*. 1st ed. Edited by C. Klüver and J. Klüver. Wiesbaden: Springer Vieweg.

Klüver, C. & Klüver, J. (2015), 'Self-enforcing networks als tools zur Auswahl eines geeigneten (ggf. Hybriden) Vorgehensmodells in IT-Projekten', in *Projektmanagement und Vorgehensmodelle 2015: Hybride Projektstrukturen erfolgreich umsetzen*. Elmshorn: Gesellschaft für Informatik e.V., pp. 139–150.

Kolltveit, B.J., Karlsen, J.T. & Grønhaug, K. (2007), 'Perspectives on project management', *International Journal of Project Management*, **25**(1), pp. 3–9.

Kuhrmann, M. & Linssen, O. (2014), 'Welche Vorgehensmodelle nutzt Deutschland?', in M. Engstler, E. Hanser, M. Mikusz, and G. Herzwurm (eds.) *Projektmanagement und Vorgehensmodelle 2014—Soziale Aspekte und Standartisierung*. Bonn: Gesellschaft für Informatik e.V., pp. 17–32.

Lagstedt, A., Dahlberg, T., Kiselev, C. & Kautz, T. (2022), 'Selection, Adaption and Use of IS and Business Development Methods in Digitalization Projects', in *Proceedings of the 55th Hawaii International Conference on System Sciences*, pp. 7486–7495.

Langer, P., Köbler, F., Berkovich, M., Weyde, F., Leimeister, J.M. & Krcmar, H. (2010), 'Vorgehensmodelle für die Entwicklung hybrider Produkte - Eine Vergleichsanalyse', in M. Schumann, L.M. Kolbe, M.H. Breitner, and A. Frerichs (eds.) *Multikonferenz Wirtschaftsinformatik 2010*. Göttingen: Universitätsverlag Göttingen, pp. 2043–2056.

Laux, H., Gillenkirch, R.M. & Schenk-Mathes, H.Y. (2018), *Entscheidungstheorie*. 10th ed. Berlin, Heidelberg: Springer Berlin Heidelberg.

Lee, G. & Xia, W. (2010), 'Toward agile: An integrated analysis of quantitative and qualitative field data on software development agility', *MIS Quarterly*, **34**(1), pp. 87–114.

Lehmann, O.F. (2016), 'An introduction to a typology of projects', *PM World Journal*, **5**(12), pp. 152–164.

Lindvall, M., Basili, V., Boehm, B., Costa, P., Dangle, K., Shull, F., Tesoriero, R., Williams, L. & Zelkowitz, M. (2002), 'Empirical findings in agile methods', *Lecture Notes in Computer Science (including subseries Lecture Notes in Artificial Intelligence and Lecture Notes in Bioinformatics)*, **2418**(May 2014), pp. 197–207.

Little, T. (2005), 'Context-adaptive agility: Managing complexity and uncertainty', *IEEE Software*, **22**(3), pp. 28–35.

MacCormack, A. & Verganti, R. (2003), 'Managing the sources of uncertainty: Matching process and context in software development', *Journal of Product Innovation Management*, **20**(3), pp. 217–232.

Moyo, B., Soganile, N., Dzawo, G., Madzima, K., Science, C. & Africa, S. (2013), 'Empirical evaluation of software development methodology selection consistency: A case study using Analytical Hierarchy Process', in *Proceedings of the 2013 International Conference on Software Engineering Research & Practice*. Athen: The Steering Committee of the World Congress in Computer Science, pp. 268–274.

Noack, J. & Schienmann, B. (1999), 'Objektorientierte Vorgehensmodelle im Vergleich', *Informatik-Spektrum*, **22**(3), pp. 166–180.

Papadakis, E. & Tsironis, L.K. (2020), 'Towards a hybrid project management framework: A systematic literature review on traditional, agile and hybrid techniques', *Journal of Modern Project Management*, **8**(2), pp. 124–139. https://doi.org/10.19255/JMPM02410.

Pearson, A.W. (1990), 'Innovation strategy', *Technovation*, **10**(3), pp. 185–192.

PMI (2021), The standard for project management and a guide to the project management body of knowledge (PMBOK® Guide). 7th ed. Chicago: Project Management Institute.

PricewaterhouseCoopers (2014), *Project Management: Improving performance, reducing risk*. https://www.pwc.com/jg/en/publications/ned-presentation-project-management.pdf. Accessed: 05/01/2022.

Ratbe, D., King, W.R. & Kim, Y.G. (1999), 'The fit between project characteristics and application development methodologies: A contingency approach', *Journal of Computer Information Systems*, **40**(2), pp. 26–33.

Recker, J., Holten, R., Hummel, M. & Rosenkranz, C. (2017), 'How agile practices impact customer responsiveness and development success: A field study', *Project Management Journal*, **48**(2), pp. 99–121.

Ribeiro, A., Amaral, A. & Barros, T. (2021), 'Project manager competencies in the context of the industry 4.0', *Procedia Computer Science*, **181**(2019), pp. 803–810.

Samuelson, W. & Zeckhauser, R. (1988), 'Status quo bias in decision making', *Journal of Risk and Uncertainty*, **1**(1), pp. 7–59.

Schütte, R. (1998), *Grundsätze ordnungsmäßiger Referenzmodellierung*. 1st ed. Wiesbaden: Gabler Verlag.

Shapiro, D.L., Kirkman, B.L. & Courtney, H.G. (2007), 'Perceived causes and solutions of the translation problem in management research', *Academy of Management Journal*, **50**(2), pp. 249–266.

Shenhar, A.J. & Dvir, D. (2007), *Reinventing project management: The diamond approach to successful growth and innovation*. 6th ed. Boston, MA: Harvard Business School Press.

Shenhar, A.J. (2001), 'One size does not fit all projects: Exploring classical contingency domains', *Management Science*, **47**(3), pp. 394–414.https://doi.org/10.1287/mnsc.47.3.394.9772

Simion, C.-P., Popa, Ştefan-C. & Albu, C. (2018), 'Project management 4.0 - Project management in the digital era', in *Proceedings of the 12th international management conference: "Management Perspectives in the Digital Era."* Bucharest, Romania, pp. 93–100.

Sommerville, I. (2018), *Software Engineering*. 10th ed. Pearson Deutschland.

Špundak, M. (2014), 'Mixed Agile/Traditional Project Management Methodology—Reality or Illusion?', *Procedia—Social and Behavioral Sciences*, **119**, pp. 939–948.

Tell, P., Klunder, J., Kupper, S., Raffo, D., MacDonell, S.G., Munch, J., Pfahl, D., Linssen, O. & Kuhrmann, M. (2019), 'What are Hybrid Development Methods Made Of? An Evidence-Based Characterization', in *2019 IEEE/ACM International Conference on Software and System Processes (ICSSP)*. IEEE, pp. 105–114. https://doi.org/10.1109/ICSSP.2019.00022.

Terlizzi, M.A., Meirelles, F. de S. & de Moraes, H.R.O.C. (2016), 'Barriers to the use of an IT Project Management Methodology in a large financial institution', *International Journal of Project Management*, **34**(3), pp. 467–479.

The Standish Group (2010), *Chaos Report*. Boston.

Turner, J.R., Anbari, F. & Bredillet, C. (2013), 'Perspectives on research in project management: the nine schools', *Global Business Perspectives*, **1**(1), pp. 3–28.

van Donk, D.P. & Molloy, E. (2008), 'From organising as projects to projects as organisations', *International Journal of Project Management*, **26**(2), pp. 129–137.

Vavpotič, D., Bajec, M. & Krisper, M. (2004), 'Software development methodology evaluation model', in H. Linger, J. Fisher, W. Wojtkowski, W.G. Wojtkowski, J. Zupančič, K. Vigo, and J. Arnold (eds.) *Constructing the Infrastructure for the Knowledge Economy*. Boston, MA: Springer US, pp. 141–153.

Wallace, L. (2015), 'IT Project Management', *Wiley Encyclopedia of Management*. Chichester, UK: John Wiley & Sons, Ltd.

Wieczorrek, H.W. & Mertens, P. (2011), *Management von IT-Projekten: Von der Planung zur Realisierung*. 4th ed. Berlin: Springer Berlin Heidelberg (Xpert.press).

Wood, S. (1979), 'A Reappraisal of the Contingency Approach to Organization', *Journal of Management Studies*, **16**(3), pp. 334–354.

Wysocki, R.K. (2019), *Effective project management: traditional, agile, extreme*. 5th ed., *Effective project management traditional, agile, extreme*. 5th ed. Indianapolis, Ind: Wiley Pub.

Zachman, J. (1987), 'A framework for information systems architecture', *IBM Systems Journal*, **26**(3), pp. 276–292.

The manufacturer's authorised representative in the EU is Springer Nature Customer Service Centre GmbH, Europaplatz 3, 69115 Heidelberg, Germany. If you have any concerns regarding our products, please contact ProductSafety@springernature.com

Printed and bound by CPI Group (UK) Ltd, Croydon, CR0 4YY
30/09/2026
02225573-0012